D1765961

WITHDRAWN

Programming Languages and Methodologies

Robert J. Schalkoff
Clemson University

JONES AND BARTLETT PUBLISHERS
Sudbury, Massachusetts
BOSTON TORONTO LONDON SINGAPORE

World Headquarters
Jones and Bartlett Publishers
40 Tall Pine Drive
Sudbury, MA 01776
978-443-5000
info@jbpub.com
www.jbpub.com

Jones and Bartlett Publishers Canada
6339 Ormindale Way
Mississauga, Ontario L5V 1J2
CANADA

Jones and Bartlett Publishers International
Barb House, Barb Mews
London W6 7PA
UK

Jones and Bartlett's books and products are available through most bookstores and online booksellers. To contact Jones and Bartlett Publishers directly, call 800-832-0034, fax 978-443-8000, or visit our website, www.jbpub.com.

Substantial discounts on bulk quantities of Jones and Bartlett's publications are available to corporations, professional associations, and other qualified organizations. For details and specific discount information, contact the special sales department at Jones and Bartlett via the above contact information or send an email to specialsales@jbpub.com.

Production Credits
Acquisitions Editor: Timothy Anderson
Editorial Assistant: Laura Pagluica
Production Director: Amy Rose
Marketing Manager: Andrea DeFronzo
Manufacturing Buyer: Therese Connell
Composition: Northeast Compositors, Inc.
Cover Design: Timothy Dziewit
Cover Image: © Alexis Puentes/ShutterStock, Inc.
Printing and Binding: Malloy Inc.
Cover Printing: Lehigh Press

Library of Congress Cataloging-in-Publication Data
Schalkoff, Robert J.
Programming languages and methodologies / Robert J. Schalkoff.
p. cm.
Includes bibliographical references and index.
ISBN-13: 978-0-7637-4059-7
ISBN-10: 0-7637-4059-4
1. Programming languages (Electronic computers) I. Title.
QA76.7.S28 2006
005.13—dc22

2006008100

6048

Printed in the United States of America
10 09 08 07 06 10 9 8 7 6 5 4 3 2 1

For Chrissie

Preface

I think there is a world market for maybe five computers.

—Thomas Watson, Chairman of IBM, 1943

What Is This Book About?

This book concerns computer programming languages and methodologies. It is intended to convey what programming means in a larger sense. It also introduces an assortment of programming paradigms. To many readers, these approaches may be considered novel and nontraditional.

There is an old adage that basically says, *"If your only tool is a hammer, every problem looks like a nail."* In the present context, it might be modified to, *"If the only programming language/paradigm you know is* x*, every problem looks like an application for* x*."*

This is not a book on learning how to program. Instead, the intent is to present a more mature viewpoint of the entire process. The major concepts covered include:

1. different programming *methodologies* (imperative, declarative, functional, object oriented, parallel, and event driven).
2. the concepts of formal grammars and syntax.
3. the concepts of scanning and parsing.
4. implementation of scanning and parsing.[1]
5. the concept of semantics.

Although this book presents the rudiments of a number of languages and paradigms, the main objective is to convey a more mature and higher-level impression of *programming as a means of human–computer interaction* in the process of developing something useful (i.e., software). It is not accidental that we call these tools programming "languages," because they, like any language, are used to facilitate communication.

[1] Thus, the book also answers the question, "What happens to my code after I give it to the compiler?"

To this end, readers may be surprised to discover:

1. there are languages other than C (or C++ or Java).
2. there are ways to approach program development other than the imperative style.
3. some programming paradigms (e.g., declarative, parallel, and event driven) require a rethinking of the traditional program development mindset.
4. there are ways to learn and describe programming language constructs other than "xx for Dummies."
5. there are many higher-level ways to explore, describe, and analyze the concept and process of programming.

Perhaps it would help to describe what this book is *not* about.[2] The focus is not about how to become a fluent programmer in a specific language (although a number of languages are introduced). Nor is it a lengthy comparison of the minutiae of (usually similar) programming languages. It is not another book that catalogs programming languages and their associated constructs. If anything, it attempts to correct the "mono-paradigm" educational approach to programming.

This book is also not focused on the *program design process*, which often leads to software engineering (SE). SE basically concerns the management of software development and software as a product. Productivity in software development is a big issue. SE is a much bigger, albeit related, issue. This book serves as a prerequisite to this subject. In addition, the material contained herein is related to SE because:

- some software engineering decisions are based upon productivity; if a specific tool for a job is more suitable than others, then productivity may be enhanced using this tool.
- correctness proofs in functional programming are straightforward.
- axiomatic semantics are a basis for correctness proofs.
- algebraic semantics lead to object-oriented programming.

There is a great deal of uncertainty as to the long-term direction and evolution of programming/software development. Arguably, one of the most discernable trends might be paraphrased as "jump on the latest bandwagon." In my opinion, no one has been particularly adept at predicting the future of this technology. This suggests that programmers should be well versed in the underpinnings of a variety of different programming methodologies, rather than in the intimate details of a group of very similar (e.g., imperative) programming languages.

Some Personal Observations, or "How I Learned Programming"

The software development process can be exhilarating (e.g., seeing a complex program graphical interface appear and work correctly for the first time). It may also be deeply frustrating (seeing the same error message for the 1000th time, seemingly independent of code revisions). The programmer's overall impression of the process also depends upon experience, maturity, compensation, and time schedules.

[2] The artificial intelligence community would call this approach *description using negative exemplars*.

What started as an almost hobby-like interest in programming over 40 years ago gradually developed into a more mature and professional interest in quantification of the underlying process. I have always been intrigued by the notion of human–computer interaction, initially in the context of programming. For me, learning and using programming languages was both intellectually stimulating and fun. One of my colleagues in the early 1980s advised me to put the qualification *"able to code 'Hello World' in more than 20 languages"* on my résumé.

I was first introduced to programmable computers in 1971, in the form of the FORTRAN language coded via punch cards. In 1972, I learned (time-shared) Basic. FORTRAN served me well until 1979, when I learned Pascal. I liked Pascal. In the early 1980s, I began a slow, reluctant, and painful transition to C. In the mid-1980s, I learned Prolog and Lisp, as well as TeX (and later LaTeX). In the early 1990s, I jumped onto the object-oriented bandwagon, and became familiar with C++ and Java. I also learned to develop scientific solutions to problems using Matlab and Maple. In the late 1990s, there were brief stints with Perl and Tk/Tcl. The advent of the graphical user interface required that I learn to program with libraries in Microsoft Windows and X Windows and the event-driven paradigm. As a byproduct of my research, it became necessary to consider the programming necessary for parallel processing. Most recently, this has been addressed using MPI.

From an engineering perspective, I see programming as a *design effort*. The process is really no different than the design of an electronic circuit to sense temperature or the design of an algorithm to process images. There is a problem, there is a body of knowledge, there is a body of tools, and there is usually some testing method, and when the process is over there is a program. Throughout the process, there are numerous possible alternatives and consequently decisions that must be made. Analytical thinking and attention to detail are required.

I also feel that aspects of programming allow a creative process or outlet. In some ways, creation of a program is similar to creation of a piece of music, a painting, or other art forms. Personally speaking, I don't think I've ever written a program that was "finished." There were always tweaks, refinements, enhancements, and other modifications that would make the program better. Thus, it is often hard to stop this creative process, although deadlines and other obligations help.

Intended Audience

This book accompanies a second course in programming languages and systems for computer engineering and science majors. It is written at a level suitable for junior- or senior-level Computer Engineering (CpE) or Computer Science (CS) students.[3] It also addresses most of the ABET criteria related to Programming Languages, with additional support for criteria concerning Programming Fundamentals. The objective is to enable a more complete understanding of programming topics and related supporting tools, including philosophy, methodology, formal syntax and semantics, and examples of languages and development approaches. Practicing professionals and graduate students may also find this information useful.

One of the most significant risks in writing a book of this sort is trying to be all things to all people. One group of users may be looking for an "in this language you have these

[3] I do not distinguish between the two audiences (CpE and CS) here, but I am aware that there are differences.

constructs" approach; another may be looking for an object-oriented programming book; yet another may be looking for a book on formal grammars and parsing; another may view all of programming as the end-product of UML.

Notes to Readers

The book presents the basic concepts that are generally considered within the domain of mainstream programming. It does not attempt to be an encyclopedia or bibliographic summary. The book is intended to be largely self-contained. The maximum benefit will be achieved if the book is accompanied by hands-on experience with the topics presented. Access to the Internet and motivation are the only real prerequisites.

Little previous experience in this area is assumed, although readers are expected to be able to program in some (usually an imperative) language. Typically, C or Java seems to be the language of familiarity.

Some Preliminary Questions

To facilitate the study of programming languages and methodologies, begin with a few introspective questions, such as:

- What am I actually doing when I program?
- Can programming be a creative, enjoyable endeavor?
- Is an algorithm always necessary?
- How many languages are there?
- How many *ways* of programming are there?

Now take a personal inventory. Consider how you would answer the following questions:

- What is your favorite programming language?
- What did you last use it for?
- Why?
- What is your favorite programming paradigm?
- What did you last use it for?
- Why?

Many readers will have a single answer to the preceding set of questions. Finally, consider some quasi-technical questions:

- How did you learn to develop software to solve problems (program)?[4]
- How do you choose a programming language?
- How do you tell someone about a programming language?
- How do you describe what a program does?
- How do you describe what a program is supposed to do?

[4]You should reflect upon your own programming evolution.

Part of the motivation of this book is to allow the reader to develop more mature, more elaborate, and more experienced answers to the preceding questions.

Notes to Instructors

1. To borrow from another domain, I hope the students will leave a course based upon this text (and the accompanying assignments) with three attributes related to software development: *perspective, perspective, and perspective.*

2. It is not necessary to use the book sequentially. Some semesters I start with event-driven programming; other times I start with Prolog (or Lisp). Sometimes I start with parallel programming. Most reasonable sequences seem to work.

3. The book contains much more material than can be reasonably covered in a single semester. I can usually cover about 65% of the material in 14 weeks.

4. In order to provide as much flexibility as practical, many programming topics and paradigms are treated in multiple, alternative ways. For example, in order to study event-driven/GUI-based programming, instructors may present the material using:

    - Microsoft Windows and the MFC
    - X windows
    - wxWidgets
    - the Palm OS

    Similarly, object-oriented and functional programming may be presented using:

    - Common Lisp and the CLOS
    - ML
    - CAML

    Parsing may be shown using:

    - Prolog and the LGN
    - `flex` and `bison`

5. The study of programming can and should be quantitative, but experimental or hands-on experience is also necessary to gain perspective. The worst course I can imagine is the survey course where students spend a semester comparing control constructs in an imperative language. I do several variations on a semester-long project theme involving realistic applications. Application domains include computer music, dive computers, or gas-mixing programs. The Instructors Manual provides details.

6. There is a large body of supporting software and notes available to instructors. E-mail the author `rjschal@clemson.edu` or the publisher for more information.

7. The costs of courseware and other academic resources can be reduced by taking advantage of resources available from the Internet. Instructors using this book can support their entire course on PCs with Linux, Mac OS X, or Windows OS at no cost. For illustration, the book uses software that is:

   - Free to students—that is, in the public domain or GPLed.
   - Available on multiple platforms. Windows, MAC OS X, and Linux seem to be the most popular.

8. Feedback is always welcome.

Acknowledgments

I would like to thank Tim Anderson at Jones and Bartlett for believing in this project.

In addition, thanks are due to Amy Rose and the Jones and Bartlett staff for converting 417 LaTeX files into a polished, readable text. Constructive comments from several reviewers helped to improve the manuscript. The trials of students in ECE 352 at Clemson University who used earlier versions of the text are appreciated.

Finally, the recognition of those who consider textbook production a bona fide and respectable academic venture is especially appreciated.

Acknowledgments

About the Author

Robert J. Schalkoff is currently Professor of Electrical and Computer Engineering at Clemson University. His primary scholarly interests are in intelligent systems and computing. He is also the author of *Digital Image Processing and Computer Vision, Artificial Intelligence: An Engineering Approach, Pattern Recognition: Statistical, Syntactic and Neural Approaches,* and *Artificial Neural Networks.* He received his Ph.D. in Electrical Engineering from the University of Virginia.

Contents

Preface v

Acknowledgments xi

About the Author xiii

1 Introduction: Programming Concepts and Languages 1

1.1 Overview 1
1.1.1 What Is a Program (Programming Language)? 1
1.1.2 What Is a Program? 1
1.1.3 What Is Programming? 1
1.1.4 How Do We Articulate the Desired Computation? 2
1.1.5 Motivation to Study Programming Paradigms and Language Concepts 2
1.1.6 Looking Ahead (the Grammatical Viewpoint) 3
1.1.7 Choices, Choices, Choices 3
1.1.8 Language Popularity 3
1.1.9 The Times They Are A-Changin (Specifying Languages by Law) . 6
1.1.10 The Concept and Use of an API 7
1.1.11 Common "Revelations" Regarding Programming 8
1.1.12 The Value of Software 8
1.1.13 Programming (Software Development) Trends 9
1.2 Productivity and Moore's Law 11
1.2.1 Is There a Perfect (or Best) Programming Language? 12
1.2.2 Language Evaluation Criteria 13
1.2.3 The Level of a Programming Language 13
1.2.4 Example of Language Distinctions: Parameter Passing Mechanisms 13
1.2.5 The Concept of Language Construct Orthogonality 14
1.3 Programming History: From Gears to Software Objects 14
1.3.1 Hardware and Software Co-Evolution 14
1.3.2 A Point of Departure 16
1.3.3 Language Chronology 17
1.4 Programming Paradigms and Possible Language Taxonomies 18
1.4.1 Paradigms 18
1.4.2 Selected Language Paradigms: Taxonomy and Differences 18
1.4.3 Other Programming Language Classifications and Examples 23

1.4.4 Remarks 28
1.5 Introduction to a More Formal Viewpoint 28
1.5.1 A Sample Code Fragment and Corresponding Questions 28
1.5.2 Programming Language Quantitative Specification 29
1.5.3 Formal Grammars and Productions 30
1.5.4 Syntactic Description Example 30
1.5.5 Generation and Recognition, Part 1 30
1.6 Programming Tools 31
1.6.1 Programming in the Small 31
1.6.2 Reading Code Is Good for You 31
1.6.3 IDEs and Editors 31
1.6.4 Code Beautifiers and Other Tools 33
1.6.5 Search and Regular Expressions 36
1.6.6 What's the Difference? 36
1.7 Coding Standards and Conventions 36
1.7.1 Elements of Coding Style 37
1.7.2 Documentation (and Comments) 38
1.8 Some Humor: The Evolution of a Programmer 38
1.9 Bibliographical Remarks and References 40
1.9.1 Books and Journals 40
1.9.2 Web-Based References 42
1.10 Exercises 42

2 From Formal Grammars to Programming Languages 47
2.1 Prelude 47
2.2 A Syntactic Viewpoint: Programs are Strings 47
2.3 Formal Grammars 48
2.3.1 Example: English-Language Sentence Formation via Productions (Rewrite Rules) 48
2.3.2 Programming Language Syntax Specification and Productions . . . 49
2.3.3 What Does This Have to Do With a Programming Language Compiler? 49
2.3.4 Strings: Definitions and Conventions 49
2.3.5 Grammar: Formal Definition 51
2.3.6 Constraining Grammar Productions 52
2.3.7 Grammar Application Modes 52
2.3.8 Languages, Possible Strings, and $L(G)$ 52
2.3.9 String Grammar Types 53
2.3.10 A Sample G: Determining Grammar Type and $L(G)$ 56
2.3.11 Representation/Parsing Tradeoffs 56
2.3.12 The Non-uniqueness of G, Given L 57
2.4 Using Grammars: Derivation Trees and Ambiguity 57
2.4.1 The Derivation (or Parse) Tree 57
2.4.2 Derivation Tree Example 58
2.4.3 Grammatical or Syntactic Ambiguity 60
2.5 BNF and Alternatives 60
2.5.1 Alternatives to BNF for Syntax Specification 60
2.5.2 Graphical Descriptions of Syntax 60

2.5.3 Definition: Regular Expressions 61
2.5.4 Regular Expressions and Languages 62
2.5.5 RE Application to Description of Syntax 63
2.6 Bibliographical Remarks and References 64
2.7 Exercises 64

3 Programming in Prolog **75**
3.1 Introduction 75
3.1.1 Getting Started with Prolog Programming: Resources 75
3.1.2 The Prolog Incremental Development Cycle 75
3.1.3 Language Background 76
3.1.4 Hello World in Prolog 76
3.1.5 Prolog `help` Notation 77
3.2 Prolog Syntax and Use 77
3.2.1 Predicates, Clauses, Facts, Rules, and Goals 77
3.2.2 The Prolog Programming Concept as Description 81
3.2.3 Tracing Predicates 83
3.2.4 Recursion 84
3.2.5 Prolog, Variable Bindings, and `is` 87
3.2.6 Testing for Equality Versus Assignment 87
3.2.7 Prolog and Arithmetic 88
3.2.8 Lists in Prolog 93
3.2.9 Recursion and Lists: Another Example: (Recursively) Summing the Elements of a List 95
3.2.10 Input/Output in Prolog 97
3.2.11 Multiple Solutions and Backtracking 99
3.2.12 Combining `not`, `fail`, `true`, `call`, and the Cut 102
3.3 Alternate Interpretations of Prolog 103
3.3.1 Prolog from the Viewpoint of First-Order Logic 104
3.3.2 Prolog and Modus Ponens (MP) 104
3.4 Parsing (Grammatical Recognition) and Prolog 104
3.4.1 Introduction to the Prolog LGN Preprocessor 104
3.4.2 Grammar Rule Notation 105
3.4.3 Prolog and Grammars: A Short Summary 106
3.4.4 More on Grammar Rule Notation 107
3.4.5 Adding Variables in the LGN 110
3.4.6 The 'C' Predicate 110
3.4.7 Prolog and Infinite Recursion (Nontermination) 111
3.5 Prolog and Constraint Satisfaction Problems 113
3.5.1 A Constraint Satisfaction Problem 113
3.5.2 The Role of Prolog in CSPs 113
3.5.3 Example: Numerical Constraint Satisfaction 113
3.5.4 Labeling Complexity 114
3.5.5 Image Labeling Example 114
3.5.6 CSP (Labeling) in Prolog 115
3.6 Bibliographical Remarks and References 116
3.6.1 Books and Journals 116
3.6.2 Web-Based Resources 116

3.7 Exercises . . . 118

4 Sample Programming Language minic **135**
4.1 Overview . . . 135
4.2 minic (Version 1) Syntax . . . 135
4.2.1 A Language Close to a Subset of C . . . 135
4.2.2 minic BNF Description . . . 135
4.2.3 Syntax Notes . . . 136
4.2.4 minic Syntax Subdivision . . . 137
4.2.5 A minic (Version 1) Sample Program . . . 137
4.2.6 Sample Derivation Trees (Lexical Syntax) . . . 137
4.2.7 Derivation Tree for Sample Program . . . 137
4.3 Development of Parsers for minic: Basic Concerns . . . 139
4.3.1 Program Generation and Recognition in a Grammatical Context . 139
4.3.2 Parsing as a Two-Step Process . . . 139
4.3.3 Lexics from the Grammatical Viewpoint . . . 140
4.3.4 Tokens . . . 141
4.3.5 The Two Essential Processes of Syntactic Analysis . . . 141
4.4 Parsing . . . 141
4.4.1 Specification of the Parsing Problem . . . 141
4.4.2 Parsing/Generation Similarities . . . 142
4.4.3 Parsing Computational Complexity and the Decidability Problem . 142
4.4.4 Parsing Approaches . . . 142
4.4.5 Comparing Parsing Approaches . . . 143
4.4.6 The Cocke-Younger-Kasami (CYK) Parsing Algorithm . . . 143
4.5 Life After Parsing . . . 146
4.6 Bibliographical Remarks and References . . . 147
4.7 Exercises . . . 147

5 Using Prolog for Scanning and Parsing **151**
5.1 Scanner and Parser for minic Version 1: Overall Objectives . . . 151
5.1.1 Good News: The Prolog LGN Builds the Parser for Us . . . 151
5.1.2 Bad News: We Have to Build the minic Source File to Token List Scanner in Prolog . . . 151
5.1.3 Concerns with minic and Recursion . . . 151
5.1.4 Preliminary Examples . . . 152
5.2 minic Prolog Scanner . . . 153
5.2.1 Scanner Objective . . . 153
5.2.2 Prolog Predicates Related to Scanner Development . . . 153
5.2.3 Remarks on the Scanner Development . . . 153
5.2.4 What Does the Input Stream Look Like? . . . 154
5.2.5 Why Is it Necessary to Look Ahead? . . . 155
5.2.6 Exactly What Are We Looking For? . . . 155
5.2.7 Recursion within Recursion . . . 156
5.2.8 Prolog Scanner Source . . . 156
5.3 Prolog Parser . . . 161
5.3.1 Prolog Implementation . . . 161
5.3.2 Sample Parser Use . . . 163

5.4 Exercises 164

6 Scanning and Parsing minic Using flex and bison 169

6.1 Building Scanners and Parsers with flex and bison 169
6.1.1 "Compiler-Compilers" 169
6.1.2 In the Beginning: yacc and lex 169
6.2 Introduction to flex and bison 170
6.3 flex 170
6.3.1 Regular Expressions (REs) in flex 170
6.3.2 flex Input File Structure 170
6.3.3 flex Output 171
6.3.4 Example: The "Hello World" of flex 172
6.3.5 More Elaborate flex Examples 172
6.4 Applying flex to minic 172
6.4.1 A Simple Use of flex with minic 172
6.4.2 Using flex to Generate minic Tokens for Parsing 174
6.5 bison 176
6.5.1 The Pragmatics of Using bison 176
6.5.2 Overview of bison Operation 176
6.5.3 bison Parsing Strategy 177
6.6 Using flex and bison Together for minic 177
6.6.1 The bison Grammar File for minic 177
6.6.2 The Overall Project: main 180
6.6.3 Putting flex- and bison-Generated Functions Together 180
6.7 A More Complete Example 180
6.7.1 Revised Parser 181
6.7.2 Revised Scanner 182
6.7.3 Sample Operation of Revised Design 183
6.8 "Under the Hood" of bison 183
6.8.1 The Syntax of miniclite 184
6.8.2 The bison Parsing Algorithm 185
6.8.3 The -v and -g Switches in bison 186
6.8.4 Examining miniclite.output 186
6.8.5 Examining the miniclite.vcg Visualization of Compiler Graph 191
6.8.6 Following a miniclite Parse 191
6.9 Toward a More Complete Parser/Compiler 193
6.9.1 Pragmatics of Passing of Semantic Values 193
6.9.2 Using Semantic Values in flex/bison 195
6.9.3 Using a Symbol Table: Toward Context-Sensitive Parsing 199
6.10 Bibliographical Remarks and References 204
6.11 Exercises 204

7 Enhancing minic 209

7.1 minic, Version 2 209
7.1.1 Introduction and Overview 209
7.1.2 minic Version 2 Syntax 210
7.1.3 What's Changed in the Syntax? 211
7.1.4 Sample minic Version 2 Source File 211

7.1.5 An Example: Possible minic Syntax Ambiguity (Using a Modified Syntax) . . . 212
7.2 Scanning and Parsing minic Version 2 Using flex and bison . . . 213
7.2.1 flex Scanner for minic Version 2 Lexics . . . 213
7.2.2 bison Parser for minic Version 2 . . . 215
7.2.3 Pragmatics . . . 217
7.2.4 Sample Result Using the Scanner/Parser . . . 218
7.3 Scanning and Parsing minic Version 2 Using Prolog . . . 221
7.3.1 Scanner Modification/Extension . . . 221
7.3.2 Parser Modification/Extension . . . 222
7.3.3 The Initial minic Version 2 Prolog Parser . . . 222
7.3.4 Examples of Modified Parser Use . . . 226
7.3.5 Examining Intermediate Prolog Parsing Results . . . 227
7.4 Further minic Extensions (Extended Version 2) . . . 227
7.4.1 Desirable Extensions . . . 227
7.4.2 The Incremental Development Strategy . . . 228
7.4.3 The Complete Syntax and Prolog Parser for minic Enhanced Version 2 . . . 230
7.5 Scanning and Parsing minic Extended Version 2 Using flex and bison . . 232
7.5.1 flex Modifications for minic Source Code Comments . . . 234
7.5.2 flex and bison Input Files for minic Extended Version 2 . . . 234
7.5.3 minic Extended Version 2 Scan and Parse Examples Using flex and bison . . . 240
7.6 Scanning and Parsing minic Extended Version 2 Using Prolog . . . 246
7.6.1 Prolog Scanner Modifications for minic Source Comments . . . 246
7.6.2 Example of Prolog Scanning and Parsing with Comments in the minic Source . . . 246
7.6.3 Implementing Other minic Extensions in Prolog . . . 247
7.6.4 Sample minic Extended Version 2 Scanning and Parsing Results Using Prolog . . . 252
7.6.5 Listing of the Overall Prolog Scanning/Parsing Code for minic Extended Version 2 . . . 252
7.7 Considering Contextual Constraints and Typed Languages . . . 256
7.7.1 Context-Based Productions . . . 256
7.7.2 Introducing Attribute Grammars . . . 257
7.7.3 Contextual Constraints in Programming Languages . . . 257
7.7.4 Relation of Contextual Constraints to minic . . . 258
7.7.5 What Would the Problem Look Like with a "Real" C Compiler? . 258
7.7.6 Potential Approaches to Implement Type Checking . . . 259
7.8 Attribute Grammars . . . 259
7.8.1 Origins and Uses of Attribute Grammars . . . 259
7.8.2 Attaching Attributes to Symbols . . . 260
7.8.3 Synthesized Versus Inherited Attributes . . . 260
7.8.4 Passing Attributes: Which Way Do They Go? . . . 260
7.8.5 Attaching Semantic Functions (Semantic Rules) to Productions . . 261
7.8.6 Predicate Functions . . . 261
7.8.7 Extension: Attribute Grammars for Semantics . . . 261

7.8.8 Application of Attribute Grammars to minic 262
7.9 flex/bison Implementation of a minic Parser 262
7.9.1 Symbol Table: Implementation and Use 263
7.9.2 The Symbol Table 263
7.9.3 Symbol Table Implementation and Associated Functions 264
7.9.4 Revised bison Input File 267
7.9.5 Examples of Symbol Table Use with minic 272
7.9.6 An Illustrative Extension: Parsing typedef 275
7.9.7 Other Possible Extensions 276
7.10 Prolog Implementation of a minic Parser 277
7.10.1 Generating the Prolog Symbol Table 278
7.10.2 Checking the Prolog Symbol Table 279
7.10.3 Context-Capable Prolog Scanner/Parser 279
7.10.4 minic Type Checking Examples Using the Prolog Symbol Table . 282
7.11 Bibliographical Remarks and References 288
7.12 Exercises 289

8 Functional Programming and the Lambda Calculus 305
8.1 Introduction to the Lambda Calculus and Functional Programming 305
8.1.1 Functional Programming History 305
8.1.2 A Calculus for Computation via Functions 306
8.1.3 Relations and Functions 307
8.2 The Syntax and Semantics of the Lambda Calculus 308
8.2.1 Four Productions Go a Long Way 308
8.2.2 Remarks on the Lambda Calculus 308
8.2.3 Extensions 309
8.2.4 Handworked Reduction (Evaluation) Examples 309
8.2.5 Reduction (Evaluation) Examples Using Lisp 310
8.2.6 Reduction (Evaluation) Example Using CAML 311
8.2.7 Multivariable (Multiargument) Functions 311
8.3 Functional Programming Concepts and Syntax 313
8.4 Side Effects and Functional Programming 314
8.4.1 The Notion of a Side Effect 314
8.4.2 More Formal Approach and Extensions 315
8.4.3 Referential Transparency 315
8.4.4 Why Do We Care? 316
8.5 Functional Programming with Typed Functions: A Preliminary Example Using ML 316
8.6 Bibliographical Remarks and References 317
8.7 Exercises 317

9 Lisp 319
9.1 Lisp Introduction, Pragmatics, and Resources 319
9.1.1 Ways to Approach Learning Lisp Programming 319
9.1.2 Who Uses Lisp? 319
9.1.3 Important First Principles 320
9.1.4 Programs and Data Are Lists 321
9.1.5 CommonLisp (clisp) Installation, Testing, and Customization . . 321

9.1.6 System Access . . . 322
9.1.7 Logging a Lisp Session . . . 322
9.1.8 Lisp Editors . . . 323
9.2 The Lisp Top-Level Loop (EVAL) . . . 323
9.2.1 The Behavior of EVAL . . . 323
9.2.2 Reading Lisp Source . . . 324
9.2.3 Functional Programming and Assignment . . . 324
9.2.4 Comments . . . 324
9.2.5 Numbers and Arithmetic Functions in CommonLisp . . . 325
9.2.6 Loading Source Files . . . 325
9.3 Basic CommonLisp Building Blocks . . . 326
9.3.1 S-expressions (or Forms) and Evaluation . . . 326
9.3.2 Some Special Forms . . . 326
9.3.3 Inhibiting Evaluation: The Quote . . . 327
9.3.4 Special Symbols . . . 327
9.3.5 Predicates . . . 327
9.3.6 Arrays and Strings . . . 327
9.3.7 Functions . . . 329
9.3.8 Variables . . . 332
9.4 Basic List Manipulation . . . 333
9.4.1 car and cdr . . . 333
9.4.2 The `cons` Concept . . . 333
9.4.3 List Manipulation Functions and Examples . . . 333
9.4.4 Special Definitions (Empty List) . . . 336
9.5 Lisp Booleans and Conditionals . . . 336
9.5.1 Branching in Lisp . . . 336
9.5.2 Logical Functions . . . 336
9.5.3 The All-Important `cond` . . . 337
9.5.4 Recursion . . . 338
9.5.5 `case` . . . 341
9.5.6 From `cond` to `if` . . . 341
9.5.7 `progn` Forms . . . 342
9.5.8 The Three Faces of Equality . . . 342
9.6 Scope and Iteration in Lisp . . . 343
9.6.1 Global and Local Variables . . . 343
9.6.2 `let` and `Scope` . . . 343
9.6.3 CommonLisp `print` and Examples with `let` . . . 344
9.6.4 Iteration . . . 344
9.6.5 `funcall`, `apply`, and `mapcar` . . . 346
9.7 I/O in CommonLisp . . . 347
9.7.1 `print` and Printing Control . . . 347
9.7.2 The Concept of Streams . . . 347
9.7.3 A Family of Output Functions . . . 347
9.7.4 Formatted Printing . . . 347
9.7.5 The Function `read` . . . 348
9.7.6 Using `read` in Functions . . . 348
9.8 CommonLisp Macros . . . 349

9.8.1 The General Idea of Macros . . . 349
9.8.2 Macros in CommonLisp . . . 349
9.8.3 Simple CommonLisp Macro Examples . . . 350
9.9 CommonLisp Programming Conventions . . . 351
9.10 Function (Program) Design, Implementation, and Correctness . . . 352
9.10.1 Motivation . . . 352
9.10.2 Proving Correctness . . . 353
9.10.3 Example Proof . . . 353
9.11 Extended CommonLisp Design Example . . . 353
9.11.1 Problem Overview . . . 353
9.11.2 Design Constraints . . . 353
9.11.3 Review of the Unit Equations, Training Algorithm, and Nomenclature . . . 354
9.11.4 Resulting CommonLisp Implementation of the Unit and Training . 355
9.11.5 Assessment of the Solution . . . 357
9.12 CommonLisp Functions (and Macros) You Should Know . . . 358
9.13 Bibliographical Remarks and References . . . 359
9.14 Exercises . . . 359

10 Object-Oriented Functional Programming 369
10.1 The CommonLisp Object System (CLOS) . . . 369
10.1.1 Introduction and Background . . . 369
10.2 CommonLisp Object System (CLOS) . . . 376
10.2.1 Objects and Classes in CommonLisp . . . 376
10.2.2 Elementary Class and Object Functions and Arguments . . . 376
10.2.3 CLOS Invocation . . . 376
10.2.4 CLOS Class Hierarchy Example . . . 377
10.2.5 Creating Instances in CLOS . . . 378
10.2.6 Accessing Slots in CLOS . . . 378
10.2.7 CLOS Methods and Method-Defining Functions . . . 378
10.2.8 Methods Are Specialized in CLOS—An Example . . . 379
10.2.9 Another Example of Class-Specialized Methods in CLOS . . . 380
10.3 Relation to Other Programming Languages . . . 383
10.3.1 Overview . . . 383
10.3.2 A Revised CLOS Example . . . 383
10.3.3 An Analogous Representation in C++ . . . 385
10.4 Exercises . . . 388

11 Object-Oriented, Typed Functional Programming with Modules 391
11.1 An Introduction to SML/NJ and CAML . . . 391
11.1.1 Introduction to ML (SML/NJ) and CAML . . . 391
11.1.2 Major Distinctions . . . 392
11.1.3 ML and CAML in Programming Language Evolution . . . 392
11.1.4 The ML Family Tree and Other Relatives . . . 393
11.2 The SML/NJ Language . . . 393
11.2.1 Overview of SML/NJ . . . 393
11.2.2 Noteworthy ML Features . . . 394
11.2.3 Basic Interaction with ML . . . 396

11.2.4 SML Typing and Error Reporting . . . 397
11.2.5 Exceptions . . . 397
11.2.6 SML/NJ: Function Definition . . . 398
11.2.7 ML Conditionals, Part 1 . . . 398
11.2.8 ML Conditionals, Part 2: Pattern Matching . . . 398
11.2.9 Other Selected ML Pragmatics . . . 399
11.2.10 Additional ML Language Features . . . 400
11.2.11 Exploring ML Functions, Part II . . . 404
11.2.12 Lists in SML . . . 405
11.2.13 Recursion, Pattern Matching, and Lists . . . 406
11.2.14 Extended SML Example: ANN Unit Design and Training . . . 407
11.3 CAML and `ocaml` . . . 410
11.3.1 Overview of Selected CAML Syntax and Pragmatics . . . 410
11.3.2 Defining Functions in CAML . . . 414
11.3.3 Sample CAML Interaction and an Introduction to Lists . . . 416
11.3.4 CAML I/O . . . 419
11.3.5 Recursion, Pattern Matching, Lists, and `trace` . . . 421
11.3.6 Revisiting the ANN Unit Example . . . 422
11.3.7 What's CAML Light? . . . 424
11.3.8 Overview of Objects in CAML . . . 424
11.4 Scanning and Parsing in CAML . . . 427
11.4.1 Introduction . . . 427
11.4.2 CAML Scanners (Lexers) . . . 427
11.4.3 Creating a Free-Standing Scanner (Interactive CAML Mode) . . . 428
11.5 CAML Compilation with `ocamlc` . . . 429
11.5.1 `ocamlc` Compilation Example . . . 429
11.5.2 Compiling with Libraries . . . 430
11.5.3 `ocaml` Compilation Extensions . . . 430
11.6 Bibliographical Remarks and References . . . 431
11.6.1 Books and Journals . . . 431
11.6.2 Web-Based Resources . . . 431
11.7 Exercises . . . 432

12 Abstract Syntax and Formal Approaches to Programming Language Semantics 437
12.1 Programming Language Semantics . . . 437
12.1.1 What Are Semantics and Why Study Them? . . . 437
12.1.2 A Brief History of "Reasoning About Programs" . . . 440
12.2 Semantics, Semantics, Semantics . . . 441
12.2.1 Semantics for Specific Language Types . . . 441
12.2.2 How to Do Semantics Informally . . . 442
12.2.3 Another Simple Example . . . 442
12.2.4 Semantics of Classes and Class Members . . . 443
12.3 A Quick Overview of Approaches to Semantics Formalization . . . 443
12.3.1 Self-Definition . . . 443
12.3.2 Translational Semantics . . . 443
12.3.3 Operational Semantics . . . 444
12.3.4 Denotational Semantics . . . 445

12.3.5 Axiomatic Semantics 446
12.3.6 Algebraic Semantics 446
12.4 Semantic Equivalence 446
12.5 Semantic Descriptions Using an Abstract Syntax 446
12.5.1 Abstract Syntax 446
12.5.2 Why "Abstract" Syntax? 447
12.5.3 From Concrete to Abstract Syntax 447
12.5.4 Abstract Syntax Examples for `minic` 448
12.6 Denotational Semantics 450
12.6.1 Concept and Examples 450
12.6.2 Semantic Functions 452
12.6.3 Composition 455
12.6.4 Denotational Semantic Equivalence 456
12.7 Axiomatic Semantics 458
12.7.1 Using Logic to Formalize Semantics 458
12.7.2 Axiomatic Semantics Development 458
12.7.3 Application of Axiomatic Semantics 459
12.7.4 The Basic Premise 459
12.7.5 Developing Axiomatic Semantics Descriptions 461
12.7.6 Partial and Total Correctness in Axiomatic Semantics 461
12.7.7 Lack of Uniqueness of the Axiomatic Specification 462
12.7.8 Rules of Inference: Adjunct Tools for Axiomatic Specification . . . 464
12.7.9 Proof Direction 466
12.8 Functional Programming: Semantics and Correctness 466
12.8.1 Proving Correctness Is Much Easier 467
12.8.2 Example Proof 467
12.8.3 Interpreting Functional Programming Using Axiomatic Semantics . 468
12.9 Algebraic Semantics 468
12.9.1 What Is an "Algebra?" 468
12.9.2 Algebraic Formalization for Programming Language Semantics . . 469
12.9.3 Vocabulary: Sorts, Operations, and Signatures 469
12.9.4 An Example Syntax via Algebraic Specification: Booleans 470
12.9.5 Corresponding Example Semantics for Booleans 471
12.10 Concluding Remarks 471
12.11 Bibliographical Remarks and References 471
12.12 Exercises 472

13 Event-Driven Programming, Part 1 477
13.1 Introduction 477
13.1.1 A Long Time Ago 477
13.1.2 Event-Driven Programming 478
13.2 Example: Microsoft Windows and the MFC 480
13.2.1 C++ Preliminaries and Relevant Review Topics 480
13.2.2 OO: Object-Oriented Thinking/Design 483
13.2.3 Using Classes/Methods You Did Not Write 484
13.2.4 Hello, World (File: `static1.cpp`) 486
13.2.5 A Simple Extension: A Button-Based Application 488
13.3 Example: The X Windows System 490

13.3.1 The X (Windows) Concept . . . 490
13.3.2 An Example of Programming in X/Motif . . . 491
13.3.3 Concluding Remarks . . . 494
13.4 Cross-Platform and Multi-Platform Software Development . . . 494
13.4.1 Cross-Platform Development Tools . . . 495
13.4.2 Similarity to MFC-based Coding . . . 495
13.4.3 wxWidgets Fundamentals . . . 497
13.4.4 A Dialog and Button-Based `wxWidgets` Example . . . 499
13.5 Bibliographical Remarks and References . . . 501
13.5.1 Windows Programming References and Related Resources . . . 501
13.5.2 X and Motif References and Related Resources . . . 501
13.5.3 wxWidgets Programming and Related Resources . . . 502
13.6 Exercises . . . 502

14 Event-Driven Programming, Part 2 **507**
14.1 Overview . . . 507
14.1.1 Event-Driven Programming and the Palm OS . . . 507
14.1.2 The Confluence of Four Entities . . . 508
14.1.3 Understanding (and Achieving) Palm Programming . . . 508
14.1.4 Installation Details and Important References . . . 509
14.1.5 Viewing Resources . . . 511
14.2 Palm Programming Specifics, Part I . . . 511
14.2.1 Palm Programming and Running an Application . . . 511
14.2.2 Palm Programming Is Event-Driven Programming with a Graphical User Interface (GUI) . . . 511
14.2.3 The Event Loop . . . 511
14.2.4 Creating the GUI: Specifying and Viewing Resources . . . 512
14.2.5 The First Palm GUI . . . 515
14.2.6 The First Palm Application: C Code and Analysis . . . 516
14.2.7 Events . . . 517
14.2.8 Some Important Palm OS Functions . . . 520
14.2.9 How to Compile the First Application . . . 523
14.2.10 Resultant Appearance (via the Emulator) . . . 523
14.2.11 Adding Bitmaps to the Palm Application . . . 523
14.3 A More Elaborate Example (Buttons, Multiple Forms, and a Menu) . . . 524
14.3.1 Adding and Handling Resources . . . 524
14.3.2 Specifying and Viewing Resources for the Modified Application . . 525
14.3.3 Revised Resource File Specification . . . 526
14.3.4 Modified C Code and Analysis . . . 527
14.3.5 Switching Forms . . . 527
14.3.6 New Functions (from `PalmOSReference.pdf`) . . . 528
14.3.7 The Finished (Revised) Application . . . 529
14.3.8 Using `pilrc` to Generate the Header File from a Resource Specification . . . 531
14.4 Interaction with User-Entered Data and the "Echo" Application . . . 532
14.4.1 Input and Output Fields Are ASCII Text . . . 532
14.4.2 Specifying the Application "Look and Feel" . . . 533
14.4.3 Specifying and Viewing Resources for the GUI Design . . . 533

14.4.4 Analysis of Revised C Code for the "Echo" Application 534
14.4.5 New Palm OS Functions 536
14.5 Example: Numerical Input and Computations and Interaction with Fields . 538
14.5.1 Field Handles and Dynamic Memory Allocation 538
14.5.2 Specifying and Viewing Resources for the Modified Design 539
14.5.3 Analysis of the Revised C Code 539
14.5.4 Sample Operation of the Resulting Application 543
14.5.5 New Palm OS Functions 543
14.6 Additional Palm OS Programming Notes and Features 545
14.6.1 Data Alerts 545
14.6.2 Local, Global, and Static Designators 548
14.6.3 The Application `*.def` File 548
14.6.4 Debugging 549
14.6.5 C Functions Versus the Palm OS Library 549
14.6.6 String Manager Functions 549
14.7 Implementing Databases on the Palm 550
14.7.1 Dealing with Palm Databases 550
14.7.2 An Automotive Database Application 551
14.7.3 Relevant Palm OS Database Functions 562
14.8 Bibliographical Remarks and References 563
14.8.1 Books 563
14.8.2 Palm Web-Based Resources 563
14.9 Exercises 564

15 Parallel Computing and Parallel Programming 569
15.1 Introduction 569
15.1.1 Problems, Algorithms, and Implementations 569
15.1.2 Why Is Parallel Programming a Separate Programming Issue? . . 570
15.1.3 A Simple `minic` Example 571
15.1.4 Interrelated Parallel Concepts 572
15.1.5 "Can't We Just Increase the Clock Speed?" 572
15.1.6 Computational Complexity 572
15.1.7 Space (Area)–Time Tradeoffs 574
15.1.8 Parallel Performance and Limitations 574
15.1.9 Metrics for Measuring or Predicting Speedup 575
15.2 Algorithm Decomposition Techniques and Tools 576
15.2.1 Types of Parallelism 576
15.2.2 Data Flow Graphs 576
15.2.3 Data Dependency 576
15.3 Parallelism in Declarative Programming (Prolog) 577
15.3.1 AND and OR Parallelism 577
15.3.2 Argument Dependence and Parallelism 578
15.3.3 Parallel Implementation of Unification 579
15.3.4 Parallel Prolog 579
15.4 Extension of Languages to Allow Concurrent Programming 579
15.4.1 Necessary Parallel Programming Language Extensions 580
15.4.2 Processes 580

15.5 MPI and Beowulf Cluster Programming . . . 582
15.5.1 The Beowulf Concept . . . 582
15.5.2 MPI . . . 582
15.5.3 Basic MPI Function Summaries . . . 583
15.5.4 MPI "Hello World" Example . . . 583
15.5.5 MPI and Lisp . . . 584
15.6 Extended MPI Examples . . . 585
15.6.1 1-NNR Computations and Parallel (Cluster) Processing . . . 585
15.6.2 Image Processing (Binary Morphology) . . . 595
15.6.3 Concluding Remarks . . . 613
15.7 Selected (Abbreviated) MPI and MPE `man` Pages . . . 614
15.7.1 MPI . . . 614
15.7.2 MPE . . . 619
15.8 Bibliographical Remarks and References . . . 621
15.8.1 Books and Journals . . . 621
15.8.2 Web-Based Resources . . . 621
15.9 Exercises . . . 622

Bibliography **629**

Index **633**

CHAPTER 1

Introduction: Programming Concepts and Languages

If debugging is the process of removing bugs from programs, programming must be the process of putting them in.
—Anonymous

1.1 Overview

1.1.1 What Is a Program (Programming Language)?

It is surprising how many programming language books never define their topic. Perhaps definitions of programming languages (and programs) are considered widely agreed upon and understood. We address this situation as follows: A **programming language** is a notational system intended primarily to facilitate human–machine interaction. The notation is both human- and machine-readable. From a linguistic viewpoint, a (programming) language has a **syntax**, and language elements have **semantics**.

A programming language is a tool for communication. Note that the communication, unlike "natural" languages, is between a programmer and a (target) machine. This communication is the focus of this book. Thus, it is generally not intended to be two way.

A secondary use of a programming language is to communicate algorithms and computational strategies among humans. This is seen in the (Open Source) collaboration-based development of large software projects, where, for example, changed code fragments are passed among programmers as a vehicle for articulating the code changes.

1.1.2 What Is a Program?

Using the previous definition, a **program** is relatively straightforward to define:

- A program is something that is produced using a programming language.
- A program is a structured entity with semantics.

1.1.3 What Is Programming?

Instead of a succinct and direct answer, we first note that programming is (or involves) many things. Programming is a science, because it implements algorithms described by mathematics and logic. It is a design effort, which requires skill. It is also engineering, which requires the consideration of tradeoffs of program size, speed, maintainability, and the time required for development and debugging of perhaps many possible solutions. It may even be art, since it requires the programmer to be creative, and employ imagination. It is also considered by many to be a craft.

1.1.4 How Do We Articulate the Desired Computation?

Programming is the traditional way to develop software. Our communication with a computing device is facilitated by a programming language. Just as there are many spoken languages, there are many programming languages. Some are very similar in notation and paradigm; others are very dissimilar in both. For example, to articulate our computational objective to the machine:

1. Do we say: "Do this, then do this, then do this, and if xx, do this, otherwise do this?" *This is imperative programming.*

2. Do we say: "Implement this function, which invokes a number of other functions and returns a value?" *This is functional programming.*

3. Do we say: "Here is a set of statements I know to be logically true. On this basis, is xx true?" *This is declarative programming.*

4. Do we say: "I don't know what the user will want when the program is run, but I'll give the user an interface (usually graphical or visual) and react to every possible user action through the interface?" *This is event-driven programming.*

5. Do we say: "Process x could implement this part of the computation, process y could implement another part, process z yet another?" *This is parallel programming.*

1.1.5 Motivation to Study Programming Paradigms and Language Concepts

Although this text conveys the rudiments of a number of languages, the main objective is to impart a mature or higher-level understanding of the broad notion of programming as a means for programmer-computer communication. How we articulate what we want in the way of a computation from a machine is profoundly influenced by:

1. our programming backgrounds,

2. available languages and support tools,

3. the programming objective or the problem (application),

and has profound impacts on:

1. ease of programming (communication),

2. efficiency (both programmer and machine),

3. overall outcome, both in terms of the code produced today as well as the next time we revisit the "communication" (upgrade or revise the software).

In the early days of computing, programmers used a language that was mandated, not chosen. The language often reflected the attributes and architecture of the underlying machine. Furthermore, the primary concerns were optimizing the program for speed and memory usage, because processors were (relatively) slow and memory (RAM) was scarce. Although this situation still holds today in certain embedded applications, the more typical situation is that hardware (processors and RAM) are inexpensive, capable, plentiful, and fast. Thus, modern programming concerns include choosing languages that allow fast (and correct) program development as well as long-term program maintenance.

In summary, we study programming language concepts for many reasons, including to

- become aware of language features or capabilities that could speed the development process (increased expressive capability).
- be able to intelligently choose an appropriate language.
- be able to learn new languages (more efficiently).
- understand the underlying implementation issues.
- be able to modify or design new languages.
- get credit for required college courses in computer engineering and science.

Most notably, the concepts and features embraced by a particular programming language may have a significant influence on a programmer's mindset. In other words, language design may shape a programmer's thought processes.

1.1.6 Looking Ahead (the Grammatical Viewpoint)

As we will see in Section 1.5 and subsequent chapters, a formal and quantitative characterization of a programming language is based in theory upon a formal language, which itself is based upon a formal grammar. Denote this grammar G. This viewpoint allows us to alternately and quantitatively define a program as a *sentence* or *string* produced by G, and a programming language as the set of all strings (programs) producible by G.

1.1.7 Choices, Choices, Choices

A quick Internet search will easily show that the number of programming languages available is measured at least in the hundreds. A few dozen languages arguably achieve "mainstream" status. When it comes to choosing a programming language, we might say we are potentially drowning in a sea of programming languages (Figure 1.1).

It is even debatable how to categorize programming languages; in this book, we will try several approaches. This book assumes the reader is familiar with an imperative language; usually this implies C. The question of which language or programming style is best will probably be unresolved for some time.

1.1.8 Language Popularity

Programming language choice should not be a popularity contest, but it is illustrative to consider language popularity over time. To this end, many indicators are available. For example, Tiobe Software (`http://www.tiobe.com/`) produces a monthly Programming Community Index. Search engines Google, MSN, and Yahoo! are used to calculate the

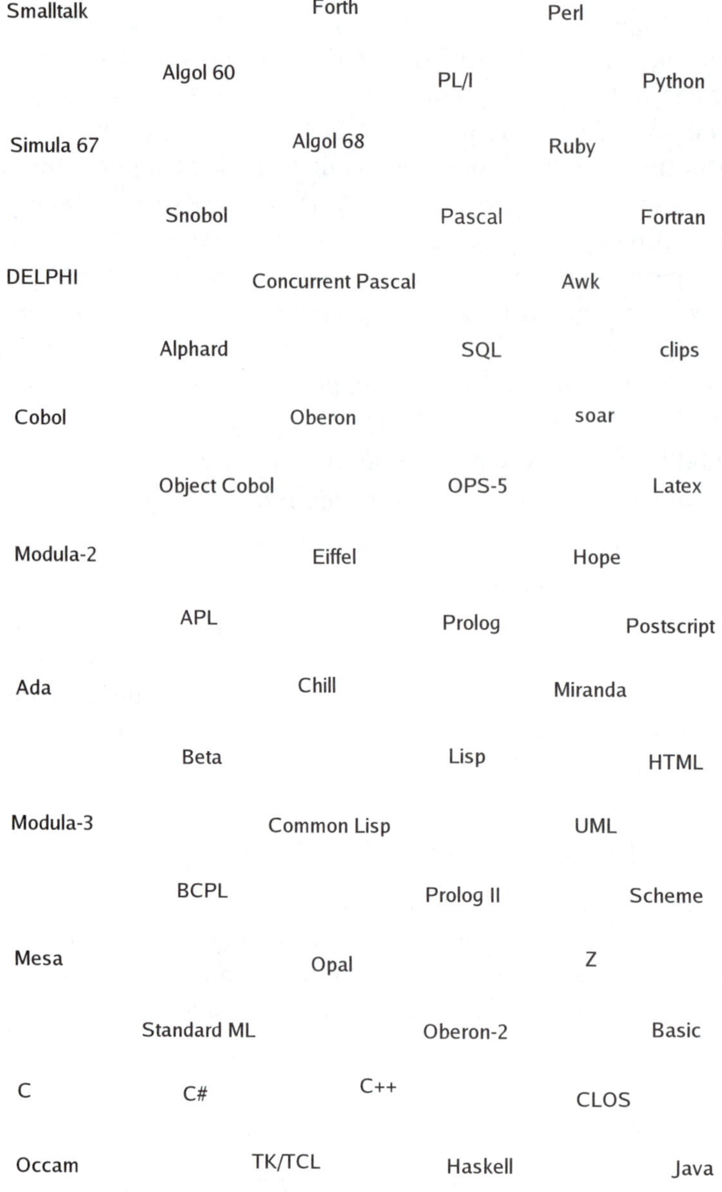

Figure 1.1 A Portion of the Sea of Languages.

ratings. Programming languages that have status "A" are considered to be mainstream languages. A status of "A–" and "A– –" indicates that a programming language is between status "A" and "B." More details on the search strategy, trends, and ranking details are provided by Tiobe.

Figures 1.2 and 1.3 indicate rankings for the top twenty and next thirty languages in September 2005. Note that the languages considered in this text appear in these tables. The Tiobe website also indicates trends in language popularity over time.

Position	(Position)	Programming Language	Ratings	(Ratings)	Status
1	↑	Java	22.442%	+6.55%	A
2	↓	C	19.160%	+2.04%	A
3	=	C++	11.168%	–3.75%	A
4	↑	Perl	9.274%	+0.31%	A
5	↑	PHP	8.895%	+0.66%	A
6	↓↓	(Visual) Basic	6.509%	–5.14%	A
7	↑↑	C#	3.290%	+1.66%	A
8	=	Python	3.032%	–2.57%	A
9	↑	JavaScript	1.768%	+0.26%	A
10	↓↓↓	Delphi/Kylix	1.670%	–4.20%	A
11	↑	SAS	1.299%	+0.65%	A
12	↓	PL/SQL	0.959%	–0.39%	A
13	=	COBOL	0.855%	+0.36%	A
14	↑↑↑	Lisp/Scheme/Dylan	0.718%	+0.40%	A
15	↓	VB.NET	0.663%	+0.18%	A--
16	↑↑	Fortran	0.600%	+0.32%	A--
17	↑↑	Ada	0.540%	+0.27%	B
18	↓↓	IDL	0.486%	+0.15%	A--
19	↓↓↓↓	Pascal	0.480%	+0.12%	B
20	↑↑	ABAP	0.396%	+0.14%	B

Figure 1.2 Top 20 Programming Languages, September 2005. Reprinted with permission by Tiobe Software (www.tiobe.com).

Position	Programming Language	Ratings
21	Awk	0.369%
22	Visual FoxPro	0.343%
23	ColdFusion	0.341%
24	ActionScript	0.327%
25	Prolog	0.325%
26	MATLAB	0.317%
27	dBASE	0.310%
28	Ruby	0.290%
29	Bash	0.278%
30	Postscript	0.241%
31	D	0.233%
32	Logo	0.215%
33	Smalltalk	0.189%
34	S-Lang	0.177%
35	Forth	0.167%
36	CL	0.600%
37	RPG	0.161%
38	Tcl/Tk	0.159%
39	LabView	0.158%
40	Lingo	0.148%
41	VBScript	0.106%
42	REXX	0.103%
43	Felix	0.102%
44	Erlang	0.100%
45	Icon	0.094%
46	OCaml	0.089%
47	ML	0.082%
48	Bourne Shell	0.074%
49	Maple	0.073%
50	Objective-C	0.066%

Figure 1.3 Table of Programming Languages, Rank 21 to 50, September 2005. Reprinted with permission by Tiobe Software (www.tiobe.com).

1.1.9 The Times They Are A-Changin' (Specifying Languages by Law)

As noted in Section 1.1.7, a given problem requiring software development for a solution might be approached with a variety of paradigms and languages. An interesting lesson was learned in the specification of the Ada programming language by the U.S. Department of Defense (DoD).

In 1991, recognition by the DoD that software costs and complexity in DoD systems were limiting factors in system reliability and maintainability led to the mandate of a programming language *by law*. Appropriations bills (passed into law in 1991, 1992, and 1993) contained language of the form shown here.[1]

> *Section 9070 of the FY 1993 DoD Appropriations Act (Public Law 102-396) contains legislation which is "permanent" (i.e., section 9070 remains in effect unless a new law is enacted to specifically repeal or revise it). This section states:*
>
> *Notwithstanding any other provision of law, after June 1991, where cost effective, all Department of Defense software shall be written in the programming language Ada, in the absence of special exemption by an official designated by the Secretary of Defense.*

It is also noteworthy that this argument was reversed a month later[2] and Ada is no longer required by law. Instead, some guidance on programming language selection for DoD projects is provided by DoD:[3]

> *Programming language selections should be made in the context of the system and software engineering factors that influence overall life-cycle costs, risks, and potential for interoperability.... Computer languages should be used in such a way as to minimize changes when compilers, operating systems, or hardware change. To maximize portability, the software should be structured where possible so it can be easily ported.*

1.1.10 The Concept and Use of an API

In many cases, "real" programming means writing code/developing software that interfaces to a substantial amount of (and investment in) existing code. The existing code was hopefully designed for this type of interface through an Application Programming Interface (API). An **application programming interface** is a set of routines (usually functions) and accompanying protocols for using these functions that provide building blocks for software development.

APIs are designed for software developers. However, APIs also tend to have a more widespread benefit in that users of the software see similar interfaces to the software, and consequently users may find it easier to learn to use new programs developed with a common API.

Examples of programming to an API include:

1. the X-windows system (common on Unix/Linux platforms).
2. Microsoft Windows (probably one of the more difficult and simultaneously popular API families).
3. the Palm OS.

---

[1] `http://unicoi.kennesaw.edu/ase/ase02_01/docs/pol_hist/policy/afmc96.htm`

[2] `http://sw-eng.falls-church.va.us/ada_law.html`

[3] From Section 2.2.2.2.1.1 "Software-Engineering Services" of the Department of Defense, Joint Technical Architecture, Joint Interoperability and Warrior Support, version 3.1, March 31, 2000 (approved for public release).

Other noteworthy examples are:

- `wine`, an open-source implementation of the Windows API built upon X and Linux.
- `cygwin`, an environment for Windows providing a Linux-like API.

1.1.11 Common "Revelations" Regarding Programming

1. There are languages other than C (or C++, Java, Visual Basic, or FORTRAN).
2. There are ways to program other than the imperative style.
3. There are ways to learn and describe programming language constructs other than "xx for Dummies."
4. There are many "higher-level" ways to explore, describe, and analyze programming.

1.1.12 The Value of Software

Computer hardware may be the raw material of computing, but it is empowered by software. Software is everywhere. Typical cell phone software consists of approximately 2 million lines of source code, and this number is expected to grow by a factor of 10 by 2010. General Motors Corporation estimates that by 2010 the average automobile will contain 100 million lines of source code.

Software "Crisis"?

The software crisis has been around since the late 1960s, although it became critical in the 1980s and 1990s. Arguably, software development will always be challenging and require skill; thus a "crisis" may always be with us. There are several reasons for this:

1. As hardware evolves, applications that were previously infeasible become feasible. For example, it was not practical to consider the digital processing of images in 1950; today it is commonplace on personal computers. *As applications become (hardware) feasible, they will require (new) software.*
2. The production of both software and hardware is limited by complexity and the management of the software development process. In fact, inability to handle software project complexity is an oft-touted reason for software failure. Sloppy development practices is another.
3. Good engineering practice places as much system complexity as possible in software as opposed to hardware.
4. Software makes hardware flexible and adaptable.
5. There are many potential applications (e.g., vision, speech, robotics) where the only impediment to achieving successful systems is our inability to write the appropriate programs. In other words, hardware complexity is not the limitation.

1.1.13 Programming (Software Development) Trends

Arguably, there are three paradoxical trends in software development:

1. It is always changing. New languages and development environments appear frequently and adopt a small following. A few achieve mainstream status.

2. It is fairly static. The number of available paradigms does not appear to be changing, and the widespread use of imperative languages for the solution of mainstream problems has not significantly changed since 1960.

3. A significant desire is that the software development process (and the resulting software itself) become more efficient[4] and robust.

The following list describes some observed trends in software development. The list is admittedly incomplete and in no special order. Investigation of any one topic (this is left to the reader) will almost certainly spawn considerable debate.

- Writing code at a higher level rather than a lower level (subject to debate)
- Very large to huge software projects
- Porting and upgrading software, as opposed to development from scratch (see "Software Refactoring" later in the chapter)
- Reusable/extendible software
- Building-block software development approaches
- Extensive use of APIs
- Emerging dichotomies between programming by/for users and programming by/for professionals, and between programmers and software engineers
- Jumping on the latest bandwagon
- Software as a long-term investment
- The dichotomy between software as property and the emerging Open Source movement
- Multiprogrammer software projects
- Recognition that multipurpose languages may not be
- Multilanguage development
- Software standardization
- Tool integration (debuggers, editors, and integrated development environments)
- Perceived shortage of programmers
- Analysis and design prior to programming
- Programming and specification considered together
- Programming and testing (validation) considered together
- The quest for "correctness"
- Less distinction between hardware and software

[4]Or programmers become more abundant and much less expensive.

"To Engineer or Not To Engineer"

Note that many of the topics just listed refer not to a specific programming language or paradigm but to the *program or software development process.* This process, of course, includes programming. In the early days of modern computing, software was conceived as a mathematical artifact. British mathematician Alan Turing formalized the concept of an algorithm and its corresponding implementation via the so-called Turing machine. Today, software is both indispensible and an industry.

A very significant trend is the continued search for ways to structure and formalize this process (e.g., software engineering, agile and extreme programming). The overall objective is to develop methods to produce the highest-quality software at the lowest long-term cost.[5]

Because there are alternative approaches, it is no surprise that controversy and debate have ensued (for about thirty years). Those advocating the "craft-based" (also known as the "agile" or "extreme" approach) are pitted against the "traditional" (software engineering) group. About all the two groups can agree on is that software development methods need improvement. See the URL `www.extremeprogramming.org` for more details on agile programming.

"It Has Already Been Written"

Another common theme in the preceding list of topics is software maintenance, upgrading (or extension), and reuse. *Most software systems are not new.*

Reusable software assets are either the existing software itself or the software-related knowledge used to produce the software. **Software reuse** is the use of this existing software (or software knowledge) to produce new software.

The availability of robust, standardized software libraries (through an API) is an obvious contributor to software reuse. A common task involving software reuse is to continually rewrite and update an existing piece of software, sometimes in a more current language. For example, the OPS5 Production System development environment was initially written in Lisp, later ported to `C` (as `clips`), and since ported to `Java` (as `Jess`). Another approach is to develop the software in a language that facilitates subsequent revision; this is one of the benefits claimed for the object-oriented paradigm.

Software Refactoring

Automation of the concepts mentioned leads to the concept of **refactoring**, a systematic technique for restructuring existing code by altering (improving) its internal structure without changing external behavior. Refactoring is a type of source-to-source program transformation that changes code, but preserves semantics. This is much deeper than the simple reformatting of source code.[6] At this point in time, there is much research on the refactoring of programs written in many languages.[7]

---

[5]We refrain here from quantifying quality, cost, or any other quantitative aspect of software. This is left to software engineers.

[6]Code beautifiers such as `indent` (see Section 1.6.4) are available for this type of transformation.

[7]See `http://www.refactoring.com/`

"It Has Already Been Designed or Solved"

Reuse of software (design) knowledge leads to the concept of **design patterns**. Experienced programmers often experience a sense of déjà vu in tackling new software challenges. From this, the reuse of a previous design approach, or design pattern, is suggested. The concept of design patterns applies to many problem domains; we restrict our discussion to the software domain.

We might say that a design pattern is to software design what a class library is to coding. It is also important to note that the design pattern is not the code itself.

Design patterns are usually the result of years of experience, collaboration, and refinement. They may be classified using multiple criteria, but the most common classification is according to the basic problem they address. Accordingly, design pattern categories include:

- structural patterns.
- behavioral patterns.
- concurrency patterns.
- event-handling patterns.
- architectural patterns.

Grand Research Challenges and Software

Finally, although prediction is risky, it is nonetheless important to mention some grand challenges. The Computing Research Association, with financial assistance from the National Science Foundation, hosted a conference series on Grand Research Challenges in Computer Science and Engineering. In 2002, a group convened to discuss specific research challenges for computing systems of the future. The resulting document is available at:

`http://www.cra.org/Activities/grand.challenges/`

Many of the conclusions regarding technical objectives and directions in computing are related to the objectives of this book. This includes building self-sustaining software as well as increased emphasis on programming languages and computational models. One particularly noteworthy remark from the 'Grand Challenges' document is:

> *The limiting factor is software, not hardware... Software is still being written at the same manual pace and has progressed only incrementally since the 1950s. Software organization hits a "complexity barrier" somewhere above 10 million lines of code. Without better ways of producing and structuring software, the complexity barrier will constrain our ambitions for system behaviors.*

1.2 Productivity and Moore's Law

Moore's law, stated in 1965 by Gordon Moore, postulates a doubling in computer hardware performance (measured by component density or gates on a chip) roughly every 18 months. This translates into a factor of 100 every 10 years. Although Moore's law is not a law of physics, it has been reasonably accurate in predicting combined computer processing, storage, and communication capabilities for several decades.

There does not appear to be a corollary to Moore's law for software. In fact, there is evidence that software quality and productivity have remained relatively constant over the decade.[8]

Other related remarks are:

1. Moore also predicted his law would no longer be applicable in 2017, a point in time when he predicted the limits of transistor miniaturization would be reached. Many observers believe that the end of Moore's law is imminent; others consider this unlikely, suggesting alternative processing technologies and paradigms will enable the trend to continue.

2. Parallel processing research shows that more and more hardware does not always guarantee a faster computation; many algorithms have inherently serial paths.

Thus, one viewpoint (see also Section 1.3.2) is that future gains in computing will be primarily through software, including:

- More efficient *production* of the software (especially through the development of new tools and the rediscovery of others).
- Enhanced *software capabilities.* This includes advanced user interfaces and probably requires future algorithm advancements in a number of areas, including intelligent systems.

Another viewpoint related to the software/hardware issue is postulated by the agile programming enthusiasts:

> *A typical project will spend about twenty times as much on people as on hardware.*

In this case, "people" refers predominantly to programmers. Regardless of whether the exact ratio is 20:1, in many applications it is noteworthy that the value added is due to software, because the hardware is nearly a commodity. The possible corollary to this argument is that development costs are dominated by software.

1.2.1 Is There a Perfect (or Best) Programming Language?

Any useful programming language should facilitate both description (in the sense that programs may be written and read by programmers) and computation. Other attributes, such as portability and efficiency, should be considered.

Like any sort of tool, a programming language is probably used most efficiently if it is well suited for a specific task. For example, business applications are often written in COBOL, beginners to programming often choose Basic, and scientific processing is often undertaken with either FORTRAN, Pascal, or C. Few people would cut their lawns with scissors when a lawn mower is available; similarly, few artificial intelligence applications are written in assembly language.

[8] In 1992, the DoD designed the Software Inspection Lab, which implemented the so-called National Software Quality Experiment. The objective was to reduce software problems by a factor of 10 by the year 2001. A decade later, no appreciable changes in either productivity or quality are evident.

1.2.2 Language Evaluation Criteria

The following list of attributes is incomplete, but conveys an idea of relevant measures for programming language evaluation.

- **Readability.** This measure reflects lexical simplicity and programmer ease in reading source code.
- **Orthogonality.** See Section 1.2.5.
- **Applicability.** This is best stated as "use the right tool for the job."
- **Writability.** This includes simplicity and orthogonality and support for abstraction.
- **Reliability.** This includes type checking and exception handling.
- **Cost.** Costs associated with a programming language are many, including programmer learning cost, programmer writing (design) productivity, compilation cost (arguable), execution cost (most critical in real-time systems), debugging cost, and maintenance cost.
- **Other.** Other criteria include the flexibility of control statements and the availability of (perhaps predefined) data structures.

1.2.3 The Level of a Programming Language

Programming in different languages may involve programming at different "levels." For example, even simple tasks (e.g., addition of two numbers) require a considerable number of program statements (instructions) in assembly language, whereas these same tasks may be accomplished with a single statement in a high-level language. Thus, assembly language is considered low(er) level.

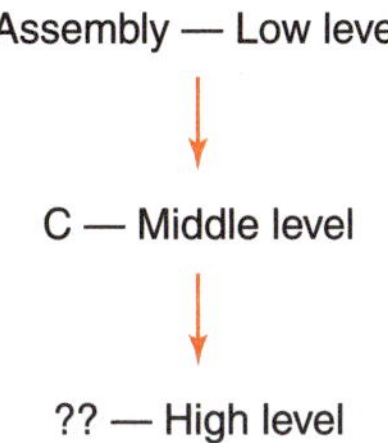

1.2.4 Example of Language Distinctions: Parameter Passing Mechanisms

When invoking functions or procedures, languages vary on how the arguments are used.

- **Pass (call) by value.** Arguments are considered expressions that are evaluated at the time of the procedure or function call. These values are used during the execution of the procedure or function.
- **Pass (call) by reference.** Arguments are variables with previous memory allocation(s). The location, or address of the variable, is passed to the procedure or function. For example, in C arrays must be passed by reference. The programmer has a choice with other data types.

1.2.5 The Concept of Language Construct Orthogonality

Definition and Significance

The property of orthogonality means many things in many different contexts. It is generally a concept borrowed from mathematics, usually implying independence in direction. A major concern in programming language design and use is that language constructs *do not behave differently* in different contexts. Thus, in terms of programming languages, we define **orthogonality** in the following way:

> *In an orthogonal programming language, language constructs may be combined in any meaningful way, without restrictions (or unexpected behavior) due to the context of usage.*

Alternately, context-sensitive restrictions on language constructs are "nonorthogonalities" in the language. For historical reference, Algol 68 (1963 to 1968) was a completely orthogonal language.

Nonorthogonality by Example

It is probably easier to convey the concept by negative examples. Here are a few:

- **The Equality operator** (=). In Pascal and C, this operator may be applied to scalars, pointers, and sets, but not to arrays, records, or structs.
- **Returned values.** In C, all data types *except array types* may be returned from a function call.
- **Parameter Passing.** In C, parameter passing results in nonorthogonal behavior. All parameters may be passed by value *except* arrays, which must be passed by reference.

Part of the (non)orthogonality concept is philosophical; there are lots of times that certain constructs and data types are incomparable. For example, consider the fragments:

```
file_1 > file_2
```

or

$$\begin{pmatrix} x \\ y \\ z \end{pmatrix} < \begin{pmatrix} 6 \\ 7 \\ 8 \end{pmatrix}$$

Overloading of functions (C++, for example) is one way to overcome this problem.

1.3 Programming History: From Gears to Software Objects

1.3.1 Hardware and Software Co-Evolution

It is not surprising that the concept of programming languages grew simultaneously with the evolution of computer hardware. In the earliest days of computing, software did not exist. However, some means to control or instruct the computing device was necessary. Charles Babbage's difference engine, invented in 1822, could execute different computational tasks by changing the gears that executed the calculations. This difference engine

Figure 1.4 The Mechanical Difference Engine Computer. (And you thought software development in Linux was difficult?). Reprinted with permission by Doran D. Swade.

is shown in Figure 1.4. One might refer to this concept as **mechanical programming**. It is also representative of an era of machines without languages.[9]

Similarly, the U.S. Government fostered development of the ENIAC (Electronic Numerical Integrator and Computer) in the early to mid- 1940s. ENIAC, although hardly user friendly, typified the notion of a general-purpose electronic digital computer. ENIAC was controlled or programmed by presetting switches and patch cords, and required rewiring the device for each new calculation. This process was, at best, very tedious and inefficient. For reference, ENIAC was comprised of 18,000 tubes, 70,000 resistors, 10,000 capacitors, 1,500 relays, and 6,000 manual switches and consumed 140 kilowatts of power while filling a 20-foot by 40-foot room (Figure 1.5). Similarly, fifty-some years ago, Remington Rand's new UNIVAC weighed 29,000 pounds and required 125 kilowatts. Technicians could walk into it to work on the 5,200 vacuum tubes. An excellent visual archive of early computing history is found online at the IEEE Virtual Museum. The URL is `www.ieee-virtual-museum.org`.

The notion of programming and computing machines evolving together is shown in Figure 1.6. Early computing devices were programmed with cables, or in machine code. As the architecture changed, so did the programming technique. New "translators" were necessary. As machines became more computationally powerful, languages were developed to take advantage of the new capabilities. A good example is display capabilities; once the graphical user interface (GUI) became possible it was necessary to develop or ex-

[9]In addition, we could postulate one or more eras of languages without machines; for example, the lambda calculus (the underpinnings of functional programming) was pioneered before machines were available to implement functional programming languages.

Figure 1.5 The ENIAC Computer, circa 1945. ENIAC contained 20 electronic accumulators, each capable of storing a 10-digit decimal number, and had a read-only memory of about 300 numbers. (U.S. Army photo.)

tend programming tools for display programming. As networking hardware became more ubiquitous, Web-based programming was introduced.

Hardware	"Software"
Gears	Changing gears
Relays/vacuum tubes	Switches, cables, machine code
Discrete transistors	Assemblers
LSI	Higher-level dev. systems
VLSI	Paradigms chosen by *application*

Figure 1.6 Language Generations Parallel Hardware Evolution

1.3.2 A Point of Departure

Today, however, the situation is one of significantly greater independence. Computing hardware generally supports a number of operating systems and development tools, including language interpreters and compilers for many different programming languages. Typically, language choice is independent of hardware.

More notable, however, is the observation that there has not been the same magnitude of advancements or breakthroughs in software as in hardware. The hardware function of relays or vacuum tubes has been reduced in measures of physical scale and electrical power consumption to an almost astonishing degree. Much of the software practice, however, remains (at least by paradigm) surprisingly similar to that used in Algol in 1958. This

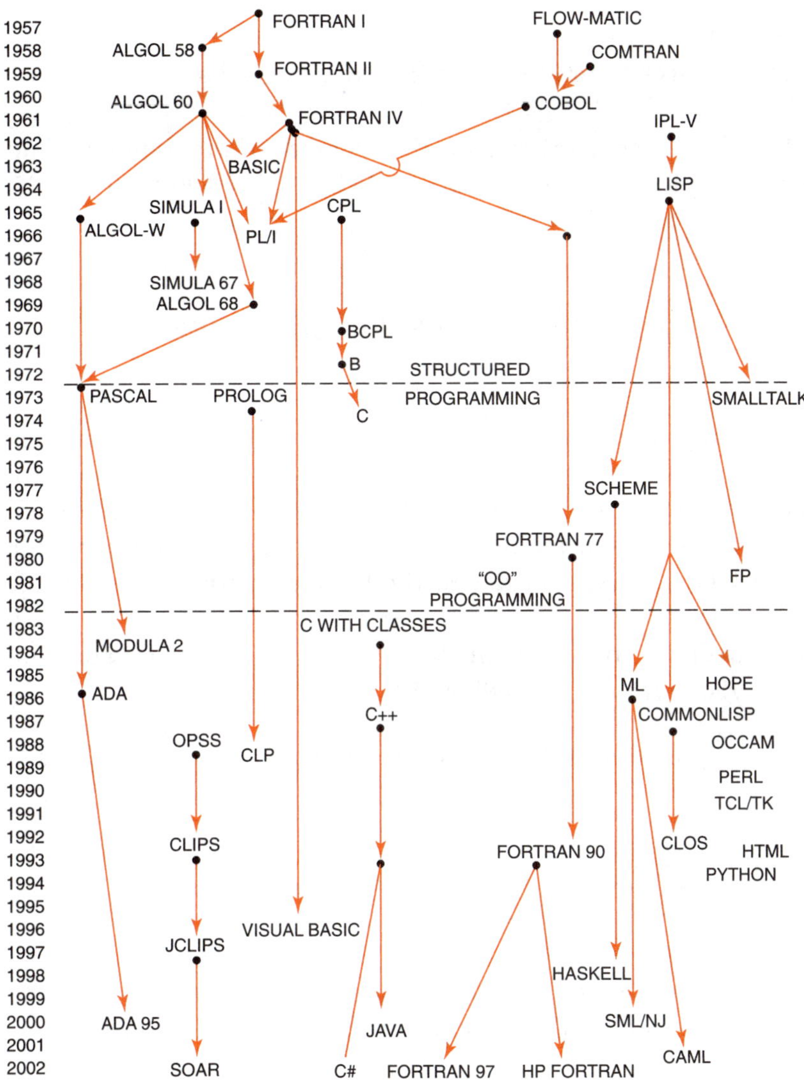

Figure 1.7 Programming Language Evolution.

reasoning leads to the arguable, but plausible, assertion that software, not hardware, is holding back advances in computing.

1.3.3 Language Chronology

The earliest programming languages were developed with one simple goal in mind: to provide a flexible mechanism to direct the operation of a computer. As noted, the first languages reflected the structure of the underlying machines. Early programming was done in machine code or primitive assembly language. In the late 1950s, a number of high-level programming languages appeared, including FORTRAN.

A chronology of selected languages illustrates a number of things, including:

- evolution within a language.
- evolution into new languages.

- the creation of new languages.
- the cross-fertilization of languages to produce new (hybrid) languages.

This is shown in Figure 1.7. Note that many long-lasting families of programming languages are evident. Examples are FORTRAN I, FORTRAN IV, (ANSI) FORTRAN 77, and FORTRAN 90.

1.4 Programming Paradigms and Possible Language Taxonomies

1.4.1 Paradigms

The spectrum of programming approaches, and the even larger spectrum of programming languages, is wide and growing wider. Many different languages share a common programming approach. Imperative languages, as a class, are an example of this. Although we could study the similarities and differences among constructs (e.g., control constructs, built-in data structures, and I/O) in these languages, the basic **paradigm** used by the programmer is similar.

It seems more meaningful to discuss programming languages by approach or paradigm. A number of programming paradigms exist, including:

1. procedural or imperative (probably the best-known; found in languages such as C and Java).
2. functional (or applicative).
3. declarative.
4. object oriented (allows complex systems to be modeled as modular components, which can be easily reused to model other systems or to create new components).
5. rule based.
6. event driven.
7. parallel or concurrent (this paradigm is applicable when parts of the computation may be executed independently. Many languages have extensions to facilitate this. Familiarity with the concepts of a process or other hardware abstractions is necessary for this type of programming).

1.4.2 Selected Language Paradigms: Taxonomy and Differences

Imperative Languages

Briefly, imperative languages are characterized by the following features. Imperative programs emphasize the "tell what to do" model of computing.[10] They focus on evaluating

[10] This also arises from the somewhat misguided (or at least inaccurate) notion that a program is "a description of a set of actions that we want a computer to carry out."

expressions and storing results in a variable (memory location). The most common imperative languages are comprised of sequences of statements such as:

```
a = 10;
b = 20;
c = a + b;
```

Furthermore, imperative programs focus on the concept of memory and are usually compiled.

Examples of languages used in the imperative style include:

- Assembly language
- COBOL
- FORTRAN
- Pascal
- C and C++
- Java

Furthermore, imperative languages are characterized as having an implicit state that is modified by constructs (causing side effects) or "commands" in the language. Consequently, imperative languages generally rely strongly on the notion of a sequence of commands that permit precise and deterministic control over the state. Many of the popular languages in existence today are imperative, or have a strong imperative component.

Functional Languages

Functional (or applicative) languages are languages whose underlying model of computation is the *function*. Key aspects of functional languages are:

- a focus on applying functions to (evaluated) arguments.
- the ability to implement mathematical functions.
- minimal (strictly speaking, no) use of variables or assignment statements.
- programs as function definitions and function applications.
- basing the language on a few (about eight to ten) primitive functions or building blocks. Complex functions are built up from these primitive functions.
- recursion (not iteration) occurs naturally.
- a theoretical basis in the lambda calculus.

Examples of functional languages include Haskell, (Common) Lisp, Scheme, Hope, Miranda, Standard ML (SML), and CAML. A fragment of Lisp, a functional language, is shown here.

```
(defun recur (alist)
  (cond
    ( (not (null (cdr alist)))
      (recur (cdr alist)) )
    ( t alist ) ) )
```

Declarative Languages

Declarative languages are often described as expressing *what is* rather than *how to.* Salient attributes include:

- description or specification (often with logical or numerical constraints) of a situation.
- use in an interpreted mode (with a compilation option).

In a declarative language, looping is accomplished via recursion rather than by sequencing or iteration. Perhaps the best declarative language example is Prolog (PROgramming in LOGic), whose syntax is the modified predicate calculus. Declarative languages are very useful in *constraint satisfaction problems.* A sample Prolog clause is shown here.

```
factorial(N,Result) :- Imin1 is N-1,
factorial(Imin1,Fmin1),
Result is N*Fmin1.
```

Object-Oriented Language

Object-oriented (OO) programming is based upon the concept of an object, which may be conceptualized as a data structure (abstract data type) with a related set of methods. Objects are instances of a class, and classes may be arranged in a class hierarchy. This allows inheritance of both methods and class attributes. Examples of object-oriented languages include Eiffel, Simula 67,[11] C++, CLOS, OCAML, and Java.

The object-oriented (OO) computing and object-oriented programming (OOP) paradigms are significant concepts. Object-oriented programming is one software technology to receive massive attention as the cure-all for many programming and software development ills. Note that the complexity of OO programming may not always be warranted.[12] In terms of programming systems and techniques, OOP is a direct descendant of abstract data type (ADT) research efforts.

Key Elements Key attributes of OO programming include:

1. classes and class hierarchies.
2. instances of classes.
3. inheritance.
4. methods.
5. access to values of object slots and object methods.

A Software Object An abstract view of a software object is shown in Figure 1.8. Observe that data and methods (functions) are encapsulated inside the object, in order to hide implementation details (which could change) from the outside world. The messages sent to the object may contain the name of the object to receive the message, the action to perform (method(s) to be used) and additional parameters necessary for the method.

[11] Yes, there really was an OO language in 1967.

[12] Do we really need objects to print "Hello World"?

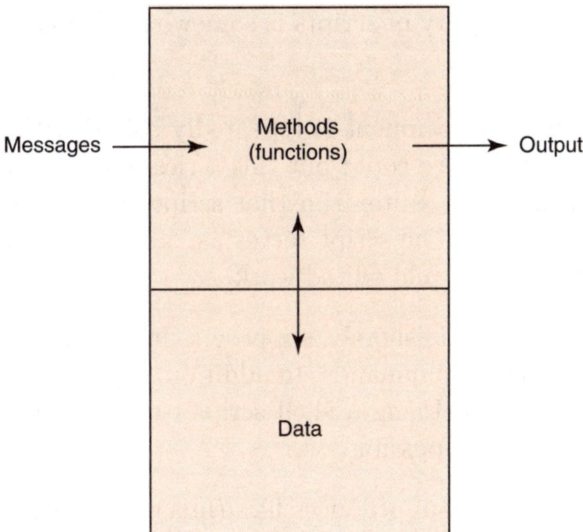

Figure 1.8 Model for a Software 'Object.'

Applications Numerous examples of OOP application appear throughout this text, including:

- the use of the Microsoft Foundation Classes for OO-based Windows programming (Chapter 13).
- the use of C++ for event-driven/GUI-based program design using `wxWidgets` (Chapter 13).
- the use of the Common Lisp Object System for OO and functional Programming (Chapter 10).
- the use of the object-oriented features of CAML, leading to OCAML (Chapter 11, Section 11.3.8).

In addition, Chapter 13 summarizes a number of OO concepts using C++.

Scripting Languages

Overview A scripting language, or what is often called a glue language, loosely refers to any language that is weakly typed or untyped and has little or no provision for complex data structures. A program in a scripting language is called a script. A script is typically interpreted.

Scripts usually interact either with other programs or with a set of functions provided by the script interpreter. These functions may include operating system function calls. Prototypical scripting languages are bash (for creating bash "shell" scripts), Perl, sed/awk, Python, Tk/Tcl, and the interpreter for MSDOS batch files.

Scripting languages have evolved into much richer languages that provide (in many cases) all of the functionality provided by the more traditional programming languages. Moreover, as the programmable features of shells become more and more powerful, as with the Bourne Again Shell (bash), they begin to resemble traditional interpreted languages.

Examples The notion and utility of scripts is somewhat obvious. We illustrate the case with four examples:

1. Consider a case where a document is repeatedly edited with the same (sequential) set of editing commands. We could put this series of editing commands or "script" in a file and then have the editor run that script as if those commands had been typed while in the editor. The script serves as "glue," invoking the various editing actions and producing the final edited work.
2. As we'll show in an example shortly, suppose a number of files are to be processed with a similar sequence of commands. In addition, suppose we have a file containing the location of these files. Using a shell script to process this input file, and thus process each of the files, is possible.
3. Suppose a particular program produces files (image files in this case) with a naming convention that is unsuitable (e.g., 8.3 names are desired) for some subsequent application. We would like to convert the unsuitable names into similar, but suitable, names. While we could rename the selected files by hand, if there are hundreds of files this process is impractical and error prone.
4. Suppose we wish to execute a sequence of commands necessary to build a Palm application.

Bash and Examples Arguably one of the most common scripting languages is the bash shell. The following file (`makeshell2`) is used as a script to build a Palm application using the gcc toolchain:

```
m68k-palmos-gcc -c -g -Wall $1.c
m68k-palmos-gcc $1.o -lm -g -Wall -o $1
pilrc -q $1.rcp
build-prc $1.def $1 *.bin
```

In Unix-like OS (including Linux and Mac OS X), if the first two bytes of an executable file are `#!`, this "magic number" (or sha-bang or shebang) is a special marker that designates this file as an executable shell script. Immediately following the sha-bang, and everything up to the first whitespace, is the path to the program that interprets the commands in the script, whether it is a shell, a programming language, or a utility. For example, if the first line of an executable[13] is

```
#!/usr/bin/perl
```

the script will be treated as a Perl script. In bash, the `#!` can be omitted if the script consists only of a set of generic system commands, using no internal shell directives. This is shown in the previous example.

Bash shell scripts may use environment variables as well as input parameters. Two examples with the same intent follow. Suppose a set of files is to be processed in a similar manner. The file names, including paths, are contained in a text file. The first example copies all of these files to a new directory, preserving the relative paths and directory structure.

[13]Assuming this is the location of the Perl executable.

```
#!/bin/bash
filefile=$1
for i in $( cat $filefile );
do
echo copying $i
cp --parents $i ./allBookFiles
done
```

The second example is similar, except that each file is treated as an image and edge enhanced:

```
#!/bin/bash
# rem use -x for debugging
filefile=$1
for i in $( cat  $filefile );
do
echo processing $i
#cp $i $i.testme
convert -edge 1 $i $i.enh
echo produced $i.enh
done
```

Perl and Examples The first Perl example is quite simplistic:

```
#!/usr/bin/perl
print "Hello, Bob!\n";
```

The next example script (`dc280.perl`) is quite handy when dealing with Kodak digital cameras and software. It also illustrates the conciseness of the language in iteration and search/replace operations using regular expressions.

```
#!/usr/bin/perl
# to convert DC280 files
while (<*.JPG>) {
$oldname = $_;
s/DCP_//;
s/\.JPG$/\.jpg/;
rename $oldname, $_;
                }
```

To illustrate the operation of this Perl script, look at the before and after contents of the sample directory "test":

```
$ cd ./test
$ ls
dc280.perl  DCP_0505.JPG  DCP_0518.JPG  DCP_0519.JPG  DCP_0520.JPG
$ ./dc280.perl
$ ls
0505.jpg  0518.jpg  0519.jpg  0520.jpg  dc280.perl
```

1.4.3 Other Programming Language Classifications and Examples

Rule-Based Languages

Rule-based languages focus on programming using rules, which allow knowledge to be represented as a set of preconditions that must hold and, if so, a set of actions to be performed.

```
(defrule determine-knocking-cause
   (working-state engine unsatisfactory)
   (working-state fuel-quality satisfactory)
   (not (repair ?))
   =>
   (if (yes-or-no-p "does the engine knock (yes/no)? ")
       then
       (assert (repair "suggest timing adjustment"))))
```

(a) Automotive Diagnosis Example

```
(defrule assess_teach_perf
   (faculty (name ?W) (lecture_prep yes))
   (faculty (name ?W) (lecture_quality good))
   (faculty (name ?W) (teaching_evals good))
=>
   (assert (teaching_performance (name ?W) (rating acceptable))))
```

(b) Faculty Teaching Evaluation Example

Figure 1.9 Two Examples of Rule-Based Programming (`clips`).

OPS5, `clips`, and Soar are three of the better-known rule-based languages. Rule-based languages find significant application in developing expert or intelligent systems, as shown in Figure 1.9.

Bondage-and-Discipline Languages

This descriptor may mean anything from strongly typed to nearly impossible to use. Another characterization[14] is "a language ... that, though ostensibly general-purpose, is designed so as to enforce an author's theory of 'right programming' ...." These languages are abbreviated B&D. Perhaps the two most notorious B&D languages are Ada and ML.

Prototyping Languages

These are used for quickly writing exploratory and/or proof-of-concept software prototypes.

Extension Languages

An extension language is a language (usually interpreted) that is embedded within a program to allow future behavior of the program to be modified even after the program has been distributed in binary form. In the simplest case, we might argue that configuration files comprise a crude extension language. However, these files merely control already defined program options (or user preferences) and enable little actual *extension* of the program. On the other hand, the ability to create and execute scripts or macros made up of program commands from within a program (examples are found in Microsoft Word and the `vi` editor) is closer to the idea of an extension language.

Many extension languages are relatively simple and not overflowing with features. However, very useful and sophisticated examples exist. For example, the GNU `Emacs` editor allows extension at a higher level through a built-in scripting language in the form of a

[14] From the Free On-line Dictionary of Computing (March 13, 2001).

dialect of Lisp. Through this extension language, users may achieve substantial program functionality not envisioned by the original program designers. Many computer games incorporate scripting languages to allow users to create new scenarios or situations. Finally, the emerging `Guile`[15] language is intended to facilitate the creation of programs that allow software *plugins* for enhanced functionality.

Architecture Definition Languages

Typified by APL and HDL, these languages may be used for hardware description.

Metalanguages

A metalanguage is a language used for the formal description of another language.

Intermediate Languages

An intermediate language is a language used in an intermediate stage of compilation.

Toy Languages

This is sometimes a negative connotation. A toy language may be useful for instructional purposes, but inadequate for general-purpose programming. Pascal is occasionally referred to as a toy language; in this text `minic` is a toy language.

Visual Programming Languages

These languages support "point and click programming" and programming by nonprogrammers. The "visual programming" moniker is a catch-all for a number of things, including:

- Languages intended to develop programs to be used with a graphical user interface (GUI), such as Windows. In these languages, specification of, and interaction with, visual resources (buttons, windows, menus, and so on) is often a significant part of the program development effort. Visual Basic is perhaps the best example of this paradigm.
- Integrated development environments (IDEs), which facilitate much of the programming effort with visual displays. This includes visual debuggers and resource editors.
- True visual programming environments, in which programs are created and exist in a visual form. An example is the Cantata extension to Khoros, which allows "drag and drop" creation of image-processing algorithms. High-level image processing functions are provided as "glyphs," or visual representations of functions with image input and (possibly) image output. Glyphs are chosen, arranged, and connected visually to achieve an overall computation. An example is shown in Figure 1.10. Note the possible analogy with the patch-cord-programming based strategies of very early computers in Section 1.3.1.

[15]GNU Ubiquitous Intelligent Language Extension.

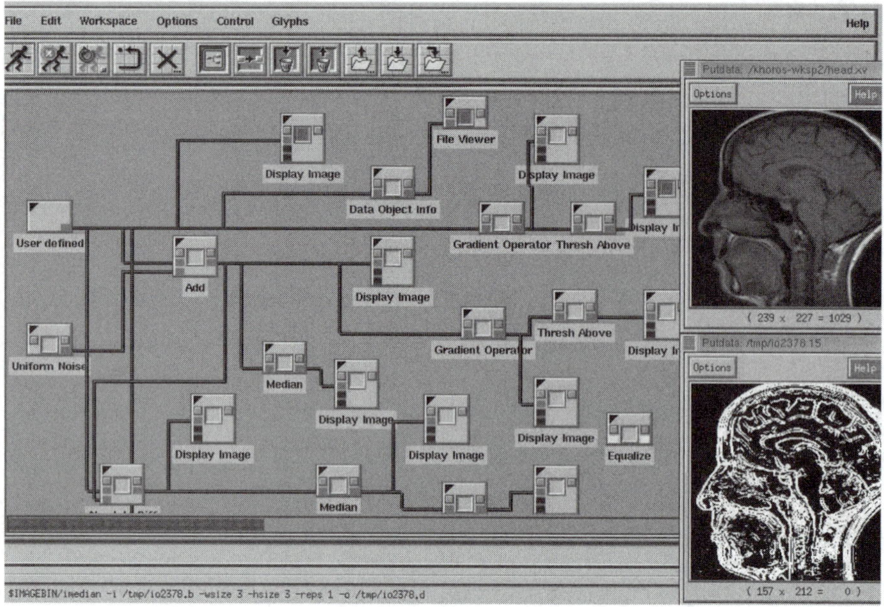

Figure 1.10 Example of Visual Programming Using the Khoros Cantata System for the Implementation of Image Processing Algorithms.

Specification Languages

Specification languages provide a formalism for expressing a hardware or software design. These include VHDL and UML.

Query Languages

These are typically used to implement an interface to a database.

Assembly Language

Assembly language is basically a symbolic representation of the machine language of a specific computer.

Markup Languages

In a markup language, special characters are used to mark the data in a document and indicate its structure. Most often, the markup is used to control the visual appearance of the document. Commonly, a markup language is text-(file) based and must be both human- and machine-readable.

Markup languages include LaTeX, HTML, SGML, and others. HTML (Hypertext Markup Language) is a markup language used to create hypertext documents that are platform independent. It has been in use by the World Wide Web (WWW) global information initiative since 1990. HTML uses tags that surround blocks of text to control the document's appearance. HTML has a fixed set of tags. A simple example of HTML is shown in Figure 1.11.

LaTeX is an important markup language used for typesetting (including this book). A simple example of LaTeX is shown in Figure 1.12.

```
<html>
<head>
<title>Course Materials -- Fall 2003 --- (Private)</title>
</head>
<body>
Course Materials Download Page<br>
</body>
</html>
```

Figure 1.11 Simple Example of a HTML Document.

```
\documentclass[12pt,oneside]{book}
\usepackage{fancybox,verbatim,shapepar,amsmath}
\usepackage[dvips]{graphicx}
\makeindex
\pagestyle{plain}
\setcounter{tocdepth}{3}

\begin{document}
\title{{\Huge Programming Languages and Methodologies}}
\author{Robert J. Schalkoff \\ Clemson University}
\date{\copyright 2002-2005 RJ Schalkoff \\
All Rights Reserved \\
revised \today \\ ECE352, Spring 2005\\
\vspace{1in} {\em For Chrissie}}

\frontmatter

\maketitle
\tableofcontents
\listoffigures

\include{/ece352/newbook/prefacer}

\mainmatter

\include{/ece352/introduction/introductionr}

\include{/ece352/formal-grammars/formal-grammarsr}

%% here is index
\input{plm.ind}

\end{document}
```

Figure 1.12 Simple Example of a LaTeX Source File.

SGML (Standard Generalized Markup Language, ISO 8879) is an international standard metalanguage for markup languages.

XML.

Perhaps one of the most important and prevalent markup languages is the extensible markup language, or XML. XML is platform independent. Via markup using tags, XML facilitates the representation of data in a hierarchical structure. The XML standard is controlled by the World Wide Web Consortium (W3C). XML is like HTML, but far more powerful. Whereas HTML is used for display, XML is used for data structuring. Both use tags, however, XML does not have a fixed or finite set of possible tags like HTML. XML allows the programmer to create new tags. Finally, XML has a much more strictly enforced set of syntactic and semantic rules. Many dialects of XML exist.

And Thousands of Others . . .

Many other possible classifications of programming languages exist, often by application. This includes:

1. general-purpose languages.
2. systems programming languages.
3. artificial intelligence languages.
4. GUI programming and graphics languages.
5. typesetting languages.
6. game programming languages.

1.4.4 Remarks

Many programming languages share attributes from several paradigms or taxonomies. Thus, the classification of programming languages is often difficult unless "fuzzy" boundaries are allowed. For example, imperative languages usually provide some support for functional programming (problems arise, however, when restrictions on the type of returned values are enforced). Additionally, functional languages often include some imperative language features (e.g., variables, assignment, iteration), and to a more limited extent, so do declarative languages. Visual programming environments are used to support both functional and declarative paradigms. Event-driven and concurrent programming applications may use imperative, declarative, or functional paradigms.

1.5 Introduction to a More Formal Viewpoint

1.5.1 A Sample Code Fragment and Corresponding Questions

Let's start with a simple (and hopefully familiar) snippet of code, as shown in Figure 1.13.

```
int main(void)
{
int t1,t2,kt,ans;
t1=10;
t2=3;
kt=10;
ans=t1 + t2 + kt;
return(ans);
}
```

Figure 1.13 A Snippet of `minic` Code.

Suppose we interpret (or compile) and then execute this code fragment.[16] Some relatively obvious questions arise:

- Did it compile (why or why not)?
- What does/did the program do?
- What was it supposed to do?
- Did it do it?

1.5.2 Programming Language Quantitative Specification

There exist many ways to quantitatively describe a programming language. Three are of special significance, and shown in the following sections.

Syntax

Programming language syntax defines the allowable arrangement of symbols in programs, especially program fragments. For example, the syntax may constrain fragments to have matching parentheses; in `minic` we might have:

```
<main-decl> ::= <type> main <arg>
<type> ::= int | void
<arg> ::= lparens <type> rparens
```

where `lparens` denotes "(" and `rparens` denotes ")".

Syntax also catalogs the basic elements of the language, most importantly the **structure** of the language. Syntax is often specified by a metalanguage,[17] such as the language of regular expressions or BNF.

Syntactic descriptions may be either **concrete** or **abstract**. Initially, we consider the concrete case, because that is required by the parser. Abstract syntax may be ambiguous and is of primary interest in attaching semantic descriptions to abstract syntax fragments.

Although they are highly interrelated, it is nevertheless convenient to divide the overall syntax or the syntactic specification of a language into two parts:

- The lexical structure, which indicates the constraints on the **tokens**, or lexical units, which define the basic "words" or symbols of the language. This includes reserved words and symbols (e.g., `void`, `while`, `if`, {, }, `;`) as well as user-defined words such as variable and function names. (More on this later).
- The (remaining) syntactic structure, which is then input to the grammatical recognizer, or **parser**. In fact, it is common to distinguish between *lexical rules* or productions and *syntactic rules* or productions.

Semantics

Roughly, semantics means "meaning." The language semantics define the meaning of program fragments or the overall program written in the language. Semantics are usually only considered after a program is deemed syntactically correct. In exploring semantics, we may use either formal or informal approaches.

---

[16]This is left to the reader.

[17]As noted in Section 1.4.3, a metalanguage is a language used to quantify another language.

Pragmatics

Pragmatics defines the usage and features of the language.

1.5.3 Formal Grammars and Productions

Programming languages are, formally speaking, languages, and therefore invoke the concept of formal grammars. Central in our look at formal grammars is the notion of a *production*, or a formal expression of how language fragments may be produced. In many implementations of a production, the notion of *replacement* is key.

The syntax of a language is usually expressed in a formal notation, usually in BNF (Backus's 1959/Naur's 1960 notation "form" or language). EBNF (Extended Backus Naur Form) is an extension of BNF and adds the regular expression syntax to the BNF notation, in order to allow very compact specifications. There is an ISO standard for EBNF.

Although BNF notation can be explained in a few sentences, the definition of EBNF requires more explanation, and therefore frequently only BNF is used. The use of regular expressions and graphical approaches as alternative for syntax description is described later.

1.5.4 Syntactic Description Example

Here we begin our look at a simple, imperative language derived from C hereafter referred to as `minic`. The very simple sample syntactic description shown in Figure 1.14 uses BNF.[18] Using the rules or productions described in the language syntax, many program fragments may be produced (see Figure 1.13).

```
<transunit> ::= <main-decl> <body>
<main-decl> ::= <type> main <arg>
<type> ::= int | void
              /* must specify input and returned type */
<arg> ::= lparens <type> rparens
<body> := lbrace <decl> <statseq> rbrace
              /* forces declarations, if any,  first and only once */
<decl> ::= e | <type> <variable-list>;
              /* uses <variable list> (not shown)*/
<statseq> ::= e | <command-seq>; <return-stat>
              /* uses <command-seq> (not shown) */
<return-stat> ::= return <return-arg>;
              /* no optional return  statement */
<return-arg> ::= lparens <variable> rparens
              /* no expression evaluation in the return */
```

Figure 1.14 Sample (Portion) of `minic` Syntax.

1.5.5 Generation and Recognition, Part 1

Language utility involves both generation and recognition. In the case of a spoken language, consider a speaker and a listener. One generates sentences in the language; the other recognizes them (otherwise the conversation is at best one sided). *In the case of*

[18]The comments shown using `/*` and `*/` are for readability only; they are not part of the syntax. Note also this syntactic description is incomplete; the most glaring omission is absence of the lexical part of the syntax.

a programming language, generation typically occurs in the process of writing (or creating) the program; recognition is what is done by the parser (usually the front end of the interpreter or compiler).

1.6 Programming Tools

There has probably never been a time in history where more tools are available to the programmer. Some are good; some are difficult to learn; some are crutches to allow non-programmers to develop programs. A complete listing of available tools for all languages is impractical. We highlight a few tools and related approaches to give readers the impression that more than an editor is available and useful for software development.

1.6.1 Programming in the Small

The current trend in software development may be characterized as "programming in the large." Consequently, many tools are aimed at large, multifile (perhaps multilanguage), multi-programmer projects. Many of these tools work on programs at the lexical (source code) level. Our objective in this book is to develop small coding examples with various paradigms. This might be characterized as "programming in the small." However, many features of the tools described are still useful to us.

1.6.2 Reading Code Is Good for You

Professional software developers spend a significant fraction of their time not in actually writing code, but instead in reading, understanding, and modifying existing code. The intricacies and realities of modern software projects suggest this ability is essential. An emerging notion is that learning how to produce good code is based upon reading good code.[19] This viewpoint is, in some respects, an extension of the concepts of informal operational semantics (Chapter 8) and the process of code inspections (used in structured software development). Lots of Open Source code corresponding to popular programs such as Web browsers, graphics file manipulation programs, language interpreters/compilers, and even entire operating systems is available for reading and review. This available code includes many different languages and programming styles. Note that a key element for the success of this approach is the ability to distinguish good from not so good programming practices.

1.6.3 IDEs and Editors

The notion of an integrated development editor (IDE) is appealing to programmers and involves combining an editor, a source compiler (or interpreter), debugging, revision control, and project management, all in one application. Some may argue that this is not necessary with a customizable, multiple-window GUI or desktop; this is a personal decision.

A popular IDE is the MS Visual Studio for Windows platform. Other examples are Open Perl, an IDE for writing and debugging Perl scripts,[20] and Anjuta,[21] an IDE for C and C++ on GNU/Linux systems with the GNOME desktop. The Mac OS X includes

[19] Spinellis, Diomidis. *Code Reading: The Open Source Perspective.* Boston: Addison-Wesley, 2003.

[20] `http://open-perl-ide.sourceforge.net/`

[21] `http://anjuta.sourceforge.net/`

the Xcode-based IDE. Finally, the Red Hat Source Navigator[22] is a multiplatform coding tool that provides a graphic framework for understanding and reengineering large or complex software projects. It includes parsers for C, C++, Java, Tcl, FORTRAN, COBOL, and assembly programs. Included tools such as `cscope` and `cbrowser` facilitate C code scanning.

The availability of editors that allow language-specific syntax highlighting, customization of commands, multiple windows, scripting, and shelling out to access system services (and run other programs) blurs the distinction between IDEs and editors. In fact, sometimes `vi` and `emacs` are referred to as Unix-style IDEs.

vi(m)

`vi` is a visual editor developed by Bill Joy. Although not as intuitive as editors like `WordPad` or `gedit`, it is very well suited to software development. A modern incarnation of this useful editor is `vim`. `vim` is available for many platforms and in source form.[23] It is distributed free as "charityware."

Line Numbering Most importantly, `vi` supports line numbering. While this may seem insignificant, it is absolutely essential for error identification and correction when used in conjunction with compilers and interpreters that generate line-specific error messages and warnings. The `gcc` compiler, the `clisp` CommonLisp interpreter, the SML/NJ ML interpreter, and the SWI Prolog interpreter all have the ability to indicate line-number-specific errors and warnings. In this way, the programmer may immediately go to the offending line of source code and fix the problem. Many IDEs employ this feature.

Finding Matching Delimiters That Occur in Pairs Perhaps the second most useful feature of `vi` is the use of the `%` command. The matching item for the delimiter under the cursor is identified (if one exists) and the cursor jumps to the match. This is invaluable in locating matching parentheses, brackets, and braces in C programs. It is also useful in determining the extent of complicated lists in Lisp.

Invoking `vi` Depending upon the distribution, `vim` may be invoked in a number of ways. In addition, a number of useful command line arguments are available. For example, `vi +n` invokes `vi` and places the cursor at line *n*. `vi -R` invokes `vi` in the read-only mode (often implemented as `view` on some systems). `vi -l` invokes `vi` in lisp mode, which is equivalent to using the `:set lisp` and `:set showmatch`. The combination of these switches enables `vi` to automatically indent lines and show matching parentheses, braces, and brackets upon text insertion. This is invaluable in composing Lisp source. Graphical versions of `vim` are invoked using `gvim` or `vim -g`.

Color Syntax Highlighting In addition, `vim` expands upon `vi` functionality with language-specific and customizable color syntax highlighting (see Section 1.6.3). Syntax files are available for C, C++, Lisp, Prolog, SML, OCAML, PASCAL, XML, HTML, PERL, and so on.

[22] `http://sourcenav.sourceforge.net/`
[23] `http://www.vim.org/`

Shelling Out This is done via the `:sh` command.

Syntax Highlighting Syntax highlighting is quite useful in developing and analyzing source code. `vim` supports this for a variety of languages with a command syntax of the form:

```
:set syntax=<language>
:syntax enable
```

Most `vim` distributions include syntax files for popular languages. It is also possible to develop your own.

1.6.4 Code Beautifiers and Other Tools

Code Beautifiers

Properly formatted source code makes code reading more efficient. Early Unix C code beautifiers were `cb` and `vgrind`. Today, many alternatives exist. `indent` is a beautifier included with many linux distributions. A before and after example using `indent` is shown in Figure 1.15.

Unformatted Source Code

```
/* test-noindent.c */

int process(void){
/* now  process data  */
for(i=0;i<dim_m;i++) for(j=0;j<dim_n;j++) imageout[i][j]=0;

for(i=bM/2;i<dim_m-bM/2;i++) for(j=bN/2;j<dim_n-bN/2;j++) { contained=1;
    for(bi=0;bi<bM;bi++) for(bj=0;bj<bN;bj++) compute_contained();
    if(contained) imageout[i][j]=255;  else imageout[i][j]=0; }

printf("processed image\n"); return(0);
}

int main(void){ process(); output_image("image2ero5x5.pgm"); return(0);
} /* main */
```

Formatted Source Code

```
/* test-indent.c */
  int
process (void)
{

/* now  process data  */
    for (i = 0; i < dim_m; i++)
    for (j = 0; j < dim_n; j++)
      imageout[i][j] = 0;
```

Figure 1.15 Example of Formatting Using `indent`. Note the visual effect.

```
  for (i = bM / 2; i < dim_m - bM / 2; i++)
    for (j = bN / 2; j < dim_n - bN / 2; j++)
      {
contained = 1;
for (bi = 0; bi < bM; bi++)
  for (bj = 0; bj < bN; bj++)
    compute_contained ();
if (contained)
  imageout[i][j] = 255;
else
  imageout[i][j] = 0;
      }
  printf ("processed image\n");
  return (0);
}
int
main (void)
{
  process ();
  output_image ("image2ero5x5.pgm");
  return (0);
} /* main */
```

Figure 1.15 (continued)

Compiler Help

In addition to generating errors and warnings, certain compilers may facilitate the analysis of source code. A useful feature of `gcc`, for example, is the ability to show the resulting source when compiler directives are replaced. This is accomplished with the `-E` compiler switch, wherein the source file is passed through the preprocessor. Sample results are shown in Figure 1.16.

An Overlooked "Tool"

The possibility of using an executable version of the source code as a tool for understanding, development, and debugging should not be overlooked. Interpreting or compiling the source code (before modification) may help in understanding the effect of changing inputs, arguments, and other program or code parameters. Overuse of an executable as a development tool may lead to the "it worked for one case, therefore it is correct" syndrome.

Other Tools for Code Development

Other useful tools include:

`gprof`: A code profiler. Use of this tool is shown in Chapter 11.

`cdecl`: Sometimes the understanding of source code requires deciphering complex type declarations. `cdecl`, for C source, may help in this process. An example, taken from the parallel image dilation code of Chapter 11, is shown here.

```
cdecl> explain int (*imagein)[]
declare imagein as pointer to array of int
```

The syntax of the grammar for `cdecl` is considered in a problem in Chapter 2.

Compiler Directives Replaced

```
FILE *imagefileptr;
int n=200;
int imagein[200][200];
int imageout[200][200];
int dim_m,dim_n,max_val;
int i,j,bi,bj;
int b[5][5]={1,1,1,1,1,
               1,1,1,1,1,
               1,1,1,1,1,
               1,1,1,1,1,
               1,1,1,1,1};

int process(void){

for(i=5/2;i<dim_m-5/2;i++)
   for(j=5/2;j<dim_n-5/2;j++)

   {
    contained=1;
    for(bi=0;bi<5;bi++)
       for(bj=0;bj<5;bj++)
          compute_contained();
    if(contained) imageout[i][j]=255;
          else imageout[i][j]=0;
   }

printf("processed image\n");
return(0);
}
```

Source Code with Compiler Directives

```
#define N 200
#define bM 5
#define bN 5

FILE *imagefileptr;
int n=N;
int imagein[N][N];
int imageout[N][N];
int dim_m,dim_n,max_val;
int i,j,bi,bj;
int b[bM][bN]={1,1,1,1,1,
               1,1,1,1,1,
               1,1,1,1,1,
               1,1,1,1,1,
               1,1,1,1,1};

int process(void){

for(i=bM/2;i<dim_m-bM/2;i++)
   for(j=bN/2;j<dim_n-bN/2;j++)
/* arbitrary sized B (bM,bN) loop */
   {
    contained=1;
    for(bi=0;bi<bM;bi++)
       for(bj=0;bj<bN;bj++)
          compute_contained();
    if(contained) imageout[i][j]=255;
          else imageout[i][j]=0;
   }

printf("processed image\n");
return(0);
}
```

Figure 1.16 Example of Using Compiler (`gcc -E`) Directives with Source Code.

`RCS` and `CVS`: These are tools for the management of multiprogrammer projects and keeping track of revisions of source code.

`strace (linux)` and `API Spy (Windows)`: These tools facilitate checking on operating system calls and may be used to check or debug an executable.

`gctags` and `ctags`: Large software projects often spread declarations and definitions throughout a number of files. These code-reading utilities help to find declarations and definitions, and produce output compatible with the regular expression search facility in `vi`.

`hexedit`: Binary editors such as `hexedit` are useful for examining object code, exploring binary data structures, and deciphering non-ASCII image files.

`Cygwin libraries for Windows Users`: POSIX is an operating system interface standardized by ISO/IEC, IEEE, and the Open Group. Cygwin is a port of POSIX.1/90 system calls to Win32. Using this library, numerous Unix utilities are available to the Windows user.

1.6.5 Search and Regular Expressions

In addition to providing an alternative syntax representation (Chapter 2), regular expressions are very useful in search. Most computer users are familiar with the rudiments of regular expressions; however, their power is in enabling more focused searches. Programs such as `grep` use regular expressions for searching, as do the `vi` and `vim` editors.

1.6.6 What's the Difference?

In modifying code, or comparing different versions of a source file, determining what has changed in a file or what is different between two (or more) files is often necessary or useful. It is seldom practical (or possible) to spot differences in large source code files. For this reason, utilities such as `diff` and `diff3` (allows three files) are popular. An example is shown in Figures 1.17 and 1.18.

Graphical tools related to `diff` are popular. MS Visual Studio comes with a graphical tool `Windiff` for displaying file differences, and `vim` has a similar feature.

1.7 Coding Standards and Conventions

In software development, coding standards and conventions are used to provide stylistic guidance to programmers. This often increases code readability, fosters multiprogrammer efforts, and may help in long-term code maintainability. Examples of commonly used conventions are:

- the GNU coding standards advocated by Stallman
  (`www.gnu.org/prep/standards_toc.html`)
- the Hungarian naming convention advocated by Simonyi and used in many MS Windows development efforts
  (`http://msdn.microsoft.com/library/default.asp?url=/library/en-us/dnvsgen/html/HungaNotat.asp`)

file: `lilo.conf.laptop`

```
prompt
timeout=50
default=linux
boot=/dev/hda

image=/boot/vmlinuz-2.4.20-8
     label=linux
     initrd=/boot/initrd-2.4.20-8.img
     read-only
     root=/dev/hdb2

image=/dev/hda1
     label=winXP
     table=/dev/hda
```

file: `lilo.conf.presario`

```
prompt
timeout=50
default=linux
boot=/dev/hda
map=/boot/map
install=/boot/boot.b
message=/boot/message
lba32

image=/boot/vmlinuz-2.4.7-10
label=linux
initrd=/boot/initrd-2.4.7-10.img
read-only
root=/dev/hdb2
append="hdd=ide-scsi"

other=/dev/hda1
optional
label=Win2K
```

Figure 1.17 Files for Illustrating `diff`.

```
[rjschal@seahunt rjschal]$ diff -b -y --left-column lilo.conf.laptop lilo.conf.presario
prompt                                                      (
timeout=50                                                  (
default=linux                                               (
boot=/dev/hda                                               (
                                                            > map=/boot/map
                                                            > install=/boot/boot.b
                                                            > message=/boot/message
                                                            > lba32
                                                            (
image=/boot/vmlinuz-2.4.20-8                                | image=/boot/vmlinuz-2.4.7-10
     label=linux                                            (
     initrd=/boot/initrd-2.4.20-8.img                       |         initrd=/boot/initrd-2.4.7-10.img
     read-only                                              (
     root=/dev/hdb2                                         (
                                                            >         append="hdd=ide-scsi"
                                                            (
image=/dev/hda1                                             | other=/dev/hda1
     label=winXP                                            |         optional
     table=/dev/hda                                         |         label=Win2K
```

Figure 1.18 A `diff` Application to the Files of Figure 1.17.

1.7.1 Elements of Coding Style

More generally, conventions may be used to constrain many aspects of program development. This includes, but is not limited to:

1. Consistent use of abbreviations.

2. Naming conventions for user-chosen entities (e.g., variables, functions, predicates). This is often related to the use of case. Microsoft's Charles Simonyi introduced an identifier naming convention that adds a prefix to the identifier name to indicate the functional type of the identifier.

3. The use of case. In some instances (e.g., Prolog[24]) this is constrained by the language syntax. In other cases, options exist. It is typical for programmers to name descriptors (identifiers) after more abstract concepts. For example, in Lisp a list comprised of all binding lists might be named `all-binding-lists`, `list-of-all-binding-lists`, `allbindinglists`, `AllBindingLists`, or `allBindingLists`. The last option is often preferable in that it follows the convention that each new or distinct word in an identifier is capitalized.

4. The use of indentation and whitespace, including tabs.[25]

5. The structure and placement of comments (more on this below).

6. Formatting of program statements. An example is placement of curly braces for C statements such as function definitions and nested `for` loops.

---

[24]Variables must begin with an uppercase letter, predicates must not.

[25]Note that this may not always be just a stylistic feature; for example, a required and often overlooked tab in Makefiles often causes much trauma for beginners. Furthermore, tab use is somewhat controversial due to the often editor-specific definition of tabs.

7. Placement of comments and comment structure. Comments are generally useful if they are understandable, accurate, and do not overwhelm the source code.[26] Comments may be used to indicate changes, revisions and places to add features, extensions, and enhancements. Comments may even include ASCII art and mathematical derivations. This is closely related to documentation conventions, as described next.

1.7.2 Documentation (and Comments)

Software documentation is a part of the software engineering process and varies by project, objectives, resources, specification, and custom. It is not uncommon to use a large section of source file comments to indicate legal (copyright and licensing) constraints and disclaimers. It is useful to indicate basic usage (and perhaps compilation) information in source comment-based documentation, although large projects would include a Makefile and freestanding documentation. In addition, documentation often includes a change log describing changes made to program source files.

Freestanding documentation is often in the form of "man" pages. For example, according to the GNU convention, a manual should serve both as tutorial and program reference.

1.8 Some Humor: The Evolution of a Programmer

The following "Internet humor" is also a test for language familiarity—can you identify each programming approach?

High School/Junior High

```
10 PRINT "HELLO WORLD"
20 END
```

First Year in College

```
program Hello(input, output)
  begin
    writeln('Hello World')
  end.
```

Senior Year in College

```
(defun hello
  (print
    (cons 'Hello (list 'World))))
```

New Professional

```
#include
void main(void)
{
  char *message[] = {"Hello ", "World"};
  int i;
```

[26] This author is a major offender here.

```
  for(i = 0; i < 2; ++i)
    printf("%s", message[i]);
  printf("\n");
}
```

Seasoned Professional

```
class string
{
private:
  int size;
  char *ptr;

public:
  string() : size(0), ptr(new char('\0')) {}

  string(const string &s) : size(s.size)
  {
    ptr = new char[size + 1];
    strcpy(ptr, s.ptr);
  }

  ~string()
  {
    delete [] ptr;
  }

  friend ostream &operator <<(ostream &, const string &);
  string &operator=(const char *);
};

ostream &operator<<(ostream &stream, const string &s)
{
  return(stream << s.ptr);
}

string &string::operator=(const char *chrs)
{
  if (this != &chrs)
  {
    delete [] ptr;
   size = strlen(chrs);
    ptr = new char[size + 1];
    strcpy(ptr, chrs);
  }
  return(*this);
}

int main()
{
  string str;

  str = "Hello World";
  cout << str << endl;

  return(0);
}
```

Apprentice Hacker

```
#!/usr/local/bin/perl
$msg="Hello, world.\n";
if ($#ARGV >= 0) {
  while(defined($arg=shift(@ARGV))) {
    $outfilename = $arg;
    open(FILE, ">" . $outfilename) ||
         die "Can't write $arg: $!\n";
    print (FILE $msg);
    close(FILE) || die "Can't close $arg: $!\n";
  }
} else {
  print ($msg);
}
1;
```

Experienced Hacker

```
#include
#define S "Hello, World\n"
main(){exit(printf(S) == strlen(S) ? 0 : 1);}
```

New Manager

```
10 PRINT "HELLO WORLD"
20 END
```

Middle Manager

```
mail -s "Hello, world." bob@b12
Bob, could you please write me a program
that prints "Hello, world."?
I need it by tomorrow.
^D
```

Senior Manager

```
% zmail jim
I need a "Hello, world." program by
this afternoon.
```

Chief Executive

```
% letter
letter: Command not found.
% mail
To: ^X ^F ^C
% help mail
```

1.9 Bibliographical Remarks and References

1.9.1 Books and Journals

The history of programming, as we have shown, parallels that of machine computation. As such, it is an extraordinarily broad and well-covered topic. Excellent historical references are [Weg76, Wex81, BG96]. For a more recent historical perspective on software

http://www.cs.cmu.edu/afs/cs.cmu.edu/user/mleone/web/language/publications.html	Programming Language Journals, Books, and Publishers
http://www.cs.iastate.edu/~leavens/teaching-prog-lang/home.html	The Teaching About Programming Languages Project
http://perso.wanadoo.fr/levenez/lang/	Computer Languages History
http://dmoz.org/Computers/Programming/Languages/	Open Directory - Computers: Programming: Languages
http://merd.net/pixel/language-study/index.html	programming languages study
http://web.cs.mun.ca/~ulf/pld/pls.html	Ulf's Programming Language List
http://cui.unige.ch/OSG/info/Langlist/intro.html	Introduction to The Language List
http://www-2.cs.cmu.edu/~mleone/language-research.html	Resources for Programming Language Research
http://allserv.rug.ac.be/~vfack/files/proglan.html	Programming Languages
http://www.cs.cmu.edu/afs/cs.cmu.edu/user/mleone/web/language-research.html	Resources for Programming Language Research
http://www.csci.csusb.edu/dick/languages.html	Computer Languages Page
http://www.icnet.net/~timtroyr/funhouse/beer.html	99 Bottles of Beer on the Wall
http://www.hypernews.org/HyperNews/get/computing/lang-list.html	Hypernews Computing Languages List
http://www.uni-karlsruhe.de/~uu9r/lang/html/lang.en.html	Examples of programs in different programming languages
http://users.erols.com/ziring/dopl.html	Dictionary of Programming Languages
http://src.doc.ic.ac.uk/bySubject/Computing/Languages.html	On-line reference information about computer languages
http://directory.google.com/Top/Computers/Programming/Languages/	General place to start

Table 1.1 Selected Internet Sites for Programming Language References.

development, see [Eis02]. For a comprehensive history of selected computing machines, applications, and companies, the *IEEE Annals of the History of Computing* is hard to beat.

1.9.2 Web-Based References

The Internet provides a rich source of information on the history, current status, examples, and trends in programming language development. Table 1.1 is a useful starting point for Web-based programming language references.

1.10 Exercises

1. Programming languages are often compared and contrasted with so-called natural languages (used for human-human interaction). On the basis of your understanding of both, how are they similar (and different)?

2. Here is an (admittedly incomplete) list of languages. Your mission is to find out something about each one and answer the following questions. The presentation and content of your solution are both important. Cite your references or sources used.

    - What is it intended for? Who are the primary users?
    - How are its syntax/semantics described?
    - What are its strengths?
    - Who uses it?
    - What is its origin/history?
    - What type of language is it (imperative, declarative, functional, OO, scripting, other)?
    - Is it usually used in interpretive mode or is it compiled?
    - What does a code fragment look like?
    - What constructs in this language are worth special note?
    - Is it a special-purpose language?
    - Is it a high-performance language, (i.e., is it fast)?
    - Any other significant attributes?
    - What OS support it?

    (a) Ada
    (b) APL
    (c) Basic
    (d) BLISS
    (e) COBOL
    (f) Fortran
    (g) Forth
    (h) Hope
    (i) HTML
    (j) Java

(k) LaTeX
(l) LOGO
(m) Matlab
(n) Pascal
(o) Perl
(p) Python
(q) Scheme
(r) SQL(99)
(s) Tcl
(t) XML

3. The history of programming languages is rich with anecdotal entertainment. Here is some programming language trivia. See if you can name (or uncover) the language.

   - The "Green Project" team accidentally developed a programming language. What is it's name?
   - For the above "Green Team language," what was the planned name?
   - The creator of this language, in submitting it to the Internet Software Consortium, claimed it was a replacement for awk and sed. What is it?
   - This text-processing language was written in 1977 at AT&T Bell Labs and is named after its creators.
   - Many students come to believe that this language stands for Lots of Irritating Silly Parentheses.
   - The author of this language was a fan of a BBC comedy show from the 1970s that starred Graham Chapman, John Cleese, and Eric Idle. He named the language after the show.[27]
   - This was perhaps the first list processing language, intended for Rand Corporation's Johnniac computer. Hint: it is not Lisp.
   - The current version of this language is asymptotically approaching π.
   - Grace Hopper's research on early languages eventually led to the language FLOW-MATIC, which was the precursor of this language.

4. Eric Raymond's *The Cathedral and the Bazaar*, available at:

   `http://tuxedo.org/~esr/writings/cathedral-bazaar/`

   describes one form of an open software development model (the bazaar), as well as interesting notes on the evolution of Linux and hackerdom. It is required reading for aspiring software developers. After reading it, determine which of the following assertions are made in *The Cathedral and the Bazaar*:

   (a) The costs of duplicated work tend to scale linearly with team size.

[27] This is probably too easy.

(b) The open-source community can only be relied on to do work that is “sexy” or technically sweet; anything else will be left undone (or done only poorly) unless it is churned out by money-motivated cubicle peons with managers cracking whips over them.

(c) Provided the development coordinator has a medium at least as good as the Internet, and knows how to lead without coercion, many heads are inevitably better than one.

(d) To solve an interesting problem, start by finding a problem that is interesting to you.

(e) Release early. Release often. And listen to your customers.

(f) Perfection (in design) is achieved not when there is nothing more to add, but rather when there is nothing more to take away.

(g) The next best thing to having good ideas is recognizing good ideas from your users. Sometimes the latter is better.

(h) If you treat your beta-testers as if they are your most valuable resource, they will respond by becoming your most valuable resource.

(i) Smart data structures and dumb code work a lot better than the other way around.

(j) Good programmers know what to rewrite (and reuse). Great ones know what to write.

5. Section 1.6 illustrated the utility of a number of commonly used tools to enhance programming productivity. Shell scripts for program building were shown. Another very useful tool, especially for large software projects, is `make`. The operation of `make` is directed by a specially structured file called (and named as) a `Makefile`. A simple Makefile sample is shown in Figure 1.19.

   (a) Using the `GNU Make Manual` or `info make` (on a Unix system), show the role of each line in this file.

   (b) Suppose source code file `ga11.c` consists of a single text file that only includes the following `c` files:

   ```
   #include <stdlib.h>
   #include <stdio.h>
   #include <time.h>
   #include <math.h>
   ```

   Based upon your previous answer, how would the function of this Makefile be replaced by a single call to `gcc`? Specifically, what are the `gcc` parameters and switches necessary to produce an executable?

6. (This problem may be expanded into an excellent project.) One of the more interesting ways to become familiar with similarities and differences in programming languages is to consider *language translators*, software that converts (rewrites) a program written in one language (e.g., Pascal) into another (e.g., C). One such translator is `ptoc` (or `p2c`), which converts dialects of Pascal into C. Download a copy, install it, and see how it works.

```
#
# makefile for problem
#

CXX = gcc

PROGRAM = ga11

OBJECTS = $(PROGRAM).o

# implementation

.SUFFIXES: .o .c

.c.o :
$(CXX) -c -Wall -o $@ $<

all:    $(PROGRAM)

$(PROGRAM): $(OBJECTS)
$(CXX) -o $(PROGRAM) $(OBJECTS) -lm

clean:
rm -f *.o $(PROGRAM)
```

Figure 1.19 A Simple Makefile.

7. Many programs allow *plugins* for program extension. An example is the GNU Image Manipulation Program (GIMP). Discuss whether plugins of this sort should be considered extension languages.

8. Both SGML and XML are markup languages. Using the Web as a resource, determine the main features of each.

   (a) What are the differences between SGML and XML?

   (b) When would you choose one over the other?

9. Many (often interrelated) concerns influence the design of a programming language. Good judgment and compromise are essential.

   (a) These concerns include reserved words and symbols. Why is the asterisk used to indicate multiplication? For this problem, consider the FORTRAN (I) control statement:

   ```
   IF <arithmetic expression> n1, n2, n3
   ```

   which differs significantly from the C control construct syntax:

   ```
   if <condition> <statement>
   ```

   Because these syntactic fragments have a similar purpose, one might ask why this distinction is necessary. Was it just an arbitrary design decision? See if you can use an Internet search engine to cast some light on this historically significant decision.

(b) Other design decisions are more significant, and often controversial. Often the language design process concerns decisions about what to *leave out*, as well as what to include. For example, should a programming language allow or facilitate low-level memory management? Again, use the Internet as a research vehicle and explore both sides of this issue.

CHAPTER 2

From Formal Grammars to Programming Languages

High thoughts must have a high language.

—Aristophanes c. 450–385 BC

2.1 Prelude

In this chapter, we relate the syntax of a programming language to a formal grammar. Specifically, we cast the notions of programming and machine recognition of a program as the use of a grammar in the generative and recognition (parsing) modes, respectively.

2.2 A Syntactic Viewpoint: Programs are Strings

Consider the following code fragment:

```
void main(void)
  {
    char *message[] = {"Hello ", "World"};
    int i;

    for(i = 0; i < 2; ++i)
      printf("%s", message[i]);
    printf("\n");
}
```

Although the structure and intent of this code are apparent to C programmers, two somewhat subtle points need to be made:

- *In the context of our discussion, the end-user or "consumer" of this code is not a programmer, but rather a compiler.* The compiler will attempt to determine if the code is syntactically correct, and if so, will determine the semantics of the constructs used by the programmer. Following that, the "back end" of the compiler will produce machine code for a target machine.
- The code or program may be visualized as a string of terminals or "tokens."

Thus, from the compiler viewpoint, the code might as well appear as follows:

```
void main(void) { char *message[] = {"Hello ", "World"}; int i; for(i = 0;
i < 2; ++i) printf("\%s", message[i]); printf("\n"); }
```

To illustrate further, consider another simple C function:

```
int square (int x)
{
    return x * x;
}
```

The compiler (to be precise, the scanner) sees this code fragment with whitespace (e.g., line feeds, tabs, spaces) removed, as the string:

```
i n t s q u a r e ( i n t x ) { r e t u r n x * x ; }
```

Thus, from the viewpoint of machine interpretation, the visual formatting of the two previous examples is essentially irrelevant. Apparently, the structure of the desired computation is conveyed independently of "pretty printing." In these examples, all the high-level meaning a reader might attribute to the code is lost. The source code is merely a sequence of symbols. *This sequence (string, actually) is characterized via formal grammars.* The programming language that allows production of these strings exists to facilitate communication between the programmer and the compiler.

2.3 Formal Grammars

We first develop a general and formal mathematical description of the notion of a **language**, L. The descriptors "language" and "sentence" connote a far broader meaning than spoken words. In very general terms, a language is a mechanism that permits the expression of general ideas. We are careful to note: *Languages are generated by grammars.* Most importantly, the syntax of a programming language may be described through specification of a grammar. There are many different types of grammars.

2.3.1 Example: English-Language Sentence Formation via Productions (Rewrite Rules)

We begin a study of formal definitions of grammars and parsing approaches with a simple example. Consider the following English-language sentence:[1] "The quarterback throws accurately."

This sentence could have been produced using the following sequence of "rewriting" rules:

1. <sentence>
2. <noun phrase> <verb phrase>
3. <article>[2] <noun> <verb phrase>
4. The <noun> <verb phrase>

---

[1]Temporarily ignore the significance of the capital letter at the beginning and the period at the end and concentrate on the formation and structure of this sentence.

[2]Also referred to as a "determiner"; may be an adverb or adjective.

5. The quarterback <verb phrase>
6. The quarterback <verb> <adverb>
7. The quarterback throws <adverb>
8. The quarterback throws accurately.

Note the gradual elimination of intermediate and relatively nonspecific entities such as "noun" and "adverb." The sequence that led to the production of the above sentence could be cataloged according to the above sequence of rewrites or substitutions. We will later develop a graphical tool, the derivation tree, for this purpose.

2.3.2 Programming Language Syntax Specification and Productions

Typically, the syntax of a programming language may be written using a set of reserved words (primitives or tokens) and rules (productions) for combining these reserved words to form programs. For example, a part of the lexical syntax of Pascal may be shown in BNF (Backus Naur Form):

$$\begin{aligned} function - identifier &::= identifier \\ identifier &::= letter\{letter - or - digit\}^* \\ letter &::= a|b|c|\ldots|z|\ldots|A|\ldots|Z \\ digit &::= 0|1|2|3|4|\ldots|9 \\ letter - or \;-\; digit &::= letter|digit \end{aligned}$$

where ::= means "is defined as" or "may be replaced by," | denotes "or," and $\{\}^*$ indicates items that may be repeated zero or more times.

2.3.3 What Does This Have to Do With a Programming Language Compiler?

Part of a compiler is a *grammatical recognizer* or *parser*. Here we make two important points:

- A compiler or interpreter for a (higher-level) language attempts to generate lower-level machine instructions by determining the desired structure of the input high-level language program. An initial step is *parsing* the input or source code.
- The compiler or interpreter begins with processing the program as an input string, and this processing is based on a formal specification of the programming language syntax. In our case, the specification will be through a formal grammar.

2.3.4 Strings: Definitions and Conventions

An Alphabet

An **alphabet** (V) is a finite, nonempty set of *symbols*, for example

$$V = \{a, b, c, \ldots z\}$$

The concatenation of a and b, denoted $a \circ b$, produces a sequence of two symbols simply denoted hereafter as ab.

Forming Strings

A **string** or sentence over V is either a single symbol from V or a sequence of symbols formed by concatenation of zero or more symbols from V. Therefore, using the V shown above, a ab az and $azab$ are strings or sentences over V.

String Length

The length of (or number of symbols in) string s is denoted $|s|$. A string has a natural ordering of elements from left to right. Often it is convenient to denote a string like $x = aaa \ldots a$, where a symbol (or sequence of symbols) is repeated n times as $x = a^n$. For example:

$$aabbbcccc = a^2b^3c^4$$

The Null String and Closure

The empty string or empty sentence, denoted ϵ or λ, has the property that for any string

$$x \circ \epsilon = \epsilon \circ x = x$$

and also

$$|\epsilon| = 0$$

Derivable (Unconstrained) Strings

Denoting

$$V \circ V = V^2$$

as the set of all strings of length 2 derivable from V, and

$$V \circ V \circ V = V^3$$

as the set of all strings of length 3, we may continue this process up to V^n.

The Closure Set

Define V^+ as

$$V^+ = V \cup V^2 \cup V^3 \cup \ldots$$

V^+ is the set of all nonempty sentences producible using V. Adding the empty string to V^+ produces V^*, that is,

$$V^* = \{\epsilon\} \cup V^+$$

V^* is denoted the closure (set) of V and $V^+ = V^* - \{\epsilon\}$ is often called the *positive closure* of V. The sentences produced using these sets need not be finite in length.

Languages, Grammars, and Strings

The following is very important:

Grammars are used with V to give some meaning to a subset of strings, $L \subseteq V^*$.

L is called a language. Furthermore:

- Languages are generated by grammars.
- Another viewpoint is that a grammar restricts the production of strings from V.
- Grammars are used to recognize (parse) elements of a language.

Union, Concatenation, and Iterates

Given two languages, L_1 and L_2, over some alphabet V (i.e., $L_1 \subseteq V^*$ and $L_2 \subseteq V^*$),

1. The **union** of L_1 and L_2 is
$$L_1 \cup L_2 = \{s|s \in L_1 \textit{ or } s \in L_2\}$$
2. The **concatenation**, denoted $\circ$, of L_1 and L_2 is
$$L_1 \circ L_2 = \{s|s = s_1 s_2 \text{ where } s_1 \in L_1 \text{ and } s_2 \in L_2\}$$
3. The **iterate** of L_1, denoted $L_1^{iterate}$ is
$$L_1^{iterate} = \{s|s = s_1 s_2 \ldots s_n,\ n \geq 0 \text{ and } s_i \in L_1\}$$

For strings $x, y \in V^*$, string y is a *substring* of x if V^* contains strings u and v such that
$$x = uyv$$

2.3.5 Grammar: Formal Definition

A **grammar**
$$G = (V_T, V_N, P, S)$$
consists of the following four entities:

1. A set of terminal or primitive symbols (primitives), denoted V_T (or, alternately, Σ). These are the elemental "building blocks" of the grammar (and corresponding language).
2. A set of nonterminal symbols, *or* variables, which are used as intermediate quantities in the generation of an outcome consisting solely of terminal symbols. This set is denoted as V_N (or, alternately, N).

   Note that V_T and V_N are disjoint sets, that is, $V_T \cap V_N = \emptyset$.
3. A set of **productions**, or production rules or rewriting rules, which govern how strings may be formed. It is this set of productions, coupled with the terminal symbols, that principally gives the grammar its structure. The set of productions is denoted P.
4. A starting (or root) symbol, denoted S. $S \in V_N$.

2.3.6 Constraining Grammar Productions

Given V_T and V_N, the productions, P, place restrictions on the formation of strings using G. For example, it is reasonable to constrain elements of P to the form[3]

$$\alpha \rightarrow \beta$$

where

$$\alpha \in (V_N \cup V_T)^+ - V_T^+$$

and

$$\beta \in (V_N \cup V_T)^*$$

Thus, string α must consist of at least one member of V_N, (i.e., a non-terminal), and string β is allowed to consist of any arrangement of terminals and nonterminals. This is a partial characterization of **phrase structure grammar**.

2.3.7 Grammar Application Modes

A grammar may be used in one of two modes:

1. *Generative:* The grammar is used to create a string of terminal symbols using P; a *sentence* in the language of the grammar is thus generated.

2. *Analytic:* Given a sentence (possibly in the language of the grammar), together with specification of G, one seeks to determine:

   (a) if the sentence was generated by G; and if so,

   (b) the structure (usually characterized as the sequence of productions used) of the sentence. This is where we begin to consider semantics.

2.3.8 Languages, Possible Strings, and $L(G)$

Any subset $L \subseteq V_T^*$ is a *language*. If $|L|$ is finite, the language is called finite; otherwise it is infinite.

The *language generated by grammar G*, denoted $L(G)$, is the set of all strings that satisfy these conditions:

1. Each string consists solely of terminal symbols from V_T of G.

2. Each string was produced from S using P of G.

The use of graphical constructs for a grammar in either the generative or analytic mode is common. In the generative mode we may show a *derivation tree*, whereas in the analytic mode we may use a *parse tree*. These are treated in Section 2.4.

---

[3]Meaning string α replaces string β. Recall BNF uses the notation `::=` in place of the arrow.

2.3.9 String Grammar Types

We use the following formal notation:

1. Symbols beginning with a capital letter (e.g., S_1 or S) are elements of V_N.
2. Symbols beginning with a lowercase letter (e.g., a or b) are elements of V_T.
3. n denotes the length of string s, that is,

$$n = |s|$$

4. Greek letters (e.g., α, β) represent (possibly empty) strings, typically comprised of terminals and/or nonterminals.

Constraining Productions in String Grammars

Constraints on the production or rewrite rules, P, in string grammar G are explored by considering the general production form:

$$\alpha_1 \to \beta_2 \tag{2.1}$$

which means string α_1 is replaced by string β_2. In general, α_1 and β_2 may contain terminals and/or nonterminals.

Four types of grammars have been delineated by Chomsky.

Type 0 or T_0: Free or Unrestricted A T_0 grammar has no restrictions on the rewrite rules, and is of little practical significance.

Type 1 or T_1: Context-Sensitive A T_1 or context-sensitive (CS) grammar restricts productions to the form:

$$\alpha\alpha_i\beta \to \alpha\beta_i\beta$$

meaning β_i replaces α_i *in the context of* α *and* β, where $\alpha,\ \beta \in (V_N \cup V_T)^*, \alpha_i \in V_N$, and $\beta_i \in (V_N \cup V_T)^* - \{\epsilon\}$. Note that α or β (or both) may equal ϵ.

Context-sensitive grammars allow the production of the empty string,[4] but with restrictions.

Type 2 or T_2: Context Free In a T_2 or context-free grammar (CFG), the production restrictions, using equation 2.1, are:

$$\alpha_1 = S_1 \in V_N$$

that is, α_1 *must be a single nonterminal* for every production in P:

$$|S_1| \le |\beta_2|$$

---

[4]Question for the reader: Why do you think we care about restrictions on producing ϵ in a programming language?

An alternate characterization of a T_2 grammar is that every production must be of the form:

$$S_1 \rightarrow \beta_2$$

where $\beta_2 \in (V_N \cup V_T)^+$. Note that a CFG production allows S_1 to be replaced by string β_2 *independently or irrespective of the context in which* S_1 *appears.* Context-free grammars and the class of context-free languages they generate are paramount in the study of programming languages, because they are reasonably adequate for describing the syntax of many programming languages. More on this later.

Notice that T_1 and T_2 grammars can generate a string of terminals and/or nonterminals in a single production. Moreover, productions of the form $A \rightarrow \alpha A \beta$ are allowed. This is an example of grammars that are *self-embedding.*

It is also worth noting:

- Context-free grammars are important because they are the most descriptively versatile grammars for which effective (and efficient) parsers are available.
- *The production restrictions increase in going from context-sensitive (T_1) to context-free (T_2) cases.*

Type 3 or T_3: Finite-State or Regular Regular or finite-state grammars are common. The production restrictions in a T_3 grammar are, using the notation of equation 2.1, those of a T_2 grammar, plus the additional restriction that *at most one nonterminal symbol is allowed on each side of the production.* That is,

$$\alpha_1 = S_1 \in V_N$$

$$|S_1| \leq |\beta_2|$$

and productions are restricted to:

$$A_1 \rightarrow a$$

or

$$A_1 \rightarrow aA_2$$

Finite-state grammars are parsed or recognized with finite state machines.

Phrase-Structure Grammars

A *phrase-structure grammar* constrains productions as follows:

$$\alpha \rightarrow \beta$$
$$\alpha \neq \epsilon$$

or more specifically,

$$\alpha \in \{V_T \cup V_N\}^* - \{\epsilon\} - \{V_T\}$$

Thus, string α must consist of at least one element of V_N. The constraint on β is:

$$\beta \in \{V_T \cup V_N\}^*$$

Regular Languages

A language is *regular* if:

1. L is finite; *or*
2. $L \in L_1 \cup L_2$, where L_1 and L_2 are regular; *or*
3. $L \in L_1 \circ L_2$ (concatenation) and L_1 and L_2 are regular; *or*
4. $L \in L_1^{iterate}$ where L_1 is regular.

Recursive and Definite Grammars

G is **recursive** if it allows at least one derivation of the form

$$S_1 \Rightarrow \alpha S_1 \beta$$

where $S_1 \in V_N$ and $\alpha, \beta \in (V_T \cup V_N)^*$. A recursive grammar, G_R, generates a $L(G_R)$ where $|L(G_R)| = \infty$. Recursive grammars often yield compact representations for class-specific pattern generation. If G is not recursive, G is said to be a **definite** grammar. $|L(G)|$ is finite for a definite grammar.

Right- and Left-Linear Languages

Subclasses of context-free grammars, known as linear grammars, are important. A **right-linear language** denoted $LR(k)$, is generated by a right-linear grammar, where P has the following production restrictions:

$$A \rightarrow bC$$

or

$$A \rightarrow b$$

where

$$A \in V_N$$
$$b \in V_T \cup \{\epsilon\}$$

Similarly, a **left-linear language**, denoted $LL(k)$, constrains P to productions of the form:

$$A \rightarrow Ab$$

or

$$A \rightarrow c$$

$$S \rightarrow AB$$
$$S \rightarrow C$$
$$A \rightarrow C$$
$$A \rightarrow a$$
$$B \rightarrow b$$
$$B \rightarrow c$$
$$C \rightarrow d$$

(a) Formal Notation

```
<s> ::= <a><b> | <c>
<a> ::= <c> | a
<b> ::= b | c
<c> ::= d
```

(b) BNF

Figure 2.1 Productions for Sample Grammar, G_s.

2.3.10 A Sample G: Determining Grammar Type and $L(G)$

Suppose we had the set of productions for a grammar, G_s, shown in Figure 2.1. Note that the formal representation of the productions is shown along with a BNF version.

Assuming S is the starting symbol and that V_T and V_N may be inferred from the productions, we can formally characterize G_s. Now suppose we ask the following questions:

1. What type(s) of grammar do we have?
2. What is $L(G_s)$ corresponding to G_s?

To answer the first question, note that any grammar is a free or T_0 grammar. Also note (the reader should verify this) that the production constraints for a context-sensitive and context-free grammar are satisfied. Other types are considered in the exercises. To answer the second question, we could speculatively produce strings of terminals. This is left to the reader; we will use Prolog to do this as well.

2.3.11 Representation/Parsing Tradeoffs

Returning to a slight modification of the simple example syntax shown previously, consider the following two productions from a CFG grammar in BNF form:

```
<decl> ::= <type> <variable>;
<return-arg> ::= lparens <variable> rparens
```

Assuming a nonempty declaration of some integer variable, such as `t`, we could produce code of the form:[5]

```
int main(void)
{
 int t;
 t=10.0101;
 return(void);
}
```

Although the CFG syntax of the language would allow production of this code, notice that we are violating type specifications in two places. This is allowable, at the syntactic

[5]Not all of the syntax that would allow this is shown.

level, because the CFG productions do not require a variable name, declared to be of some type, to keep this type in subsequent appearances. Additional shortcomings of CFGs will be cited later. Thus, a strong case can often be made for the use of context-sensitive grammars for programming language description.[6]

In progressing from a T_0 to a T_4 grammar, notice that as production restrictions increase, representational power decreases. At the same time, increasing production restrictions leads to simpler parsers. In parsing strings in a T_1 grammar, the number of contextual possibilities for each of the rewrite rules would need to be considered. The number of recognition steps in such a parser becomes combinatorially explosive.

Parsing complexity in a T_2 grammar is a linear function of the number of rewrite rules in a derivation. As shown, using CFGs may result in syntactically correct programs with nonsense semantics. Similarly, a CFG, although perhaps more descriptively versatile than a finite-state grammar, requires a more complex parser than that of a finite-state machine.

Denoting $L(T_i)$ as the class of language generated by grammar T_i, the preceding restrictions indicate:

$$L(T_3) \subset L(T_2) \subset L(T_1) \subset L(T_0)$$

2.3.12 The Non-uniqueness of G, Given L

Grammars generate languages, but there is no unique relationship between a given language and a grammar. In other words, a language L may be generated by several different grammars, that is, $L = L(G_1) = L(G_2)$. This raises interesting questions in the design of grammars for programming.

Equivalence of Grammars Two grammars, G_1 and G_2 are *equivalent* if $L(G_1) = L(G_2)$. Grammar equivalence has the following ramifications:

1. If G_1 and G_2 are finite-state grammars, an algorithm to determine if they are equivalent exists.

2. If G_1 and G_2 are context-free grammars, a general algorithm to test for equivalence does not exist.

Another important observation is that two different and non-equivalent grammars may generate one or more identical strings.

2.4 Using Grammars: Derivation Trees and Ambiguity

2.4.1 The Derivation (or Parse) Tree

The use of a sequence of specific productions in a formal language G may be cataloged in graphical form as a **derivation tree**. Because the parsing process attempts to "invert" the use of the grammar in generative mode, this tree is also referred to as a *parse tree*. The class of derivation trees described next is restricted to context-free grammars.

A derivation or parse tree, T, has the following characteristics:

1. The root of T is the starting symbol $S \in V_N$.

2. Leaf nodes of T are terminals $\in V_T$.

[6] Aside: How would you enforce context using a context-sensitive grammar?

3. Interior[7] nodes are nonterminals $\in V_N$.

4. The children of any nonleaf node[8] represent the right-hand side (RHS) of some production in P, where the parent node represents the corresponding left-hand side (LHS) of the production.

Note that the production, and consequent parsing, of any given string, $x \in L(G)$, may occur with a nonunique sequence of productions. At any given time in the generation of the string (program?), several alternative productions may be employed for replacement of nonterminals. Derivation trees are particularly important when cataloging the production of x, because except in cases of grammatical ambiguity they allow us to see the structure of x *independently of the possible sequences.* This is best seen with an example.

2.4.2 Derivation Tree Example

Recall the productions in an earlier grammar:

$$S \rightarrow AB$$
$$S \rightarrow C$$
$$A \rightarrow C$$
$$A \rightarrow a$$
$$B \rightarrow b$$
$$B \rightarrow c$$
$$C \rightarrow d$$

First, we show the derivation of string dc. Before drawing the tree, we see this string could be produced by the following sequence of replacements (the reader should identify the corresponding production sequence):

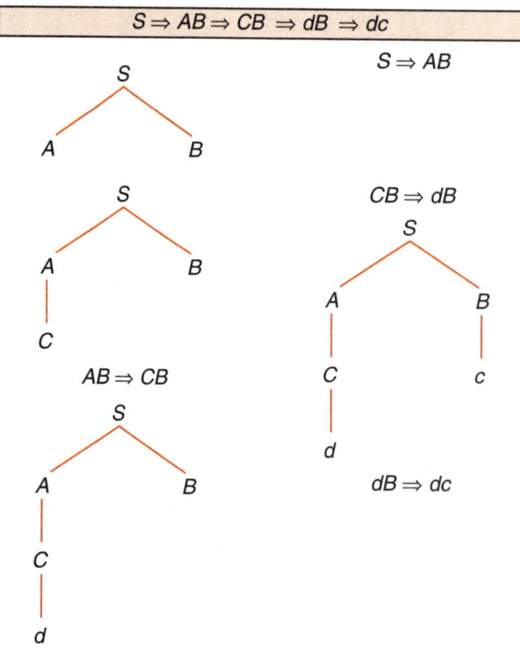

[7]Neither root nor leaf.

[8]Recall leaf nodes have no children.

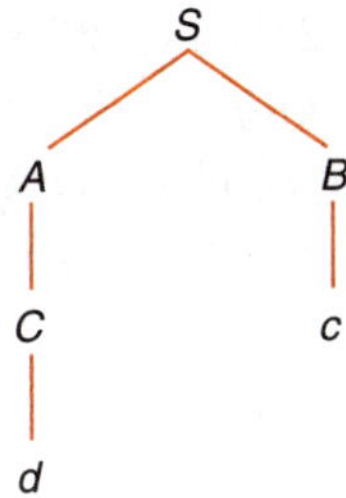

Figure 2.2 Derivation Tree Using the Production Sequence $S \Rightarrow AB \Rightarrow CB \Rightarrow dB \Rightarrow dc$.

Figure 2.2 shows the final derivation tree corresponding to this sequence of productions.

Now consider an alternative derivation *sequence* for the same string:

$$S \Rightarrow AB \Rightarrow Ac \Rightarrow Cc \Rightarrow dc$$

Development of the derivation tree with this sequence proceeds as follows:

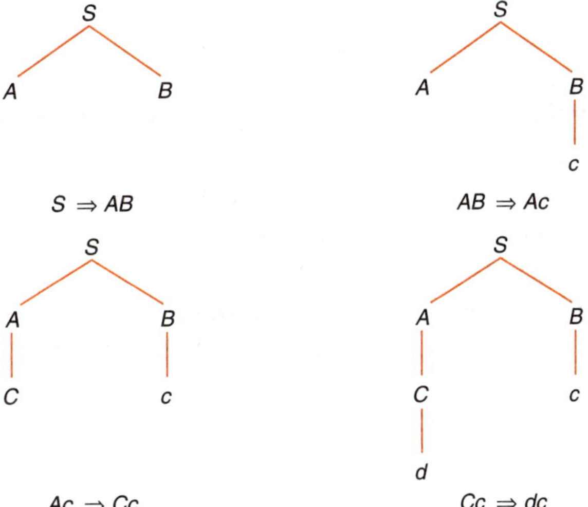

Figure 2.3 shows the corresponding final tree for this different production *sequence*.

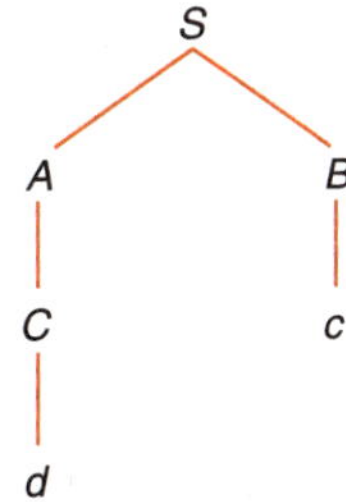

Figure 2.3 Derivation Tree Using the Production Sequence $S \Rightarrow AB \Rightarrow Ac \Rightarrow Cc \Rightarrow dc$.

Remark It is apparent that Figures 2.2 and 2.3 show the same (final) derivation tree. *Note that a different sequence (of the same productions) yielded the same derivation tree. This illustrates the importance of the derivation tree in providing a sequence-independent, graphical depiction of the derivation (or parse) of a string* $\in L(G)$.

2.4.3 Grammatical or Syntactic Ambiguity

With the definition of a derivation tree, the concept of grammar ambiguity may be phrased another way:

> *A grammar is ambiguous if any string in* $L(G)$[9] *has two or more distinct derivation trees.*

We will explore possible grammatical ambiguity in the syntax of a language using `minic` later.

Classic Examples of Ambiguity Classic examples of potential ambiguity encountered in programming languages include the following:

- Strings employing binary mathematical operators. For example, what is the underlying structure of:

$$a = b + c * a$$

  Of course, specification of operator precedence together with the syntax specification may eliminate this problem.
- The use of nested "if-then-(optional) else" constructs. This is a major source of potential ambiguity, and so the syntax specification is usually augmented with a description of the corresponding interpretation algorithm.
- Confusion between function invocation and array use. For example, how would you interpret: $a(2)$? Is this function a called with argument 2 or the second (or third) element of array a?

2.5 BNF and Alternatives

As noted previously, the syntax of a programming language is expressed in a formal notation, most often the metalanguage[10] of Backus Naur Form (BNF).

2.5.1 Alternatives to BNF for Syntax Specification

Although BNF syntax descriptions are ubiquitous, there are alternatives, including graphical approaches and the use of regular expressions. We show examples of both.

2.5.2 Graphical Descriptions of Syntax

Productions may be represented using directed graphs (digraphs). Using digraphs, visual presentation of the programming language syntax is often easier to understand.

[9]The language generated by grammar G.

[10]A metalanguage is a language used to describe another language.

Pascal

The Pascal programming language provides an excellent example of visual presentation of language syntax. Figures 2.4 and 2.5 show representations for the syntax corresponding to nonterminals <`program`> and <`block`>, respectively.

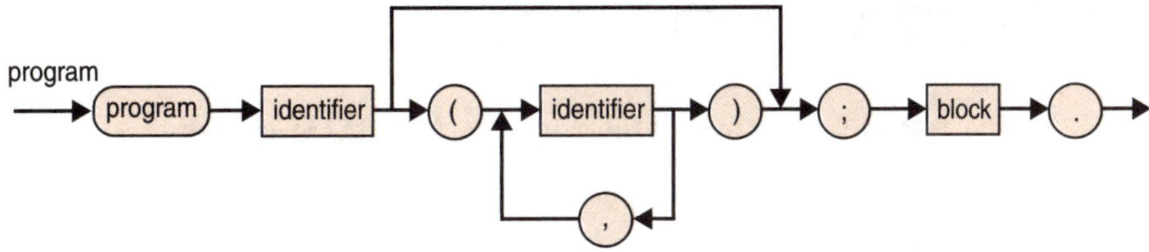

Figure 2.4 Syntax Diagram for Pascal `program`.

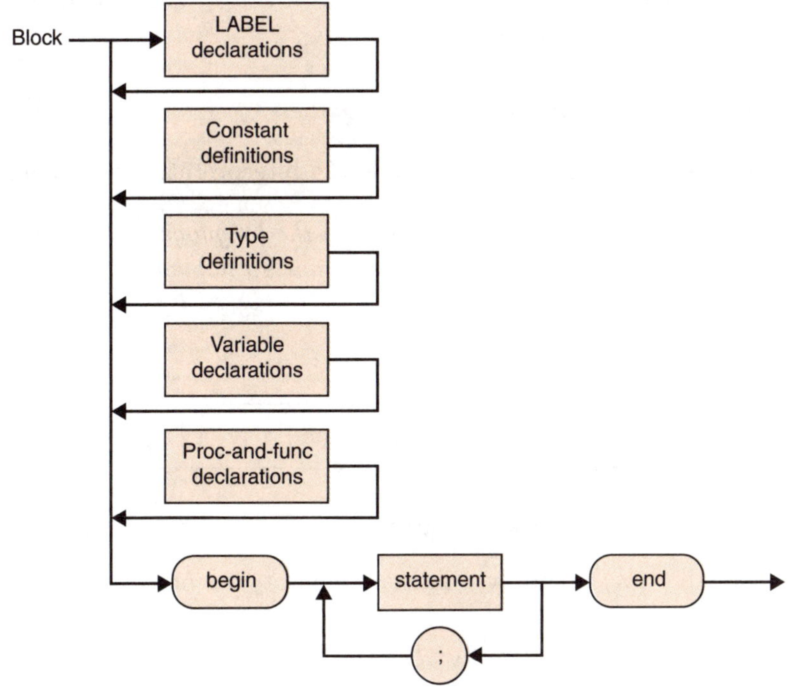

Figure 2.5 Syntax Diagram for Pascal `block`.

Ada

Similarly, a digraph for the representation of the Ada `if` statement is shown in Figure 2.6.

2.5.3 Definition: Regular Expressions

A **regular expression** (RE) may be characterized in many ways. For one, a RE is shorthand for abbreviating a pattern or set of patterns. For our purposes, a regular expression is an alternative for describing the syntax of a language. Regular expressions are typically constructed by using various operators to combine smaller regular expressions. Thus, they are often considered building blocks.

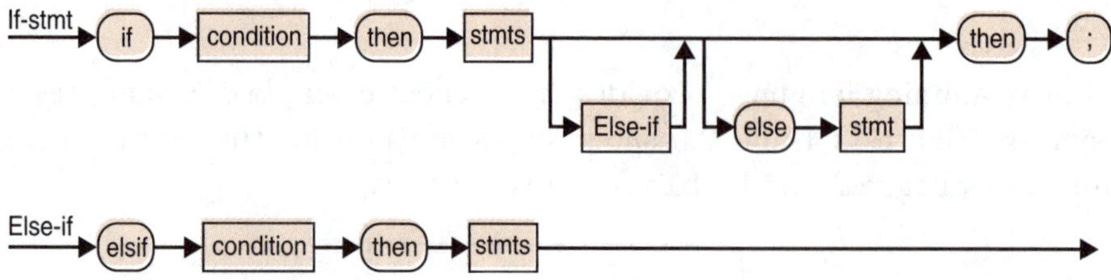

Figure 2.6 Syntax Diagram for Ada `if` Statement.

Aside: Regular Expressions and UNIX In a UNIX environment, one popular concept (a tool, actually) is the RE. A variety of UNIX tools and commands use REs. For example, GNU `grep` is a general RE parser and search engine used to perform free-text searches. In other tools, REs are often provided as "power user" options. For example, the editor `vi` allows patterns of character strings to be input as REs so that it can either display or modify the occurrences of that pattern.

2.5.4 Regular Expressions and Languages

When a set of REs is used to define a language, the interpretation is straightforward.

> *If a regular expression represents a pattern in the language, strings that match the pattern are in the language, and strings that do not match the pattern are not in the language.*

We now get more formal.

A regular expression, E defines a language $L(E)$, over V_T.

Primitive Regular Expressions and Notation

Recall that an alphabet (V) is simply a finite, nonempty set of symbols, such as

$$V = \{a, b, 1, 2, +, -, \dots\}$$

In our approach to formal grammars, we have defined strings (programs and program fragments) over some alphabet, V_T or Σ. In terms of REs:

1. The empty string or "empty sentence" is denoted ϵ.
2. No string is indicated by $\emptyset$.
3. The concatenation of a and b, denoted $a \circ b$, produces a sequence of two symbols often simply denoted as the string ab.
4. The choice of either symbol a or b, denoted $a|b$ or $a + b$, produces either a or b.

The fundamental building blocks are the regular expressions that match a single character. Most characters, including all letters and digits, are regular expressions (which match themselves).

RE	Correspondıng Language, $L\,(RE)$
$\emptyset$	$\emptyset$
ϵ	$\{\epsilon\}$
x	$\{x\}$

Table 2.1 Primitive Languages.

Three Primitive REs

Regular expressions are typically constructed by using various operators to combine smaller regular expressions.

Two of the three primitive REs are the empty string, ϵ, and the empty set, $\emptyset$. Furthermore, for each element, x, of the alphabet V_T, that is, $x \in V_T$, x is an RE. This yields the corresponding languages shown in Table 2.1.

Composite REs

Using recursion, we now "bootstrap" our way to a richer set of regular expressions. Note that x^* denotes zero or more repetitions of x, for example, the language $\{\epsilon, x, xx, xxx, \dots\}$ (or $\{\epsilon, x, x \circ x, x \circ x \circ x, \dots\}$).

Let RE be any RE, generating the corresponding language $L(RE)$. E^* denotes zero or more repetitions of E.

Regular Expression	Corresponding Language, $L\,(RE)$	Comments
x^*	$\{L\,(x)\}^* = \{\epsilon, x, xx, xxx, ...\}$	Zero or more x
$x \circ y$	$L\,(x) \circ L\,(y) = \{x \circ y\}$	
E	$L\,(E)$	
E^*	$\{L\,(E)\}^*$	
$E \circ F$	$L\,(E) \circ L\,(F) = L\,(E)\,L\,(F)$	$\{x, y \mid x \in L\,(E) \cap y \in L\,(F)\}$
$E \mid F = E + F$	$L\,(E) + L\,(F)$	$\{x \mid x \in L\,(E) \cup x \in L\,(F)\}$
$E^+ = E \circ E^*$		No empty (one or more) strings
$E^? = \epsilon \mid E$		Empty or one string
E^n		nEs

2.5.5 RE Application to Description of Syntax

Consider the self-embedding BNF production below. This is used to define a portion of the lexical syntax of a language.

$$< numeral > ::= < digit > \mid < digit >< numeral >$$

Using this production, (assuming **<digit>** is defined to produce the set of digits $1 \dots 9$), we are able to produce the following strings from **<numeral>**:

$$1 \qquad 12 \qquad 123 \qquad 123123$$

Alternately, as an RE, the previous production may be represented as:

$$< numeral > ::= < digit > \circ < digit >^*$$

or

$$< numeral > ::= < digit >^+$$

2.6 Bibliographical Remarks and References

Early attempts to characterize languages via a taxonomy are due to Chomsky [Cho57]. Useful introductions to formal grammars are [HU69], [AU72], and [RMK88]. Note that the use of formal grammars extends beyond programming languages; for example, they play an important role in syntactic pattern recognition [Sch92], and even music [Roa79].

2.7 Exercises

1. Consider the syntax of a favorite programming language, specifically the *underlying grammar*. What type of a grammar is it?

2. Given $V = \{a, b\}$, show V^2, V^3, and V^4.

3. Distinguish between, or relate, a phrase structure grammar and

   (a) A free grammar.

   (b) A context-sensitive grammar.

4. A part of the lexical syntax for `minic` is shown below in Figure 2.7. Show a derivation (series of replacements) and the derivation tree for the `<identifier>` "himom."

```
/* lexical part (user identifiers and numerals)
   of the syntax */

<identifier> ::= <letter> | <identifier> <letter>
                          |  <identifier> <digit>

<letter> ::= a | b | c | d | e | f | g | h | i | j
               | k | l | m | n | o | p | q | r | s
               | t | u | v | w | x | y | z

<numeral> ::= <digit> | <digit> <numeral>

<digit> ::= 0|1|2|3|4|5|6|7|8|9
```

Figure 2.7 Portion of Lexical Syntax of `minic`

5. Which of the following are true?

   (a) A regular grammar is a context-free grammar.

   (b) A regular grammar is a free grammar.

   (c) A context-free grammar is a context-sensitive grammar.

   (d) A context-sensitive grammar is a context-free grammar.

6. Show that the following grammar can be used to generate the language of equilateral triangles, that is, $L(G) = \{a^n b^n c^n \text{ for } n > 1\}$.

$$\begin{aligned} S &\rightarrow aSBA|aBA \\ AB &\rightarrow BA \\ bB &\rightarrow bb \\ bA &\rightarrow bc \\ cA &\rightarrow cc \\ aB &\rightarrow ab \end{aligned}$$

   What type(s) of grammar is this grammar?

7. Suppose you are given the language, L, where $L = \{a^n b | n = 1, 2, \dots\}$. Derive three different types of grammars that generate L.

8. Define a grammar that produces the language

$$L = \{a^n b^{n+1} | n > 0\}$$

9. Given $V_T = \{a, b\}$ and $V_N = \{F, G\}$, determine $(V_N \cup V_T)^*$ and $(V_N \cup V_T)^* - V_T^*$.

10. Given a grammar G_{BIN}, where

$$G_{BIN} = \{V_T^{BIN}, V_N^{BIN}, P^{BIN}, S^{BIN}\}$$

   with

$$\begin{aligned} V_T^{BIN} &= \{0, 1\} \\ V_N^{BIN} &= \{S\} = S^{BIN} \\ P^{BIN} &= \{S \rightarrow 0 \\ S &\rightarrow 0S \\ S &\rightarrow 1 \\ S &\rightarrow 1S \\ S &\rightarrow \epsilon\} \end{aligned}$$

   Determine $L(G_{BIN})$.

11. Consider the grammar, G_{test}, shown in Figure 2.8, with starting nonterminal S.

    (a) What type(s) of grammar is G_{test}?

    (b) Is the string $abcd \in L(G_{test})$?

$$V_n = \{S, A, B, C, D, E, F, G\}, \quad V_r = \{a, b, c, d\}$$

and P:

$S \rightarrow aAB$,	$DB \rightarrow FB$,	$dFB \rightarrow dFd$
$A \rightarrow aAC$,	$ED \rightarrow Gd$,	$dFd \rightarrow Fdd$
$A \rightarrow D$,	$cG \rightarrow Gc$,	$cF \rightarrow Fc$
$Dc \rightarrow cD$,	$dG \rightarrow Gd$,	$bF \rightarrow bbc$
$Dd \rightarrow dD$,	$aG \rightarrow abcD$,	$aF \rightarrow ab$
$DC \rightarrow EC$,	$bG \rightarrow bbcD$,	$bB \rightarrow bcd$
$EC \rightarrow Ed$		

Figure 2.8 Production in Grammar G_{test}.

12. Given G_{test2}, where

$$G_{test2} = \{\Sigma = (a, b, c), N = (S, A, B, C, D, E), P, S\}$$

with productions P:

$$S \rightarrow aAB$$
$$S \rightarrow aB$$
$$A \rightarrow aAC$$
$$A \rightarrow aC$$
$$B \rightarrow Dc$$
$$CD \rightarrow CE$$

(a) What type(s) of grammar(s) is G_{test2}?

(b) Which of the following strings are $\in L(G_{test2})$, (starting from the nonterminal S):

(i) aab

(ii) baC

(iii) aa

13. Given G_{test3}, where $G_{test3} = \{V_T = (a, b, c), V_N = (S, A, B, C, D, E), P, S\}$ with productions P:

$$S \rightarrow aAS$$
$$S \rightarrow aB$$
$$AS \rightarrow aAC$$
$$C \rightarrow S$$
$$SA \rightarrow aC$$
$$B \rightarrow Dc$$
$$D \rightarrow E$$
$$E \rightarrow b$$

Which of the following strings are $\in L(G_{test3})$, (starting from the nonterminal S):

(i) aab
(ii) ba
(iii) aC
(iv) bca

14. Given G_{rjs}, where $G_{rjs} = \{V_T = (a, b, c), V_N = (S, T, O), P, S\}$ with productions P:

$$\begin{aligned} S &\rightarrow abc|aTbc \\ Tb &\rightarrow bT \\ Tc &\rightarrow Obcc \\ aO &\rightarrow aa|aaT \\ bO &\rightarrow Ob \end{aligned}$$

(a) What type(s) of a grammar is G_{rjs}?
(b) Which of the following strings are $\in L(G_{rjs})$, (starting from the nonterminal S):

(i) aa
(ii) abc
(iii) $aOOa$
(iv) ab
(v) $aaabbbccc$

15. A sample grammar (used to show the CYK parsing algorithm) is given below.

$$\begin{aligned} S &\rightarrow AB|BB \\ A &\rightarrow CC|AB|a \\ B &\rightarrow BB|CA|b \\ C &\rightarrow BA|AA|b \end{aligned}$$

Show the derivation tree for the string $x = aabb$.

16. Using the graphical representation for the Ada **if** statement from Section 2.5.2 and shown in Figure 2.6, derive the corresponding BNF description.

17. True or False. If a right-linear language is restricted to $b \in V_T$, a right-linear grammar becomes a FSG.

18. Below are the productions (using BNF) for a grammar denoted $G_{problem}$. Recall in BNF that angular brackets, as in <**f**>, denote a nonterminal $\in V_N$, whereas a symbol without brackets, e.g., **f**, denotes a terminal $\in V_T$.

```
<a> ::= <b> <c>

<b> ::= <d> d <e>
```

```
<d> ::= a | e

<e> ::= l <d> r

<c> ::= m <f> n

<j> ::= b

<f> ::= <g> | <h> s <g>

<h> ::= <i> | <i> s <h>

<i> ::= <j> q <k>

<g> ::= f <l> s

<l> ::= l <j> r

<k> ::= c
```

(a) What type(s) of grammar is $G_{problem}$?

(b) Consider the following string:

```
a d l e r m b q c s f l b r s n
```

Prove that this string is an element of $L(G_{problem})$, where the starting symbol (S) is <a>. Recall that there are two constraints that must be satisfied. If you show this by a succession of strings derived from <a>, only show one replacement per line.

19. `cdecl`, a utility for decyphering and creating complex type declarations in `C`, was mentioned in Chapter 1. Inquiries at the operating system prompt (`$`) are of the form:

    `$ cdecl <program>`

    where <`program`> is the user query in an English-like language. For example, the user might phrase the inquiry[11] as:

    `$ cdecl declare myptr as pointer to char`

    wherein the `cdecl` utility responds with the desired `C` declaration:

    `char *myptr`

    The syntax of the grammar used for forming queries (derived from <`program`>) in `cdecl` is shown in the following modified man page excerpt.

```
The following grammar describes the language.  Words in "<>"  are non-terminals,
bare lower-case words are terminals that stand for themselves.
Bare upper-case words are other lexical tokens:
       NOTHING  means  the empty string;
       NAME means a valid C identifier;
       NUMBER means a string of decimal digits; and
       NL means the new-line or semi-colon characters.
```

[11] Assume all inquiries are terminated by a new-line character.

```
<program> ::= NOTHING
     | <program> <stmt> NL
<stmt>    ::= NOTHING
     | declare NAME as <adecl>
     | declare <adecl>
     | cast NAME into <adecl>
     | cast <adecl>
     | explain <optstorage> <ptrmodlist> <type> <cdecl>
     | explain <storage> <ptrmodlist> <cdecl>
     | explain ( <ptrmodlist> <type> <cast> ) optional-NAME
     | set <options>
     | help | ?
     | quit
     | exit
<adecl>   ::= array of <adecl>
     | array NUMBER of <adecl>
     | function returning <adecl>
     | function ( <adecl-list> ) returning <adecl>
     | <ptrmodlist> pointer to <adecl>
     | <ptrmodlist> pointer to member of class NAME <adecl>
     | <ptrmodlist> reference to <adecl>
     | <ptrmodlist> <type>
<cdecl>   ::= <cdecl1>
     | * <ptrmodlist> <cdecl>
     | NAME :: * <cdecl>
     | & <ptrmodlist> <cdecl>
<cdecl1>  ::= <cdecl1> ( )
     | <cdecl1> ( <castlist> )
     | <cdecl1> [ ]
     | <cdecl1> [ NUMBER ]
     | ( <cdecl> )
     | NAME
<cast>    ::= NOTHING
     | ( )
     | ( <cast> ) ( )
     | ( <cast> ) ( <castlist> )
     | ( <cast> )
     | NAME :: * <cast>
     | * <cast>
     | & <cast>
     | <cast> [ ]
     | <cast> [ NUMBER ]
<type>    ::= <typename> | <modlist>
     | <modlist> <typename>
     | struct NAME | union NAME | enum NAME | class NAME
<castlist>     ::= <castlist> , <castlist>
     | <ptrmodlist> <type> <cast>
     | <name>
<adecllist>    ::= <adecllist> , <adecllist>
     | NOTHING
     | <name>
     | <adecl>
     | <name> as <adecl>
<typename>     ::= int | char | double | float | void
<modlist> ::= <modifier> | <modlist> <modifier>
<modifier>     ::= short | long | unsigned | signed | <ptrmod>
<ptrmodlist>   ::= <ptrmod> <ptrmodlist> | NOTHING
<ptrmod>  ::= const | volatile | noalias
```

```
<storage> ::= auto | extern | register | auto
<optstorage>    ::= NOTHING | <storage>
<options> ::= NOTHING | <options>
     | create | nocreate
     | prompt | noprompt
     | ritchie | preansi | ansi | cplusplus
     | debug | nodebug | yydebug | noyydebug
```

On the basis of this syntax, determine which of the following are syntactically correct inquiries. (Extra credit: for each syntactically correct inquiry, what is returned by `cdecl`?)

```
$ cdecl declare imagein as pointer to array 100 of int

$ cdecl declare mychar as array of char

$ cdecl declare mystruct as array of struct

$ cdecl explain struct mystruct yourstruct

$ cdecl declare myint as int
```

20. Refer to the sample grammar G_s in Section 2.3.10.

    (a) In terms of grammar type:

        i. Is G_s a phrase structure grammar?

        ii. Is $L(G_s)$ a regular language?

        iii. Is $L(G_s)$ a right-linear or a left-linear language?

    (b) Can you enumerate $L(G_s)$?

21. If every production of a CFG has the form

$$A_1 \rightarrow \alpha B_1 \beta$$

or

$$A_1 \rightarrow \alpha$$

where $\alpha, \beta \in V_T^*$, $A_1, B_1 \in V_N$, and α and β are not *both* the empty string, a *linear grammar* results. Using this definition, show an example of a CFG that is not a linear grammar

22. One interesting and allowable aspect of a T_0 grammar is the possibility of "erasing productions," because the constraint $|\alpha_1| \leq |\beta_2|$ does not exist.

    How would this feature of a T_0 grammar make grammatical recognition (parsing) of a programming language virtually impossible?

23. MIDI is shorthand for Musical Instrument Digital Interface, a communications protocol that allows electronic musical instruments to communicate with each other. The MIDI protocol has been widely accepted and used by musicians and hardware developers. A proposed BNF specification for MIDI Streams is shown on the next page.[12]

[12]The leftmost number (e.g., "1," "2," "3,") for each BNF production is just for ease in referring to the production; it is not a part of the syntax.

```
1.  <MIDI Stream> ::=           <MIDI msg> < MIDI Stream>

2.  <MIDI msg> ::=              <sys msg> | <chan msg>

3.  <chan msg> ::=              <chan 1byte msg> | <chan 2byte msg>

4.  <chan 1byte msg> ::=        <chan stat1 byte> <data singlet> <running singlets>

5.  <chan 2byte msg> ::=        <chan stat2 byte> <data pair> <running pairs>

6.  <chan stat1 byte> ::=       <chan voice stat1 nibble> <hex nibble>

7.  <chan stat2 byte> ::=       <chan voice stat2 nibble> <hex nibble>

8.  <chan voice stat1 nibble>::= C | D

9.  <chan voice stat2 nibble>::= 8 | 9 | A | B | E

10. <hex nibble> ::=             0 | 1 | 2 | 3 | 4 | 5 | 6 | 7 |
                                | 8 | 9 | A | B | C | D | E | F

11. <data pair> ::=             <data singlet> <data singlet>

12. <data singlet> ::=          <realtime byte> <data singlet> |<data byte>

13. <running pairs> ::=         e | <data pair> <running pairs>

14. <running singlets> ::=      e |<data singlet> <running singlets>

15. <data byte> ::=             <data MSD> <hex nibble>

16. <data MSD> ::=              0 | 1 | 2 | 3 | 4 | 5 | 6 | 7

17. <realtime byte> ::=         F8 | FA | FB | FC | FE | FF

18. <sys msg> ::=               <sys common msg> | <sysex msg> | <sys realtime msg>

19. <sys realtime msg> ::=      <realtime byte>

20. <sysex msg> ::=             <sysex data byte> <data singlet> <running singlets> <eox byte>

21. <sysex stat byte> ::=       F0

22. <eox byte> ::=              F7

23. <sys common msg> ::=        <song position msg> | <song select msg> | <tune request>

24. <tune request> ::=          F6

25. <song position msg> ::=     <song position stat byte> <data pair>

26. <song select msg> ::=       <song select stat byte> <data singlet>

27. <song position stat byte>::=F2

28. <song select stat byte> ::= F3
```

(Note: the empty string is denoted `e`, as in the `minic` syntax.)

(a) Is the string:
`C 8 7 F`

a syntactically correct MIDI message (e.g., `S = <MIDI msg>`)? Why or why not?[13]

(b) Is the string:

`8 0 0 F 0 F`

a syntactically correct MIDI message (e.g., `S = <MIDI msg>`)? Why or why not?

24. Suppose we had the set of productions for a grammar, G_s, shown below. S, V_T, and V_N are obvious.

$$S \rightarrow AB$$
$$S \rightarrow C$$
$$A \rightarrow C$$
$$A \rightarrow a$$
$$B \rightarrow b$$
$$B \rightarrow c$$
$$C \rightarrow d$$

Draw the derivation tree for string ac.

25. Given grammar G_{01}, where

$$G_{01} = \{\Sigma = (a, b, c), N = (S, A, B, C), P, S\}$$

with productions P:

$$S \rightarrow AB$$
$$S \rightarrow C$$
$$A \rightarrow c$$
$$A \rightarrow a$$
$$B \rightarrow b$$
$$B \rightarrow c$$
$$C \rightarrow cC$$
$$C \rightarrow c$$

(a) What type(s) of grammar is G_{01}?

(b) Enumerate $L(G_{01})$.

(c) Show a derivation tree for the string:

$$x = ac$$

(d) Is G_{01} ambiguous? Justify your answer.

[13]No credit without justification.

26. Suppose we had the set of productions for a grammar, G_s, shown below. S, V_T, and V_N are obvious.

$$\begin{aligned} S &\rightarrow AB \\ S &\rightarrow C \\ A &\rightarrow C \\ A &\rightarrow a \\ B &\rightarrow b \\ B &\rightarrow c \\ C &\rightarrow d \end{aligned}$$

We would like to modify G_s to form G_{mod} so that

$$L(G_{mod}) = L(G_s) \cup \{da, dd\} - \{d\}$$

that is, the only effects of the modification are to add strings da and dd to the language and to remove string d from the language. Moreover, this must be done by *change* of a single production, and without the use of "or" ($|$).

(a) Which *single* production should be *changed* to achieve this?

(b) What is the exact change (the revised production)?

(c) With this change, show the derivation of strings da and dd.

(d) How do you know that no other modifications to $L(G_s)$ have occurred?

CHAPTER 3

Programming in Prolog

To be or not to be is true.
—G. Boole

3.1 Introduction

This chapter introduces declarative programming using Prolog. The first part of the chapter is an overview of the declarative programming paradigm, Prolog syntax, Prolog semantics, and the development cycle. The latter part deals with the Prolog Language Grammar Notation extension (LGN). The LGN is used in the development of parsers for `minic`. In addition, we illustrate an equally important Prolog application to constraint satisfaction problems (CSPs).

3.1.1 Getting Started with Prolog Programming: Resources

SWI-Prolog is used as an example of a Prolog programming environment. It has been available for a number of years and has a considerable following. SWI-Prolog is quite stable and standardized,[1] is usable with a number of operating systems, and is licensed under the Lesser GNU Public License. The GUI-based help and tracing available with recent versions is a handy tool for the Prolog developer.

Section 3.6.2 lists the SWI (and GNU Prolog) Web home pages. Binaries for `Windows`, `Linux`, and Mac OS X platforms are available, as well as the SWI-Prolog source in `C`.

3.1.2 The Prolog Incremental Development Cycle

Typically, development in Prolog proceeds iteratively, with creation of the Prolog database (using an editor) as a file or set of files, interpretation of the source file(s), execution of the program (query), source file modifications, reinterpretation of the source, execution of the program, and so forth. Although not absolutely necessary, there are IDEs that help this process.

[1]SWI-Prolog includes a comprehensive set of built-in predicates that conform to the ISO and Edinburgh Prolog standards.

3.1.3 Language Background

Prolog is a declarative language, as opposed to the more traditional imperative programming languages (e.g., C). This often causes some difficulty for beginners, because good Prolog programmers have mastered the art of developing Prolog descriptions and letting the unification mechanism in Prolog solve the problem, without forcing or dictating the solution (as in imperative approaches).

Both the Lisp and Prolog languages originated in academia. Lisp origins may generally be traced to universities in the United States, whereas Prolog has origins in Canada, France, and Great Britain.

Although the declarative concept is straightforward, when actually employing Prolog, the consequences of:

- the goal-satisfaction or unification mechanism (including backtracking);
- the computational requirements of depth-first search;
- advanced Prolog constructs such as lists and the cut; and
- recursion

need to be considered. Two points are intended to help with the introduction:

1. *Prolog is a useful language when the solution to a problem involves satisfaction of a number of constraints relating problem variables.*

2. *In Prolog, the programmer does not concentrate on the specification of a program execution sequence, but rather attempts to specify the problem (or situation) through development of a database consisting of clauses. Clauses may be either facts or rules. Given a goal, it is then left for the Prolog unification mechanism to provide a solution, if one exists.*

3.1.4 Hello World in Prolog

We visit this application as an overall introduction to Prolog. Unfortunately, the simplicity of the first example might suggest interpretation as an imperative process.

Prolog Source File

```
%% hello world program
%% hello.pro

go :- nl, write('hello, ece352 world'), nl.
```

The above Prolog source code consists of two lines of comments and a single Prolog clause. Note that Prolog allows two forms of comments, which we use freely in this and subsequent chapters. The first is the "end-of-line" form, beginning with a % and ending with the end of line character(s). The second is the variable-length comment, delineated by /* and */. The latter is familiar to C programmers.

Using the Program (Invoking the Goal)

To see the utility of this Prolog database, it is first necessary to start the Prolog interpreter, and then interpret the source file in Prolog. Following this, the source file contents (without comments) are the current Prolog database.

```
?- consult('hello.pro').
hello.pro compiled, 0.00 sec, 532 bytes.

Yes
?- listing(go).

go :-
        nl,
        write('hello, ece352 world'),
        nl.

Yes
?- go.

hello, ece352 world

Yes
?- halt.
```

After the database is consulted, querying the Prolog interpreter with the goal `go` causes Prolog's unification mechanism to search for a response to the query. Although a general description of the working of this mechanism is deferred until Section 3.2.1, we postulate that if the goal matches the head of a Prolog clause in the database, the tail of the clause (`nl, write('hello, ece352 world'), nl` in this case) is taken as a new set of subgoals. Subgoals are explored in the order in which they appear in the tail. Each of the three subgoals is separated by the comma, indicating conjunction or AND. Therefore all three must be successful for the Prolog system to report TRUE or "yes." Quite simply, `nl` always succeeds with the side effect of generating a cr/lf (newline) on the standard output, and `write` succeeds with the side effect of sending the string `'hello, ece352 world'` to the standard output.

3.1.5 Prolog `help` Notation

In predicate descriptions obtained via SWI `help(<pred-name>)` or in the SWI manual, predicates are shown along with the corresponding arity. For example, in describing (built-in) predicate `member`, the notation `member/2` is used to indicate the arity of the `member` predicate (number of arguments) is 2. Furthermore, `help(member)` indicates the type of arguments to `member`, e.g.,

```
member(?Elem, ?List)
```

followed by a description. In this commonly used notation,

- `+Argument` means input (i.e., the argument is bound before invoking the predicate).
- `-Argument` means output (i.e., the argument is bound to a value, if possible, in the process of finding a solution).
- `?Argument` means either (works both ways).

3.2 Prolog Syntax and Use

3.2.1 Predicates, Clauses, Facts, Rules, and Goals

Predicate A predicate consists of a name and an optional set of arguments. The number of arguments is the **arity** of the predicate.

Clause The basic statement in Prolog is the clause. A Prolog program is a set of Prolog clauses. Clauses are either rules or facts. Clauses are built using predicates and logical connectives and allowed to contain variables that are assumed universally quantified.

- A Prolog clause is comprised of a head and an (optional) body or tail.
- If the body is empty, the clause is a fact, which is interpreted to be true.
- The period (.) ends the clause.

Facts As noted, a fact is a rule with an empty tail. Although this is acceptable notation, in practice facts have the typical form:

```
predicate_name(term1, term2,...,termn).
```

where the period (.) terminates the clause. The following is an example of a database of Prolog facts:

```
is_fact (arg1, arg2).
a_fact_too (Y).
equal (X, X).
another_fact.
wheel_is_round.
round (wheel).
wheel (round).
```

Rules A rule is a clause with a non-empty head and a tail. Rules have the typical form (logical representation):

```
predicate_name1(arg1, arg2,...) :-
                predicate_name2(arg1, arg2,...),
                                ...
                predicate_nameR(arg1, arg2,...).
```

The predicate arguments `argi` above may be constants, variables (capitalized), lists, or functors. The following example is a clause that is a rule:

```
has(X, door) :- is_house (X).
```

Rules are seldom as simple as the previous examples. For example, consider a clause with a body of the form:

```
pc(Arg) :- pa1(Arg),pa2(Arg),...,pan(Arg).
```

where the comma (**,**) indicates conjunction. To logically infer that pc(Arg) (the head) is TRUE or satisfied requires Prolog to verify that pa1(Arg) and pa2(Arg) . . . pan(Arg) are true or satisfied. Predicates pa1 . . . pan therefore become subgoals, each of which must be satisfied or verified. A subgoal is satisfied if it is unifiable with the database.

Conjunction and Disjunction The use of the comma (,) in Prolog to separate clauses indicates that the conjunction (AND) of these clauses (subgoals) must be satisfied. Prolog also provides the disjunction (OR) operator (;). For example, given

```
goal :- a;b.
```

either clause a or clause +b+ must succeed. This may be rewritten as the logically equivalent pair of clauses:

```
goal :- a.
goal :- b.
```

Variables

All variables in Prolog begin with a capital (uppercase) letter.

The Anonymous Variable

The anonymous variable is used to represent universal quantification–that is, any instantiation of the variable will suffice. It is not necessary to give this variable a name; instead the underbar (_) is used. It is noteworthy that several anonymous variables in the same clause need not be given consistent interpretations.

```
matchany(_).
```

is an example of a Prolog database fact using predicate name `matchany` (arity=1), where any argument to predicate `matchany()` will cause the predicate to succeed or be true.

Goals

A Prolog program requires specification of a goal. A goal, entered at the interpreter prompt (`?-` in what follows), is a Prolog clause, which may be comprised of subgoals and logical connectives and may contain variables. The Prolog system attempts to unify this goal with the database. An example of a simple goal used to query the Prolog database might be:

```
?-has(What, door).
```

Unification = Solution = Search

Perhaps the most important conceptual characteristic of Prolog is the operation of the built-in mechanism that, given a database of facts and rules, and a goal (i.e., a statement whose validity is to be verified), employs repeated variable instantiation in order to return consistent values of the variables. This process is referred to as the **unification mechanism**.

> *An understanding of the operation of the Prolog unification mechanism is fundamental to success in developing practical Prolog programs.*

The rules for unification in Prolog are:

1. Clauses are tested in the order in which they appear in a program (the database).

2. When a subgoal matches the left side (head) of a rule, the right side (tail) becomes a new set of subgoals to unify. Because the tail of a rule may contain the conjunction or disjunction of a number of predicates,[2] it is at this stage that the complexity of the solution search becomes an issue.

3. The unifier proceeds from left to right in attempting to satisfy (unify) the predicates in the tail of a rule. Each of these predicates represents a subgoal. When a subgoal is spawned, the unification/search process described in Point 1, repeats.

4. A goal is satisfied when a matching fact (a grounded predicate) is found in the database for all the leaves of the goal tree.

5. When two or more clauses in the database with the same predicate name are identified as possible matches, the first clause in the database is chosen (first) for attempted unification. The second (and third, etc.) are marked as points for possible backtracking, and are investigated subsequently if a previous choice fails to unify.

Unification Example

Using the rule from the previous section, to unify `is-house (X)` with one (or more) database statements, a variable substitution for `X` is sought. If the database contains

```
is_house (my_house).
```

the substitution

```
my_house/X
```

results. This is shown below.

Sample House Database

```
/* simple Prolog representation */
/* file: house.pro  */

has_part(X,door) :- is_house(X).
is_house(my_house).
```

Using Prolog with the Sample Database

```
?- ['house.pro'].
% house.pro compiled 0.00 sec, 0 bytes

Yes
?- has_part(What,door).

What = my_house

Yes
?- has_part(What,fence).

No
?- has_part(What,Item).
```

[2]Each of which may, in turn, be the head of one or more rules in the database.

```
What = my_house
Item = door

Yes
```

"Moving Around" in Prolog

There are many built-in Prolog predicates, which may be used as goals with useful side effects. For example, to display or change the working Prolog directory, `pwd` and `cd` are used.

Logging a Prolog Session

SWI-Prolog allows logging the interactive session in a file using the `protocol` predicate. All Prolog interaction, including warnings and tracer output, are written on the protocol file. The basic syntax for this family of predicates is:

```
protocol(+File)
     Start protocolling on file File. If there is already
a protocol file open then close it first.
If File exists it is truncated.

noprotocol
     Stop making a protocol of the user interaction.
Pending output is flushed on the file.
```

3.2.2 The Prolog Programming Concept as Description

Prolog programs and programmers focus on description. For example, specification of a procedure to find the factorial of a number is shown below. Note that the mathematical description of factorial is inherently recursive, thus we have our first glimpse of recursion in Prolog.

`factorial` Description in Prolog

```
/* a simple fact (factorial(1)=1) */
/* file: fact.pro  */

factorial(1,1).

/* a rule to recursively define (or describe) 'factorial'  */

factorial(N,Result) :- Imin1 is N-1,
factorial(Imin1,Fmin1),
Result is N*Fmin1.
```

`factorial` Database Use

```
?- consult('fact.pro').
fact.pro compiled, 0.00 sec, 408 bytes.

Yes
?- listing.
```

```
factorial(1, 1).
factorial(A, B) :-
        C is A - 1,
        factorial(C, D),
        B is A * D.

Yes
?- factorial(4, What).

What = 24

Yes
```

Notice that the specification does not indicate how to compute factorial, but rather what factorial is. It also does not guarantee that a solution exists. To a beginning programmer, particularly one familiar with imperative languages, the following observations are the most startling discovery about Prolog.

1. It is fundamental to note that there is no emphasis placed on the imperative language assignment operator (e.g., the "=" or ":=" symbol in C or Pascal, respectively) in Prolog. The Prolog `is` infix operator, which forces assignment, is available, but is generally used to facilitate evaluation of arithmetic expressions. Assignment of values to variables in Prolog takes place principally through the unification mechanism, the operation of which is, in the execution of a Prolog program, left to the Prolog system.
2. Note that successful interpretation of Prolog only assumes syntactic correctness; it does not imply run-time correctness.

In the previous example, the reader may be interested in the behavior of the Prolog system when a goal such as

```
?- factorial(-4, What).
```

is invoked.

Another Example of the Declarative Programming Process

Consider the development of a Prolog expert system to replace a college dean. The dean, among other things, is charged with determining which faculty members in his or her college receive tenure, or lifetime employment. We begin the development of a Prolog representation for this decision capability with the following dialog between a typical dean (DEAN) and the Prolog software developer (PSD).

The Development Process Suppose the following dialog occurs:

```
PSD: Dean, tell me how you decide who gets tenure.

DEAN: That's easy. I award tenure to my faculty who publish, get research, and teach well.

PSD: Am I correct in my understanding that they must do all three of these?

DEAN: That's right.
```

```
PSD: How does a faculty member "publish"?

DEAN: The faculty member conducts research and documents the research.

PSD: How does the faculty member get research?

DEAN: The faculty member writes research proposals which subsequently become funded.

PSD: What does it mean for a faculty member to teach well?

DEAN: That's easy. A good teacher prepares lectures, delivers the lecture well, and gets
good evaluations from the students.

PSD: Is that all there is to it?

DEAN: That's right.

PSD: Thanks for your time and expertise, Dean.
```

Corresponding Prolog Representation Strategy The previous dialog may be represented in Prolog as follows.

```
gets_tenure(Faculty) :- publishes(Faculty),
                            gets_research(Faculty),
                                teaches_well(Faculty).

publishes(Professor) :- does_research(Professor),
                          documents_research(Professor).

gets_research(Researcher) :- writes_proposals(Researcher),
                                 gets_funded(Researcher).

teaches_well(Educator) :- prepares_lectures(Educator),
                             lectures_well(Educator),
                               gets_good_evaluations(Educator).
```

3.2.3 Tracing Predicates

It is useful for both debugging and illustration to trace certain predicates in a Prolog database. This may be done, as shown in the following examples, with the `trace` predicate. A more elaborate debugging facility is provided by the SWI Prolog `guitracer` and `spy` predicates and corresponding GUI, as shown in the following goal for the database of Section 3.2.2.

```
goal :-
spy(gets_tenure),  % set spy points
spy(publishes),
spy(gets_research),
spy(teaches_well),
spy(does_research),
spy(documents_research),
spy(writes_proposals),
spy(gets_funded),
```

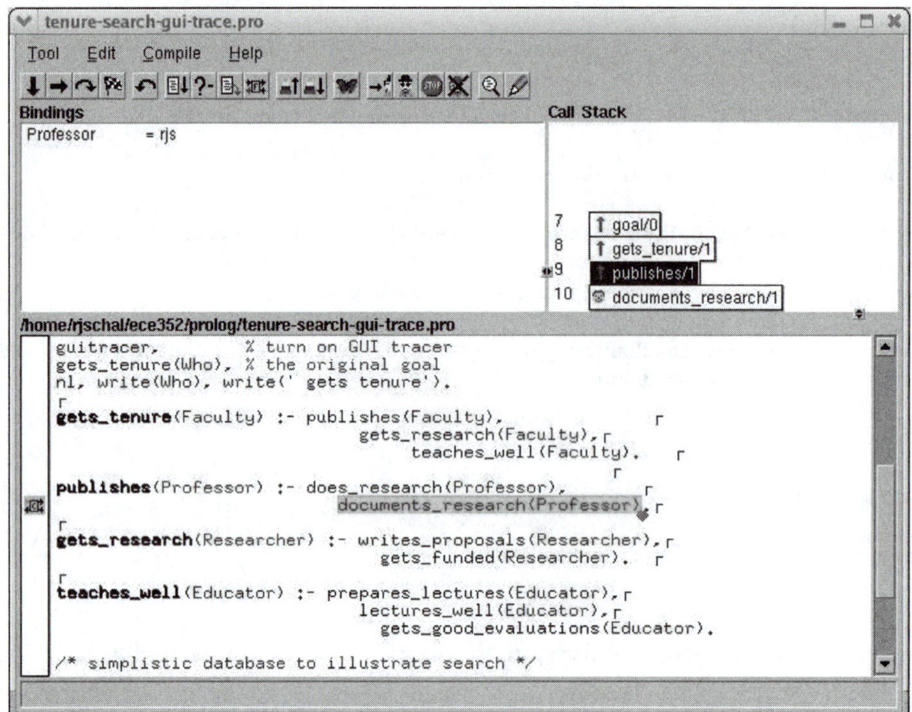

Figure 3.1 Use of the SWI Prolog Graphical Tracer.

```
spy(prepares_lectures),
spy(lectures_well),
spy(gets_good_evaluations),
guitracer,         % turn on GUI tracer
gets_tenure(Who), % the original goal
nl, write(Who), write(' gets tenure').
```

Figure 3.1 shows the Prolog graphical tracer for this example.

3.2.4 Recursion

Recursion is often used in Prolog, and manifests itself as a goal that (perhaps indirectly, that is, through other clauses) invokes itself.

An Example of Recursion

```
/* 99 bottles of (root) beer in Prolog */
/* hope we don't offend anyone */
/* file: rootbeer.pro */

/* the (recursive) clauses */
/* note that order is important */

   bottles(1) :-
     write('1 bottle of root beer on the wall, '),nl,
     write('1 bottle of root beer...'),nl,
     write('take one down and pass it around...'),nl,nl,
     write('Thats All Folks!').
```

```
   bottles(X):-
     nl,
     write(X),write(' bottles of root beer on the wall,'),nl,
     write(X),write(' bottles of root beer...'),nl,
     write('take one down and pass it around,'), nl,
     X1 is X - 1,   /* note the infix notation */
     write(X1),write(' bottles of root beer on the wall.'), nl,nl,
     write('------------- pause -----------------'),nl,nl,
     bottles(X1).     /* here's the (direct) recursion */

/* the goal */
/* only use if you want lots of output */

   root_beer_goal :- bottles(99).
```

Corresponding (Abbreviated) Output

```
?- consult('rootbeer.pro').

Yes
?- bottles(3).

3 bottles of root beer on the wall,
3 bottles of root beer...
take one down and pass it around,
2 bottles of root beer on the wall.

------------- pause -----------------


2 bottles of root beer on the wall,
2 bottles of root beer...
take one down and pass it around,
1 bottles of root beer on the wall.

------------- pause -----------------


1 bottle of root beer on the wall,
1 bottle of root beer...
take one down and pass it around...

Thats All Folks!

Yes
```

Using Care with Recursion

Prolog, although relentless in its search for a solution, is not able to detect problems with recursion. Especially significant is *infinite recursion*. Consider the following input file:

```
/* inf-recur-ex.pro */

a:-a.

a.
```

Based upon our discussion in Section 3.2.1, we note that Prolog will endlessly "loop" through the first database clause (rule). Here is a trace of the corresponding Prolog output:

```
?- ['inf-recur-ex.pro'].
% inf-recur-ex.pro compiled 0.01 sec, 0 bytes

Yes
?- listing(a).

a :-
a.
a.

Yes
?- a.
ERROR: Out of local stack
   Exception: (39,067) a ? abort
Yes

?- trace(a).
%         a/0: [call, redo, exit, fail]

Yes
[debug]  ?- a.
 T Call: (7) a
 T Call: (8) a
 T Call: (9) a
 T Call: (10) a
 T Call: (11) a
 T Call: (12) a
 T Call: (13) a
 T Call: (14) a
 T Call: (15) a
 T Call: (16) a
 T Call: (17) a
 T Call: (18) a
 T Call: (19) a
 T Call: (20) a
 T Call: (21) a
< some time later ...>
 T Call: (39,274) a
 T Call: (39,275) a
 T Call: (39,276) a
 T Call: (39,277) a
 T Call: (39,278) a
 T Call: (39,279) a
 T Call: (39,280) a
 T Call: (39,281) a
 T Call: (39,282) a
 T Call: (39,283) a
 T Call: (39,284) a
 T Call: (39,285) a
 T Call: (39,286) a
 T Call: (39,287) a
 T Call: (39,288) a
 T Call: (39,289) a
 T Call: (39,290) a
ERROR: Out of local stack
```

3.2.5 Prolog, Variable Bindings, and `is`

Typically, variables get bindings in Prolog via the unification process. There are exceptions, however, especially when arithmetic is involved. Prolog provides **`is`** for these cases. The prototypical use of **`is`** in Prolog is to *force assignment of an expression to a variable.*[3] **`is`** uses infix notation with the prototype:

```
-Number is +Expr
```

In SWI-Prolog, if **`Expr`** evaluates to a float that can be represented using an integer (that is, the value is an integer and within the range that can be described by Prolog's integer representation), **`Expr`** is unified with the integer value. Normally **`is`** is used with an unbound left operand. For example, if equality is to be tested, the connective "=" would be used. Similarly, if numerical (arithmetic) equality is to be tested, "`=:=`" is more appropriate.

3.2.6 Testing for Equality Versus Assignment

In imperative programming languages, forcing a variable binding and testing for equality are fundamentally different concepts. However, in Prolog there is some commonality, because variables may be unbound when compared. Some examples and distinctions follow.

Examples of `is`, =, and `equal`

```
/* equality vs. is vs. equality as a predicate (fact) */
/* file: equals-is.pro  */

test-is(A,B) :- A is B.

test-eq(A,B) :- A = B.

equal(X,X).

equal(X,X,X).  /* w/o testing transitivity of binary =  */
               /* also shows defns. w/ different arity "overloading" */

?- ['equals-is.pro'].
% equals-is.pro compiled 0.00 sec, 0 bytes

Yes
?- test-is(A,5).

A = 5
Yes
?- test-eq(A,5).

A = 5
Yes
?- equal(A,5).

A = 5
Yes
```

[3] Note that this is somewhat at odds with Prolog's mindset, which is not imperative programming.

```
?- test-is(5,A).
ERROR: Arguments are not sufficiently instantiated
   Exception: (6) test- (5 is _G211) ?
creep
?- test-eq(5,A).

A = 5
Yes
?- equal(5,A).

A = 5
Yes
?- test-is(5,5).

Yes
?- test-eq(5,5).

Yes
?- equal(5,5).

Yes
?- test-is(A,A).
ERROR: Arguments are not sufficiently instantiated
   Exception: (6) test- (_G210 is _G210) ?
creep
?- test-eq(A,A).

A = _G210
Yes
?- equal(A,A).

A = _G198
Yes

?- test-eq(A,B),test-eq(B,5).

A = 5
B = 5
Yes
?- equal(A,B,5).

A = 5
B = 5
Yes
?- equal(1,2,3).

No
?- equal(5,B,5).

B = 5
Yes
?-
```

3.2.7 Prolog and Arithmetic

Although Prolog is not designed as a number-crunching language, arithmetic capability is provided. However, the availability of arithmetic operators varies among implementations. Arithmetic involves predicates that implement both floating-point and integer arithmetic, as appropriate. As mentioned, one very noteworthy aspect of arithmetic in Prolog is that *infix notation is used (allowed)* for a number of arithmetic operators. This greatly improves the readability of the Prolog code that concerns arithmetic. Furthermore, for obvious reasons, arithmetic is not done by unification. In most implementations, general arithmetic predicates are compiled.

A Note about SWI-Prolog and Arithmetic Conversions

SWI-Prolog tries to minimize the apparent differences between integer arithmetic and floating-point arithmetic to the Prolog user. Arithmetic is done as integer arithmetic as long as possible, and converted to floating-point arithmetic whenever one of the arguments or the combination of them requires it. If a function returns a floating-point value that is whole, it is automatically transformed into an integer.

Sample Arithmetic Operators

The basic arithmetic operators are +, -, *, / (floating point division), // (integer division), and mod. Here are some simple examples:

```
?- Y is (3/4+1).

Y = 1.75

Yes
?- Y is (3//4+1).

Y = 1

Yes
?- Y is (4/4+1).

Y = 2

Yes
?- Y is (4.0/4+1).

Y = 2

Yes
?- Y is (4.0/4+1.0).

Y = 2

Yes
?- Y is .21.
ERROR: Syntax error: Operator expected
ERROR: Y is .
ERROR: ** here **


ERROR: 21 .
?- Y is 0.21.

Y = 0.21

Yes
```

<	Arithmetic less than
=:=	Arithmetic equal
=<	Arithmetic less than or equal
=\=	Arithmetic not equal
>	Arithmetic greater than
>=	Arithmetic greater than or equal
*	Multiplication
**	Power function
+	Addition
-	Subtraction
/	Division
//	Integer division
/\	Bitwise and
<<	Bitwise left shift
>>	Bitwise right shift
^	Power function
is	assignment

Table 3.1 Arity 2 Arithmetic Predicates.

The samples below show some of the additional arithmetic predicates. Suppose we query the SWI Prolog system with:

```
?- apropos(arithmetic).
```

This brings up another window with information regarding arithmetic-based predicates. Typically used arity 2 predicates are summarized in Table 3.1.

Similarly, Table 3.2 lists some useful arity 1 arithmetic predicates.

Predicates to Verify the Type of a Term

Prolog provides a number of predicates for this purpose, including:

```
var(+Term)
```

-	Unary minus
abs	Absolute value
acos	Inverse (arc) cosine
asin	Inverse (arc) sine
ceil or ceiling	Smallest integer larger than arg
cos	Cosine
exp	Exponent (base e)

Table 3.2 Arity 1 Arithmetic Predicates.

which succeeds if `Term` currently is a free (unbound) variable. Similarly,

```
nonvar(+Term)
```

succeeds if `Term` is currently not a free variable. For arithmetic types,

```
integer(+Term)
```

succeeds if `Term` is bound to an integer, whereas

```
float(+Term)
```

succeeds if Term is bound to a floating-point number.

Other available tests of variable type are implemented using predicates such as:

```
number(+Term)
```

which succeeds if `Term` is bound to an integer or a floating-point number,

```
atom(+Term)
```

which succeeds if `Term` is bound to an atom, and

```
string(+Term)
```

which succeeds if `Term` is bound to a string. Other type-checking predicates are available (see the problems).

Ambiguity (and Prolog Operator Precedence)

An ambiguous statement, in the context of a grammar, means that more than one valid parse of the statement exists. The syntax of Prolog allows certain binary operators (e.g., = , ; * +) to be written using infix notation. For example, consider the tails of the following two Prolog clauses:

```
testl(A,B,C,D,E) :- A = B ; C , D, not(E).

testn(A,B,C,D,E) :- A is B - C * D + E.
```

The first sample clause involves logical connectives, and the second is a numerical example. Potential ambiguity is present in both. In the first example, do we mean

```
A = (B ; C , D, not(E))
```

or

```
(A = B) ; (C , D, not(E))
```

or

```
(A = B ; C) , D, not(E)
```

or

```
(A = B ; C , D), not(E)
```

(in the last case the meaning of A = B ; C , D is still in question). Similar questions arise for the second (numerical) example. One way in which this type of ambiguity is removed is by rules that establish *operator precedence.* Another is by the use of parentheses.

Precedence	Type	Name
1200	xfx	`-->, :-`
1200	fx	`?-`
1100	xfy	`;`
1000	xfy	`,`
954	xfy	`\`
900	fy	`not`
700	xfx	`<, =, =.., =:=, =<, ==, =\=, >, >=, \=, \==, is`
500	yfx	`+, -, /\, \/, xor`
500	fx	`+, -`
400	yfx	`*, /, //, <<, >>, mod, rem`
200	xfx	`^`

Table 3.3 Precedence of Operators in SWI-Prolog.

Defining Operator Precedence and Rules to Eliminate Ambiguity

Operator precedence may be checked (and revised) in Prolog using the predicate

```
op(+Precedence, +Type, :Name)
```

which declares `Name` to be an operator of type `Type` with precedence `Precedence`. The value of `Precedence` is an unsigned integer of a range determined by the specific Prolog implementation. Higher values of `Precedence` correspond to higher precedence. Table 3.3 shows the (default) order of precedence of selected SWI-Prolog operators. (Note that predefined Prolog operators may be redefined by the user, although it is uncommon and probably unwise.) The representational challenge occurs with operators of the same precedence, as will be described next.

To indicate operator precedence with infix operators, a special notation for `Type` is used. `Type` may assume the values xfx, xfy, yfx, or yfy for infix operators, and xf, yf, fy, or fx for postfix and prefix operators, respectively. The f indicates the position of the operator and x and y indicate the position of the arguments. Any ambiguities in expressions are cleared up with the following rules:

1. A y indicates that this argument may contain operators of the same or lower precedence as f.

2. An x indicates that any operators in this argument must have precedence (strictly) lower than that of f.

For example, yfx indicates that the left argument to infix operator f may contain operators with precedence equal to that of f, but the right argument must contain operators of strictly lower precedence. This is best seen with an example.[4] Suppose `Expr` were

```
3 * 4 + 1 * 4
```

[4] Although it is unlikely that anyone would actually write Prolog expressions without using parentheses or brackets to make the expression clear.

Is the value of **Expr** 52, 60, or 16? To determine this, note that the precedence of + is higher than that of *. Furthermore, consider the association

```
3 * (4 + 1 * 4)
```

With this interpretation, f is *, y is 3, and x is 4 + 1 * 4. This is not possible, because x would contain *, which is not of strictly lower precedence. Alternately, consider

```
(3 * 4 + 1) * 4
```

This is ruled out, because y contains an operator (+) of higher precedence than *. Finally, consider the possible association where f is +:

```
(3 * 4) + (1 * 4)
```

This satisfies the `Type` of `+` being yfx, and thus is the correct (and only) interpretation. The reader should determine (and check, using Prolog) that the value of the disambiguated **Expr** is 16.

3.2.8 Lists in Prolog

Lists in Prolog consist of elements separated by commas and enclosed in brackets `[ ]`. So

```
[a, b, c, d]
```

is a four-element list of the elements a to d. Lists may be used as arguments to predicates. A list is a single argument to a predicate, *regardless of the length of the list.* Lists may be comprised of variables, constants, and other lists.
The head (X) and tail (Y) of a list are denoted in Prolog statements using the notation:

```
[X | Y]
```

The head is the first element; the tail is the list with the head removed. The empty list is a list without any elements and denoted `[ ]`.

List Membership Example

Consider a simple, recursive, and complete definition of list membership:

> *X is a member of a list if it is in the head (the first element) of the list or it is a member of the tail (the rest) of the list.*

The first part of the description allows us to write the Prolog description:

```
member(X, [X|_]).
```

that is, predicate **member** succeeds if X is the first element of the list. (Note the use of the anonymous variable in the formulation.) To test for membership in the tail of the list, we employ the second part of the description and use recursion:

```
member(X, [_|Y]) :- member(X,Y).
```

Note that the second clause, when invoked recursively, involves a shorter list at each invocation. Again, the anonymous variable is used in matching the head of the list in the second case.

member1 Declaration

We use the predicate name member1 instead of simply member, because member is usually a built-in or system predicate and often the Prolog system will, at best, complain about redefinition of built-in or system predicates.

```
/* member-ex.pro    */
/* example of lists, recursion */

member1(X,[X|_]).
member1(X,[_|Y]) :- member1(X,Y).
```

member1 Use and Tracing

```
?- ['member-ex.pro'].
member-ex.pro compiled, 0.00 sec, 476 bytes.

Yes
?- listing(member1).

member1(A, [A|B]).
member1(A, [B|C]) :-
        member1(A, C).

Yes
?- member1(3, [1,3,4,5]).

Yes
?- member1(6, [1,3,4,5]).

No
?- trace(member1).
        member1/2: call redo exit fail

Yes
[debug]  ?- member1(3, [1,2,3,4,5]).
T Call:  (  7) member1(3, [1, 2, 3, 4, 5])
T Call:  (  8) member1(3, [2, 3, 4, 5])
T Call:  (  9) member1(3, [3, 4, 5])
T Exit:  (  9) member1(3, [3, 4, 5])
T Exit:  (  8) member1(3, [2, 3, 4, 5])
T Exit:  (  7) member1(3, [1, 2, 3, 4, 5])

Yes

?- member(3, [1,3,4,5]).

Yes
?- member(6, [1,3,4,5]).

No
?-
```

With Unification, You Often Get More Than You Pay For

Because Prolog works by unification, many times predicates will have additional functionality. An example, using member, is shown below. Instead of using the predicate to ascertain list membership, we leave the first argument variable and thus let Prolog, through unification, indicate all possible bindings on variable `What`.

```
?- member(What, [1,2,3]).

What = 1 ;

What = 2 ;

What = 3 ;

No
```

3.2.9 Recursion and Lists: Another Example: (Recursively) Summing the Elements of a List

Here is an example that illustrates the use of recursion in Prolog descriptions in order to accomplish what might otherwise be considered an imperative, iterative task. Several design decisions are shown.

The Goal and Assumed Input Structure

Suppose our goal is to design a Prolog predicate with prototype `sumoflist(List, Sum)`, whose `List` argument takes the form of an arbitrarily long list of lists,

```
[[1],[2],[3],[4],[5],...]
```

This predicate should succeed with argument `Sum` bound to the sum of the values found in all the sublists (i.e., the integer 15 in the above five-element input list example).

Declarative Programming-Based Design

We note that the sum of a single element of the top-level list is the element value itself, that is,

```
sumoflist([[X]],X).
```

The process may be described recursively as:

```
sumoflist([A|B], Sum) :- sumoflist([A],I),sumoflist(B,J),Sum is I+J.
```

Prolog Source

```
/* sum of list of lists example */
/* sumoflist.pro  */
/* predicate format:
      sumoflist(List, Sum)
   sample list format (any length):
   [[1],[2],[3],[4],[5],...]
                                        */
/* sum of a single element of the top-level list
     is the element itself; note
     the assumed input list structure    */

sumoflist([[X]],X).
```

```
/* alt to above:
sumoflist([[X]],Sum) :- Sum is X.
*/

sumoflist([A|B], Sum) :- sumoflist([A],I),sumoflist(B,J),Sum is I+J.

/* thats all folks */
```

Results (with Errors, for Illustration)

```
?- ['sumoflist.pro'].
% sumoflist.pro compiled 0.01 sec, 744 bytes

Yes
?- sumoflist([[9]],What).

What = 9

Yes

%%% here's where it doesn't work due to head of list structure incompatible
%% with fact structure
%% i.e., sumoflist([A|B], Sum) :- sumoflist(A,I),sumoflist(B,J),Sum is I+J.

?- sumoflist([[2],[3]], What).

No
?- trace(sumoflist).
%         sumoflist/2: [call, redo, exit, fail]

Yes
[debug]  ?- sumoflist([[2],[3]], What).
 T Call: (6) sumoflist([[2], [3]], _G438)
 T Call: (7) sumoflist([2], _G527)
 T Call: (8) sumoflist(2, _G527)
 T Fail: (8) sumoflist(2, _G527)
 T Fail: (7) sumoflist([2], _G527)
 T Fail: (6) sumoflist([[2], [3]], _G438)

No

%%% so we fix it
%% sumoflist([A|B], Sum) :- sumoflist([A],I),sumoflist(B,J),Sum is I+J.
%% and go on

[debug]  ?- ['sumoflists.pro'].
% sumoflists.pro compiled 0.01 sec, 16 bytes

Yes
[debug]  ?- sumoflist([[2],[3]], What).
 T Call: (6) sumoflist([[2], [3]], _G438)
 T Call: (7) sumoflist([[2]], _G530)
 T Exit: (7) sumoflist([[2]], 2)
 T Call: (7) sumoflist([[3]], _G530)
 T Exit: (7) sumoflist([[3]], 3)
 T Exit: (6) sumoflist([[2], [3]], 5)

What = 5
```

```
Yes
[debug]  ?- sumoflists([[1],[2],[3
|    ],[4],[5]], Sum).
Correct to: sumoflist([[1], [2], [3], [4], [5]], Sum)? yes
 T Call: (6) sumoflist([[1], [2], [3], [4], [5]], _G534)
 T Call: (7) sumoflist([[1]], _G775)
 T Exit: (7) sumoflist([[1]], 1)
 T Call: (7) sumoflist([[2], [3], [4], [5]], _G775)
 T Call: (8) sumoflist([[2]], _G778)
 T Exit: (8) sumoflist([[2]], 2)
 T Call: (8) sumoflist([[3], [4], [5]], _G778)
 T Call: (9) sumoflist([[3]], _G781)
 T Exit: (9) sumoflist([[3]], 3)
 T Call: (9) sumoflist([[4], [5]], _G781)
 T Call: (10) sumoflist([[4]], _G784)
 T Exit: (10) sumoflist([[4]], 4)
 T Call: (10) sumoflist([[5]], _G784)
 T Exit: (10) sumoflist([[5]], 5)
 T Exit: (9) sumoflist([[4], [5]], 9)
 T Exit: (8) sumoflist([[3], [4], [5]], 12)
 T Exit: (7) sumoflist([[2], [3], [4], [5]], 14)
 T Exit: (6) sumoflist([[1], [2], [3], [4], [5]], 15)

Sum = 15

Yes
```

3.2.10 Input/Output in Prolog

Our later work in parser development will require use of Prolog's input capabilities.

Why Johnny Can Read

Reading in Prolog may be challenging. Some built-in predicates include:

```
read(-Term)
    Read the next Prolog term from the current input stream and unify
    it with Term.
name(?AtomOrInt, ?String)
    String is a list of ASCII values describing Atom. Each of the
    arguments may be a variable, but not both. When String is bound to
    an ASCII value list describing an integer and Atom is a variable
    Atom will be unified with the integer value described by String
tab(+Amount)
    Writes Amount spaces on the current output stream. Amount
    should be an expression that evaluates to a positive integer
put(+Char) (see also 'get')
    Write Char to the current output stream
```

Here is a simple example of reading (input). First, the source file:

```
example :- write('input a Prolog term from
your terminal, terminated by  a dot (.) and CR'),
nl, read(A), write(A).
```

Sample use of this predicate yields:

```
 ?- example.
input a Prolog term from
your terminal, terminated by  a dot (.) and CR
|: hi-mom.
hi-mom
Yes
```

Atoms and Subatomic Entities

In parsing our `minic` programs using Prolog, we need to look at "subatomic" entities. The Prolog `name` predicate facilitates this, as the example shows.

```
?- name(WhatIs, [104, 105, 32, 109, 111, 109]).
WhatIs = 'hi mom'
Yes
?- name('hi mom', AsciiList).
AsciiList = [104, 105, 32, 109, 111, 109]
Yes
```

The `name` predicate has the following syntax:

```
name(?AtomOrInt, ?String)
    String is a list of ASCII values describing Atom.  Each of the
    arguments may be a variable, but not both. When String is bound to
    an ASCII value list describing an integer and Atom is a variable
    Atom will be unified with the integer value described by String
    (e.g. 'name(N, "300"), 400 is N + 100' succeeds).
```

A closely related Prolog predicate is `string_to_list`. An even more basic input predicate is **get**, which reads a single character from the current input stream.

Writing (and Recursion) Example: A Prolog ASCII Table Generator

```
/* quick way to generate ASCII table */
/* ascii-gen.pro */
/* for simplicity, consider ASCII values 32-126  */
/* so we don't have to deal with unprintables */

goal :- nl, write('symbol ASCII value'), nl,
        show_table(32,126).

show_table(A,B) :- name(Symbol,[A]),
                   write(Symbol),write('     '),write(A),
                   nl, C is A + 1, C =< B, show_table(C,B).

?- ['ascii-gen.pro'].
% ascii-gen.pro compiled 0.00 sec, 1,204 bytes

Yes
```

The output is arranged in four columns to save space:

```
?- goal.                6    54     O   79     h   104
                        7    55     P   80     i   105
symbol ASCII value      8    56     Q   81     j   106
        32              9    57     R   82     k   107
!       33              :    58     S   83     l   108
"       34              ;    59     T   84     m   109
#       35              <    60     U   85     n   110
$       36              =    61     V   86     o   111
%       37              >    62     W   87     p   112
&       38              ?    63     X   88     q   113
'       39              @    64     Y   89     r   114
(       40              A    65     Z   90     s   115
)       41              B    66     [   91     t   116
*       42              C    67     \   92     u   117
+       43              D    68     ]   93     v   118
,       44              E    69     ^   94     w   119
-       45              F    70     _   95     x   120
.       46              G    71     `   96     y   121
/       47              H    72     a   97     z   122
0       48              I    73     b   98     {   123
1       49              J    74     c   99     |   124
2       50              K    75     d   100    }   125
3       51              L    76     e   101    ~   126
4       52              M    77     f   102
5       53              N    78     g   103    No
```

3.2.11 Multiple Solutions and Backtracking

Many times multiple problem solutions exist or alternative paths to be searched for a solution. In the unification process, Prolog marks potential alternatives for possible subsequent investigation. This leads to **backtracking**.

Consider the syntactically correct Prolog database below.

```
/* smpl-unify1.pro */

goal1(X,Y) :- first(X), second(Y).

goal2(X) :- first(X), second(X).

first(1).
first(2).
first(3).
second(2).
second(4).
second(6).
```

Simple query results are shown below.

```
?- consult('./smpl-unify1.pro').
% ./smpl-unify1.pro compiled 0.00 sec, 112 bytes

Yes
?- goal1(1,2).

Yes
?- goal1(2,1).
```

```
No
?- goal1(2,2).

Yes
?- goal2(1).

No
?- goal2(2).

Yes
```

We now incorporate variables into our queries. The reader should observe that there are multiple possible solutions to some queries, and thus a number of points marked as points for backtracking. Typing the ";" is equivalent to asking Prolog to display an alternative solution, determined by backtracking to the most recent[5] point marked for backtracking that enables an alternative solution. Otherwise, only the *first* one found by Prolog is shown.

```
?- goal1(A,B).

A = 1
B = 2 ;

A = 1
B = 4 ;

A = 1
B = 6 ;

A = 2
B = 2 ;

A = 2
B = 4 ;

A = 2
B = 6 ;

A = 3
B = 2 ;

A = 3
B = 4 ;

A = 3
B = 6 ;

No
?- goal2(C).

C = 2 ;

No
```

[5]In terms of the unification search strategy.

Inhibiting Backtracking and the Cut (!)

The cut (!) is used as a predicate[6] that always succeeds, but with a significant side effect: *all backtracking points (if they exist) up to the cut are erased.* Thus the cut, in a sense, forces commitment to a solution found prior to the occurrence of the cut.

Backtracking Example Here are two different versions of a Prolog database. The cut is used in the second case to restrict backtracking. First, we show an example of a database with multiple solutions from backtracking:

Here are two different versions of a Prolog database. The cut is used in the second case to restrict backtracking. First, we show an example of a database with multiple solutions from backtracking:

```
%% backtrack1.pro
%% show solutions;
%% prior to showing effect of cut

goal(A,C) :- adjacent_to(A,B),adjacent_to(B,C).

adjacent_to(r1,r2).
adjacent_to(r2,r1).
adjacent_to(r1,r3).
adjacent_to(r3,r4).
```

Here is the previous database with the cut used to inhibit backtracking after the first predicate in the tail:

```
%% backtrack2.pro
%% mod to show cut effect

goal(A,C) :- adjacent_to(A,B),!,adjacent_to(B,C).

adjacent_to(r1,r2).
adjacent_to(r2,r1).
adjacent_to(r1,r3).
adjacent_to(r3,r4).
```

We now explore the different results:

```
?- ['backtrack1.pro'].
Yes
?- goal(X,Y).

X = r1
Y = r1 ;

X = r2
Y = r2 ;

X = r2
Y = r3 ;

X = r1
Y = r4 ;

No
```

[6] With a strange notation.

The first database (without the cut) has four possible solutions.

```
?- ['backtrack2.pro'].
Yes
?- goal(X,Y).

X = r1
Y = r1 ;

No
```

Thus, the cut, by limiting backtracking, has reduced the possible solutions to one.

Recall if Prolog finds the potential for multiple solutions, candidate clauses are marked as points for possible backtracking. The use of the "`;`" at the interpreter prompt indicates that additional solutions, defined by backtracking points, are to be displayed.

3.2.12 Combining `not`, `fail`, `true`, `call`, and the Cut

The Concept of Negation as Failure

Prolog provides the `not` predicate, which must be used with care.

> *The* `not` *predicate, as would logically be expected, succeeds if unification of its argument fails.*

Thus, one aspect of Prolog that should be remembered in designing systems employing `not`:

> *Whatever is omitted from the database is treated as logically false. This is known as* ***negation-as-failure****.*

Examples using `not`

Now let's look at some help results and examples:

```
?- help(not).
not(+Goal)
    Succeeds when Goal cannot be proven.

?- true.

Yes
?- fail.

No
?- not(true).

No
?- not(fail).

Yes

?- help(call).
call(+Goal)
```

```
        Invoke Goal as a goal. Note that clauses may have variables as
        subclauses, which is identical to call/1, except when the argument
        is bound to the cut. See !/0.

Yes
?- help(!).
!
        Cut. Discard choice points of parent frame and frames created
        after the parent frame.
```

Defining `not`

Although it is built in, using the preceding predicates we may now define `not` as follows:

```
not(P) :- call (P), !, fail.
not (P).
```

Notice how the use of `call`, the cut (!), `fail`, and Prolog's backtracking mechanism (note the order of the preceding clauses) allows implementation of the `not` predicate.

3.3 Alternate Interpretations of Prolog

Although we have emphasized the declarative nature of Prolog, other viewpoints are possible and useful. Consider the Prolog clause (rule):

```
a :- b1, b2 ,..., bn
```

or the equivalent logical expression

$$b1 \cap b2 \cap \ldots bn \rightarrow a \tag{3.1}$$

Although we have concentrated on the use of Prolog as a declarative language, there are multiple viewpoints of this clause:

1. Declarative viewpoint: a is true if b1 and b2 and . . . bn are true.

2. Procedural viewpoint: to find if a is true, determine if b1 is true, and then determine if b2 is true, and so on.

3. Behavioral[7] viewpoint: process or goal a may be replaced by a set of processes/goals {b1, b2, . . . bn}.

The first two have been covered in some detail up to this point. We digress to explore the third.

---

[7]This is key to considering parallel implementation.

3.3.1 Prolog from the Viewpoint of First-Order Logic

The Implication Logical Connective

$$\{(p \rightarrow q) = (\neg p \cup q)\} = T$$

p	q	$p \rightarrow q$	$\neg p \cup q$
T	T	T	T
T	F	F	F
F	T	T	T
F	F	T	T

Prolog Notation Compared with Logic. This is shown in Table 3.4.

Connective	Logical Symbol	Prolog Syntax
Conjunction (and)	$\cap$	,
Disjunction (or)	$\cup$	;
Implication	$\rightarrow$	:-
Negation (not)	$\neg$	not()

Table 3.4 Relating Logical Connectives to Prolog Syntax.

Note the reversing of arguments in using implication, i.e., $p \rightarrow q$ corresponds to `q :- p.`

3.3.2 Prolog and Modus Ponens (MP)

From logic, the pair of statements

```
p -> q
p
```

is equivalent to the Prolog database

```
q:-p.
p.
```

3.4 Parsing (Grammatical Recognition) and Prolog

There are a number of possible approaches to developing parsers for grammar recognition. These include the CYK algorithm or the use of tools like `Bison`. These are explored in Chapter 4 and beyond.

3.4.1 Introduction to the Prolog LGN Preprocessor

Entering grammar productions directly in Prolog is facilitated by the use of a preprocessor for Logic Grammar Notation (LGN). This is also referred to as the Definite Clause Grammar (DCG). DCG handling is not part of the Prolog standard, but most Prolog implementations provide the DCG. Grammar rules in the LGN/DCG format look like ordinary clauses, but use `-->` for separating the head and tail, rather than `:-`. Expanding grammar rules is done by an internal predicate **expand_term**, which adds two additional arguments to each predicate. The **expand_term** predicate is normally invoked by the compiler/interpreter as a preprocessing step in the consulting of a file.

3.4.2 Grammar Rule Notation

Prolog has a built-in feature allowing the direct construction of parsers from CFGs by entering productions directly in *grammar rule notation*, also known as the LGN (Logic Grammar Notation). It is built around translation of the functor `-->`, which is declared to be an infix operator. The Prolog *preprocessor* converts the logic grammar notation to more traditional Prolog clauses.

First, it is assumed that the strings are represented in Prolog as lists. For example,

$$x = aabac$$

is represented in Prolog as the list

```
[a, a, b, a, c]
```

Recall that our ultimate objective is to represent our programs as lists, for example,

```
[void, main, lparens, void,
        rparens, lbrace, int, x, semicolon,
              |<more>]
```

First, consider a simple example. Suppose we had a very minimal set of productions:

$$S \rightarrow AB$$

$$A \rightarrow terma$$

$$B \rightarrow termb$$

where $S, A, B \in V_N$, and $terma, termb \in V_T$. This could be entered *directly* in Prolog LGN as:

```
s --> a, b.
a --> [terma].
b --> [termb].
```

Notice in Prolog that the *predicates* are s, a, and b. Consider the following translation and application in Prolog:

```
?- ['logicgr1.pro'].
logicgr1.pro compiled, 0.00 sec, 784 bytes.

Yes
?- listing(s).

s(A, B) :-
        a(A, C),
        b(C, B).

Yes
```

Here we see that Prolog has done all the work in converting the notation to actual predicates. What is even more important is that Prolog has built a parser for us. We will adopt a "consumption-based" interpretation of the parser operation. For example, the LGN-generated clause:

```
s(A, B) :-
        a(A, C),
        b(C, B).
```

may be interpreted as:

> A is an s with B leftover if A is an a, with C leftover and C is a b with B leftover.

Notice the shared variables and that typically B is the empty list (to require the parser to use all of the input, string, or list). Similarly,

```
?- listing(a).

a([terma|A], A).

Yes
?- listing(b).

b([termb|A], A).

Yes
```

More importantly, we can show that the string `terma termb`, that is, the list `[terma, termb]` is $\in L(G)$. Watch this:

```
?- s(All, []).

All = [terma, termb] ;

No

?- s([terma, termb], []).

Yes
```

3.4.3 Prolog and Grammars: A Short Summary

Productions	In Prolog LGN	Translation
$S \rightarrow AB$	`s --> a, b.`	`s(A, B) :- a(A, C), b(C, B).`
$A \rightarrow terma$	`a --> [terma].`	`a([terma|A], A).`

3.4.4 More on Grammar Rule Notation

Suppose we had a slightly more complex[8] set of productions:

$$S \rightarrow AB$$
$$S \rightarrow C$$
$$A \rightarrow C$$
$$A \rightarrow a$$
$$B \rightarrow b$$
$$B \rightarrow c$$
$$C \rightarrow d$$

Recall that the logic grammar representation in Prolog (below) looks slightly different due to the Prolog requirement that predicates must begin with a lowercase symbol.

This is represented in Prolog as:

```
s --> a, b.
s --> c.
a --> c.
a --> [terma].
b --> [termb].
b --> [termc].
c --> [termd].
```

Now watch what Prolog does:

```
6 ?- ['logicgr2.pro'].
logicgr2.pro compiled, 0.00 sec, 60 bytes.

Yes
7 ?- listing(s).

s(A, B) :-
        a(A, C),
        b(C, B).
s(A, B) :-
        c(A, B).

Yes
8 ?- listing(a).

a(A, B) :-
        c(A, B).
a([terma|A], A).

Yes
9 ?- listing(b).

b([termb|A], A).
b([termc|A], A).

Yes
10 ?- listing(c).
```

[8] Aside: can you determine $L(G)$?

```
c([termd|A], A).

Yes
```

Here we see again that Prolog has done all the work in converting the logic grammar notation to actual predicates. The reader should be able to generate $L(G)$ for this example. Here are some examples:

```
11 ?- s([a, b], []).

No
12 ?- s([terma, termb], []).

Yes

14 ?- s([termd], []).

Yes

15 ?- s([termd, termb], []).

Yes
16 ?- s([termb, termb], []).

No
```

Lets watch a few examples of the parse in detail:

```
18 ?- trace(s).
        s/2: call redo exit fail

Yes
19 ?- trace(a).
        a/2: call redo exit fail

Yes
20 ?- trace(b).
        b/2: call redo exit fail

Yes
21 ?- trace(c).
        c/2: call redo exit fail

Yes

22 ?- s([termd, termb], []).
T Call:  (  7) s([termd, termb], [])
T Call:  (  8) a([termd, termb], _L144)
T Call:  (  9) c([termd, termb], _L144)
T Exit:  (  9) c([termd, termb], [termb])
T Exit:  (  8) a([termd, termb], [termb])
T Call:  (  8) b([termb], [])
T Exit:  (  8) b([termb], [])
T Exit:  (  7) s([termd, termb], [])

Yes
```

```
23 ?- s([terma], []).
T Call:  (  7) s([terma], [])
T Call:  (  8) a([terma], _L144)
T Call:  (  9) c([terma], _L144)
T Fail:  (  9) c([terma], _L144)
T Redo:  (  8) a([terma], _L144)
T Exit:  (  8) a([terma], [])
T Call:  (  8) b([], [])
T Fail:  (  8) b([], [])
T Redo:  (  7) s([terma], [])
T Call:  (  8) c([terma], [])
T Fail:  (  8) c([terma], [])
T Fail:  (  7) s([terma], [])

No


24 ?- s([terma, termb], []).
T Call:  (  7) s([terma, termb], [])
T Call:  (  8) a([terma, termb], _L144)
T Call:  (  9) c([terma, termb], _L144)
T Fail:  (  9) c([terma, termb], _L144)
T Redo:  (  8) a([terma, termb], _L144)
T Exit:  (  8) a([terma, termb], [termb])
T Call:  (  8) b([termb], [])
T Exit:  (  8) b([termb], [])
T Exit:  (  7) s([terma, termb], [])

Yes
```

Let's let Prolog generate $L(G)$:

```
33 ?- s(All, []).

All = [termd, termb] ;

All = [termd, termc] ;

All = [terma, termb] ;

All = [terma, termc] ;

All = [termd] ;

No
```

If you would like to see the trace as well:

```
25 ?- s(All, []).
T Call:  (  7) s(_G155, [])
T Call:  (  8) a(_G155, _L145)
T Call:  (  9) c(_G155, _L145)
T Exit:  (  9) c([termd|_G242], _G242)
T Exit:  (  8) a([termd|_G242], _G242)
T Call:  (  8) b(_G242, [])
T Exit:  (  8) b([termb], [])
T Exit:  (  7) s([termd, termb], [])
```

```
All = [termd, termb] ;
T Redo:  (  8) b(_G242, [])
T Exit:  (  8) b([termc], [])
T Exit:  (  7) s([termd, termc], [])

All = [termd, termc] ;
T Redo:  (  8) a(_G155, _L145)
T Exit:  (  8) a([terma|_G242], _G242)
T Call:  (  8) b(_G242, [])
T Exit:  (  8) b([termb], [])
T Exit:  (  7) s([terma, termb], [])

All = [terma, termb] ;
T Redo:  (  8) b(_G242, [])
T Exit:  (  8) b([termc], [])
T Exit:  (  7) s([terma, termc], [])

All = [terma, termc] ;
T Redo:  (  7) s(_G155, [])
T Call:  (  8) c(_G155, [])
T Exit:  (  8) c([termd], [])
T Exit:  (  7) s([termd], [])

All = [termd] ;

No
```

3.4.5 Adding Variables in the LGN

Given a production in the LGN:

```
sentence --> nounphrase, verbphrase.
```

the Prolog preprocessor will automatically convert this into:

```
sentence(A, B) :-
        nounphrase(A, C),
        verbphrase(C, B).
```

Suppose we need to add another variable to the automatically translated LGN rule. Let's say that what is desired after LGN translation is:

```
sentence(N, A, B) :-
        nounphrase(N, A, C),
        verbphrase(N, C, B).
```

This is done in Prolog's LGN as follows:

```
sentence(N) --> nounphrase(N), verbphrase(N).
```

3.4.6 The 'C' Predicate

Recall in our LGN-based Prolog parser, a list is "consumed." Sometimes we mix terminals and nonterminals in a single LGN production. For example, consider the production in a formal grammar:

$$S \rightarrow AaB$$

which we convert into LGN form, as shown in the following example:

```
/* C example c-pred-ex.pro  */

s --> a, [terma], b.
```

The resulting translation appears as follows:

```
?- ['c-pred-ex.pro'].
% c-pred-ex.pro compiled 0.00 sec, 628 bytes

Yes
?- listing(s).

s(A, B) :-
        a(A, C),
        'C'(C, terma, D),
        b(D, B).

Yes
```

In translating the LGN, our listing shows a 'C' predicate. Conceptually, this strangely named "predicate"[9] is used to enforce connectivity in a string or derivation tree. The Prolog implementation of 'C' is quite simple and just requires the database *fact*:

```
?- listing('C').

'C'([A|B], A, B).
```

Sample uses of 'C' are shown below.

```
?- 'C'([a,b], a, [b]).

Yes
?- 'C'(WhatNode, the, [boy, saw, a, dog]).

WhatNode = [the, boy, saw, a, dog]

Yes
?- 'C'([the, young, boy, saw, a, dog],
          the, [boy, saw, a, dog]).

No
```

3.4.7 Prolog and Infinite Recursion (Nontermination)

How Can Infinite Recursion Occur in Prolog?

When recursion is used, either in Prolog or functional approaches, the possibility of infinite recursion exists. Often, it is simply a byproduct of developing a declarative program

[9]Note the use of the quotes, because the predicate name is uppercase.

without consideration of the order in which Prolog searches for a solution to satisfy a specified goal. Consider first the simple example below.

A Simple Example

Suppose in the development of a declarative "blocks world" model of the world it is desired to represent the symmetry of the adjacency property: "If block A is adjacent to block B, then block B must be adjacent to block A." A straightforward representation of this in Prolog might be in the form of a rule:

```
adjacent-to(A,B) :- adjacent-to(B,A).
```

The reader should verify that this Prolog representation results in non-termination. A standard solution is renaming one of the predicates to be used in the facts-based portion of the representation as follows:

```
adjacent-to(A,B) :- adj-to(A,B).
adjacent-to(A,B) :- adj-to(B,A).
```

Infinite Recursion in Productions: Solutions

As noted above, rewriting the productions to alleviate the problem may be possible. In rewriting language productions, care must be exercised in order that the two languages (the original and the one corresponding to the rewritten productions) be equivalent.[10] Left recursion in productions that are to be converted to Prolog is often handled in a manner analogous to the renaming previously used. Specifically, the database containing a left recursive production:

$$C \rightarrow Cc$$
$$C \rightarrow c$$

may be converted to the set of productions:

$$C \rightarrow cR$$
$$R \rightarrow cR$$
$$R \rightarrow \epsilon$$

Using the LGN, consider the revised database and behavior below:

```
/* Prolog database examples for non-termination */
/* recur-ex2.pro */
/* handling possible cases of left recursion */

/* case4 revisited */

c4 --> [termc4],rest_of_c4.
rest_of_c4 --> [termc4], rest_of_c4.
rest_of_c4 --> [].
?- ['recur-ex2.pro'].
% recur-ex2.pro compiled 0.00 sec, 0 bytes
```

[10]That is, $L(G_1) = L(G_2)$, where G_1 is the original, which involves left recursion, and G_2 is the rewritten form.

```
Yes
?- listing(c4).

c4(A, B) :-
        'C'(A, termc4, C),
        rest_of_c4(C, B).

Yes
?- c4([termc4,termc4,termc4],[]).

Yes
?- c4(What,[]).
ERROR: Out of local stack
```

This is explored further in the exercises.

3.5 Prolog and Constraint Satisfaction Problems

3.5.1 A Constraint Satisfaction Problem

A (binary) constraint satisfaction problem (CSP) is defined by:

- a set of variables.
- a domain of values for each variable.
- a set of constraints between each pair of variables. Often this binary constraint takes the form of a (binary) relation.

A solution of a CSP is a consistent assignment of all variables to values in such a way that all the constraints are satisfied. Note that a CSP can have zero solutions, a unique solution (one), or many solutions. Many important applications—such as planning, resource scheduling, parsing, and engineering design—can be cast within the framework of CSPs.

3.5.2 The Role of Prolog in CSPs

From the Prolog viewpoint, many CSPs may be implemented using a set of variables, and a set of predicates, the conjunction of which the instantiated variables must satisfy.

3.5.3 Example: Numerical Constraint Satisfaction

This is a familiar example. Consider the solution of a set of linear equalities of the form:

$$x + y = 6 \tag{3.2}$$

$$3x - y = 2 \tag{3.3}$$

Each of these equations constrains the numerical solution of assignment of values to variables x and y. Furthermore, each equation alone has insufficient constraint information for a unique solution. More precisely, each equation constrains the n-dimensional numerical solution space to an $n-1$ dimensional subspace. In this example, with $n = 2$ variables, each equation therefore constrains the solution to a line. The satisfaction of the conjunction (AND-ing) of these constraints (in this example, the intersection of the constraint lines), yields the global solution space. In this example, if the constraint equations are linearly independent, these constraint lines are forced to be noncollinear; thus a unique solution is obtained at their intersection. This is shown in Figure 3.2.

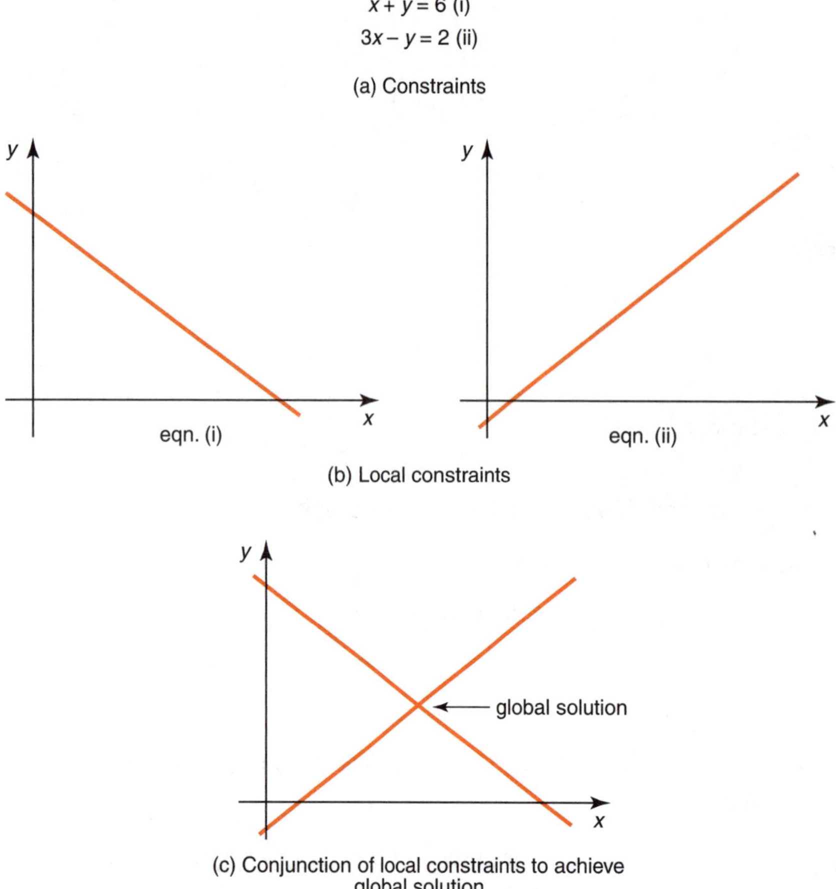

Figure 3.2 Example of a Numerical CSP.

3.5.4 Labeling Complexity

Given n objects to be labeled and the set of m possible labels on each, note that, without further constraints, m^n *possible and valid* labeling solutions exist.

3.5.5 Image Labeling Example

Assume that the input is a segmented image of the form shown in Figure 3.3. As Figure 3.3 indicates, we consider the labeling of six regions, denoted as R1, R2, . . . R6. There are five possible labels for each of these regions, or members of the set:

$$\{car, road, trees, grass, sky\}$$

Note that an exhaustive enumeration of the unconstrained labeling of these regions thus yields $5^6 = 15,625$ possibilities.

Definition: Adjacency

For simplicity, first consider a single binary constraint, namely that of region adjacency. Two regions that share a boundary are said to be adjacent. This is an easily extracted relation involving the image regions of Figure 3.3. Adjacency is a symmetric relation that is easily depicted graphically via an adjacency graph. The observed region adjacency graph (in terms of unlabeled regions R_i) for the sample segmented image of Figure 3.3 is shown.

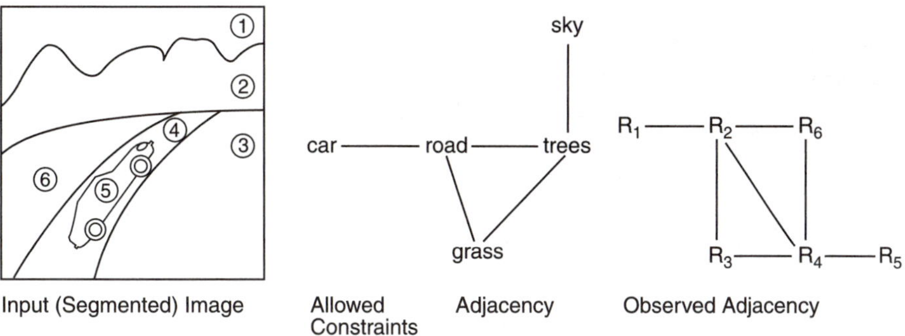

Figure 3.3 Sample Image and Labeling Constraints.

Constraints Regarding Adjacency

The next step is developing a set of constraints on allowable labels pairwise as a function of whether the regions are adjacent. For example, it makes sense to allow two adjacent regions to have the labels "car" and "road," that is, it does not violate human intuition when viewing an image wherein a car is adjacent to a road. On the other hand, if a label indicated a car was adjacent to grass (the driver is driving off the road) in the image, we would not allow this labeling.

Allowable Labels

We therefore generate the set of compatible labels given in Figure 3.4 and shown graphically in Figure 3.3. Note that adjacency is a symmetric relation.

3.5.6 CSP (Labeling) in Prolog

Initial Prolog Database and Goal

The essential database (using *only* the `adjacent-to` constraint) is shown in Figure 3.5. The reader should verify that there are 42 solutions to this problem, without any other constraints or measures to be optimized.

Revised Database (Additional Constraints)

To further reduce the number of possible solutions (and perhaps generate the solution a human observer would provide), consider the addition of two constraints and corresponding observations:

1. The region observed to be highest in the image must be labeled "sky." Region R1 was observed to be highest.

```
"car" is adjacent to "road"
"road" is adjacent to "grass"
"grass" is adjacent to "trees"
"road" is adjacent to "trees"
"sky" is adjacent to "trees"
```

Figure 3.4 Allowable Labels on Adjacent Regions (Symmetry of Relation Not Enumerated).

```
/* label.pro */
/* basic image labeling solution in Prolog */
/* database of allowed adjacency constraints */

adj-to(car,road).
adj-to(road,grass).
adj-to(road,trees).
adj-to(sky,trees).
adj-to(grass,trees).

adjacent-to(X,Y) :- adj-to(X,Y).
adjacent-to(X,Y) :- adj-to(Y,X).

/* observations of adjacency  */

goal([R1,R2,R3,R4,R5,R6]):-
adjacent-to(R1,R2),
adjacent-to(R2,R6),
adjacent-to(R2,R3),
adjacent-to(R3,R4),
adjacent-to(R2,R4),
adjacent-to(R4,R6),
adjacent-to(R4,R5).
```

Figure 3.5 Skeletal Prolog Image Labeling Formulation (Yields 42 Solutions).

2. Any region observed to be moving must be labeled "car." Region R5 was observed moving.

A Prolog database that accomplishes this is shown in Figure 3.6, and the results are shown in Figure 3.7.

3.6 Bibliographical Remarks and References

3.6.1 Books and Journals

The classic reference to the Prolog language is Clocksin and Mellish (2003). The standard is described in Ed-Dbali, Deransart, and Cervoni (1996). References to logic programming include Doets (1994), Hogger (1984), and Lloyd (1984). A more mathematical treatment can be found in Borger and Rosensweig (1994). Robinson (1965) provides a look at implementing logic as a basis for computation.

3.6.2 Web-Based Resources

SWI-Prolog implements all predicates described in *Prolog: The Standard* (Ed-Dbali, Deransart, and Cervoni, 1996), and is close to conforming with the ISO specification described in *Information Technology—Programming Languages—Prolog, Part 1: General Core*, ISO/IEC 13211-1, 1995. The SWI-Prolog homepage is:

www.swi-prolog.org

Here you will find SWI-Prolog in various forms, including a self-extracting executable for Windows and an rpm for Linux, as well as a User's Guide (pdf). You will also find various additional tools (IDEs, editors, etc.) and Prolog links.

```
/* label2.pro */
/* added 2 unary constraints and
   output display (write,fail) */

highest(sky).
moving(car).
adj-to(car,road).
adj-to(road,grass).
adj-to(road,trees).
adj-to(sky,trees).
adj-to(grass,trees).

adjacent-to(R1,R2) :- adj-to(R1,R2).
adjacent-to(R1,R2) :- adj-to(R2,R1).


goal :- highest(R1),
        moving(R5),
        adjacent-to(R1,R2),
        adjacent-to(R2,R6),
        adjacent-to(R2,R3),
        adjacent-to(R3,R4),
        adjacent-to(R2,R4),
        adjacent-to(R4,R6),
        adjacent-to(R4,R5),
        write('Solution is'),nl,nl,
        write('region 1 is bound to  '),write(R1),nl,
        write('region 2 is bound to  '),write(R2),nl,
        write('region 3 is bound to  '),write(R3),nl,
        write('region 4 is bound to  '),write(R4),nl,
        write('region 5 is bound to  '),write(R5),nl,
        write('region 6 is bound to  '),write(R6),nl,nl,
        fail.
```

Figure 3.6 Enhanced Prolog Image Labeling Formulation: Addition of Highest and Moving Constraints.

```
?- ['label2.pro'].
% label2.pro compiled 0.00 sec, 2,892 bytes

Yes
?- goal.
Solution is

region 1 is bound to  sky
region 2 is bound to  trees
region 3 is bound to  grass
region 4 is bound to  road
region 5 is bound to  car
region 6 is bound to  grass


No
?-
```

Figure 3.7 Results Using Enhanced Prolog Image Labeling Database.

Alternatives to SWI-Prolog include the GNU Prolog compiler (`gprolog`), available at:

http://www.gnu.org/software/prolog/

A description of the ISO-conformant version of the Prolog language may be found at:

http://pauillac.inria.fr/~deransar/prolog/docs.html

3.7 Exercises

1. Consider the following two database formulations in Prolog. Formulation 1:

```
father(bob, bernard).
mother(bob, anne).
father(jesse, bob).
mother(jesse, leslie).
```

   Formulation 2:

```
bernard(father, bob).
anne(mother, bob).
bob(father, jesse).
leslie(mother, jesse).
```

   Note that in both formulations, the first fact is interpreted as "bernard is the father of bob."

   In each formulation, it is desired to form a rule (or set of rules, if necessary) that allows queries to the Prolog system to determine who is the grandparent of whom. Consider the suitability of each formulation, as well as the applicable rule(s).

2. This problem provides some experience with recursive Prolog descriptions and list manipulation. It is based upon the list membership predicate `member`. Consider two possible formulations of `member`:

```
member1(X,[_|Y]) :- member1(X,Y).
member1(X,[X|_]).

member2(X,[X|_]).
member2(X,[_|Y]) :- member2(X,Y).
```

   For the inquiry

```
?- member (a, [b, c, a, d]).
```

   show, in detail, the sequence of attempted unifications. (This may be done by hand or Prolog `trace`.) In this case, is one formulation more efficient? Is this always true?

3. In our development of a predicate member, membership of item X in the head of the list was tested via:

```
member(X, [X|_]).
```

Consider the alternative formulation:

```
member(X, [Y|_]) :- X = Y.
```

Is this formulation valid? If so, comment on the practicality of this approach compared to the former.

4. Given the following Prolog database:

```
pass_exam(Who1) :- study_hard(Who1), not(fool_around(Who1)).

pass_exam(Who2) :- do_homework(Who2), fail, study_hard(Who2).

study_hard(class).
fool_around(some).
do_homework(others).
do_homework(some).
```

what is the result of querying the Prolog database with

```
?- pass\_exam(Anybody).
```

Specifically, does this goal succeed, and if so, what are the resulting bindings on variable `Anybody`?

5. Which of the following are logically valid or consistent Prolog representations?

(a)
```
q:-p.
p.
q.
```
(b)
```
q:-p.
q.
```
(c)
```
q.
q:-not(p).
p.
```
(d)
```
q:-not(p).
q.
```

6. (This problem provides valuable experience in interpreting the not and cut predicates.) Prolog provides two built-in predicates defined as follows:

var(X) succeeds if X is currently an unbound variable.

nonvar(X) succeeds if X is currently not an unbound variable (the opposite of var(X)).

In Clocksin and Mellish (1984) a Prolog description of nonvar(X) is offered as follows:

```
nonvar(X) :- var(X), !, fail.

nonvar(\_).
```

Show how the use of the cut and fail predicates, together with the anonymous variable and the correct ordering of the above two statements, leads to proper operation of predicate nonvar.

Consider instead the following:

```
nonvar(X) :- not(var(X)).
```

Does this formulation accomplish the same thing?

7. In the text example, it was indicated that the rule:

```
sumoflist([[X]],Sum) :- Sum is X.
```

is a less efficient, but logically equivalent alternate for the clause:

```
sumoflist([[X]],X).
```

Why is this so?

8. `(Prolog LGN translations for grammar parsers.)` The file below shows five syntactically correct Prolog LGN clauses. Show the translated version of each clause.

```
/* sample LGN translations in Prolog */
/* file: lgn_trans.pro */

/* case (a) */

translate1 --> first, rest.

/* case (b) */

translate2 --> first,[middle],rest.

/* case (c) */

intexpr(E) --> term(T),restint(T,E).

/* case (d) */

strongop1 --> [times].

/* case (e) */

strongop2(Times) --> [times].
```

9. More recent Prologs provide **if . . . then** and **if . . . then . . . else** type constructs. These constructs are:

- familiar to imperative language programmers as basic control constructs.
- very troublesome if used carelessly.

- In Prolog, the **if . . . then** is based upon the infix operator ->/2, and extension to an **if . . . then . . . else** form incorporates the ;/2 predicate. More importantly, the ->/2 construct commits to the choices made at its left-hand side, removing backtracking points created inside the clause (using ;), or by goals spawned by this clause.

(a) Using your knowledge of the `call()` predicate and the cut (!) operator, define the **if . . . then** construct, that is,

$$(A- > B) : - < solution >$$

(b) Repeat the previous design for the **if . . . then . . . else** form, that is,

$$(A- > B; C) : - < solution >$$

10. An ambiguous grammar is shown below.

$$S \rightarrow AB$$
$$S \rightarrow C$$
$$A \rightarrow c$$
$$A \rightarrow a$$
$$B \rightarrow b$$
$$B \rightarrow c$$
$$C \rightarrow cC$$
$$C \rightarrow c$$

Show, using derivation tree(s) for the string *cc*, why it is ambiguous.

11. As shown in Section 3.2.7, Prolog often (carefully) mixes floating-point and integer results. Test your understanding by predicting (and checking) Prolog's response to the following example queries:

```
?- 1.0 is sin(pi/2).

?- 1.0 is float(sin(pi/2)).

?- 1.0 =:= sin(pi/2).
```

12. In Section 3.2.7, a number of type-checking predicates were introduced. Using the reference manual and/or Prolog's `help` facility, determine the use of each of the following predicates:

```
atomic(+Term)

compound(+Term)

ground(+Term)
```

13. A Prolog description (database) `scuba.pro` is given below. Show the Prolog response (*all* solutions, if any) for the following queries or goals:

(a) `?-ascends_carefully(darren).`

(b) `?-can_equalize_pressure(Any).`

(c) `?-competent_diver(kim).`

```
/* Prolog scuba 'proficiency' database */
/* file: scuba.pro */

competent_diver(X) :- breathes_continuously(X),
                      obtains_neutral_buoyancy(X),
                      ascends_carefully(X),
                      descends(X, slowly).

competent_diver(Y) :- certified(Y).

breathes_continuously(D) :- not(stops_breathing(D)).

obtains_neutral_buoyancy(E) :- controls_BCD(E), not(uses_junk(E)).

can_equalize_pressure(F) :- descends_slowly(F), knows_Valsalva_tech(F), !.

can_equalize_pressure(F) :- descends_slowly(F), knows_Toynbee_tech(F), !.

can_equalize_pressure(F) :- knows__tech(F).

ascends(Who, slowly) :- false.

ascends(Who, carefully) :- ascends_carefully(_).

descends_slowly(Who) :- descends(Who, slowly).

certified(Y) :- pays_money(Z).

passes_course(darren).
passes_course(kim).

knows_Toynbee_tech(darren).
knows_Valsalva_tech(kim).

ascends_carefully(darren).
descends(darren, _).
certified(darren).
certified(kim).

stops_breathing(dead_guy).

controls_BCD(darren).

pays_money(patti).
```

14. A Prolog parser, `parser_q.pro`, is shown below. For each of the queries below, find the *first* solution returned by Prolog.

    (a) `?-parse1(vp, What, [], ShowMe).`

    (b) `?-parse2(vp, What, [], ShowMe).`

```
/* FILE NAME: parser_q.pro */
/* REVISION:  2-14-03 rjs */


parse1(sentence, Before, After, [Np_result, Vp_result]) :-
          parse1(np, Before, Not_np, Np_result),
          parse1(vp, Not_np, After, Vp_result).

parse1(np, In, Left, [Adj_result, Noun_result]) :-
          parse(det, In, Rest, Adj_result),
          parse1(modnoun, Rest, Left, Noun_result).

parse1(vp, In, Left, [Verb_result, Np_result]) :-
          parse(verb, In, Rest, Verb_result),
          parse1(np, Rest, Left, Np_result).

parse1(modnoun, In, Left, [Adj_result, Noun_result]) :-
          parse1(adj, In, Rest, Adj_result),
          parse1(noun, Rest, Left, Noun_result).

parse1(modnoun, In, Left, Mod_result) :-
          parse(noun, In, Left, Mod_result).

parse2(sentence, Before, After, [Np_result, Vp_result]) :-
          parse2(np, Before, Not_np, Np_result),
          parse2(vp, Not_np, After, Vp_result).

parse2(np, In, Left, [Adj_result, Noun_result]) :-
          parse(det, In, Rest, Adj_result),
          parse2(modnoun, Rest, Left, Noun_result).

parse2(vp, In, Left, [Verb_result, Np_result]) :-
          parse(verb, In, Rest, Verb_result),
          parse2(np, Rest, Left, Np_result).

parse2(modnoun, In, Left, [Adj_result, Noun_result]) :-
          parse(adj, In, Rest, Adj_result),
          parse(noun, Rest, Left, Noun_result).

parse2(modnoun, In, Left, Mod_result) :-
          parse(noun, In, Left, Mod_result).

parse(det,  [A|B], B, A) :- word(det,  A).
parse(noun, [C|D], D, C) :- word(noun, C).
parse(verb, [E|F], F, E) :- word(verb, E).
parse(adj,  [G|H], H, G) :- word(adj, G).

word(verb, crashes).
word(det, the).
word(noun, computer).
word(noun, program).
word(adj, faulty).
word(adj, esoteric).
```

15. What do you think that

```
sent2v(N,M) --> np2v(N,M), vp2v(N,M).
```

would translate into?

16. This problem extends the Prolog CSP example shown in Section 3.5. Using the given Prolog as a start, show a revised Prolog description that includes the additional specifications (taken individually) that there should be:

    (a) At most one region labeled "trees" in the solution.
    (b) Exactly one region labeled "car" in the solution.
    (c) At least one region labeled "trees" in the solution.

    Show your labeling results for each case.

17. Suppose you are given the grammar $L(G_{square-weave})$, where

$$G_{square-weave} = \{\Sigma, N, P, S\} \tag{3.4}$$

where $N = \{S, A\}$, $\Sigma = \{d, l, r\}$ and

$$\begin{aligned} &P = \{\\ &S \rightarrow rS\\ &S \rightarrow dA\\ &A \rightarrow lA\\ &A \rightarrow dS\\ &A \rightarrow l\\ &S \rightarrow r\ \} \end{aligned}$$

and S is the starting symbol.

    (a) What type(s) of a grammar is $G_{square-weave}$?
    (b) Is the following string an element of $L(G_{square-weave})$?
    $rrdrdr$
    (c) Is the following string an element of $L(G_{square-weave})$?
    $rrrdlldrr$
    (d) Is the following string an element of $L(G_{square-weave})$?
    $rrdldr$
    (e) Draw a derivation tree for the string rrr.

18. (a) The productions in $L(G_{square-weave})$ were shown in the previous problem. For each production, show the corresponding representation in the Prolog LGN.
    (b) Show the corresponding representation of the productions in $L(G_{square-weave})$ in BNF.

19. In Section 3.5 all the solutions to the labeling CSP were shown by adding `fail` at the end of the goal to force backtracking (and writing of the solutions). This problem suggests an alternative, using Prolog's `bagof` predicate, described as:

```
bagof(+Var, +Goal, -Bag)
    Unify Bag with the alternatives of Var, if Goal has free variables
    besides the one sharing with Var bagof will backtrack over the
    alternatives of these free variables, unifying Bag with the
    corresponding alternatives of Var.
```

Given the database shown in Section 3.5, Figure 3.5:

(a) Use `bagof` to show the 42 solutions.

(b) Use `bagof` and `length` to verify that there are 42 solutions.

20. This is an introduction to constrained optimization using Prolog. Consider two additional problem constraints for the labeling problem of Section 3.5:

    (a) Maximize the number of regions labeled "car."

    (b) Maximize the number of regions labeled "trees."

    Use only the original `adjacent-to` constraint together with these new global constraints (individually) and show *all* the resulting labelings.

21. In Section 3.2.8, we noted that unification-based problem solutions may have functionality beyond that of the original intent. To verify this, consider our design of the `member` predicate and determine and explain the Prolog response to the following goals:

    - `?- member(6, [7,8,Var1,9,Var2]).`
    - `?- member(what, What).`

22. Suppose we desire a predicate of the form:

```
append(List1, List2, Result).
```

    where Result is the list resulting from appending `List2` to the end of `List1`. Develop a Prolog representation for this predicate. Here is a hint:

```
append([], List, List).
```

23. This problem considers several rather long examples of using a Prolog database with various list structures and options.

    Consider first the use of a simplistic list structure, as shown here:

```
/* Prolog data base for example */
/* file: prolog-db-merch2a.pro */
/* this version uses (too simple) list structures */


character([desdemora,psychic,frank_bama,pilot,trevor_kane,artist,
rudy_breno,reporter,colonel_cairo,bad_guy,charlie_fabian,real_bad_guy,
root_boy,cook,root_boy,cannonball,billy_cruiser,pilot,billy_cruiser,mentor,
joe_merchant,rock_star,little_elmo,diver,blanton_meyercord,jet_ski_killer,
hoagy,dog]).

place([boomtown,rudderville,miami,havana]).

/* pay attention to the arity of the predicate and list(s) below-- */

object([plane,hemisphere_dancer],[plane,vomit_comet],[boat,cosmic_muffin],
[boat,nomad]).
```

Notice in this case the entire database consists of a single ("linear") list.

```
Yes
?- ['./prolog-db-merch2a.pro'].
% ./prolog-db-merch2a.pro compiled 0.00 sec, 2,512 bytes

Yes
?- character(billy_cruiser).

No
?- character(X), member(billy_cruiser, X).

X = [desdemora, psychic, frank_bama, pilot, trevor_kane,
artist, rudy_breno, reporter, colonel_cairo|...]
Yes
?- character(X), member(artist, X).

X = [desdemora, psychic, frank_bama, pilot, trevor_kane,
artist, rudy_breno, reporter, colonel_cairo|...]
Yes
?- place(X),member(miami,X).

X = [boomtown, rudderville, miami, havana]
Yes
?- place(X),member(clemson,X).

No
?- object(X), member(plane,X).

No
?- object(X), member([plane,Y],X).

No
?- object(X,_,_,_), member([plane,Y],X).

No
?- object(X,_,_,_), member(plane,X).

X = [plane, hemisphere_dancer]
Yes
```

The limited utility of this approach should be obvious. Consider instead the revised formulation in which we use a list structured as a list of two element sublists, namely a database in an association-list format:

```
/* Prolog data base for example */
/* file: prolog-db-merch2b.pro */
/* this version uses alternative list structures */


character([[desdemora,psychic],[frank_bama,pilot],[trevor_kane,artist],
[rudy_breno,reporter],[colonel_cairo,bad_guy],[charlie_fabian,real_bad_guy],
[root_boy,cook],[root_boy,cannonball],[billy_cruiser,pilot],[billy_cruiser,mentor],
[joe_merchant,rock_star],[little_elmo,diver],[blanton_meyercord,jet_ski_killer],
[hoagy,dog]]).

place([boomtown,rudderville,miami,havana]).
```

```
/* choice of predicate name is poor */

object([[plane,hemisphere_dancer],[plane,vomit_comet],[boat,cosmic_muffin],
[boat,nomad]]).
```

Design a Prolog predicate that allows us to query the list-based database and determine if a certain character is on the list.

24. Consider the following (ambiguous) grammar:

$$S \to AB$$
$$S \to C$$
$$A \to c$$
$$A \to a$$
$$B \to b$$
$$B \to c$$
$$C \to cC$$
$$C \to c$$

We could determine $L(G)$ by hand, but there is an easier way—we can let Prolog generate it, as shown below.

```
/* lgn-example2.pro */

s --> a,b.
s --> c.
a --> [termc].
a --> [terma].
b --> [termb].
b --> [termc].
/* observe order */
c--> [termc].
c --> [termc],c.

?- listing(s).

s(A, B) :-
a(A, C),
b(C, B).
s(A, B) :-
c(A, B).

Yes
?- listing(c).

c([termc|A], A).
c(A, B) :-
'C'(A, termc, C),
c(C, B).

Yes
?- s(LofG,[]).
```

```
LofG = [termc, termb] ;;

LofG = [termc, termc] ;;

LofG = [terma, termb] ;;

LofG = [terma, termc] ;;

LofG = [termc] ;;

LofG = [termc, termc] ;;

LofG = [termc, termc, termc] ;;

LofG = [termc, termc, termc, termc] ;;

LofG = [termc, termc, termc, termc, termc] ;;

LofG = [termc, termc, termc, termc, termc, termc] ;;

LofG = [termc, termc, termc, termc, termc, termc, termc]
Yes
?-
```

What is the problem with this grammar in the generative mode?

25. The previous problem alluded to the possibility of infinite recursion in recursive productions and Prolog LGN implementations. Here we seek to focus on the cause and look for solutions or at least preventative measures. To this end, consider the productions:

$$C \rightarrow cC$$
$$C \rightarrow c$$

The first production employs *right recursion.* For reference, the corresponding LGN representation in a Prolog database is:

```
c --> [termc],c.
c--> [termc].
```

An alternative is the set of productions:

$$C \rightarrow Cc$$
$$C \rightarrow c$$

which represent *left recursion.*

Actually there are eight cases in Prolog, depending upon the order of the two corresponding clauses in each Prolog database and whether the grammar is used in the generative or recognition (i.e., as a parser) mode.

Show the behavior for the eight combinations, and summarize the cases.

26. Look at the following Prolog code and determine what you think the operator precedence rules would yield.

```
/* examples of operator precedence in PROLOG */
/* file: predecd.pro          */

/* first some numerical examples */

testn(A,B,C,D,E) :- A is B - C * D + E.
testn2(A,B,C,D,E) :- A is (B - C * D + E).
testn3(A,B,C,D,E) :- A is (B - C) * (D + E).
testn4(A,B,C,D,E) :- A is (B - (C * D) + E).
testn5(A,B,C,D,E) :- A is B - ((C * D) + E).

goaln(Ans) :- testn(Ans,2,3,4,5).
goaln2(Ans) :- testn2(Ans,2,3,4,5).
goaln3(Ans) :- testn3(Ans,2,3,4,5).
goaln4(Ans) :- testn4(Ans,2,3,4,5).
goaln5(Ans) :- testn5(Ans,2,3,4,5).

/* now some logical examples  */

testl(A,B,C,D,E) :- A = B ; C , D, not(E).
testl1(A,B,C,D,E) :- A = B ; (C , D, not(E)).
testl2(A,B,C,D,E) :- A = B ; (C , not(D , E)).
testl3(A,B,C,D,E) :- A = (B ; C , not(D) , E).
testl4(A,B,C,D,E) :- (A = B) ; (C , D, not(E)).
testl5(A,B,C,D,E) :- (A = B ; C), D, not(E).

goall :- testl(fail,true,fail,true,fail).
goall1 :- testl1(fail,true,fail,true,fail).
goall2 :- testl2(fail,true,fail,true,fail).
goall3 :- testl3(fail,true,fail,true,fail).
goall4 :- testl4(fail,true,fail,true,fail).
goall5 :- testl5(fail,true,fail,true,fail).
```

27. The objective of this exercise is to implement a simple version of the "hangman" game in Prolog. This version does not stop after six misses, nor does it keep track of previously guessed letters. (Note: this problem is continued in the Palm development examples.) *The solution should be based upon recursion.* A list should be used to hold the database of hangman problems, the current problem, and the current problem display. Random generation of problems is required. Sample operation of the desired Prolog design is shown below.

```
?- ['hangman.pro'].
% hangman.pro compiled 0.00 sec, 5,868 bytes

Yes
?- game.


welcome to Prolog hangman
typing 0-CR ends the game and Prolog session


-- --- ---- ------
input guess followed by CR:a

you entered: a
-- a-- ---- ------
```

```
input guess followed by CR:s

you entered: s
__ as_ ____ ______
input guess followed by CR:t

you entered: t
__ as_ ____ __t___
input guess followed by CR:r

you entered: r
__ as_ ___r __t__r
input guess followed by CR:k

you entered: k
__ ask ___r __t__r
input guess followed by CR:g

you entered: g
g_ ask ___r __t__r
input guess followed by CR:o

you entered: o
go ask _o_r _ot__r
input guess followed by CR:y

you entered: y
go ask yo_r _ot__r
input guess followed by CR:u

you entered: u
go ask your _ot__r
input guess followed by CR:m

you entered: m
go ask your mot__r
input guess followed by CR:h

you entered: h
go ask your moth_r
input guess followed by CR:e

you entered: e
go ask your mother

*** CONGRATULATIONS -- YOU WON! ***
```

28. A Prolog designer was trying to develop a version of hangman that would play the game forever (unless the user forced the Prolog system to break by using CRTL-C), and therefore developed the Prolog clause shown below. Assume predicates `welcome`, `generate`, `showInitial`, and `go` (all) succeed. Will this strategy achieve the design goal?

```
game :- welcome, generate(Problem),
        showInitial(Problem,Current),
        go(Problem,Current), game.
```

29. The SWI-Prolog help predicate says the following about predicate append:

```
append(?List1, ?List2, ?List3)
    Succeeds when List3 unifies with the concatenation of List1 and
    List2. The predicate can be used with any instantiation pattern
    (even three variables).
```

On this basis, what is the Prolog response to each of the following queries:

```
?- append([1,2,3],[4,5,6],What).

?- append([1,2,3],[4,5,6],[1,2,3]).

?- append([1,2,3],What,[1,2,3]).

?- append(What,[4,5,6],[1,2,3]).

?- append(What,[4,5,6],[1,2,3,4,5,6]).
```

30. Develop both recursive and nonrecursive Prolog definitions for a predicate last that works for any length list and has behavior as follows:

```
?- last([a,s,d,f,g],Which).

Which = g

Yes
```

31. Test your understanding of the difference between Prolog is and = as well as variable scoping with the following queries:

```
?- A=B.

?- A is 10.

?- A=B.

?- A is 10,A=B.

?- A is 10, B is 20, A=B.

?- B is 20, A=B.

?- A is 25, write(A).
```

32. The Prolog tenure database in Section 3.2.2 is augmented to include the following facts:

```
prepares_lectures(_).
writes_proposals(rjs).
prepares_lectures(rjs).
```

```
gets_good_evaluations(rc).
does_research(mab).
gets_funded(mab).

documents_research(rjs).
documents_research(pw).
writes_proposals(pw).

gets_good_evaluations(pw).
gets_good_evaluations(rjs).
lectures_well(pw).

lectures_well(mab).
lectures_well(rjs).
gets_funded(rc).

gets_funded(rjs).
does_research(pw).
```

Suppose the modified database is consulted and Prolog is then given the goal:

```
?- gets_tenure(Anyone).
```

Show the response of the Prolog system to this goal, that is, all possible bindings for variable `Anyone`.

33. Develop a Prolog database for an arity 2 predicate, `third`, which returns the third element of an arbitrarily sized list as the value of the second argument. The prototype is:

```
third(?Alist,?ThirdElement).
```

with sample operation:

```
?- third([[1,2],[3,4],[5,6],[7,8]],What).

What = [5, 6]

Yes
```

Do not use any of the `nth` family of predicates.

34. Consider a syntactically correct version of the "rootbeer" Prolog database:

```
/* Modification of (root) beer in Prolog */
/* the (recursive) clauses */

   bottles(X):-
     nl,
     write(X),write(' bottles of root beer on the wall,'),nl,
     write(X),write(' bottles of root beer...'),nl,
     write('take one down and pass it around,'), nl,
     X1 is X - 1,    /* note the infix notation */
     write(X1),write(' bottles of root beer on the wall.'), nl,nl,
```

```
    write('------------- pause -----------------'),nl,nl,
    bottles(X1).     /* here's the (direct) recursion */


  bottles(1) :-
    write('1 bottle of root beer on the wall, '),nl,
    write('1 bottle of root beer...'),nl,
    write('take one down and pass it around...'),nl,nl,
    write('Thats All Folks!').
```

If the goal

```
?- bottles(1).
```

is invoked, what is the result? Be specific and show the Prolog output.

35. The following Prolog database involves lists and is syntactically correct. Assume the database has been consulted.

```
whatdoes(Huh,[Huh]).
whatdoes(Huh, [_|Whoa]) :- whatdoes(Huh,Whoa).
```

Show the Prolog response (as Prolog would) for each of the following inquiries:

```
?- whatdoes(W,[1,2,3]).
?- whatdoes(W,[3,2,1,0]).
?- whatdoes(0,[1,2,3]).
?- whatdoes(3,[3,2,1,0]).
?- whatdoes(6,[merry,Xmas]).
```

CHAPTER 4

Sample Programming Language **minic** (Version 1) and Aspects of Scanning and Parsing

If you do not work on an important problem, it's unlikely you'll do important work.

—Richard Hamming[1]

4.1 Overview

The goal in this and subsequent chapters is to introduce the "toy" language `minic` and then to develop scanners and parsers for minic. We will show this development using `flex` and `bison`, as well as using the Prolog LGN. In addition, we enhance `minic` in subsequent chapters in order to approach a more familiar and realistic programming language.

4.2 minic (Version 1) Syntax

4.2.1 A Language Close to a Subset of C

`minic` is a small (toy) language used to show both generation and recognition of a grammar. `minic` is imperative, and (not accidentally) very similar to a subset of `C`. The syntax of the initial version of `minic` is very simple. Because most of the effort in developing a scanner and parser is reflected in the simpler syntax, we use it first before adding bells and whistles.

4.2.2 minic BNF Description

The syntax of `minic` (version 1) is shown below:

```
/* first translation unit BNF */
/* minic version 1.0 */
/* file: transunit-baf1.txt        */
/* note that comments below are ONLY for readability */
/*    i.e., not part of syntax              */
```

[1]From "You and Your Research," Transcription of the Bell Communications Research Colloquium Seminar, March 7, 1986.

```
<transunit> ::= <main-decl> <body>
<main-decl> ::= <type> main <arg>
<type> ::= int | void

              /* must specify input and returned type */
<arg> ::= lparens <type> rparens
<body> ::= lbrace <decl> <statseq> rbrace

              /* forces declarations, if any, first and only once */
<decl> ::= e | <type> <variable-list>;
<variable-list> ::= <variable> | <variable> , <variable-list>
<variable> ::= <identifier>
<statseq> := <return-stat> | <command-seq>; <return-stat>
<command-seq> ::= <command> | <command>; <command-seq>
<command> ::= <variable> assign <expr>
<expr> ::= <numeral> /* may want to revise this, maybe | <variable> */
<return-stat> ::= return <return-arg>;
             /* no optional return statement or semicolon */
<return-arg> ::= lparens <variable> rparens |
                             lparens <numeral> rparens
             /* no expression evaluation in the return */



/* lexical part (user identifiers and numerals) of the syntax */


<identifier> ::= <letter> | <identifier> <letter> | <identifier> <digit>
<letter> ::= a | b | c | d | e | f | g | h | i | j | k | l | m
                 | n | o | p | q | r | s | t | u | v | w | w | x | y | z
<numeral> ::= <digit> | <digit> <numeral>
<digit> ::= 0 | 1 | 2 | 3 | 4 | 5 | 6 | 7 | 8 | 9
```

4.2.3 Syntax Notes

For clarity in illustrating the syntax, and as a prelude to the tasks of scanning and parsing, note that some terminals in the grammar are shown using very unintuitive names. Although this is not strictly necessary, we do this so that our subsequent work in scanner/parser development (in Prolog) does not confuse reserved words and symbols in `minic` with those of Prolog. Table 4.1 shows the conversion. Further ramifications of this are considered in the problems.

`minic` Terminal	Actually Used	Meaning
`lparens`	(	Left parens
`rparens`	)	Right parens
`lbrace`	{	Left brace
`rbrace`	}	Right brace
`assign`	=	Assignment

Table 4.1 Equivalent Terminals in `minic`.

4.2.4 minic Syntax Subdivision

We subdivide the `minic` syntax into three parts:

1. Productions, which fundamentally determine the structure of major constructs in the language (main declarations, statement sequence, and so forth).
2. Reserved words and symbols.
3. User-formed "pseudo-terminals"—strings formed to represent numerals and identifiers.

Reserved Words and Symbols

```
int
void
lparens
rparens
lbrace
rbrace
,
;
assign
return
a | b | c | d | e | ...
0|1|2|3|4|5|6|7|8|9
```

User Identifiers and Numerals

These are shown in the last part of the syntax.

4.2.5 A minic (Version 1) Sample Program

Even with the very simple C-like syntax specified in Section 4.2.2, generation of a number of syntactically correct programs is possible. For example, it should be possible to produce the following program[2]:

```
int main(void)
{
int t1;
t1=10;
return(t1);
}
```

4.2.6 Sample Derivation Trees (Lexical Syntax)

Sample Derivation of Identifier and Numeral Using Lexical Syntax

Derivation trees corresponding to the production of the identifier `t1` and the numeral `10` are shown in Figure 4.1.

4.2.7 Derivation Tree for Sample Program

Figure 4.2 shows the derivation tree for the simple `minic` program shown in Section 4.2.5.

[2]The reader is encouraged to determine if `gcc` is able to compile this `minic` program.

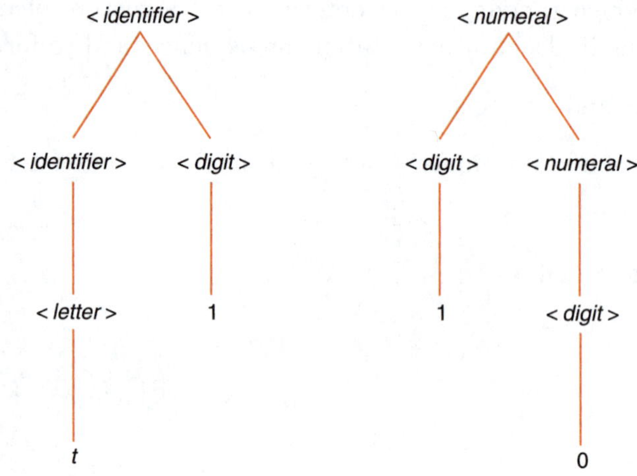

Figure 4.1 Sample Derivation Trees for Lexical Productions.

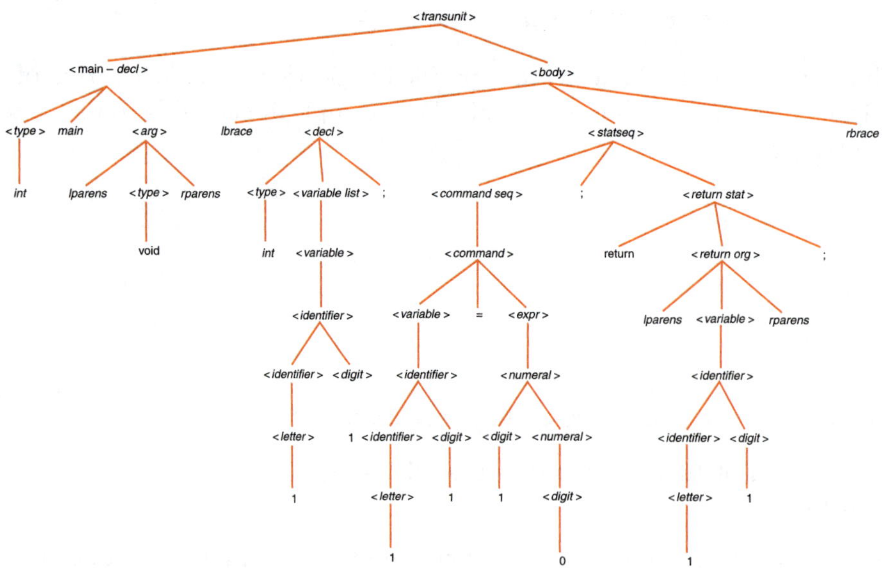

Figure 4.2 Derivation Tree for a Simple minic Program.

4.3 Development of Parsers for minic: Basic Concerns

4.3.1 Program Generation and Recognition in a Grammatical Context

Programming language utility, in the context of a grammar, involves both generation and recognition:

- Generation is the process of writing the program ("programming"). This is done by the programmer.
- Recognition is the process of translating the source code (usually as an ASCII file) into machine-level instructions, as determined by the particular program and the programming language semantics. These instructions are for a target machine, which may be virtual. Recognition is done by machine (e.g., via a compiler).

Although they are interrelated entities, it is nevertheless convenient to divide the overall syntax or the syntactic specification of a language into two parts:

- the lexical structure, which indicates the constraints on the **tokens**, or lexical units, which define the basic words or (multisymbol) terminals of the language. This includes reserved words and symbols (e.g., `void`, `while`, `if`, {, }, `;`) as well as user-defined words such as variable and function names.
- the remaining syntactic structure, which is then input to the grammatical recognizer, or **parser**. In fact, it is possible to distinguish between *lexical rules* or productions as well as *syntactic rules* or productions.

4.3.2 Parsing as a Two-Step Process

First, we digress to discuss lexical concerns, which ultimately leads to a two-part process.

The parsing process is often implemented as a two-step procedure, because that is often the most structured and efficient method. Moreover, in most modern programming languages, the existence of a number of user-specified identifiers[3] in the language specification give rise to what we may conceptualize as dynamic terminals in the underlying G.

Programming Language Lexical Constructs and Analysis

Our previous look at formal grammars considered, among other things, terminals and nonterminals. Most programming languages have a number of tokens, consisting of reserved words, special symbols, user-defined variable and procedure names, and so forth. Some examples follow.

Reserved Words

`begin, end` (Pascal)

`int, while, main, if` (C and minic)

`is, consult` (Prolog)

`defun, load, cond` (Lisp)

[3] Such as variable and function or predicate names.

Special Symbols

`!=` { } `++` (C)

`:-` , . (Prolog)

( ) (Lisp)

User-Defined Variable and Procedure Names

"my_program", "index", j, k, "find-roots"

One usual constraint is that user-defined symbol names cannot be the same as reserved words (That's why they're "reserved").

White Space

White space (whitespace) refers to characters in the ASCII source file that serve to delineate other groupings of characters, but as such have no translated counterpart after the scanning process. Most often characters taken to be whitespace include the carriage return/linefeed,[4] the tab, and extraneous spaces.

4.3.3 Lexics from the Grammatical Viewpoint

Recall that for a *grammar*, $G = (V_T, V_N, P, S)$, the specification of the terminals is via the set V_T. Consider a programming language where the user may define identifiers, such as program name, variable names, and function names. These are created in the programming process (the language-generative mode using G) and are not known in advance.

For purposes of parsing, however, it is convenient to consider these entities, once produced, as (pseudo)terminals. Consider the following fragment of `minic`:[5]

```
ans = t1 + t2 + kt;
```

Also consider a portion of the lexical syntax of `minic`:

```
<identifier> ::= <letter> | <identifier> <letter> |  <identifier> <digit>
<letter> ::= a | b | c | d | e | f | g | h | i | j | k | l | m
                 | n | o | p | q | r | s | t | u | v | w | x | y | z
<numeral> ::= <digit> | <digit> <numeral>
<digit> ::= 0|1|2|3|4|5|6|7|8|9
```

As far as the *syntactic structure* of the code fragment is concerned, the names of the variables (while important, because they correspond to specific storage locations) are not paramount. What is important is that they are allowable names, as dictated by the lexical BNF productions. We hereafter consider them tokens.

The structure of:

```
v1 = v2 + v2 + v3;
```

would be identical. Thus, in order to make the recognition/parsing process more efficient, we could first check to see if the variable names are valid—that is, if they satisfy the lexical part of the syntax—using a scanner, and if so, then parse the statement for structure.

[4]Note that Microsoft operating systems put both a carriage return and a linefeed at the end of each line in a text file. This is usually referred to as the "carriage return."

[5]As extended in Chapter 7 to allow more general expressions in statements.

4.3.4 Tokens

The `minic` tokens that are output from the scanner are recognized from the ASCII source file input. Formally:

> *Tokens are reserved words and symbols (in a converted or renamed form, if necessary) as well as anything producible via the lexical part of the minic syntax. Thus far, this includes the constructs that generate numerals and user-defined identifiers, as defined in the lexical productions.*

4.3.5 The Two Essential Processes of Syntactic Analysis

As we noted, parsing of a source file is often preceded by scanning **lexical analysis** to identify tokens. Similarly, the grammar specification often distinguishes lexical productions from the higher-level productions—for example, those involving major constructs such as:

```
<main-decl>, <body>, <statseq>, <return-stat>, <command-seq>,
```

Scanning or lexical analysis prior to parsing allows a more efficient representation of the grammar productions. The `minic` parser will reflect this structure, by proceeding in two steps:

1. **Scanning:** To see if we can recognize all terminals in the string (program). Valid identifiers are recognized and converted to "pseudoterminals."[6] At this time it is also convenient to convert the source file into **tokens** for subsequent syntactic analysis.

2. **Parsing:** To see if the string of tokens is derivable according to the (nonlexical) syntax of the language.

   In summary, grammatical recognition is often accomplished in two parts: scanning followed by parsing. This corresponds to lexical analysis followed by syntactic analysis.

4.4 Parsing

The objective of parsing is to determine if a given string is *syntactically well formed* in the context of a prespecified grammar. Parsing is accomplished by parsers, which are often referred to as syntax analyzers. To construct a parser for any language, it is first necessary to quantify the language as described previously.

Different parsing methods are used for different classes of grammars. Although we first consider building parsers for `minic` and its descendants in Prolog, we will consider a number of alternative parsing approaches. Specifically, the the use of the CYK parsing algorithm on a CFG grammar in Chomsky normal form is shown. In addition, we show the use of the GNU `flex` lexical scanner generator and the GNU `bison` compiler-generator.

4.4.1 Specification of the Parsing Problem

Given a string of terminals comprising a sentence x, and a grammar G, specified as:

$$G = (V_T, V_N, P, S) \tag{4.1}$$

[6]In the previous example, they would be output from the scanner as `ide(v1)`, `ide(v2)`, etc.

consider forming a derivation (or parse) tree. The process of creating the interior of the parse tree of productions that links S to x is called a parse. If we are successful, we have determined that x is a member of $L(G)$. If we fill the interior of the tree from the top down (i.e., from the root of the tree), a *top-down parse* results. Thus, *top-down parsing* proceeds from S to the terminals. It is an attempt to obtain a derivation of x. Alternately, if we work from the bottom (x) up—that is, begin with the terminal symbols—a *bottom-up parse* results. Thus, *bottom-up parsing* proceeds from terminals toward S.

4.4.2 Parsing/Generation Similarities

Although generation and parsing of a string are strongly related, the situation is by no means a two-way street. Application of a grammar in the generative mode is usually far easier than in the analytic mode, or parsing. Two concerns with parsing are:

1. In practice, the parser must determine the extent of the elements that are derived from nonterminals. This is not simple, given a complex grammar.

2. The parser must find a use for all of string x. It cannot simply identify parts of the string with some structure and discard the rest. Thus, in a sense, the string must be "consumed" in the parse.

4.4.3 Parsing Computational Complexity and the Decidability Problem

Parsing of sentences in formal languages involves the matching of substructures to form and recognize an overall or global structure. The potential search complexity suggests that other *a priori* information (including heuristics) may be useful in the development of practical parsers.

Given $L(G)$ and a string x, we ask:

$$x \overset{?}{\in} L(G) \tag{4.2}$$

Consider the effort required to answer this question. If an algorithm exists that answers this question in a finite amount of time, the parsing problem is said to be *fully decidable.*

4.4.4 Parsing Approaches

Top-Down Parsing Approaches

Recall that in the top-down parsing approach, we proceed from the start symbol, S, to the terminals. Two approaches (Trembly and Sorenson, 1985) are:

1. top-down with fullbackup (TDFB) (brute force): This is a depth-first expansion of nonterminals starting with the leftmost nonterminal in the expansion of goal.

2. recursive descent (RD): This approach allows no backup; it may not work on all grammars. It uses binary-valued and recursive *functions* to recognize substrings that correspond to the expansion of a specific nonterminal.

Bottom-Up Parsing Approaches

We might envision top-down parsing as the speculative application of productions, beginning with S. The alternative bottom-up approach may be viewed as the speculative "reversing" of productions. Given x, we construct a series or sequence of intermediate strings from $(V_N \cup V_T)^+$ by reversing a corresponding series of productions.

"Reversing" a Production

Given a production, $P1$

$$P1 : A \rightarrow \alpha \tag{4.3}$$

where A is a nonterminal and α is a string of terminals and nonterminals; "reversing" $P1$ means locating an occurrence of α in one of the strings in the sequence and replacing α by A. The combinatorial explosion of choices in the sequence is often a barrier to practical application. For example, given $\alpha = a$, and the string $x = aaaa$ and $P1$, possible (one-step) reverses are

$$\begin{array}{c} A\ a\ a\ a \\ a\ A\ a\ a \\ a\ a\ A\ a \\ a\ a\ a\ A \end{array}$$

Bottom-up approaches, therefore, attempt to speculatively contract the given string into nonterminals, whereas top-down are speculative, or tentative, expansions.

4.4.5 Comparing Parsing Approaches

It is difficult to comparatively assess top-down and bottom-up approaches. There are grammars that are more efficiently parsed with top-down parsers and others where bottom-up parsers are more efficient. Therefore, the choice is often grammar dependent. In addition, transformation or normalization of a given grammar may affect parsing efficiency. Unfortunately, brute force top-down and bottom-up parsing approaches have a computational complexity that, in general, may grow exponentially with $|x|$. For this reason, we seek enhancements or alternatives that yield more practical utility.

4.4.6 The Cocke-Younger-Kasami (CYK) Parsing Algorithm

Constraints on and Performance of the CYK Approach

The CYK algorithm is a parsing approach that will parse string x in a number of steps proportional to $|x|^3$. The CYK algorithm requires the CFG be in Chomsky normal form. With this restriction, the derivation of any string involves a series of binary decisions.

Chomsky Normal Form

In Chomsky Normal Form (CNF), each production of G must be in the form of either

$$A \rightarrow BC$$

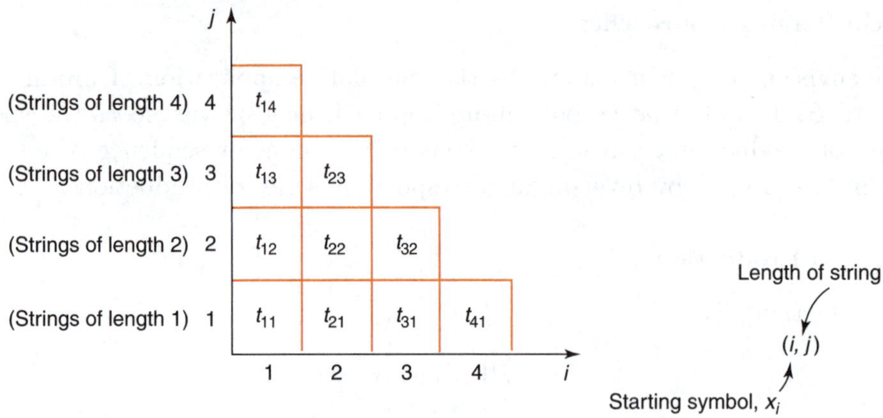

Figure 4.3 Basic Parse Table Structure for CYK Algorithm.

or

$$A \rightarrow a$$

Thus, conversion of the given grammar into this form is necessary.

The CYK Parse Table

Given string $x = x_1, x_2, \ldots x_n$, where $x_i \in V_T$, $|x| = n$, and a grammar, G, we form a triangular table with entries t_{ij} indexed by i and j where $1 \leq i \leq n$ and $1 \leq j \leq (n-i+1)$. The origin is at $i = j = 1$, and entry t_{11} is the lower left-hand entry in the table. t_{1n} is the uppermost entry in the table. This structure is shown in Figure 4.3, for the case of $n = 4$.

Forming the CYK Table

The CYK parse table is built, starting from location $(1, 1)$. *If a substring of* x*, beginning with* x_i*, and of length* j *can be derived from a nonterminal, this nonterminal is placed into cell* (i, j). If cell $(1, n)$ contains S, the table contains a valid derivation of x in $L(G)$. It is convenient to list the x_i, starting with $i = 1$, under the bottom row of the table.

Examples of the CYK Approach

The following productions are used.[7] V_N and V_T are apparent from the productions.

Sample Grammar Productions

$$\begin{aligned} S &\rightarrow AB|BB \\ A &\rightarrow CC|AB|a \\ B &\rightarrow BB|CA|b \\ C &\rightarrow BA|AA|b \end{aligned}$$

We explore the parse (derivation) of string $x = aabb$ using the CYK approach. Notice that the grammar productions are already in CNF. Conversion of productions from a general CFG form into CNF is addressed in the problems.

[7]This is a modified example of that shown in Arbib, Moll, and Kfoury (1988), p. 65.

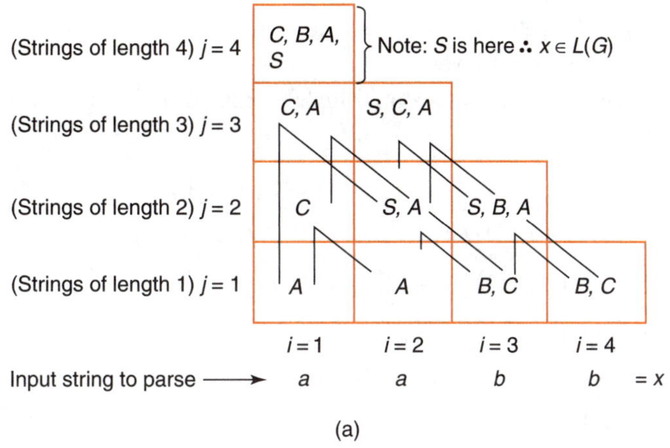

(a)

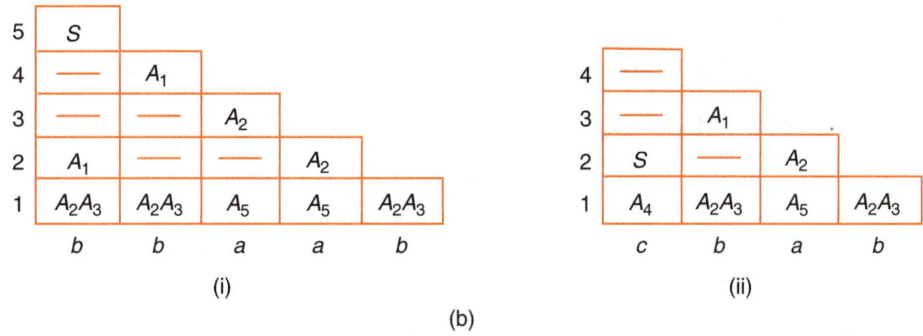

(b)

Figure 4.4 Sample Formation of the Parse Tables for Text Examples.

Construction of the CYK Parse Table

Construction of the parse table for this example is shown in Figure 4.4(a). Recall that cell entry (i, j) corresponds to the possibility of production of a string of length j, starting with symbol x_i. The table is formed from the bottom row ($j = 1$) upward. Entries for cells (1, 1), (2, 1), (3, 1), and (4, 1) are relatively easy to determine, because they each correspond to production of a single terminal. The process of completing the upper rows of this table is now detailed.

For the second ($j = 2$) row of the table, all nonterminals that could yield derivations of substrings of length 2, beginning with x_i $i = 1, 2, 3$, must be considered. For example, cell (1, 2) corresponds to production of a two-terminal long-string beginning with "a." Alternately, it is only necessary to consider nonterminals that produce AA, as shown in the $j = 1$ row of the table. From the given grammar productions, only nonterminal 'C,' in production $C \rightarrow BA|AA|b$, satisfies this.

Forming the third and fourth ($j = 3$ and $j = 4$, respectively) rows of the table is slightly more complicated. For example, cell (1, 3) corresponds to strings of length 3, beginning with terminal x_1 (a) in this case. This requires examination of cells (1, 1) and (2, 2), corresponding to producing the desired string with one nonterminal followed by two nonterminals (denoted $\{1 + 2\}$ hereafter), as well as cells (1, 2) and (3, 1), denoted the $\{2 + 1\}$ derivation. For the former, it is necessary to consider whether production of AS, AA, and nonterminal C is applicable. For the latter, the production of CB and CC is considered, yielding A. Thus, cell (1, 3) contains nonterminals C and A. Similarly, for cell (2, 3), cells (2, 1) and (3, 2) (the $\{1+2\}$ derivation) as well as (2, 2) and (4, 1) (the $\{2+1\}$ derivation) must be considered.

Finally, formation of cell (1, 4) is considered. Possible cell pairings to consider are summarized below:

$$(1,1) \text{ and } (2,3)\{1+3\} \rightarrow AS, AC, \underline{AA} : C$$
$$(1,2) \text{ and } (3,2)\{2+2\} \rightarrow CS, CB, \underline{CA} : B$$
$$(1,3) \text{ and } (4,1)\{3+1\} \rightarrow CB, \underline{CC}, \underline{AB}, AC : A, S$$

Cell pairings that yield a possible nonterminal are shown underlined. Thus, (1, 4) contains nonterminals C, B, A, S. Because this includes the starting symbol, the parse succeeds and *aabb* is a valid string in the language of this grammar. Note that because the grammar is in CNF, it is never necessary to consider more than two-cell pairings (although as we increase j the number of possible pairings increases).

Another Example of CYK Parsing

Suppose we are given the following finite state grammar (FSG):

$$S \rightarrow bA_1|cA_2$$
$$A_1 \rightarrow bA_2$$
$$A_2 \rightarrow b|aA_2$$

Converting to CNF yields

$$S \rightarrow A_3A_1$$
$$A_3 \rightarrow b$$
$$S \rightarrow A_4A_2$$
$$A_4 \rightarrow c$$
$$A_1 \rightarrow A_3A_2$$
$$A_2 \rightarrow b$$
$$A_2 \rightarrow A_5A_2$$
$$A_5 \rightarrow a$$

Parse tables for strings $x = bbaab$ and $x = cbab$ are shown in Figure 4.4(b). Note that the existence of an empty cell (other than $(1, n)$) does not necessarily lead to a failure to parse.

4.5 Life After Parsing

In many applications, such as development of compilers for programming languages, parsing is not the final step, but rather a necessary means to a larger end. In the case of a compiler, parsing is followed by conversion of the parsed program into machine instructions. This is often referred to as the compiler's "back-end," that is, the postparsing code that generates machine language specific to the architecture of a target machine.

Given a string (program) and G, parsing answers the question of whether the string is syntactically correct. In addition, and often as a direct result of the parsing process,[8] the

[8]We show this in our Prolog parser for `minic`.

structure of the string (program) is determined. Especially significant is the identification of syntactic fragments–`<command-seq>`, `<command>`, and so forth. Each of these program elements is then converted to machine code and executed (or evaluated).

4.6 Bibliographical Remarks and References

Classic references for lookahead and LR parsing are Aho and Ulman (1973), Aho and Johnson (1974), Kristensen and Madsen (1981), and DeRemer and Pennello (1982). Compiler writing and generation are treated in Trembly and Sorenson (1985) and Appel and Ginsburg (1998). A classic reference for treating semantics in CFGs is Knuth (1968).

4.7 Exercises

1. Suppose you are given the grammar $G_{square-weave}$, where

$$G_{square-weave} = \{\Sigma, N, P, S\} \tag{4.4}$$

where $N = \{S, A\}$, $\Sigma = \{d, l, r\}$ and

$$\begin{aligned}
&P = \{\\
&S \rightarrow rS\\
&S \rightarrow dA\\
&A \rightarrow lA\\
&A \rightarrow dS\\
&A \rightarrow l\\
&S \rightarrow r\}
\end{aligned}$$

and S is the starting symbol.

Using $G_{square-weave}$, show a CYK parse table for each of the strings:

(a) $rrdrdr$
(b) $rrrdlldrr$
(c) $rrdldr$

2. A sample grammar is shown below.

$$\begin{aligned}
S &\rightarrow AB|BB\\
A &\rightarrow CC|AB|a\\
B &\rightarrow BB|CA|b\\
C &\rightarrow BA|AA|c
\end{aligned}$$

Show the CYK parsing tables for the strings:

(a) $x = caab$
(b) $x = bbaa$
(c) $x = cccb$

3. Comment on each of the following assertions. Be clear and specific.

   (a) In using the CYK algorithm, if a row (e.g., row p), of the parse table becomes identically zero, i.e., $t_{ip} = 0 \quad \forall i$, the parse must fail.

   (b) In using the CYK algorithm, if a column (e.g., column p), of the parse table becomes identically zero, i.e., $t_{pi} = 0 \quad \forall i$, the parse must fail.

4. Recall G from Chapter 2:

$$S \rightarrow AB$$
$$S \rightarrow C$$
$$A \rightarrow C$$
$$A \rightarrow a$$
$$B \rightarrow b$$
$$B \rightarrow \mathrm{c}$$
$$C \rightarrow d$$

   Show CYK parse tables for the strings:

   (a) $x = dc$

   (b) $x = cd$

5. Refer to the `minic` syntax.

   (a) Using the starting nonterminal S=`<identifier>`, show a complete derivation tree for the identifier (or string):

   `ans10`

   (b) In `minic`, the BNF productions for both `<identifier>` and `<digit>` are recursive. Thus, the grammar is self-embedding. Would it make any difference with respect to the $L(G_{minic})$ if we rewrote the production:

   <numeral> ::= <digit> | <numeral> <digit>

   as follows:

   <numeral> ::= <digit> | <digit> <numeral>

   Why or why not?

   (c) Instead of the modification in part (b), what if we rewrote the single `minic` production:

   <identifier> ::= <letter> |<identifier> <letter> | <identifier> <digit>

   as:

   <identifier> ::= <letter> |<letter> <identifier> | <digit> <identifier>

   Would this change $L(G_{minic})$?

6. Which of the following three files are syntactically valid `minic` (Version 1) programs, that is, derivable from $S =$ `<transunit>`?

```
int main(void)
{
    int t1,t2;
    t1=t2;
    return(t2);
}

int main(void)
{
     int t1;
     int t2;
     t1=10;
     t2=20;
     return(t2);
}

int main(void)
{
     t2=20;
     return(t2);
}
```

7. The CYK algorithm requires productions in a CFG represented in Chomsky normal form, as defined in Section 4.4.6. Given an arbitrary set of productions in a CFG, show how these could be converted into CNF.

CHAPTER 5

Using Prolog for Scanning and Parsing

Why do programmers get Halloween and Christmas mixed up? Because
OCT(31) == DEC(25)
—Source Unknown

5.1 Scanner and Parser for minic Version 1: Overall Objectives

The minic parser development effort in this chapter involves the following tasks:

- convert each BNF production in minic to a corresponding LGN clause.
- do this without causing infinite recursion (i.e., some rewriting may be required).
- develop a scanner in Prolog that (1) recognizes the lexical part of the minic syntax (without infinite recursion); and (2) converts an ASCII source file containing a minic program into a Prolog list of tokens, for use with the resulting parser.

5.1.1 Good News: The Prolog LGN Builds the Parser for Us

As shown in Section 5.1.3, once productions from the BNF description of minic are converted into the Prolog LGN representation, the development of a parser (neglecting any problems with infinite recursion) is essentially complete. For that reason, we show several example conversions and alternatives before considering the entire parser.

5.1.2 Bad News: We Have to Build the minic Source File to Token List Scanner in Prolog

In the two-step scanning/parsing process, the conversion of the input ASCII source file to parser inputs (tokens) may be challenging. We treat this problem first.

5.1.3 Concerns with minic and Recursion

We first relate the results of Section 3.4.7 with the development of our minic parser. Several productions from the minic programming language syntax involve recursion and are converted for use with the Prolog LGN.

For example, recall the basic syntax constraint for a command sequence in minic (from Section 4.2.2) is given in BNF as:

```
<command-seq> ::= <command> | <command> ; <command-seq>
```

which is converted into:

```
cmds --> command, restcmds.
restcmds --> [semicolon], cmds.
restcmds --> [].
```

Similarly, the BNF production:

```
<variable-list> ::= <variable> | <variable> , <variable-list>
```

becomes

```
varlist --> [ide(_)], restvars.
restvars --> [comma], varlist.
restvars --> [].
```

5.1.4 Preliminary Examples

minic LGN Translation Example 1

Before proceeding to the full scanner/parser development, we look at several Prolog parsing predicates corresponding to key `minic` syntactic elements. Consider the BNF description of the `minic` production:

```
<transunit> ::= <main-decl> <body>
```

On the basis of our previous work, we could represent this production directly in the LGN as

```
transunit --> maindecl,body.
```

Looking ahead, we want a Prolog representation that not only implements the parse but also indicates key results, such as program structure. Therefore, we add another argument to the LGN description, yielding the corresponding Prolog LGN construct:

```
transunit(transunit(Maindecl, Body)) --> maindecl(Maindecl), body(Body).
```

This translates into the pure Prolog:

```
transunit(transunit(A, B), C, D) :-
        maindecl(A, C, E),
        body(B, E, D).
```

The parser for this nonterminal now indicates or "captures" the resulting structure returned from the parse using the added LGN functor with structure `transunit(Maindecl, Body)`.

minic LGN Translation Example 2

Consider the BNF description of another `minic` production:

```
<body> ::= lbrace <decl> <statseq> rbrace
```

which we represent using a corresponding Prolog LGN construct:

```
body(body(Decl, Statseq)) --> [lbrace], decl(Decl), statseq(Statseq), [rbrace].
```

This LGN fragment translates into the (pure) Prolog database clause:

```
body(body(A, B), C, D) :-
        'C'(C, lbrace, E),
        decl(A, E, F),
        statseq(B, F, G),
        'C'(G, rbrace, D).
```

We now consider the overall scanner/parser design and implementation.

5.2 minic Prolog Scanner

5.2.1 Scanner Objective

The objective of the scanner, as shown in Figure 5.1, is to convert an ASCII file containing `minic` source code into a Prolog list of tokens.

5.2.2 Prolog Predicates Related to Scanner Development

Several Prolog predicates are fundamental to the design of the scanner. A synopsis of each is provided below; more complete information is available from Prolog `help()` or the Prolog manual.

`see(+SrcDest)`: Make `SrcDest` the current input stream.

`seen`: Close the current input stream.

`tab(+Amount)`: Writes `Amount` spaces on the current output stream.

`get0(-Char)`: Read the current input stream and unify the next byte with `Char`.

`put(+Char)`: Write `Char` to the current output stream.

5.2.3 Remarks on the Scanner Development

Considerable effort is used to develop predicates that allow the identification of multicharacter reserved words and user-specified identifiers. We output the latter as an element of

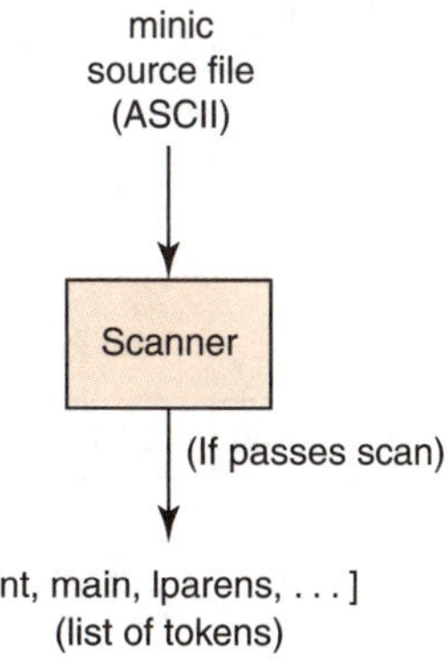

Figure 5.1 minic Scanner Objective.

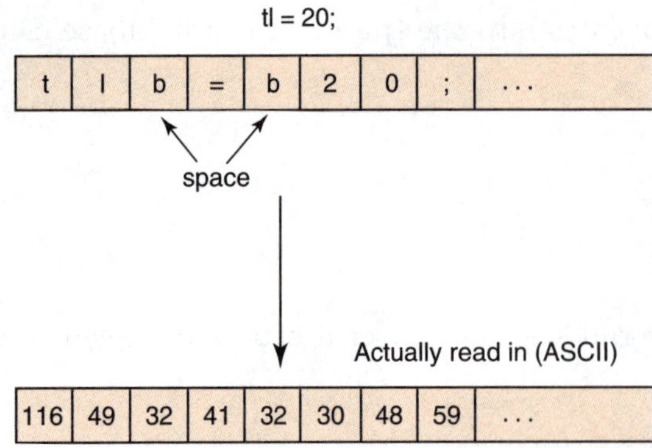

Figure 5.2 Sample input stream for t1 = 20;.

the token list using the notation ide(<name>), where <name> is the user-chosen name of the identifier.

5.2.4 What Does the Input Stream Look Like?

Understanding the format of the input stream is essential to the design of the Prolog-based lookahead scanner. Figures 5.2 and 5.3 provide two examples of this format.

White Space

Using the ASCII table, white space is easy to define in Prolog, as the following example shows.

```
space(32).
tabch(9).
endline(10).

whitespace(C) :- space(C) ; tabch(C) ; endline(C).
```

int main (void) {return(0);}

Aside: you've seen a related derivation tree for this

Conceptualize as:

i	D	1	b	m	i	j	n	(	v	o	i	d	)	b	{	x	

Actually read in (ASCII)

109	110	108	32	109	97	105	110	40	112	111	105	100	41	32	123	114	

Figure 5.3 Sample input stream for int main(void){, etc.

5.2.5 Why Is it Necessary to Look Ahead?

The previous section indicated the form of the input stream from the ASCII source file containing `minic` code. Note that this is read into Prolog using `get0()`. It is essential to note the following:

> *Once* `get0(C)` *is invoked as a subgoal, the ASCII value of the current character in the input stream becomes the binding on variable C, and this character is lost forever (in the sense that the input stream pointer is then incremented to point to the next character). Thus, once we read a character, we need to "find a use" for it.*

Although it is possible to read ahead some number of characters and figure out what to do with some portion of the input stream, it is neither efficient nor straightforward to do this. Any random fragment of the input stream may contain parts of identifiers, several reserved words or symbols, and so on. The length of this string (in characters) is variable.

This problem is a well-known one in Prolog. The solution (Clocksin and Mellish, 2003) is based upon reading ahead one character and developing recursive predicates for the entities to be recognized. Thus, we develop a scanner that identifies arbitrary-length tokens based upon the current character and at most one more (i.e., the "lookahead"). The examples that follow should help us to see the actual operation of the scanner.

5.2.6 Exactly What Are We Looking For?

Recall the role of the scanner is to convert the input ASCII file into a list of tokens. Therefore, in designing the Prolog scanner we must identify the following entities as the input source file is read (character by character):

`int` (reserved word) length = 3

`void` (reserved word) length = 4

`main` (reserved word) length = 4

`lparens` single character, ASCII 40

`rparens` single character, ASCII 41

`lbrace` single character, ASCII 123

`rbrace` single character, ASCII 125

`assign` single character, ASCII 61

`<identifier>` any length, but with production constraints

`<numeral>` any length, but with production constraints

`,` single character, ASCII 44

`;` single character, ASCII 59

`return` (reserved word) length = 5

Note also that the length of these entities varies, especially user-chosen numerals and identifiers. The BNF syntax of the lexical part of the `minic` grammar places constraints on the allowable ASCII values used, but not the length. Conversely, a number of these entities are relatively easy to recognize (especially single-character reserved symbols) by simply matching ASCII values.

5.2.7 Recursion within Recursion

We employ recursion in our Prolog description of the scanner predicates at two levels:

1. The first recursion occurs in the recognition of a *single* multiple-character reserved word, user identifier, or numeral. See predicate `gettoken`.

2. The second level of recursion is over the entire source file, to find *all* tokens. See predicate `restprog`.

5.2.8 Prolog Scanner Source

Reading and Lookahead

The development of the scanner follows the strategy of Clocksin and Mellish (2003) for reading English sentences in Prolog. The approach is based upon attempted reading or recognition of a single word, using single-character lookahead. The basis is the description of the arity 3 predicate `readword(C,W,C1)`, wherein `C` is a single character, `W` is the symbolic representation of the resulting word, and `C1` is the next or lookahead character. The reader is referred to Clocksin and Mellish for further details.

The Design of Predicate `gettoken(C,T,D)`

Referring to the source listing, note that the predicate

```
gettoken(C,T,D)
```

which is analogous to `readword(C,W,C1)`, forms the heart of the lookahead process. In every case `gettoken` is invoked as a subgoal, it is preceded by a call to `get0` (through `getch`). Thus, when invoked as a subgoal, `gettoken(C,T,D)` has its first argument, denoted C here, bound to the current character under consideration. Arguments T and D are presently unbound.

For illustration, let us assume we are beginning the scanning process. The recognition of a single token is shown. Recall that the process is recursively implemented in order to recognize all input file tokens. Thus, we employ the following decision strategies, depending upon the outcome of the following (sequential[1]) tests:

1. *C is the end-of-file character.* We add a special token (the list [eop]) to the end of the token list. We are done scanning.

2. *C is unifiable (recognizable) as a single character reserved symbol.* We add the token corresponding to this single character to the token list. For example, if C were bound

[1]The reader should observe that the order of these tests is a direct consequence of the ordering of the clauses in the scanner Prolog database shown in Section 5.2.5.

to the ASCII representation of "=" (61), we add the token "assign" to the token list. Notice that C is recognized as this token from the Prolog database rule

```
gettoken(C, T, D) :- single(C,T), getch(D).
```

which then unifies with the fact

```
single(61,assign).
```

3. *C is the start of an identifier string or a multicharacter reserved word.* In this case, the first subgoal in the tail of the rule:

   ```
   gettoken(C, T, E) :- lower(C), getch(D), restid(D, Lc, E),
                        name(I, [C|Lc]), (reswd(I),T=I ; T=ide(I)).
   ```

   is satisfied, because only lowercase characters are permitted in the lexical syntax. We then acquire the next input character, and invoke the subgoal

   ```
   restid(D, Lc, E)
   ```

   starting with this character. There are two possible clauses to satisfy this subgoal, namely,

   ```
   restid(C, [C|Lc], E) :- idchar(C), getch(D),restid(D,Lc,E).
   restid(C, [],     C).
   ```

   The former clause above checks to see if a multicharacter identifier string continues; the latter indicates the end of the identifier if C is not an identifier character (i.e., `idchar(C)` fails) and backtracking takes us to the clause `restid(C, [], C).`, wherein Lc is bound to the empty list. Once all the characters in this token have been scanned (`restid(D,Lc,E)` succeeds), the remaining subgoals are:

   ```
   name(I, [C|Lc]), (reswd(I),T=I ; T=ide(I))
   ```

   Recall predicate `name` converts the ASCII list to a string and the string is then recognized as either a reserved word *or* an identifier. It is then appended to the token list.

4. *C is the start of a numeral string.* The analysis is similar to that in the case of an identifier, described previously.

5. *C is whitespace.* It is echoed, but not used in token formation.

6. *C is none of the above.* It is therefore an unrecognizable character and the scanning process terminates due to the input string containing a terminal $\notin V_T$.

Extended Example: The Scan of a Sample Source Code Fragment

The reader is advised to follow this description using the code in Section 5.2.5. Consider the scanning of the input stream (`minic` program fragment)

```
t1 = 20;
```

The conceptual view of this stream is shown in Figure 5.2. The first significant subgoal is predicate `scan`, which invokes `getch`, which in turn invokes `get0`,[2] which in turn spawns subgoal `gettoken`. The structure of unifications related to `gettoken` was described in Section 5.2.8; here we consider the path of Prolog's unification process using specific ASCII characters in the input stream.

After the first input stream character is read, we have subgoal

```
gettoken(116,T,D)
```

Because the character "t" (ASCII value 116) is not an end-of-file marker and not a recognizable single reserved word, but is lowercase (predicate `lower` succeeds), subgoal `getch(D)` is invoked, yielding `getch(49)` or `getch('1')`, where "1" is the the next character (ASCII value 49). The next subgoal spawned is `restid(49,Lc,E)`, which is then unified with clause head `restid(49,[49|Lc],E)` from the clause:

```
restid(C, [C|Lc], E) :- idchar(C), getch(D),restid(D,Lc,E).
```

Because subgoal `idchar(49)` succeeds, `getch(D)` binds D to the next input stream character (ASCII value 32, or the space), and the subgoal `restid(32, Lc,E)` is spawned.

The unification of subgoal `restid(32, Lc,E)` requires checking two clauses in the scanner database:

```
restid(C, [C|Lc], E) :- idchar(C), getch(D),restid(D,Lc,E).
restid(C, [],      C).
```

Because `idchar(32)` fails, `restid(32, Lc,E)` unifies with the second[3] clause, that is, the fact `restid(C, [], C)`. Thus, the earlier subgoal `restid(32, Lc,E)` succeeds, with `Lc` bound to `[]`; thus clause head `restid(C, [C|Lc], E)` succeeds with `[C|Lc]` bound to `[116,49]`, and `E` is bound to the last character read (but not used to form the current token), namely the space with ASCII value 32. At this point, the remaining subgoals are

```
name(I, [C|Lc]), (reswd(I),T=I ; T=ide(I))
```

which the user may verify are satisfied with `I` bound to the string `t1`, and (because `t1` is not a reserved word), `T` bound to `ide(t1)`. This satisfies the initial call of the `gettoken` predicate, that is,

```
gettoken(116,ide(t1),32)
```

which, in clause

```
scan([T|Lt]) :- tab(4), getch(C), gettoken(C,T,D), restprog(T, D, Lt).
```

then spawns subgoal `restprog(ide(t1), 32, Lt)`. This token (variable `T`) then becomes the head of the list of tokens (note that in this example it was assumed initially empty), and the process continues.

[2]Or `get0sim`, if the input stream simulator is used.

[3]Remember how backtracking occurs in Prolog.

Source Listing

The Prolog source for the scanner follows.

```
% File: cscanv1r4.pro
% DOS and unix version
% scanner for minic ver 1 translational unit
%------------------------------------------------------------------------------

scan-goal :-
      nl,write('---- minic (ver 1) scanner  ----'), nl, nl,
      write('Enter name of source file:  '), nl,
      getfilename(File), nl,
      see(File),
      scan(Tokens),
      seen,
      write('Scan successful'),
      nl, nl,
      write(Tokens),
      nl.

%------------------------------------------------------------------------------

lower(C) :- 97=<C,C=<122.       % a-z
digit(C)  :- 48=<C,C=<57.       % 0-9

% ASCII characters of special significance

space(32). tabch(9). period(46).
cr(13).  lf(10).  endfile(26).   endfile(-1).
endline(C) :- lf(C).  % for both DOS and UNIX

whitespace(C) :- space(C) ; tabch(C) ; cr(C) ; lf(C).

idchar(C) :- lower(C) ; digit(C).

% read the filename--inelegant, but easy (see the problems)

getfilename(W) :- nl,write('input the source filename IN QUOTES'),nl,
                     write('followed by a . and CR'),nl,
                     read(X),nl, name(W,X).

%------------------------------------------------------------------------------
%---------  Scanner  -----------------------------------------------------------

scan([T|Lt]) :- tab(4), getch(C), gettoken(C,T,D), restprog(T, D, Lt).

getch(C) :- get0(C), (endline(C),nl,tab(4) ; endfile(C),nl ; put(C)).

restprog(eop, _, []).        % end of file reached with previous character
restprog(_, C, [U|Lt]) :- gettoken(C, U, D), restprog(U, D, Lt).

gettoken(C, eop, 0) :- endfile(C).
gettoken(C, T, D) :- single(C,T), getch(D).
gettoken(C, T, E) :- lower(C), getch(D), restid(D, Lc, E),
                     name(I, [C|Lc]), (reswd(I),T=I ; T=ide(I)).

restid(C, [C|Lc], E) :- idchar(C), getch(D),restid(D,Lc,E).
restid(C, [],     C).   % end identifier if C is not id character
```

```
gettoken(C, num(N), E) :- digit(C), getch(D), restnum(D, Lc, E),
                          name(N, [C|Lc]).
restnum(C, [C|Lc], E) :- digit(C), getch(D), restnum(D, Lc, E).
restnum(C, [],     C).    % end number if C is not digit

gettoken(C, T, E) :- whitespace(C), getch(D), gettoken(D,T,E).
gettoken(C, _, _) :- write('This character is not in the lexical syntax: '),
                     put(C), write('Bye'), nl, abort.

%%  the reserved words and symbols (tokens) for minic ver 1:

reswd(main). reswd(void). reswd(int). reswd(return).

single(123, lbrace). single(125, rbrace).  single(40,lparen).
single(41,rparen).   single(44,comma). single(59,semicolon).
single(61,assign).

%% thats all folks!
```

Sample `minic` Program to Be Scanned

```
int main(void)
{
int t1;
t1=10;
return(t1);
}
```

Scanner Results for Sample Program

```
?- ['cscanv1r4.pro'].
% cscanv1r4.pro compiled 0.00 sec, 7,680 bytes

Yes
?- scan-goal.

---- minic (ver 1) scanner  ----

Enter name of source file:

input the source filename IN QUOTES
followed by a . and CR
|: "minicex1.mc".


    int main(void)
    {
     int t1;
     t1=10;
     return(t1);
    }
Scan successful

[int, main, lparen, void, rparen, lbrace, int, ide(t1),
semicolon, ide(t1), assign, num(10), semicolon, return,
lparen, ide(t1), rparen, semicolon, rbrace, eop]

Yes
```

5.3 Prolog Parser

Now that the scanner design and implementation are complete, our attention focuses on the minic Prolog parser implementation.

5.3.1 Prolog Implementation

The conversion of the minic BNF from Section 4.2.2 to Prolog LGN representation is straightforward, and shown below. Note the rewriting of self-embedding productions to eliminate the possibility of infinite recursion.

```
% File: cscanpv1r4.pro
% DOS and unix version
% uses minic ver 1.0 bnf syntax from transunit-bnf1.txt


%--------- minic translational unit parser -----------------------

transunit(transunit(Maindecl, Body)) --> maindecl(Maindecl), body(Body).

maindecl(maindecl(Type, Arg)) --> type(Type), [main], marg(Arg).

type(int) --> [int].
type(void) --> [void].

marg(mainarg(Arg)) --> [lparen], type(Arg), [rparen].

body(body(Decl, Statseq)) --> [lbrace], decl(Decl), statseq(Statseq), [rbrace].

decl([]) --> [].

decl(decl(Type, Vars)) --> type(Type), varlist(Vars), [semicolon].

statseq(statseq(Cmdseq, Retstat)) --> cmdseq(Cmdseq), [semicolon], retstat(Retstat).

statseq(statseq([], Retstat)) --> retstat(Retstat).

/* notice allows empty command sequence and requires return */

retstat(retstat(Returnarg)) --> [return], returnarg(Returnarg), [semicolon].

returnarg(ide(Returnarg)) --> [lparen], [ide(Returnarg)], [rparen].

returnarg(num(Returnarg)) --> [lparen], [num(Returnarg)], [rparen].

varlist(Vars) --> [ide(Var)], restvars(Var,Vars).
  restvars(Var,[Var|Vars]) --> [comma], varlist(Vars).
  restvars(Var,[Var])      --> [].

cmdseq(Cmds) --> command(Cmd), restcmds(Cmd,Cmds).
  restcmds(Cmd,[Cmd|Cmds]) --> [semicolon], cmdseq(Cmds).
  restcmds(Cmd,[Cmd])      --> [].

command(assign(ide(V),expr(N))) --> [ide(V)], [assign], expr(N).

expr(N) --> [num(N)].

parse-goal :-
```

```
     nl,write('>>> Scanning and parsing minic (ver 1.0) <<<'), nl, nl,
     write('Enter name of source file:  '), nl,
     getfilename(File), nl,
     see(File), scan(Tokens), seen, write('Scan successful'), nl, nl,
     write(Tokens), nl,nl, !,
     transunit(Parse,Tokens,[eop]), write('Parse successful'), nl,!,
     write(Parse), nl, !.

%--------- Scanner -------------------------------------------------------

lower(C) :- 97=<C,C=<122.        % a-z
digit(C)  :- 48=<C,C=<57.        % 0-9

% ASCII characters of special significance

space(32). tabch(9). period(46).
cr(13).  lf(10).  endfile(26).   endfile(-1).
endline(C) :- lf(C).  % for both DOS and UNIX

whitespace(C) :- space(C) ; tabch(C) ; cr(C) ; lf(C).

idchar(C) :- lower(C) ; digit(C).

% read the filename--inelegant, but easy (see the problems)

getfilename(W) :- nl,write('input the source filename IN QUOTES'),nl,
                  write('followed by a . and CR'),nl,
                  read(X),nl, name(W,X).


scan([T|Lt]) :- tab(4), getch(C), gettoken(C,T,D), restprog(T, D, Lt), !.

getch(C) :- get0(C), (endline(C),nl,tab(4) ; endfile(C),nl ; put(C)).

restprog(eop, _, []).          % end of file reached with previous character
restprog(_,    C, [U|Lt]) :- gettoken(C, U, D), restprog(U, D, Lt).

gettoken(C, eop, 0) :- endfile(C).
gettoken(C, T, D) :- single(C,T), getch(D).

gettoken(C, T, E) :- lower(C), getch(D), restid(D, Lc, E),
                     name(I, [C|Lc]), (reswd(I),T=I ; T=ide(I)).
restid(C, [C|Lc], E) :- idchar(C), getch(D),restid(D,Lc,E).
restid(C, [],     C).    % end identifier if C is not id character

gettoken(C, num(N), E) :- digit(C), getch(D), restnum(D, Lc, E),
                          name(N, [C|Lc]).
restnum(C, [C|Lc], E) :- digit(C), getch(D), restnum(D, Lc, E).
restnum(C, [],     C).    % end number if C is not digit

gettoken(C, T, E) :- whitespace(C), getch(D), gettoken(D,T,E).
gettoken(C, _, _) :- write('This character is not in the lexical syntax: '),
                     put(C), write('Bye'), nl, abort.

%% here are the reserved words (tokens) for minic:

reswd(main). reswd(void). reswd(int). reswd(return).
```

```
single(123, lbrace). single(125, rbrace). single(40,lparen).
single(41,rparen).

single(44,comma). single(59,semicolon). single(61,assign).

%% thats all folks!
```

5.3.2 Sample Parser Use

Two examples of the parser use are shown next. The first example shows most of the allowable constructs in this version of `minic`. Many extensions are developed and implemented in the next chapter. The second example shows a very minimal use of `minic`. The reader is encouraged to generate and explore others.

```
?- parse-goal.

>>> Scanning and parsing minic (ver 1.0) <<<

Enter name of source file:

input the source filename IN QUOTES
followed by a . and CR
|: "minicex1.mc".


    int main(void)
    {
     int t1;
     t1=10;
     return(t1);
    }
Scan successful

[int, main, lparen, void, rparen, lbrace, int, ide(t1),
semicolon, ide(t1), assign, num(10), semicolon, return,
lparen, ide(t1), rparen, semicolon, rbrace, eop]

Parse successful
transunit(maindecl(int, mainarg(void)),
body(decl(int, [t1]), statseq([assign(ide(t1), expr(10))],
retstat(ide(t1)))))

Yes
?- parse-goal.

>>> Scanning and parsing minic (ver 1.0) <<<

Enter name of source file:

input the source filename IN QUOTES
followed by a . and CR
|: "minicex1r.mc".


    int main(void)
    {
     return(10);
    }
```

```
Scan successful

[int, main, lparen, void, rparen, lbrace,
return, lparen, num(10), rparen, semicolon,
rbrace, eop]

Parse successful
transunit(maindecl(int, mainarg(void)),
body([], statseq([], retstat(num(10)))))

Yes
```

5.4 Exercises

1. A good bit of the complexity of the minic Prolog scanner is due to the tedious task of reading a minic source file character-by-character in Prolog. Because it is somewhat difficult to trace the behavior of the predicate get0(C), the simple utility shown below may help. It is useful for checking the behavior of the scanner when entering code fragments and checking for results. The reader is encouraged to verify the operation of this utility with examples. Simply replace all occurrences of Prolog's low-level character reader get0 with get0sim.

```
/* get0sim, the character-by-character simulator */
/* file get0sim.pro */

init :- assert(current(0)). %% current position in input stream

sample_input(A) :- name('testfile.source',A). % data in ASCII

get0sim(Char) :- sample_input(A), current(X), nth0(X,A,Char),
                 retract(current(X)),Next is X+1,assert(current(Next)).
```

2. SWI-Prolog includes a predicate for character reading peek_char, with the description of this predicate as follows:

```
peek_char(-Char)
    Reads the  next input character like get_char/1,  but does not remove
    it from the input stream.
```

   Discuss how this influences the lookahead design of the scanner. Using this predicate, rewrite the relevant portions of the scanner.

3. It is often claimed that the use of or (;) in Prolog clause tails yields potential difficulties in debugging. Therefore, a student decided to rewrite a portion of the minic scanner replacing the original description of getch in Prolog, that is,

```
getch(C) :- get0(C), (endline(C),nl,tab(4) ; endfile(C),nl ; put(C)).
```

   with the or expanded into three clauses as follows:

```
getch(C) :- get0(C), endline(C),nl,tab(4).

getch(C) :- get0(C), endfile(C),nl.

getch(C) :- get0(C), put(C).
```

(a) Comment on the wisdom of this.

(b) Implement the change in Prolog and check if the rewriting is acceptable.

4. The first LGN-based `minic` Version 1.0 scanner and parser followed the BNF syntax specification for the declaration of `main` in the translational unit. The type of `main` may be either `int` or `void`. Revise the scanner/parser such that the type of `main` may only be `void`.

5. The preliminary lexical analysis of `minic` Version 1.0 in Section 4.2.3 required that we "rename" certain terminals as tokens with a different name to avoid confusion between reserved words and symbols in `minic` and those of Prolog. This included `assign` versus =, `lbrace` versus }, and so on. Consider an alternative for token representation in Prolog that allows dual naming, the token list might look like:

```
[int, main, '(', void, ')', ...]
```

Comment on this approach versus the one used in the text.

6. Prolog solutions are based upon unification. In the introductory Prolog chapter, we observed a "you get more than you pay for" effect in the design of certain predicates. For example, we saw that a Prolog parser for a simple grammar was also able to serve as a language generator. On this basis, we investigate this situation with our current `minic` parser, and generate the following trace:

```
?- transunit(What,Aprogram,[eop]).

ERROR: Out of local stack
```

Why does this happen?

7. Suppose you are given the grammar $G_{square-weave}$, from Chapter 4, where

$$G_{square-weave} = \{\Sigma, N, P, S\} \tag{5.1}$$

where $N = \{S, A\}$, $\Sigma = \{d, l, r\}$ and

$$\begin{aligned} &P = \{\\ &S \rightarrow rS\\ &S \rightarrow dA\\ &A \rightarrow lA\\ &A \rightarrow dS\\ &A \rightarrow l\\ &S \rightarrow r\ \} \end{aligned}$$

and S is the starting symbol.

(a) First, answer each of the following questions:

Is the following string an element of $L(G_{square-weave})$?
$rrdrdr$

Is the following string an element of $L(G_{square-weave})$?
$rrrdlldrr$
Is the following string an element of $L(G_{square-weave})$?
$rrdldr$

(b) For each production, show the corresponding representation in the Prolog LGN.

(c) Using the Prolog parser provided by the LGN, check your answers to the preceding parsing questions posed.

8. Consider the `minic` grammar production from the lexical part of the syntax:

   <identifier> ::= <letter> | <identifier> <letter> | <identifier> <digit>

   This involves left recursion. If this production is rewritten as:

   <identifier> ::= <letter> | <letter><identifier> | <digit><identifier>

   does an equivalent grammar/language result?

9. Consider the following:

```
/* Examples of alternative Prolog LGN representations
   corresponding to the minic production:
   <command-seq> ::= <command> | <command> ; <command-seq> */

/* one strategy */
cmdseq1 --> command, restcmdseq1.
restcmdseq1 --> [semicolon], cmdseq1.
restcmdseq1 --> [].


/* an alternative */
cmdseq2 --> command.
cmdseq2 --> command, [semicolon], cmdseq2.


/* single command for simplicity */
command --> [cmd].
```

   Show the behavior of each LGN-translated predicate (`cmdseq1` and `cmdseq2`) as a command-sequence parser.

10. A new (contextual) constraint might be that the declared type of the translational unit must match the type returned by the `return` statement. For purposes of this problem, type `void` is a type to be checked. Since we are working with Version 1.0 of `minic`, assume that an identifier or numeral is declared of type `int`.

    For example, consider the following cases:

```
int main(void)         void main(void)        int main(void)
{                      {                      {
int t1;                int t1;                int t1;
t1=10;                 t1=10;                 t1=10;
return(t1);            return(t1);            return(void);
}                      }                      }
```

VALID	INVALID	INVALID

```
void main(void)       void main(void)       void main(void)
{                     {                     {
int t1;               int t1;               int t1;
t1=10;                t1=10;                t1=10;
return(100);          return(void);         return();
}                     }                     }
```

INVALID VALID VALID

Revise the Version 1.0 Prolog scanner/parser to implement this constraint. If the parse is successful, the behavior should be as before. If the constraint is violated (and the parse would otherwise succeed), the parse should fail; state why.

11. This chapter developed a parser for `minic` using the LGN. The purpose of this problem is to consider alternative Prolog-based approaches, as shown in the following Prolog source code. A simple subset of the `minic` syntax is used.

```
/* file: parser-goal1r.pro */
/* to illustrate simplistic Prolog implementation
   of the minic constructs:

<main-decl> ::= <type> main <arg>
<type> ::= int | void
<arg> ::= lparens <type> rparens

*/

/* first, simple but limited and arity limitation */

main_declaration1(int, main, lparens, void, rparens).
main_declaration1(void, main, lparens, void, rparens).
main_declaration1(int, main, lparens, int, rparens).
main_declaration1(void, main, lparens, int, rparens).

/* a step in the right direction-- use a list */

main_declaration2([int, main, lparens, void, rparens]).
main_declaration2([void, main, lparens, void, rparens]).
main_declaration2([int, main, lparens, int, rparens]).
main_declaration2([void, main, lparens, int, rparens]).

/*  further progress; start using variables for some nonterminals  */

main_declaration3([Type, main, lparens, Type, rparens]) :-
                                is_type(Type).
is_type(int).
is_type(void).

/* now enhance previous predicate to allow for different types */

main_declaration4([Type1, main, lparens, Type2, rparens]) :-
                                is_type(Type1), is_type(Type2).
```

Show, using examples and in Prolog, the corresponding use of the simplistic parsing predicates shown previously. Comment on the generality and structure in these approaches.

12. Given the following alternative Prolog “filename reader,” show, via examples and the use of predicate `trace`, the operation of the reader.

```
/* file: filename.pro     */
/* example of reading filename */
/* as part of scanner operation */

lower(C) :- 97=<C,C=<122.          % a-z
upper(C) :- 65=<C,C=<90.           % A-Z allowed for filenames
digit(C)  :- 48=<C,C=<57.          % 0-9

period(46).
slash(47).


filechar(C) :- lower(C) ; upper(C) ; digit(C) ; period(C) ; slash(C).

/* ---reading the file name ----------------------*/

getfilename(W) :- get0sim(C),restfilename(C,Cs),name(W,Cs).
  restfilename(C,[C|Cs]) :- filechar(C),get0sim(D),restfilename(D,Cs).
  restfilename(C,[]).


/* simulation utility from file get0sim.pro  */
/* need to invoke goal 'init' before starting */
/* or put in top-level goal */

init :- assert(current(0)). %% current position in input stream

sample_input(A) :- name('/this/is/my/sourcefile.mc',A). % data in ASCII

get0sim(Char) :- sample_input(A), current(X), nth0(X,A,Char),
                 retract(current(X)),Next is X+1,assert(current(Next)).

%% thats all folks!
```

CHAPTER 6

Scanning and Parsing `minic` Using `flex` and `bison`

You have a hardware or a software problem.

—Service manual for Gestetner 3240

6.1 Building Scanners and Parsers with `flex` and `bison`

In this section, we show the use of the **flex** and **bison** tools for **minic** (Version 1.0) scanning and parsing. As in our Prolog approach, the effort involves scanning a source code file for tokens, and providing these tokens to the parser.

6.1.1 "Compiler-Compilers"

Many tools exist that facilitate development of scanners and parsers. Because many of these tools are actually designed to produce compilers, they are often referred to as compiler-compilers (CC).

The first compilers appeared in the late 1950s. Credit is often given to FORTRAN as the first successfully compiled language. At that time, compiler development was slow and tedious because the languages were being designed at the same time compilers were being implemented, the translation process was not well understood, and tools to facilitate compiler development (compiler-compilers) did not yet exist.

6.1.2 In the Beginning: `yacc` and `lex`

One of the most recognizable compiler-compilers is yacc (yet another compiler compiler), written by Steve Johnson (1975). It is part of many Unix implementations. Free and compatible versions are available, including Berkeley yacc and GNU bison. Each offer slight improvements and additional features, but the concept remains the same.

Yacc requires input in the form of tokens produced by a scanner (which is not a part of yacc). The tokens are extracted from an ASCII input stream contained in a source file (just as in the Prolog implementation). Perhaps the best-known "classical" scanner-generator is lex, (lexical analyzer generator) by Lesk and Schmidt. lex usually accompanies yacc in most distributions.

lex produces a program, often in C or C++, that recognizes tokens resulting from parsing regular expressions. The more modern version of lex is flex, a tool for generating scanners. Both lex and yacc, and their modern, GNU counterparts, flex and bison, *produce programs* for scanning and parsing, respectively. The IEEE POSIX P1003.2 standard defines the functionality and requirements for both lex and yacc.

6.2 Introduction to flex and bison

In its most general form, **flex** is a tool for generating programs that perform pattern-matching on text. **bison** is a parser-generator. As noted, **flex** and **bison** are the updated and GNU versions of **lex** and **yacc**. They are backward compatible with their respective **lex** and **yacc** counterparts.

In what follows, we show the utility of **flex** and **bison** in building a parser for a simplified version of **minic**. Understanding this process first requires an understanding of the operation of **flex** and **bison** individually. Following this, we show how they are combined to produce a C compiler for **minic**.

6.3 flex

As noted, **flex** produces a lexical analyzer (scanner) in C. Using **flex** requires:

1. familiarity with the concept of regular expressions. They are the basis for conveying lexical syntax to **flex**.
2. understanding the **flex** input file structure and format.
3. knowing what to do with the resulting C source file.

We will consider each of these sequentially.

6.3.1 Regular Expressions (REs) in flex

Regular expressions[1] are commonly used in **bash**, **grep**, and **vi**. Most importantly, they form the basis for the token recognizer implemented in **flex**. Patterns to be recognized by **flex** in the input are denoted using extended regular expressions. The basic building blocks are summarized in Table 6.1.

The fundamental RE building blocks are regular expressions that match a single character. Most characters, including all letters and digits, are considered regular expressions that match themselves. When necessary, a meta character with special meaning may be quoted by preceding it with a backslash, as shown in Table 6.1.

A bracketed entity denotes a regular expression that matches any single character enclosed in the brackets. Within a bracketed expression, two characters separated by a hyphen denote a range expression. Any single character in the range constitutes a match.[2] If the first character in the range is a caret (^) then the bracketed entity matches any character not in the following range.

In Table 6.1, the REs are listed in terms of decreasing precedence. Note that the repetition designators (*, +, etc.) only apply to the immediately preceeding regular expression. Parentheses may be used on expressions to override this precedence.

6.3.2 flex Input File Structure

The regular expressions to be matched against input are specified by the user in a **flex** source file (with the extension .in, by convention). This file consists of regular expressions to be matched against the input file together with corresponding **flex** actions. This file

[1] And extended regular expressions.

[2] Note that this assumes a character ordering.

Character	Action (Matches)
x	Match the character x
.	Match any character except newline
[xyz]	Match either an x, a y, or a z
[j-o]	Match any letter from j through o
[^A-Z]	Match any character except an uppercase letter
[^A-Z\n]	Match any character except an uppercase letter or a newline
R*	Match zero or more R, where R is a regular expression
R+	Match one or more R
R?	Match zero or one R
R{2,5}	Match from two to five R
"[xyz]"	Match the enclosed string *literally*, i.e., match [xyz]
\X	Match the c interpretation of \X if X is a, b, f, n, r, t, or v
(R)	Match R using parens to denote precedence
R | S	Match regular expression R or regular expression S

Table 6.1 Primitive **flex** RE Building Blocks.

is translated by **flex** into a C program that reads an input character stream, and, where possible,[3] converts the input into tokens that match the specified regular expressions.

The **flex** input file consists of up to three sections, separated by a line containing the single (two-character) token %% with the form:

```
definitions
%%
rules
%%
user code
```

Definitions are described in the following sections. The rules section of the input file contains a sequence of *pattern-action* specifications, *where the pattern must be unindented and the action must begin on the same line.* Rules are checked in the order in which they appear; the significance of this is explored in the exercises. By default, any text not matched by the **flex** scanner is copied to the output. This is sometimes referred to as the default rule. The user code section is optional; we will show how it is used shortly. Comments in the **flex** input file follow the C style.

6.3.3 flex Output

The output of **flex** is a file, `lex.yy.c`, containing C source for a scanner. The scanning function within this file is denoted **yylex**. This process is shown here:

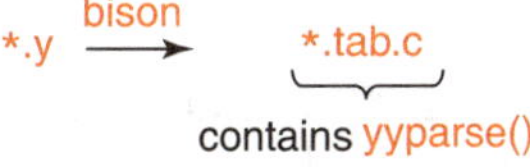

[3]As dictated by the lexical syntax enumerated by the REs.

`lex.yy.c` may be compiled into a freestanding executable using `gcc` with the `-lfl` library specification.

6.3.4 Example: The "Hello World" of flex

Figure 6.1 shows a simple example. In this case, the only rule in the `flex` input file looks for occurrences of the string hello and prints another string, as shown. All other characters are echoed. In Figure 6.1, note that the `flex` output file `lex.yy.c` is compiled into a freestanding executable.

```
%%
hello printf("hello bobby!");
}
```

Input file hello.in

```
$ cat hello.in
%%
hello printf("hello bobby!");

$ flex hello.in

$ gcc lex.yy.c -lfl -o flex-hello

$ ./flex-hello
hi mom
hi mom
hello world
hello bobby! world
bye
bye
```

Use of flex and resulting executable

Figure 6.1 Hello World, `flex` Version

6.3.5 More Elaborate flex Examples

Here we show a series of examples with increasing complexity in using `flex` to recognize automobile license plates. Suppose the constraint is that a valid plate must contain three letters followed by three digits. The first digit may not be a zero. We show several variations on the solution, beginning with the simplest formulation. The result is shown in Figures 6.2 through 6.4.

The third example in Figure 6.4 shows the use of variable and values available from the `flex`-generated scanner, specifically the variable `yytext`. In `flex`, following the match of an RE, the text corresponding to the match (in the case of `minic`, a token) is made available through the predefined global character pointer `yytext`. The length of the token is available in another global integer variable, `yyleng`.

6.4 Applying flex to minic

6.4.1 A Simple Use of flex with minic

We now work our way up to a general `minic` scanner, beginning with a few straightforward examples. The `minic` input source file used in the examples is shown in Figure 6.5. Note we have already shown this file is syntactically correct.

```
%%
[a-z][a-z][a-z][1-9][0-9][0-9]  printf(" valid license plate");
```

Input file license1.in

```
$ flex license1.in
$ gcc lex.yy.c -lfl -o license1
$ ./license1
123qwe
123qwe
qwe123
 valid license plate
asdf12
asdf12
as1234
as1234
aaa000
aaa000
aaa111
 valid license plate
```

Use of flex and resulting executable

Figure 6.2 Simple flex License Plate Recognizer.

```
%%
[a-z]{3}[1-9][0-9]{2}  printf(" valid license plate");
```

Input file license2.in

```
$ flex license2.in
$ gcc lex.yy.c -lfl -o license2
$ ./license2
asd345
 valid license plate
asd034
asd034
xxx100
 valid license plate
```

Use of flex and resulting executable

Figure 6.3 Second flex License Plate Recognizer.

```
%%
[a-z]{3}[1-9][0-9]{2}\n  printf(" --->>> %s is a valid license plate", yytext);
```

Input file license3.in

```
$ cat license3.in
%%
[a-z]{3}[1-9][0-9]{2}\n  printf(" --->>> %s is a valid license plate", yytext);
$ flex license3.in
$ gcc lex.yy.c -lfl -o license3
$ ./license3
asd455
 --->>> asd455
 is a valid license plate

qwe001
qwe001
```

Use of flex and resulting executable

Figure 6.4 Third flex License Plate Recognizer.

```
int main(void)
{
int t1;
t1=10;
return(t1);
}
```

Figure 6.5 minic Input (Source) File Used for Examples.

Figure 6.6 shows the first flex-based scanner for minic tokens. In the scanner based upon the flex input file of Figure 6.6, the corresponding action is to simply print the recognized token. In addition, the definition part of the flex input file has been used to "name" regular expressions. In the example of Figure 6.6, ID and NUM are used as names for the regular expressions corresponding to identifier and numeral, respectively. Notice that these names are later expanded in the rules section of the flex input file, where, for example, {ID} indicates the expansion of the ID definition.

Also notice that in this case whitespace has been retained from the minic input source file. Although this helps in understanding scanner action and visualizing the results, recall whitespace is irrelevant in terms of the parse. To alleviate this, consider the approach of Figure 6.7, where an additional RE is used to identify (and not print) whitespace. Note that spaces in the resulting output are produced as part of the printf strings; they are not echoed.

6.4.2 Using flex to Generate minic Tokens for Parsing

The previous examples are based upon replacement of recognized characters with strings and showing the replacement using printf. We now want to consider flex-based generation of tokens for the parser that are compatible with bison. This is done through the flex-created function yylex(). To show this, we must first digress to introduce bison, because the bison parser, implemented as function yyparse, expects tokens to be returned from the flex-generated scanner upon demand.

```
/* this version does not gobble up whitespace */
ID [a-z][a-z0-9]*
NUM [0-9]+
%%
"(" printf(" lparens ");
")" printf(" rparens ");
"{" printf(" lbrace ");
"}" printf(" rbrace ");
"=" printf(" assign ");
";" printf(" semicolon ");
int printf(" int ");
void printf(" void ");
main printf(" main ");
return printf(" return ");
{ID} printf(" ide(%s) ",yytext);
{NUM} printf(" num(%s) ",yytext);
```

Input file minicex0.in

```
 int   main  lparens  void  rparens
 lbrace
 int   ide(t1)  semicolon
 ide(t1)  assign  num(10)  semicolon
 return  lparens  ide(t1)  rparens  semicolon
 rbrace
```

Use of flex: Resulting file of tokens

Figure 6.6 First Use of flex to Recognize minic Tokens.

```
/* this version gobbles up whitespace */
ID [a-z][a-z0-9]*
NUM [0-9]+
%%
[ \r\t\n]+ /* whitespace */
"(" printf(" lparens ");
")" printf(" rparens ");
"{" printf(" lbrace ");
"}" printf(" rbrace ");
"=" printf(" assign ");
";" printf(" semicolon ");
int printf(" int ");
void printf(" void ");
main printf(" main ");
return printf(" return ");
{ID} printf(" ide(%s) ",yytext);
{NUM} printf(" num(%s) ",yytext);
```

Input file minicex0a.in

```
 int  main  lparens  void  rparens  lbrace  int  ide(t1)
semicolon  ide(t1)  assign  num(10)  semicolon  return
lparens  ide(t1)  rparens  semicolon  rbrace
```

Use of flex: Resulting file of tokens (wordwrapped for illustration)

Figure 6.7 Using flex for minic: Elimination of Whitespace.

6.5 bison

bison is the GNU[4] version of the yacc parser generator. Like yacc, bison is a general-purpose parser generator that converts a grammar description for an LALR(1) context-free grammar into C (or C++) code to parse that grammar. bison is upward compatible with yacc. Note that neither bison nor yacc generates a complete executable (freestanding) program. bison produces the function yyparse. The user needs to also provide "wrapper" code (i.e., main), an error-reporting function that the parser calls to report an error, as well as a lexical analyzer. Fortunately, the last task is not difficult due to the use of flex. We show all of this in the subsequent development of a series of minic scanners and parsers.

Sources

bison and additional accompanying software are available at:

http://www.gnu.org/software/bison/bison.html

Furthermore, bison and flex are found in most recent Linux distributions.

6.5.1 The Pragmatics of Using bison

Using bison to generate a working parser from a grammar specification usually consists of the following steps:

1. Specify the grammar in one or more bison grammar files.
2. Write or generate a lexical analyzer to process source code input and pass tokens to the parser.
3. Write a function that calls the bison-generated parser.
4. Write error-reporting routines.
5. Run bison on the grammar to produce the parser function (yyparse).
6. Compile yyparse with other source files and link the object files to produce the overall parser.

6.5.2 Overview of bison Operation

By convention, bison input files have the extension y. This process is shown below:

*.y --bison--> *.tab.c (contains yyparse())

Note that the bison-generated C function yyparse calls yylex to provide tokens. bison may also be used with the -d option, in which case a file *.tab.h is generated for use with flex. This process is shown here:

*.y --bison -d--> { *.tab.c, *.tab.h }

[4]The Free Software Foundation.

6.5.3 bison Parsing Strategy

The `bison` parser generator requires input in the form of a context-free, LALR(1) grammar. In brief, this means that *it must be possible to parse any portion of an input string with single-token lookahead.*[5]

Conveying the Grammar to bison

For `bison` to generate the parsing program, the grammar syntax must be input in the form of a `bison` grammar file. A number of conventions are used:

- A nonterminal symbol in the formal grammar is represented in `bison` input as an identifier, which by bison convention, must be in lowercase (i.e., all characters); for example, `expr`.
- The `bison` representation for a terminal (also called a token type) is in uppercase, e.g., (`IDENTIFIER`). A terminal symbol that stands for a particular keyword in the language should be named after that keyword is converted to uppercase.

Specifying (Compiler) Actions

Our initial concern is simply to develop a scanner and parser for the syntax of `minic`. However, `bison` is designed to facilitate the implementation of semantics and machine translation (not just simple syntax checking or parsing). Therefore, a grammar rule input to `bison` may have an associated action. The typical purpose of the associated action is to compute a *semantic value* of the whole construct from the semantic values of its parts. Suppose the grammar to be recognized by `bison` includes a rule that says an expression can be the sum of two expressions. If the parser successfully recognizes the syntax of such a sum expression, and each of the subexpressions also has a semantic value, the action of the rule might be to determine the resulting semantic value for the newly recognized larger expression. For example, the following is a rule (similar to that of the extended `minic` syntax) that allows a nonterminal expression to be the sum of two expressions:

```
expr: expr '+' expr  $$ = $1 + $3;
```

The associated action, indicated by `$$ = $1 + $3`, defines the semantic value of the expression, which is defined to be the sum of the values of the two expressions.

6.6 Using flex and bison Together for minic

6.6.1 The bison Grammar File for minic

The application of `flex` and `bison` for `minic` (Version 1.0) scanning and parsing is straightforward. Figure 6.8 shows the `bison` input file for the non-lexical part of the grammar.

[5] Actually, this is a description of an LR(1) grammar. LALR(1) involves additional restrictions that are rarely violated.

```
#include <stdio.h>
#include <ctype.h>
int yylex (void);
int yyerror (char *s);
%}

%token INT
%token VOID
%token MAIN
%token LPARENS
%token RPARENS
%token LBRACE
%token RBRACE
%token ASSIGN
%token SEMICOLON
%token COMMA
%token RETURN
%token NUM
%token IDE

%%  /* Grammar rules */

transunit: maindecl body
;
maindecl: type MAIN arg
;
type: INT | VOID
;
arg: LPARENS type RPARENS
;
body: LBRACE decl statseq RBRACE
;
decl:  /* empty */
     | type variablelist SEMICOLON
;
variablelist: variable
             | variable COMMA variablelist
;
statseq: returnstat
        | commandseq SEMICOLON returnstat
;
commandseq: command
           | commandseq SEMICOLON command
;
command: variable ASSIGN expr
;
variable: IDE
;
expr: NUM
;
returnstat: RETURN returnarg SEMICOLON
;
returnarg: LPARENS IDE RPARENS | LPARENS NUM RPARENS
;
%%
```

Figure 6.8 bison Input File minicex1.y.

```
%{
#include "minicex1.tab.h"
%}
ID [a-z][a-z0-9]*
A_NUM [0-9]+
%%
[ \r\t\n]+ /* whitespace */
"(" return LPARENS;
")" return RPARENS;
"{" return LBRACE;
"}" return RBRACE;
"=" return ASSIGN;
";" return SEMICOLON;
"," return COMMA;
int return INT;
void return VOID;
main return MAIN;
return return RETURN;
{ID} return IDE; /* more later */
{A_NUM} return NUM;
%%
```

Figure 6.9 Corresponding `flex` Input File `minicex1.in`.

```
#ifndef BISON_MINICEX1_TAB_H
# define BISON_MINICEX1_TAB_H

# ifndef YYSTYPE
#  define YYSTYPE int
#  define YYSTYPE_IS_TRIVIAL 1
# endif
# define INT 257
# define VOID 258
# define MAIN 259
# define LPARENS 260
# define RPARENS 261
# define LBRACE 262
# define RBRACE 263
# define ASSIGN 264
# define SEMICOLON 265
# define COMMA 266
# define RETURN 267
# define NUM 268
# define IDE 269


extern YYSTYPE yylval;

#endif /* not BISON_MINICEX1_TAB_H */
```

Figure 6.10 Resulting `bison`-Generated Header File `minicex1.tab.h`.

The corresponding `bison`-generated header file is shown in Figure 6.10. Figure 6.9 shows the corresponding `flex` input file used to generate the scanner.

By convention, the `bison` input file[6] ends in `.y` and the corresponding parser created by `bison` is contained in the `C` file with extension `tab.c`.

---

[6]This file should be a Unix-formatted file.

```
int yyerror (s)  /* Called by yyparse on error */
     char *s;
{
  printf ("%s\n", s);
  return(-1);
}
```

Figure 6.11 Error Handling Function yyerror.c.

Error Handling

It is appropriate to include a function that will be called for error handling. An example is shown in Figure 6.11.

6.6.2 The Overall Project: main

Recall that flex generates the C-based scanner in lex.yy.c and bison generates the parser in minicex1.tab.c. More importantly, "wrapper" code is necessary to integrate these functions to achieve a scanner/parser executable. An example is shown in Figure 6.12.

```
#include "minicex1.tab.c"
#include "lex.yy.c"
#include "yyerror.c"
#define YYERROR_VERBOSE

int main ()
{
  yyparse ();
  return(1);
}
```

Figure 6.12 Overall Project Source File minicex1.c.

6.6.3 Putting flex- and bison-Generated Functions Together

Compiling the scanner/parser and sample operation is shown in the following:

```
$ gcc minicex1.c -lfl -o minicex1
$ ./minicex1 <minicex1.mc
$
```

In this case, the parse was successful, although it is not immediately apparent from the scarce output.

6.7 A More Complete Example

The yes-no answer provided by the scanner-parser in the previous section is illustrative, but insufficient for two reasons:

1. We do not see much of the scanning and parsing action.

2. The parser does not use the input semantic values to accomplish any significant actions. In this and the following sections, we enhance the previous parser design to address these shortcomings.

6.7.1 Revised Parser

The bison grammar file is revised to include actions indicating the successful parsing or selected nonterminals. This is shown in Figure 6.13.

```
%{
#include <stdio.h>
#include <ctype.h>
int yylex (void);
int yyerror (char *s);
%}

%token INT
%token VOID
%token MAIN
%token LPARENS
%token RPARENS
%token LBRACE
%token RBRACE
%token ASSIGN
%token SEMICOLON
%token COMMA
%token RETURN
%token NUM
%token IDE

%%  /* Grammar rules */

transunit: maindecl body
           {printf("\n***** congratulations *****\n\
***** parse for transunit successful *****\n");}
;

maindecl: type MAIN arg
          {printf(" => found main declaration\n");}
;

type: INT | VOID
;

arg: LPARENS type RPARENS
;

body: LBRACE decl statseq RBRACE
      {printf(" => found body\n");}
;

decl:  /* empty */
     | type variablelist SEMICOLON
       {printf(" => found declaration\n");}
;
```

Figure 6.13 Revised bison Grammar File minicex2.y.

```
variablelist: variable
             | variable COMMA variablelist
;

statseq: returnstat
        | commandseq SEMICOLON returnstat
        {printf(" => found statseq\n");}
;

commandseq: command
          | commandseq SEMICOLON command
         {printf(" => found command seq.");}
;

command: variable ASSIGN expr
;

variable: IDE
;

expr: NUM
;

returnstat: RETURN returnarg SEMICOLON
            {printf(" => found return statement\n");}
;

returnarg: LPARENS IDE RPARENS | LPARENS NUM RPARENS
;
%%

/* Lexical analyzer */

/* error handling */
```

Figure 6.13 (continued)

6.7.2 Revised Scanner

The revised `flex` input file used to generate the `minic` scanner is shown in Figure 6.14. Note that actions in this scanner design include both returning the appropriate tokens for `yyparse` as well as printing the corresponding recognized source code symbol. The latter action is just for illustration.

```
/* this version prints the recognized tokens */
/* and associated semantic values  */
%{
#include "minicex2.tab.h"
YYSTYPE yylval;
%}
ID [a-z][a-z0-9]*
A_NUM [0-9]+
%%
[ \r\t\n]+ /* whitespace */
```

Figure 6.14 Revised `flex` Input File `minicex2.in`.

```
"(" { printf("'(' \n");
      return LPARENS; }

")" { printf("')' \n");
      return RPARENS;}

"{" { printf("'{' \n");
      return LBRACE;}

"}" { printf("'}' \n");
      return RBRACE;}

"=" { printf("'=' \n");
      return ASSIGN;}

";" { printf("';' \n");
      return SEMICOLON;}

"," { printf("',' \n");
      return COMMA;}

int { printf("'int' \n");
        return INT;}

void { printf("'void' \n");
         return VOID;}

main { printf("'main' \n");
         return MAIN;}

return { printf("'return' \n");
           return RETURN;}

{ID} { printf("ide(%s) \n", yytext);
       return IDE; }

{A_NUM} { printf("num(%s)=%d \n", yytext,
                yylval=atoi(yytext));
          return NUM;}
%%
```

Figure 6.14 (continued)

6.7.3 Sample Operation of Revised Design

Using the `minic` input file `minicex1.mc`, the operation is shown in Figure 6.15. Note that in this design, the result of each call to the scanner as well as successful parses for major syntactic components are reported. In addition, semantic values are reported.

6.8 "Under the Hood" of `bison`

In this section we look at the operation of the `bison` parsing algorithm. In addition, a number of optional `bison` features are examined. These features are useful for understanding `bison` operation as well as for debugging `bison` grammar files. To facilitate our inquiry, a very minimal version of `minic` (hereafter referred to as `"miniclite"`) is used.

```
$ gcc minicex2.c -lfl -o minicex2
$ ./minicex2 <minicex1.mc
'int'
'main'
'('
'void'
')'
 => found main declaration
'{'
'int'
ide(t1)
';'
 => found declaration seq
ide(t1)
'='
num(10)=10
';'
'return'
'('
ide(t1)
')'
';'
 => found return statement
 => found statseq
'}'
 => found body

***** congratulations *****
***** parse for transunit successful *****
$
```

Figure 6.15 Operation of Revised minic Scanner/Parser Design.

6.8.1 The Syntax of miniclite

miniclite uses a simplified syntax to illustrate bison, not the features of a programming language. The bison input grammar file is shown in Figure 6.16.

```
%{
#include <stdio.h>
#include <ctype.h>
int yylex (void);
int yyerror (char *s);
%}

%token INT
%token VOID
%token MAIN
%token LPARENS
%token RPARENS
%token LBRACE
%token RBRACE
%token SEMICOLON
%token RETURN
%token NUM
%% /* Grammar rules */
```

Figure 6.16 bison Input for miniclite Grammar.

```
transunit: maindecl body
;
maindecl: type MAIN arg
;
type: INT | VOID
;
arg: LPARENS type RPARENS
;
body: LBRACE statseq RBRACE
;
statseq: returnstat
;
returnstat: RETURN returnarg SEMICOLON
;
returnarg: LPARENS NUM RPARENS
;
%%
```

Figure 6.16 (continued)

6.8.2 The bison Parsing Algorithm

As we have seen, there are many different parsing approaches for context-free grammars. Parsers that attempt to construct the derivation tree bottom-up[7] are, for historical reasons, called LR parsers. The "L" denotes "left-to-right scan of the input," and the "R" denotes "rightmost derivation." LR parsers are suited for use in compilers for many programming languages based upon context-free grammars.

At each step in the parse, the parser is in some state determined solely by the part of the sentence it has parsed thus far. Reading and then pushing tokens onto a stack is called *shifting*; a single read/push thus defines a *shift*.

A context-free grammar is LR(1) if it can be parsed by a shift-reduce parser that only requires the next input token to decide which parsing action to take. In other words, it only needs one token lookahead—thus the (1) denotation.

LR Parsing Actions

There are only four parsing actions possible in an LR parser:

- **Shift:** Accept the next input token.
- **Reduce:** Replace the sequence of symbols corresponding to the right part of some production by the nonterminal on the left of that production.
- **Accept:** Announce completion of parse.
- **Report error in parsing.**

A subset of the lookahead LR(1) grammars is LALR(1) grammars. A quick, precise definition of an LALR(1) grammar is difficult. Basically, it involves merging (perhaps an impractically large set of) states from a LR(1) parser into a more compact-state machine.

A bison-generated parser is based upon shift/reduce operations and the constraint of an LALR(1) grammar. `yyparse()` thus implements a state machine wherein the parser operation is solely dependent upon the current state and the next or look-ahead token.

[7] From the leaves to the root of the derivation of parse tree.

6.8.3 The -v and -g Switches in bison

Two very useful features of bison are the ability to provide verbose output and to create a graphical rendition of the parser state machine. Use of the -v switch generates a file with the extension *.output. This file is very illustrative and useful for debugging. An example follows.

Invoking bison with the -g switch instructs bison to create a *visualization of compiler graph* (*.vcg) file. This file may be viewed using the xvcg viewer:

```
xvcg -silent -psoutput miniclite.ps miniclite.vcg
```

A sample corresponding to the miniclite parser is shown in Figure 6.17.

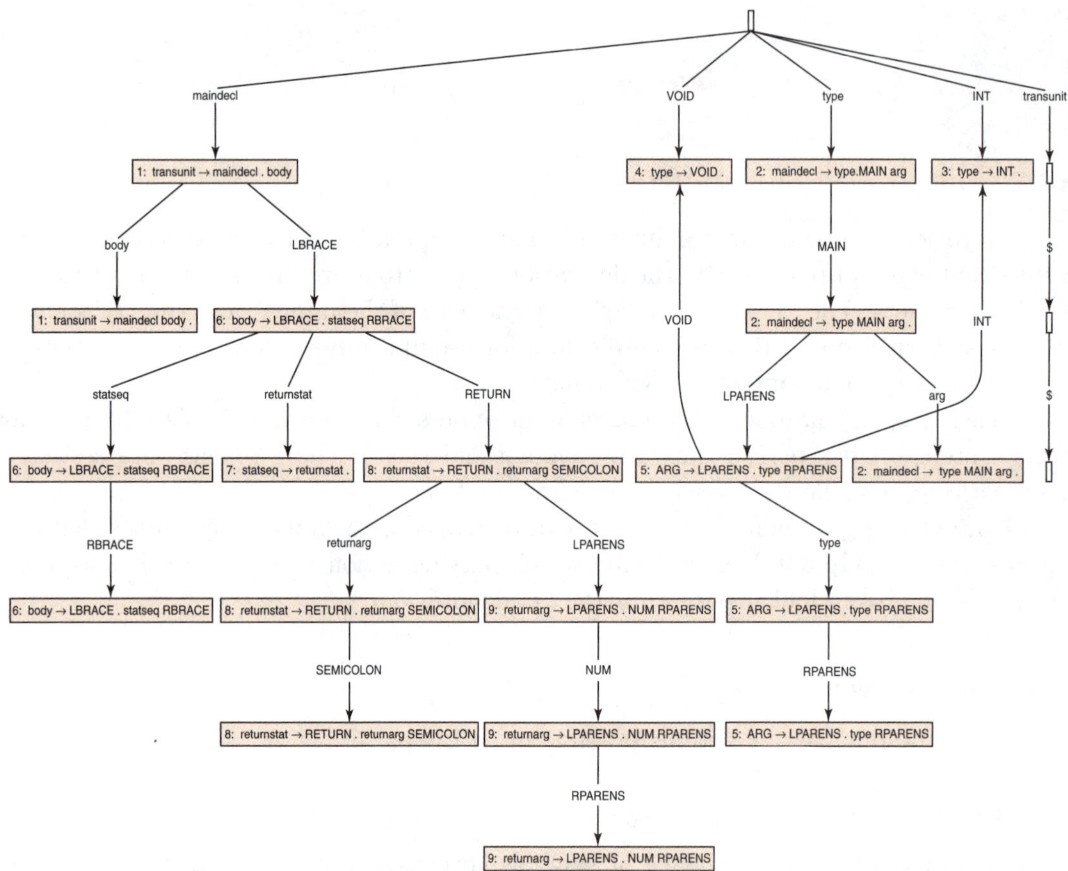

Figure 6.17 Graphical View of the bison-Created Parser State Machine.

6.8.4 Examining miniclite.output

```
Grammar

  Number, Line, Rule
    1  21 transunit -> maindecl body
    2  23 maindecl -> type MAIN arg
    3  25 type -> INT
```

```
    4  25 type -> VOID
    5  27 arg -> LPARENS type RPARENS
    6  29 body -> LBRACE statseq RBRACE
    7  31 statseq -> returnstat
    8  33 returnstat -> RETURN returnarg SEMICOLON
    9  35 returnarg -> LPARENS NUM RPARENS


Terminals, with rules where they appear

$ (-1)
error (256)
INT (257) 3
VOID (258) 4
MAIN (259) 2
LPARENS (260) 5 9
RPARENS (261) 5 9
LBRACE (262) 6
RBRACE (263) 6
SEMICOLON (264) 8
RETURN (265) 8
NUM (266) 9


Nonterminals, with rules where they appear

transunit (13)
    on left: 1
maindecl (14)
    on left: 2, on right: 1
type (15)
    on left: 3 4, on right: 2 5
arg (16)
    on left: 5, on right: 2
body (17)
    on left: 6, on right: 1
statseq (18)
    on left: 7, on right: 6
returnstat (19)
    on left: 8, on right: 7
returnarg (20)
    on left: 9, on right: 8


state 0

    INT  shift, and go to state 1
    VOID shift, and go to state 2

    transunit go to state 21
    maindecl go to state 3
    type go to state 4

state 1

    type  ->  INT .   (rule 3)

    $default reduce using rule 3 (type)
```

```
state 2

    type  ->  VOID .   (rule 4)

    $default reduce using rule 4 (type)



state 3

    transunit  ->  maindecl . body   (rule 1)

    LBRACE shift, and go to state 5

    body go to state 6



state 4

    maindecl  ->  type . MAIN arg   (rule 2)

    MAIN shift, and go to state 7



state 5

    body  ->  LBRACE . statseq RBRACE   (rule 6)

    RETURN shift, and go to state 8

    statseq go to state 9
    returnstat go to state 10

state 6

    transunit  ->  maindecl body .   (rule 1)

    $default reduce using rule 1 (transunit)



state 7

    maindecl  ->  type MAIN . arg   (rule 2)

    LPARENS shift, and go to state 11

    arg  go to state 12



state 8

    returnstat  ->  RETURN . returnarg SEMICOLON   (rule 8)

    LPARENS shift, and go to state 13

    returnarg go to state 14
```

```
state 9

    body  ->  LBRACE statseq . RBRACE   (rule 6)

    RBRACE shift, and go to state 15



state 10

    statseq  ->  returnstat .   (rule 7)

    $default reduce using rule 7 (statseq)

state 11

    arg  ->  LPARENS . type RPARENS   (rule 5)

    INT  shift, and go to state 1
    VOID shift, and go to state 2

    type go to state 16



state 12

    maindecl  ->  type MAIN arg .   (rule 2)

    $default reduce using rule 2 (maindecl)



state 13

    returnarg  ->  LPARENS . NUM RPARENS   (rule 9)

    NUM  shift, and go to state 17



state 14

    returnstat  ->  RETURN returnarg . SEMICOLON   (rule 8)

    SEMICOLON shift, and go to state 18



state 15

    body  ->  LBRACE statseq RBRACE .   (rule 6)

    $default reduce using rule 6 (body)
```

```
state 16

    arg  ->  LPARENS type . RPARENS   (rule 5)

    RPARENS shift, and go to state 19

state 17

    returnarg  ->  LPARENS NUM . RPARENS   (rule 9)

    RPARENS shift, and go to state 20



state 18

    returnstat  ->  RETURN returnarg SEMICOLON .   (rule 8)

    $default reduce using rule 8 (returnstat)



state 19

    arg  ->  LPARENS type RPARENS .   (rule 5)

    $default reduce using rule 5 (arg)



state 20

    returnarg  ->  LPARENS NUM RPARENS .   (rule 9)

    $default reduce using rule 9 (returnarg)



state 21

    $     go to state 22



state 22

    $     go to state 23



state 23

    $default accept
```

6.8.5 Examining the miniclite.vcg Visualization of Compiler Graph

The graph corresponding to the parser defined in Section 6.8.4 is shown in Figure 6.17. The reader should pay particular attention to the mapping of the state transitions indicated by the parser output file in Section 6.8.4 and their graphical counterparts presented in Figure 6.17.

6.8.6 Following a miniclite Parse

Using a modified version (miniclite2, as shown in Figure 6.18) of the bison-created parser, consider the first few steps of the parse of the following simple minic(lite) program:

```
int main(void)
{
 return(10);
}
```

```
%{
#include "miniclite2.tab.h"
%}
A_NUM [0-9]+
%%
[ \r\t\n]+ /* whitespace */
"(" { printf("token is: '(' \n");
      return LPARENS; }
")" { printf("token is: ')' \n");
      return RPARENS;}
"{" { printf("token is: '{' \n");
      return LBRACE;}
"}" { printf("token is: '}' \n");
      return RBRACE;}
";" { printf("token is: ';' \n");
      return SEMICOLON;}
int { printf("token is: 'int' \n");
        return INT;}
void { printf("token is: 'void' \n");
         return VOID;}
main { printf("token is: 'main' \n");
         return MAIN;}
return { printf("token is: 'return' \n");
           return RETURN;}
{A_NUM} { printf("token is: %s \n", yytext);
          return NUM;}
%%

%{
#include <stdio.h>
#include <ctype.h>
int yylex (void);
int yyerror (char *s);
%}
```

Figure 6.18 miniclite2 *.in and *.y Files Used to Show bison Parse.

```
%token INT
%token VOID
%token MAIN
%token LPARENS
%token RPARENS
%token LBRACE
%token RBRACE
%token SEMICOLON
%token RETURN
%token NUM

%%  /* Grammar rules */

transunit: maindecl body
          {printf(" => reduced transunit\n");}
;
maindecl: type MAIN arg
          {printf(" => reduced maindecl\n");}
;
type: INT
      {printf(" => reduced type\n");}
      | VOID
      {printf(" => reduced type\n");}
;
arg: LPARENS type RPARENS
          {printf(" => reduced arg\n");}
;
body: LBRACE statseq RBRACE
          {printf(" => reduced body\n");}
;
statseq: returnstat
          {printf(" => reduced statseq\n");}
;
returnstat: RETURN returnarg SEMICOLON
          {printf(" => reduced returnstat\n");}
;
returnarg: LPARENS NUM RPARENS
          {printf(" => reduced returnarg\n");}
;
%%
```

Figure 6.18 (continued)

This is shown in the following output from the miniclite2 parser:

```
$ gcc miniclite2.c -lfl -Wall -o miniclite2
lex.yy.c:1035: warning: `yyunput' defined but not used
$ ./miniclite2 < minicliteex1.mc
token is: 'int'
token is: 'main'
token is: '('
token is: 'void'
 => reduced type
token is: ')'
 => reduced arg
 => reduced maindecl
token is: '{'
token is: 'return'
token is: '('
```

```
token is: 10
token is: ')'
 => reduced returnarg
token is: ';'
 => reduced returnstat
 => reduced statseq
token is: '}'
 => reduced body
 => reduced transunit
```

The reader should use Figure 6.17 and the `flex`-generated tokens to verify this parse.

6.9 Toward a More Complete Parser/Compiler

6.9.1 Pragmatics of Passing of Semantic Values

In Section 6.7 we noted that semantic values were not used in the parser. Implementation of this requires careful attention to the passing of values from `yylex` to `yyparse`. This is accomplished by using a number of global variables that are available to both functions. We begin with a simple example based upon the simple (nonunion) use of global variable `yylval`, as shown in Figures 6.19 to 6.21. In this example, only the semantic value of token `NUM` (defined as the integer value of the `NUM`) is used.

```
/* this version extends ver 2 by using
the recognized token NUM semantic (numerical) value
passing via yylval.
In this example, the return argument is only
allowed to be a NUM */
%{
#include <stdio.h>
#include <ctype.h>
int yylex (void);
int yyerror (char *s);
%}

%token INT
%token VOID
%token MAIN
%token LPARENS
%token RPARENS
%token LBRACE
%token RBRACE
%token ASSIGN
%token SEMICOLON
%token COMMA
%token RETURN
%token NUM
%token IDE

%%  /* Grammar rules */

transunit: maindecl body
           {printf("\n***** parse for transunit successful *****\n");}
```

Figure 6.19 `bison` Grammar File `minicex3.y` for Use of Token Semantic Value as Returned Value of Program.

```
;
maindecl: type MAIN arg
;
type: INT | VOID
;
arg: LPARENS type RPARENS
;
body: LBRACE decl statseq RBRACE
;

decl:  /* empty */
     | type variablelist SEMICOLON
;
variablelist: variable
             | variable COMMA variablelist
;
statseq: returnstat
         | commandseq SEMICOLON returnstat
;
commandseq: command
           | commandseq SEMICOLON command
;
command: variable ASSIGN expr
;
variable: IDE
;
expr: NUM
;
returnstat: RETURN returnarg SEMICOLON
            {printf("\nin the return statement\n");}
;
returnarg: LPARENS NUM RPARENS
           {$$=$2;
            printf("the value returned by 'transunit' is %d", $$);
           }
;
%%
```

Figure 6.19 (continued)

```
/* this version shows passing semantic values from yylex
and the printing of recognized tokens is removed
except for ide() and num                              */
%{
#include "minicex3.tab.h"
int yylval;
%}
ID [a-z][a-z0-9]*
A_NUM [0-9]+
%%
[ \r\t\n]+ /* whitespace */

"("  return LPARENS;
```

Figure 6.20 Revised `flex` Input File `minicex3.in` for Passing Token Semantic (Numerical) Value to `yyparse`.

```
")" return RPARENS;

"{" return LBRACE;

"}" return RBRACE;

"=" return ASSIGN;

";" return SEMICOLON;

"," return COMMA;

"int" return INT;

"void" return VOID;

"main" return MAIN;

"return" return RETURN;

{ID} { printf("ide(%s) \n", yytext);
       return IDE; }

{A_NUM} { printf("num(%s)=%d \n", yytext,
                 yylval=atoi(yytext));
          return NUM;}
%%
```

Figure 6.20 (continued)

```
$ ./minicex3 <minicex0a.mc
ide(t1)
ide(t1)
num(10)=10
num(1)=1
the value returned by 'transunit' is 1
in the return statement

***** parse for transunit successful *****
```

Figure 6.21 Sample Operation: Passing Token (`NUM`) Semantic Value Using `minic` Source File `minicex0a.mc` (Shown in Figure 6.24).

6.9.2 Using Semantic Values in `flex/bison`

Figure 6.22 shows the `bison` input file further enhanced with actions to use semantic values. The corresponding modifications to the `flex` input file are shown in Figure 6.23. In this example, we show the use of semantic values for both user identifiers (recall the form is `ide(<name>)`) and the token `NUM`. Especially significant is what action we would define for parsing of nonterminal `variable`.

```
/* ex3a: this version extends ver 3 by using
the recognized tokens semantic values,
passing via yylval and using in bison
action pseudo-variables
need to define token semantic values as a
union to allow int and string */
%{
#include <stdio.h>
#include <ctype.h>
#include<string.h>
int yylex (void);
int yyerror (char *s);
%}
%union{
int numval;
char *ideptr;
}

%token INT
%token VOID
%token MAIN
%token LPARENS
%token RPARENS
%token LBRACE
%token RBRACE
%token ASSIGN
%token SEMICOLON
%token COMMA
%token RETURN
%token <numval> NUM
%token <ideptr> IDE
%type <numval> returnarg
%type <numval> returnstat
%type <numval> expr
%type <numval> command
%type <numval> commandseq
%type <numval> statseq
%type <ideptr> variable
%type <ideptr> variablelist

%%  /* Grammar rules */

transunit: maindecl body
           {printf("\n***** parse for transunit successful *****\n");}
;
maindecl: type MAIN arg
;
type: INT | VOID
;
arg: LPARENS type RPARENS
;
body: LBRACE decl statseq RBRACE
;
decl:  /* empty */
     | type variablelist SEMICOLON
```

Figure 6.22 bison Grammar File minicex3a.y for Enhanced Use of Semantic Values.

```
;
variablelist: variable
            | variable COMMA variablelist
;
statseq: returnstat {$$=$1}
        | commandseq SEMICOLON returnstat {$$=$3}
;
commandseq: command
          | commandseq SEMICOLON command
;
command: variable ASSIGN expr  /* put value $3 into symtable
                                  for value $1 */
         {printf("--> a variable named: %s\n",$1);
          printf("later will be put into symbol table with value: %d\n",$3);
          $$=$3;}
;
variable: IDE /* yytext put into symtable */
          {printf("parsed variable with name %s\n",$1);}
;
expr: NUM /* note the default action will put
             $$=$1=yylval.numval (from the scan)*/
;
returnstat: RETURN returnarg SEMICOLON
            {$$=$2;}
;
returnarg: LPARENS NUM RPARENS
           {$$=$2;
            printf("the value returned by 'transunit' is %d", $$);
           }
;
returnarg: LPARENS IDE RPARENS
           {printf("to do: look up the value of variable %s\n",$2);
            $$=-1; /* temp measure */
            printf("the value returned by 'transunit' is %d", $$);
           }
;
%%
```

Figure 6.22 (continued)

```
/* this version shows passing semantic values from yylex
and the printing of recognized tokens is removed
except for ide() and num                              */
/* use array to preserve yytext values */
%{
#include "minicex3a.tab.h"
%}
ID [a-z][a-z0-9]*
A_NUM [0-9]+
%%
[ \r\t\n]+ /* whitespace */

"("  return LPARENS;
```

Figure 6.23 Revised `flex` Input File `minicex3a.in` for Passing Token Semantic Values to `yyparse`.

```
")" return RPARENS;

"{" return LBRACE;

"}" return RBRACE;

"=" return ASSIGN;

";" return SEMICOLON;

"," return COMMA;

"int" return INT;

"void" return VOID;

"main" return MAIN;

"return" return RETURN;

{ID} { yylval.ideptr=(char *) strdup(yytext);
       printf("scanned: ide(%s) \n", yylval.ideptr);
       return IDE; }

{A_NUM} { printf("scanned: num(%s) with value=%d\n", yytext,
                yylval.numval=atoi(yytext));
          return NUM;}
%%
```

Figure 6.23 (continued)

```
int main(void)
{
        int t1;
        t1=10;
        return(1);
}
```

Figure 6.24 minic Input File for the Examples of Figs. 6.21 and 6.25.

```
$ ./minicex3a <minicex0a.mc
scanned: ide(t1)
parsed variable with name t1
scanned: ide(t1)
parsed variable with name t1
scanned: num(10) with value=10
--> a variable named: t1
later will be put into symbol table with value: 10
scanned: num(1) with value=1
the value returned by 'transunit' is 1
***** parse for transunit successful *****
```

Figure 6.25 Sample Operation: Using Semantic Values.

```
int main(void)
{
        int t1,t2,t3;
        t1=5;
        t2=6;
        t3=7;
        return(t1);
}
```

Figure 6.26 `minic` Input File for the Example of Figs. 6.27 and 6.31.

```
$ ./minicex3a <minicex0f.mc
scanned: ide(t1)
parsed variable with name t1
scanned: ide(t2)
parsed variable with name t2
scanned: ide(t3)
parsed variable with name t3
scanned: ide(t1)
parsed variable with name t1
scanned: num(5) with value=5
--> a variable named: t1
later will be put into symbol table with value: 5
scanned: ide(t2)
parsed variable with name t2
scanned: num(6) with value=6
--> a variable named: t2
later will be put into symbol table with value: 6
scanned: ide(t3)
parsed variable with name t3
scanned: num(7) with value=7
--> a variable named: t3
later will be put into symbol table with value: 7
scanned: ide(t1)
to do: look up the value of variable t1
the value returned by 'transunit' is -1
***** parse for transunit successful *****
```

Figure 6.27 Sample Operation: Using Semantic Values with Source File `minicex0f.mc`.

6.9.3 Using a Symbol Table: Toward Context-Sensitive Parsing

Figure 6.28 shows an enhanced `bison` input file, wherein a rudimentary symbol table is used to store and check semantic values for the recognized tokens. This effort is the beginning of work on a context-sensitive parser, which is considered in the next chapter. The `C` functions necessary to supplement the scanner and parser design are shown in Figure 6.30.

```
/* ex4: this version extends version 3 by using
a rudimentary symbol table and
the recognized tokens semantic values */
/* need to define token semantic values as a
union to allow int and string */
%{
#include <stdio.h>
#include <ctype.h>
#include "symbTableIncl.c"
int yylex (void);
int yyerror (char *s);
%}
%union{
int numval;
char *ideptr;
}

%token INT
%token VOID
%token MAIN
%token LPARENS
%token RPARENS
%token LBRACE
%token RBRACE
%token ASSIGN
%token SEMICOLON
%token COMMA
%token RETURN
%token <numval> NUM
%token <ideptr> IDE
%type <numval> returnarg
%type <numval> returnstat
%type <numval> expr
%type <numval> command
%type <numval> commandseq
%type <numval> statseq
%type <ideptr> variable
%type <ideptr> variablelist

%%  /* Grammar rules */

transunit: maindecl body
           {printf("\n***** parse for transunit successful *****\n");}
;
maindecl: type MAIN arg
;
type: INT | VOID
;
arg: LPARENS type RPARENS
;
body: LBRACE decl statseq RBRACE
```

Figure 6.28 bison Grammar File minicex4.y for More Extensive Use of Semantic Values, Including Forming a Rudimentary Symbol Table.

```
;
decl:  /* empty */
     | type variablelist SEMICOLON
;
variablelist: variable
             | variable COMMA variablelist
;
statseq: returnstat {$$=$1}
        | commandseq SEMICOLON returnstat {$$=$3}
;
commandseq: command
          | commandseq SEMICOLON command
;
command: variable ASSIGN expr  /* put value $3 into symtable
                                  for value $1 */
          {util_ptr=getsymval($1);
           printf("--> for variable named: %s\n",util_ptr->idename);
           putsymval($1, $3);
           util_ptr=getsymval($1);
           printf("I put symbol table value: %d\n",util_ptr->numval);
           $$=$3;}
;
variable: IDE /* put semantic value into symtable (if not there) */
          {if((symrec *)0==getsymval($1)) {
                        putsymval($1, 0);
                        util_ptr=getsymval($1);
                        $$=util_ptr->idename;
                        printf("into symbol table -->\
 variable with name %s\n",$$);            }
          }
;
expr: NUM {$$=$1;} /* the default action */
;

returnstat: RETURN returnarg SEMICOLON
            {$$=$2;}
;
returnarg: LPARENS NUM RPARENS
           {$$=$2;
            printf("the value returned by 'transunit' is %d", $$);
           }
;
returnarg: LPARENS IDE RPARENS
           {util_ptr=getsymval($2);
            printf("I looked up the value of variable %s\n",util_ptr->idename);
            printf("And found the value %d\n",util_ptr->numval);
            $$=util_ptr->numval;
            printf("the value returned by 'transunit' is %d", $$);
           }
;
%%
```

Figure 6.28 (continued)

```
/* ex4: this version shows passing semantic values from yylex
and the printing of recognized tokens is removed
except for ide() and num                                 */
/* use %array to preserve yytext values */
%{
#include "minicex4.tab.h"
%}
ID [a-z][a-z0-9]*
A_NUM [0-9]+
%%
[ \r\t\n]+ /* whitespace */

"("  return LPARENS;

")" return RPARENS;

"{" return LBRACE;

"}" return RBRACE;

"=" return ASSIGN;

";" return SEMICOLON;

"," return COMMA;

"int" return INT;

"void" return VOID;

"main" return MAIN;

"return" return RETURN;

{ID} { yylval.ideptr=(char *) strdup(yytext);
       printf("scanned: ide(%s) \n", yylval.ideptr);
       return IDE; }

{A_NUM} { printf("scanned: num(%s) with value=%d\n", yytext,
                yylval.numval=atoi(yytext));
          return NUM;}
%%
```

Figure 6.29 Revised flex Input File minicex4.in for Passing Token Semantic Values to yyparse.

```
/* minic (example4) symbol table implementation */
/* and manipulation */

#include <stdlib.h>
#include <string.h>

/* simple data structure for singly-linked list */
typedef struct symrec
{
char *idename;
int numval;
struct symrec *next;
}
symrec;

/* declare and initialize sym_table */
symrec *sym_table = (symrec *)0;

/* utility pointer  */
symrec *util_ptr;

/* manipulation functions */
/* puts on front of linked list */
symrec *putsymval(const char *idename, int value)
{
   symrec *ptr;
   ptr = (symrec *) malloc (sizeof (symrec));
   ptr->idename = (char *) malloc (strlen (idename) + 1);
   strcpy (ptr->idename, idename);
   ptr->numval = value; /* use 0 value for declaration purposes */
   ptr->next = (struct symrec *)sym_table;
   sym_table = ptr;
   return ptr;
}

symrec *getsymval(const char *idename)
{
   symrec *ptr;
   for (ptr = sym_table; ptr != (symrec *)0;
            ptr = (symrec *)ptr->next)
         if (strcmp (ptr->idename,idename) == 0)
           return ptr;
       return 0;
}
```

Figure 6.30 Implementation of a Symbol Table for Manipulation of Semantic Values in yyparse.

```
$ ./minicex4<minicex0f.mc
scanned: ide(t1)
into symbol table --> variable with name t1
scanned: ide(t2)
into symbol table --> variable with name t2
scanned: ide(t3)
into symbol table --> variable with name t3
scanned: ide(t1)
scanned: num(5) with value=5
--> for variable named: t1
I put symbol table value: 5
scanned: ide(t2)
scanned: num(6) with value=6
--> for variable named: t2
I put symbol table value: 6
scanned: ide(t3)
scanned: num(7) with value=7
--> for variable named: t3
I put symbol table value: 7
scanned: ide(t1)
I looked up the value of variable t1
And found the value 5
the value returned by 'transunit' is 5
***** parse for transunit successful *****
```

Figure 6.31 Sample Operation Using Symbol Table and Semantic Values.

This effort is continued in Chapter 7 to implement type checking in an expanded version of `minic` and leads to the concept of an underlying attribute grammar.

6.10 Bibliographical Remarks and References

The `man` pages for GNU `flex` and GNU `bison` are essential and relatively complete references for these tools. In addition, Web references for GNU `flex` and `bison`, including downloads of the executables and extensive documentation in various formats, may be found at:

```
http://www.gnu.org/software/flex/
http://www.gnu.org/software/flex/manual/
http://www.gnu.org/software/bison/bison.html
http://www.gnu.org/software/bison/manual/
```

6.11 Exercises

1. After studying the `man` page for `flex`, extend the formulation of the valid license plate scanner to recognize the alternative South Carolina license plate, namely one that simply reads: "tag applied for." Any number of spaces between words is allowed. (Extra credit: can you further revise the scanner to allow the most likely misspelling of the three words?)

2. In Section 6.3.2 it was noted that the order of rules in a `flex` input file was significant. To get some experience with this, consider the following `flex` input file:

```
/* to show the significance of rule order */
```

```
%%
a printf("I found an 'a'\n");
[a]+ printf("I found a string of 'a's'\n");

[b]+ printf("I found a string of 'b's'\n");
b printf("I found a 'b'\n");
```

Determine the `flex` response for the inputs `a`, `aaa`, `b`, and `bbb` and explain the behavior.

3. The simple, sample grammar G_s was introduced in Section 2.3.10, and consisted of the productions:

$$S \to AB$$
$$S \to C$$
$$A \to C$$
$$A \to a$$
$$B \to b$$
$$B \to c$$
$$C \to d$$

For this grammar:

(a) Develop the `flex` input file for the lexical portion of G_s.

(b) Compile the `flex` output and test the scanner. Name the freestanding scanner "sab-scan." Use an input file consisting of ASCII characters to hold the input string; name the file after the string. For example, file `fd` contains (only) the string `fd`. Sample use is shown here:

```
$ ./sab-scan < aa

$ ./sab-scan < f
f
$ ./sab-scan < dc

$ ./sab-scan < dd
```

(c) Develop the corresponding `bison` input file.

(d) Put the previous results together to develop a scanner/parser. Name the executable "sab." Sample use is shown here:

```
$ ./sab < ab
```

```
***** congratulations *****
***** parse for S successful *****

$ ./sab < aa
parse error
$ ./sab < f
f
parse error
$ ./sab < dc

***** congratulations *****
***** parse for S successful *****

$ ./sab < dd
parse error
```

(e) Test the scanner/parser using both strings $\in L(G_s)$ and those that are not.

4. This is an extension of the previous problem. Suppose that the scanner is based upon recognition of, and returning the relevant tokens corresponding to, just the terminals $\in V_T$. For example:

```
$ ./sab-scan < fd
f
```

This yields the corresponding parser result:

```
$ ./sab < fd
f

***** congratulations *****
***** parse for S successful *****
```

(a) Is this correct (`flex/bison`) behavior?

(b) Is this desired behavior?

(c) How would you modify the `flex/bison` input files to achieve the desired parsing capability?

5. Suppose a recent visit to a state motor vehicle agency yielded the following examples of allowable license plates:

```
1H 9870

QWY 762

ALGT 709

MG 2008

SG 1009

UTW 966

FZBT 394

ABC 1945
```

Using these examples, show the **flex** input file for recognition of allowable license plates. Note: only the *structure* of the alphanumeric pattern is significant; specific letters or numbers are not. Case and spaces matter.

6. Below are the productions (using BNF) for the grammar denoted $G_{problem}$. Recall in BNF that angular brackets, for example, `<f>`, denote a nonterminal $\in V_N$, whereas a symbol without brackets, for example, `f`, denotes a terminal $\in V_T$. The starting symbol (S in the formal notation) is `<a>`.

```
<a> ::= <b> <c>

<b> ::= <d> d <e>

<d> ::= a | e

<e> ::= l <d> r

<c> ::= m <f> n

<j> ::= b

<f> ::= <g> | <h> s <g>

<h> ::= <i> | <i> s <h>

<i> ::= <j> q <k>

<g> ::= f <l> s

<l> ::= l <j> r

<k> ::= c
```

For this grammar, develop the corresponding **flex** and **bison** input files, and the **flex**- and **bison**-generated scanner and parser. Show sample use. For example, show the result of an attempted scan/parse of the following string:

```
a d l e r m b q c s f l b r s n
```

7. Referring to the example of Figure 6.4, modify the **flex** input file to indicate an invalid license plate, for example, to achieve the behavior shown here:

```
]$ ./license3problem
xyz101
 --->>> xyz101
 is a valid license plate
abcd20
 --->>> abcd20
 NOT valid license plate
```

8. Consider the use of regular expressions and **flex** to recognize valid playing cards. The following syntactically correct **flex** input file is developed:

```
/* flex file for problem */
RANK 2|3|4|5|6|7|8|9|10|J|Q|K|A
SUIT spades|clubs|diamonds|hearts
%%
\n /* gobble up CR */
({RANK}[ ]*{SUIT}[ ]*)+ printf(" valid hand: (%s) \n",yytext);
([0-9]|[ ]|[A-Z]|[a-z])* printf(" garbage: (%s) \n",yytext);
.* printf(" real garbage: (%s) \n",yytext);
```

This file is processed by `flex` and compiled into an executable. Given the following inputs, show the resulting `flex`-generated scanner output (indicated as `<response #X>`):

```
$ ./flexquiz
asdf
<response #1>
2 spades
<response #2>
J hearts
<response #3>
1 diamonds
<response #4>
A hearts
<response #5>
333 diamonds
<response #6>
K queens
<response #7>
A spades J diamonds
<response #8>
J       diamonds
<response #9>
8 clubs
<response #10>
```

9. (a) The following recursive BNF production:

```
<h> ::= <i> | <i> s <h>
```

if directly translated into a `bison` input file rule, that is,

```
h: i | i S h
;
```

causes some difficulty and concerns.

What is the `bison` reaction (message)?

Why does it occur? Be specific.

Show how the production could be rewritten in BNF and subsequently coded as a `bison` production to avoid this problem.

Does a similar problem occur using the Prolog LGN?

(b) Suppose instead the production was:

```
<h> ::= <i> | <i> s <g>
```

How do your answers to the preceding question change?

CHAPTER 7

Enhancing `minic`: Control Statements, Iterative Constructs, Comments, and Type Checking

WARNING—Your Keyboard Cable is Disconnected. Press F1 for Help.

—Seen on a Computer Screen

7.1 `minic`, Version 2

7.1.1 Introduction and Overview

Chapters 4 to 6 considered a very simple syntax for Version 1 of a `C`-like programming language named `minic`. This allowed us to explore the concepts of scanning and parsing and corresponding Prolog and `flex`/`bison` implementations of these processes. In this chapter, we expand this rudimentary syntax of `minic`, yielding `minic` Version 2. The extensions are shown and scanners/parsers are implemented using both `flex/bison` and Prolog.

Following this, other `minic` extensions are introduced piecemeal, first as extensions or enhancements to the BNF productions, and then the corresponding scanner and parser modifications are shown. This leads to `minic` Extended Version 2. These extensions include control and iteration constructs and allow comments of different forms in the source file. Again, both Prolog and `flex`/`bison` implementations of the resulting scanner/parser are shown.

In addition, we consider the addition of more complex and typed expressions. Type checking and variable declaration is then enforced in the scanning/parsing process. These modifications yield a more syntactically rich language and lead to both contextual and semantic concerns.

Chapters 5 and 6 considered separately the scanner/parser implementations in Prolog and `flex`/`bison`, respectively, for the `minic` Version 1 syntax of Chapter 4. This chapter considers subsequent scanner/parser modifications using both `flex/bison` and Prolog for implementation. The developments are essentially independent; readers interested in only one of the approaches need only skip to the relevant sections. The exercises at the end of this chapter consider further syntax extensions and added features for `minic`.

7.1.2 minic Version 2 Syntax

The BNF description of the revised minic grammar is shown here.

```
/* enhanced minic translational unit grammar */
/* Version 2 */
/* file: transunit-bnf2.txt  */

<transunit> ::= <main-decl> <body>
<main-decl> ::= <type> main <arg>
<type> ::= int | void | boolean
<arg> ::= lparens <type> rparens

<body> ::= lbrace <dec-seq> <statseq> rbrace

<dec-seq> ::= e | <decl> <dec-seq>
<decl> ::= <type> <variable-list>;
<variable-list> ::= <variable> | <variable> , <variable-list>
<variable> ::= <identifier>

<statseq> ::= <return-stat> | <command-seq>; <return-stat>

<command-seq> ::= <command> | <command> ; <command-seq>
<command> ::= <simple-assignment>      /* leaves room for expansion */

<simple-assignment> ::= <identifier> = <expr>
<expr> ::= <integer-expr> | <boolean-expr>
<integer-expr> ::= <simple-integer-expr> | <comp-integer-expr>
<boolean-expr> ::= <simple-boolean-expr> | <comp-boolean-expr>
<comp-integer-expr> ::= <integer-expr> <int-oper> <integer-expr>
<boolean-expr> ::= ! <boolean-expr>
<comp-boolean-expr> ::= <integer-expr> <bool-oper> <integer-expr>
<simple-integer-expr> ::= <identifier> | <integer-const>
<simple-boolean-expr> ::= <identifier> | <boolean-const>
<integer-const> ::= <numeral>
<int-oper> ::= * | / | + | -
<bool-oper> ::= < | <= | == | !=
<boolean-const> ::= true | false

<return-stat> ::= return <return-arg>;
<return-arg> ::= lparens <variable> rparens
                 | lparens <numeral>  rparens
                 | lparens <boolean-const>  rparens

/* end of updated syntax  */

/* lexical part for identifiers and numerals */

<identifier> ::= <letter> | <identifier> <letter> |  <identifier> <digit>
<letter> ::= a | b | c | d | e | f | g | h | i | j | k | l | m
                   | n | o | p | q | r | s | t | u | v | w | x | y | z
<numeral> ::= <digit> | <digit> <numeral>
<digit> ::= 0|1|2|3|4|5|6|7|8|9
```

7.1.3 What's Changed in the Syntax?

Structural Changes

Structural changes include:

1. the new type `boolean` and related boolean expressions. This is a prelude to adding other new statements that use boolean predicates. Note also we are beginning to diverge from `C` in the sense that `C` has no predefined boolean type;[1]

2. incorporation of the important concept of an expression (integer or boolean), whose value may be assigned to a variable. (This is a semantic interpretation). For example, integer expressions may now be of the form:

   ans=t1 + t2 + t3 / t4 + ...;

3. the use of a declaration *sequence*, as opposed to a single declaration.

Note that many of the changes to `minic`, resulting in Version 2, allow the creation of expressions that are syntactically correct but whose interpretation may be (semantically) ambiguous. This is further addressed on page 210.

Lexical Changes

The revised syntax shows the addition of new reserved symbols:

```
*  /  +  -
<  <=  ==  !=
true  false
!
```

Even more reserved words and symbols will be added later in the chapter (and problems).

Version 2 Expressions and Operator Precedence

Note from Section 7.1.3 that the revised `minic` syntax makes it possible to generate and parse syntactically correct and (grammatically) unambiguous strings that are more complex and theoretically infinite in length. These are derived from the recursive use of productions from nonterminal `<expr>`. For example, a syntactically correct integer expression is:

```
t1 = 20 + 40 / 20;
```

Subsequent interpretation of the semantics or meaning of this string, however, yields problems. Is the semantic interpretation of variable `t1` above the value 3, or the value 22? It is necessary to semantically disambiguate the parsed string to determine subsequent processing. In many programming languages, this disambiguation is accomplished using disambiguation rules. Such rules are often based upon the concept of operator precedence.

7.1.4 Sample minic Version 2 Source File

The following source file may be generated with the `minic` Version 2 syntax. Note that we still have not defined semantics for the various syntactic constructs used. However,

[1] Although C99 specifies type `bool` as shown in section 7.7.5.

by ascribing C semantics to the sample source, the reader will probably find the syntax familiar.

```
int main(void)
{
 int t1,t2,kt,ans;
 t1=10;
 t2=3;
 kt=10;
 ans=t1 + t2 + kt;
 return(ans);
}
```

7.1.5 An Example: Possible minic Syntax Ambiguity (Using a Modified Syntax)

Prior to developing scanners and parsers for minic Version 2, we digress to reconsider the issue of grammatical ambiguity. In designing the syntax of a language, we need to be careful not to create an ambiguous grammar.

It is not always easy to see ambiguity creep into the syntax, as the following example shows. Below is a (carelessly) modified version of the minic syntax. *The reader should note the changes that were made.*

```
<command> ::= <simple-assignment>
<simple-assignment> ::= <identifier> = <expr>
<expr> ::= <primary-expr> | <compound-expr>
<compound-expr> ::= <integer-expr> | <boolean-expr>
<integer-expr> ::= <simple-integer-expr> | <mult-expr> | <add-expr>
<boolean-expr> ::= <simple-boolean-expr> | <relational-expr> | <equality-expr>
<mult-expr> ::= <integer-expr> * <integer-expr> | <integer-expr> / <integer-expr>
<add-expr> ::=  <integer-expr> + <integer-expr> | <integer-expr> - <integer-expr>
<relational-expr> ::= <integer-expr> < <integer-expr> | <integer-expr> <= <integer-expr>
<equality-expr> ::= <integer-expr> == <integer-expr> | <integer-expr> != <integer-expr>
<simple-integer-expr> ::= <identifier> | <integer-const>
<simple-boolean-expr> ::= <identifier> | <boolean-const>
<primary-expr> ::= <identifier> | <constant>
<constant> ::= <boolean-const> | <integer-const>
<integer-const> ::= <numeral>
<boolean-const> ::= true | false
```

An important note is that this version allows **ambiguity**; notice that there are two trees for derivations starting at <simple-assignment>. For example, consider production of the string:

$$k = 6$$

As shown in the following diagram, two distinct derivation trees exist.

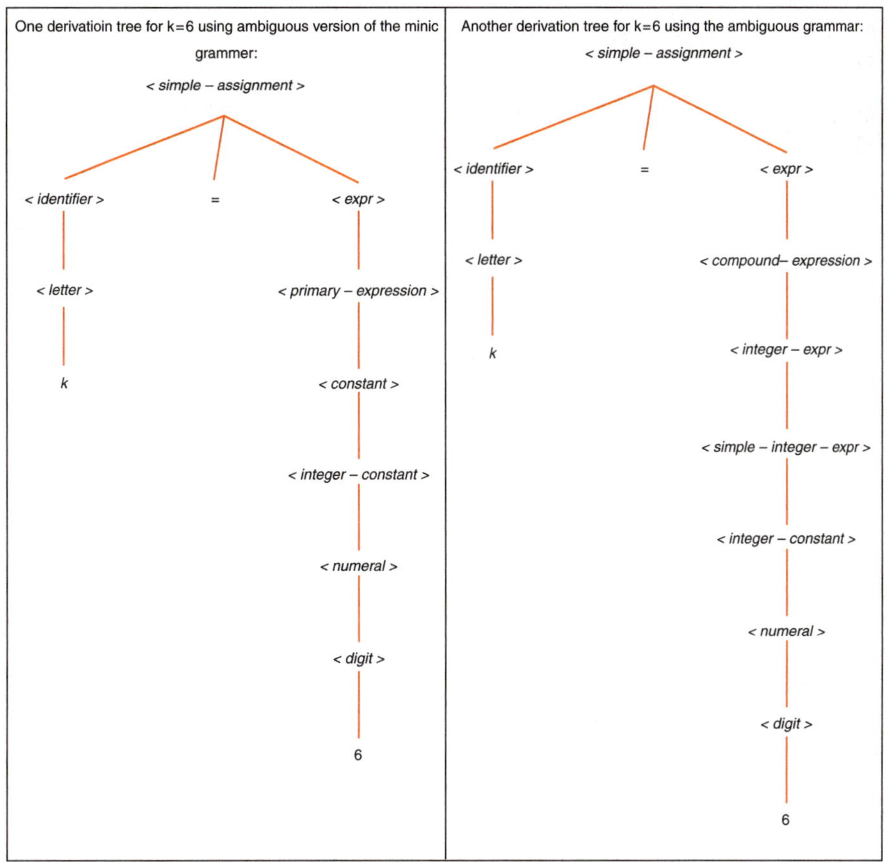

7.2 Scanning and Parsing minic Version 2 Using flex and bison

The development of a scanner and parser for **minic** Version 2 using **flex** and **bison**, respectively, is straightforward. First, we show the individual components, and then we test the completed effort.

7.2.1 flex Scanner for minic Version 2 Lexics

The **flex** input file used to build the scanner is shown here.

```
/* this version is for 'basic' minic version 2 */
/* it prints the recognized tokens */
%{
#include "minicv2.tab.h"
YYSTYPE yylval;
%}
ID [a-z][a-z0-9]*
A_NUM [0-9]+
%%
[ \r\t\n]+ /* whitespace */

"(" { printf("'(' \n");
      return LPARENS; }
```

```
")" { printf("')' \n");
      return RPARENS;}

"{" { printf("'{' \n");
      return LBRACE;}

"}" { printf("'}' \n");
      return RBRACE;}

"==" { printf("'==' \n");
      return EQUAL;}

"=" { printf("'=' \n");
      return ASSIGN;}

"<=" { printf("'<=' \n");
      return LEQ;}

"<" { printf("'<' \n");
      return LESS;}

"!=" { printf("'!=' \n");
      return NEQUAL;}

";" { printf("';' \n");
      return SEMICOLON;}

"," { printf("',' \n");
      return COMMA;}

"*" { printf("'*' \n");
      return TIMES;}

"/" { printf("'/' \n");
      return DIV;}

"+" { printf("'+' \n");
      return PLUS;}

"-" { printf("'-' \n");
       return MINUS;}

true { printf("'true' \n");
       return TRUE;}

false { printf("'false' \n");
       return FALSE;}

int { printf("'int' \n");
        return INT;}

boolean { printf("'boolean' \n");
         return BOOLEAN;}

void { printf("'void' \n");
         return VOID;}

main { printf("'main' \n");
```

```
         return MAIN;}

return { printf("'return' \n");
           return RETURN;}

{ID} { printf("ide(%s) \n", yytext);
       return IDE; }

{A_NUM} { printf("num(%s)=%d \n", yytext,
                 yylval=atoi(yytext));
          return NUM;}
%%
```

7.2.2 bison Parser for minic Version 2

The bison input file used to build the parser is shown here.

```
%{
#include <stdio.h>
#include <ctype.h>
int yylex (void);
int yyerror (char *s);
%}

%token INT
%token BOOLEAN
%token VOID
%token MAIN
%token LPARENS
%token RPARENS
%token LBRACE
%token RBRACE
%token ASSIGN
%token SEMICOLON
%token COMMA
%token RETURN
%token NUM
%token IDE
%token TIMES
%token DIV
%token PLUS
%token MINUS
%token TRUE
%token FALSE
%token LESS
%token LEQ
%token EQUAL
%token NEQUAL

%%  /* Grammar rules */

transunit: maindecl body
           {printf("\n***** congratulations *****\n\
***** parse for transunit successful *****\n");}
;

maindecl: type MAIN arg
          {printf(" => found main declaration\n");}
;
```

```
type: INT | BOOLEAN | VOID
;

arg: LPARENS type RPARENS
;

body: LBRACE decseq statseq RBRACE
      {printf(" => found body\n");}
;

decseq:   /* empty */
        | decseq decl
       {printf(" => found declaration seq\n");}
;

decl: type variablelist SEMICOLON
;

variablelist: variable
            | variable COMMA variablelist
;

statseq: returnstat
         | commandseq SEMICOLON returnstat
         {printf(" => found statseq\n");}
;

commandseq: command
           | commandseq SEMICOLON command
          {printf(" => found command seq.\n");}
;

command: simpleassignment
;

simpleassignment: variable ASSIGN expr
         {printf(" => found simple assignment\n");}
;

booleanexpr: simplebooleanexpr | compbooleanexpr
;

compbooleanexpr: simpleintegerexpr booloper simpleintegerexpr
;

simplebooleanexpr: booleanconst
;

booloper: LESS | LEQ | EQUAL | NEQUAL
;

booleanconst: TRUE | FALSE
;

variable: IDE
;

expr: integerexpr | booleanexpr
      {printf(" => found expr.\n");}
;
```

```
integerexpr: simpleintegerexpr | compintegerexpr
      {printf(" => found integer expr.\n");}
;

compintegerexpr: simpleintegerexpr intoper restintegerexpr
      {printf(" => found compound integer expr.\n");}
;

restintegerexpr: simpleintegerexpr | compintegerexpr
;

simpleintegerexpr: variable | integerconst
      {printf(" => found simple integer expr.\n");}
;

integerconst: NUM
;

intoper: TIMES | DIV | PLUS | MINUS
;

returnstat: RETURN returnarg SEMICOLON
            {printf(" => found return statement\n");}
;

returnarg: LPARENS IDE RPARENS
         | LPARENS NUM RPARENS
         | LPARENS booleanconst RPARENS
;
%%

/* Lexical analyzer */

/* error handling */
```

7.2.3 Pragmatics

The C file containing main is shown here.

```
#include "minicv2.tab.c"
#include "lex.yy.c"
#include "yyerror.c"

int main ()
{
  yyparse();
  return(1);
}
```

The overall scanner/parser is built as shown:

```
#include "minicv2.tab.c"
#include "lex.yy.c"
#include "yyerror.c"

int main ()
{
  yyparse();
  return(1);
}
```

7.2.4 Sample Result Using the Scanner/Parser

Using the minic input file shown in Section 7.1.4, sample results are shown here.

```
$ ./minicv2 <minicex2.mc
'int'
'main'
'('
'void'
')'
 => found main declaration
'{'
'int'
ide(t1)
','
ide(t2)
','
ide(kt)
','
ide(ans)
';'
 => found declaration seq
ide(t1)
'='
num(10)=10
 => found simple integer expr.
';'
 => found simple assignment
ide(t2)
'='
num(3)=3
 => found simple integer expr.
';'
 => found simple assignment
 => found command seq.
ide(kt)
'='
num(10)=10
 => found simple integer expr.
';'
 => found simple assignment
 => found command seq.
ide(ans)
'='
ide(t1)
'+'
ide(t2)
'+'
ide(kt)
';'
 => found compound integer expr.
 => found compound integer expr.
 => found integer expr.
 => found simple assignment
 => found command seq.
'return'
'('
ide(ans)
')'
```

```
';'
 => found return statement
 => found statseq
'}'
 => found body

***** congratulations *****
***** parse for transunit successful *****
```

In addition, consider a differerent `minic` input file:

```
boolean main(void)
{
 int t1,t2,t3;
 boolean b1;
 t1=10;
 t2=3;
 t3=t2*t1;
 b1=t2<t3;
 return(b1);
}
```

Application of the scanner/parser to this file yields:

```
$ ./minicv2 <minicex2.mc
'int'
'main'
'('
'void'
')'
 => found main declaration
'{'
'int'
ide(t1)
','
ide(t2)
','
ide(kt)
','
ide(ans)
';'
 => found declaration seq
ide(t1)
'='
num(10)=10
 => found simple integer expr.
';'
 => found simple assignment
ide(t2)
'='
num(3)=3
 => found simple integer expr.
';'
 => found simple assignment
 => found command seq.
ide(kt)
'='
num(10)=10
```

```
 => found simple integer expr.
';'
 => found simple assignment
 => found command seq.
ide(ans)
'='
ide(t1)
'+'
ide(t2)
'+'
ide(kt)
';'
 => found compound integer expr.
 => found compound integer expr.
 => found integer expr.
 => found simple assignment
 => found command seq.
'return'
'('
ide(ans)
')'
';'
 => found return statement
 => found statseq
'}'
 => found body

***** congratulations *****
***** parse for transunit successful *****
```

Finally, consider the (syntactically incorrect) input file:

```
int main(void)
{
 int t1,t2,kt,ans;
 t1=10;
 t2=3;
 kt=10;
 ans=t1 + t2 + kt;
}
```

with corresponding scan/parse result:

```
$ ./minicv2 <minicex2b.mc
'int'
'main'
'('
'void'
')'
 => found main declaration
'{'
'int'
ide(t1)
','
ide(t2)
','
```

```
ide(kt)
','
ide(ans)
';'
 => found declaration seq
ide(t1)
'='
num(10)=10
 => found simple integer expr.
';'
 => found simple assignment
ide(t2)
'='
num(3)=3
 => found simple integer expr.
';'
 => found simple assignment
 => found command seq.
ide(kt)
'='
num(10)=10
 => found simple integer expr.
';'
 => found simple assignment
 => found command seq.
ide(ans)
'='
ide(t1)
'+'
ide(t2)
'+'
ide(kt)
';'
 => found compound integer expr.
 => found compound integer expr.
 => found integer expr.
 => found simple assignment
 => found command seq.
'}'
syntax error
```

7.3 Scanning and Parsing minic Version 2 Using Prolog

The Prolog scanner/parser effort of Chapter 5 is used as a basis. However, a number of modifications and extensions are necessary.

7.3.1 Scanner Modification/Extension

A number of the required modifications appear straightforward, such as adding the new reserved words/symbols. However, in the scanner design using one-character lookahead, a subtle problem arises: *certain characters have a dual role.* Examples are found when looking at the terminals: `=`, `<`, `<=`, `==`, and `!=`.

To accommodate characters that are used either singly or as part of a pair (double), we define a double predicate:

```
double(60,less).  % <
double(61, assign). % =
```

And indicate character pairs using:

```
pair(60,61,leq).          % <=
pair(61,61,equal).        % ==
```

Furthermore, to check for dual-use characters, we define another case for success using lookahead predicate `gettoken`. If a character with dual use (satisfying predicate `double`) is encountered in the scanning process, it is first checked to see if it is part of a pair; otherwise it is considered a valid single token. This is achieved using the enhanced Prolog description:

```
gettoken(C, T, E) :- double(C,U),getch(D),(pair(C,D,T),getch(E) ; T=U,E=D).
```

7.3.2 Parser Modification/Extension

Syntax Rewriting to Avoid Nontermination

A straightforward translation of the Version 2 `minic` syntax of Section 7.1.2 yields a parser with a problem in nontermination due to some of the newly added recursive (or self-embedding) productions. Thus, we rewrite some the Version 2 productions prior to development of the parser. For example, we rewrite

```
<comp-integer-expr> ::= <integer-expr> <int-oper> <integer-expr>
```

as

```
 /* here's the 'no infinite recursion' version of the
     updated part of the syntax  */

<comp-integer-expr> ::= <simple-integer-expr> <int-oper> <rest-integer-expr>
<rest-integer-expr> ::= <simple-integer-expr> | <comp-integer-expr>
```

Note no further scanner modifications are necessary to accommodate this version of the syntax revision.

7.3.3 The Initial minic Version 2 Prolog Parser

Note that the addition of extra arguments and functors to the LGN leads to parse results that show the structure of the `minic` program. The Prolog source for the initial parser is shown here.

```
% File: cscanpv2r4.pro
% uses minic version 2 BNF syntax from transunit-bnf2nir.txt
% this version has more variables and functors as addl arguments
%      to illustrate parse structure and results


%--------- version 2 translational unit (transunit) parser -------------------------

transunit(transunit(Maindecl, Body)) --> maindecl(Maindecl), body(Body).

maindecl(maindecl(Type, Arg)) --> type(Type), [main], marg(Arg).

type(int) --> [int]. type(void) --> [void]. type(bool) --> [boolean].

marg(mainarg(Arg)) --> [lparen], type(Arg), [rparen].

body(body(Decseq, Statseq)) --> [lbrace], decseq(Decseq), statseq(Statseq), [rbrace].

%%---------- declaration sequence -------------------------

decseq([]) --> [].
decseq([Dec|Decs]) --> decl(Dec), decseq(Decs).
decl(decl(Type, Vars)) --> type(Type), varlist(Vars), [semicolon].

%%----------- statement sequence ------------------------------

statseq(statseq(Cmdseq, Retstat)) --> cmdseq(Cmdseq), [semicolon], retstat(Retstat).

statseq(statseq([], Retstat)) --> retstat(Retstat).

retstat(retstat(Returnarg)) --> [return], returnarg(Returnarg), [semicolon].

returnarg(ide(Returnarg)) --> [lparen], [ide(Returnarg)], [rparen].


returnarg(num(Returnarg)) --> [lparen], [num(Returnarg)], [rparen].
returnarg(boolconst(Returnarg)) --> [lparen], [boolconst(Returnarg)], [rparen].

varlist(Vars) --> [ide(Var)], restvars(Var,Vars).
  restvars(Var,[Var|Vars]) --> [comma], varlist(Vars).
  restvars(Var,[Var])      --> [].

cmdseq(Cmds) --> command(Cmd), restcmds(Cmd,Cmds).
  restcmds(Cmd,[Cmd|Cmds]) --> [semicolon], cmdseq(Cmds).
  restcmds(Cmd,[Cmd])      --> [].

command(sassign(X,E)) --> simpleassign(X,E).

simpleassign(X,E) --> identifier(X), [assign], expr(E).

expr(E) --> intexpr(E).   expr(E) --> boolexpr(E).

intexpr(E) --> simpleintexpr(E).  intexpr(E) --> compintexpr(E).

boolexpr(E) --> simpleboolexpr(E).
boolexpr(E) --> compboolexpr(E).
boolexpr(not(E)) --> [not], boolexpr(E).
```

```
compintexpr(compintexpr([E,Op,R])) --> simpleintexpr(E), intoper(Op), restintexpr(R).
restintexpr(R) --> simpleintexpr(R).
restintexpr(compintexpr([Er,Opr,Rr])) --> compintexpr(compintexpr([Er,Opr,Rr])).

compboolexpr(compbool(A,B,C)) --> simpleintexpr(A), booloper(B), simpleintexpr(C).

simpleintexpr(E) --> identifier(E).   simpleintexpr(E) --> intconst(E).

simpleboolexpr(E) --> identifier(E).  simpleboolexpr(E) --> boolconst(E).

intoper(times) --> [times]. intoper(times) --> [div].
intoper(plus) --> [plus]. intoper(minus) --> [minus].

booloper(less) --> [less]. booloper(leq) --> [leq].
booloper(equal) --> [equal]. booloper(nequal) --> [nequal].

intconst(E) --> numeral(E).
boolconst(true) --> [true].  boolconst(false) --> [false].

identifier(ide(V)) --> [ide(V)].
numeral(num(N)) --> [num(N)].


parse-goal :- nl,write('>>> Scanning and parsing minic (ver 2) <<<'), nl, nl,
      write('Enter name of source file:  '), nl,
      getfilename(File), nl,
      see(File), scan(Tokens), seen, write('Scan Results'), nl, nl,
      write(Tokens), nl, nl, !,
      transunit(Parse,Tokens,[eop]), write('Parse Results'), nl, nl,!,
      write(Parse), nl, !.

%---------  Scanner  -----------------------------------------------------

lower(C) :- 97=<C,C=<122.       % a-z
digit(C)  :- 48=<C,C=<57.       % 0-9

% ASCII characters of special significance

space(32). tabch(9). period(46).
cr(13).  lf(10).  endfile(26).   endfile(-1).
endline(C) :- lf(C).  % for both DOS and UNIX

whitespace(C) :- space(C) ; tabch(C) ; cr(C) ; lf(C).

idchar(C) :- lower(C) ; digit(C).

getfilename(W) :- nl,write('input the source filename IN QUOTES'),nl,
                  write('followed by a . and CR'),nl,
                  read(X),nl, name(W,X).

scan([T|Lt]) :- tab(4), getch(C), gettoken(C,T,D), restprog(T, D, Lt), !.

getch(C) :- get0(C), (endline(C),nl,tab(4) ; endfile(C),nl ; put(C)).

restprog(eop, _, []).        % end of file reached with previous character
restprog(_,   C, [U|Lt]) :- gettoken(C, U, D), restprog(U, D, Lt).

gettoken(C, eop, 0) :- endfile(C).
gettoken(C, T, D) :- single(C,T), getch(D).
```

```
%% check for dual-use chars
%% if double, check if pair, otherwise it is a single token
gettoken(C, T, E) :- double(C,U),getch(D),(pair(C,D,T),getch(E) ; T=U,E=D).

gettoken(C, T, E) :- lower(C), getch(D), restid(D, Lc, E),
                     name(I, [C|Lc]), (reswd(I),T=I ; T=ide(I)).
  restid(C, [C|Lc], E) :- idchar(C), getch(D),restid(D,Lc,E).
  restid(C, [],     C).    % end identifier if C is not id character
gettoken(C, num(N), E) :- digit(C), getch(D), restnum(D, Lc, E),
                          name(N, [C|Lc]).
  restnum(C, [C|Lc], E) :- digit(C), getch(D), restnum(D, Lc, E).
  restnum(C, [],     C).    % end number if C is not digit
gettoken(C, T, E) :- whitespace(C), getch(D), gettoken(D,T,E).
gettoken(C, _, _) :- write('This character is not in the lexical syntax: '),
                     put(C), write('Bye'), nl, abort.

%% here are the revised reserved words (tokens) for ver 2 of minic:

reswd(main).
reswd(void).
reswd(int).
reswd(return).

%% new


reswd(boolean).
reswd(true).
reswd(false).

single(123, lbrace).
single(125, rbrace).
single(40,lparen).
single(41,rparen).
single(44,comma).
single(59,semicolon).

%% new

single(42,times).
single(47,div).
single(43,plus).
single(45,minus).

%% single chars that are used either singly or as
%% part of a pair (double)

double(60,less).  % <
double(61, assign). % =
double(33, not).  % !

%% character pairs

pair(60,61,leq).        % <=
pair(61,61,equal).      % ==
pair(33,61,nequal).     % !=

%% thats all folks!
```

7.3.4 Examples of Modified Parser Use

Using the minic Version 2 parser, two examples of sample output are shown here. The second example involves boolean expressions.

```
?- parse-goal.

>>> Scanning and parsing minic (ver 2) <<<

Enter name of source file:

input the source filename IN QUOTES
followed by a . and CR
|: "minicex2.mc".

    int main(void)
    {


     int t1,t2,kt,ans;
     t1=10;
     t2=3;
     kt=10;
     ans=t1 + t2 + kt;
     return(ans);
    }

Scan Results

[int, main, lparen, void, rparen, lbrace, int, ide(t1), comma, ide(t2), comma,
ide(kt), comma, ide(ans), semicolon, ide(t1), assign, num(10), semicolon,
ide(t2), assign, num(3), semicolon, ide(kt), assign, num(10), semicolon,
ide(ans), assign, ide(t1), plus, ide(t2), plus, ide(kt), semicolon,
return, lparen, ide(ans), rparen, semicolon, rbrace, eop]

Parse Results

transunit(maindecl(int, mainarg(void)), body([decl(int, [t1, t2, kt, ans])],
statseq([sassign(ide(t1), num(10)), sassign(ide(t2), num(3)),
sassign(ide(kt), num(10)), sassign(ide(ans),
compintexpr([ide(t1), plus, compintexpr([ide(t2), plus, ide(kt)])]))],
retstat(ide(ans)))))

Yes
?- parse-goal.

>>> Scanning and parsing minic (ver 2) <<<

Enter name of source file:

input the source filename IN QUOTES
followed by a . and CR
|: "minicex3.mc".
```

```
    boolean main(void)
    {
     int t1,t2,t3;
     boolean b1;
     t1=10;
     t2=3;
     t3=t2*t1;
     b1=t2<t3;
     return(b1);
    }

Scan Results

[boolean, main, lparen, void, rparen, lbrace, int, ide(t1), comma, ide(t2),
comma, ide(t3), semicolon, boolean, ide(b1), semicolon, ide(t1),
assign, num(10), semicolon, ide(t2), assign, num(3), semicolon,
ide(t3), assign, ide(t2), times, ide(t1), semicolon, ide(b1), assign, ide(t2),
less, ide(t3), semicolon, return, lparen, ide(b1), rparen, semicolon, rbrace, eop]

Parse Results

transunit(maindecl(bool, mainarg(void)),
body([decl(int, [t1, t2, t3]), decl(bool, [b1])],
statseq([sassign(ide(t1), num(10)), sassign(ide(t2), num(3)),
sassign(ide(t3), compintexpr([ide(t2), times, ide(t1)])),
sassign(ide(b1), compbool(ide(t2), less, ide(t3)))],
retstat(ide(b1)))))

Yes
```

7.3.5 Examining Intermediate Prolog Parsing Results

The reader is encouraged to consult and run the Prolog scanner/parser implementation. To help in an understanding of the parser operation, it is useful to look at intermediate parsing results. For example, using the token list from the previous example, we can check:

```
?- boolexpr(What,[ide(t2),less,num(10)],[]).
What = compbool(ide(t2), less, num(10))
```

7.4 Further `minic` Extensions (Extended Version 2)

7.4.1 Desirable Extensions

Here we begin the enhancement of the parser for other extensions to the `minic` syntax. Some are left as exercises. Desirable modifications include:

1. extending the scanner to allow for comments in the source code.
2. addition of `if` and other branching/conditionals.
3. adding `reading` and `writing` (I/O) capabilities.
4. allowing functions/subroutines/procedures.

5. adding user-defined data types.

6. implementing type checking (this leads to attribute grammars in Section 7.8).

7.4.2 The Incremental Development Strategy

In the revisions that follow, we adopt the following development strategy.

1. We show an example or examples of the desired `minic` extension.

2. We indicate the new construct prototype.

3. We develop the BNF description(s) of the new feature. (This provides a basis to modify the scanner and/or parser to accommodate the new BNF description.)

4. finally, we test the resulting modification.

Adding Comments to minic Source Files

The ability to put comments in `minic` source files is both useful to the programmer[2] and a good test of our understanding of the Prolog implementation of the scanner. There are many ways to designate comments in programming languages, as summarized in Table 7.1. We will focus on the two forms used in `C` and `C++`.

Comment Style			Language
/*		*/	C
	//		C++
	%		LaTeX
	;		Lisp
/*		*/	Prolog ('var-length')
	%		Prolog ('end-of-line')
<!--		-->	HTML
	#		bash shell script

Table 7.1 Sample Comment Styles.

C++ Style Comments Although there are a variety of widely used comment formats, we initially concentrate on the `C++` syntax: *a comment begins with // and ends with the end of the line.* A sample `minic` program with comments is shown here.

```
boolean main(void)
{
 int t1,t2,t3;
 // here is a boolean
```

[2] Although it is sometimes abused.

```
 boolean b1;
 t1=10; // comment after statement
 t2=3;
 t3=t2*t1;
 b1=t2<t3;
// time to return something
 return(b1);
}
```

Because *comments do not generate tokens*, we do not explicitly add the comment structure to the syntax. However, we must modify the scanner to accommodate this enhancement.

C Style Comments Here we modify the scanner to allow minic source code comments, using the comment notation or form of C, that is,

```
/* <comment body> */
```

Thus, two new pairs of input ASCII symbols become important, namely /* and */. Comments are allowed to span multiple lines. At this time, we do not attempt to facilitate nested comments. This is left to the exercises.

Adding Iteration Statements to minic

We add two commonly used forms of iteration statements to minic, namely while and for. Both are derived from nonterminal <command>, and follow the C syntax.

while The while construct has the form:

```
while(<boolean-expr>) <command>
```

More specifically, the while BNF syntax is as follows:

```
<command> ::= while(<boolean-expr>) <command>
```

The semantics of while are that <command> is executed repeatedly as long as <boolean-expr> is true. The test on <boolean-expr> takes place before each execution of <command>.

for The for structure is as follows:

```
for(<expr1> ; <expr2>  ; <expr3> ) <command>
```

where <expr1> and <expr3> are derived from <simple-assignment> and <expr2> is derived from <boolean-expr>. The semantics of for are that <expr1> is evaluated before the first iteration. After each iteration,<expr3> is evaluated. All arguments are optional.

Both `<expr1>` and `<expr3>` may be omitted. If `<expr2>` is omitted, it is assumed to be `true`. This gives rise to the "forever" construct:

```
for(;;;) //forever
```

`<command>` is executed repeatedly until the value of `<expr2>` is `false`. The test on `<expr2>` occurs before each execution of `<command>`.

Note we create the nonterminals `<expr1>`, `<expr2>`, and `<expr3>` simply to facilitate the description of the semantics of this syntactic fragment (in order to avoid referring to the "first argument," "second argument," and so on).

The actual syntactic description to be added to `minic` is:

```
<command> ::=
  for(<simple-assignment> ; <boolean-expr>  ; <simple-assignment> ) <command>
```

Adding `if` to `minic`

It is desired to add an `if` construct (derived from `<command>`) to the syntax of `minic`. Specifically, we follow the `C` syntax,

```
if <expression> <statement>
```

where `<statement>` is a single statement (command). If the `if <expression>` evaluates to anything other than 0, then `<statement>` is executed. At this point we ignore implementation of an `else` part to the syntax, as well as allowing `<statement>` to be a command sequence. This is left to the problems.

Adding Function Invocation (Calls) to `minic`

Another useful extension to `minic` is the ability to invoke (predefined) functions, such as `sin(x)`. The following are modifications to the syntax (BNF) of `minic` to allow for expressions involving `square(x)`and `cube(x)`, where `x` is an integer variable. In addition, we develop and test the corresponding scanner/parser modifications.

Adding (Integer) Functions to the `minic` BNF Syntax

The additions are straightforward, as shown here:

```
<integer-expr> ::= <function-appl>
<function-appl> ::= <function-name> <fn-args>
<fn-args> ::= lparens <identifier> rparens | lparens <numeral> rparens
```

7.4.3 The Complete Syntax and Prolog Parser for `minic` Enhanced Version 2

```
/* minic translational unit grammar w/ o inf. recursion */
/* Version 4.1 with many new constructs */
/* for use in parser development  */
/* file: transunit-bnf4r2nir.txt  */
```

```
<transunit> ::= <main-decl> <body>
<main-decl> ::= <type> main <arg>
<type> ::= int | void | boolean
<arg> ::= lparens <type> rparens
<body> ::= lbrace <dec-seq> <statseq> rbrace

<dec-seq> ::= e | <decl> <dec-seq>
<decl> ::= <type> <variable-list>;
<variable-list> ::= <variable> | <variable> , <variable-list>
<variable> ::= <identifier>

<statseq> ::= <return-stat> | <command-seq>; <return-stat>
<command-seq> ::= <command> | <command> ; <command-seq>

/* new commands */

<command> ::= <simple-assignment> | <while> | <for> | <if>

<while> ::= while lparens <boolean-expr> rparens <command>
/* note arguments to for optional */

<for> ::= for lparens <for-simple-assignment> ;
                        <for-boolean-expr>  ;
                        <for-simple-assignment>
                        rparens <command>

<if> ::= if lparens <expr> rparens <command>

<for-simple-assignment> ::= <simple-assignment> | e
<for-boolean-expr> ::= <boolean-expr> | e

<simple-assignment> ::= <identifier> = <expr>
<expr> ::= <integer-expr> | <boolean-expr>

<integer-expr> ::= <simple-integer-expr> | <comp-integer-expr>

<integer-expr> ::= <function-appl>
<function-appl> ::= <function-name> <fn-args>
<fn-args> ::= lparens <identifier> rparens | lparens <numeral> rparens

<boolean-expr> ::= <simple-boolean-expr> | <comp-boolean-expr>

<comp-integer-expr> ::= <simple-integer-expr> <int-oper> <rest-integer-expr>
<rest-integer-expr> ::= <simple-integer-expr> | <comp-integer-expr>
/* note to disambiguate need operator precedence rules */

<comp-boolean-expr> ::= <simple-integer-expr> <bool-oper> <simple-integer-expr>
/* not fancy but usable  */

<simple-integer-expr> ::= <identifier> | <integer-const>
<simple-boolean-expr> ::= <identifier> | <boolean-const>
<integer-const> ::= <numeral>
<int-oper> ::= * | / | + | -
<bool-oper> ::= < | <= | == | !=
<boolean-const> ::= true | false

<return-stat> ::= return <return-arg>;
<return-arg> ::= lparens <variable> rparens
```

$P \in G$	BNF	LGN	bison
$S \rightarrow AB$	<s> ::= <a><b>	s --> a,b	s: a b ;
$S \rightarrow aB$	<s> ::= a<b>	s --> [a],b	s: A b ;

Table 7.2 Relating Productions in a Formal Grammar, BNF, Prolog LGN and bison.

```
                | lparens <numeral>  rparens
                | lparens <boolean-const>  rparens

/* end of updated syntax  */
/* lexical part for identifiers and numerals */

<identifier> ::= <letter> | <identifier> <letter> |  <identifier> <digit>
<letter> ::= a | b | c | d | e | f | g | h | i | j | k | l | m
                   | n | m | o | p | q | r | s | t | u | v | w | x | y | z
<numeral> ::= <digit> | <digit> <numeral>
<digit> ::= 0|1|2|3|4|5|6|7|8|9
```

7.5 Scanning and Parsing minic Extended Version 2 Using flex and bison

In this section, we show the use of the **flex** and **bison** tools for the expanded **minic** (Extended Version 2) scanning and parsing. We follow the development strategy used for **minic** Version 1. The reader may wish to review relevant sections of Chapter 6 regarding the structure or format of **flex** and **bison** input files and the interaction between the C files generated by these programs and the ultimate scanner/parser before proceeding. Especially significant is the passing of semantic values described in Section 6.9.3.

A Review of Productions and flex/bison

Table 7.2 reviews and unifies our look at sample productions in G, BNF, Prolog LGN(considered later), and **bison**. Note the different uses of case in specifying nonterminals and terminals.

Although the **flex** and **bison** manuals should be consulted before use, the following summarizes important concepts of these tools:

1. In a successful match, the **text**[3] corresponding to the match (i.e., the token) is available via the global pointer **yytext**. Note the C pointer-array mechanism allows this text to be accessed also as an array of characters. The length of the token is available as the value of the global integer **yyleng**.

2. Each **flex** pattern rule may have corresponding actions. An example is conversion of the recognized text to an integer.

3. **flex** produces the C function **yylex()**. **bison** invokes this function to acquire the next token. **yylex()** is expected to return the type of the next token, as well as any semantic value in global variable **yylval**.

4. **bison** expects an unambiguous context-free grammar.

[3] Note that anything recognized is considered text (prior to possible conversion).

5. Nonterminals in `bison` grammar rules are lowercase; terminals (tokens) are uppercase.

6. Each token has a type, and may have a semantic value. For example, the token `WHILE` probably does not have a value, but `NUM` probably does. When the parser accepts the token, it keeps track of the token's semantic value (if any).

7. `bison` grammar rules may have associated (semantic) actions that are comprised of `C` statements. An action may be to compute the semantic value of the parsed nonterminal from the component semantic values in the rule. These semantic values are held and passed using the `bison` variables `$$`, `$1`, `$2`, and so forth. For example, using an example from the `bison` rule for `minic` Version 1 in Chapter 4:

```
returnstat: RETURN returnarg SEMICOLON
            {$$=$2;}
;
```

   we note that the semantic value corresponding to nonterminal `returnstat`, that is, `$$`, is formed by assigning it the semantic value of the second component of the RHS side of the rule, that is, nonterminal `returnarg`, with value `$2`. If an action is not specified, the default `bison` action is `$$=$1`.

8. The variables `$$` through `$n`, where `n` corresponds to the nth component of the rule, are available for use in the `C` functions comprising the rule actions.

9. Because it is often the case that semantic values are of various types, `bison` provides the `%union` and `%type` constructs, which are illustrated in the following Chapter 4 excerpt:

```
%union{
int numval;
char *ideptr;
}

%token <numval> NUM
%token <ideptr> IDE
%type <numval> returnarg
%type <numval> returnstat
%type <ideptr> variable
%type <ideptr> variablelist
```

   Here we are able to declare terminal `NUM` and nonterminals `returnarg` and `returnstat` as having semantic values of type `numval`, whereas terminal `IDE` and nonterminals `variable` and `variablelist` have semantic values of type `ideptr`. Of course, additional types may be added to the union.

10. A parser must know the grammar's starting symbol, or S. `bison`'s default is to assume the start symbol for the grammar is the *first nonterminal* specified in the grammar specification section.

11. `bison` produces a function `yyparse`. Because many of the identifiers used by `flex` and `bison` begin with `yy` or `YY`, the user is encouraged to use other choices in naming variables.

```
%%
"//".*\n         {
 printf("--> I ate a c++ comment\n");}
"/*"[^"*/"]*"*/" {
 printf("--> I ate a c comment");}
```

flex Input File for C++-Style Comments

```
$ ./commentEater2<minicex0ac.mc
int main(void) --> I ate a c++ comment
{
--> I ate a c comment
        int t1;
        t1=10; --> I ate a c++ comment
        return(1);
--> I ate a c comment
}
```

Sample Use with Comments

```
int main(void) // returns int
{
/* here's the declaration */
         int t1;
         t1=10; // simple assignment
return(1);
/* that's all folks! */
}
```

Sample minic Source with Comments

Figure 7.1 Using flex for Eliminating C++-Style Comments.

12. Numerous bison macros are available. For example, invoking the macro YYABORT causes parse to return immediately and report parser failure. This macro is used in some of our examples.

13. bison requires an error function named yyerror. This is written by the user. In the examples in Chapter 4 of this chapter, this function is very simple.

Review of Pragmatics

- bison takes an input grammar file *.y and produces a file *.tab.c (and *.tab.h if the -d switch is used) containing the parser yyparse.
- flex takes an input file *.in and produces a file lex.yy.c, containing the scanner function yylex().
- The user then writes C function main and the error-handling function yyerror. main invokes yyparse, which in turn invokes yylex.
- These are then compiled to yield the scanner/parser.

7.5.1 flex Modifications for minic Source Code Comments

We modify the scanner to allow C and C++-style comments. In either case, the use of REs in flex makes the effort quite simple, as shown by the example of Figure 7.1.

7.5.2 flex and bison Input Files for minic Extended Version 2

As in the previous development, we proceed by generating input files corresponding to the lexical syntax of minic Extended Version 2 (for flex) and the remaining minic grammar (for bison). These are shown in Figures 7.2 and 7.3. The grammar shown in BNF of Section 7.4.3 is used.

```
%{
#include <stdio.h>
#include <ctype.h>
int yylex (void);
int yyerror (char *s);
%}

%token INT
%token BOOLEAN
%token VOID
%token MAIN
%token LPARENS
%token RPARENS
%token LBRACE
%token RBRACE
%token ASSIGN
%token SEMICOLON
%token COMMA
%token RETURN
%token NUM
%token IDE
%token TIMES
%token DIV
%token PLUS
%token MINUS
%token WHILE
%token FOR
%token IF
%token TRUE
%token FALSE
%token LESS
%token LEQ
%token EQUAL
%token NEQUAL
%token FN  /* function name */


%%  /* Grammar rules */

transunit: maindecl body
           {printf("\n***** congratulations *****\n\
***** parse for transunit successful *****\n");}
;

maindecl: type MAIN arg
          {printf(" => found main declaration\n");}
;

type: INT | BOOLEAN | VOID
;

arg: LPARENS type RPARENS
;
```

Figure 7.2 bison Input Grammar File minicv2r1.y for minic Extended Version 2.

```
body: LBRACE decseq statseq RBRACE
      {printf(" => found body\n");}
;

decseq:   /* empty */
        | decseq decl
       {printf(" => found declaration seq\n");}
;

decl: type variablelist SEMICOLON
;

variablelist: variable
            | variable COMMA variablelist
;

statseq: returnstat
         | commandseq SEMICOLON returnstat
         {printf(" => found statseq\n");}
;

commandseq: command
           | commandseq SEMICOLON command
          {printf(" => found command seq.\n");}
;

command: simpleassignment | while | for | if
;

simpleassignment: variable ASSIGN expr
         {printf(" => found simple assignment\n");}
;

while: WHILE LPARENS booleanexpr RPARENS command
         {printf(" => found while\n");}
;

for: FOR LPARENS forsimpleassignment SEMICOLON
                 forbooleanexpr SEMICOLON
                 forsimpleassignment RPARENS command
         {printf(" => found for\n");}
;

if: IF LPARENS expr RPARENS command
         {printf(" => found if\n");}
;

forsimpleassignment: /* empty */
                    | simpleassignment
;

forbooleanexpr: /* empty */
                | booleanexpr
;
```

Figure 7.2 (continued)

```
booleanexpr: simplebooleanexpr | compbooleanexpr
;

compbooleanexpr: simpleintegerexpr booloper simpleintegerexpr
;

simplebooleanexpr: booleanconst
;

booloper: LESS | LEQ | EQUAL | NEQUAL
;

booleanconst: TRUE | FALSE
;

variable: IDE
;

expr: integerexpr | booleanexpr
      {printf(" => found expr.\n");}
;

integerexpr: simpleintegerexpr | compintegerexpr
      {printf(" => found integer expr.\n");}
;

compintegerexpr: simpleintegerexpr intoper restintegerexpr
      {printf(" => found compound integer expr.\n");}
;

restintegerexpr: simpleintegerexpr | compintegerexpr
;

/* includes function invocation */

simpleintegerexpr: variable | integerconst
      {printf(" => found simple integer expr.\n");}
;

simpleintegerexpr: functionappl
      {printf(" => found function application\n");}
;

functionappl: fnname fnargs
;

fnargs: LPARENS IDE RPARENS
;

fnargs: LPARENS integerconst RPARENS
;

fnname: FN
;
```

Figure 7.2 (continued)

```
integerconst: NUM
;

intoper: TIMES | DIV | PLUS | MINUS
;

returnstat: RETURN returnarg SEMICOLON
            {printf(" => found return statement\n");}
;

returnarg: LPARENS IDE RPARENS
         | LPARENS NUM RPARENS
         | LPARENS booleanconst RPARENS
;
%%

/* Lexical analyzer */

/* error handling */
```

Figure 7.2 (continued)

```
/* this version is for minic version 2 */
/* it prints the recognized tokens */
%{
#include "minicv2r1.tab.h"
YYSTYPE yylval;
%}
ID [a-z][a-z0-9]*
A_NUM [0-9]+
%%
[ \r\t\n]+ /* whitespace */

"/*"[^"*/"]*"*/"  /* (loose) c style comments */

"//".*\n /* c++-style comments */

"(" { printf("'(' \n");
      return LPARENS; }

")" { printf("')' \n");
      return RPARENS;}

"{" { printf("'{' \n");
      return LBRACE;}

"}" { printf("'}' \n");
      return RBRACE;}

"==" { printf("'==' \n");
      return EQUAL;}
```

Figure 7.3 Corresponding `flex` Input File `minicv2r1.in` for minic Extended Version 2.

```
"=" { printf("'=' \n");
      return ASSIGN;}

"<=" { printf("'<=' \n");
      return LEQ;}

"<" { printf("'<' \n");
      return LESS;}

"!=" { printf("'!=' \n");
      return NEQUAL;}

";" { printf("';' \n");
      return SEMICOLON;}

"," { printf("',' \n");
      return COMMA;}

"*" { printf("'*' \n");
      return TIMES;}

"/" { printf("'/' \n");
      return DIV;}

"+" { printf("'+' \n");
      return PLUS;}

"-" { printf("'-' \n");
       return MINUS;}

true { printf("'true' \n");
       return TRUE;}

false { printf("'false' \n");
       return FALSE;}

while { printf("'while' \n");
       return WHILE;}

for { printf("'for' \n");
       return FOR;}

if { printf("'if' \n");
       return IF;}

int { printf("'int' \n");
        return INT;}

boolean { printf("'boolean' \n");
         return BOOLEAN;}

void { printf("'void' \n");
         return VOID;}
```

Figure 7.3 (continued)

```
main { printf("'main' \n");
         return MAIN;}

return { printf("'return' \n");
           return RETURN;}

square { printf("square");
           return FN;}

cube { printf("cube");
           return FN;}

{ID} { printf("ide(%s) \n", yytext);
       return IDE; }

{A_NUM} { printf("num(%s)=%d \n", yytext,
                yylval=atoi(yytext));
          return NUM;}
%%
```

Figure 7.3 (continued)

The Overall Project: `main`

Recall that `flex` generates the C-based scanner in `lex.yy.c` and `bison` generates the parser in `minicex1.tab.c`. More importantly, as shown in the previous chapter, "wrapper" code is necessary to integrate these functions to achieve a scanner/parser executable. An example is shown in Figure 7.4.

```
#include "minicv2r1.tab.c"
#include "lex.yy.c"
#include "yyerror.c"
#define YYERROR_VERBOSE

int main ()
{
  yyparse ();
  return(1);
}
```

Figure 7.4 Overall Project Source File `minicv2r1.c`.

7.5.3 `minic` Extended Version 2 Scan and Parse Examples Using `flex` and `bison`

Sample operation of the `flex` and `bison`-based scanner/parser is shown in Figures 7.5 to 7.7.

```
int main(void)
{
int t1,t2,kt,ans;
t1=10;
t2=3;
kt=10;
ans=t1 + t2 + kt;
return(ans);
}
```

Sample minic Source

```
$ ./minicv2r1 <minicex2.mc
'int'
'main'
'('
'void'
')'
 => found main declaration
'{'
'int'
ide(t1)
','
ide(t2)
','
ide(kt)
','
ide(ans)
';'
 => found declaration seq
ide(t1)
'='
num(10)=10
 => found simple integer expr.
';'
ide(t2)
'='
num(3)=3
 => found simple integer expr.
';'
 => found command seq.
ide(kt)
'='
num(10)=10
 => found simple integer expr.
';'
 => found command seq.
ide(ans)
'='
ide(t1)
'+'
ide(t2)
'+'
ide(kt)
';'
 => found compound integer expr.
 => found compound integer expr.
 => found integer expr.
 => found command seq.
'return'
'('
ide(ans)
')'
';'
 => found return statement
 => found statseq
'}'
 => found body

***** congratulations *****
***** parse for transunit successful *****
```

Corresponding Scan/Parse

Figure 7.5 flex- and bison-based Scanner/Parser Example 1.

```
int main(void)
{
int t1,t2;
t2=3;
for(t1=10;t1<20;t1=t1+1)
             while(t2<10) t2=t2+2;
return(t2);
}
```

Sample minic Source

```
$ ./minicv2r1 <minicex7.mc
'int'
'main'
'('
'void'
')'
 => found main declaration
'{'
'int'
ide(t1)
','
ide(t2)
';'
 => found declaration seq
ide(t2)
'='
num(3)=3
 => found simple integer expr.
';'
 => found simple assignment
'for'
'('
ide(t1)
'='
num(10)=10
 => found simple integer expr.
';'
 => found simple assignment
ide(t1)
'<'
num(20)=20
 => found simple integer expr.
';'
ide(t1)
'='
ide(t1)
'+'
num(1)=1
 => found simple integer expr.
')'
 => found compound integer expr.
 => found integer expr.
 => found simple assignment
'while'
'('
ide(t2)
'<'
num(10)=10
 => found simple integer expr.
')'
ide(t2)
'='
ide(t2)
'+'
num(2)=2
 => found simple integer expr.
';'
 => found compound integer expr.
 => found integer expr.
 => found simple assignment
 => found while
 => found for
 => found command seq.
'return'
'('
ide(t2)
')'
';'
 => found return statement
 => found statseq
'}'
 => found body

***** congratulations *****
***** parse for transunit successful *****
```

Corresponding Scan/Parse

Figure 7.6 flex- and bison-based Scanner/Parser Example 2.

```
// file: minicn2.mc
boolean main(void)
{
    int t1,t2,t3;
    boolean b1,b2;
    b1=true; b2=true;
    t1=10; t2=0;
/*  while and for */
    while(t2 <= 5)
       for(t2=0; t2<5; t2=t2+1) t2=t2+t1;
    t2=cube(t1);
    t1=square(t2);
    t3=t1*t2;
    if(t2!=t1) b2=false;
    return(true);
}
```

Sample minic Source

```
$ ./minicv2r1 <minicn2.mc
'boolean'
'main'
'('
'void'
')'
 => found main declaration
'{'
'int'
ide(t1)
','
ide(t2)
','
ide(t3)
';'
 => found declaration seq
'boolean'
ide(b1)
','
ide(b2)
';'
 => found declaration seq
ide(b1)
'='
'true'
 => found expr.
 => found simple assignment
';'
ide(b2)
'='
'true'
 => found expr.
 => found simple assignment
 => found command seq.
';'
```

Figure 7.7 flex- and bison-based Scanner/Parser Example 3.

```
ide(t1)
'='
num(10)=10
 => found simple integer expr.
';'
 => found simple assignment
 => found command seq.
ide(t2)
'='
num(0)=0
 => found simple integer expr.
';'
 => found simple assignment
 => found command seq.
'while'
'('
ide(t2)
'<='
num(5)=5
 => found simple integer expr.
')'
'for'
'('
ide(t2)
'='
num(0)=0
 => found simple integer expr.
';'
 => found simple assignment
ide(t2)
'<'
num(5)=5
 => found simple integer expr.
';'
ide(t2)
'='
ide(t2)
'+'
num(1)=1
 => found simple integer expr.
')'
 => found compound integer expr.
 => found integer expr.
 => found simple assignment
ide(t2)
'='
ide(t2)
'+'
ide(t1)
';'
 => found compound integer expr.
 => found integer expr.
 => found simple assignment
 => found for
```

Figure 7.7 (continued)

```
 => found while
 => found command seq.
ide(t2)
'='
cube'('
ide(t1)
')'
 => found function application
';'
 => found simple assignment
 => found command seq.
ide(t1)
'='
square'('
ide(t2)
')'
 => found function application
';'
 => found simple assignment
 => found command seq.
ide(t3)
'='
ide(t1)
'*'
ide(t2)
';'
 => found compound integer expr.
 => found integer expr.
 => found simple assignment
 => found command seq.
'if'
'('
ide(t2)
'!='
ide(t1)
 => found expr.
')'
ide(b2)
'='
'false'
 => found expr.
 => found simple assignment
 => found if
 => found command seq.
';'
'return'
'('
'true'
')'
';'
 => found return statement
 => found statseq
'}'
 => found body

***** congratulations *****
***** parse for transunit successful *****
```

Corresponding Scan/Parse

Figure 7.7 (continued)

7.6 Scanning and Parsing minic Extended Version 2 Using Prolog

7.6.1 Prolog Scanner Modifications for minic Source Comments

The reader may wish to consider each of the scanner modifications to allow comments separately. The relevant new or revised code that implements both forms follows.

```
%% check for dual-use chars
%% if double, see if pair, see if comment(s), otherwise it is a single token
%% since comment should not generate a token,
%%     after comment look for next real token
%% both c and c++ style comments handled

gettoken(C, T, E) :- double(C,U),getch(D),
      (pair(C,D,begincomment),getch(F),restcommentc(F,K),gettoken(K,T,E);
       commentline(C,D,comment),getch(F),restcomment(F,H),gettoken(H,T,E);
       pair(C,D,T),getch(E);
       T=U,E=D).

/* no need to keep track of comment body chars  */
/* c++ comment ends with endline; c style ends with endcomment pair */

/* recognize end of c style comment or keep reading chars */
restcommentc(F,E) :- getch(G),(pair(F,G,endcomment),getch(E);restcommentc(G,E)).

/* recognize end of c++ style comment (new line) or keep reading comment chars */
restcomment(F,F) :- endline(F).
restcomment(_,H) :- getch(G), restcomment(G,H).

%% lexical modifications for scanner--
%% single chars that are used either singly or as
%% part of a pair (double)

double(60,less).  % <
double(61, assign). % =
double(47, div). % /
double(33,not). % ! unary operator

%% character pairs
pair(60,61,leq).        % <=
pair(61,61,equal).      % ==
pair(33,61,nequal).     % !=


pair(47,42,begincomment).       % /*
pair(42,47,endcomment).         % */

commentline(47,47,comment).  % //
```

7.6.2 Example of Prolog Scanning and Parsing with Comments in the minic Source

An example that mixes C and C++-style comments follows. In addition, examples of integer and boolean expressions are shown.

```
?- parse-goal.

>>> Scanning and parsing minic (ver 4.6) <<<

Enter name of source file:

input the source filename IN QUOTES
followed by a . and CR
|: "minicex4b.mc".


    boolean main(void)
    {
    /* here are the declarations  */
     int t1,t2,t3;
     boolean b1; // here is a boolean
     t1=10;
     t2=3;
     /* here are expressions */
     t3=t2*t1;
     b1=t2<t3;
    // return the value of b1
     return(b1);
    }

Scan Results

[boolean, main, lparen, void, rparen, lbrace, int, ide(t1), comma, ide(t2), comma,
ide(t3), semicolon, boolean, ide(b1), semicolon, ide(t1), assign, num(10), semicolon,
ide(t2), assign, num(3), semicolon, ide(t3), assign, ide(t2), times, ide(t1), semicolon,
ide(b1), assign, ide(t2), less, ide(t3), semicolon, return, lparen, ide(b1),
rparen, semicolon, rbrace, eop]

Parse Results

transunit(maindecl(bool, mainarg(void)), body([decl(int, [t1, t2, t3]), decl(bool, [b1])],
statseq([sassign(ide(t1), num(10)), sassign(ide(t2), num(3)), sassign(ide(t3),
compintexpr([ide(t2), times, ide(t1)])), sassign(ide(b1), compbool(ide(t2), less, ide(t3)))],
retstat(ide(b1)))))

Yes
```

7.6.3 Implementing Other minic Extensions in Prolog

Adding while and for to the minic Scanner/Parser

Modifications to both the scanner and parser are necessary. *Note that all of the arguments to* for *are considered optional.* This adds slight complexity to the Prolog LGN implementation.

Because for and while represent new reserved words, the scanner must be revised. The modifications are shown here.

```
/* modifications for while and for with optional for arguments */

command(while(Cond,Cmd)) --> [while],[lparen],boolexpr(Cond),[rparen],command(Cmd).

command(for(init(A,B),test(Cond),update(C,D),Cmd)) --> [for],[lparen],
                    forsimpleassign(A,B),[semicolon],forboolexpr(Cond),[semicolon],
                    forsimpleassign(C,D),[rparen],command(Cmd).
```

```
forsimpleassign(X,E) --> simpleassign(X,E).
forsimpleassign(none,opt) --> [].

forboolexpr(E) --> boolexpr(E).
forboolexpr(none) --> [].

%% new scanner clauses

reswd(while).
reswd(for).
```

while and for Prolog Parsing Examples

Four examples of the operation or use of the revised Prolog minic scanner/parser follow.

```
?- parse-goal.

>>> Scanning and parsing minic (ver 4.6) <<<

Enter name of source file:

input the source filename IN QUOTES
followed by a . and CR
|: "minicex5.mc".
    int main(void)
    {
     int t1,t2;
     t2=3;
     for(t1=10;t1<20;t1=t1+1) t2=t2+2;
     return(t2);
    }

Scan Results

[int, main, lparen, void, rparen, lbrace, int, ide(t1), comma, ide(t2), semicolon,
ide(t2), assign, num(3), semicolon, for, lparen, ide(t1), assign, num(10), semicolon,
ide(t1), less, num(20), semicolon, ide(t1), assign, ide(t1), plus, num(1), rparen,
ide(t2), assign, ide(t2), plus, num(2), semicolon, return, lparen, ide(t2), rparen,
semicolon, rbrace, eop]

Parse Results

transunit(maindecl(int, mainarg(void)), body([decl(int, [t1, t2])],
statseq([sassign(ide(t2), num(3)), for(init(ide(t1), num(10)),
test(compbool(ide(t1), less, num(20))), update(ide(t1),
compintexpr([ide(t1), plus, num(1)])), sassign(ide(t2),
compintexpr([ide(t2), plus, num(2)])))], retstat(ide(t2)))))

Yes
?- parse-goal.

>>> Scanning and parsing minic (ver 4.6) <<<

Enter name of source file:

input the source filename IN QUOTES
followed by a . and CR
```

```
|: "minicex6.mc".


    int main(void)
    {
     int t2;
     t2=3;
     while(t2<10) t2=t2+2;
     return(t2);
    }

Scan Results

[int, main, lparen, void, rparen, lbrace, int, ide(t2), semicolon,
ide(t2), assign, num(3), semicolon, while, lparen, ide(t2), less, num(10), rparen,
ide(t2), assign, ide(t2), plus, num(2), semicolon, return,
lparen, ide(t2), rparen, semicolon, rbrace, eop]

Parse Results

transunit(maindecl(int, mainarg(void)), body([decl(int, [t2])],
statseq([sassign(ide(t2), num(3)), while(compbool(ide(t2), less, num(10)),
sassign(ide(t2), compintexpr([ide(t2), plus, num(2)])))], retstat(ide(t2)))))

Yes
?- parse-goal.

>>> Scanning and parsing minic (ver 4.6) <<<

Enter name of source file:

input the source filename IN QUOTES
followed by a . and CR
|: "minicex7.mc".


    int main(void)
    {
     int t1,t2;
     t2=3;
     for(t1=10;t1<20;t1=t1+1)
               while(t2<10) t2=t2+2;
     return(t2);
    }

Scan Results

[int, main, lparen, void, rparen, lbrace, int, ide(t1), comma, ide(t2), semicolon,
ide(t2), assign, num(3), semicolon, for, lparen, ide(t1), assign, num(10), semicolon,
ide(t1), less, num(20), semicolon, ide(t1), assign, ide(t1), plus, num(1), rparen,
while, lparen, ide(t2), less, num(10), rparen, ide(t2), assign, ide(t2), plus,
num(2), semicolon, return, lparen, ide(t2), rparen, semicolon, rbrace, eop]

Parse Results

transunit(maindecl(int, mainarg(void)), body([decl(int, [t1, t2])],
statseq([sassign(ide(t2), num(3)), for(init(ide(t1), num(10)),
```

```
test(compbool(ide(t1), less, num(20))), update(ide(t1),
compintexpr([ide(t1), plus, num(1)])), while(compbool(ide(t2), less, num(10)),
sassign(ide(t2), compintexpr([ide(t2), plus, num(2)]))))], retstat(ide(t2)))))

Yes
?- parse-goal.

>>> Scanning and parsing minic (ver 4.6) <<<

Enter name of source file:

input the source filename IN QUOTES
followed by a . and CR
|: "minicex8.mc".


    int main(void)
    {
     int t1,t2;
     t2=3;
     for(;;) t1=t2+1; //forever
     return(t2);
    }

Scan Results

[int, main, lparen, void, rparen, lbrace, int, ide(t1), comma, ide(t2), semicolon,
ide(t2), assign, num(3), semicolon, for, lparen, semicolon, semicolon, rparen,
ide(t1), assign, ide(t2), plus, num(1), semicolon, return, lparen, ide(t2), rparen,
semicolon, rbrace, eop]

Parse Results

transunit(maindecl(int, mainarg(void)), body([decl(int, [t1, t2])],
statseq([sassign(ide(t2), num(3)), for(init(none, opt), test(none),
update(none, opt), sassign(ide(t1), compintexpr([ide(t2), plus, num(1)])))],
retstat(ide(t2)))))

Yes
```

Prolog Scanner/Parser Implementation of `if`

To avoid rewriting the entire source code for the scanner/parser, we simply show the required modifications here.

Prolog Lexical (Scanner) Modifications.

Modification to accommodate `if` only requires addition of the following to the scanner:

```
reswd(if).
```

Prolog Parser Modifications

Because `if` is a command, the Prolog parser modification is as follows:

```
command(if(E,S)) --> [if],[lparen],expr(E),[rparen],statement(S).
                              /* note no braces, only single command */

statement(S) --> command(S).
```

Prolog Parsing Examples

The following provides a simple test of the ability to parse `if` statements in `minic`. Note also the ability for handling comments in the "traditional" `C` format.

```
?- parse-goal.

>>> Scanning and parsing minic (ver 4.6) <<<

Enter name of source file:

input the source filename IN QUOTES
followed by a . and CR
|: "minicif1.mc".


    int main(void)
    {
    /* here is a comment */
     int t1,t2;
     t1=10;
    /* here is an if statement  */
        if(t1) t2=3;
        return(t2);
    }

Scan Results

[int, main, lparen, void, rparen, lbrace, int, ide(t1), comma, ide(t2), semicolon,
ide(t1), assign, num(10), semicolon, if, lparen, ide(t1), rparen, ide(t2),
assign, num(3), semicolon, return, lparen, ide(t2), rparen, semicolon, rbrace, eop]

Parse Results

transunit(maindecl(int, mainarg(void)), body([decl(int, [t1, t2])],
statseq([sassign(ide(t1), num(10)), if(ide(t1), sassign(ide(t2), num(3)))],
retstat(ide(t2)))))

Yes
```

Prolog LGN Modifications for User-Defined Function Syntax

```
/* here's the function invocation */

simpleintexpr(E) --> functionappl(E).
functionappl(fn(A,B)) --> fnname(A),fnargs(B).
fnargs(B) --> [lparen],identifier(B),[rparen].
fnargs(B) --> [lparen],intconst(B),[rparen].
fnname(A) --> [fn(A)].

/* modification for predefined function name */
gettoken(C, T, E) :- lower(C), getch(D), restid(D, Lc, E),
                     name(I, [C|Lc]), (reswd(I),T=I;
                                      functionname(I),T=fn(I);
                                      T=ide(I)).
```

```
/* here's the (predefined) function names */

functionname(square).
functionname(cube).
```

7.6.4 Sample minic Extended Version 2 Scanning and Parsing Results Using Prolog

```
?- parse-goal.

>>> Scanning and parsing minic (ver 4.6) <<<

Enter name of source file:
|: minicfn1.mc

    int main(void)
    {

    // example of function invocation

        int t1,t2;
        t1 = 10;
        t2 = square(t1);
        return(t2);
    }
Scan Results

[int, main, lparen, void, rparen, lbrace, int, ide(t1),
comma, ide(t2), semicolon, ide(t1), assign, num(10),
semicolon, ide(t2), assign, fn(square), lparen, ide(t1),
rparen, semicolon, return, lparen, ide(t2), rparen,
semicolon, rbrace, eop]

Parse Results

transunit(maindecl(int, mainarg(void)),
body([decl(int, [t1, t2])], statseq([sassign(ide(t1), num(10)),
sassign(ide(t2), fn(square, ide(t1)))], retstat(ide(t2)))))

Yes
```

7.6.5 Listing of the Overall Prolog Scanning/Parsing Code for minic Extended Version 2

```
% revised scanner/parser for minic translational unit
% File: cscanpv4r6.pro
% uses minic ver 4.2 bnf syntax from transunit-bnf4r2nir.txt
% allows declaration sequence, c and c++ style comments, while, for, if
% and functions like square(x)
% arguments to for are optional ('forever')
% this version has more variables or functors as addl arguments
%     to indicate parse results


%---------  translational unit parser -----------------------------

transunit(transunit(Maindecl, Body)) --> maindecl(Maindecl), body(Body).
```

```
maindecl(maindecl(Type, Arg)) --> type(Type), [main], marg(Arg).

type(int) --> [int].  type(void) --> [void]. type(bool) --> [boolean].

marg(mainarg(Arg)) --> [lparen], type(Arg), [rparen].

body(body(Decseq, Statseq)) --> [lbrace], decseq(Decseq), statseq(Statseq), [rbrace].

%%---------- declaration sequence -------------------------

decseq([]) --> [].
decseq([Dec|Decs]) --> decl(Dec),decseq(Decs).
decl(decl(Type, Vars)) --> type(Type), varlist(Vars), [semicolon].

%%----------- statement sequence -------------------------------

statseq(statseq(Cmdseq, Retstat)) --> cmdseq(Cmdseq), [semicolon], retstat(Retstat).
statseq(statseq([], Retstat)) --> retstat(Retstat).

retstat(retstat(Returnarg)) --> [return], returnarg(Returnarg), [semicolon].
returnarg(ide(Returnarg)) --> [lparen], [ide(Returnarg)], [rparen].
returnarg(num(Returnarg)) --> [lparen], [num(Returnarg)], [rparen].
returnarg(boolconst(Returnarg)) --> [lparen], [boolconst(Returnarg)], [rparen].

varlist(Vars) --> [ide(Var)], restvars(Var,Vars).
  restvars(Var,[Var|Vars]) --> [comma], varlist(Vars).
  restvars(Var,[Var])      --> [].

cmdseq(Cmds) --> command(Cmd), restcmds(Cmd,Cmds).
  restcmds(Cmd,[Cmd|Cmds]) --> [semicolon], cmdseq(Cmds).
  restcmds(Cmd,[Cmd])      --> [].

command(sassign(X,E)) --> simpleassign(X,E).
simpleassign(X,E) --> identifier(X), [assign], expr(E).

/* modifications for while and for with optional for arguments */

command(while(Cond,Cmd)) --> [while],[lparen],boolexpr(Cond),[rparen],command(Cmd).

command(for(init(A,B),test(Cond),update(C,D),Cmd)) --> [for],[lparen],
                  forsimpleassign(A,B),[semicolon],forboolexpr(Cond),[semicolon],
                  forsimpleassign(C,D),[rparen],command(Cmd).

forsimpleassign(X,E) --> simpleassign(X,E).
forsimpleassign(none,opt) --> [].

forboolexpr(E) --> boolexpr(E).
forboolexpr(none) --> [].

command(if(E,S)) --> [if],[lparen],expr(E),[rparen],statement(S).
                              /* note no braces, only single command */

statement(S) --> command(S).

expr(E) --> intexpr(E).
expr(E) --> boolexpr(E).
```

```
intexpr(E) --> simpleintexpr(E).
intexpr(E) --> compintexpr(E).

boolexpr(E) --> simpleboolexpr(E).
boolexpr(E) --> compboolexpr(E).
boolexpr(not(E)) --> [not], boolexpr(E).

/* to allow (predefined) function invocation */

simpleintexpr(E) --> functionappl(E).
functionappl(fn(A,B)) --> fnname(A),fnargs(B).
fnargs(B) --> [lparen],identifier(B),[rparen].
fnargs(B) --> [lparen],intconst(B),[rparen].
fnname(A) --> [fn(A)].

compintexpr(compintexpr([E,Op,R])) --> simpleintexpr(E), intoper(Op), restintexpr(R).
restintexpr(R) --> simpleintexpr(R).
restintexpr(compintexpr([Er,Opr,Rr])) --> compintexpr(compintexpr([Er,Opr,Rr])).

compboolexpr(compbool(A,B,C)) --> simpleintexpr(A), booloper(B), simpleintexpr(C).

simpleintexpr(E) --> identifier(E).
simpleintexpr(E) --> intconst(E).

simpleboolexpr(E) --> identifier(E).
simpleboolexpr(E) --> boolconst(E).
/* note that identifier is not typed in either case */

intoper(times) --> [times]. intoper(times) --> [div].
intoper(plus) --> [plus]. intoper(minus) --> [minus].

booloper(less) --> [less]. booloper(leq) --> [leq].
booloper(equal) --> [equal]. booloper(nequal) --> [nequal].

intconst(E) --> numeral(E).
boolconst(true) --> [true]. boolconst(false) --> [false].

identifier(ide(V)) --> [ide(V)].
numeral(num(N)) --> [num(N)].

parse-goal :- nl,write('>>> Scanning and parsing minic (ver 4.6) <<<'), nl, nl,
      write('Enter name of source file:  '), nl,
      getfilename(File), nl,
      see(File), scan(Tokens), seen, write('Scan Results'), nl, nl,
      write(Tokens), nl, nl, !,
      transunit(Parse,Tokens,[eop]), write('Parse Results'), nl, nl,!,
      write(Parse), nl, !.


%--------- Scanner ---------------------------------------------------------

lower(C) :- 97=<C,C=<122.       % a-z
digit(C)  :- 48=<C,C=<57.       % 0-9

% ASCII characters of special significance
```

```
space(32). tabch(9). period(46).
cr(13).  lf(10).  endfile(26).   endfile(-1).
endline(C) :- lf(C).  % for both DOS and UNIX

whitespace(C) :- space(C) ; tabch(C) ; cr(C) ; lf(C).

idchar(C) :- lower(C) ; digit(C).

getfilename(W) :- nl,write('input the source filename IN QUOTES'),nl,
                     write('followed by a . and CR'),nl,
                     read(X),nl, name(W,X).

scan([T|Lt]) :- tab(4), getch(C), gettoken(C,T,D), restprog(T, D, Lt), !.

getch(C) :- get0(C), (endline(C),nl,tab(4) ; endfile(C),nl ; put(C)).

restprog(eop, _, []).        % end of file reached with previous character
restprog(_,   C, [U|Lt]) :- gettoken(C, U, D), restprog(U, D, Lt).

gettoken(C, eop, 0) :- endfile(C).
gettoken(C, T, D) :- single(C,T), getch(D).

%% check for dual-use chars
%% if double, see if pair, see if comment(s), otherwise it is a single token
%% since comment should not generate a token,
%%     after comment look for next real token
%% both c and c++ style comments handled

gettoken(C, T, E) :- double(C,U),getch(D),
      (pair(C,D,begincomment),getch(F),restcommentc(F,K),gettoken(K,T,E);
       commentline(C,D,comment),getch(F),restcomment(F,H),gettoken(H,T,E);
       pair(C,D,T),getch(E);
       T=U,E=D).

/* no need to keep track of comment body chars  */
/* c++ comment ends with endline; c style ends with endcomment pair */

/* recognize end of c style comment or keep reading chars */
restcommentc(F,E) :- getch(G),(pair(F,G,endcomment),getch(E);restcommentc(G,E)).

/* recognize end of c++ style comment (new line) or keep reading comment chars */
restcomment(F,F) :- endline(F).
restcomment(_,H) :- getch(G), restcomment(G,H).

/* modification for predefined function name */
gettoken(C, T, E) :- lower(C), getch(D), restid(D, Lc, E),
                     name(I, [C|Lc]), (reswd(I),T=I;
                                       functionname(I),T=fn(I);
                                       T=ide(I)).

  restid(C, [C|Lc], E) :- idchar(C), getch(D),restid(D,Lc,E).
  restid(C, [],     C).   % end identifier if C is not id character
gettoken(C, num(N), E) :- digit(C), getch(D), restnum(D, Lc, E),
                          name(N, [C|Lc]).
  restnum(C, [C|Lc], E) :- digit(C), getch(D), restnum(D, Lc, E).
  restnum(C, [],     C).   % end number if C is not digit
gettoken(C, T, E) :- whitespace(C), getch(D), gettoken(D,T,E).
```

```
/* when all else fails, say so ...  */
gettoken(C, _, _) :- write('This character is not in the lexical syntax: '),
                     put(C), write('Bye'), nl, abort.


%% here are the revised reserved words (tokens) for minic:

reswd(main). reswd(void). reswd(int). reswd(return).
reswd(boolean). reswd(true). reswd(false).

/* control and iteration constructs */

reswd(while). reswd(for). reswd(if).

/* here's the (predefined) function names */

functionname(square). functionname(cube).


single(123, lbrace). single(125, rbrace). single(40,lparen).
single(41,rparen). single(44,comma). single(59,semicolon).
single(42,times). single(43,plus). single(45,minus).

%% single chars that are used either singly or as
%% part of a pair (double)

double(60,less).  % <
double(61, assign). % =
double(47, div). % /
double(33,not). % ! unary operator

%% character pairs
pair(60,61,leq).          % <=
pair(61,61,equal).        % ==
pair(33,61,nequal).       % !=
pair(47,42,begincomment).        % /*
pair(42,47,endcomment).          % */

commentline(47,47,comment).  % //

%% thats all folks!
```

7.7 Considering Contextual Constraints and Typed Languages

7.7.1 Context-Based Productions

Consider a simplistic grammar intended to facilitate English-language sentence production[4] with a sample production of the form:

$$S \rightarrow NVO$$

where $S, N, V, O \in V_N$. The alternative BNF representation might be:

```
<sentence> ::- <noun> <verb> <object>
```

[4]Here S represents "sentence," N represents "noun," V represents "verb," and O represents "object."

Nonterminal	Attribute
N	Something used for computing
V	An action allowed in computing
O	The result of a computing action

Table 7.3 Example of Nonterminal Attributes for Context-Sensitive Parse.

In using productions in this context-free grammar, there is no need for the noun, verb, and object of the sentence to have any meaningful relationship; that is, it is possible to produce sentences like:

computers eat ladders
ladders hate computers
books study students

Such sentences, although *syntactically correct*, are *semantically meaningless*. To rectify this situation, we seek two things:

1. a way to "globally" constrain the allowable replacements, rather than simply allowing any joint set of values that results from *independent* replacement of N, O, V.

2. a way to accomplish the preceding item without using a context-sensitive grammar.

7.7.2 Introducing Attribute Grammars

To solve this problem, consider the possibility that the nonterminals N, O, V used in the first list item have properties or *attributes* available for use during the generation or recognition phases of the grammar use. These attributes are shown in Table 7.3.

Suppose before allowing the generation or parse of an expression using these nonterminals, a function is available for checking attribute compatibility. In our example the check (in words) might be: "This production may be used if the attributes of all nonterminals involve computing." Although a simplistic example, it nonetheless conveys the idea that to effect contextual constraints, attributes are generated and checked during the parsing process.

7.7.3 Contextual Constraints in Programming Languages

The issue of handling contextual constraints in programming languages is analogous to the problem introduced in Section 7.7.1. One of the most common constraints is that of *enforcing variable declarations and type checking*. Because many languages are typed, how do we enforce type checking in the parsing process? First, we elaborate on the problem. Consider two program fragments-

```
int t1;
t1=10;
```

vs.

```
int t1;
t1=10.00001;
```

Assume the lexical part of the `minic` language is enhanced to allow production of 10.00001. Without modification, our previous `minic` grammar and parser cannot distinguish between these cases, both of which would be considered syntactically correct. This occurs because, in the `minic` syntax:

```
<decl> ::= e | <type> <variable-list>;
<variable-list> ::= <variable> | <variable> , <variable-list>
<variable> ::= <identifier>
<command> ::= <variable> = <expr>
```

there is no checking to see if the type of `<expr>` matches the type declaration for the variable identifier used.

7.7.4 Relation of Contextual Constraints to minic

Given our understanding of the *syntax* of `minic` up to this point, we ask, what is wrong with the syntax of the following `minic` translational unit?

```
// miniccontext1.mc
boolean main(void)
{
boolean b1,b2;
int t2;
t2=true;
t3=t4+b3+20;
b2 = b1 + 20;
while(b2<t3) b2=t2+2;
return(t2);
}
```

The (hopefully not too surprising) answer is "nothing." The astute reader may question numerous perceived violations of variable and expression typing, including the appearance of undeclared variables, the assignment of boolean values to variables declared as `int`, variables used but not declared, mixing `int` and `boolean` types, and so forth. *This is a result of familiarity with* `C`, *not minic.* We have not (yet) incorporated these contextual constraints in the `minic` parser. A scan/parse of this file also confirms the syntactic correctness of this file.[5] Clearly, it is desirable to enforce type constraints in `minic`, and we show how this may be accomplished in the following sections.

7.7.5 What Would the Problem Look Like with a "Real" C Compiler?

To further illustrate the problem and our objectives, consider a `C` formulation[6] of the preceding `minic` file:

```
// from miniccontext1.mc
#include<stdbool.h>
typedef bool boolean;
boolean main(void)
{
boolean b1,b2;
int t2;
```

[5]This is left to the reader.

[6]Here we use the C99 extension for type `bool`.

```
t2=true;
t3=t4+b3+20;
b2 = b1 + 20;
while(b2<t3) b2=t2+2;
return(t2);
}
```

Using `gcc`, this `C` source generates the following warnings.

```
bash-2.02$ gcc miniccontext1r.c -Wall
miniccontext1r.c:5: warning: return type of 'main' is not 'int'
miniccontext1r.c: In function 'main':
miniccontext1r.c:9: 't3' undeclared (first use in this function)
miniccontext1r.c:9: (Each undeclared identifier is reported only once
miniccontext1r.c:9: for each function it appears in.)
miniccontext1r.c:9: 't4' undeclared (first use in this function)
miniccontext1r.c:9: 'b3' undeclared (first use in this function)
```

7.7.6 Potential Approaches to Implement Type Checking

In the parsing process, we must enforce the type of `<expr>` to match the type declaration for the variable identifier used. This is sometimes easier said than done. Historically, solutions to this problem include:

1. Lexical restrictions on identifier names for each type (e.g., "all integers begin with i, j, or k").
2. Constrain the production(s) involving `<variable>` in

   ```
   <decl> ::= <type> <variable-list>;
   <variable-list> ::= <variable>
   ```

   to be somehow constrained by the other production:

   ```
   <command> ::= <variable> = <expr>
   ```

   This suggests that the second production could only be used *in the context* of the first set of productions, that is,

   ```
   <decl> <command> ::= <type> <variable>; <variable> = <expr>
   ```

   As the preceding BNF-form production indicates, we have just entered the world of context-sensitive grammars.
3. Use an attribute grammar.

7.8 Attribute Grammars

7.8.1 Origins and Uses of Attribute Grammars

Attribute grammars (Knuth, 1968) are modified (or augmented) context-free grammars. Historically, they were intended to facilitate semantic descriptions of program fragments as a means for conveying semantics. In our present discussion, we consider attribute grammars first as a vehicle to represent and consequently enforce context constraints in `minic`. The complete study of attribute grammars is beyond the scope of this text, and the present coverage is only intended to illustrate the concept.

Definition

An attribute grammar is a context-free grammar augmented with attributes and semantic functions. Attributes are attached to terminal and nonterminals, and semantic functions are used in the attribute grammar productions.

Recall a context-free grammar is given by:

$$G = \{V_T, V_N, P, S\} \tag{7.1}$$

and a sample production in G is written:

$$X_0 \rightarrow X_1\ X_2\ \ldots\ X_n$$

where $n \geq 1$, $X_0 \in V_N$, and $X_k \in V_N \cup V_T$ for $k = 1, 2, \ldots, n$.

Given G, a derivation or parse tree T, has the following characteristics:

1. the root of T is the starting symbol $S \in V_N$.
2. leaf nodes (nodes having no children) of T are terminals $\in V_T$.
3. interior (neither root nor leaf) nodes are nonterminals $\in V_N$.
4. the children of any nonleaf node represent the right hand side (RHS) of some production in P, where the parent node represents the corresponding LHS of the production.

7.8.2 Attaching Attributes to Symbols

Each $X \in V_N \cup V_T$ is associated with disjoint, finite sets $I(X)$ and $S(X)$ of *inherited* and *synthesized* attributes, respectively. For $X = S$ (the start symbol), and for $X \in V_T$, we require that $I(X) = \emptyset$. Furthermore, we define the total set of attributes for symbol X as $A(X) = I(X) \cup S(X)$.

7.8.3 Synthesized Versus Inherited Attributes

In the generative or parse mode of the grammar, attributes of symbols must be generated or checked. Oftentimes, the meaning of the descriptors on attributes (synthesized or inherited) is not clear. It is not, strictly speaking, necessary that children inherit the parents' attributes and parents synthesize children's attributes. A third possibility is for children to inherit attributes from each other. This kills the familiar notion of inheritance.

Attribute Utility

The attributes of a symbol X could characterize its "meaning." For example, this meaning could be a measure of its length (the a's example) its type, (type checking), or some other values.

7.8.4 Passing Attributes: Which Way Do They Go?

> *Inherited attributes transmit information down the parse tree toward the leaves, while synthesized attributes transmit information up the tree toward the root.*

The starting symbol, S, may not have inherited attributes because it has no ancestor. Terminals[7] (leaf nodes) may have no inherited attributes. Values of a terminal symbol's synthesized attributes are often set by the scanner. In general, some nonterminals X may inherit attributes and some may synthesize them. We will look at this situation more fully after considering the `minic` grammar and implications of attributes.

7.8.5 Attaching Semantic Functions (Semantic Rules) to Productions

For each production $p \in P$, there is an associated set $F(p)$ of semantic functions or semantic rules. For the production:

$$X_0 \rightarrow X_1\ X_2\ \ldots\ X_n$$

the synthesized attributes of X_0 are computed by a function

$$S(X_0) = f_S(A(X_1), A(X_2),\ \ldots\ , A(X_n))$$

and the inherited attributes of X_k, $k = 1, 2,\ \ldots\ , n$ are computed by a function f_{I_k}, that is,

$$I(X_k) = f_{I_k}(A(X_0) \quad k = 1, 2,\ \ldots\ , n$$

7.8.6 Predicate Functions

Once we have the semantic functions f_S and f_{I_k}, it is possible to use them to place conditions or constraints on attribute values in

$$A(X_0) \cup A(X_1) \cup A(X_2), \ldots\ , \cup A(X_n)$$

For each production $\in P$, predicate functions are formed as boolean expressions on the overall attribute set $A(X_0) \cup A(X_1) \cup A(X_2),\ \ldots\ , \cup A(X_n)$.

Basically, *semantic rules (further) use these predicate functions to constrain the use of the production.* In other words, the production

$$X_0 \rightarrow X_1\ X_2\ \ldots\ X_n$$

may only be used in a parse or derivation tree if the corresponding predicate functions are satisfied.

7.8.7 Extension: Attribute Grammars for Semantics

Recall that an attribute grammar is an extended context-free grammar. Another use of an attribute grammar is to specify the "meaning" or semantics of each symbol in the language. Each grammar symbol has an associated set of attributes, and each production rule is provided with a corresponding semantic rule expressing the relationships between the attributes of the symbols in the production. To find the meaning of a string (program), we first generate its parse tree and then determine the values of all the symbol attributes in the parse tree. This is shown later in this chapter using `bison`.

---

[7]Tokens, in the `minic` application.

7.8.8 Application of Attribute Grammars to minic

minic Context Constraints

Contextual constraints that might be implemented using an attribute grammar include:

1. Each variable and its type must be declared in the declaration sequence prior to use in the body. (In our enforcement of this constraint, neglecting to do this in the `minic` source causes a parser failure.)
2. Each variable in the body may only be assigned an expression of the same type as the declared type of the variable. (In our enforcement of this constraint, a warning is generated if this constraint is violated.)
3. The declared type of the translational unit must match the type returned by the return statement. Note that `void` is considered a type to be checked.
4. Each variable must be declared exactly once.

In what follows, we show the implementation of the first two constraints; the rest are left as exercises.

Relationship to the minic Parser "Symbol Table"

A commonly used data structure for storage of attributes is the *symbol table*. Most compilers (and some debuggers) use this structure to keep track of symbols (including names of variables, functions, and corresponding types) defined in a program. The symbol table may be implemented in many ways—for example, as a list, linked list, array, set, hash table, or tree.

Sometimes the symbol table is considered to represent a third class of attributes called *intrinsic attributes*. These are synthesized attributes determined outside the parse tree. Typically, these attributes are the result of a previous declaration of type, perhaps in another program block. We employ the symbol table concept in using attribute grammars for the enforcement of `minic` contextual constraints.

Defining the Auxiliary Functions for the Symbol Table

Desired operations on the symbol table are:

1. creation (initialization) of the table in a desired format.
2. adding declared variables and corresponding types.
3. checking (for both declared type as well as the possibility of redeclaration).

7.9 flex/bison Implementation of a minic Parser Using Attribute Grammars and a Symbol Table

In this section, we implement a context-sensitive scanner and parser for `minic` using `flex` and `bison`. In addition, we introduce the implementation of semantics for specific elements of the parse, as a prelude to Chapter 12. The overall development is shown in four sequential phases. Each version builds upon (and thus includes elements of) the previous version.

This section extends our understanding of the parsing process, contextual constraints, and elementary semantics. C data structures and related functions are introduced to efficiently implement a symbol table for the parse. The reader is encouraged to review linked lists, enumerations, and unions in C before proceeding.

7.9.1 Symbol Table: Implementation and Use

Constraints to be Enforced

This effort involves implementation of a symbol table and enforcing contextual constraints. These are similar to those used in the Prolog implementation (see Section 7.10), with the parsing constraints as follows:

1. Each variable and its type must be declared in the declaration sequence prior to use in the body. *We synthesize the symbol table in a successful parse of the declaration sequence.*

2. Each variable must be declared exactly once.

3. In our enforcement of these constraints, neglecting to do this in the minic source causes a parser failure. This is shown in the examples. Note we are not checking and comparing types (yet), but rather just that a variable has been previously declared. A default value of -1 is used in the symbol table to indicate declaration of the variable without assignment of a (more meaningful) value. (Note that minic cannot produce a numeral with this value.)

A Note about void

In our development of minic up to this point, void is a syntactically valid type. In "real" C, there are no objects of type void, that is,

```
void t;
```

yields an error. In other words, void is useful in declaring functions that do not return a value and in specifying an empty argument list. From this point on, we will only consider void in these circumstances; that is, main is the only function whose returned value may be void or one of the true types, namely boolean or integer. Variables may only be declared as one of the true types.

7.9.2 The Symbol Table

The symbol table is a singly linked list in C. In parsing a single declaration involving multiple variables (of the same type), a second list to hold the variable names is used. Sample contents of the symbol table (in tabular form) corresponding to a parse of the minic declaration sequence

```
int t1;
boolean b1;
```

yields the desired symbol table structure shown in Table 7.4. Note that in the table we use the name `integer` to represent the declared type. This representation is purely symbolic and left up to the table designer; `int` would also suffice. We use `integer` here, as one of the ennumerated types in the `C` implementation.

Initial Symbol Table Entries		
t1	Integer	-1
b1	Boolean	-1

Table 7.4 Initial `bison` Parser Symbol Table Following Parse of Declaration Sequence.

With these declarations, and the subsequent commands:[8]

```
t1=10;
b1=true;
```

the updated symbol table would appear as shown in Table 7.5.

Updated Symbol Table Entries		
t1	Integer	10
b1	Boolean	true

Table 7.5 Updated `bison` Parser Symbol Table Following Assignment of Values to Declared Variables.

7.9.3 Symbol Table Implementation and Associated Functions

The symbol table is an enhanced version of that introduced in Chapter 6 and is shown here.

```
/* enhanced symbol table implementation
   accommodates typdefs and main returned value
   also includes another linked list for storing
   values in variablelist.
   Note: malloc-ed memory should be released in main.
   file: EnhancedSymbolTable5Incl.c  */

#include <stdlib.h>
#include <string.h>
#include <stdbool.h>

enum mctypes {integer, boolean, declaration} thetype;

union mcvalues
{int intval;
 bool boolval;
 enum mctypes mctype;  /* allows transitivity */
} thevalue;
```

[8]The propagation of semantic values using `bison` is left as an exercise for Chapter 8.

```
/* simple data structure for singly-linked list
   to be called the symbol table          */
typedef struct symrec
{
char *idename;
enum mctypes type;
union mcvalues value;
struct symrec *next;
}
symrec;

/* declare and initialize global sym_table */
symrec *symb_table = (symrec *)0;

symrec *util_ptr;

/* symbol table manipulation functions */
symrec *getsymval(const char *idename)
{
   symrec *ptr;
   for (ptr = symb_table; ptr != (symrec *)0;
            ptr = (symrec *)ptr->next)
         if (strcmp (ptr->idename,idename) == 0) /* it is there */
            return ptr;
       return 0; /* not there */
}

/* put on front of linked list after check */

symrec *putsymval(const char *idename,
                  enum mctypes type,
                  union mcvalues value)
{
   symrec *ptr;
   if((ptr=getsymval(idename))==0)
    { /* not there */
     ptr = (symrec *) malloc (sizeof (symrec));
     ptr->idename = (char *) malloc (strlen (idename) + 1);
     strcpy (ptr->idename, idename);
     ptr->type=type;
     ptr->value = value;
     ptr->next = (struct symrec *)symb_table;
     symb_table = ptr;
     return ptr;
    }
   else
    {if(value.intval==-1) /* use -1 as value for declaration */
      printf("\n WARNING: identifier %s is already in symbol table "
             "(no modification)\n",idename);
     return symb_table;
    }
}

int printLookupResult(char *idename)
{
symrec *util_ptr;
```

```
if((util_ptr=getsymval(idename))==0)
  {
  printf("\n !!!! UNDECLARED VARIABLE: variable %s IS NOT IN THE SYMBOL "
         "TABLE !!!!\n",idename);
  return (0);
  }
  else{
       printf("\nfor identifier %s (found in symbol table)\n",
              util_ptr->idename);
      switch(util_ptr->type){
      case integer:
        printf("the type is INT, with value %d\n",
                util_ptr->value.intval);
      break;
      case boolean:
        if(util_ptr->value.boolval==true)
         printf("the type is BOOLEAN, with value TRUE\n");
         else
         printf("the type is BOOLEAN, with value FALSE\n");
      break;
      case declaration:
        printf("the type is a TYPEDEF, with value ");
         switch (util_ptr->value.mctype){
           case integer:
           printf("INT\n");
           break;
           case boolean:
           printf("BOOLEAN\n");
           break;
           default:
             printf("\n problem with symbol table\n");
                                       }
      break;
      default:
        printf("\n big problem with symbol table\n");
                            }
  return(1);
       }
}

/* another data structure for singly-linked list
   to be used for parsing variablelist         */

typedef struct varlist
{
char *idename;
struct varlist *next;
}
varlist;
varlist *var_ptr;

/* declare and initialize variable name table */
varlist *var_table = (varlist *)0;

varlist *getvar()
{
   varlist *ptr;
   ptr = var_table;
```

```
    if(ptr != (varlist *)0){
             ptr = (varlist *)ptr->next;
             return ptr;    }
    return 0;
}

/* put variable name on front of linked list after check */

varlist *putvarname(const char *idename)
{
    varlist *ptr;
      ptr = (varlist *) malloc (sizeof (varlist));
      ptr->idename = (char *) malloc (strlen (idename) + 1);
      strcpy (ptr->idename, idename);
      ptr->next = (struct varlist *)var_table;
      var_table = ptr;
      return ptr;
}
```

7.9.4 Revised bison Input File

The enhanced version of the bison parser follows the structure introduced in Chapter 6 and is shown here.

```
/* minicv2r6.y
this version creates and uses the
symbol table and the recognized tokens semantic values */
%{
#include <stdio.h>
#include <ctype.h>
#include "EnhancedSymbTable5Incl.c"
int yylex (void);
int yyerror (char *s);
%}
%union{
int numval;
char *ideptr;
}

%token INT
%token BOOLEAN
%token VOID
%token MAIN
%token LPARENS
%token RPARENS
%token LBRACE
%token RBRACE
%token ASSIGN
%token SEMICOLON
%token COMMA
%token RETURN
%token <numval> NUM
%token <ideptr> IDE
%token TIMES
%token DIV
%token PLUS
%token MINUS
%token WHILE
```

```
%token FOR
%token IF
%token <numval> TRUE
%token <numval> FALSE
%token LESS
%token LEQ
%token EQUAL
%token NEQUAL
%token FN  /* function name */
%token TYPEDEF
%type <numval> decl
%type <numval> realtype
%type <numval> returnarg
%type <numval> returnstat
%type <numval> expr
%type <numval> command
%type <numval> commandseq
%type <numval> statseq
%type <ideptr> variable
%type <ideptr> variablelist
%type <ideptr> restvars
%type <numval> simpleassignment
%type <numval> forsimpleassignment
%type <numval> integerconst
%type <numval> while
%type <numval> for
%type <numval> if
%type <numval> integerexpr
%type <numval> booleanexpr
%type <numval> forbooleanexpr
%type <numval> booleanexpr
%type <numval> simplebooleanexpr
%type <numval> compbooleanexpr
%type <numval> simpleintegerexpr
%type <numval> booleanconst
%type <numval> restintegerexpr
%type <numval> compintegerexpr

%%  /* Grammar rules */

transunit: typedefs maindecl body
           {printf("\n***** congratulations *****\n\
***** parse for transunit successful *****\n");}
;

maindecl: type MAIN arg
          {printf(" => found main declaration\n");}
;

typedefs: /* empty */
         | typedef typedefs
;

typedef: TYPEDEF realtype IDE SEMICOLON
         /* here update symbol table for typedef
            do not check for redeclaration      */
         {printf(" => found typedef\n");
          thevalue.mctype=$2;  /* consistent with enum */
```

```
          symb_table=putsymval($3, declaration, thevalue);
         /* now check it */
          printLookupResult($3);}
;

realtype: INT
          {$$=0} /* consistent with enum */
         | BOOLEAN
           {$$=1}
;

type: INT | BOOLEAN | VOID
;

arg: LPARENS type RPARENS
;

body: LBRACE decseq statseq RBRACE
      {printf(" => found body\n");}
;

decseq:   /* empty */
        | decseq decl
       {printf(" => found a declaration\n");}
;

/* symbol table synthesized from next two */

decl: realtype variablelist SEMICOLON
      /* declaration of variables (all one type) ----
         put value (names, i.e., <ideptr>) of all
         variables on the VARIABLELIST on the symboltable
         with type which is value of realtype.
         Here the realtype value is consistent with the
         enum declaration     */
      {thevalue.intval=-1;
      /* put all of variable list into symbol table  */
      for (var_ptr = var_table; var_ptr != (varlist *)0;
                             var_ptr = (varlist *)var_ptr->next)
       {
       symb_table=putsymval(var_ptr->idename, $1,thevalue);
       /* now check it */
       util_ptr=getsymval(var_ptr->idename);
       printf("In symbol table --> put\
 variable with name %s and type %d\n",util_ptr->idename,util_ptr->type);
       }
      /* reinitialize the variable list for the next declaration*/
       var_table = (varlist *)0;
       $$=0}
;

decl: IDE variablelist SEMICOLON    /* for typedef */
      {thevalue.intval=-1;
       util_ptr=getsymval($1);
      /* put all of variable list into symbol table
         with the real type   */
      for (var_ptr = var_table; var_ptr != (varlist *)0;
                             var_ptr = (varlist *)var_ptr->next)
```

```
        {
        symb_table=putsymval(var_ptr->idename, util_ptr->value.mctype, thevalue);
        /* now check it */
        util_ptr=getsymval(var_ptr->idename);
        printf("In symbol table --> put\
 variable with name %s and type %d\n",util_ptr->idename,util_ptr->type);
        }
       /* reinitialize the variable list for the next declaration*/
        var_table = (varlist *)0;
        $$=0}
;

variablelist: variable
              {var_table=putvarname($1);
               printf("** Put a variable named %s on the VARIABLE list\n",$1);}
               restvars
               {$$=0}
;
restvars:      COMMA variablelist
               {$$=0}
;

restvars:      /* empty */
               {printf("** No more variables for the VARIABLE list\n\n");$$=0}
;

statseq: returnstat
         | commandseq SEMICOLON returnstat
         {printf(" => found statseq\n");}
;

commandseq: command
           | commandseq SEMICOLON command
          {printf(" => found command\n");}
;

command: simpleassignment | while | for | if
;

simpleassignment: variable ASSIGN expr
         {printf(" => found simple assignment\n");
          if(printLookupResult($1)==0) YYABORT}
;

while: WHILE LPARENS booleanexpr RPARENS command
         {printf(" => found while\n");}
;

for: FOR LPARENS forsimpleassignment SEMICOLON
                 forbooleanexpr SEMICOLON
                 forsimpleassignment RPARENS command
         {printf(" => found for\n");}
;

if: IF LPARENS expr RPARENS command
         {printf(" => found if\n");}
;
```

```
forsimpleassignment: /* empty */ {$$=0}
                   | simpleassignment
;

forbooleanexpr: /* empty */ {$$=0}
              | booleanexpr
;


booleanexpr: simplebooleanexpr | compbooleanexpr
;

compbooleanexpr: simpleintegerexpr booloper simpleintegerexpr
;

simplebooleanexpr: booleanconst
;

booloper: LESS | LEQ | EQUAL | NEQUAL
;

booleanconst: TRUE | FALSE
;

variable: IDE
          {$$=$1}
;

expr: integerexpr | booleanexpr
      {printf(" => found expr.\n");}
;

integerexpr: simpleintegerexpr | compintegerexpr
      {printf(" => found integer expr.\n");}
;

compintegerexpr: simpleintegerexpr intoper restintegerexpr
      {printf(" => found compound integer expr.\n");}
;

restintegerexpr: simpleintegerexpr | compintegerexpr
;

/* includes function invocation */

simpleintegerexpr: variable
                   {$$=0; /* fix with symbol table */
                    printf(" => found simple integer expr. (i.e, variable)\n");
                    if(printLookupResult($1)==0) YYABORT}
                 | integerconst
      {printf(" => found simple integer expr. (i.e., constant)\n");}
;

simpleintegerexpr: functionappl
      {printf(" => found function application\n");}
;
```

```
functionappl: fnname fnargs
;

fnargs: LPARENS variable RPARENS
        {if(printLookupResult($2)==0) YYABORT;}
;

fnargs: LPARENS integerconst RPARENS
;

fnname: FN
;

integerconst: NUM {$$=$1;} /* the default action */
;

intoper: TIMES | DIV | PLUS | MINUS
;

returnstat: RETURN returnarg SEMICOLON
            {printf(" => found return statement\n");}
;

returnarg: LPARENS variable RPARENS
           {if(printLookupResult($2)==0) YYABORT; $$=0}  /* fix in symbol table */
         | LPARENS NUM RPARENS
           {$$=$2}
         | LPARENS booleanconst RPARENS
           {$$=2}
;
%%

/* Lexical analyzer */

/* error handling */
```

7.9.5 Examples of Symbol Table Use with minic

Figure 7.8 shows the formation of the symbol table for a simple **minic** program primarily consisting of variable declarations. Figures 7.9 and 7.10 show both the formation and checking of the symbol table (*for declaration only*) for other sample **minic** programs. In checking for prior declaration of a variable, the (previous) value found on the symbol table, as well as the declared variable type, are printed for illustration.

```
// file: minicn1t2.mc
/* to show forming symbol table */
boolean main(void)
{
    int t1,t2;
    boolean b1,b2;
    return(true);
}
```

```
$ ./minicv2r6 <minicn1t2.mc
 >>> parsing minic version 2 rev. 6 <<<<<<

 => found main declaration


scanned: ide(t1)
** Put a variable named t1 on the VARIABLE list
scanned: ide(t2)
** Put a variable named t2 on the VARIABLE list
** No more variables for the VARIABLE list

In symbol table --> put variable with name t2 and type 0
In symbol table --> put variable with name t1 and type 0
 => found a declaration

scanned: ide(b1)
** Put a variable named b1 on the VARIABLE list
scanned: ide(b2)
** Put a variable named b2 on the VARIABLE list
** No more variables for the VARIABLE list

In symbol table --> put variable with name b2 and type 1
In symbol table --> put variable with name b1 and type 1
 => found a declaration

 => found return statement

 => found body

***** congratulations *****
***** parse for transunit successful *****
```

Figure 7.8 Using minic Source and flex/bison Scanner/Parser Creation of Corresponding Symbol Table.

```
int main(void)
{
// file: minicfn1.mc

// example of function invocation

    int t1,t2;
    t1 = 10;
    t2 = square(t1);
    return(t2);
}


./minicv2r6 <minicfn1.mc
```

```
 >>> parsing minic version 2 rev. 6 <<<<<<
 => found main declaration
scanned: ide(t1)
** Put a variable named t1 on the VARIABLE list
scanned: ide(t2)
** Put a variable named t2 on the VARIABLE list
** No more variables for the VARIABLE list

In symbol table --> put variable with name t2 and type 0
In symbol table --> put variable with name t1 and type 0
 => found a declaration

scanned: ide(t1)
scanned: num(10) with value=10
 => found simple integer expr. (i.e., constant)
 => found simple assignment

for identifier t1 (found in symbol table)
the type is INT, with value -1

scanned: ide(t2)
scanned: ide(t1)

for identifier t1 (found in symbol table)
the type is INT, with value -1
 => found function application
 => found simple assignment

for identifier t2 (found in symbol table)
the type is INT, with value -1
 => found command

scanned: ide(t2)

for identifier t2 (found in symbol table)
the type is INT, with value -1
 => found return statement
 => found statseq

 => found body

***** congratulations *****
***** parse for transunit successful *****
```

Figure 7.9 `flex/bison` Sample Use of Symbol Table for Checking Variable Declarations. Note: The Symbol Table Is *Not* Updated with Variable Values (yet).

```
int main(void)
// file: minict6.mc
boolean main(void)
{
    int t2;
    boolean b1;
    b1=true;
    t2=0;
    t3=square(10);
    return(b2);
}
$ ./minicv2r6 <minict6.mc

 >>> parsing minic version 2 rev. 6 <<<<<<
 => found main declaration


scanned: ide(t2)
** Put a variable named t2 on the VARIABLE list
** No more variables for the VARIABLE list

In symbol table --> put variable with name t2 and type 0
 => found a declaration

scanned: ide(b1)
** Put a variable named b1 on the VARIABLE list
** No more variables for the VARIABLE list

In symbol table --> put variable with name b1 and type 1
 => found a declaration

scanned: ide(b1)
 => found expr.
 => found simple assignment

for identifier b1 (found in symbol table)
the type is BOOLEAN, with value FALSE

scanned: ide(t2)
scanned: num(0) with value=0
 => found simple integer expr. (i.e., constant)
 => found simple assignment

for identifier t2 (found in symbol table)
the type is INT, with value -1
 => found command

scanned: ide(t3)
scanned: num(10) with value=10
 => found function application
 => found simple assignment

 !!!! UNDECLARED VARIABLE: variable t3 IS NOT IN THE SYMBOL TABLE !!!!
```

Figure 7.10 Enhanced flex/bison Scanner/Parser Failure Due to Missing Variable Declaration.

7.9.6 An Illustrative Extension: Parsing typedef

In implementing typedef, we follow the C convention. The prototype for typedef is:

```
typedef <type> <newname>;
```

and sample use is shown here.

```
typedef int myint;
.
.
.
```

```
myint t12;
.
.
.
t12=12;
```

In our syntax extension, multiple `typedef`s are allowed and they must precede the main declaration. An example code fragment follows, with the corresponding symbol table in Table 7.6.

```
typedef int myint;
typedef boolean mybool;
.
.
.
myint t1;
mybool b1;
.
.
.
t1=10;
b1=true;
```

Figure 7.11 shows the symbol table use (*declaration only*) in this case. Note that the process involves two parts:

1. The `typedef` is recorded in the symbol table, and
2. variables are then put into the symbol table with the real (not derived) type, by consulting the symbol table in parsing of the declaration for the real type.

7.9.7 Other Possible Extensions

Other extensions are left as exercises and include:

1. Enforce the contextual constraint that the declared type of the translational unit must match the type returned by the return statement. Note that `void` is considered a type to be checked. *The symbol table data structure should be enhanced (and used) for this purpose.*

Symbol Table Entries		
myint	declaration	integer
mybool	integer	boolean
t1	integer	10
b1	boolean	true

Table 7.6 Sample `bison` Parser Symbol Table Using `typedef`.

```
// file: minicp3t1.mc
typedef int myint;
typedef boolean mybool;
boolean main(void)
{   int t5;
    mybool b100;
    t5=10;
    return(b100);
}
```

```
$ ./minicv2r6 <minicn5t2.mc

 >>> parsing minic version 2 rev. 6 <<<<<<
scanned: ide(myint)
 => found typedef

for identifier myint (found in symbol table)
the type is a TYPEDEF, with value INT

 => found main declaration

scanned: ide(myint)
scanned: ide(t5)
** Put a variable named t5 on the VARIABLE list
** No more variables for the VARIABLE list

In symbol table --> put variable with name t5 and type 0
 => found a declaration

scanned: ide(t5)
scanned: num(10) with value=10
 => found simple integer expr. (i.e., constant)
 => found simple assignment

for identifier t5 (found in symbol table)
the type is INT, with value -1

scanned: ide(t5)

for identifier t5 (found in symbol table)
the type is INT, with value -1
 => found return statement
 => found statseq

 => found body

***** congratulations *****
***** parse for transunit successful *****
```

Figure 7.11 `flex/bison` Symbol Table Use with `typedef`. (Left, minic source; right, parse.)

2. Enforce the constraint that each variable in the body may only be assigned an expression of the same type as the declared type of the variable. (In our enforcement of this constraint, a warning is generated if this constraint is violated.)

3. Attributing semantics to selected nonterminals and implementing the evaluation of these semantics. This is left to Chapter 8.

7.10 Prolog Implementation of a `minic` Parser Using Attribute Grammars and a Symbol Table

Recall that to effect contextual constraints, attributes are generated and checked during the parse. We show the design of the Prolog code for this task.

7.10.1 Generating the Prolog Symbol Table

We adopt a structure for the symbol table in an association-list format as follows:

```
[[type1,name1],[type2,name2],...]
```

For example, given the `minic` declaration sequence:

```
int t1,t2,t3;
boolean b1;
```

the resulting association list would be:

```
[[bool, ide(b1)], [int, ide(t1)], [int, ide(t2)], [int, ide(t3)]]
```

Note that the order of entries is not significant. The modified code to accomplish this, and other context checking, is shown here. For simplicity, only the modifications are shown.

```
transunit(transunit(Maindecl, Body),SymbolTable) --> maindecl(Maindecl),
                                                     body(Body,SymbolTable).

% initial symbol table inherited by decseg (from body)
% symbol table synthesized by decseq (from children)
% symbol table inherited by statseq

body(body(decseq,Statseq),SymbolTable) --> {initsymboltable(InitSymbolTable)},
                           [lbrace], decseq(InitSymbolTable, SymbolTable),
                           statseq(Statseq,SymbolTable), [rbrace].

initsymboltable([]).

%%---------- declaration sequence modifications ----------------------

decseq(SymbolTable, SymbolTable) --> [].

decseq(InitSymbolTable, SymbolTable) --> decl(Type,Vars),
                               {updatesymboltable(InitSymbolTable,Type,Vars,SymbolTable1),
                                write('symbol table so far is:'),nl,nl,
                                write(SymbolTable1), nl,nl}, %% for illustration
                               decseq(SymbolTable1, SymbolTable).

%% here's the simplistic symbol table updating

updatesymboltable(InitSymbolTable,Type,Vars,SymbolTable1) :-
                           formaddltable(Type,Vars,Addl),
                           append(Addl,InitSymbolTable,SymbolTable1).

formaddltable(Type,[F|S],[[Type,F]|Rest]) :- formaddltable(Type,S,Rest).

formaddltable(_,[],[]).


decl(Type, Vars) --> type(Type), varlist(Vars), [semicolon].

varlist([ide(Var)|Rest]) --> [ide(Var)], restvars(Rest).
  restvars(Rest) --> [comma], varlist(Rest).
  restvars([]) --> [].
```

```
%----------------------modified goal predicate ----------------------------------------

parse-goal :- nl,write('>>> Scanning and parsing minic (symboltable version) <<<'), nl, nl,
      write('Enter name of source file:  '), nl, getfilename(File), nl,
      see(File), scan(Tokens), seen, write('Scan Results'), nl, nl,
      write(Tokens), nl, nl, nl, !,
      transunit(Parse,SymbolTable,Tokens,[eop]),
      write('the final symbol table for this transunit is:'),nl,nl,
      write(SymbolTable),nl,nl, %% for illustration
      write('Parse Results'), nl, nl,!,
      write(Parse), nl, !.
```

Of particular significance is the predicate **formaddltable**, defined as:

```
formaddltable(Type,[F|S],[[Type,F]|Rest]) :-
                        formaddltable(Type,S,Rest).
formaddltable(_,[],[]),
```

which takes single declarations of multiple variables of the form

```
int t1,t2,t3;
```

and converts them into the desired symbol table additions

```
[int,t1],[int,t2],[int,t3]
```

Also note from the preceding Prolog code modifications that after each declaration is parsed, the current symbol table may be printed. (This is not illustrated in the following examples.) Alternative structures for the symbol table are considered in the exercises.

7.10.2 Checking the Prolog Symbol Table

Once the symbol table has been synthesized, the parsing process relies on checking for declared variables, recognition of composite expressions that are type-compatible (i.e., all subexpressions are of appropriate types), and have a resulting type, as well as matching of expression type to variables in assignment statements. We show the code to accomplish this in stages.

First, a predicate for accessing the symbol table is necessary. The design of a recursive predicate to accomplish this is straightforward, and shown here.

```
%% symbol table as an assoc list
%% form:
%% [[type1,name1],[type2,name22],...]
%% corresponding access predicate:
%% assoc(key,  list,  type)

assoc(Key, [[Type, Key]|_], Type).

assoc(Key, [_|Rest], Type) :- assoc(Key,Rest,Type).
```

7.10.3 Context-Capable Prolog Scanner/Parser

The context-capable Prolog parser that incorporates the symbol table and associated predicates follows. For brevity, the scanner is not shown.

```
% File: cscanp2r2-symboltable2.pro
% revised minic translational unit parser with
% ** incorporation of symbol table **
% uses minic ver 2.1 bnf syntax from transunit-bnf2nir.txt
% scanner ommitted for brevity
%% notice parse fails for non-declaration, else report errors ('warnings')

%---------  translational unit parser ----------------------------

transunit(transunit(Maindecl, Body),SymbolTable) --> maindecl(Maindecl),
                                                     body(Body,SymbolTable).

maindecl(maindecl(Type, Arg)) --> type(Type), [main], marg(Arg).

type(int) --> [int]. type(void) --> [void]. type(bool) --> [boolean].

marg(mainarg(Arg)) --> [lparen], type(Arg), [rparen].

% initial (empty) symbol table
% SymbolTable synthesized by decseq (from children)
% SymbolTable inherited by statseq

body(body(decseq,Statseq),SymbolTable) --> {initsymboltable(InitSymbolTable)},
                           [lbrace], decseq(InitSymbolTable, SymbolTable),
                           statseq(Statseq,SymbolTable), [rbrace].

initsymboltable([]).

%%---------- declaration sequence ----------------------

decseq(SymbolTable, SymbolTable) --> [].

decseq(InitSymbolTable, SymbolTable) --> decl(Type,Vars),
                              {updatesymboltable(InitSymbolTable,Type,Vars,SymbolTable1)},
                              decseq(SymbolTable1, SymbolTable).

%% here's the simplistic symbol table updating
%% may be modified (see text) to show creation
%%    of the symboltable

updatesymboltable(InitSymbolTable,Type,Vars,SymbolTable1) :-
                            formaddltable(Type,Vars,Addl),
                            append(Addl,InitSymbolTable,SymbolTable1).

formaddltable(Type,[F|S],[[Type,F]|Rest]) :- formaddltable(Type,S,Rest).
formaddltable(_,[],[]).


decl(Type, Vars) --> type(Type), varlist(Vars), [semicolon].


%%----------- statement sequence ------------------------------
%% add symbol table passing (inheritence) using 3rd argument

statseq(statseq(Cmdseq, Retstat),SymbolTable) --> cmdseq(Cmdseq,SymbolTable), [semicolon],
                                                  retstat(Retstat,SymbolTable).
statseq(statseq([], Retstat),SymbolTable) --> retstat(Retstat,SymbolTable).
```

```
%% presently no checking of type of returned value; left as exercise
%% requires adding type of transunit to symbol table and checking

retstat(retstat(Returnarg),_) --> [return], returnarg(Returnarg), [semicolon].
returnarg(ide(Returnarg)) --> [lparen], [ide(Returnarg)], [rparen].
returnarg(num(Returnarg)) --> [lparen], [num(Returnarg)], [rparen].
returnarg(boolconst) --> [lparen], [boolconst], [rparen].

varlist([ide(Var)|Rest]) --> [ide(Var)], restvars(Rest).
  restvars(Rest) --> [comma], varlist(Rest).
  restvars([]) --> [].


%------------- command sequence and expressions ---------------------

%% symbol table as an assoc list
%% [[type1,name1],[type2,name2],...]
%% form: assoc(key,  list,  type)
%% access and checking via assoc

assoc(Key, [[Type, Key]|_], Type).
assoc(Key, [_|Rest], Type) :- assoc(Key,Rest,Type).

cmdseq(Cmds,SymbolTable) --> command(Cmd,SymbolTable), restcmds(Cmd,Cmds,SymbolTable).
  restcmds(Cmd,[Cmd|Cmds],SymbolTable) --> [semicolon], cmdseq(Cmds,SymbolTable).
  restcmds(Cmd,[Cmd],_)      --> [].

command(sassign,SymbolTable) --> simpleassign(SymbolTable).

simpleassign(SymbolTable) --> identifier(ide(Vname)), [assign], expr(Etype,SymbolTable),
 {checkexprcompat(Vname,Etype,SymbolTable)}.

%% note any missing declaration causes parse failure in assoc
%% otherwise we issue a warning

checkexprcompat(Vname,Etype,SymbolTable) :- assoc(ide(Vname),SymbolTable,Vtype),
                                      (Vtype \== Etype, nl,
                                      write('Warning:'),nl,
                                      write('********'), write(Vname),
                                      write(' and the expression are different types'),
                                      nl, write('********'),nl;
                                      true).

expr(int,SymbolTable) --> intexpr(int,SymbolTable).
expr(bool,SymbolTable) --> boolexpr(bool,SymbolTable).

intexpr(int,SymbolTable) --> simpleintexpr(int,SymbolTable).
intexpr(int,SymbolTable) --> compintexpr(int,SymbolTable).

boolexpr(bool,SymbolTable) --> simpleboolexpr(bool,SymbolTable).
boolexpr(bool,SymbolTable) --> compboolexpr(bool,SymbolTable).
boolexpr(bool,SymbolTable) --> [not], boolexpr(bool,SymbolTable).

compintexpr(int,SymbolTable) --> simpleintexpr(int,SymbolTable),
                              intoper, restintexpr(int,SymbolTable).

restintexpr(int,SymbolTable) --> simpleintexpr(int,SymbolTable).
restintexpr(int,SymbolTable) --> compintexpr(int,SymbolTable).
```

```
compboolexpr(bool,SymbolTable) --> simpleintexpr(int,SymbolTable),booloper,
                                   simpleintexpr(int,SymbolTable).

simpleintexpr(Type,SymbolTable) --> identifier(ide(Name)),
{assoc(ide(Name),SymbolTable,Type)}.
%% note any missing declaration or mismatch here causes parse failure

simpleintexpr(int,_) --> intconst.

simpleboolexpr(Type,SymbolTable) --> identifier(ide(Name)),
{assoc(ide(Name),SymbolTable,Type)}.
%% note any missing declaration or mismatch causes parse failure

simpleboolexpr(bool,_) --> boolconst.

intoper --> [times]. intoper --> [div].
intoper --> [plus]. intoper --> [minus].

booloper --> [less]. booloper --> [leq].
booloper --> [equal]. booloper --> [nequal].

intconst --> numeral. boolconst --> [true].
boolconst --> [false].

identifier(ide(V)) --> [ide(V)].
numeral --> [num(_)].

parse-goal :- nl,write('>>> Scanning and parsing minic (symbol table ver) <<<'), nl, nl,
      write('Enter name of source file:  '), nl, getfilename(File), nl,
      see(File), scan(Tokens), seen, write('Scan Results'), nl, nl,
      write(Tokens), nl, nl, nl, !,
      transunit(Parse,SymbolTable,Tokens,[eop]),
      write('the final symbol table for this transunit is:'),nl,nl,
      write(SymbolTable),nl,nl, %% for illustration only
      write('Parse Results'), nl, nl,!,
      write(Parse), nl, !.
```

7.10.4 minic Type Checking Examples Using the Prolog Symbol Table

The following are several sample applications of the new, attribute-grammar (and symbol-table) based parser. The reader should first check the input minic file for syntax errors (especially related to contextual constraints), and then verify the corresponding output of the enhanced parser.

```
?- parse-goal.

>>> Scanning and parsing minic (symbol table ver) <<<

Enter name of source file:
|: minicex1.mc

    int main(void)
    {
     int t1;
     t1=10;
     return(t1);
    }
```

```
Scan Results

[int, main, lparen, void, rparen, lbrace, int, ide(t1), semicolon,
ide(t1), assign, num(10), semicolon, return, lparen,
ide(t1), rparen, semicolon, rbrace, eop]


the final symbol table for this transunit is:

[[int, ide(t1)]]

Parse Results

transunit(maindecl(int, mainarg(void)),
body(decseq, statseq([sassign], retstat(ide(t1)))))

Yes
?- parse-goal.

>>> Scanning and parsing minic (symbol table ver) <<<

Enter name of source file:
|: minicex1b.mc

    int main(void)
    {
     int t1;
     t2=10;
     return(t1);
    }

Scan Results

[int, main, lparen, void, rparen, lbrace, int, ide(t1), semicolon,
ide(t2), assign, num(10), semicolon, return, lparen, ide(t1),
rparen, semicolon, rbrace, eop]



No
?- parse-goal.

>>> Scanning and parsing minic (symbol table ver) <<<

Enter name of source file:
|: minicex1c.mc

    int main(void)
    {
     int t1;
     t1=true;
     return(t1);
    }

Scan Results

[int, main, lparen, void, rparen, lbrace, int, ide(t1), semicolon,
ide(t1), assign, true, semicolon, return, lparen, ide(t1), rparen,
semicolon, rbrace, eop]
```

```
Warning:
********t1 and the expression are different types
********
the final symbol table for this transunit is:

[[int, ide(t1)]]

Parse Results

transunit(maindecl(int, mainarg(void)),
body(decseq, statseq([sassign], retstat(ide(t1)))))

Yes
?- parse-goal.

>>> Scanning and parsing minic (symbol table ver) <<<

Enter name of source file:
|: minicex1d.mc

    int main(void)
    {
     int t1,t2;
     t1=10;
      t2=t1;
     return(t1);
    }

Scan Results

[int, main, lparen, void, rparen, lbrace, int, ide(t1),
comma, ide(t2), semicolon, ide(t1), assign, num(10), semicolon,
ide(t2), assign, ide(t1), semicolon, return,
lparen, ide(t1), rparen, semicolon, rbrace, eop]


the final symbol table for this transunit is:

[[int, ide(t1)], [int, ide(t2)]]

Parse Results

transunit(maindecl(int, mainarg(void)),
body(decseq, statseq([sassign, sassign],
retstat(ide(t1)))))

Yes
?- parse-goal.

>>> Scanning and parsing minic (symbol table ver) <<<

Enter name of source file:
|: minicex1e.mc

    boolean main(void)
    {
     int t1;
```

```
      boolean b1;
     b1=false;
      t1=b1;
     return(b1);
    }

Scan Results

[boolean, main, lparen, void, rparen, lbrace, int, ide(t1), semicolon,
boolean, ide(b1), semicolon, ide(b1), assign, false, semicolon,
ide(t1), assign, ide(b1), semicolon, return, lparen, ide(b1), rparen,
semicolon, rbrace, eop]



Warning:
********t1 and the expression are different types
********
the final symbol table for this transunit is:

[[bool, ide(b1)], [int, ide(t1)]]

Parse Results

transunit(maindecl(bool, mainarg(void)),
body(decseq, statseq([sassign, sassign],
retstat(ide(b1)))))

Yes
?- parse-goal.

>>> Scanning and parsing minic (symbol table ver) <<<

Enter name of source file:
|: minicex1f.mc

    boolean main(void)
    {
     int t1;
      boolean b1;
     b1=10+3;
     return(b1);
    }

Scan Results

[boolean, main, lparen, void, rparen, lbrace, int, ide(t1), semicolon,
boolean, ide(b1), semicolon, ide(b1), assign, num(10), plus, num(3),
semicolon, return, lparen, ide(b1), rparen, semicolon, rbrace, eop]



Warning:
********b1 and the expression are different types
********
```

```
Warning:
********b1 and the expression are different types
********
the final symbol table for this transunit is:

[[bool, ide(b1)], [int, ide(t1)]]

Parse Results

transunit(maindecl(bool, mainarg(void)),
body(decseq, statseq([sassign], retstat(ide(b1)))))

Yes
?- parse-goal.

>>> Scanning and parsing minic (symbol table ver) <<<

Enter name of source file:
|: minicex1g.mc

    int main(void)
    {
     int t1,t2;
     t1=10;
      t2=20;
     return(t1);
    }

Scan Results

[int, main, lparen, void, rparen, lbrace, int, ide(t1), comma,
ide(t2), semicolon, ide(t1), assign, num(10), semicolon,
ide(t2), assign, num(20), semicolon, return, lparen, ide(t1), rparen,
semicolon, rbrace, eop]


the final symbol table for this transunit is:

[[int, ide(t1)], [int, ide(t2)]]

Parse Results

transunit(maindecl(int, mainarg(void)),
body(decseq, statseq([sassign, sassign],
retstat(ide(t1)))))

Yes
?- parse-goal.

>>> Scanning and parsing minic (symbol table ver) <<<

Enter name of source file:
|: minicex1h.mc

    int main(void)
    {
     int t1,t2;
```

```
        t2=t1;
     return(t1);
    }

Scan Results

[int, main, lparen, void, rparen, lbrace, int, ide(t1), comma,
ide(t2), semicolon, ide(t2), assign, ide(t1), semicolon,
return, lparen, ide(t1), rparen, semicolon, rbrace, eop]


the final symbol table for this transunit is:

[[int, ide(t1)], [int, ide(t2)]]

Parse Results

transunit(maindecl(int, mainarg(void)),
body(decseq, statseq([sassign],
retstat(ide(t1)))))

Yes
?- parse-goal.

>>> Scanning and parsing minic (symbol table ver) <<<

Enter name of source file:
|: minicex2.mc

    int main(void)
    {
     int t1,t2,kt,ans;
     t1=10;
     t2=3;
     kt=10;
     ans=t1 + t2 + kt;
     return(ans);
    }

Scan Results

[int, main, lparen, void, rparen, lbrace, int, ide(t1), comma,
ide(t2), comma, ide(kt), comma, ide(ans), semicolon,
ide(t1), assign, num(10), semicolon, ide(t2), assign, num(3), semicolon,
ide(kt), assign, num(10), semicolon, ide(ans), assign, ide(t1),
plus, ide(t2), plus, ide(kt), semicolon,
return, lparen, ide(ans), rparen, semicolon, rbrace, eop]


the final symbol table for this transunit is:

[[int, ide(t1)], [int, ide(t2)], [int, ide(kt)], [int, ide(ans)]]

Parse Results

transunit(maindecl(int, mainarg(void)),
body(decseq, statseq([sassign, sassign, sassign, sassign],
retstat(ide(ans)))))
```

```
Yes
?- parse-goal.

>>> Scanning and parsing minic (symbol table ver) <<<

Enter name of source file:
|: minicex3.mc

    boolean main(void)
    {
     int t1,t2,t3;
     boolean b1;
     t1=10;
     t2=3;
     t3=t2*t1;
     b1=t2<t3;
     return(b1);
    }

Scan Results

[boolean, main, lparen, void, rparen, lbrace, int, ide(t1), comma,
ide(t2), comma, ide(t3), semicolon, boolean, ide(b1), semicolon,
ide(t1), assign, num(10), semicolon, ide(t2), assign, num(3), semicolon,
ide(t3), assign, ide(t2), times, ide(t1), semicolon,
ide(b1), assign, ide(t2), less, ide(t3), semicolon,
return, lparen, ide(b1), rparen, semicolon, rbrace, eop]



Warning:
********b1 and the expression are different types
********
the final symbol table for this transunit is:

[[bool, ide(b1)], [int, ide(t1)], [int, ide(t2)], [int, ide(t3)]]

Parse Results

transunit(maindecl(bool, mainarg(void)),
body(decseq, statseq([sassign, sassign, sassign, sassign],
retstat(ide(b1)))))

Yes
```

Note that we are not yet finished with the revisions to the parser to incorporate all the contextual constraints. For example, the type of the returned value is not checked. This is left as an exercise.

7.11 Bibliographical Remarks and References

A classic reference for the extended scanning and parsing concepts considered in this chapter is Aho and Johnson (1974). Early works on attribute grammars for contextual parsing as well as formal descriptions of semantics are Knuth (1971), Kennedy and Ramanathan (1979), and Wilner (1972).

7.12 Exercises

1. An alternative to the approach shown for adding comments to the syntax of `minic` is shown here. Comment on the wisdom of this approach.

```
/* attempt at minic comment effort */
/* for exercises */
/* file: mcomment1.pro */

comment --> [begincomment],commentbody,[endcomment].
commentbody --> [_],commentbody.
commentbody --> [].
?- ['mcomment1.pro'].
% mcomment1.pro compiled 0.00 sec, 0 bytes

Yes
?- comment([begincomment,this,is,my,first,comment,endcomment],[]).

Yes
?- comment([begincomment,this,is,my,first,comment],[]).

No
?- comment([begincomment,endcomment],[]).

Yes
?- comment([begincomment,_,endcomment],[]).

Yes
?- comment([begincomment,this,is,begincomment,a,
              endcomment,nested,comment,endcomment],[]).

Yes
```

2. In adding an `if` construct to the syntax of `minic` in Section 7.4.2, we created the `C`-like syntax

```
if <expression> <statement>
```

We ignored implementation of an `else` part to the syntax. Consider instead the syntax

```
if <expression> <statement>
else <statement>
```

Modify the minic scanner/parser for this case. Can you also make the `else` part optional?

3. Which of the following strings may be produced in `minic` Version 2 starting from the nonterminal <expr>:

   (a) $v1 + v2 + v3$;

   (b) $v1 + (v2 + v3)$;

4. Extend the scanner to allow for nested comments in the source code, using the comment notation or form of C or C++. Show the code used and a display of the results that shows the task was accomplished.

5. Try your revised parser (with comments) on each of the files that follow. Are they syntactically correct translational units? Comment on the results.

```
boolean main(void)
// minicex9.mc
{
    int t1,t2;
    t2=3;
    return(t2);
}
boolean main(void)
// here's minicex10.mc
{
    int t1,t2;
    t2=3;
    return(t2);
}
boolean main(void)
// minicex11.mc
{
    int t1,t2;
    boolean b3;
    t1=12;t2=3;b3=t2!=t1;
    return(b3);
}
```

6. This exercise is a useful prelude to the design of a full-fledged scanner/parser for "real" programming languages. We seek to modify our earlier results and develop a scanner/parser capable of parsing files containing multiple translational units. For example, consider the following minic source file comprised of five separate minic transunit files:

```
// Source file 1:
boolean main(void)
{
int t1,t2,t3;
// here is a boolean
boolean b1;
t1=10; // comment after statement
t2=3;
t3=t2*t1;
b1=t2<t3;
// time to return something
return(b1);
}
// Source file 2:
int main(void)
{
int t1,t2;
t2=3;
for(t1=10;t1<20;t1=t1+1) t2=t2+2;
return(t2);
}
```

```
// Source file 3:
int main(void)
{
int t1,t2;
t2=3;
for(t1=10;t1<20;t1=t1+1)
while(t2<10) t2=t2+2;
return(t2);
}
// Source file 4:
int main(void)
{
int t1,t2;
t2=3;
for(;;) t1=t2+1; //forever
return(t2);
}
// Source file 5:
boolean main(void)
// minicex11.mc
{
int t1,t2;
boolean b3;
t1=12;t2=3;b3=t2!=t1;
return(b3);
}
```

Desired behavior of the modified scanner/parser (using the preceding input file) is shown here:

```
?- parse-goal.

>>> Scanning and parsing minic (multiple files -- ver 3.2) <<<

Enter name of source file:
|: rev5files.mc

    // Source file 1:
    boolean main(void)
    {
    int t1,t2,t3;
    // here is a boolean
    boolean b1;
    t1=10; // comment after statement
    t2=3;
    t3=t2*t1;
    b1=t2<t3;
    // time to return something
    return(b1);
    }
    // Source file 2:
    int main(void)
    {
    int t1,t2;
    t2=3;
    for(t1=10;t1<20;t1=t1+1) t2=t2+2;
    return(t2);
    }
```

```
    // Source file 3:
    int main(void)
    {
    int t1,t2;
    t2=3;
    for(t1=10;t1<20;t1=t1+1)
    while(t2<10) t2=t2+2;
    return(t2);
    }
    // Source file 4:
    int main(void)
    {
    int t1,t2;
    t2=3;
    for(;;) t1=t2+1; //forever
    return(t2);
    }
    // Source file 5:
    boolean main(void)
    // minicex11.mc
    {
    int t1,t2;
    boolean b3;
    t1=12;t2=3;b3=t2!=t1;
    return(b3);
    }
Scan successful

[boolean, main, lparen, void, rparen, lbrace, int, ide(t1), comma,
ide(t2), comma, ide(t3), semicolon, boolean, ide(b1), semicolon,
ide(t1), assign, num(10), semicolon, ide(t2), assign, num(3), semicolon,
ide(t3), assign, ide(t2), times, ide(t1), semicolon, ide(b1),
assign, ide(t2), less, ide(t3), semicolon, return, lparen, ide(b1), rparen,
semicolon, rbrace, int, main, lparen, void, rparen, lbrace, int,
ide(t1), comma, ide(t2), semicolon, ide(t2), assign, num(3), semicolon,
for, lparen, ide(t1), assign, num(10), semicolon, ide(t1), less, num(20),
semicolon, ide(t1), assign, ide(t1), plus, num(1), rparen, ide(t2),
assign, ide(t2), plus, num(2), semicolon, return, lparen, ide(t2), rparen,
semicolon, rbrace, int, main, lparen, void, rparen, lbrace, int, ide(t1),
comma, ide(t2), semicolon, ide(t2), assign, num(3), semicolon,
for, lparen, ide(t1), assign, num(10), semicolon, ide(t1), less, num(20),
semicolon, ide(t1), assign, ide(t1), plus, num(1), rparen, while,
lparen, ide(t2), less, num(10), rparen, ide(t2), assign, ide(t2),
plus, num(2), semicolon, return, lparen, ide(t2), rparen, semicolon,
rbrace, int, main, lparen, void, rparen, lbrace, int, ide(t1),
comma, ide(t2), semicolon, ide(t2), assign, num(3), semicolon,
for, lparen, semicolon, semicolon, rparen, ide(t1), assign,
ide(t2), plus, num(1), semicolon, return, lparen, ide(t2),
rparen, semicolon, rbrace, boolean, main, lparen, void, rparen,
lbrace, int, ide(t1), comma, ide(t2), semicolon, boolean,
ide(b3), semicolon, ide(t1), assign, num(12), semicolon,
ide(t2), assign, num(3), semicolon, ide(b3), assign,
ide(t2), nequal, ide(t1), semicolon, return, lparen,
ide(b3), rparen, semicolon, rbrace, eop]


Parse successful
```

```
transunit(maindecl(bool, mainarg(void)),
body([decl(int, [t1, t2, t3]), decl(bool, [b1])],
statseq([sassign(ide(t1), num(10)),
sassign(ide(t2), num(3)), sassign(ide(t3),
compintexpr([ide(t2), times, ide(t1)])),
sassign(ide(b1), compbool(ide(t2), less, ide(t3)))],
retstat(b1))))

Remainder of token list is:

[int, main, lparen, void, rparen, lbrace, int, ide(t1),
comma, ide(t2), semicolon, ide(t2), assign, num(3),
semicolon, for, lparen, ide(t1), assign, num(10),
semicolon, ide(t1), less, num(20), semicolon, ide(t1),
assign, ide(t1), plus, num(1), rparen, ide(t2),
assign, ide(t2), plus, num(2), semicolon, return,
lparen, ide(t2), rparen, semicolon, rbrace, int, main,
lparen, void, rparen, lbrace, int, ide(t1),
comma, ide(t2), semicolon, ide(t2), assign, num(3),
semicolon, for, lparen, ide(t1), assign, num(10),
semicolon, ide(t1), less, num(20), semicolon, ide(t1),
assign, ide(t1), plus, num(1), rparen, while,
lparen, ide(t2), less, num(10), rparen, ide(t2),
assign, ide(t2), plus, num(2), semicolon, return,
lparen, ide(t2), rparen, semicolon, rbrace, int,
main, lparen, void, rparen, lbrace, int, ide(t1),
comma, ide(t2), semicolon, ide(t2), assign, num(3),
semicolon, for, lparen, semicolon, semicolon,
rparen, ide(t1), assign, ide(t2), plus, num(1),
semicolon, return, lparen, ide(t2), rparen, semicolon,
rbrace, boolean, main, lparen, void, rparen,
lbrace, int, ide(t1), comma, ide(t2), semicolon,
boolean, ide(b3), semicolon, ide(t1), assign, num(12),
semicolon, ide(t2), assign, num(3), semicolon, ide(b3),
assign, ide(t2), nequal, ide(t1), semicolon, return,
lparen, ide(b3), rparen, semicolon, rbrace, eop]

Parse successful

transunit(maindecl(int, mainarg(void)),
body([decl(int, [t1, t2])], statseq([sassign(ide(t2), num(3)),
for(init(ide(t1), num(10)), test(compbool(ide(t1), less, num(20))),
update(ide(t1), compintexpr([ide(t1), plus, num(1)])),
sassign(ide(t2), compintexpr([ide(t2), plus, num(2)])))],
retstat(t2))))

Remainder of token list is:

[int, main, lparen, void, rparen, lbrace, int, ide(t1),
comma, ide(t2), semicolon, ide(t2), assign, num(3),
semicolon, for, lparen, ide(t1), assign, num(10),
semicolon, ide(t1), less, num(20), semicolon, ide(t1),
assign, ide(t1), plus, num(1), rparen, while,
lparen, ide(t2), less, num(10), rparen, ide(t2),
assign, ide(t2), plus, num(2), semicolon, return,
lparen, ide(t2), rparen, semicolon, rbrace, int, main,
lparen, void, rparen, lbrace, int, ide(t1), comma, ide(t2),
semicolon, ide(t2), assign, num(3), semicolon, for, lparen,
```

```
semicolon, semicolon, rparen, ide(t1), assign, ide(t2),
plus, num(1), semicolon, return, lparen, ide(t2), rparen,
semicolon, rbrace, boolean, main, lparen, void, rparen,
lbrace, int, ide(t1), comma, ide(t2), semicolon, boolean,
ide(b3), semicolon, ide(t1), assign, num(12),
 semicolon, ide(t2), assign, num(3), semicolon, ide(b3),
assign, ide(t2), nequal, ide(t1), semicolon, return,
lparen, ide(b3), rparen, semicolon, rbrace, eop]

Parse successful

transunit(maindecl(int, mainarg(void)),
body([decl(int, [t1, t2])], statseq([sassign(ide(t2), num(3)),
for(init(ide(t1), num(10)), test(compbool(ide(t1), less, num(20))),
update(ide(t1), compintexpr([ide(t1), plus, num(1)])),
while(compbool(ide(t2), less, num(10)), sassign(ide(t2),
compintexpr([ide(t2), plus, num(2)]))))],
retstat(t2))))

Remainder of token list is:

[int, main, lparen, void, rparen, lbrace, int, ide(t1),
comma, ide(t2), semicolon, ide(t2), assign, num(3),
semicolon, for, lparen, semicolon, semicolon, rparen,
ide(t1), assign, ide(t2), plus, num(1), semicolon,
return, lparen, ide(t2), rparen, semicolon, rbrace,
boolean, main, lparen, void, rparen, lbrace, int, ide(t1),
comma, ide(t2), semicolon, boolean, ide(b3), semicolon,
ide(t1), assign, num(12), semicolon, ide(t2), assign, num(3),
semicolon, ide(b3), assign, ide(t2), nequal, ide(t1),
semicolon, return, lparen, ide(b3), rparen, semicolon,
rbrace, eop]

Parse successful

transunit(maindecl(int, mainarg(void)),
body([decl(int, [t1, t2])], statseq([sassign(ide(t2), num(3)),
for(init(none, opt), test(none), update(none, opt), sassign(ide(t1),
compintexpr([ide(t2), plus, num(1)])))], retstat(t2))))

Remainder of token list is:

[boolean, main, lparen, void, rparen, lbrace, int, ide(t1),
comma, ide(t2), semicolon, boolean, ide(b3), semicolon,
ide(t1), assign, num(12), semicolon, ide(t2), assign, num(3),
semicolon, ide(b3), assign, ide(t2), nequal, ide(t1), semicolon,
return, lparen, ide(b3), rparen, semicolon, rbrace, eop]

Parse successful

transunit(maindecl(bool, mainarg(void)),
body([decl(int, [t1, t2]), decl(bool, [b3])],
statseq([sassign(ide(t1), num(12)), sassign(ide(t2), num(3)),
sassign(ide(b3), compbool(ide(t2), nequal, ide(t1)))],
retstat(b3))))
```

```
Remainder of token list is:

[eop]


No
```

7. As noted, another contextual constraint might be that the declared type of the translational unit must match the type returned by the return statement. For purposes of this problem, type `void` is a type to be checked.

   Revise the parser to check this constraint. This requires both an addition to the symbol table, as well as a check during the parse of `retstat`.

8. The purpose of this exercise is to consider and implement a different symbol table structure. Recall the structure used in Section 7.10.1. Consider the alternative structure, wherein a separate part of the symbol table is allocated and used for each different type; that is, the structure is:

```
[...[int,[ide(t1),ide(t2),...],[boolean,[ide(b1),ide(b2),...], [void,[...],...]
```

   Revise the parser functions to accommodate this structure.

9. An extension for the symbol–table based parser is to constrain a variable to be declared only once. Implement this extension.

10. Show why the "blind" use of `append` that follows will cause problems.

```
?-append([ide(t3),integer],[[ide(t2),integer],[ide(b1),boolean],[ide(t1),integer]],
NewSymbolTable).
```

11. Section 7.4.2 illustrates the modifications and additions necessary to the scanner that allow comments in `C++` or `C` style in `minic`. This problem considers a slightly different strategy for the scanner, namely to report the recognition of a comment by adding a token `comment` to the scanner output list, and then removing this token prior to parsing. For example, using the following `minic` source code:

```
int main(void)
{/* declare the ints */
    int t1,t2;
/* set t1 to 10 */
    t1=10;
/* now the if  */
    if(t1) t2=3;
/* return something */
    return(t2);
}
```

   The desired output is:

```
Yes
?- parse-goal.

>>> Scanning and parsing minic (ver 4.4) <<<
```

```
Enter name of source file:
|: minicif2prob1.mc

    int main(void)
    {/* declare the ints */
        int t1,t2;
    /* set t1 to 10 */
        t1=10;
    /* now the if  */
        if(t1) t2=3;
    /* return something */
        return(t2);
    }
Scan successful

[int, main, lparen, void, rparen, lbrace, comment, int, ide(t1),
comma, ide(t2), semicolon, comment, ide(t1), assign, num(10),
semicolon, comment, if, lparen, ide(t1), rparen, ide(t2),
assign, num(3), semicolon, comment, return, lparen, ide(t2),
rparen, semicolon, rbrace, eop]


Parse successful
transunit(maindecl(int, mainarg(void)), body([decl(int, [t1, t2])],
statseq([sassign(ide(t1), num(10)), if(ide(t1),
sassign(ide(t2), num(3)))], retstat(t2))))

Yes
?- noprotocol.
```

Modify the `minic` scanner/parser to achieve this.

12. Do the modifications to `minic` in Section 7.4.2 allow nested comments (of either type)? Looking at the scanner/parser implementation, predict an answer and test your hypotheses with examples.

13. A desirable extension to the `minic` syntax is that of input/output constructs—reading and writing. Referring to the syntax of `C`, develop LGN representations for an input construct and an output construct. Map these into the scanner/parser implementation and show your results.

14. Another desirable extension to the `minic` syntax is to allow the translational unit (derived from `<transunit>`) to have arguments[9]—that is, we could produce program main declarations that are no longer simply `int` or `void`, but of the more general[10] form:

```
int main(int arg1, int arg2)
```

Modify the `minic` LGN representation for this and develop and test the corresponding scanner/parser Prolog implementation.

---

[9]Note that we do not follow the `C` syntax here, due to the need to add pointers and so forth.
[10]Only two arguments are shown here.

15. As noted in Section 7.1.3, it is possible to generate and parse syntactically correct and (grammatically) unambiguous strings whose subsequent interpretation or semantics are ambiguous. Given the `minic` syntax, suggest rules to disambiguate the semantics or interpretation of strings derived from `<expr>` that involve the following operators:

```
*  /  +  -
<  <=  ==  !=
```

16. In Section 7.10, the Prolog modifications to the `minic` scanner and parser necessary to enforce contextual constraints were shown. Attributes derived from declared variables were cataloged in the symbol table. Attributes derivable in the parse of `<expr>` were also implemented, along with checks.

    The purpose of this problem is to test your understanding of the attribute grammar Prolog implementation and the difference between inherited and synthesized attributes. Refer to Table 7.7 (on page 298). Using the parser revisions shown in Sections 7.10.1 and 7.10.2, show $S(X)$ and $I(X)$ for each nonterminal.

17. Show the required modifications to the Prolog code of Sections 7.10.1 and 7.10.2 to enforce the constraint that each variable must be declared exactly once.

18. Show the required modifications to the Prolog code of Sections 7.10.1 and 7.10.2 to enforce the constraint that the type used in the `return` statement matches the type declaration of `main`.

19. As an alternative to the synthesis of expression type shown in Section 7.10.2, consider a method for determining the overall expression type based upon operator type. Show the required modifications to the Prolog code of Section 7.10.2.

20. Add a `switch` construct to `minic`. The form follows that of `C`, that is,

```
switch (expr) {
   case const1: statement1 break;
   case const2: statement2 break;
   .
   .
   .
   default: statement
           }
```

21. `minic` (v4r6) has no input/output (I/O) constructs. The purpose of this problem is to add both input and output to the syntax, and thus to the scanner/parser.

    The form of each construct roughly follows that of `C`, but is simplified and is shown here:

```
printf("print-format-string",arg1,arg2,...,argn);
scanf("scan-format-string", name1, name2, ..., namen);
```

    where (for our simplified implementation) `"print-format-string"` consists of lowercase alphabetical characters, digits, spaces, and three special two-character designators (described on the next page) to indicate the printing of integer or boolean

Nonterminal	$S(X)$	$I(X)$
<transunit>		
<main-decl>		
<body>		
<dec-seq>		
<decl>		
<variable-list>		
<variable>		
<identifier>		
<statseq>		
<return-stat>		
<command>		
<simple-assignment>		
<lvalue>		
<expr>		
<integer-expr>		
<boolean-expr>		
<simple-integer-expr>		
<simple-integer-expr>		
<comp-integer-expr>		
<boolean-expr>		
<simple-boolean-expr>		
<comp-boolean-expr>		
<integer-const>		
<boolean-const>		
<numeral>		
<int-oper>		
<bool-oper>		
<boolean-const>		
<lvalue>		
<return-stat>		
<return-arg>		

Table 7.7 `minic` Nonterminals with Possible Attributes.

values or printing of a linefeed. These are designated by `\i`, `\b`, and `\n`, respectively.[11] As the following examples indicate, they are the only special two-character symbols allowed in the string. Similarly, `"scan-format-string"` consists of lowercase alphabetical characters, digits, spaces, and special designators to indicate the reading of integer or boolean values.

Each construct should allow an arbitrary number of arguments to be scanned or printed. Follow the development procedure indicated in Section 7.4.2: show examples of the desired `minic` extension, then indicate the new construct prototype, then develop the BNF description(s) of the new feature, then modify the scanner and parser to accommodate the new BNF description, and test your results.

[11] Note that they vary from their `C` counterparts.

Some examples are shown here to aid in development. First, some scans and parses that succeed:

```
?- parse-goal.

>>> Scanning and parsing minic (I/O-- ver 4.7) <<<

Enter name of source file:
|: minicpr1.mc

    // minicpr1.mc
    int main(void)
    {
     int t1;
     t1=352;
            printf("hi mom\n");
     return(t1);
    }

Scan Results

[int, main, lparen, void, rparen, lbrace, int, ide(t1), semicolon,
ide(t1), assign, num(352), semicolon, printf, lparen, string("hi mom\n"), rparen,
semicolon, return, lparen, ide(t1), rparen, semicolon, rbrace, eop]

Parse Results

transunit(maindecl(int, mainarg(void)),
body([decl(int, [t1])], statseq([sassign(ide(t1), num(352)),
printf(format("hi mom\n"), [])], retstat(ide(t1)))))

Yes
?- parse-goal.

>>> Scanning and parsing minic (I/O-- ver 4.7) <<<

Enter name of source file:
|: minicpr2.mc

    // minicpr2.mc
    int main(void)
    {
     int t1;
     boolean b1;
     t1=352;
     b1=false;
            printf("the values are \i and \b \n", t1, b1);
     return(t1);
    }

Scan Results

[int, main, lparen, void, rparen, lbrace, int, ide(t1), semicolon,
boolean, ide(b1), semicolon, ide(t1), assign, num(352), semicolon,
ide(b1), assign, false, semicolon,
printf, lparen, string("the values are \i and \b \n"), comma, ide(t1),
comma, ide(b1), rparen, semicolon, return, lparen, ide(t1),
rparen, semicolon, rbrace, eop]
```

```
Parse Results

transunit(maindecl(int, mainarg(void)),
body([decl(int, [t1]), decl(bool, [b1])],
statseq([sassign(ide(t1), num(352)), sassign(ide(b1), false),
printf(format("the values are \i and \b \n"), printargs([t1, b1]))],
retstat(ide(t1)))))

Yes
?- parse-goal.

>>> Scanning and parsing minic (I/O-- ver 4.7) <<<

Enter name of source file:
|: minicpr3.mc
    //minicpr3.mc
    int main(void)
    {
     int t1,t2;
     t2=3;
     for(t1=10;t1<20;t1=t1+1) printf("t1 is \i t2 is \i\n",t1,t2);
     return(t2);
    }

Scan Results

[int, main, lparen, void, rparen, lbrace, int, ide(t1), comma,
ide(t2), semicolon, ide(t2), assign, num(3), semicolon,
for, lparen, ide(t1), assign, num(10), semicolon,
ide(t1), less, num(20), semicolon, ide(t1),
assign, ide(t1), plus, num(1), rparen,
printf, lparen, string("t1 is \i t2 is \i\n"), comma, ide(t1), comma, ide(t2),
rparen, semicolon, return, lparen, ide(t2), rparen, semicolon, rbrace, eop]

Parse Results

transunit(maindecl(int, mainarg(void)),
body([decl(int, [t1, t2])], statseq([sassign(ide(t2), num(3)),
for(init(ide(t1), num(10)), test(compbool(ide(t1), less, num(20))),
update(ide(t1), compintexpr([ide(t1), plus, num(1)])),
printf(format("t1 is \i t2 is \i\n"), printargs([t1, t2]))))],
retstat(ide(t2)))))

Yes
?- parse-goal.

>>> Scanning and parsing minic (I/O-- ver 4.7) <<<

Enter name of source file:
|: minicpr4.mc

    //minicpr4.mc
    int main(void)
    {
     int t1,t2,t3;
     scanf("\i  \i", t2,t3);
     for(t1=t2;t1<t3;t1=t1+1) printf("t1 is \i \n\n",t1);
```

```
    return(t2);
   }
```

```
Scan Results

[int, main, lparen, void, rparen, lbrace, int, ide(t1), comma, ide(t2),
comma, ide(t3), semicolon, scanf, lparen, string("\i  \i"), comma,
ide(t2), comma, ide(t3), rparen, semicolon,
for, lparen, ide(t1), assign, ide(t2), semicolon, ide(t1), less, ide(t3), semicolon,
ide(t1), assign, ide(t1), plus, num(1), rparen,
printf, lparen, string("t1 is \i \n\n"), comma, ide(t1), rparen, semicolon,
return, lparen, ide(t2), rparen, semicolon, rbrace, eop]

Parse Results

transunit(maindecl(int, mainarg(void)),
body([decl(int, [t1, t2, t3])],
statseq([scanf(format("\i  \i"), inputargs([t2, t3])),
for(init(ide(t1), ide(t2)), test(compbool(ide(t1), less, ide(t3))),
update(ide(t1), compintexpr([ide(t1), plus, num(1)])),
printf(format("t1 is \i \n\n"), printargs([t1])))], retstat(ide(t2)))))

Yes
```

Note the following behavior is not allowed:

```
?- parse-goal.

>>> Scanning and parsing minic (ver 4.7) <<<

Enter name of source file:
|: minicpr5.mc

    //minicpr5.mc
    int main(void)
    {
        int t1,t2,t3;
        scanf("\\\\i  \i", t2,t3);
        for(t1=t2;t1<t3;t1=t1+1) printf("t1 is\\\\v \i \n\n",t1);
        return(t2);
    }

Scan Results

[int, main, lparen, void, rparen, lbrace, int, ide(t1), comma,
ide(t2), comma, ide(t3), semicolon, scanf, lparen, string("\\\\i  \i"),
comma, ide(t2), comma, ide(t3), rparen, semicolon,
for, lparen, ide(t1), assign, ide(t2), semicolon, ide(t1),
less, ide(t3), semicolon, ide(t1), assign, ide(t1), plus, num(1), rparen,
printf, lparen, string("t1 is\\\\v \i \n\n"), comma, ide(t1), rparen, semicolon,
return, lparen, ide(t2), rparen, semicolon, rbrace, eop]

Parse Results

transunit(maindecl(int, mainarg(void)),
body([decl(int, [t1, t2, t3])],
statseq([scanf(format("\\\\i  \i"), inputargs([t2, t3])),
for(init(ide(t1), ide(t2)), test(compbool(ide(t1), less, ide(t3))),
update(ide(t1), compintexpr([ide(t1), plus, num(1)])),
```

```
printf(format("t1 is\\\\v \i \n\n"), printargs([t1]))],
retstat(ide(t2)))))

Yes
```

Thus, here are examples where the parse should fail:

```
?- parse-goal.

>>> Scanning and parsing minic (I/O-- ver 4.7) <<<

Enter name of source file:
|: minicpr5.mc

    //minicpr5.mc
    int main(void)
    {
     int t1,t2,t3;
     scanf("\\cannot interpret this character: "
% Abort: closed stream '$stream'(1968642)
?- parse-goal.

>>> Scanning and parsing minic (I/O-- ver 4.7) <<<

Enter name of source file:
|    minicpr5r.mc

    //minicpr5r.mc
    int main(void)
    {
        int t1,t2,t3;
        scanf("\i  \i", t2,t3);
        for(t1=t2;t1<t3;t1=t1+1) printf("t1 is \\cannot interpret this character: "
% Abort: closed stream '$stream'(8199170)
% Execution Aborted
?- parse-goal.

>>> Scanning and parsing minic (I/O-- ver 4.7) <<<

Enter name of source file:
|: minicpr5r2.mc

    //minicpr5r2.mc
    int main(void)
    {
        int t1,t2,t3;
        scanf("\fcannot interpret this character: "
% Abort: closed stream '$stream'(8199170)
% Execution Aborted
```

22. Revise the scanner/parser for a more general and "block-oriented" implementation of the `while` and `for` constructs that allows iteration over a `<command-seq>`, rather than just a single `<command>`.

23. It may surprise the reader to discover that the BNF syntax for the extended `minic` in Section 7.4.3 (syntax contained in `file:transunit-bnf4r2nir.txt`) *is ambiguous.* Although subtle, it is nonetheless an important concern. To this end:

(a) Determine the source of the ambiguity through examination of the BNF syntax.

(b) Let `bison` detemine the ambiguity via development of a `bison` grammar file for the BNF specification. (Note: the use of the `-v` switch is recommended.)

(c) Suggest a modification to eliminate this ambiguity.

24. Develop a `flex` input file that can recognize `C++`-style comments, but distinguish between DOS-formatted files and Unix-formatted ASCII files.

25. Following the added syntax of Section 7.4.2, revise the `flex` and `bison` input files to accommodate the scanning and parsing of `minic` source containing *user-defined* functions.

26. Revise the `bison`-based parser to enforce the contextual constraint that the declared type of the translational unit must match the type returned by the `return` statement. For this problem to make sense, it is necessary to revise the `minic` Version 2 syntax to make the `return` statement optional. This situation is consistent when main is declared to return `void`. The symbol table data structure should be enhanced (and used) for this purpose.

27. In the `minic` scanner/parser enhancements shown in Section 7.9, parse failure resulted from the use of undeclared variables. Consider the opposite problem,[12] namely the declaration of variables that are never used. Implement a suitable warning by modification of the `bison` input file.

[12] Which is implemented in `gcc` using the `-Wall` switch.

CHAPTER 8

Functional Programming and the Lambda Calculus

There are known knowns.
There are things we know we know.
We also know
There are known unknowns.
That is to say
We know there are some things
We do not know.
But there are also unknown unknowns

—Donald Rumsfeld, quoted in 'The Existential Poetry of Donald H. Rumsfeld,' H. Seely, The Free Press, 2003.

8.1 Introduction to the Lambda Calculus and Functional Programming

We will now consider the foundations of another programming paradigm, namely **functional programming**. Not surprisingly, the basis for the paradigm is the implementation of functions. First, we introduce the lambda calculus. The lambda calculus has a very simple syntax with very powerful semantics. We will consider both the syntax of the lambda calculus and the evaluation of syntactically correct expressions in this syntax. In addition, we introduce Lisp (and ML and OCAML in the next chapter) as "sugared" implementations and extensions of the lambda calculus and examples of functional programming.

8.1.1 Functional Programming History

The evolution of functional languages has been influenced by many sources. One of the most significant resulted from the work of Alonzo Church in developing the lambda calculus (Manzano, 1997). Although many consider the lambda calculus to be the first functional language, it is noteworthy that there were no (digital) computers at the time of its introduction. Thus, there was no way to run (or evaluate) functional programs, or any programs. Modern functional languages such as Lisp and ML may be thought of as extensions of the lambda calculus.

The Roots of Functional Programming (Lisp)

In a seminal paper published in 1960, John McCarthy showed how a small number of (possibly recursive) functions and a data structure (a list) for both code and data could form the basis for a programming language. A remarkable corollary to this result is the fact that these functions (alone) allow one to write an interpreter for Lisp *in Lisp*. This is an example of the *self-definition* of the semantics of a programming language. McCarthy's aim was to develop a programming system to facilitate manipulating symbolic expressions representing declarative and imperative expressions for an application dubbed "Advice Taker." However, Lisp may be studied within the framework of the lambda calculus. Note also that Lisp has had a significant impact on the subsequent development of other functional languages, such as ML and Haskell.

8.1.2 A Calculus for Computation via Functions

Church's work was motivated by the desire to create a calculus[1] that incorporated the computational aspect of functions. Furthermore, Church's lambda calculus is based upon a very interesting property, namely that functions may be applied to themselves. Thus, recursion occurs naturally in the lambda calculus (and consequently in functional programming). Note that in theories of functions as set mappings, this interpretation is impossible because it requires a set to contain itself, resulting in well-known paradoxes.

As will be shown, the lambda calculus enjoys a very simple syntax, consisting of only four productions. However, recognition and reduction (evaluation) of phrases in the lambda calculus can still be challenging.

The Turing Machine Analogy to Computation

Most computer science/engineering students are familiar with the concept of a sequential (or finite-state) machine. This class of machines produces output based upon current state and external stimuli (inputs). These machines are **non-writing**, since they cannot determine or change their own inputs. A finite-state machine that is able to influence its own inputs is referred to as a **writing machine**.

In 1936, British mathematician Alan Turing proposed an idealized mathematical structure for a writing machine. The Turing machine is one of the key abstractions used in modern computability theory.[2] Turing machine operations are limited to reading and writing symbols on a tape, or moving along the tape to the left or right. The tape is subdivided into cells, each of which can be filled with at most one symbol. At any given time, the Turing machine can only read or write on one of these cells.

A Turing machine has a finite number of states and is in exactly one of these states at any given time. Associated with these states are instructions telling the machine what action to perform if it is currently scanning a particular symbol, and what state to go into after performing this action.

Most importantly, the Turing machine provides a formalism for expressing (procedural) computation.

---

[1]That is, a syntax for terms and a set of rewriting rules for manipulating terms.

[2]Basically, the study of what computers can and cannot do.

The Lambda Calculus Analogy to Functional Programming

By analogy, the lambda calculus provides a formalism for the expression of a computation in a purely functional language.

8.1.3 Relations and Functions

Recall that a (binary) relation is a mapping between elements of two sets:

$$R:\ A \rightarrow B$$

A function is a special case of a relation:

$$f:\ X \rightarrow Y$$

such that for each $x \in X$ we can specify a unique element in Y, denoted y or $f(x)$. It is useful to expand our thinking beyond numerical functions and remember that functions can return objects (a larger class than numbers), which can be almost anything—for example, sets, lists, strings, function definitions, or void.

Example 1 Consider the (numerical) function *square*, with signature:

$$square:\ Integer \rightarrow Integer$$

which is commonly written as $square(n) = n^2$. In this case, the function is given a name ($square$).

Alternately, consider the definition of an anonymous function (a function with no name) that has the same input–output mapping. It takes n as input and returns n^2. We can write this in the syntax of the lambda calculus[3] as:

$$\lambda n.n^2$$

Example 2 Consider the function abstraction:

$$(\lambda n.n)$$

This anonymous function represents the identity mapping—that is, it returns the input value. For example, the combination

$$((\lambda n.n)\ 4)$$

returns the value 4, whereas

$$((\lambda n.n)\ 'hi\ mom')$$

returns the string *hi mom*. Note that the function does not need to know the type of the input, yet behaves similarly in both cases. Such behavior is called *polymorphic*.

[3]Temporarily ignoring missing parentheses and the n^2 notation, which is not permitted by the syntax in Section 8.2.1.

Looking Ahead

Although our immediate interest in functions is motivated by the lambda calculus and functional programming, in Chapter 9 we will again return to the notions of functions as mappings and function signatures. Semantic functions will be used to map syntactically correct phrases into objects in a semantic domain to indicate "meaning."

8.2 The Syntax and Semantics of the Lambda Calculus

8.2.1 Four Productions Go a Long Way

The lambda-calculus syntax is very simple, consisting of only four productions. Note that in the syntactic specification, the parentheses are not for clarity of reading; *they are part of the syntax.* The syntax of any expression producible in the lambda calculus is given here.

<expression> ::=
<variable>
| **<constant>**
| (**<expression>** **<expression>**)
| (λ **<variable>** . **<expression>**)

Note the self-embedding or recursive nature of the last two productions. Variables are denoted by *lowercase* letters. We will show some examples of each in Section 8.2.4, but digress to introduce two particularly important forms.

The Combination

The third production option, namely

<expression> ::= (**<expression>** **<expression>**)

is denoted a *combination* and yields strings of the overall form:

```
(expression1 expression2)
```

where `expression1` and `expression2` are each derived from `<expression>`. The corresponding semantics of this string indicate application of `expression1` to `expression2`. Often, `expression1` is referred to as the **operator** (or **rator**), and `expression2` is referred to as the **operand** (or **rand**). `expression1` must be (or evaluate to) a function, either predefined (constant) or an abstraction. This was shown in Example 2.

The Abstraction

The fourth production is an example of a **lambda abstraction** or (anonymous) function definition. More is said on this in the following section.

8.2.2 Remarks on the Lambda Calculus

There are a few important things to note about the lambda calculus, including the notation used.

1. The role of a variable in the lambda calculus is quite different from the notion of a variable as used in an imperative language. In (purely) functional programming, variables only serve to indicate function parameters, whereas in imperative programming, in a statement such as:

$$x = 6;$$

variable `x` corresponds to a memory location occupied with value 6.

2. The set of constants includes the names of (assumed) built-in functions, such as **`add`** or $+$.

3. Because we adopt a functional representation, we use prefix notation; for example, the infix-based expression $n{+}1$ is denoted $(+\ n\ 1)$ or $(+\ 1\ n)$. We almost immediately run into difficulty expressing simple functions of two variables, because we have not defined any extensions to the lambda calculus that would allow two-input functions. Thus, we cannot visualize this notation as a subcase of the application of a two-input function +—that is, $(+\ x\ y)$.

   Instead, consider a predefined function (as noted, considered a constant) +1, which adds 1 to its argument when applied.[4] Thus, (+1 2) evaluates to 3. Borrowing from the preceding, consider a more general function $+x$, which adds x to its argument. A sample reduction[5] is:

$$((\lambda x.(+x)\ 3)) \Rightarrow (+x\ 3)$$

   In what follows, we will simply write this as $(+\ x\ 3)$.

8.2.3 Extensions

One topic we have overlooked is recursive function abstraction and evaluation in the lambda calculus. This is treated in the references.

8.2.4 Handworked Reduction (Evaluation) Examples

Simple Example

Consider the reduction of an *abstraction* applied to an expression, that is, a *combination* of the form:

$$((\lambda n.\ (+n\ 1))\ 5)$$

The first thing to do is to recognize the overall (two-part) form, from the syntax specification in Section 8.2.1. Thus the reduction is:

$$((\lambda n.\ (+n\ 1))\ 5) \Rightarrow (+\ 5\ 1) \Rightarrow 6$$

[4]Also known as the successor function.

[5]Notice that we use the notation ⇒ to signify "reduces to."

A More Challenging Reduction

Consider a systematic reduction of the following lambda calculus expression:

$$(((\lambda f.(\lambda x.(f(f\ x))))\ square)\ 2)$$

where *square* is assumed to be the predefined squaring function. First, we recognize this string in the lambda calculus language as an (overall) *combination* of the form:

```
(<expresson> <expression>)
```

specifically $((\lambda f.(\lambda x.(f(f\ x))))\ square)$ applied to 2. The former is itself a *combination* that evaluates to an *abstraction*. In other words, in $((\lambda f.(\lambda x.(f(f\ x))))\ square)$, the "outer" abstraction involving the λ function with argument f has the corresponding expression $(\lambda x.(f(f\ x)))$, and is applied to the expression *square*. Evaluation of this part yields:

$$((\lambda f.(\lambda x.(f(f\ x))))\ square) \Rightarrow (\lambda x.(square\ (square\ x)))$$

The resulting *abstraction* is then applied to 2, yielding:

$$((\lambda x.(square(square\ x)))\ 2) \Rightarrow (square\ (square\ 2)) \Rightarrow (square\ 4) \Rightarrow 16$$

So the overall reduction shown in this case is:

$$\begin{aligned}&(((\lambda f.(\lambda x.(f(f\ x))))\ square)\ 2) \Rightarrow\\ &\quad((\lambda x.(square(square\ x)))\ 2) \Rightarrow\\ &\qquad(square\ (square\ 2)) \Rightarrow (square\ 4) \Rightarrow 16\end{aligned}$$

Notice that this example also shows that arguments to lambda functions may be the names of other functions.

8.2.5 Reduction (Evaluation) Examples Using Lisp

Although we have yet to introduce the syntax of CommonLisp, we now show a few examples of using CommonLisp to implement the lambda calculus. For example, to define a lambda function with the abstraction $(\lambda x.(+\ 3\ x))$ in Lisp we write:

```
> (lambda (x) (+ 3 x))
#<closure :lambda (x) (+ 3 x)>
```

Lisp calls this a *lexical closure*. Now we show a combination using the preceding abstraction. Recall that the lambda calculus syntax for this is $((\lambda x.(+\ 3\ x))\ 9)$. In Lisp this becomes:

```
> ((lambda (x) (+ 3 x)) 9)
12
```

Finally, we show one more single-variable example. Consider the abstraction $(\lambda n.n^3)$. The Lisp is:

```
> ((lambda (n) (* n n n)) 3)
27
```

8.2.6 Reduction (Evaluation) Example Using CAML

Consider the following anonymous function definition and application in CAML:

```
# ((function x -> x+1) 4);;
- : int = 5
```

8.2.7 Multivariable (Multiargument) Functions

What Is the Problem?

Suppose we want to represent a very simple two-variable function

$$f(a,b) = a + b$$

in the lambda calculus. Unfortunately, the syntax does not allow the production of the string or *abstraction*[6]

$$(\lambda a, b.(+\ a\ b))$$

To make the lambda-calculus useful, this apparent limitation must be addressed.

Currying

One solution, which is probably the most commonly cited, is from the mathematician Haskell B. Curry, and is called "currying" the function. Each variable in the multivariable function $f(a, b, c, \ldots)$ needs its own binding (λ). Curry suggested that we view a solution to this representational problem using the form:

$$(\lambda a.(\lambda b.(\lambda c ...)))$$

This can be viewed as defining an anonymous function of the variable a that has as its value a function of the variable b, and so on. One point is that a higher-order function has been reduced to an abstraction where each of the arguments may be considered and evaluated separately. There are subtle distinctions in representing this mapping.

$$R \times R \times R \rightarrow R$$

versus

$$R \rightarrow R \rightarrow R \rightarrow R$$

Notice that we can view

$$((+\ x)\ 3)$$

as a *combination* that applies conversly, a function, $(+\ x)$ to the value 3.

$$(+\ x\ 3)$$

is prefix notation for a 2-argument function, $+$, with arguments x and 3.

[6]Although it is often used as shorthand for a legal interpretation, as explained later.

Example 1 This is an example of two-operand multiplication using the curried abstraction:

$$(\lambda x.(\lambda y.((* \ x) \ y)))$$

Applied to a single argument, this yields:

$$((\lambda x.(\lambda y.((* \ x) \ y))) \ 5) \Rightarrow (\lambda y.((* \ 5) \ y))$$

The result is an abstraction for a second function that multiplies its argument by 5. We usually simplify this to mean $(\lambda y.(* \ 5 \ y))$

Example 2 In this example, we show currying the two-operand addition function +.

$$(\lambda a.(\lambda b.(+ \ a) \ b))$$

is an abstraction for two functions, used in succession. $(+ \ a)$ is the function that adds a to something. We often skip this and thus just write $(\lambda a.(\lambda b.(+ \ a) \ b))$ as:

$$(\lambda a.(\lambda b.(+ \ a \ b)))$$

Similarly, $((+ \ a) \ b)$ is simply written as $(+ \ a \ b)$.

This reasoning leads to the simplified abbreviation for multivariable functions involving an expression, E:

$$(\lambda x.(\lambda y.(\lambda z.E))) \rightarrow (\lambda xyz.E)$$

which is shown in Lisp in the next section.

Multivariable Lambda Functions in Lisp

The basic strategy is easy to see, and is illustrated in the following examples. First we show some surprising unary uses of binary functions.

```
lisp> (* 3)
3
lisp> (+ 3)
3
lisp> (* (+ 3) 3)
9
```

Here's a lambda function with values, that is, a combination:

```
lisp> ((lambda (x y) (+ (* 3 x) (* y y))) 1 2)
7
```

Another Lisp example leads to the naming of a function, so that it is no longer anonymous. First:

```
lisp> ((lambda (x y) (+ (* y y) x)) 3 4)
19
```

As a look ahead, lets give the function a name, using the Lisp function **defun**:

```
lisp> (defun named (x y) (+ (* y y) x))
NAMED
lisp> (named 3 4)
19
```

Finally, we show some polymorphic behavior of a function in Lisp.

```
lisp> (lambda (x) x)
#<closure :lambda (x) x>
lisp> ((lambda (x) x) 4)
4
lisp> ((lambda (x) x) "hi mom")
"hi mom"
lisp> ((lambda (x) x) '(a b c d))
(a b c d)
```

For comparison, here are the uncurried and curried versions of a lambda expression:

```
lisp> ((lambda (r s) (- r s)) 5 3)
2
lisp> ((lambda (r) ((lambda (s) (- r s)) 3)) 5)
2
```

The reader should be sure to see the difference between the two preceding forms. Finally, we show how currying works for more than two arguments.

```
lisp> (* 5 (- 6 3))
15
lisp> ((lambda (x y z) (* x (- y z)) ) 5 6 3)
15
lisp> ((lambda (x) ((lambda (y) ((lambda (z) (* x (- y z))) 3)) 6)) 5)
15
```

Multivariable Lambda Functions in CAML

ML and CAML allow either curried function arguments or tuples. The following is a four-augument CAML function definition example where the CAML interpreter indicates the resulting currying.

```
# (fun a b c d -> a+b+c+d);;
- : int -> int -> int -> int -> int = <fun>
#  (fun a b c d -> a+b+c+d) 1 2 3 4;;
- : int = 10
```

8.3 Functional Programming Concepts and Syntax

The notion of a function is familiar in the mathematical[7] sense: given input, a value is returned. A more general interpretation is shown in Figure 8.1. Possible side effects are shown; this is explored in Section 8.4. Most programmers are used to the notation for function evaluation (and subsequent assignment of the result to a named variable) using the form:

$$output = f(input);$$

[7] Typically numerical.

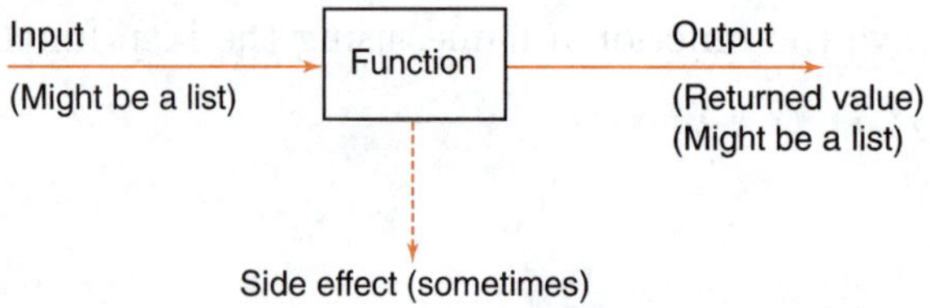

Figure 8.1 General Concept of a Function.

In Lisp, for example, this function evaluation is indicated using the list structure:

```
(f input)
```

or, if assignment to a variable is necessary, the form:

```
(setq output (f input))
```

is used. There is no general need for assignment of the output value to a named variable. We have shown it here to illustrate the notational difference between Lisp and an imperative language statement.

Thus, it is important to distinguish between (perhaps familiar) notation for a function evaluation—for example, `fun1(v1,v2)`—and the Lisp counterpart, `(fun1 v1 v2)`. Typing expressions such as `fun1(v1 v2)` or `fun1(v1,v2)` at the Lisp prompt is a sure way to generate error messages.

Because most programming is unlikely to be accomplished with a single function, the notion of a composite function is important. This is shown in Figure 8.2. Finally, Figure 8.3 illustrates a more complicated composite function evaluation. In Lisp, this would be indicated as:

```
(fnk (fnk-1 ...(fn2 (fn1 input))...)
```

8.4 Side Effects and Functional Programming

8.4.1 The Notion of a Side Effect

Up to this point, we have used the term "side effect" numerous times in describing aspects of functional programming. Recall that our concept of functional programming (with origins in the lambda calculus) only allowed a function to have arguments and return a value. Thus, a side effect is some effect of a function *other than just returning a value.* Some common side effects are assignment (or modification) of values to global variables,[8] printing, and loading files.

[8]By far the most common "offender."

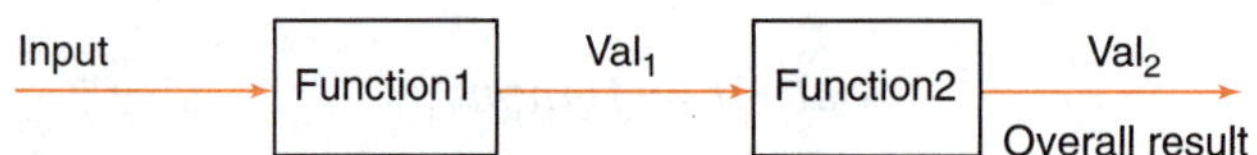

Figure 8.2 Typical Composition of Functions to Achieve an Output.

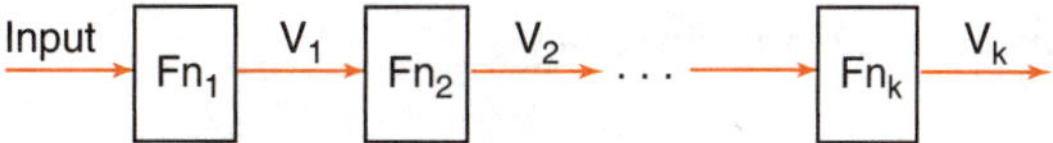

Figure 8.3 General Form of a Composite Function.

8.4.2 More Formal Approach and Extensions

Another definition of a language construct that contains a side effect is one that modifies the state of the system.

The most common side effects are assignment, input, and output. A language without side effects is purely functional; execution consists of the evaluation of an expression or series of expressions. All subexpressions are referentially transparent.

8.4.3 Referential Transparency

In a **referentially transparent** function, the value returned by the function is determined solely by the values of the arguments. It is independent of the state of the system or any previous history of function evaluations.

"The evaluation of a function with the same arguments produces the same result each time the function is invoked."

The most common example of nonreferentially transparent behavior involves global variables.

Examples

The following are some example functions, with and without referential transparency:

```
;; file: ref-trans-ex.l
;; examples involving referential transparency in lisp

(defun ref-trans (x)
   (+ x 5)
)

(defun not-ref-trans1 (x)
   (+ x y) ;relies on global variable y having a value
)

; the next one is even worse

(defun not-ref-trans2 (x)
   (setq y (+ x y))
)

;; here's a fix

(defun not-ref-trans1-fixed (x y)
   (+ x y) ; now y is an argument
)
```

The reader should study what happens when these functions are used:

```
lisp> (load ''ref-trans-ex.l'')
;; Loading file ref-trans-ex.l ...
```

```
;; Loading of file ref-trans-ex.l is finished.
t
lisp> (setq y 10)
10
lisp> (ref-trans 4)
9
lisp> (ref-trans 5)
10
lisp> (ref-trans 4)
9
lisp> (not-ref-trans1 4)
14
lisp> (not-ref-trans1 5)
15
lisp> (setq y 5)
5
lisp> (not-ref-trans1 4)
9
lisp> (not-ref-trans1 5)
10
lisp> (not-ref-trans2 4)
9
lisp> (setq y 10)
10
lisp> (not-ref-trans2 4)
14
lisp> (not-ref-trans2 4)
18
lisp> (not-ref-trans2 4)
22
lisp> (not-ref-trans1-fixed 4 5)
9
lisp> (not-ref-trans2 4)
26
lisp> (not-ref-trans1-fixed 4 5)
9
lisp>
```

8.4.4 Why Do We Care?

Pure functional languages achieve referential transparency by forbidding assignment to global variables. Each expression is a constant or a function application whose evaluation has no side effect—that is, it only returns a value and that value depends only on the definition of the function and the values of its arguments.

In general, referentially transparent programs are more amenable to formal methods and easier to reason about because the meaning of an expression depends only on the meaning of its subexpressions and not on the order of evaluation or side effects of other expressions.

8.5 Functional Programming with Typed Functions: A Preliminary Example Using ML

The previously introduced lambda calculus makes no mention of typing of variables, and therefore could be called the "untyped" lambda calculus. Note also that Lisp is not typed.

The functional programming language ML is a recent functional language that is strongly typed. The lambda calculus may be expanded to notate this typing as shown in the following example abstraction:

$$(\lambda x : N.\lambda y : N.(x\ +\ y))$$

where the type of the result is inferred from the types (N) of the arguments.

The following is a simple ML session illustrating the definition and use of typed functions in ML:

```
$ sml
Standard ML of New Jersey, Version 110.0.7, September 28, 2000 [CM; autoload enabled]

- fun addTyped (x:int, y:int) = x + y;
val addTyped = fn : int * int -> int

- addTyped(5,6);
val it = 11 : int
```

8.6 Bibliographical Remarks and References

The history and evolution of functional programming is well and thoroughly covered in Hudak (1989). However, the original McCarthy (1960) paper on Lisp makes extremely interesting reading. A readable history of the lambda calculus is given in Rosser (1984), and a history of the use of recursive functions is presented in Kleene (1981). Backus (1978) provides an interesting look at the distinction between imperative and functional programming styles.

Although it is a challenge (for a nonmathematician) to read any of the works of Church or Curry, Manzano (1997) and Enderton (1995) provide some perspective.

8.7 Exercises

1. Which of the following are syntactically correct lambda expressions?[9]

$$(\lambda x.(-\ (+\ (*\ x\ x)(*\ 3\ x))\ 5))$$
$$(\lambda a(-\ (+1\ 3))\ 5)$$
$$(\lambda x.((+\ x)\ 3))$$
$$(\lambda b.(*\ b\ b))$$
$$\lambda n.(+\ n\ 1)$$

2. Reduce each of the following strings in the language of the lambda calculus.

$$((\lambda x.x)\ y)$$
$$(+\ (*\ 5\ 6)\ (*\ 8\ 3))$$

3. Reduce each of the following strings in the language of the lambda calculus.

$$((\lambda x.(\lambda y.(*\ x\ y)))\ 5)$$
$$((\lambda x.(-\ (+\ (*\ x\ x)(*\ 3\ x))\ 5))\ 1)$$
$$((\lambda a.(\lambda b.(+\ a\ b))\ 5)\ 12)$$

[9]Where necessary, assume built-in functions such as $+$, $-$, $*$.

4. Given the following lambda calculus expression:

$$((\lambda\, n.(+\ n\ 1))\ 5)$$

   (a) Evaluate (reduce) it by hand.

   (b) Convert this expression to a CommonLisp s-expression that may be input to `EVAL`.

5. Here is an expression in dire need of parentheses:

$$\lambda x\ .\ x\ \lambda y\ .\ y\ z$$

   (a) Add parentheses to obtain a syntactically correct lambda expression.

   (b) Reduce the syntactically correct lambda expression, if possible.

   (c) Is there more than one solution to this problem—that is, is the expression *ambiguous*?

CHAPTER 9

Lisp

Before software can be reusable it first has to be usable.

—Ralph Johnson

9.1 Lisp Introduction, Pragmatics, and Resources

9.1.1 Ways to Approach Learning Lisp Programming

There are many ways to approach learning the syntax and semantics of Lisp, including:

- as a list-manipulation language.
- as an example of functional programming.
- as an implementation of the extended lambda calculus.
- via programming by example.

Our strategy is as follows:

- assume or provide lots of built-in (predefined) functions.
- use them to build up any computation desired in succession.
- provide a function to name lambda functions.
- provide an environment to interact with the function evaluator.

With this, we have created Lisp. Much of the introduction is conveyed by examples. Note that it is impractical to individually consider every possible Lisp function (that is what references are for). Instead, we attempt to convey the Lisp programming concept and principal function groups.

9.1.2 Who Uses Lisp?

Two popular misconceptions about Lisp are:

1. Lisp is only used by artificial intelligence (AI) researchers. Although Lisp is commonly used to implement AI systems (and for good reason), AI is only one application domain. This is illustrated with the examples on the next page.

2. Lisp is old and therefore useless. Again, see the examples on the next page.

Sample Lisp Applications

Lisp applications include the following:

1. AutoDesk uses Lisp in the CAD program Autocad.
2. Yahoo Store (implemented as Viaweb Store) uses Lisp to configure "online stores" for its customers. This application is one of the best high-profile Lisp success stories.
3. Sony, Electronic Arts, and Nintendo use a graphics system written in Lisp for advanced three-dimensional graphics in game systems.
4. GNU Emacs, the GNU version of the Emacs editor, allows programs in the Lisp language to be run by Emacs's own Lisp interpreter. This allows customization and extension.[1] Most (not all) of the editing commands of Emacs are written in Lisp.[2]
5. Scheme is a dialect of Lisp. It has been used as an embedded language. For example, see The Gimp, which uses Scheme to process images automatically. Another example is GNU Guile, a Scheme interpreter used in the Gnome desktop.
6. The Sawfish window manager is implemented using a Lisp-based scripting language. All high-level window manager functions are implemented in Lisp to allow extensibility or redefinition. User-configuration is possible by writing Lisp code in a personal `.sawfishrc` file.

9.1.3 Important First Principles

The acronym Lisp originally stood as an abbreviation for for **list** **p**rocessing. One (more modern?) view of Lisp might be through a revision of the acronym: *l*ots of *i*rritating *s*illy *p*arentheses. However, Lisp does not need to be traumatic for newcomers. A few simple guidelines may help:

1. The basic data structures are lists, atoms, and strings.
2. The basic concept is **function application**, that is, applying **functions** to these basic data structures. This involves defining (or at least identifying) functions, with particular care to specify **arguments** and function **returned values**.
3. Lisp provides lots of built-in functions (see Section 9.13 for a complete listing). The Lisp programmer achieves additional functionality by using these to define new functions.
4. In a "pure" Lisp, assignment would not be used. Values would be passed through the use of function parameters and returned values. However, for practical purposes, assignment is provided.
5. Frequently **recursion** is used because it is natural in functional programming and often leads to compact implementations.
6. Like Prolog, the reader should learn to think like a language interpreter (EVAL—the Lisp read-eval-print loop).

---

[1] To learn Emacs Lisp programming, see *Introduction to Emacs Lisp* by Robert J. Chassell, published by the Free Software Foundation.

[2] For example, typing `CTRL-x CTRL-e` in any buffer evaluates the Lisp form contained in the text immediately before the cursor and prints its value in the echo area.

7. Proof of correctness of a (functional) program is straightforward.

8. Because the language name is derived from "list processing," it is not surprising that numerous list-manipulation functions are provided. In addition, many of the "lists" are, in fact, function definitions and applications that enable use of the **functional programming** paradigm.

9. *Incremental program development*—that is, developing a single function at a time—is highly recommended.

10. Our examples and applications are based upon an interpreter; `clisp` has a compiler (as do most Lisps).

9.1.4 Programs and Data Are Lists

Note that every one of the following examples involves a *list*. Some lists are function definitions, some are function applications, and so forth. Combinations of these Lisp expressions form programs. The basic data structure is the list. It is for this reason we cite the very important point:

In Lisp, there is no difference between programs and data.

A Lisp program is therefore Lisp data (or so-called "s-expressions"), which may be manipulated by Lisp. This makes (intentionally) self-modifying code easily possible.

9.1.5 CommonLisp (`clisp`) Installation, Testing, and Customization

All of the examples shown in this chapter are based upon `clisp`. `clisp` is a multiplatform implementation of CommonLisp. On-line sources of information and distributions are:

http://clisp.cons.org/

http://clisp.sourceforge.net/

Testing the Initial Installation

The CommonLisp specification defines a number of miscellaneous features, including functions and variables to indicate machine type and software versions. Some examples are shown in Figure 9.1. Note that the responses may vary by `clisp` version and platform.

```
lisp> (lisp-implementation-type)
"CLISP"
lisp> (machine-type)
"I686"
lisp> (software-type)
"ANSI C program"
lisp> (lisp-implementation-version)
"2.30 (released 2002-09-15) (built on localhost [127.0.0.1])"
lisp> *features*
(:clos :loop :compiler :clisp :ansi-cl :common-lisp :lisp=cl :interpreter
 :sockets :generic-streams :logical-pathnames :screen :ffi :unicode
 :base-char=character :syscalls :pc386 :unix)
```

Figure 9.1 Implementation-Related Functions.

Limited Help

clisp does not contain built-in help. However, there is a limited amount of information (which would serve as a pointer into the documentation) on various topics available via the apropos function. An example, related to lisp prompt customization, follows in clisp.

```
lisp> (apropos 'prompt-string)
prompt-string
system::prompt-string1                          function
system::prompt-string2                          function
system::prompt-string3                          function
```

Alternatives to clisp

There are a number of alternatives to clisp. Some are commercial products (e.g, see http://www.franz.com/); others, like clisp, are covered under the GNU license. This includes gcl[3] (see http://www.gnu.org/software/gcl/) and CMUCL.

9.1.6 System Access

Most development environments let you "shell out" to get OS functions. The clisp function (shell) invokes the operating system shell (Windows or Linux). exit gets you back to the Lisp interpreter from the shell.

9.1.7 Logging a Lisp Session

Recall the use of predicate protocol in Prolog for logging a session. clisp has a similar function, named dribble. Sample behavior is shown in Figure 9.2. The figure shows the session and then the log file.

```
lisp> (dribble "lisplog1.lsp")
#<string-char-file-stream #"lisplog1.lsp" @1>
lisp> (print "Hi Mom!")

"Hi Mom!"
"Hi Mom!"
lisp> (car '(a s d f))
a
lisp> (dribble)
#<closed string-char-file-stream #"lisplog1.lsp" @1>
```

Now the contents of the logged file:

```
#<string-char-file-stream #"lisplog1.lsp" @1>
lisp> (print "Hi Mom!")

"Hi Mom!"
"Hi Mom!"
lisp> (car '(a s d f))
a
lisp> (dribble)
```

Figure 9.2 Logging a Lisp Session with dribble.

---

[3]gcl is the official CommonLisp for the GNU project. It is available on eleven GNU/Linux architectures (x86, powerpc, s390, sparc, arm, alpha, ia64, hppa, m68k, mips, mipsel) and for Windows. Also noteworthy is the availability of xgcl, a Lisp interface to the X Windows system, and pargcl, an MPI extension enabling Lisp programs to run in parallel on clusters.

9.1.8 Lisp Editors

Developing and editing longer Lisp function definitions and list-based data structures often requires finding matching parentheses. Editors that facilitate this are quite useful; one such editor (noted in Chapter 1) is `vim`.[4] Details on and distributions of `vim` may be found at `http://www.vim.org`.

9.2 The Lisp Top-Level Loop (EVAL)

9.2.1 The Behavior of EVAL

In this chapter, we only consider the use of Lisp in interpreted mode. The `read-eval-print` loop (`EVAL`) evaluates what you type at the interpreter prompt (sometimes called a "form") and acts accordingly:

1. If it is an atom with a value, the value is returned.

   ```
   lisp> pi
   3.1415926535897932385L0
   ```

2. If it is a list, the `car` of the list is assumed to be the name of a function, which is then applied to the evaluation of the rest of the list elements.[5]

   ```
   lisp> (exp 1)
   2.7182817
   ```

3. If `EVAL` can't figure out what you want to do,[6] you are sent to the debugger (numerous examples follow that show this and how to recover).

   ```
   lisp> (ln (exp 1))

   *** - eval: the function ln is undefined
   1. Break lisp> abort

   lisp> (log (exp 1))
   0.99999994
   ```

   Notice in the preceding example that the `abort` command is used to recover from an error.

4. The quote (`'`) inhibits evaluation by `EVAL`, as shown in the following example. Also refer to Section 9.3.3.

   ```
   lisp> pi
   3.1415926535897932385L0
   lisp> 'pi
   pi
   lisp> (quote pi)
   pi
   ```

---

[4]Another is `emacs`.

[5]Some functions (special forms) such as `setq` inhibit evaluation of one or more of their arguments.

[6]For example, atoms with no value are entered, or function names that do not correspond to a known follow that are entered.

```
lisp> (setq tom 10)
10
lisp> (setq gary tom)
10
lisp> gary
10
lisp> (setq gary 'tom)
tom
lisp> gary
tom
lisp> (eval gary)
10
```

Figure 9.3 Simple Assignment, Evaluation, the Quote, and `eval`.

9.2.2 Reading Lisp Source

When faced with reading unfamiliar Lisp source code, the following approach is recommended:

1. Find the functions. Make sure you understand the operation of each built-in or user-defined function, including returned values and possible side effects.

2. Find the function arguments.

3. Determine the returned value.

4. Be aware of any special data (list) structures used or assumed.

5. Think like `EVAL`.

9.2.3 Functional Programming and Assignment

Unfortunately, it is necessary to introduce the (nonfunctional) idea of creating variables and giving them values, principally using `setq`. Notice that `(setq arg value)` is equivalent to `set (quote arg value)`, that is, it does not evaluate its first argument. It is critical to distinguish variable names from values, as the examples in Figure 9.3 show.

9.2.4 Comments

The ; is Lisp's comment delimiter. Everything from ; to the end of line is ignored by the `read-eval-print` loop. Comments may be included at the interpreter prompt and in Lisp source files. Many examples of the latter are shown throughout. Here is an example of comments when interacting with `EVAL`:

```
lisp> (setq a 10)        ;create variable and give it a value
10
lisp> a                  ;evaluate variable
10
lisp> (+ a 1)            ;use value of variable as function argument
11
```

```
lisp> (- 16 9)
7
lisp> (* 2 3 4 5)
120
lisp> (max (+ 5 8) (* 6 3) (- 20 1))
19
lisp> (sqrt 100)
10
lisp> (setq pi 3.14159)
3.14159
lisp> (sin pi)
2.5351817E-6
lisp> (sin (/ pi 2))
1.0
```

Figure 9.4 Lisp Math Examples.

9.2.5 Numbers and Arithmetic Functions in CommonLisp

Numbers evaluate to their numerical value. An integer is defined as a string of digits optionally preceded by + or −. A real number looks like an integer, except that it has a decimal point and optionally can be written in scientific notation. A rational looks like two integers with a / between them. Lisp supports complex numbers, which are written #c(r i) (where r is the real part and i is the imaginary part). A number is any of the preceding entities.

Arithmetic Functions in CommonLisp

CommonLisp has a rich library of mathematical functions; an example is shown in Figure 9.4.

9.2.6 Loading Source Files

Source files are loaded with the `load` function, with syntax:

```
lisp>(load "<filename>")
```

The file must be in the CommonLisp path, which includes the current directory. In Figures 9.5 and 9.6 we show an extended example of list manipulation functions and how we load Lisp source from a file.

```
;; examples using lists
;; file: list_ex.l

(setq alist '(this is a list))

(setq blist '(this (is a list)))

(setq clist '((this) is a list))

(setq dlist '((this) (is a list)))

(setq elist '(first second))
```

Figure 9.5 Sample Lisp Source (in File).

```
lisp> (load "list_ex.l")
;; Loading file list_ex.l ...
;; Loading of file list_ex.l is finished.
t
lisp> alist
(this is a list)
lisp> blist
(this (is a list))
lisp> (car alist)
this
lisp> (cdr alist)
(is a list)
lisp> (car blist)
this
lisp> (cdr blist)
((is a list))
lisp> (car clist)
(this)
lisp> (cdr clist)
(is a list)
lisp> (car dlist)
(this)
lisp> (cdr dlist)
((is a list))
lisp> elist
(first second)
lisp> (car (cdr elist))
second
lisp> (nth 0 elist)
first
lisp> (nth 1 elist)
second
lisp> (nth 2 elist)
nil
lisp> (nth 0 (cdr elist))
second
```

Figure 9.6 Results of Loading File and Sample (List) Function Evaluations.

9.3 Basic CommonLisp Building Blocks

We now refine our look at the syntax and semantics of Lisp.

9.3.1 S-expressions (or Forms) and Evaluation

In general, a *form or an s-expression* is either an atom or a list. As noted, if the s-expression is an atom, Lisp evaluates it. *Note that integers and strings evaluate to themselves.* If the s-expression is a list, the first element (the `car` of the list) is assumed to be the name of a function. The evaluated remaining list elements (the `cdr` of the list) are then passed to the function as arguments.

9.3.2 Some Special Forms

There are a number of special forms in CommonLisp that look like function calls but, strictly speaking, aren't.[7] These include control constructs such as `if` and `do`, definitions

[7]This is treated in more detail in Section 9.8.

```
lisp> (if t 5 6)
5
lisp> (if nil 5 6)
6
lisp> (if 4 5 6)
5
```

Figure 9.7 Use of Predicates and a "Mini" `if` Example.

using `defun` and `defstruct`, and binding constructs such as `let`. It probably doesn't hurt us to ignore their special significance and just look at them as if they were functions (usually with side effects).

9.3.3 Inhibiting Evaluation: The Quote

We have seen several examples of inhibiting `EVAL` in the previous examples. These involved the special form called the `quote`. `quote` prevents its argument from being evaluated. Note that `'a` is an abbreviation for `(quote a)`. A simple way to visualize the behavior involving the quote is that `EVAL` simply removes the quote and returns (verbatim) what is quoted.

9.3.4 Special Symbols

There are two special symbols, `t` and `nil`. The value of `t` is defined always to be `t`, and the value of `nil` is defined always to be `nil`. Symbols like `t` and `nil` are called self-evaluating symbols, because they evaluate to themselves. There is a whole class of self-evaluating symbols called keywords; any symbol whose name starts with a colon is a keyword.

Lisp uses `t` and `nil` in conjunction with predicates to represent true and false. An example using the `if` statement (described later) is shown in Figure 9.7.

9.3.5 Predicates

The example of Figure 9.7 illustrates the use of predicates in Lisp and introduces an important concept: `nil` *means false, and anything else is non-*`nil`. Predicate behavior is determined using `nil` and non-`nil`. Note that there is a significant distinction between logical `true` and non-`nil`.

9.3.6 Arrays and Strings

Arrays

The function `make-array` creates an array. The `aref` function (along with `setf`) is used to access array elements. All elements of an array are initially set to `nil`. For example:

```
lisp> (make-array '(3 3))
#2a((nil nil nil) (nil nil nil) (nil nil nil))
lisp> (aref * 1 1)
nil
lisp> (make-array 4)        ;1D arrays don't need the extra parens
#(nil nil nil nil)
```

Array indices always start at 0. Further array examples follow.

```
lisp> (setf first-array (make-array '(2 2) :initial-contents
'((1 2) (3 4)) ))
#2A((1 2) (3 4))
lisp> first-array
#2A((1 2) (3 4))
lisp> (aref first-array 1 1)
4
lisp> (array-element-type first-array)
t
lisp> (array-rank first-array)
2
lisp> (array-dimensions first-array)
(2 2)
lisp> (setf (aref first-array 1 1) nil)
nil
lisp> (setf (aref first-array 0 0) t)
t
lisp> first-array
#2A((t 2) (3 nil))
```

Strings and Sequence Functions

In CommonLisp, a string is displayed as a sequence of characters between double quotes, that is, "   ". Internally, Lisp represents a string as a specialized vector (or one-dimensional array) whose elements are characters. In Lisp notation, `#\c` denotes the character "c". Sample functions used with strings follow:

```
lisp> (concatenate 'string "abcd" "efg")
"abcdefg"
lisp> (char "abc" 1)
#\b
lisp> (aref "abc" 1)
#\b
lisp> (stringp '(1 2 3))
nil
lisp> (stringp "123")
t
```

The so-called generic-sequence functions operate on strings. In addition to those used in the previous examples, this set of functions includes **`reverse`**, **`map`**, **`remove`**, **`length`**, **`position`**, **`substitute`**, and **`replace`**. For example, **`concatenate`** (shown in the previous example) may be used with other types of sequences, as shown in the following example:

```
lisp> (concatenate 'string '(#\a #\b) '(#\c))
"abc"
lisp> (concatenate 'list "abc" "de")
(#\a #\b #\c #\d #\e)
lisp> (concatenate 'vector '#(3 3 3) '#(3 3 3))
#(3 3 3 3 3 3)
```

As another example, consider

```
(remove item sequence)
```

which returns a copy of `sequence` from which all elements `eql` to `item` have been removed, that is,

```
lisp> (remove #\a "asdfasdf")
"sdfsdf"
```

Similarly, `position` shows the index of a character in the string (or array); for example:

```
lisp> (position #\s "asdf")
1
lisp> (position #\f "asdf")
3
```

9.3.7 Functions

Many of the functions that follow have been introduced, some implicitly.

Basic Function Groups

1. Assignment: (`setf, setq, defvar`).
2. List manipulation (`car, cdr, nth, cons, append, assoc`).
3. Sequence (string and array) manipulation (`concatenate, subseq, substitute, position`).
4. Predicates (evaluate and return "non-`nil`" or `nil`).
5. Control/branching (`cond, if`).
6. Sequential evaluation and iteration (`let, do, mapcar`).
7. I/O (`read, print, load`).
8. Math and logical functions (`and, or, *, +`).
9. Function defining functions (`defun`).
10. Tracing/debugging/system calls (`trace`).

Function Application Example

```
lisp> (+ 3 4 5 6)  ; the + function takes any number of arguments
18

lisp> (+ (* 3 4) (- 5 6) (+ (* 2 3) 4)) ; note the expression structure
21
```

Defining Common Lisp Functions: `defun`

Lisp would not be of much use (or at least not extendible) if we could not define our own functions. `defun` is the built-in Lisp function used for this purpose. From the point of view of functional programming, we could view **defun** as itself a function[8] that defines functions. Let's define a function using **defun**:

```
lisp> (defun first-one (x)
     (car x)
             )
first-one
```

Notice the value returned by **defun**. Now let's try it out:

```
lisp>(setq a '(my dog has fleas))

lisp> (first-one a)
my

lisp> (first-one (cdr a))
dog
```

Comment Syntax and Documentation Strings

A relatively complicated function definition may only make sense to the original programmer. In addition to using comments, we can enhance a function definition with an optional documentation string, as shown in the following example:

```
lisp> (defun first-one (x)
 "this is our first function
it returns the car of a list"
(car x))
first-one

lisp> (documentation 'first-one 'function)
"this is our first function
it returns the car of a list"
```

Now let's try defining the function and loading it from a file. Here's the file:

```
;; file: firstone.l
;; function first-one:
;;   args: a list
;;   returns: the car of the list
;;   side effects: none

(defun first-one (x)
"  function definition
   file: firstone.l
   revised
   use: (first-one arg)
   arguments: a list
   returns: the car of the list
   side effects: none "
(car x))
```

Now let's load it and use it. Notice that the following example shows that Lisp uses different namespaces for functions and variables.

[8]With this view, what does it return and what are the side effects?

```
lisp> (load 'firstone.l)
;; Loading file FIRSTONE.L ...
;; Loading of file FIRSTONE.L is finished.
T

lisp> (documentation 'first-one 'function)
"  function definition
   file: firstone.l
   revised
   use: (first-one arg)
   arguments: a list
   returns: the car of the list
   side effects: none "

lisp> (first-one '(anybody for windsurfing?))
anybody

lisp> (setq first-one '(lets go windsurfing))
(lets go windsurfing)

lisp> (first-one first-one)
lets
```

Another Example

Here's an even simpler example:

```
lisp> (defun a (b)
"just return (evaluated) b"
b)
a

lisp> (a '(a b c d))
(a b c d)

lisp> (documentation 'a 'function)
"just return (evaluated) b"
```

Optional Function Arguments, Default Values, and &rest

Functions may be designed with optional arguments. An argument after the parameter `&optional` is optional, as shown in the following example:

```
lisp> (defun optarg (x &optional y) (if y y x))
optarg
lisp> (optarg 1)
1
lisp> (optarg 1 2)
2
```

Default Values

A function may be designed to accept any number of arguments[9] by ending its argument list with an `&rest` parameter. When the function is invoked, all arguments beyond

[9]And many built-in Lisp functions are so designed.

the "non-rest" arguments are converted into a list, which is then bound to the **&rest** parameter. This is shown in the following examples.

```
lisp> (defun restall (x &rest y) (list x y))
restall
lisp> (restall 'a)
(a nil)
lisp> (restall 'a 'b 'c)
(a (b c))
lisp> (defun optargdef (&optional (x 1) (y 2)) (+ x y))
optargdef
lisp> (optargdef)
3
lisp> (optargdef 5)
7
lisp> (optargdef 5 10)
15
```

9.3.8 Variables

We create a variable and give it a value with function `setq`.

```
lisp> (setq a '(my dog has fleas))
(my dog has fleas)

lisp> a
(my dog has fleas)
```

Setf

In the `setf` form, the first argument defines a *place* (in memory). The second argument is evaluated, and `setf` stores the resulting value in the defined memory location. `setf` *is the only way to set the fields of a structure or the elements of an array.* For example,

```
lisp> (setq a (make-array 3))
#(NIL NIL NIL)
lisp> (aref a 1)
NIL
lisp> (setf (aref a 1) 3)
3
lisp> a
#(NIL 3 NIL)
lisp> (aref a 1)
3
```

Global Variables and Documentation

By *convention* global variables begin and end with the character `*`. Instead of using `setq`, global variables are handled by `defvar`, as shown.

```
lisp> (defvar *alpha-list* '(a b c d e f)
"the first 6 alphabetical characters as a list")
*alpha-list*

lisp> *alpha-list*
(a b c d e f)
```

```
lisp> (documentation '*alpha-list* 'variable)
"the first 6 alphabetical characters as a list"

"the first 6 alphabetical characters as a list"
```

9.4 Basic List Manipulation

9.4.1 car and cdr

At this point, functions to manipulate lists are introduced. The two essential list manipulation functions are `car` and `cdr`. Their use and returned values are easily shown by example.

```
lisp> (setq a '(my dog has fleas))
(my dog has fleas)
lisp> (car a)
my
lisp> (cdr a)
(dog has fleas)
```

9.4.2 The cons Concept

A `cons` is a two-field structure. Usually[10] a `cons` involves a list as the second argument.

```
lisp> (cons 'a 'b)
(a . b)
lisp> (cons 'a (list 'b))
(a b)
lisp> (cons 'a '( b c d))
(a b c d)
lisp> (setq e (cons 'a '( b c d)))
(a b c d)
lisp> (car e)
a
lisp> (cdr e)
(b c d)
```

Notice the "inverse" behavior of `cons` and `car` and `cdr`.

9.4.3 List Manipulation Functions and Examples

append

`append` expects each argument to be a list and returns a (linear) list that is the concatenation of its arguments. For example:

```
lisp>(append '(a b c) '(d e f) '() '(g)) => (a b c d e f g)
```

[10] The exception is most often due to a programming error.

list

`list` returns a list of its arguments. `list` and `cons` are quite different. For example:

```
lisp> (setq newlist '(n1 n2 n3))
(n1 n2 n3)
lisp> (setq oldlist '(o1 o2 o3 o4))
(o1 o2 o3 o4)
lisp> (list newlist oldlist)
((n1 n2 n3) (o1 o2 o3 o4))
lisp> (length oldlist)
4
lisp> (length newlist)
3
lisp> (length (list newlist oldlist))
2
lisp> (cons newlist oldlist)
((n1 n2 n3) o1 o2 o3 o4)
lisp> (length (cons newlist oldlist))
5
```

cons and list Distinctions in CommonLisp

The following examples further show the difference between a `cons` cell and a (true) `list`.

```
lisp> (equal nil ())
t
lisp> (setq a-cons '( a b . (c d)))
(a b c d)
lisp> (car a-cons)
a
lisp> (cdr a-cons)
(b c d)
lisp> (cdr (cdr a-cons))
(c d)
lisp> (listp a-cons)
t
;; Now a cons-

lisp> (setq a-cons2 '(a . b))
(a . b)
lisp> (listp a-cons2)
t
lisp> (car a-cons2)
a
lisp> (cdr a-cons2)
b
lisp> a-cons
(a b c d)
lisp> (cdr (cdr (cdr (cdr a-cons))))
nil
lisp> (cdr (cdr (cdr (cdr a-cons2))))

*** - cdr: b is not a list
1. Break> abort
lisp> (cons 'a 'b)
(a . b)
lisp> (cons 'a '(b))
```

```
(a b)
lisp> (cons 'a (list 'b))
(a b)
lisp> (cons 'a '(b . nil))
(a b)
lisp> (list-length '(a b))
2
lisp> (list-length '(a . b))

*** - list-length: A true list must not end with b
1. Break> abort
```

assoc and Association Lists

```
 ; sample use of assoc function
     ; prelude to matching
     ; file assoc-ex2.l

     (setq rjs-assoc-list '(
          (buoyancy-compensator tusa)
          (regulator   dacor)
          (guages suunto)
          (knife performance)
          (mask seaquest)
          (wetsuit oneil)
                                 ))
```

A sample operation follows.

```
lisp> (assoc 'mask rjs-assoc-list)
(mask seaquest)
lisp> (assoc 'regulator rjs-assoc-list)
(regulator dacor)
lisp> (assoc 'speargun rjs-assoc-list)
nil
```

Some Other Family Members

```
lisp> (member 'a '(f g h a s d))
(a s d)

lisp> (find 'a '(f g h a s d))
a

lisp> (count 'a '(f g h a s d))
1

lisp> (position 'a '(f g h a s d))
3

lisp> (append (list 'z) '(f g h a s d))
(z f g h a s d)

lisp> (append '(f g h a s d) (list 'z))
(f g h a s d z)

lisp> (reverse '(f g h a s d))
(d s a h g f)
```

Other Useful List Functions

```
lisp> (reverse '(1 2 3))           ;reverse the elements of a list
(3 2 1)
lisp> (find 'a '(b d a c))         ;another way to do list membership
a
lisp> (intersection '(a b c) '(b))  ;set intersection
(b)
```

9.4.4 Special Definitions (Empty List)

For reasons that will become more apparent in dealing with recursive operations on lists, the `car` and `cdr` of `nil` are defined to be `nil`.

9.5 Lisp Booleans and Conditionals

9.5.1 Branching in Lisp

Recall the notion of implementing a function in Lisp from Section 8.3. Inputs yield returned values. We may need tests to determine how the output is produced, as a function of the value of the input. This statement may at first sound silly, given that just about any useful function has a returned value that depends upon the input. The major distinction here is that entirely different function application branches may be selected. In this section, we explore Lisp's functions/macros that permit "branching," in the sense that control over alternative function applications or returned values is provided.

Branching is controlled by predicates. Lisp predicate functions rely on tests of whether something is `nil` or not (`nil`). In the sense of logic,[11] Lisp provides the special symbol `nil` to mean false. Anything other than `nil` means "not `nil`." Not `nil` does not imply true. In Lisp, the self-evaluating symbol `t` indicates true.

The two major functions/macros of interest are `cond` and `if`. They facilitate building much more complex functions. Note that regardless of whether we call them constructs, macros, or functions,[12] they have arguments, return values, and may have side effects.

9.5.2 Logical Functions

Lisp provides a standard set of logical functions, including `and`, `or`, and `not`. The functions `and` and `or` employ lazy evaluation—`and` does not evaluate any arguments to the right of the first one that evaluates to `nil`, whereas `or` does not evaluate any arguments to the right of the first one that evaluates to `t`.

```
lisp> (and t 13 "himom")
"himom"
lisp> (and pi (print "hi mom"))

"hi mom"
"hi mom"
lisp> (and nil pi (print "hi mom"))
nil
```

[11] Note that `nil` also denotes the empty list.

[12] The reference manual can help sort this out.

9.5.3 The All-Important cond

Programmers familiar with the Pascal **case** statement or C's **switch** should find the **cond** construct in Lisp familiar. Consider a **cond** with the typical form:

```
(cond
   (<pred1> <expr1>)
   (<pred2> <expr2>)
   (<pred3> <expr3>)
         .
         .
         .
   (<predn> <exprn>)
   )
```

Many functions are written with this form. Each argument to the **cond** is a list of the form **(<predi> <expri>)**. The semantics are relatively simple—this cond form *tests its arguments sequentially* and finds the first argument whose **<predi>** evaluates to non-**nil** and then evaluates the corresponding **<expri>**, returning this evaluation as the value of the **cond**.

More generally, a **cond** consists of the symbol **cond** followed by a number of arguments, each of which is a list. The **car** of each argument to the **cond** is considered a predicate. The **cond** form *tests its arguments sequentially* and finds the first argument whose predicate (i.e., **car**) evaluates to non-**nil**, and then evaluates each of the remaining elements of this argument list, returning the result of the last evaluation. Thus a more general **cond** structure is:

```
(cond
   (<predi> <expr1i> <expr2i> <expr3i> . . . <exprqi>)
   (<predj> <expr1j> <expr2j> <expr3j> . . . <exprpj>)
   .
   .
   .
   )
```

That is, if **<predi>** evaluates to non-**nil**, **<expr1i> <expr2i> <expr3i> . . .<exprqi>** are sequentially evaluated and the value returned by the **cond** is the value of **<exprqi>**. Notice these points:

1. This form allows a **cond** to implement sequential evaluation, as indicated in the preceding example.

2. In this case, the only role of the evaluations **<expr1i> <expr2i> <expr3i> . . .** is for side effects. Typically these are assignments, printing, input, and so on.

cond Examples

Most often, **cond** is found in the body of a function. However, for illustration, we show a few **cond** examples:

```
lisp> (setq my-list '(1 2 3))
(1 2 3)
lisp> (cond ((equal (car my-list) 2) (cdr my-list)) (t (car my-list)))
1
```

```
lisp> (setq my-list '(2 1 3))
(2 1 3)
lisp> (cond ((equal (car my-list) 2) (cdr my-list)) (t (car my-list)))
(1 3)
```

Note that when a `cond` "runs out of arguments" (i.e., none of the predicates evaluate to non-`nil`), `nil` is returned. However, good programming practice suggests that the behavior of the `cond` accommodate all the cases that are likely to occur. For this reason, it is typical to add a final argument with a non-`nil` predicate to the `cond` indicating a "bailout," "drop-thru," or default returned value.[13]

9.5.4 Recursion

Recursion is both natural and typical in functional programming. *Direct recursion* occurs when the body of a function definition invokes the function itself (with modified arguments). A number of examples follow.

Recursion/cond (Factorial) Example

The well-known recursive definition of the factorial function lends itself to direct implementation in functional programming, as shown in the following example.

Source File

```
;; function: factorial
;; file: factorial.l
;; input: (n) integer >= 1 (LAE to fix this limitation)
;; factorial(n)
;; side effects: none

(defun factorial (n)
(cond
   ((equal n 1) 1)
   (t (* n (factorial (- n 1)))))
)
```

Results A sample use follows, along with an illustration of the utility of the `trace` function.

```
lisp> (load ''factorial.l'')
;; Loading file factorial.l ...
;; Loaded file factorial.l
t
lisp> (factorial 4)
24
lisp> (trace factorial)
;; Tracing function factorial.
(factorial)
lisp> (factorial 3)

1. Trace: (factorial '3)
2. Trace: (factorial '2)
3. Trace: (factorial '1)
```

[13]Other than nil.

```
3. Trace: factorial ==> 1
2. Trace: factorial ==> 2
1. Trace: factorial ==> 6
6
```

Recursion Example with a Trace

Here is a second example of a file containing a recursive function, along with a trace of the function use:

```
; FILE NAME: recur.l
; CONTENT: recursive function example

(setq friends '(D1 D2 D3))

; FUNCTION:

; Name:           recur
; Input:          list of atoms
; Returned Value: a list of the last element of input list
; Side Effects:   none

(defun recur (alist)
  (cond
    ( (not (null (cdr alist)))
      (recur (cdr alist)) )
    ( t alist ) ) )
```

```
Common LISP session for "recur.l".


> (load "recur.l")
;;; Loading source file "recur.fcl"

> friends
(D1 D2 D3)

> (recur friends)
(D3)

> (trace recur)
(RECUR)

> (recur friends)
1 Enter RECUR (D1 D2 D3)
| 2 Enter RECUR (D2 D3)
|   3 Enter RECUR (D3)
|   3 Exit RECUR (D3)
| 2 Exit RECUR (D3)
1 Exit RECUR (D3)
(D3)

> (abort)
```

List Membership via Recursion

Another example of using `cond` and recursion through the definition of the list-membership function[14] follows:

```
; function: member2
; input:    item - list element
;           alist - list
; output:   sublist with item as car
;                  - if item in alist
;           nil - otherwise
; note:     uses "equal" to test

(defun member2 (item alist)
    (cond
       ((null alist) nil)
       ((equal item (car alist)) alist)
       (t (member2 item (cdr alist)))))
```

A sample use of the `member2` function follows:

```
lisp> (member2 'has '(my dog has fleas))
(has fleas)
lisp> (member2 'brains '(my dog has fleas))
nil
```

Recursive List Reversal

Function Design Consider the definition of a CommonLisp function for list element reversal. The desired functionality follows:

$$(1\ 2\ 3\ 4\ 5) \Rightarrow (5\ 4\ 3\ 2\ 1)$$

We approach the recursive design of this function by looking at three examples of the desired behavior:

$$(1) \Rightarrow (1)$$
$$(1\ 2) \Rightarrow (2\ 1)$$
$$(1\ 2\ 3 \Rightarrow ((reverse(2\ 3)\ 1) \Rightarrow (3\ 2\ 1)$$

Notice from the first case, if the `cdr` of the list is empty, the list is either a single element or itself empty. In this case, the reverse of the list is the list itself. In the second case, we form the returned value by appending the `cdr` of the list to a list comprised of the `car` of the list. Finally, in the third example, we recursively reverse the `cdr` of the list and append this to the list consisting of the `car` of the input list. This reasoning leads to the following function definition.

`reverse2` Function Definition

```
;; example of recursion
;; list reversal
;; file: reverse2.l
```

[14] This is built-in as `member`.

```
(defun reverse2 (alist)
 (cond
    ((null (cdr alist)) alist)
    (t (append (reverse2 (cdr alist)) (list (car alist))))
))
```

Sample Use

```
lisp> (reverse2 '(1))
(1)
lisp> (reverse2 '(1 2 3))
(3 2 1)
lisp> (trace reverse2)
;; Tracing function reverse2.
(reverse2)
lisp> (reverse2 '(1 2 3))

1. Trace: (reverse2 '(1 2 3))
2. Trace: (reverse2 '(2 3))
3. Trace: (reverse2 '(3))
3. Trace: reverse2 ==> (3)
2. Trace: reverse2 ==> (3 2)
1. Trace: reverse2 ==> (3 2 1)
(3 2 1)
```

9.5.5 case

The Lisp `case` statement is like a C `switch` statement, and is illustrated as follows:

```
lisp> (setq test 'ok)
ok
lisp> (case test
        (nil 10)
        (( a b) -10)
        (ok "the input was ok")
        (otherwise -1)
      )
"the input was ok"
```

The `otherwise` clause at the end is the default or bailout case, which in this example causes the `case` statement to return -1.

9.5.6 From cond to if

Many times the use of a `cond` takes the following form:

```
(cond
   (a b)
   (t c)
   )
```

Our previously developed understanding of `cond` suggests that this construct is implementing an `if-then-else` form; that is, if `a` evaluates to non-`nil`, the evaluation of `b` is returned, otherwise the evaluation of c is returned. Lisp provides the if macro/function/construct, which facilitates a clearer[15] representation of this type of a cond with the form:

```
(if a b c)
```

Thus, in the if construct (which usually expands into the previously-cited cond form), the first argument determines whether the second or third argument will be evaluated. Other examples were shown in Section 9.3.4. Two related forms are when and unless.

9.5.7 progn Forms

progn is used to implement sequential evaluation of s-expressions. It is also used frequently in an attempt to make functional programming look like imperative programming. progn executes each statement in its body and returns the value of the last evaluation. An example follows:

```
lisp> (progn
      (setq a 10)
      (setq b (+ 2 a))
      (setq c (* a b))
      )
120
```

9.5.8 The Three Faces of Equality

Many predicates tests involve equality. Lisp allows different notions of equality. Numerical equality is denoted by =. Two symbols are eq if and only if they are identical. Two copies of the same list are not eq, but they are equal. Some examples follow.

```
lisp> (eq 'a 'a)
t
lisp> (setq b 'a)
a
lisp> b
a
lisp> (eq 'a 'b)
nil
lisp> (eq 'a b)
t
lisp> (equal 'a b)
t
lisp> (= 'a b)

*** - argument to = should be a number: a
1. Break lisp> abort

lisp> (= 10 (+ 2 8))
t
lisp> (setq alist '(a s d))
(a s d)
lisp> (eq alist '(a s d))
nil
lisp> (equal alist '(a s d))
t
```

[15] To the programmer.

```
lisp> (eql 'a 'a)
t
lisp> (eql 10 10)
t
```

The `eql` predicate function is equivalent to `eq` for symbols and to `=` for numbers. The `equal` predicate is equivalent to `eql` for symbols and numbers.

9.6 Scope and Iteration in Lisp

9.6.1 Global and Local Variables

Scope

The scope of a variable defines where references to the variable may be made. Within the scope of variable v, we may assign v values or get v's value, that is, evaluate v. Outside the scope of v, it does not make sense to refer to v.

Local Variables

Variables created in the argument list to `defun` are local to the function; that is, the scope of the variable is limited to the duration of the function call. These are usually called local variables. Note also that CommonLisp does not permit function a's local variables to be used during execution of a function b, which is invoked inside function a, *unless they are passed to function b as part of the argument list to b.* The following example may help.

```
lisp> (defun scopex (v) (car v))
scopex
lisp> (scopex '(y i p))
y
lisp> v

*** - EVAL: variable v has no value
1. Break lisp> abort
```

Variables that are not local are considered global, that is, their scope is not restricted to any single function in the Lisp source. Usually `setq` is involved. Another example may help.

```
lisp> (defun scopex2 (v) (setq g (car v)))
scopex2
lisp> g

*** - EVAL: variable g has no value
1. Break lisp> abort

lisp> (scopex2 '(y i p))
y
lisp> g
y
```

9.6.2 `let` and Scope

Using `setq` on an undeclared variable inside a function makes it a global variable, which is generally considered undesirable. A global variable has dynamic scoping: once a value has been assigned to a dynamically scoped variable, every evaluation of that variable returns that value until another value is assigned to the same variable. In Lisp, dynamically scoped global variables should be declared using the `defvar` form.

Special form `let` is used to enable serial evaluation and declare local variables. Another viewpoint is that `let` provides lexical scoping. For example, C is lexically scoped.

The structure of `let` is:

```
(let  (<var-binding-pairs>) <body>)
```

where `<var-binding-pairs>` is a set of lists, each of the form:

```
(var1 value1)
(var2 value2)
...
(var-n value-n)
```

and `<body>` is a sequence of s-expressions to be sequentially evaluated. A variable declaration can be either a variable name or a list of variable name and initial value. The body is a sequence of s-expressions that are serially evaluated. `let` returns the value of the last form in the body of code.

9.6.3 CommonLisp `print` and Examples with `let`

Here's an example of both `print` and `let`:

```
> (defun my_let () ;no local vars or initialization
   (let ((var1 1) (var2 2)) ;local vars: var1=1, var2=2
     (print 'var1=) (print var1) (terpri)
     (print 'var2=) (print var2) (terpri)
     (print "this is the value of print,
                 and the value let returns")
        ) ;let
        ) ;defun
MY_LET
```

Here's an example of their use:

```
lisp> (my_let)

VAR1=
1

VAR2=
2

"this is the value of print, and the value let returns"
"this is the value of print, and the value let returns"
```

9.6.4 Iteration

As noted, *recursion is natural in functional programming*; iteration is not. However, Lisp provides constructs that facilitate iteration.

do

do may be viewed as an extension of let with the structure:

```
(do (<var-init-val-mod>)
    (<end-test>)
    <body> )
```

where <var-init-val-mod> is an extension of the <var-binding-pairs> structure found in let and is of the form:

```
(var1 init1 step1)
(var2 init2 step2)
...
(var-n init-n step-n)
```

The evaluation of a do is as follows:

1. (Local) variables in the (var-n init-n step-n) forms are created and initialized.

2. The (<end-test>) argument to do is evaluated; the rule here is exactly like that of an argument to cond. If the car of (<end-test>) evaluates to non-nil, the cdr of (<end-test>) is sequentially evaluated and the value of do is the value of the last evaluation.

3. If the car of (<end-test>) evaluates to nil, the s-expressions in <body> are sequentially evaluated (as in let).

4. Then the local variables are each updated according to the step-n. The process then continues in Step 2.

A do Example

```
lisp> (defun do_test (limit)
   (do ((index 1 (+ 1 index))) ;loc. var index, updated by 1
     ((equal index limit) ;here's the end-test
             (print "this is over")
              t)  ; returned value and side-effect
      (print index) ; the body of the do
     ) ;do
    ) ; defun
DO_TEST
```

The result of using this function follows.

```
lisp> (do_test 5)
1
2
3
4
"this is over"
T
```

Nonlocal exits from a do are possible (but not encouraged) using the return special form.

9.6.5 funcall, apply, and mapcar

Overview

Some functions take functions as arguments. For example:

```
lisp> (funcall '+ 3 4)
7
lisp> (apply '+ 3 4 '(3 4))
14
```

`funcall` calls its first argument on its remaining arguments. `apply` is just like `funcall`, except that its final argument should be a list; the elements of that list are treated as if they were additional arguments to a `funcall`.

Mapping of Functions Over Lists

Mapping is a type of iteration in which a function is successively applied to elements of one or more sequences. Lisp (and ML, as we will see in the next chapter) supports this capability. The result of the iteration is a sequence containing the respective results of the function applications. The CommonLisp function `mapcar` operates on successive elements of a list.[16] First the function is applied to the `car` of each list, then to the `cadr` of each list, and so on. `mapcar` is often referred to as "implied iteration."

`mapcar` Example 1

```
lisp> (setq list1 '(a b c))
(a b c)
lisp> (setq list2 '(1 2 3))
(1 2 3)
lisp> (setq list3 '("hey" "joe" "where"))
("hey" "joe" "where")
lisp> (setq big-list (list list1 list2 list3))
((a b c) (1 2 3) ("hey" "joe" "where"))
lisp> (mapcar 'cdr big-list)
((b c) (2 3) ("joe" "where"))
```

`mapcar` Example 2

```
lisp> (defun addtwo (x) (+ 2 x))
addtwo
lisp> (addtwo 3)
5
lisp> (setq somelist '( 1 2 3 4 5))
(1 2 3 4 5)
lisp> (addtwo somelist)

*** - +: (1 2 3 4 5) is not a number
1. Break lisp> abort

lisp> (mapcar 'addtwo somelist)
(3 4 5 6 7)
```

[16] There is a broader definition that allows operation on multiple lists.

9.7 I/O in CommonLisp

9.7.1 print and Printing Control

The variable ***print-case*** controls the case of the display. Some examples follow.

```
lisp> *print-case*
:UPCASE
lisp> (setq a-list '( a s d f))
(A S D F)
lisp> a-list
(A S D F)
lisp> (setq *print-case* :downcase)
:downcase
lisp> a-list
(a s d f)
lisp> (setq *print-case* :capitalize)
:Capitalize
lisp> '(this was the input list)
(This Was The Input List)
```

9.7.2 The Concept of Streams

A **stream** is a channel for input and output. CommonLisp has predefined streams for standard output and standard input. These are used as the defaults if stream name arguments are omitted in I/O functions. You can look at these defaults via predefined variables, as shown:

```
lisp> *standard-input*
#<io synonym-stream *terminal-io*>
lisp> *standard-output*
#<io synonym-stream *terminal-io*>
```

9.7.3 A Family of Output Functions

The basic printing functions are `print` and `prin1`. The function `terpri` is used for formatting.

Prototypes

```
(prin1 object &optional output-stream)
(print object &optional output-stream)
```

`prin1` outputs the printed representation of object to output-stream and returns the object as its value. `print` (used in many examples in this chapter) is similar to `prin1` except that the printed representation of object is preceded by a newline and followed by a space. Similarly, `print` returns object. Formatted output is possible with the function `format`.

9.7.4 Formatted Printing

`format` allows more formatted output. For example:

```
lisp> (format t "An atom: ~S~%and a list: ~S~%and an integer: ~D~%" nil (list 'a) 6)
An atom: nil
and a list: (a)
and an integer: 6
nil
```

The first argument to format is either `t`, `nil`, or a stream. `t` specifies the output should be sent to the terminal. `nil` means not to print anything but to return a string containing the output (which would then be used by another function). The second argument is a formatting template, which is a string optionally containing formatting directives. All remaining arguments are referred to by the formatting directives. Lisp will replace the directives with some appropriate characters based on the arguments to which they refer, and then print the resulting string.

Returned Value from `format`

`format` always returns `nil` unless its first argument is `nil`, in which case it prints nothing and returns the produced string.

There are three different directives in the preceding example: `~S`, `~D`, and `~%`. The first one accepts any Lisp object and is replaced by a printed representation of that object (the same representation produced by print). The second one accepts only integers. The third one does not refer to an argument, but is replaced by a carriage return. The formatting directive `~~` is replaced by a single `~`.

Another simple example follows.

```
lisp> (setq *facts* '(a b c))
(a b c)
lisp> (setq new-fact 'd)
d
lisp> (format t
     "~%~%fact ~S is added to *facts* => ~%     the new fact list is ~S~%"
         new-fact
         (setq *facts* (append *facts* (list new-fact))))


fact d is added to *facts* =>
     the new fact list is (a b c d)
nil
```

9.7.5 The Function `read`

`read` reads one data object from the standard input and returns this as the value of `read`. Optional parameters are available. Examples are:

```
lisp> (read) ; then type CR and 'hi'
hi ; then type CR
hi ; value returned by read
lisp> (read) ; then type CR and the list
(this is what read sees) ; then type CR
(this is what read sees) ; value returned by read
```

9.7.6 Using `read` in Functions

A sample function that incorporates `read` follows.

```
lisp> (defun a-reading-fn2 ()
    (let ((what-was-read))
```

```
        (print "type in something, then CR => ")
        (setq what-was-read (read))
        (print what-was-read)
        t)
)
a-reading-fn2
lisp> (a-reading-fn2)

"type in something, then CR => " "Hi Mom"

"Hi Mom"
t
lisp> (a-reading-fn2)

"type in something, then CR => " (Hi Mom)

(hi mom)
t
```

9.8 CommonLisp Macros

9.8.1 The General Idea of Macros

Many languages implement the notion of a macro, that is, a fragment of code that is later replaced by something else.

An Example: C's `#define`

Macros are commonly used in C and (to a lesser extent) C++. The C preprocessor serves as the macro processor and implements the substitutions.

In C the use of macros is relatively simple and based upon simple string substitution. The `#define` directive is used with the syntax:

```
#define macro-name repl-string
```

to replace `macro-name` with `repl-string`. C has numerous tests, often applied in the header files of large projects, to see if a macro with a particular name exists.

Macros in C can also take arguments. This leads to macros appearing like functions. Many times C programs use macro substitutions instead of function definitions and use. Although this may appear to yield speed advantages (because no function overhead is required), the actual code may become bloated in size due to the (often) duplicated macro code.

9.8.2 Macros in CommonLisp

`defmacro`

CommonLisp provides `defmacro`, the macro-defining macro (i.e., it is a macro itself) that handles processing of the macro form. `defmacro` has essentially the same syntax as defun: `name` is the symbol whose macro definition we are creating, `lambda-list` is similar in form to the lambda-list used in `defun`, and the body of the macro is considered to be an "expander" function that is applied to the *unevaluated* arguments to the macro.

Macro Expansion

When a macro is invoked, the macro call consists of passing the expander function, the macro body, and the list of (unevaluated) argument forms to `apply`.

Macro Arguments Are Not Evaluated

CommonLisp macros provide a very powerful and flexible method of extending Lisp syntax. We are comfortable with the typical CommonLisp function interface—when the function is invoked, arguments are evaluated and passed to the body of the function to return a value. However, there are times where it is desirable to have functions that do not evaluate their arguments. `defmacro` can help here.

Macros in CommonLisp can do something that functions cannot: they can control when the arguments get evaluated. Recall that functions evaluate all of their arguments before entering the body of the function. This is probably best seen by example.

Many Macros Are Built-in

In fact, many CommonLisp constructs (which we have been looking at, somewhat incorrectly, as "functions") are in fact macros that expand into other CommonLisp code.

9.8.3 Simple CommonLisp Macro Examples

The following examples may help to explain the use of macros and the differences between macros and functions.

First, here's a macro that looks like a function:

```
lisp> (defmacro cube (x) (* x x x))
cube
lisp> (cube 3)
27
lisp> (macroexpand '(cube 3))
27 ;
t
```

Here's more of the macro flavor:

```
lisp> (defmacro cube2 (x) '(* x x x))
cube2
lisp> (cube2 3)

*** - EVAL: variable x has no value
1. Break lisp> abort

lisp> (macroexpand '(cube2 (x)))
(* x x x) ;
t
```

Now look at the difference between a function (`multf`) and a macro (`multm`):

```
lisp> (defmacro multm (a) (* (car a) (cadr a)))
multm
lisp> (multm (3 4))
12
```

```
lisp> (defun multf (a) (* (car a) (cadr a)))
multf
lisp> (multf (3 4))

*** - eval: 3 is not a function name
1. Break lisp> abort
lisp> (multf '(3 4))
12
```

9.9 CommonLisp Programming Conventions

General CommonLisp programming style rules include:

1. Design relatively short functions, where each function provides a single, well-defined operation. Small functions are much easier to read, write, test, debug, and understand than functions whose definition extends over multiple pages.

2. Use descriptive variable and function names.

3. Use documentation strings, where appropriate. In function definitions and the corresponding source file, it is useful to include:

   - The objective of the function
   - Inputs and outputs
   - Side effects
   - Programmer name and date/time of last edit

4. *Don't try to program with an imperative style in Lisp.*

5. Use indentation to show the structure of your definitions.

6. Use whitespace appropriately—for example, to separate distinct code segments.

   ```
   GOOD:
         (defun ece442 (x y)
           (let ((z (+ x y 10)))
             (* z z)))

   BAD:
         (defun ece442 (x y)(let((z(+ x y 10)))(* z z)))
   ```

   Although `EVAL` doesn't care which form is used, most programmers find the first example easier to read than the second.

7. Where possible, use `cond` or `case` instead of nested `if` constructs. *Be sure to check for unreachable cases.*

8. By convention, the names of special (global) variables begin and end with an asterisk (*).

9.10 Function (Program) Design, Implementation, and Correctness

9.10.1 Motivation

Much has been studied concerning program correctness. This example provides interesting (recursive) function design. It could probably be done iteratively in most imperative languages. Consider programming the function a^b. Specifically, consider the following recursive decomposition:

$$a^b = \begin{cases} 1 & \text{if } b = 0 \\ a^{b/2}a^{b/2} & \text{if } b \text{ is even} \\ aa^{b-1} & \text{if } b \text{ is odd} \end{cases}$$

A CommonLisp implementation is shown next, followed by some examples and a discussion about "correctness."

CommonLisp Function Definition Source

```
;; file: expr1-cond.l
;; a to the b
;; no side effects

(defun expr (a b)
(cond ((zerop b) 1)
      ((evenp b) (expr (* a a) (/ b 2)))
      (t (* a (expr a (- b 1))))
))
```

Function Application Examples

```
lisp> (expr 2 3)
8
lisp> (expr 3 2)
9
lisp> (expr 3 0)
1
lisp> (trace expr)
;; Tracing function expr.
(expr)
lisp> (expr 2 3)

1. Trace: (expr '2 '3)
2. Trace: (expr '2 '2)
3. Trace: (expr '4 '1)
4. Trace: (expr '4 '0)
4. Trace: expr ==> 1
3. Trace: expr ==> 4
2. Trace: expr ==> 4
1. Trace: expr ==> 8
8
lisp> (expr 3 2)

1. Trace: (expr '3 '2)
2. Trace: (expr '9 '1)
3. Trace: (expr '9 '0)
3. Trace: expr ==> 1
```

```
2. Trace: expr ==> 9
1. Trace: expr ==> 9
9
lisp> (expr 3 0)

1. Trace: (expr '3 '0)
1. Trace: expr ==> 1
1
```

9.10.2 Proving Correctness

Correctness of programs in imperative languages is difficult to prove because:

- execution depends on the contents of each memory cell (each variable).
- loops must be mentally executed.
- the progress of the computation is measured by snapshots of the state of the computer after every instruction.

Programs in functional languages are much easier to evaluate concerning correctness, especially when referential transparency holds, because *only those values immediately involved in a function application need be considered*. Programs defined as recursive functions usually can be proved correct by an induction proof. An example follows.

9.10.3 Example Proof

```
(defun expr (a b)
(if (zerop b) 1
        (if (evenp b) (expr (* a a) (/ b 2))
              (* a (expr a (- b 1))))))
```

- Precondition: $b \geq 0$
- Postcondition: `(expr a b)` $= a^b$
- Proof by induction on b

9.11 Extended CommonLisp Design Example: Implementing and Training a Single Artificial Neural Unit

9.11.1 Problem Overview

The topic of artificial neural networks is both important and complex (Schalkoff, 1997). In this section, we show the straightforward design using a purely functional paradigm for the implementation of a single unit. This example is continued in the following chapter using SML.

The unit is trained using gradient descent; the training set indicates a two-bit D/A converter is desired. Both cases of a unit with and without a bias input are considered. Thus, the neuron will "learn" to be a two-bit D/A converter.

9.11.2 Design Constraints

The most important constraint in this problem (other than the obvious constraint that functions must return the correct values) is that *functions must not have side effects.*[17]

[17] An exception is in the squashing function, wherein an error message is printed. This is easily removed.

In addition, functions that facilitate the creation and use of local variables and/or iteration are not used to give readers a feel for "pure" functional approaches. Recursion is freely used where necessary. Furthermore, the unit has an *arbitrary* number of inputs and (equal) number of weights. Note that this purely recursive implementation has practical limitations; this is explored in the problems.

9.11.3 Review of the Unit Equations, Training Algorithm, and Nomenclature

The following are defined:

The unit input (vector), $\underline{i}$, is denoted

$$\begin{pmatrix} i_1 \\ i_2 \\ \vdots \\ i_d \end{pmatrix}$$

$o = f(net)$ corresponding unit output or response using squashing function f,

The unit weight vector is given by:

$$\underline{w} = \begin{pmatrix} w_1 \\ w_2 \\ \vdots \\ w_d \end{pmatrix}$$

t is the desired (or target) unit output, and

$net = \Sigma_j i_j w_j$ is the unit net activation.

Activation functions are sigmoid, linear, and `tanh`:

Sigmoid

$$o = \frac{1}{1 + e^{-net}} \tag{9.1}$$

Linear

$$o = net \tag{9.2}$$

`tanh` Built-in in CommonLisp.
The unit inputs and weights are denoted by lists in CommonLisp.
The training set is defined as:

$$H = \{(\underline{i}^p, t^p)\} \; p = 1, 2, \dots, n \tag{9.3}$$

Training of the ith weight is accomplished using:

$$w_i^{n+1} = w_i^n - \rho(o - t)o(1 - o)i_i \tag{9.4}$$

or

$$w_i^{n+1} = w_i^n + \rho\delta i_i \tag{9.5}$$

where

$$\delta = (t - o)o(1 - o) \tag{9.6}$$

Training is pattern-by-pattern over H. After each input has been used to adjust the unit weights (see Equation 9.4), these weights are the new unit weights and used in subsequent training. Two solutions (with assessment) are desired: with and without unit bias. Here are the respective training sets:

```
lisp> H
(((0.0 0.0) 0.25) ((0.0 1.0) 0.5) ((1.0 0.0) 0.75) ((1.0 1.0) 1.0))
lisp> HBias
(((0.0 0.0 1.0) 0.25) ((0.0 1.0 1.0) 0.5) ((1.0 0.0 1.0) 0.75)
 ((1.0 1.0 1.0) 1.0))
```

Initial weights are determined by the respective functions:

```
lisp> (weightInit)
(0.1 -0.1)

lisp> (weightInitBias)
(0.1 -0.1 0.2)
```

Unit net activation is the inner product of the input and weight vectors (here, lists) and are computed *recursively* for a *variable* number of inputs.

9.11.4 Resulting CommonLisp Implementation of the Unit and Training

```
;; file: annUnit.lisp
;; train single artificial unit with GDR

;; the constant part of the correction, delta

(defun delta (output target)
  (* (- target output ) output (- 1.0 output)))

;; single pattern training

(defun trainUnitPattern (input target inWeights rho)
" returns the modified unit weight list resulting from
  training over a single input pattern"
 (trainUnitInputRecur input inWeights (delta (unit input inWeights) target) rho)
)

(defun trainUnitInputRecur (input weights delta rho)
" forms w_i^{n+1}=w_i^n + rho * delta *i_i
i.e., doesn't require reforming delta for each component"
 (cond
   ((null weights) nil)
   (t (cons (+ (car weights)
               (* rho delta (car input)))
      (trainUnitInputRecur (cdr input) (cdr weights) delta rho))))
)
```

```
;; one pass over H

(defun trainUnitAll (H inWeights rho)
" returns the modified unit weight list resulting from
  one pass of training over H
  inputs: H inWeights rho
  value returned: modified unit weight list
  side effects: none"
 (cond
   ((not (null H))
      (trainUnitAll (cdr H)
                    (trainUnitPattern (nth 0 (car H)) (nth 1 (car H))
                    inWeights
                    rho)
                    rho))
   (t inWeights))
)

;; n passes over H

(defun trainMultiple (H inWeights rho n)
" implements n training passes (via recursion) over H
  and returns the modified unit weight list
  inputs: H inWeights rho n
  value returned: modified unit weight list
  side effects: none"
(cond
   ((> n 0) (trainMultiple H (trainUnitAll H inWeights rho) rho (- n 1)))
   ((equal n 0) inWeights))
)

;; initialization w/o bias

(defun weightInit ()
"weight initialization function"   ;; later make random
 '(0.1 -0.1))

(setq H '(
         ((0.0 0.0) 0.25)
         ((0.0 1.0) 0.5)
         ((1.0 0.0) 0.75)
         ((1.0 1.0) 1.0)
         )
)

;; initialization w/ bias

(setq HBias '(
         ((0.0 0.0 1.0) 0.25)
         ((0.0 1.0 1.0) 0.5)
         ((1.0 0.0 1.0) 0.75)
         ((1.0 1.0 1.0) 1.0)
         )
)

(defun weightInitBias ()
"weight initialization function"   ;; make random
 '(0.1 -0.1 0.2))
```

```
;; artificial neuron unit model and supporting fns.

(defun unit (inputs weights)
"implements single ANN unit
 input: inputs weights
 value returned: unit output (squashed)
 side effects: none"
 (squash (calcNet inputs weights)))

;; artificial neuron activation (squashing) function

(defun squash (net &optional choice)
"activation function implementation
 inputs: net choice (optional: sigmoid, tanh, linear)
 returns: squashed net (default is sigmoid)
 side effects: print on error"
 (cond
  ((equal choice 'sigmoid) (/ 1.0 (+ 1.0 (exp (* -1.0 net)))))
  ((equal choice 'tanh) (tanh net))
  ((equal choice 'linear) net)
  ((not (equal choice nil)) (print "sorry; not yet implemented") nil)
  (t (/ 1.0 (+ 1.0 (exp (* -1.0 net))))))
)

;; artificial neuron net activation computation

(defun calcNet (inputs weights)
"(recursively) compute unit net activation from inputs
 and (current) weights
 input: inputs, weights
 value returned: net activation
 side effects: none"
 (cond
   ((and (null inputs) (null weights)) 0.0)
   (t (+ (* (car inputs) (car weights))
        (calcNet (cdr inputs) (cdr weights))))
))
```

9.11.5 Assessment of the Solution

Results After 500 Iterations

```
lisp> (setq weights1 (trainMultiple H (weightInit) 0.25 500))
(1.7252052 0.22829074)
lisp> (unit (car (nth 0 H)) weights1)
0.5
lisp> (unit (car (nth 1 H)) weights1)
0.5568261
lisp> (unit (car (nth 2 H)) weights1)
0.8487981
lisp> (unit (car (nth 3 H)) weights1)
0.8758274
lisp> (setq weights2 (trainMultiple HBias (weightInitBias) 0.25 500))
(2.3117676 1.1563605 -1.0863377)
lisp> (unit (car (nth 0 HBias)) weights2)
0.25230855
lisp> (unit (car (nth 1 HBias)) weights2)
0.51749855
```

```
lisp> (unit (car (nth 2 HBias)) weights2)
0.7730177
lisp> (unit (car (nth 3 HBias)) weights2)
0.9154281
```

Results After 5000 Iterations

```
lisp> (setq weights1 (trainMultiple H (weightInit) 0.25 5000))
(1.7720206 0.21115907)
lisp> (unit (car (nth 0 H)) weights1)
0.5
lisp> (unit (car (nth 1 H)) weights1)
0.5525945
lisp> (unit (car (nth 2 H)) weights1)
0.8547088
lisp> (unit (car (nth 3 H)) weights1)
0.8790197
lisp> (trainMultiple HBias (weightInitBias) 0.25 5000)
(2.4983277 1.3233764 -1.249157)
lisp> (setq weights2 (trainMultiple HBias (weightInitBias) 0.25 5000))
(2.4983277 1.3233764 -1.249157)
lisp> (unit (car (nth 0 HBias)) weights2)
0.22284609
lisp> (unit (car (nth 1 HBias)) weights2)
0.51854634
lisp> (unit (car (nth 2 HBias)) weights2)
0.7771563
lisp> (unit (car (nth 3 HBias)) weights2)
0.92907375
```

9.12 CommonLisp Functions (and Macros) You Should Know

1. `defun`
2. `set`, `setq`, `setf`, and family
3. `car`, `cdr`, `nth`, and relatives
4. `cond`
5. `if`
6. `let`, `do`
7. `print`, `format`, `terpri`, `read`
8. `and`, `or`, `not`, `null`
9. `* + - /` and relatives
10. `> < > =` and relatives
11. `equal` and relatives
12. `cons`, `append`, `list`, `member`, `length`, and relatives
13. `assoc`

14. eval

15. mapcar

16. defvar

17. trace, untrace

18. load, dribble, cd

19. exit

9.13 Bibliographical Remarks and References

The Association of Lisp Users maintains a Web page at: http://www.lisp.org/alu/home containing pointers to much useful Lisp information. A good (generic) CommonLisp resource is: http://www-2.cs.cmu.edu/afs/cs.cmu.edu/project/ai-repository/ai/html/cltl/cltl2.html. This contains an online version of *Common Lisp: The Language*, 2nd edition, which also may be downloaded. Another online/downloadable book is: *Common Lisp: A Gentle Introduction to Symbolic Computation*, available at http://www-2.cs.cmu.edu/~dst/LispBook/index.html.

In addition, the CommonLisp Hyperspec document is a substantial online reference to the functions available in CommonLisp and is available at: http://www.lisp.org/HyperSpec/FrontMatter/index.html. It is possible to download the Hyperspec for local use; see: http://www.lispworks.com/reference/HyperSpec/.

Another Web resource that provides many good starting points is http://clisp.cons.org/resources.html. For clisp development and history, see the Web page at http://clisp.sourceforge.net/. Notes on clisp implementation specifics are available at: http://clisp.cons.org/impnotes.html#references.

9.14 Exercises

1. (Lambda-calculus and Lisp).

   (a) Evaluate:

$$((\lambda x.\ (-\ (+\ (*\ x\ x)(*\ 2\ x))\ 4))\ 2)$$

   (b) Convert this expression to a CommonLisp s-expression that may be input to EVAL.

2. Determine the response from the Lisp read-eval-print loop (EVAL) for each of the following inputs:[18]

```
> (sqrt (* 5 20))

> (-16 9)

> (defun test21 (x y z)
```

[18] Assume that there are no functions defined other than those available in the CommonLisp system when started.

```
(setq result (+ x (*y z))))

> (test21 '(2 3 4))

>  ((lambda (x y) (+ (* y y) x)) 5 4)

> (defun expr (a b)
(if (zerop b) 1
        (if (evenp b) (expr (* a a) (/ b 2))
              (* a (expr a (- b 1))))))

> (expr (cdr '(4 5 6)))

> (expr (car '(2 3 4 5)) (car '(3 4 5)))
```

Note: If the system reports an error, simply write ERROR and indicate (specifically) what the error was.

3. (CommonLisp). Consider the following CommonLisp s-expressions, which are sequentially input to the `read-eval-print` loop. Show the system response (returned value) for each. Indicate an error simply as "ERROR," and explain the error.

```
> (defun my (a-list)
(nth 2 a-list))

> (setq test-list '(dog has fleas))

> (defun dog ()
(return 'no))

> (setq fleas 'yes)

> (setq my 'no)

> (defun test (ans arg-list)
(setq ans (my arg-list)))

> (test '(my dog has fleas) test-list)

> (test test-list '(my dog has fleas))
```

4. The following is loaded into the CommonLisp system. For each s-expression input to `EVAL`, show the corresponding returned value, and side effects, if any. In other words, fill in the response from the Lisp `read-eval-print` loop (`EVAL`) directly below each.

   Note: If the system reports an error, simply write ERROR; you do not need to indicate what the error is.

```
>(setq result '(hi mom))

> (cons (cdr result) (list (car result)))

> (setq result2  (cons (cdr result) (list (car result))))

> (defun test21 (x y z)
(setq result (+ x (*y z))))

> (test21 '(2 3 4))

>  ((lambda (x y) (+ (* y y) x)) 5 4)
```

5. Suppose the following set of (syntactically correct) functions and related data are loaded into the CommonLisp system:

```
(defun what-is (a l)
(cond
((equal a (car l)) (a1 (cdr l) (list a)))
(t (what-is a (a1 (cdr l) (list (car l)))))))

(defun a1 (x y)
(append x y))

(setq l1 '(a b c d))

(setq l2 'c)
```

What are the results of the following evaluations?

```
>(what-is l1 l2)


>(what-is l2 l1)
```

6. (a) Show the response from `EVAL` (*in exactly the format `EVAL` would use*) for each of the following (sequentially entered) s-expressions. If you think an error results, simply write "ERROR."

```
> (setq a '(q w e r t y))

> (print (cdr a))

> (print (nth 2 (cdr a)))

> (member 'a a)

> (list 'a)
```

(b) Here's a syntactically correct function definition:

```
(defun quiz2prob (x y)
(cond
  ((cons x y) (cdr (cons x y)))
  (t (print "this can't be done")))
)
```

Show what is returned by EVAL for each of the following uses of function quiz2prob. If you think an error results, simply write "ERROR."

```
> (quiz2prob 'a '(b c d))
```

```
> (quiz2prob '(b c d) (list 'a))
```

7. Here are the results of a number of evaluations by EVAL on some list named testlist:

```
> (car (cdr testlist))
(B C)
> (cdr (cdr (cdr testlist)))
NIL
> (nth 0 testlist)
A
> (car (nth 2 testlist))
D
> (cdr (nth 2 testlist))
(E)
```

What is (the value of) testlist?

8. The following syntactically correct file contains a recursive function definition in Lisp:

```
; FILE NAME: recur2.l
; VARIABLES:

(setq friends1 '(D1 D2 D3))
(setq friends2 '(D1 D2 D3 D4))

(defun recur2 (alist)
  (cond
    ( (not (null (cdr alist)))
      (nth 2 (cdr alist))  )
    ( t (recur2 (cdr alist))) )
)
```

What is returned by EVAL for each of the following uses of recur2 with the given data:

```
> (recur2 friends1)
```

```
> (recur2 friends2)
```

9. This problem explores Lisp syntax and derivation trees. Here is a simplified description of the syntax of Lisp:

```
/* rules for <s_expression> */

<s_expression> ::= <atomic_symbol> | <list>
      | ( <s_expression>.<s_expression> )    /* allows dotted pair notation */

/* rules for <list> */

<list> ::= nil | () | (<non_empty>)

<non_empty> ::= <s_expression> | <non_empty> <s_expression>

/* lexical part of syntax  */

<atomic_symbol> ::= <letter> <atom_part>

<atom_part> ::= <letter> <atom_part> | <number> <atom_part>

<letter> ::= a | b | ... | z

<number> ::= 1 | 2 | ... | 9

/* reserved words (symbols); basic version  */

(
)
.       /* used in dotted pair notation */
1 2 ... 9
a b ... z
+ - * / /* and other misc symbols*/
nil     /* () = nil and nil is reserved symbol for predicate use */
```

Using this syntactic description, show a complete derivation tree for the following s-expression. For simplicity, however, exclude the lexical derivations, that is, stop at leaves denoting `<atomic_symbol>`. Just indicate the final symbol name directly under `<atomic_symbol>` in the derivation tree.

```
(defun first-one (x)
    (car x) )
```

10. Two lists, `a-list` and `b-list`, are created as follows.

```
> (setq a-list '(a (b c) d (e)))
(A (B C) D (E))
> (setq b-list '((e) d (b) c)))
((E) D (B) C)
```

Thereafter, the following ten s-expressions are input to `EVAL` (`EVAL` prompt is not shown). Below each input to `EVAL` are three possible returned values. **Circle** the correct response (returned value) from each input to `EVAL`. There is no significance to case. Recall that `nth` indexes lists starting from 0. *If you feel none of the options are correct, do not circle any.*

(a)

(car (cdr a-list))		
(B C)	B C	((B C))

(b)

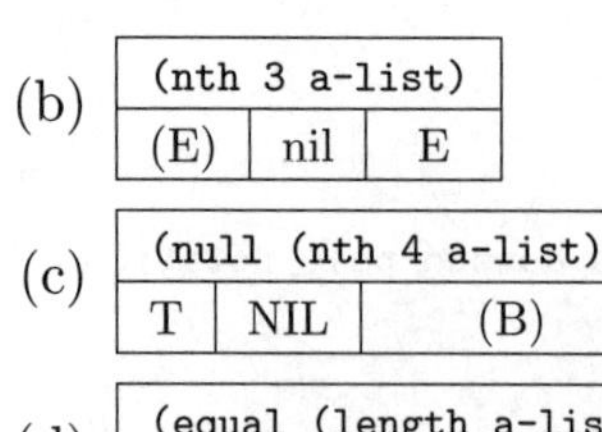

(nth 3 a-list)		
(E)	nil	E

(c)

(null (nth 4 a-list))		
T	NIL	(B)

(d)

(equal (length a-list) (length b-list))		
T	NIL	4

(e)

(and t (not (null cdr (cdr b-list)))))		
T	NIL	(B) C

(f)

(and t (not (null (cdr (cdr b-list)))))		
T	NIL	(B) C

(g)

(if (null b-list) a-list b-list))		
((E) D (B) C)	(A (B C) D (E)))	NIL

(h)

(cons a-list b-list)		
((A (B C) D (E)) (E) D (B) C)	((A B C D E)) (E D B C)	(A B C D E E D B C)

(i)

(member 'e (append a-list b-list))		
NIL	T	((E) D (B) C)))

(j)

(list (car a-list))		
(A)	(A (B C) D (E))	((E) D (B) C)

11. Which of the following functions have side effects?

    (a) `load`
    (b) `dribble`
    (c) `defvar`
    (d) `defun`
    (e) `print`
    (f) `set`
    (g) `let`
    (h) `cons`
    (i) `append`
    (j) `null`

12. For each input to `EVAL` that follows, show the corresponding *terminal output*, that is, the response you would see from `EVAL`. Assume the s-expressions are evaluated sequentially. If you think an error results, simply answer "error."

```
lisp> (setq testlist '(a1 b2 c3 d4))


lisp> (cdr (cdr (cdr testlist)))


lisp> (listp (car testlist))
```

```
lisp> (defun testfn (something) (car (cdr something)))


lisp> (testfn (car testlist))


lisp> (mapcar 'testfn '((1 2) (3 4) (5 6)))


lisp> (cons 'new (cons 'newer testlist))


lisp> (if testlist "yes" "no")


lisp> (print testlist)


lisp> (print "testlist")
```

13. Suppose we `defun` the following function:

```
(defun atestfn (x)
     (cond
           ((not (null x)) 100)
           ( t (cons (car x) (atestfn (cdr x))))))
```

What is the result of the following evaluation? (If you think an error results, simply answer "error"). `testlist` was defined in the preceding problem.

```
lisp> (atestfn testlist)
```

14. The CommonLisp implementation of `factorial` in Section 9.5.4, as noted in the function source code definition comments, has several limitations. Revise and test the CommonLisp implementation of `factorial` such that:

    (a) `(factorial 0)` is defined.

    (b) Attempts to use `factorial` with negative integers are identified and the function terminates.

15. This problem considers side effects and referential transparency. Five function definitions in Lisp follow, each indexed by a number in the `EVAL` prompt. The purpose of this problem is to determine which functions are referentially transparent or have side effects. Fill in the table below with each entry either Y (yes) or N (no).

```
[1]> (defun fun1 (a b c)
(cons (cdr a) (list (car b) (car c))))


[2]> (defun fun2 ()
(setq b '(1 2 3 4)))
```

```
[3]> (defun fun3 (help me)
(cond
(help (print me))
(t t)))
```

```
[4]> (defun fun4 (alist)
(reverse alist))
```

```
[5]> (defun fun5 (x y)
(let ((a x) (b y))
(+ a b)
(- a b)
(* a b)
(/ a b)))
```

Function Number	Side Effects?	Referentially Transparent?
1		
2		
3		
4		
5		

16. As an alternative to the cond-based implementation of a^b in Section 9.10, consider the following:

```
;;file: expr1.l

(defun expr (a b)
(if (zerop b) 1
        (if (evenp b) (expr (* a a) (/ b 2))
              (* a (expr a (- b 1))))))
```

(a) Does this function compute a^b?

(b) Is it equivalent to the function shown in Section 9.10?

17. This problem presents a challenge in recursive function design. The objective is to develop a CommonLisp function, **permute2**, along with a set of supporting functions, which takes as input a list (of anything) and returns a list of **all** permutations of the input list. The real challenge is to do this without side effects and to maximize the use of recursion. A sample operation follows.

```
lisp> (load "perm4.l")
;; Loading file perm4.l ...
;; Loading of file perm4.l is finished.
t

lisp> (permute2 '(a b))
((b a) (a b))
```

```
lisp> (permute2 '(1 2 3))
((3 2 1) (3 1 2) (2 1 3) (2 3 1) (1 3 2) (1 2 3))

lisp> (permute2 '(1 c 2 b))
((b 2 c 1) (b 2 1 c) (b c 1 2) (b c 2 1) (b 1 2 c) (b 1 c 2) (2 c 1 b)
 (2 c b 1) (2 1 b c) (2 1 c b) (2 b c 1) (2 b 1 c) (c 1 b 2) (c 1 2 b)
 (c b 2 1) (c b 1 2) (c 2 1 b) (c 2 b 1) (1 b 2 c) (1 b c 2) (1 2 c b)
 (1 2 b c) (1 c b 2) (1 c 2 b))

lisp> (documentation 'permute2 'function)
"function: permute2
 input: a list
 returned value: a list-of-lists, where each element
    is a permutation of the input list
 side effects: none"
```

Design and implement, in CommonLisp, a function **permute2**, which takes as input a list and returns a list consisting of all permutations of this input list (each as a list). Use recursion where possible.

Apply your function to the inputs that follow. Show your results (returned values) with the following function invocations:

```
lisp> (permute2 '( 1 2 3))

lisp> (permute2 '(1 2 3 4))

lisp> (length (permute2 '(1 2 3 4)))

lisp> (permute2 '(1 (2 3)))

lisp> (permute2 '(1 2 3 4 5 6))

lisp> (length (permute2 '(1 2 3 4 5 6)))

lisp> (permute2 '(1 2 3 4 5 6 7 8))

lisp> (permute2 '(1 2 3 4 5 6 7 8 9 10 11))
```

Comment on the results.

18. Two versions of a Lisp function for computing ANN unit net activation are shown in Figure 9.8. Compare and contrast the two functions.

19. The ANN unit formulation of Section 9.11 was based purely upon recursion. Using very large numbers of passes over H (i.e., n), show a limitation of this strategy.

```
;; artificial neuron net activation

(defun calcNet (inputs weights)
 (cond
   ((and (null inputs) (null weights)) 0.0)
   (t (+ (* (car inputs) (car weights))
         (calcNet (cdr inputs) (cdr weights))))
))

;; some test values
(setq input1 '(1 0 1))

(setq weight1 '(-0.1 0.0 0.2))
```

Function calcNet.lisp

```
;; artificial neuron net activation
;; calcnet2.lisp version for illustration

(defun calcNet2 (inputs weights)
 (cond
   ((and (null (cdr inputs)) (null (cdr weights)))
      (* (car inputs) (car weights)))
   (t (+ (* (car inputs) (car weights))
         (calcNet2 (cdr inputs) (cdr weights))))
))

;; some test values
(setq input1 '(1 0 1))

(setq weight1 '(-0.1 0.0 0.2))
```

Function calcNet2.lisp

Figure 9.8 Two Lisp Functions for Computing ANN Unit Net Activation.

CHAPTER 10

Object-Oriented Functional Programming: The CommonLisp Object System

Good programmers know what to write. Great ones know what to rewrite (and reuse).
—Eric Steven Raymond, *The Cathedral and the Bazaar*

In this chapter, we consider extension of the functional programming (FP) paradigm and CommonLisp to an object-oriented framework. This yields the CommonLisp Object System, or CLOS.

10.1 The CommonLisp Object System (CLOS)

10.1.1 Introduction and Background

In this section, the plan of study is in three sequential phases of concentration:

1. Introduction to CommonLisp structures.
2. Exploration of operations on CommonLisp structures (accessor functions).
3. Object-oriented programming (OOP) and the CommonLisp Object System (CLOS).

This chapter assumes the reader has been exposed to the relevant C++ object-oriented concepts.

Important CommonLisp Functions

There are a couple of important, general-purpose CommonLisp functions that are relevant to the study of CLOS.

`setf` The first is the `setf` macro, which is sort of the most general `setq`. It has the prototype:

```
(setf <place> <expression>)
```

that is, the "universal setter" **setf** puts the value of <**expression**> in <**place**>. For example, simple use looks like:

```
>(setf x '(a b c d))
(a b c d)
```

which makes it look like setq. However, consider an extension of the previous example with a more powerful effect:

```
>(setf (car x) 'change))
change
>x
(change b c d)
```

defvar Another function is the special form defvar, which is used to define global variables. It has the prototype:

```
(defvar <var> <init-value>)
```

and the <init-value> argument is optional. We will use this in CLOS.

CommonLisp Structures: A Prelude to Classes

Structures provide a prelude to the more general concepts of classes and objects (and OOP). In most languages, including CommonLisp, a **structure** is a collection of data. The structure is declared and names are assigned to parts (fields or slots) of the structure.

Digression: A Couple of C struct Examples

The C programming language makes rich use of structures. For example, a perusal of the source code for the Linux kernel illustrates massive use of pointers to structures to implement just about everything from process tables to modular hardware drivers. Here are two simple examples:

```
#include <stdio.h>
#include <string.h>

/* simple c programming using structures */

void main(void)
{
struct human {
char last[25];
char first[25];
char address[25];
int phone;
};

struct human prof = {"Schalkoff", "Robert", "EIB334", 5913};

printf("%s %s spends too much time in %s and on the phone line ext %d \n",
prof.first, prof.last, prof.address, prof.phone);
} /* end main */
```

Here is a little more complicated example for the pointer crowd:

```
#include <stdio.h>
#include <string.h>

/* c programming */
/* structures example using pointers and arrow operator */

void main(void)
{
struct human {
char last[25];
char first[25];
char address[25];
int phone;
};

struct human aprof = {"Schalkoff", "Robert", "EIB334", 5913};

struct human *prof;

prof = &aprof;

/* here is the -> notation */

printf("%s %s spends too much time in %s and on the phone line ext %d \n",
prof->first, prof->last, prof->address, prof->phone);
} /* end main */
```

Defining and Accessing CommonLisp Structures

In CommonLisp, a lot goes on behind the scenes in the form of associated function creation and a structure hierarchy. `defstruct` is used for structure definition. Here is a very simple example of the creation of a structure called `vehicle` with slot names `name`, `manufacturer`, and `power`:

```
> (defstruct vehicle
     name
     manufacturer
     power
     )
vehicle
>
```

Note that this just defined a new data type `vehicle`, but did not create anything (yet) of this type. In other words, no "vehicle" instances exist, and the slots `name`, `manufacturer`, and `power` have no values. Also note the returned value.

Suppose we wanted to give the slots values at the time the structure type `vehicle` was declared. An example is:

```
> (defstruct vehicle
    (name "somebody's ride")
    (manufacturer 'microsoft)
    (power 'unlimited))
vehicle
```

But Look What Else You Get . . .

When structure type `vehicle` is created, a number of ancillary functions are also created for you by CommonLisp. Especially interesting is the function `make-vehicle`, which facilitates creation of data objects of the type `vehicle`. For example,

```
> (setq bobs-vehicle (make-vehicle
))
#S(vehicle :name "somebody's ride" :manufacturer microsoft :power unlimited)
```

creates an instance of structure type `vehicle`, now referred to as `bobs-vehicle`.[1] `make-vehicle` is a so-called constructor for the `vehicle` structure, and takes the following keyword parameters

```
:name
:manufacturer
:power
```

in case we want to set the slot values at the time the instance was created. Because we did not do this, the *default* parameters, if any, which were specified by `defstruct`, are used. We access them using other so-called slot access functions created by CommonLisp for our use after `defstruct`, specifically:

```
vehicle-name
vehicle-manufacturer
vehicle-power
```

For example:

```
> (vehicle-name bobs-vehicle)
"somebody's ride"
> (vehicle-manufacturer bobs-vehicle)
microsoft
> (vehicle-power bobs-vehicle)
unlimited
```

Let's try using the `make-vehicle` function with the keywords and values:

```
> (setq bobs-vehicle (make-vehicle
      :name "sailboard"
      :manufacturer 'bic
      :power 'wind))
#S(vehicle :name "sailboard" :manufacturer bic :power wind)

>(vehicle-manufacturer bobs-vehicle)
bic

> (vehicle-power bobs-vehicle)
wind
```

[1]Note that the name of the structure instance and the slot name are different.

In addition, a type predicate, in this example named **vehiclep**, is automatically created to check if an object is of the type `vehicle`; for example,

```
> (vehicle-p bobs-vehicle)
t
```

Finally, let's use the slot access functions **vehicle-name, vehicle-manufacturer**, and **vehicle-power**, together with **setf** to set the values of slots:

```
> (setf (vehicle-name bobs-vehicle) "my bike")
"my bike"
> (setf (vehicle-manufacturer bobs-vehicle) 'KHS)
khs
> (setf (vehicle-power bobs-vehicle) 'pedals)
pedals>
```

leading to

```
> (vehicle-name bobs-vehicle)
"my bike"
> (vehicle-manufacturer bobs-vehicle)
khs
```

and so on.

A Step Toward Object-Oriented Programming (OOP)

Most importantly, as a prelude to CLOS, structure type automatically becomes part of the Lisp type hierarchy. Any structure defined with `defstruct` is automatically a subtype of the built-in type `structure`. In addition, we can define a structure hierarchy that supports *inheritance*. Let's work this out with an example. Recall our original type declaration of `vehicle`. The `:include` construct specifies that one structure is a subtype of another. For example:

```
> (defstruct (boat (:include vehicle))
     (floats 'yes)
)
boat
> (defstruct (sailboat (:include boat))
      sailtype
      keel
)
sailboat
```

We create some instances:

```
> (setq bobs-sailboat (make-sailboat
        :sailtype 'dacron
        :keel 'no))
#S(sailboat :name "somebody's ride" :manufacturer microsoft :power unlimited
   :floats yes :sailtype dacron :keel no
  )
```

Notice that the structure value returned has things not specific to the instance of `sailboat` known as `bobs-sailboat`. Now let's watch (single) inheritance:

```
> (vehicle-name bobs-sailboat)
"somebody's ride"
> (vehicle-manufacturer bobs-sailboat)
microsoft
> (boat-floats bobs-sailboat)
yes
> (sailboat-sailtype bobs-sailboat)
dacron
```

As you can see, lots of values have been *inherited* from types of which `bobs-sailboat` is a subtype (or, strictly speaking, "sub-subtype").

CommonLisp Packages and Examples of Package Use

Packages are a way to allow large program development in CommonLisp without the nightmare of conflicting symbol names. For example, imagine a project with 25 programmers, each writing functions and defining variables. Unfortunately, the use of a single namespace for all symbols has the potential for confusion of multiple functions and variables with the same name. This leads us to some way to associate symbols with code modules, and the concept of a package.

Basic Packages

You have, without thinking much about it, been working in the CommonLisp USER package. There are actually four basic packages:

- User package
- Lisp package
- Keyword package
- System package

and extensions such as the OPS(5) package and the CLOS package (descriptions follow). CommonLisp provides the global variable `*package*`, whose value is a package data structure, specifically the current package. You can check this via:

```
> *package*
#<PACKAGE USER>
```

In the user package (which is the package typically used by, not surprisingly, the user), `EVAL` refers to this package for symbol evaluation. The package notation can sometimes be a little daunting. The value of a package is denoted with:

```
#< . . . >
```

where the `. . .` is system-specific output. An example was shown previously.

Checking Symbols

Symbols may also be checked using `describe`.

```
lisp> (describe 'car)

car is the symbol car, lies in #<package common-lisp>,
is accessible in the packages CLOS, COMMON-LISP, COMMON-LISP-USER,
EXT, FFI, LDAP, POSIX, SCREEN, SYSTEM,
names a function, has the properties system::instruction,
system::setf-expander.

>(setq a '(a d f ( d f g (g h t y))))
(A D F (D F G (G H T Y)))

> (describe a)

Description of
(A D F (D F G (G H T Y)))
This is a list of length 4.

> (symbol-function 'car)
#<SYSTEM-FUNCTION CAR>
```

Other examples of package use and manipulation are:

- the function `find-package`, which facilitates *package input*

  ```
  > (find-package 'user)
  #<
  ```

  by translating a package name into a package.
- changing the global value of `*package*` via

  ```
  >(setq *package* (find-package 'lisp))
  ```

- the function `package-use-list`, which returns a list of other packages (known by the system) that use a symbol name. For example:

  ```
  > (package-use-list 'user)
  (#<PACKAGE LISP>)
  ```

- a way to see all currently available packages:

  ```
  > (list-all-packages)
  (#<PACKAGE FFI> #<PACKAGE SCREEN> #<PACKAGE CLOS> #<PACKAGE KEYWORD>
    #<PACKAGE SYSTEM> #<PACKAGE USER> #<PACKAGE LISP> #<PACKAGE COMMON-LISP>
    #<PACKAGE COMMON-LISP-USER>
  ```

You can also check to see if the CLOS package is available by checking `*features`:

```
> *features*
(CLOS LOOP COMPILER CLISP CLTL1 COMMON-LISP INTERPRETER CLISP2
  LOGICAL-PATHNAMES FFI PC386 UNIX
```

Although it can get lots more complicated, this should suffice for our purposes.

10.2 CommonLisp Object System (CLOS)

10.2.1 Objects and Classes in CommonLisp

To begin with, we must invoke the CLOS package via:

```
(use-package "CLOS")
```

10.2.2 Elementary Class and Object Functions and Arguments

Function defclass

`defclass` has the prototype:[2]

```
(defclass <class-name> (<supers-list>)
<slotlist>)
```

Of course, there is a lot of variation possible in individual uses of `slot-list`. A fairly typical prototype (without a lot of optional arguments) is:

```
(defclass <class-name> (<supers-list>)
(<slotname> :initform <value> :type <type> :initarg <arg> :accessor <name>)
(:documentation "<doc-string")
)
```

The `<supers-list>` names superclasses of this class, and therefore defines a class hierarchy. This hierarchy allows inheritance as well as multiple inheritance. A brief look at each of the slot components follows.

`:initform` provides a way to specify a default value for the slot in instances of the object class.

`:initarg` is a way to allow overwriting of initializations when creating instances.

`:accessor` automatically creates a slot accessor function with `<name>`.

`:documentation` is a way to provide built-in documentation.

10.2.3 CLOS Invocation

```
(use-package "CLOS")

(defclass vehicle ()
((name :accessor name :initform 'batmobile)
 (manufacturer :accessor manufacturer)
 (make :accessor make)
 (wheels :initform 4 :type 'integer :initarg wheels)
 (power :accessor power :initarg power))
(:documentation
        "general vehicle class"))


(defclass boat (vehicle)
((capacity :accessor capacity)
 (use ))
```

[2]We'll keep it simple for now.

```
(:documentation
        "general boat class"))

(defclass bicycle (vehicle)
((wheels :initform 2)
 (power :initform 'legs))
(:documentation
        "general bicycle class"))


(defclass sailboat (boat)
((capacity :accessor capacity)
 (use :initarg use)
 (sailtype :initform 2 :initarg sailtype))
(:documentation
        "sailboat class"))

(defclass jetski (boat)
((capacity :accessor capacity)
 (use :initform 'annoyance))
(:documentation
        "jetski boat class"))

(defclass hybrid-bicycle (bicycle)
()
(:documentation
        "hybrid bicycle class"))
```

The reader should pay particular attention to the class hierarchy created in the preceding example, and should be able to predict inherited values.

10.2.4 CLOS Class Hierarchy Example

Figure 10.1 gives an example of a CLOS class hierarchy.

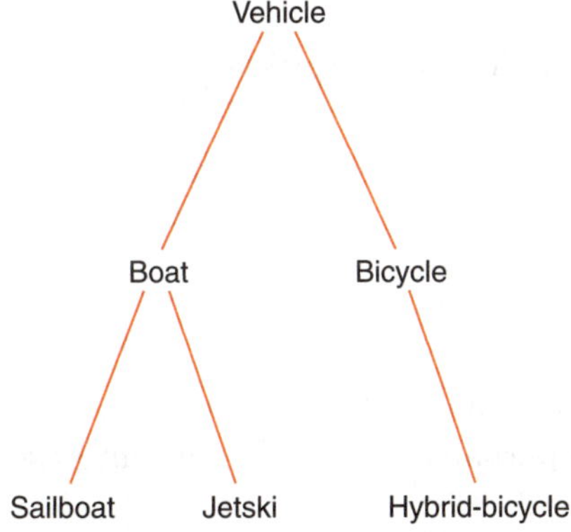

Figure 10.1 Class Hierarchy Example. (Note: No object instances have yet been created.)

10.2.5 Creating Instances in CLOS

Function `make-instance` is provided to create instances in CLOS. Here is an example:

```
> (setq my-bike (make-instance 'hybrid-bicycle))
#<HYBRID-BICYCLE #x000001D0>
```

10.2.6 Accessing Slots in CLOS

Slots are usually accessed by methods, but there is a direct way using `slot-value`:

```
> (slot-value my-bike 'wheels)
2
> (slot-value my-bike 'name)
BATMOBILE
```

Note how the name slot of `my-bike` got a value through the use of inheritance.

10.2.7 CLOS Methods and Method-Defining Functions

`defmethod`, the bigger brother of `defun`, is used for methods and method-defining functions. The prototype is:

```
(defmethod <method-name> <formal parameters>
<body>)
```

Thus, it looks like `defun`. However, `<formal parameters>` has a form that may be customized to specific classes.[3] For example, a typical body would look like:

```
Examples of Package Use
(defmethod change-name1 ((named bicycle) newname)
(setf (slot-value named 'name) newname))
```

with use:

```
> (defmethod change-name1 ((named bicycle) newname)
(setf (slot-value named 'name) newname))
#<STANDARD-METHOD (#<STANDARD-CLASS BICYCLE> #<BUILT-IN-CLASS T>)>

>  (setq my-bike (make-instance 'hybrid-bicycle))
#<HYBRID-BICYCLE #x00000060>

> (change-name1 my-bike 'llbean)
LLBEAN
> (slot-value my-bike 'name)
LLBEAN
```

In addition, the CommonLisp CLOS provides the built-in function `with-slots` to make `defmethod` use cleaner, and perhaps clearer. In the interest of brevity, we show this by example:

```
(defmethod change-name ((named bicycle) newname)
(with-slots (name) named (setf name newname)))
```

---

[3] And more than one class at a time, thus allowing *multimethods*.

The method is **change-name**, and it works with instances of class **bicycle**. The other argument, **newname**, is used to set the new name of the slot **name**, in the body. The body

```
(with-slots (name) named (setf name newname)))
```

is based upon **with-slots**, which has the prototype:

```
(with-slots <list-of-slots-to-access> <object> <expressions to evaluate>)
```

Here is an example of the use:

```
> (defmethod change-name ((named bicycle) newname)
(with-slots (name) named (setf name newname)))
#<STANDARD-METHOD (#<STANDARD-CLASS BICYCLE> #<BUILT-IN-CLASS T>)>
> (change-name my-bike 'khs)
KHS
> (slot-value my-bike 'name)
KHS
```

Of course, we can do without methods (directly and somewhat indiscriminately) via:

```
> (setf (slot-value my-boat 'name) 'leakyII)
LEAKYII
```

10.2.8 Methods Are Specialized in CLOS—An Example

Continuing the previous CLOS development, let's add to the hierarchy:

```
> (setq my-boat (make-instance 'sailboat))
#<SAILBOAT #x0000026C>
> (slot-value my-boat 'name)
BATMOBILE
```

Notice (again) that the name is inherited from "vehicle." Suppose we try to change the name. Look what happens:

```
> (change-name my-boat 'queen-elizabeth)

*** - NO-APPLICABLE-METHOD: When calling #<GENERIC-FUNCTION CHANGE-NAME> with
1. Break> abort
```

Recall that the **change-name** method was defined to be applicable to the **bicycle** class, but we are trying to apply it to a superclass of **bicycle**. We fix this via a more powerful method:

```
> (defmethod change-name ((named vehicle) modname)
(with-slots (name) named (setf name modname)))
```

Now the behavior is:

```
> (slot-value my-boat 'name)
BATMOBILE
> (change-name my-boat 'queen-elizabeth)
QUEEN-ELIZABETH
> (slot-value my-boat 'name)
QUEEN-ELIZABETH
```

10.2.9 Another Example of Class-Specialized Methods in CLOS

CLOS Source

```
;;; tank CLOS class example
;;; rjs 11-11-02
;;; file:tank-example.cl

(use-package "CLOS")

(defclass tank ()
((material)
 (initial-psi)
 (capacity)
 (current-psi)
 (hydro-date))
)

(defclass nitrox-tank (tank)
((o2-percent)
 (marked))
)

(defclass o2-clean-nitrox-tank (nitrox-tank)
((max-o2-percent))
)

(defclass o2-blend-nitrox-tank (nitrox-tank)
((max-o2-percent))
)

(defclass air-tank (tank)
()
)

(defmethod fill-tank ((any tank))
(print "this method fills any tank")
 t)

(defmethod fill-air-tank ((any air-tank))
(print "this method fills air tanks")
 t)

(defmethod fill-nitrox-tank ((any nitrox-tank))
(print "this method fills nitrox tanks")
 t)

(defmethod fill-o2-clean-nitrox-tank ((any o2-clean-nitrox-tank))
(print "this method fills o2 clean nitrox tanks")
 t)

;; some objects to use

(setq generic-tank (make-instance 'tank))

(setq air-1 (make-instance 'air-tank))
```

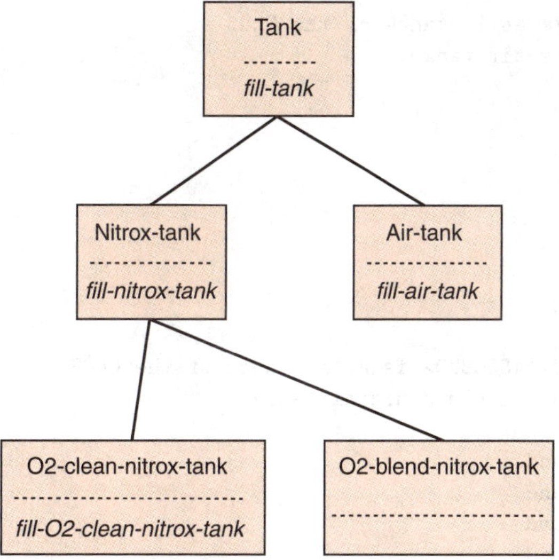

Figure 10.2 Class Hierarchy for Tanks Example.

```
(setq nitrox-1 (make-instance 'nitrox-tank))

(setq nitrox-c (make-instance 'o2-clean-nitrox-tank))

(setq nitrox-b (make-instance 'o2-blend-nitrox-tank))
```

The reader should observe the class hierarchy and class-specialized methods shown in Figure 10.2.

Results

From the sample CommonLisp session that follows, observe the specialization of methods—that is, the limitation of method applicability to the class for which it is defined and subsequent subclasses.

```
lisp> (describe generic-tank)

#<tank #x1A505B89> is an instance of the CLOS
class #1=#<standard-class tank>.
Slots:
   material     unbound
   initial-psi  unbound
   capacity     unbound
   current-psi  unbound
   hydro-date   unbound

lisp> (describe air-1)
```

```
#<air-tank #x1A5076F5> is an instance of the CLOS
class #1=#<standard-class air-tank>.
Slots:
   material     unbound
   initial-psi  unbound
   capacity     unbound
   current-psi  unbound
   hydro-date   unbound

lisp> (describe nitrox-b)

#<o2-blend-nitrox-tank #x1A50C889> is an instance of the CLOS
class #1=#<standard-class o2-blend-nitrox-tank>.
Slots:
   max-o2-percent  unbound
   o2-percent      unbound
   marked          unbound
   material        unbound
   initial-psi     unbound
   capacity        unbound
   current-psi     unbound
   hydro-date      unbound

lisp> (fill-tank generic-tank)

"this method fills any tank"
t
lisp> (fill-tank air-1)

"this method fills air tanks"
t
lisp> (fill-tank nitrox-c)

"this method fills any tank"
t
lisp> (fill-nitrox-tank generic-tank)

*** - no-applicable-method: When calling
#<generic-function fill-nitrox-tank> with
arguments (#<tank #x1A505B89>), no method is applicable.
1. Break lisp> abort

lisp> (fill-nitrox-tank nitrox-1)

"this method fills nitrox tanks"
t
lisp> (fill-nitrox-tank nitrox-c)

"this method fills nitrox tanks"
t
lisp> (fill-nitrox-tank air-1)

*** - no-applicable-method: When calling
#<generic-function fill-nitrox-tank> with
arguments (#<air-tank #x1A5076F5>), no method is applicable.
1. Break lisp> abort

lisp> (fill-o2-clean-nitrox-tank nitrox-c)
```

```
"this method fills o2 clean nitrox tanks"
t
lisp> (fill-o2-clean-nitrox-tank nitrox-1)

*** - no-applicable-method: When calling
#<generic-function fill-o2-clean-nitrox-tank>
with arguments (#<nitrox-tank #x1A5091E1>), no method is applicable.
1. Break lisp> abort
```

10.3 Relation to Other Programming Languages

10.3.1 Overview

Perhaps the best OOP example is C++. It is also noteworthy that the designers of a competing OO language, Java, chose not to implement structures or pointers, instead concentrating on classes.

In Java, a class is declared via:

```
class  <identifier> {
                     <body>}
```

The hierarchy is achieved via "derived" classes, for example

```
class <identifier> extends <superclass> {
                           <body> }
```

Creation of instances (objects) of a class is done by creation methods inside class declarations, but using the form:

```
<classtype> <instance-name> = new <classname>;
```

10.3.2 A Revised CLOS Example

Let's put the previous example together, for reference.

```
;; CLOS example
;; file: closex2.cl

(use-package "CLOS")

(defclass vehicle ()
((name :accessor name :initform "a vehicle")
 (manufacturer :accessor manufacturer)
 (make :accessor make)
 (wheels :initform 4 :initarg wheels)
 (power :accessor power :initarg power)
 (iq-of-operator :initform 'unknown :initarg iq-of-operator))
;;end of slots, now optional args, i.e., documentation
(:documentation
        "the most general vehicle class"))


(defclass boat (vehicle)
((capacity :accessor capacity)
 (wheels :initform 'none)
 (use :initarg use))
```

```
(:documentation
"general boat class"))

(defclass bicycle (vehicle)
((wheels :initform 2)
 (power :initform 'legs)
 (gears :initform 21 :initarg gears)
 (tires :initarg tires))
(:documentation
"general bicycle class"))


(defclass sailboat (boat)
((capacity :accessor capacity)
 (use :initform 'recreation)
 (sail-number :initform 2 :initarg sail-number)
 (sail-type :initform 'dacron :initarg sail-type))
(:documentation
        "sailboat class"))

(defclass jetski (boat)
((capacity :accessor capacity)
 (use :initform 'annoyance)
 (iq-of-operator :initform 'very-low))
(:documentation
        "jetski boat class"))

(defclass hybrid-bike (bicycle)
((iq-of-operator :initform 'varies)
 (use :initform '(commuting recreation)))
(:documentation
        "hybrid bicycle class"))

(defclass mountain-bike (bicycle)
((iq-of-operator :initform 'average)
 (tires :initform 'knobby)
 (shocks :initform 'probably))
(:documentation
        "mountain bicycle class"))

(defclass laser (sailboat)
 ((use :initform 'racing))
(:documentation "a C15 sailboat"))

(defclass sailboard (sailboat)
 ((use :initform 'recreation)
 (volume :initarg volume))
(:documentation "generic sailboard"))

(defclass longboard (sailboard)
((volume :initform '2351)
 (skill :initform 'minimal))
(:documentation "long sailboard"))

(defclass shortboard (sailboard)
 ((volume :initform '1501)
 (alias :initform 'sinker :initarg alias)
 (power :initform '(waves wind))
```

```
 (skill :initform '(medium high)))
(:documentation "short sailboard"))

;; create some instances

(setq b1 (make-instance 'boat))

(setq b2 (make-instance 'boat))

(setq b3 (make-instance 'sailboat))

(setq b4 (make-instance 'jetski))

(setq b5 (make-instance 'mountain-bike))

(setq b6 (make-instance 'longboard))

(setq b7 (make-instance 'shortboard))

(setq b8 (make-instance 'hybrid-bike))


;; some methods to use

(defmethod cbn ((object bicycle) newname)
(with-slots (name) object (setf name newname)))

(defmethod csn ((object sailboat) newname)
(with-slots (name) object (setf name newname)))

(defmethod chbo ((object hybrid-bike) change)
(with-slots (iq-of-operator) object (setf iq-of-operator change)))

(defmethod csbv ((object shortboard) new-volume)
(with-slots (volume) object (setf volume new-volume)))

(defmethod csbs ((object shortboard) skill-level)
(with-slots (skill) object (setf skill skill-level)))


;; example activity with the methods

(cbn b5 "stump-jumper")

(csn b3 'mylar)

(chbo b8 'low)

(csbv b7 '(high medium))

(csbs b7 175)
```

10.3.3 An Analogous Representation in C++

For reference, the following is the approximate analogy of the CLOS example in Section 10.3.2 in C++.

```
// this is  a c++ example
// corresponds to CommonLISP CLOS example
```

```
// file: closex3.cpp

#include <iostream.h>
#include "stdio.h"
#include <string.h>


class vehicle {
public:
 char name[80];
 char manufacturer[80];
 char make[80];
 int wheels;
 char power[80];
 char iq_of_operator[80];
 char documentation[80];
 vehicle(void); //constructor, no return value
 void get_manufacturer(void);  // declared here; defined below
 int get_wheels(void);
 //
};

// here's the vehicle constructor:

vehicle::vehicle(void)
{
// first the strings "symbolic quantities"
 strcpy(name,"a vehicle");
 strcpy(manufacturer,"microsoft");
// numerical values
 wheels=4;
 //printf("vehicle initialized\n");
 }

// here's two accessors:

void vehicle::get_manufacturer(void)
    {printf("manufacturer is: %s \n", manufacturer);}

int vehicle::get_wheels(void) {return wheels;}


class boat: public vehicle {
public:
 int capacity;
 int wheels;
 char use[80];
 char iq_of_operator[80];
 char documentation[80];

 boat(void); //constructor, no return value
 int get_wheels(void);
};


// boat constructor
boat::boat(void)
{
```

```
strcpy(use, "recreation");
strcpy(iq_of_operator, "usually ok");
strcpy(documentation, "general boat class");
wheels=0;
capacity=2;
   // cout << "boat initialized\n";
}

int boat::get_wheels(void) {return wheels;}

class sailboat: public boat {
public:
 //int wheels;
 int sail_number;
 char sail_type[80];
 sailboat(void); //constructor
 void access_manufacturer(int choice);
 void access_manufacturer(int choice, char *manufacturer);
 };

// here's the sailboat constructor:

sailboat::sailboat(void)
{
// first the strings "symbolic quantities"
 strcpy(name,"my sailboat");
 strcpy(manufacturer,"laser");
 strcpy(sail_type, "dacron");
// numerical values
 sail_number=2;
 //wheels=0;
// cout << "sailboat initialized\n";
 }

// here's an accessor
//example of overloaded fn

void sailboat::access_manufacturer(int choice)

{
 if (choice == 1) // read option
 cout << "sailboat manufacturer is---" << manufacturer << "\n";
}

void sailboat::access_manufacturer(int choice, char *manufacturer)

{
 if (choice == 2) //write option
 cout << "this is the write option...\n";;
}

// and, of course, main():

void main(void)
{
 int choice;
// instance creation
```

```
vehicle example1;

// check some values:

// example1.get_manufacturer();
// cout << "the example vehicle has " << example1.get_wheels() << " wheels \n";
// cout << "and the name is " << example1.name <<"\n";

// create boat instance and check some values

boat my_boat;
// cout << "my boat's use is:    " <<my_boat.use << "\n";

// create sailboat instance and use accessor

sailboat my_sail_boat;
choice=1;
// my_sail_boat.access_manufacturer(choice);
// my_sail_boat.access_manufacturer(2, "bogus argument");

// now lets explore the objects and hierarchy further
// and somewhat randomly

//cout <<  "\n\nnow lets explore the objects and hierarchy further\n";

//cout << "the boat instance name is: " << my_boat.name << "\n";
//cout << "my sailboat name is: " << my_sail_boat.name << "\n";
//cout << "the boat instance operator IQ is: " << my_boat.iq_of_operator << "\n";
//cout << "my sailboat has " << my_sail_boat.sail_number << " sails\n";
//cout << "and they are made of " << my_sail_boat.sail_type << "\n";

// test function inheritence

cout << "\nnow let's test test function inheritence\n\n";
cout << "first notice that my_boat.wheels is reporting:\n";
cout << my_boat.wheels <<"\n";
cout << "also notice that my_sail_boat.wheels is reporting:\n";
cout << my_sail_boat.wheels <<"\n";
cout << "using my_boat.get_wheels \n";
cout << "the number of wheels on my boat is reported as: \n";
cout << my_boat.get_wheels() <<"\n";
cout << "using my_sail_boat.get_wheels \n";
cout << "the number of wheels on my sailboat is reported as: \n";
cout << my_sail_boat.get_wheels() <<"\n";
cout << "finally, using example1.get_wheels \n";
cout << "the number of wheels on the vehicle instance is reported as: \n";
cout <<  example1.get_wheels() <<"\n";
}
```

10.4 Exercises

1. For the CLOS class example defined in Section 10.2.9, draw the class hierarchy.

2. This problem tests your comfort level with CLOS. Consider the Lisp code using the CLOS extensions shown in Figure 10.3. This file loads in `clisp` without any errors or warnings.

```
(defclass food () ())

(defclass fruit (food)
  ((color :initarg :color
          :accessor fruit-color)
   (price :initarg :price
          :accessor fruit-price
          :initform 'inexpensive)))

(defclass apple (fruit)
  ((apple-color :accessor apple-color
                :initform 'red)))

(defclass orange (fruit) ())

(defclass seafood (food) ())

(defclass shrimp (seafood) ())

(defclass prawn (shrimp) ())

(defmethod prepare ((item apple))
 (core item))

(defmethod prepare ((item orange))
 (peel item))

(defmethod core (item)
 (format nil "~&coring ~S~%" item))

(defmethod peel (item)
 (format nil "~&peeling ~S~%" item))

(defmethod wash (item)
 (format nil "~&washing ~S~%" item))

(defmethod cook ((item food) (time integer))
  (format nil "~&cooking ~S ~S seconds~%"
          item time))

(setq ece352-apple (make-instance 'apple))

(setq ece352-fruit (make-instance 'fruit))

(setq ece352-shrimp (make-instance 'shrimp))
```

Figure 10.3 CLOS Fruit Example.

(a) Draw the class hierarchy.

(b) Note the use of function **format** in this code. **format** has the syntax:

```
format destination control-string &rest arguments
```

format is used to produce formatted output. **format** outputs the characters of **control-string**, except that a tilde (~)introduces a directive. The character after the tilde, possibly preceded by prefix parameters and modifiers, specifies what kind of formatting is desired. The output is sent to **destination**. If destination is nil, a string is created that contains the output; this string is returned as the value of the call to format.

For example:

```
> test-item
"apple"
> (format nil "~&Peeling ~S~%" test-item)
"Peeling \"apple\"
"
```

(c) For each of the following evaluations, show the returned value below the read-eval-print input. If an error results, simply answer "ERROR".

```
> (setq ece352-apple2 (make-instance 'apple) :apple-color 'green)


> (slot-value ece352-shrimp 'color)


> (setq my-apple (make-instance apple))


> (prepare ece352-apple)


> (prepare shrimp)


> (core ece352-shrimp)


> (slot-value price ece352-shrimp)


> (peel ece352-apple)


> (slot-value ece352-shrimp 'price)


> (prepare ece352-shrimp)
```

3. Using your favorite C++ compiler, compile and run the sample C++ code in Section 10.3.3.

CHAPTER 11

Object-Oriented, Typed Functional Programming with Modules: ML and CAML

The concern for man and his destiny must always be the chief interest of all technical effort. Never forget it between your diagrams and equations.
—Albert Einstein

11.1 An Introduction to SML/NJ and CAML

In this chapter, we consider further extensions to the functional programming (FP) paradigm and introduce ML and a popular dialect, CAML. Specifically, we consider:

- strongly typed functional languages. A good example is ML.
- object-oriented and strongly typed functional languages. OCAML, derived from CAML, is an example.

11.1.1 Introduction to ML (SML/NJ) and CAML

ML and CAML are similar to Lisp in that the basic paradigm is that of functional programming. Thus, we are familiar with the processes of defining and using functions, recursion, and so forth. In this chapter, SML/NJ (Standard ML of New Jersey) is used. Key features of SML/NJ and CAML are:

- SML/NJ is a functional language.
- SML/NJ is strongly typed, with a polymorphic type system and user-defined types.
- An interactive mode is used for development.
- SML/NJ supports a modules facility for large-scale program development.
- **ML is implemented in ML!** (Self-definition.)
- ML has imperative features (recall that Lisp did also).

- Many enhancements to SML/NJ are available; in particular those necessary to generate parsers.[1] For example, ML-Yacc is a parser generator for Standard ML modeled after the Yacc parser generator, and ML-Lex is a variant of Lex for the ML programming language.
- The efficiency of compiled (S)ML code is comparable to that of C.

CAML pragmatics are similar to those of Lisp and ML, in the sense that:

- interactive use is typical and used for incremental program development.
- a compiler (`ocamlc`) is available.
- a top-level loop is used that performs type checking, argument evaluation (call by value), code compilation, evaluation, and printing of the result.
- the language is based upon a *core language*, supplemented by a module system.
- a rich set of resources is provided to program with exceptions.

11.1.2 Major Distinctions

However, two major distinctions differentiate ML and CAML from Lisp:

1. ML and CAML are strongly typed. Compared to CommonLisp, this restricts the choices of input and returned values in functions. For example, in CommonLisp a function could be defined to return either the integer 3 or the value `t`. In ML and CAML, a function declared with return type of either type integer or boolean would not be allowed to return such a mixed type (without defining new types).

2. Lists (and consequently parentheses) are less significant, both as a data structure and a part of the language syntax.

Secondary distinctions are:

1. ML and CAML are based upon a set of strongly typed basis functions, arranged in a hierarchical (Standard Basis Function) library. *For this reason, the notion of* **function signatures** *is both important and quite useful.*

2. ML and CAML have many other features that are useful for large scale programming efforts and that facilitate the production of "correct" code.

11.1.3 ML and CAML in Programming Language Evolution

Figure 1.8 of Section 1.3.3 in Chapter 1 shows a long "functional path" from Lisp to ML. ML is a typed functional language. Standard ML or SML is a standardization of ML. SML/NJ is an implementation of SML pioneered by Bell Labs (Lucent Technologies) in conjunction with several universities.

[1] Recall the LGN in Prolog.

11.1.4 The ML Family Tree and Other Relatives

Numerous variants and extension to ML exist, as the following annotated list indicates.

1. Standard ML of New Jersey (SML/NJ).
2. CAML is a strongly typed functional programming language from the ML family. Objective CAML and CAML Light are two open-source implementations of CAML developed at INRIA.
3. Objective CAML is an implementation of the ML language, based on the CAML Light dialect extended with class-based objects and a powerful module system. Objective CAML comprises two compilers. One generates bytecode, which is then interpreted by a C program.
4. CAML Light is a subset of Objective CAML, especially designed for teaching and learning the art of programming. CAML Light use is shown in Section 11.3.7.
5. Moscow ML is a lightweight implementation of Standard ML (SML).
6. Poplog (ML) is an interesting attempt to be all things to all people. It is a multi-language, virtual machine-based programming environment that includes many features, including the languages Pop-11, ML, CommonLisp (including CLOS), and Prolog. Poplog was developed at the University of Sussex and is distributed free of charge.

   Sources are available at:

   `http://openpoplog.sourceforge.net/`

   and

   `http://www.cs.bham.ac.uk/research/poplog/freepoplog.html`

7. Haskell is a polymorphically typed, lazy, purely functional language, named after the mathematician Haskell Brooks Curry.[2] Haskell is based on the lambda calculus. Because Haskell is based on open-source software, there are implementations available for most mainstream operating systems. More details are available at the Haskell home page:

   `http://www.haskell.org/`

A number of unsupported and somewhat obsolete SML/NJ ports also exist.

11.2 The SML/NJ Language

11.2.1 Overview of SML/NJ

> *Standard ML (SML) is a safe, modular, strict, functional, polymorphic programming language with compile-time type checking and type inference, garbage collection, exception handling, immutable data types and updatable references, abstract data types, and parametric modules. It has efficient implementations and a formal definition with a proof of soundness.*

[2]Whose work in mathematical logic led to the "currying" concept.

11.2.2 Noteworthy ML Features

ML (SML/NJ) was designed to be safe, in the sense that a program that passes the type-checker cannot dump core, access private fields of abstract data types, mistake integers for pointers, and so on. ML is modular; the Standard ML module system supports modules (called structures) and interfaces (called signatures). This concept is strongly related to our look at algebraic semantics in Chapter 12. Each module is specified by a signature and a structure. In this way, the language is extensible. For example, Figure 11.1 shows the signature for a random number generator module, and Figure 11.2 shows snippets of the actual implementation. SML/NJ also provides the *compilation manager*, a utility for loading and managing modules and module dependencies. The reader should also consult the basis library pages for further examples.

```
(* random-sig.sml
 *
 * COPYRIGHT (c) 1993 by AT&T Bell Laboratories.  See COPYRIGHT file for details.
 *)

signature RANDOM =
  sig

    type rand
(* the internal state of a random number generator *)

    val rand : (int * int) -> rand
(* create rand from initial seed *)

    val toString : rand -> string
    val fromString : string -> rand
        (* convert state to and from string
         * fromString raises Fail if its argument
         * does not have the proper form.
         *)

    val randInt : rand -> int
(* generate ints uniformly in [minInt,maxInt] *)

    val randNat : rand -> int
(* generate ints uniformly in [0,maxInt] *)

    val randReal : rand -> real
(* generate reals uniformly in [0.0,1.0) *)

    val randRange : (int * int) -> rand -> int
(* randRange (lo,hi) generates integers uniformly [lo,hi].
 * Raises Fail if hi < lo.
 *)

  end; (* RANDOM *
```

Figure 11.1 Example of SML/NJ Module Signature (Random).

```
(* random.sml
 *
 * COPYRIGHT (c) 1993 by AT&T Bell Laboratories.  See COPYRIGHT file for details.
 *
 * This package implements a random number generator using a subtract-with-borrow
 * (SWB) generator as described in Marsaglia and Zaman, "A New Class of Random Number
 * Generators," Ann. Applied Prob. 1(3), 1991, pp. 462-480.
     .
     .
     .
structure Random : RANDOM =
  struct
    structure A   = Array
    structure LW  = LargeWord
    structure W8A = Word8Array
    structure W8V = Word8Vector
    structure P   = Pack32Big
     .
     .
     .
    val nbits = 31                                       (* bits per word *)
    val maxWord : Word31.word = 0wx7FFFFFFF              (* largest word *)
    val bit30 : Word31.word   = 0wx40000000
    val lo30 : Word31.word    = 0wx3FFFFFFF

    val N = 48
    val lag = 8
    val offset = N-lag
     .
     .
     .
    fun rand (congy, shrgx) = let
          fun mki (i,c,s) = let
                val c' = lcg c
                val s' = xorb(s, s << 0w18)
                val s'' = xorb(s', s' >> 0w13)
                val i' = (lo30 & (i >> 0w1)) ++ (bit30 & xorb(c',s''))
                in (i',c',s'') end
  fun iterate (0, v) = v
    | iterate (n, v) = iterate(n-1, mki v)
          fun mkseed (congx,shrgx) = iterate (nbits, (0w0,congx,shrgx))
          fun genseed (0,seeds,congx,_) = (seeds,congx)
            | genseed (n,seeds,congx,shrgx) = let
                val (seed,congx',shrgx') = mkseed (congx,shrgx)
                in genseed(n-1,seed::seeds,congx',shrgx') end
          val congx = ((Word31.fromInt congy & maxWord) << 0w1)+0w1
          val (seeds,congx) = genseed(N,[],congx, Word31.fromInt shrgx)
          in
            RND{vals = A.fromList seeds,
                index = ref 0,
                congx = ref congx,
                borrow = ref false}
          end
```

Figure 11.2 Snippets of an SML/NJ Module Implementation (Random).

ML has higher-order functions–that is, functions can be passed as arguments, stored in data structures, and returned as results of function calls. Function calls in ML, like those of C and C++, evaluate their arguments before entering the body of the function. Thus, ML uses *call-by-value.*

Furthermore, ML supports polymorphic functions and data types. Thus, a single type declaration (such as "list") may be used to describe lists of integers, lists of strings, lists of lists of integers, and so on. This is shown in the examples. The SML compiler can determine many types from context. This is also shown in the examples. ML has an exception-handling mechanism similar to those of C++ and Java.

The ML language is clearly specified in Harper, Milner, Tofte, and MacQueen (1997).

11.2.3 Basic Interaction with ML

SML/NJ incorporates a "read-eval-print" loop (like Lisp). The basics of this interaction are dictated by:

- is SML's prompt

; is an input to SML (appearing at the end of an expression), which means:

1. Perform type checking and other static analysis on the expression.
2. Compile the expression.
3. Evaluate (some documentation refers to this as "execute") the expression.
4. Print the result.

`it` is the last thing you typed

This is probably best shown with a few simple examples:

```
- 9*8        (Nothing happens)
= ;
val it = 72 : int

- 10 < 11;
val it = true : bool

- "Hi Mom!" ;
val it = "Hi Mom!" : string

- 3.14159;
val it = 3.14159 : real

- val x1 = 7*9;
val x1 = 63 : int

- x1;
val it = 63 : int
```

Several aspects of the preceding examples are important:

1. SML/NJ expressions are evaluated following the ;.

2. Where possible, SML/NJ infers the type of the result from the input context.

3. `val` is similar to Lisp's `setq`.

4. The returned type (as well as a value) is reported.

11.2.4 SML Typing and Error Reporting

The following example shows SML's response when attempting to use incompatible types:

```
- true;
val it = true : bool
- false;
val it = false : bool
- 3;
val it = 3 : int
- 3-true;
stdIn:23.1-23.7 Error: operator and operand don't agree [literal]
  operator domain: int * int
  operand:         int * bool
  in expression:
    3 - true
```

Note, therefore, that type conversion does not occur automatically (like the type coercion in C); however, functions are available to facilitate this (where and when absolutely necessary).

11.2.5 Exceptions

A function must return a value. An extension to this concept is to allow a function to return an exception instead. An exception typically indicates a problem encountered during function evaluation (at so-called run-time). SML allows handling of exceptions; in fact, any of the built-in ML functions have associated exceptions.

An exception is declared using the syntax shown in the following example:

```
-exception BigProblem;
exception BigProblem
```

An exception is *raised* using `raise` as shown in the following example:

```
- if (true) then raise BigProblem else 1.0;

uncaught exception BigProblem
  raised at: stdIn:26.22-26.32
```

Notice that the exception was not caught; this is the role of `handle`. Suppose `<expression>` raises an exception. It is handled with the syntax:

```
<expression> handle <match>
```

where `<match>` is of the form:

```
<pattern> => <expression>
```

`<pattern>` is an exception and `<expression>` is the corresponding action; for example:

```
BigProblem => print "big problem!";.
```

11.2.6 SML/NJ: Function Definition

One of the most important aspects of a functional language is the creation of functions. Here is an example of both creation and use of a SML/NJ function:

```
- fun twice x:int = 2 * x;
val twice = fn : int -> int

- twice 5;
val it = 10 : int

- twice(3*4);
val it = 24 : int
```

In the preceding function definition example we see the appearance of a *function signature*, that is, `twice = fn : int -> int`. Here is another simple example:

```
- fun cube (x:int) = x*x*x;
val cube = fn : int -> int

- cube(3);
val it = 27 : int
```

11.2.7 ML Conditionals, Part 1

ML (SML/NJ) has two ways to allow conditional processing:

1. With an `if-then-else` construct, as shown in the following example.
2. With a pattern-matching facility, described later.

```
- fun fact x = if x=0 then 1 else x*fact(x-1);
val fact = fn : int -> int

- fact(4);
val it = 24 : int
```

11.2.8 ML Conditionals, Part 2: Pattern Matching

Conditional constructs are also available in SML/NJ using a pattern-matching mechanism. This is similar to the `case` construct found elsewhere. For example, consider an alternative recursive definition of a factorial function as the contents of file `fact2.sml`:

```
fun fact2 0 = 1
| fact2 x = x*fact2(x-1);
```

with ML interpreter response:

```
- use "fact2.sml";
[opening fact2.sml]
val fact2 = fn : int -> int
val it = () : unit
- fact2(4);
val it = 24 : int
```

11.2.9 Other Selected ML Pragmatics

Loading ML Source from a File

The function `use`, with signature:

```
use: string -> unit
```

will load a file containing SML source code if applied to a string containing the name of the file. For example:

```
use ''ece352ex.sml'';
```

would cause the contents of the file to be loaded into the top-level interactive system. The modules and module-management facility is typically used for big projects. For example, consider the contents of file `fact.sml`:

```
fun fact x = if x=0 then 1
else x*fact(x-1);
```

This file is loaded via:

```
- use "fact.sml" ;
[opening fact.sml]
val fact = fn : int -> int
val it = () : unit
```

after which the function `fact` is available for use:

```
- fact (2);
val it = 2 : int
```

Using SML/NJ Directory Manipulation Functions

Here we first notice the effect of the Standard Basis Function library and how functions are invoked from this library.

```
- OS.FileSys.getDir();
val it = "C:\\ece352\\ML" : string

- OS.FileSys.chDir("c:/");
val it = () : unit

- OS.FileSys.getDir();
val it = "c:\\" : string
```

Here is a second example:

```
- OS.FileSys.getDir();
val it = "C:\\WINNT\\Profiles\\rjschal\\Desktop" : string
- OS.FileSys.chDir("d:\\ece352");
val it = () : unit
- OS.FileSys.getDir();
val it = "d:\\ece352" : string
- OS.FileSys.chDir("ML");
val it = () : unit
- OS.FileSys.getDir();
val it = "d:\\ece352\\ML" : string
```

ML Source Comments

Comments begin with `(*` and end with `*)`.

Ending an SML/NJ Session (Cleanly)

Typing the EOF character at the interactive top level will quit SML/NJ. The EOF key is typically ctrl-D under Unix and ctrl-Z under Windows. It is also necessary to press the return/enter key to make it take effect. Another method is to call the function `OS.Process.exit`.

SML Compilers

SML/NJ provides a compiler and programming environment for the ML language. However, a number of other compilers are noteworthy.

MLton MLton is an optimizing compiler for the Standard ML programming language. As such, an interactive mode is not used, but rather user source to be compiled and executed is entered from a file. MLton runs on a variety of platforms, including Linux and Windows (using `cygwin`). MLton supports the full SML 97 version of the ML language and is available at:

`http://www.mlton.org/`

Other compilers are available. For example, MLJ is a compiler for Standard ML that produces Java bytecode. SML.NET is a compiler for Standard ML that targets the .NET Common Language Runtime and that supports language interoperability features for easy access to .NET libraries. It is available at:

`http://www.cl.cam.ac.uk/Research/TSG/SMLNET/`

11.2.10 Additional ML Language Features

`val` (Like CommonLisp's `setq`)

When val is used, SML/NJ reports `val` <**name**> `= etc.` rather than `it`.

```
- 2;
val it = 2 : int

- val ece352 = 2;
val ece352 = 2 : int
```

Four Basic Types in ML

The ML Basis Library provides four built-in types: `int`, `bool`, `real` (equivalent to float in C), and `string`.

Note that no automatic coercion (as in many languages, such as C) is used; this must be done via type conversion functions, as shown in the following example:

```
- 2;
val it = 2 : int
- real 2;
```

```
val it = 2.0 : real
- floor 3.14159;
val it = 3 : int
-  3.14159 - 2;
stdIn:27.2-27.13 Error: operator and operand don't agree [literal]
  operator domain: real * real
  operand:         real * int
  in expression:
    3.14159 - 2
- 3.14159 - Real.fromInt(2);
val it = 1.14159 : real
```

The Type `unit`

The type `unit` is akin to C's `void` and CommonLisp's `nil`. It is used when the value of an expression is immaterial, or when a function has no arguments. Functions returning `unit` are typically used for side effects. Several examples appear in these notes.

User-Defined Input Types

The ML construct `type` handles user-defined input types, which may then be used in function definitions. Here is a simple example:

```
- type intpair = int * int;
type intpair = int * int

- fun addpair ((x,y) : intpair) = x + y;
val addpair = fn : intpair -> int

- addpair(3,5);
val it = 8 : int
```

Returned Values and `fun`

Notice that for a nonfunction, SML/NJ returns its value. For a function, *the type of the function* is the value returned.[3] As noted, functions can also return **exceptions**.

Simple Printing with ML

SML provides the `print` function, with signature:

```
- print;
val it = fn : string -> unit
```

Thus, the argument to `print` must be of type `string`. For example:

```
- print ("Hello World\n");
Hello World
val it = () : unit
```

[3] Recall that Lisp returns the function name as the value of a `defun`.

`Real.toString` and `Real.fromString` To print entities that are not strings, conversion is required. A typical problem is the printing of real numbers. First, some function signatures:

```
- Real.toString;
val it = fn : real -> string

- Real.fromString;
val it = fn : string -> real option

- Real.==;
val it = fn : real * real -> bool
```

Now, some applications:

```
- Real.==(4.5,4.5);
val it = true : bool

- Real.toString(5.6);
val it = "5.6" : string

- print(Real.toString(5.6));
5.6val it = () : unit

- print(Real.toString(5.6)^"\n\n");
5.6

val it = () : unit

- Real.fromString("5.6");
val it = SOME 5.6 : real option

- Real.fromInt(99);
val it = 99.0 : real
```


```
- Real.toString(5.6);
val it = "5.6" : string

- print(Real.toString(5.6));
5.6val it = () : unit

- print(Real.toString(5.6)^"\n\n");
5.6

val it = () : unit

- Real.fromString("5.6");
val it = SOME 5.6 : real option

- Real.fromInt(99);
val it = 99.0 : real
```


Strings and Characters in ML

Although strings and characters are different types, we describe both together because they are often used together.

Characters `#"a"` denotes the character a. Conversely, `"a"` denotes the string a. Special characters such as LF are represented using the familiar C notation. The basis library provides many manipulation functions. The use of several follows:

```
- ord(#''\n''); (* to ASCII value *)
val it = 10 : int
- chr(10);
val it = #"\n" : char
- chr(ord(#"\n"));
val it = #"\n" : char
- Char.toString(#"\n");
val it = "\\n" : string
- print("\n\n\n\n");
val it = () : unit
- chr 42;
val it = #"*" : char
- Char.contains  "m* d*g h** fl***" #"*";
val it = true : bool
- Char.contains  "my dog has fleas" #"a";
val it = true : bool
- size "my dog has fleas";
val it = 16 : int
- val chlist = explode "my dog has fleas";
val chlist = [#"m",#"y",#" ",#"d",#"o",#"g",#" ",#"h",#"a",#"s",#" ",#"f",...]
  : char list
- chlist;
val it = [#"m",#"y",#" ",#"d",#"o",#"g",#" ",#"h",#"a",#"s",#" ",#"f",...]
  : char list
- List.hd chlist;
val it = #"m" : char
- List.tl chlist;
val it = [#"y",#" ",#"d",#"o",#"g",#" ",#"h",#"a",#"s",#" ",#"f",#"l",...]
  : char list
```

String concatenation is accomplished using ^, as the following example shows.

```
- "HI" ^ "Mom!";
val it = "HIMom!" : string
```

String-to-list conversion, as shown previously, is done using explosion. Here is another example:

```
- explode "Hi Mom!";
val it = [#"H",#"i",#" ",#"M",#"o",#"m",#"!"] : char list
```

Printing a List

The following is another example of a recursive function used to convert a real list into a string list and then, using `print`, to print the list.

```
fun stringList(inList: real list) =
if
not(null(inList))
 then Real.toString(hd(inList))^"  "^stringList(tl(inList))
 else "\n";
```

The use of this function in conjunction with `print` yields the following behavior:

```
- print (stringList([1.0, 2.0, 3.0, 4.0]));
1.0  2.0  3.0  4.0
val it = () : unit
```

11.2.11 Exploring ML Functions, Part II

Currying and Tuples

SML/NJ views every operator or function as applied to a single operand. (Recall the lambda calculus concept of currying.) However, an argument (operand) may be input as a tuple, that is, multiple arguments enclosed in parentheses and separated by commas. However, these may not be mixed.

An example of a two-argument function `power`, with input tuple `(x,0)`, follows.

```
- fun power(x, 0) = 1.0
    | power(x, n) = x * power(x,n-1) ;
val power = fn : real * int -> real

- val a = (2.0, 3);
val a = (2.0,3) : real * int

- power a;
val it = 8.0 : real

- power(4.0, 2);
val it = 16.0 : real
```

Polymorphic Behavior and Signatures

In SML, a signature is a set of types for values in the structure. In addition to being fundamental to the modular description of SML, signatures are informative for the programmer. A polymorphic function signature uses `'a`, where `'a` is a "type variable" in the signature to denote "any type."

```
- fun examp2 (x) = x;
val examp2 = fn : 'a -> 'a

(* compare with a typed definition *)

- fun examp3 (x) :real = x;
val examp3 = fn : real -> real

(* some application examples *)

- examp2(1.0);
val it = 1.0 : real

- examp2(1);
val it = 1 : int

- examp2("1");
val it = "1" : string

- examp2(true);
val it = true : bool
```

The reader is encouraged to repeat the preceding evaluations using function `exampl3`.

Local Variables and `let`

As in CommonLisp, `let` is provided to allow the definition and subsequent use of local variables without global side effects. An example of the syntax and use follows.

```
fun main((mix_total_p, xx, yy, i02, ii): realinputs)
= let
   val r = maincalcsandchecks (mix_total_p, xx, yy, i02, ii);
   val error = ~1.0;
in
if Real.==(r, error)
  then
    print("Sorry, no solution or out of bounds\n")
  else
    print("The psi of 02 to be added is " ^ Real.toString(r) ^"\n")
end;
```

Function Polymorphism

Utility A polymorphic function is usable with more than one class of type. Typically, the behavior of a polymorphic function is "uniform" over different types. For example, the type list is a primitive and important type whose elements are required to be all of the same type. However, the type may be `string`, `real`, or `int` (or other derived types). Thus we may have `int` lists, `real` lists, and `string` lists. The list manipulation functions such as `hd` and `tl` behave similarly on lists of each of these types. For example, `hd` returns the head of the list, regardless of whether it is `int`, `char`, `string`, or `real`.

Examples Many of the previous SML examples have shown the polymorphic behavior of SML functions. Additional examples follow.

```
- m;
val it = [1,2,3,4] : int list

- val n = [true, true, false];
val n = [true,true,false] : bool list

- tl m;
val it = [2,3,4] : int list

- tl n;
val it = [true,false] : bool list
```

11.2.12 Lists in SML

As the examples that follow indicate, notation of a list in ML is similar to Prolog.

In untyped languages (e.g., CommonLisp), lists are just collections. In typed languages, lists are collections of the same type. Thus, a very important distinction is: *In ML, all members of a list must have the same type.* This is due to the polymorphic behavior of list manipulation functions in the List Basis Function Library.

The functions `hd` and `tl` are similar to their Lisp counterparts. List construction is accomplished using `::`, as shown next:

```
- val m = [1,2,3,4];
val m = [1,2,3,4] : int list
```

```
- hd m;
val it = 1 : int

- tl m;
val it = [2,3,4] : int list

- null m;
val it = false : bool

- null [];
val it = true : bool

- 0 :: m;
val it = [0,1,2,3,4] : int list

- val m = [2,3,4];
val m = [2,3,4] : int list

- 1 :: m;
val it = [1,2,3,4] : int list

- m :: 1;
stdIn:22.1-22.7 Error: operator and operand don't agree [literal]
  operator domain: int list * int list list
  operand:         int list * int
  in expression:
    m :: 1
```

11.2.13 Recursion, Pattern Matching, and Lists

As a further example of pattern matching and recursion in SML, we revisit a recursive formulation of a polymorphic member function definition:

```
fun member (x,[]) = false
| member (x,h::t) =
    if (h=x) then true
             else member (x,t);
```

The SML use of this function follows:

```
]$ sml
Standard ML of New Jersey, Version 110.0.7, September 28, 2000 [CM; autoload enabled]
- use "member.sml";
[opening member.sml]
val member = fn : ''a * ''a list -> bool
val it = () : unit
- member("a", ["c";"b";"a"]);
stdIn:18.17 Error: syntax error found at SEMICOLON
- member("a", ["c","b","a"]);
val it = true : bool
- member("d", ["c","b","a"]);
val it = false : bool
- member(1, ["c","b","a"]);
stdIn:20.1-20.25 Error: operator and operand don't agree [literal]
  operator domain: int * int list
  operand:         int * string list
  in expression:
    member (1,"c" :: "b" :: <exp> :: <exp>)
```

The reader should compare this formulation with the CAML formulation in Section 11.3.5.

11.2.14 Extended SML Example: ANN Unit Design and Training

To illustrate ML program design and provide a comparison to CommonLisp, the following shows the single ANN unit implementation and training from Chapter 9 in SML/NJ.

Overall SML/NJ Program

```
(* file: annUnit.sml *)
(* rev 11-17-03  *)

(* Note: to run --
     change into directory containing file via:
       OS.FileSys.chDir(<wherever>)
     and use "annUnit.sml"   *)

(* follows structure of CommonLISP solution *)
(* uses recursion, no local variables, etc. *)

(* data and functions for unit *)

val H = [[[0.0, 0.0], [0.25]],
         [[0.0, 1.0], [0.50]],
         [[1.0, 0.0], [0.75]],
         [[1.0, 1.0], [1.00]]];

val HBias = [[[0.0, 0.0, 1.0], [0.25]],
             [[0.0, 1.0, 1.0], [0.50]],
             [[1.0, 0.0, 1.0], [0.75]],
             [[1.0, 1.0, 1.0], [1.00]]];

(* initialization w/o and w/ bias *)

fun weightInit () = [0.1, ~0.1];

fun weightInitBias () = [0.1, ~0.1, 0.2];

(* recursively) compute unit net activation from inputs
   and (current) weights
   value returned: net activation
   note: function below is slightly inefficient for clarity *)

fun calcNet (inputs: real list, weights: real list) =
if null(inputs) andalso null(weights) then 0.0
   else
   hd(inputs) * hd(weights) + calcNet(tl(inputs), tl(weights));


(* artificial neuron activation (squashing) function *)

fun squash (net: real) =
1.0 / (1.0 + (Math.exp (~1.0 * net)))


(* single ANN unit
   value returned: unit output (squashed) *)
```

```
fun unit (inputs: real list, weights: real list) =
 squash(calcNet(inputs, weights));


(* the constant part of the correction, delta *)

fun delta (output: real, target: real) =
  (target - output) * output * (1.0 - output);


(* form w_i^{n+1}=w_i^n + rho * delta *i_i
   don't require reforming delta for each component *)

fun trainUnitInputRecur (input: real list, weights: real list,
                         delta: real, rho: real)  =
if null(weights) then nil
                 else
    (hd(weights) + (rho * delta * hd(input))) ::
    trainUnitInputRecur(tl(input), tl(weights), delta, rho);


(* fn to return the modified unit weight list resulting from
   training over a single input pattern *)

fun trainUnitPattern(input: real list, target: real,
                     inWeights: real list, rho: real) =
 trainUnitInputRecur(input, inWeights, delta(unit(input,inWeights),target),rho);

(* we're almost there -- one pass over H *)

fun trainUnitAll(H: real list list list,
                 inWeights: real list, rho: real) =
if
  not(null(H))
then
  trainUnitAll(tl(H), trainUnitPattern(List.nth(hd(H),0),
                                  hd(List.nth(hd(H),1)),
                                  inWeights,rho), rho)
else
  inWeights;


(* finally, n passes over H *)

fun trainMultiple(H:real list list list,
                  inWeights: real list, rho: real, n: int) =
if
n > 0 then
      trainMultiple(H, trainUnitAll(H,inWeights,rho),rho,n-1)
      else
(* assumes n = 0 *)
     inWeights;
```

Sample Results

The results that follow should be compared to those of Chapter 9.

```
$ sml
Standard ML of New Jersey, Version 110.0.7, September 28, 2000 [CM; autoload enabled]
- use "annUnit.sml";
```

```
[opening annUnit.sml]
val H =
  [[[0.0,0.0],[0.25]],[[0.0,1.0],[0.5]],[[1.0,0.0],[0.75]],[[1.0,1.0],[1.0]]]
  : real list list list
GC #0.0.0.0.1.16:   (0 ms)
val HBias =
  [[[0.0,0.0,1.0],[0.25]],[[0.0,1.0,1.0],[0.5]],[[1.0,0.0,1.0],[0.75]],
   [[1.0,1.0,1.0],[1.0]]] : real list list list
val weightInit = fn : unit -> real list
val weightInitBias = fn : unit -> real list
type twolists = real list * real list
val calcNet = fn : real list * real list -> real
val squash = fn : real -> real
val unit = fn : real list * real list -> real
val delta = fn : real * real -> real
GC #0.0.0.0.2.55:   (0 ms)
val trainUnitInputRecur = fn : real list * real list * real * real -> real list
val trainUnitPattern = fn : real list * real * real list * real -> real list
val trainUnitAll = fn : real list list list * real list * real -> real list
val trainMultiple = fn
  : real list list list * real list * real * int -> real list
val it = () : unit

- val weights1 = trainMultiple(H,weightInit(),0.25,5000);
val weights1 = [1.77202999343,0.211156291066] : real list
- unit(hd(List.nth(H,0)),weights1);
val it = 0.5 : real
-  unit(hd(List.nth(H,1)),weights1);
val it = 0.552593801269 : real
- unit(hd(List.nth(H,2)),weights1);
val it = 0.854709938943 : real
- unit(hd(List.nth(H,3)),weights1);
val it = 0.879020412253 : real
- GC #0.0.0.0.3.163:   (0 ms)

- val weights2 = trainMultiple(HBias, weightInitBias(),0.25,5000);
val weights2 = [2.49834802227,1.32339097977,~1.24917390228] : real list
- unit(hd(List.nth(HBias,0)),weights2);
val it = 0.222843173053 : real
- unit(hd(List.nth(HBias,1)),weights2);
val it = 0.518545757382 : real
- unit(hd(List.nth(HBias,2)),weights2);
val it = 0.77715686465 : real
- unit(hd(List.nth(HBias,3)),weights2);
val it = 0.929074908599 : real

- trainMultiple(HBias, weightInitBias(), 0.25,1);
val it = [0.138894636265,~0.0734323900275,0.219071373386] : real list
```

Additional Results Using an SML File and use

To facilitate additional results (function evaluations), the following file is created:

```
val weights1 = trainMultiple(H,weightInit(),0.25,500);

unit(hd(List.nth(H,0)),weights1);

unit(hd(List.nth(H,1)),weights1);
```

```
unit(hd(List.nth(H,2)),weights1);

unit(hd(List.nth(H,3)),weights1);

val weights2 = trainMultiple(HBias, weightInitBias(),0.25,500);

unit(hd(List.nth(HBias,0)),weights2);

unit(hd(List.nth(HBias,1)),weights2);

unit(hd(List.nth(HBias,2)),weights2);

unit(hd(List.nth(HBias,3)),weights2);
```

Using this file results in the following:

```
- use "annUnit-alternative-soln.sml";
[opening annUnit-alternative-soln.sml]
val weights1 = [1.72520525302,0.228290679431] : real list
val it = 0.5 : real
val it = 0.556826085272 : real
val it = 0.848798091527 : real
val it = 0.875827337589 : real
val weights2 = [2.31176853291,1.15636076197,~1.08633798024] : real list
val it = 0.252308487621 : real
val it = 0.517498546126 : real
val it = 0.773017813595 : real
val it = 0.915428220005 : real
val it = () : unit
```

11.3 CAML and `ocaml`

Researchers from several universities, Bell Labs, and INRIA developed Standard ML. Thereafter, a variant (actually a dialect) called CAML was developed at INRIA and elsewhere. This version, enhanced with OO capabilities, has become known as Objective CAML, or OCAML.[4] As shown later, another (simpler) dialect of CAML is CAML Lite.

11.3.1 Overview of Selected CAML Syntax and Pragmatics

Introductory Points

A few noteworthy introductory points regarding CAML:

1. The command-line version of CAML is invoked by typing `ocaml` at the command prompt. Input is case-sensitive.

2. Comments follow the same format as in SML, beginning with `(*` and ending with `*)`.

3. All variable names must begin with a lowercase letter. Names beginning with a capital letter are reserved for constructors for user-defined data structures.

[4]Here we use capitals to indicate the CAML language (derived from ML); `ocaml` is an implementation of the OO version, as well as the name of the distribution. As a practical matter, the OCAML language implementation is freely available; it is up to the user to decide if the OO extensions are to be used.

4. The CAML syntax provides several ways to define functions. This is shown in Section 11.3.2. For multiargument functions; both tuples and currying are supported.

5. CAML allows the use of `if-then` constructs as well as pattern matchers for conditional statements. This is shown in several examples that follow. The CAML interpreter will check for unchecked input cases.

6. Integer and floating-point operations are distinguished by separate symbols. Integer operations such as addition and multiplication are designated `+` and `*`, respectively. The floating point counterparts are designated `+.` and `*.`, respectively. Note how this differs from SML and CommonLisp, wherein the respective operator (function) is overloaded.

7. The interactive system prompt is the `#` character, and a pair of semicolons is the CAML expression terminator. After an expression is entered, the system compiles it, evaluates it, and prints the outcome of the evaluation.

8. CAML phrases are either simple expressions or `let` definitions of identifiers that may be either values or functions.

9. Like ML, explicit type declaration of function parameters is not necessary. CAML will try to infer the type from usage in the function body.

10. Recursive functions (many examples are shown in the following) *must* be defined with the `let rec` binding.

11. Typing a function name without arguments at the command line causes `ocaml` to return the function signature. For example:

```
\# abs;;

- : int -> int = <fun>
```

The Interactive (Top-Level) CAML System

Like Lisp and ML, program (function) development in CAML is typically done interactively and incrementally. Section 11.5 discusses compilation.

In the interactive `ocaml` system, the user enters CAML expressions, terminated by `;;`. The `#` symbol is the `ocaml` prompt. The system compiles and evaluates the expression and prints the result of the evaluation. Note that the CAML system, like ML, computes and returns information on both the value and the type for each expression.

Function parameters need no explicit type declaration: the system infers their types from their usage in the function. Notice also that integers and floating-point numbers are distinct types, with distinct operators: `+` and `*` operate on integers, but `+.` and `*.` operate on floats. There is no coercion of type; CAML functions must be explicitly used for type conversion. For example, the Pervasives library contains the functions `float_of_int`, used to convert an `int` into a `float`, as well as `truncate` (or `int_of_float`), used for `float` to `int` conversion. Similarly, the Pervasives module contains elementary number to string conversion functions, including `string_of_int` for `int` to `string` conversion as well as `int_of_string` for `string` to `int` conversion.

Simple Interaction

For illustration and introduction, a short `ocaml` interaction follows.

```
#1+2*3;;
- : int = 7

#let pi = 4.0 *. atan 1.0;;
val pi : float = 3.14159265359

#let square x = x *. x;;
val square : float -> float = <fun>

#square(sin pi) +. square(cos pi);;
- : float = 1
```

Building a Custom Top-Level System

`ocaml` provides the ability to build a custom top-level system. Suppose the `ocaml` Unix library was frequently used. Instead of using `#use` or `#load` directives every time the interactive system was invoked, `ocamlmktop` could be used to build a custom top-level system where this library was included (much like the Pervasives library). To build this custom top-level `ocaml` system (named here `myocaml`) we use:

```
ocamlmktop -o myocaml unix.cma
```

This top-level system is now started via the command `./mytop` (as opposed to `ocaml`, used previously).

`ocaml` Top-Level Directives

`ocaml` top-level directives (commands) control the top level-behavior and provide useful functionality for interactive development. As shown in the numerous examples in this chapter, directives start with the `#` character. For example, typing `#quit;;` will exit the top-level `ocaml` interpreter. Some useful directives include:

`#cd`: Change the current working directory.

`#load`: Load a bytecode object file.

`#use`: Read, compile, and execute CAML source statements from a file.

`#trace`: Trace a designated function (`#untrace` stops tracing).

CAML Programming Environment Structure: Functions, Modules, and Libraries

The CAML programming environment structure is similar to that of ML in the sense that both are dependent upon a core language supported by one or more *basis libraries* and set of additional libraries containing modules of functions and data.

In `ocaml`, data, data structures, and associated functions are bundled into `modules`. Libraries contain one or more modules. For example, the `ocaml` core library provides a number of elementary data types, including the types `int`, `float`, `bool`, `list`, and `string` as well as predefined exceptions. The core library also includes the Pervasives module, which is the initially opened `ocaml` module. This module contains many useful functions

Operator Symbol	Meaning
`~-`	Unary integer negation
`+`	Integer addition
`-` (infix)	Integer subtraction
`-` (prefix)	Integer negation
`*`	Integer multiplication
`/`	Integer division
`~-.`	Unary floating-point negation
`+.`	Floating-point addition
`-.` (infix)	Floating-point subtraction
`-.` (prefix)	Floating-point negation
`*.`	Floating-point multiplication
`/.`	Floating-point division
`**`	Floating-point exponentiation
`::`	List "cons-ing"
`@`	List concatenation
`<`	Test "less than"
`<=`	Test "less than or equal to"
`>`	Test "greater than"
`>=`	Test "greater than or equal to"

Table 11.1 Elementary CAML Operators.

for use with the core library data types, including `min`, `max`, `not`, `or`, `+`, `*`, `sqrt`, `log`, and so on. (For a complete listing of libraries and associated module contents, consult the reference manual.)

Abbreviated Table of Basic CAML Operators

Table 11.1 summarizes a few simple CAML operators. Note that in CAML it is possible to redefine any of these symbols.

CAML Extensions

The CAML language and the associated `ocaml` implementation/distribution also provide:

1. a CAML-based lexer and parser generators (appropriately named `ocamllex` and `ocamlyacc`).
2. a built-in documentation generator (`ocamldoc`), which makes special use of comments delineated by `(**` and `**)`.
3. a language module browser `ocamlbrowser`,[5] which provides a quick, on-line reference to the modules and libraries as well as an IDE.
4. OO programming extensions (via `ocaml`).

[5]This requires `Tk/Tcl`.

11.3.2 Defining Functions in CAML

Function Definition Alternatives

CAML provides at least two syntactic forms to define functions. First, we provide an overview of the syntax.

Pattern-Match Version The first "pattern-match" based version has the syntax:

```
function pattern_1 -> expr_1
       | ...
       | pattern_n -> expr_n
```

When this (as yet unnamed) function of a single argument is given a value for the argument, the value is matched against each pattern in the function definition. The *first* of these matches that succeeds causes the corresponding expression to be evaluated and returned as the function value. The `ocaml` interpreter checks to be sure the pattern match defined by the function is exhaustive; if there are input patterns not recognized by the function, the interpreter will point them out. For example, consider the following anonymous function and the `ocaml` response:

```
# (function 1 -> "one" | 2 -> "two" | 3 -> "three");;
Warning P: this pattern-matching is not exhaustive.
Here is an example of a value that is not matched:
0
- : int -> string = <fun>
#
```

Using `fun` The second form of function definition uses the keyword `fun`:

```
fun parameter_1 . . . parameter_n -> expr
```

and is equivalent to the curried form:

```
fun parameter_1 -> . . . fun parameter_n -> expr
```

For example, consider the following anonymous function definition and application:

```
# (fun a b c d -> a+b+c+d);;
- : int -> int -> int -> int -> int = <fun>
#  (fun a b c d -> a+b+c+d) 1 2 3 4;;
- : int = 10
```

The result of a function invocation (as long as it is type compatible) may be used in another expression; for example:

```
# ((function x -> x+1) 4) + 7;;
- : int = 12
```

Naming Functions

The `let` keyword is used to associate a variable (name) with a function. For example:

```
# let afun = function x -> x * x;;
val afun : int -> int = <fun>
# afun 10;;
- : int = 100
```

It is worth remembering that named functions with recursive definitions must use the `rec` keyword.

Function Definitions and `let`: A Possible Source of Confusion

`ocaml` provides an alternate syntax that is commonly used to bind a variable's name to a function. The syntax:

```
let identifier = fun parameter_1 . . . parameter_m -> expr
```

is equivalent to the simpler form:

```
let identifier parameter_1 . . . parameter_m = expr
```

Thus, the preceding example may also be defined without the `function` keyword and the `->` and subsequently applied as shown:

```
# let afun x = x * x;;
val afun : int -> int = <fun>
# afun 10;;
- : int = 100
```

Currying Versus Tuples

Native CAML functions with multiple arguments are defined by currying. CAML also allows multivariable functions to be defined using **tuples**. A tuple is zero or more values enclosed in parentheses and separated by commas. Although CAML allows multiple-argument functions to be represented in either curried or tuple form, *if a function is defined using tuples, tuple notation must be used in the function invocation.* In other words, currying cannot be interchanged with tuples in the function interface. As the examples that follow indicate, the forms cannot be mixed; otherwise an error results.

```
# let calc input1 input2 = List.hd input1 * List.hd input2;;
val calc : int list -> int list -> int = <fun>
(* notice curried form above *)

# calc [1;2;3] [3;2;1];;
- : int = 3

# let calc2 (input1,input2) = List.hd input1 * List.hd input2;;
val calc2 : int list * int list -> int = <fun>
(* notice tuple form above *)

# calc2 ([1;2;3],[3;2;1]);;
- : int = 3

(* now some errors mixing curried and tuples *)

# calc ([1;2;3],[3;2;1]);;
This expression has type int list * int list but is here used with type
  int list

# calc2 [1;2;3] [3;2;1];;
This function is applied to too many arguments, maybe you forgot a ';'
```

Polymorphic Function Behavior

In CAML, a user-defined function will be polymorphic if the body only contains polymorphic functions and operators. Many native CAML functions are polymorphic (with somewhat nonintuitive extensions to types not normally used). This is shown on the next page.

```
# min;;
- : 'a -> 'a -> 'a = <fun>
# min "hi mom" "hi mommy";;
- : string = "hi mom"
# max "hi mom" "hi mommy";;
- : string = "hi mommy"
# min [1;2;3;4] [3;4];;
- : int list = [1; 2; 3; 4]
# max [1;2;3] [3;4;5];;
- : int list = [3; 4; 5]
# false;;
- : bool = false
# true;;
- : bool = true
# min false true;;
- : bool = false
# min true true;;
- : bool = true
```

11.3.3 Sample CAML Interaction and an Introduction to Lists

```
# let calc input = List.hd(input);;
val calc : 'a list -> 'a = <fun>
# calc([1;2;3]);;
- : int = 1
```

CAML List Syntax and Functions

CAML uses the semicolon to delineate list elements. To enable the polymorphic behavior of many list functions, lists must have all elements of the same type. The List module (part of the standard library) provides a rich source of useful list-manipulation functions.

```
(* Caml list examples *)

# List.hd [1;2;3];;
- : int = 1

# 1::[2;3;4];;
- : int list = [1; 2; 3; 4]

# List.append [1;2;3] [4;5;6];;
- : int list = [1; 2; 3; 4; 5; 6]

# [1;2;3]@[4;5;6];;
- : int list = [1; 2; 3; 4; 5; 6]

# List.length [1;2;3;4;5;6];;
- : int = 6

# List.nth [1;2;3;4;5;6] 3;;
- : int = 4

# let alist = [3;6;2;1;5;4];;
val alist : int list = [3; 6; 2; 1; 5; 4]

# List.nth alist 0;;
- : int = 3
```

```
# nth alist 0;;
Unbound value nth

# open List;;

# nth alist 0;;
- : int = 3

# List.sort compare alist;;
- : int list = [1; 2; 3; 4; 5; 6]

# List.nth alist 0;;
- : int = 3

# let alistsorted = List.sort compare alist;;
val alistsorted : int list = [1; 2; 3; 4; 5; 6]

# let minalist = List.nth alistsorted 0;;
val minalist : int = 1

# let maxalist = List.nth alistsorted ((List.length alist) - 1);;
val maxalist : int = 6
#
```

Example: A Recursive Function to Reverse the Elements of a List

Recursion occurs naturally in functional programming; iteration does not. Although CAML provides the `rev` function, we show a definition to illustrate the use of recursion. First, observe that the reverse of a single-element list is the list itself. On this basis, consider the recursive reversal of the list, in `ocaml` "pseudo"-notation of `[1;2;3]`:

```
[1; 2; 3]           (* original list *)
[(rev [2:3]); 1]    (* head of input to rev is now last element of returned list *)
[(rev [3]); 2; 1]   (* head of input to rev is again last element of returned list *)
[3; 2; 1]           (* reversed list *)
```

A CAML function to accomplish this follows. Notice that the function is polymorphic.

```
(* list reversal function in ocaml *)
(* file: rev.caml *)

let rec rev = fun aList ->
if ((List.tl aList) == []) then aList
 else (rev (List.tl aList)) @ [List.hd aList];;
```

Sample use follows:

```
# #use "rev.caml";;
val rev : 'a list -> 'a list = <fun>
# rev [1; 2; 3];;
- : int list = [3; 2; 1]
# rev ["one"; "two"; "three"];;
- : string list = ["three"; "two"; "one"]
```

Example: Ways to Find the Minimum Element of a List

In this example; we show numerous ways to define and use CAML functions to return the minimum element of a list. Two main strategies are used:

1. One approach based upon sorting. This is admittedly inefficient.
2. Another approach that uses recursion and either **if/then/else** constructs or pattern matchers follows.

The reader should study the following function definitions and results carefully. First, a number of functions are defined.

```
(* min and max examples *)

let rec listMin alist =
  match alist with
  [] -> failwith "listMin should not be used on an empty list"
  | [x] -> x
  | x :: t -> min x (listMin t);;

(* using the shorthand version of the syntax *)

let rec listMinP = function
 [] -> failwith "listMinP should not be used on an empty list"
|[x] -> x
| x::t -> min x (listMinP t);;

(* here's where Caml shows an inexhaustive patttern match *)

let rec listMinrev = function x::y ->
if y==[] then x
else min x (listMinrev y);;

let rec listMinrev2 = function x ->
if x==[] then
     failwith "listMinrev2 should not be used on an empty list"
              else
               if List.tl(x)==[] then List.hd(x)
               else min (List.hd x) (listMinrev2 (List.tl x));;

(* don't make polymorphic *)

let rec listMinrev3 = function (x: int list) ->
if x==[] then
     failwith "listMinrev3 should not be used on an empty list"
              else
               if List.tl(x)==[] then List.hd(x)
               else min (List.hd x) (listMinrev3 (List.tl x));;

(* some max examples *)

(* change max from curried to tuple  since
# max;;
- : 'a -> 'a -> 'a = <fun>
*)
```

```
let my_max = function x,y ->
if x < y then y else x ;;

let rec listMax =  function l ->
if List.tl(l) = [] then List.hd(l)
else  my_max (List.hd(l), listMax (List.tl(l)));;
```

Here is the sample use of these functions:

```
# #use "listmin.caml";;
val listMin : 'a list -> 'a = <fun>
val listMinP : 'a list -> 'a = <fun>
File "listmin.caml", line 18, characters 21-79:
Warning: this pattern-matching is not exhaustive.
Here is an example of a value that is not matched:
[]
val listMinrev : 'a list -> 'a = <fun>
val listMinrev2 : 'a list -> 'a = <fun>
val listMinrev3 : int list -> int = <fun>
val my_max : 'a * 'a -> 'a = <fun>
val listMax : 'a list -> 'a = <fun>

# let alist = [3;6;2;1;5;4];;
val alist : int list = [3; 6; 2; 1; 5; 4]

# listMin alist;;
- : int = 1

# listMinrev alist;;
- : int = 1

# listMinrev2 alist;;
- : int = 1

# listMinrev3 alist;;
- : int = 1

# let blist=[3.0;6.0;2.0;1.0;5.0;4.0];;
val blist : float list = [3.; 6.; 2.; 1.; 5.; 4.]

# listMin blist;;
- : float = 1.

# listMinrev3 blist;;
This expression has type float list but is here used with type int list
#

# listMax alist;;
- : int = 6
```

11.3.4 CAML I/O

Channels, Pervasives Printing and Scanning Functions, and the Scanf and Printf Modules

Many CAML functions for input and output are provided. Input and output are specified by input and output channels `in_channel` and `out_channel`, respectively. The defaults are `stdin` and `stdout`.

Functions for input contained in the Pervasives module include `read_line`, `read_int`, and `read_float`. These functions assume the standard input channel.

Output functions for use on the standard output channel are included in the Pervasives module and include `print_string` with signature `string -> unit`. This function prints an argument string on the standard output (a side effect) and returns type `unit`. Similarly, functions `print_int`, `print_float`, and `print_newline` are also provided.

The `Printf` module contains a number of more powerful printing functions intended for formatted printing, including function `printf`. A formatted string (called a `format`) is used. The structure of this string is similar to the arguments used in the C `printf` function.

The following examples show the use of the `Printf` and `Scanf` module functions.

Examples of CAML I/O

The following shows examples of CAML I/O.

```
$ ocaml
        Objective Caml version 3.08.1

# stdin;;
- : in_channel = <abstr>
# stdout;;
- : out_channel = <abstr>
# stderr;;
- : out_channel = <abstr>
# open_out;;
- : string -> out_channel = <fun>
# open_in;;
- : string -> in_channel = <fun>
# close_out;;
- : out_channel -> unit = <fun>
# close_in;;
- : in_channel -> unit = <fun>
# Printf.fprintf;;
- : out_channel -> ('a, out_channel, unit) format -> 'a = <fun>
# Scanf.fscanf;;
- : in_channel -> ('a, Scanf.Scanning.scanbuf, 'b) format -> 'a -> 'b = <fun>
# Printf.fprintf stdout "Hi Bob\n";;
Hi Bob
- : unit = ()
# stdout;;
- : out_channel = <abstr>

(* here is a file writing example *)

# let my_chan = open_out "camlTest.out";;
val my_chan : out_channel = <abstr>

# Printf.fprintf my_chan "Hi Bob\n";;
- : unit = ()

(* still nothing in file-- until-- *)

# flush my_chan;;
- : unit = ()

(* now contents written to file
further extension----  *)
```

```
# Printf.fprintf my_chan "\n %d   %d  %s\n" 10 20 "done";;
- : unit = ()
# flush my_chan;;
- : unit = ()

(* here are file contents so far: *)

Hi Bob

 10   20  done

(* examples of caml input *)

here is a file: camlTest.in:

10 20
20 30
30 40


(* Caml somewhat crude reading *)

# let my_in = open_in "camlTest.in";;
val my_in : in_channel = <abstr>
# input_line my_in;;
- : string = "10 20"
#  input_line my_in;;
- : string = "20 30"
#  input_line my_in;;
- : string = "30 40"
#  input_line my_in;;
Exception: End_of_file.

(* a solution to the EOF exception is: *)

try
  while true do
    print_string (input_line my_in ^ "\n")
  done
with
| End_of_file -> ()
```

11.3.5 Recursion, Pattern Matching, Lists, and `trace`

CAML `trace`

The CAML `trace` function is useful in debugging. The syntax is:

```
#trace <function>
```

As a further example of pattern matching and recursion in CAML, consider a recursive formulation of a polymorphic member function definition:

```
let rec member = function
    (x, []) -> false
  | (x, h::t) ->
      if (h = x)
```

```
        then true
        else member (x, t) ;;
```

contained in the file `member.caml`. The use and tracing of this CAML function follows:

```
# #use "member.caml";;
val member : 'a * 'a list -> bool = <fun>
# #trace member;;
member is now traced.
# member("a",["c";"b";"a"]);;
member <-- (<poly>, [<poly>; <poly>; <poly>])
member <-- (<poly>, [<poly>; <poly>])
member <-- (<poly>, [<poly>])
member --> true
member --> true
member --> true
- : bool = true
#
```

The reader should compare this formulation with the SML formulation in Section 11.2.13.

11.3.6 Revisiting the ANN Unit Example

The implementation and training of a single ANN unit to become a two-bit D/A converter was shown in CommonLisp in Chapter 6, as well as in SML/NJ in Section 11.2.14. Here we show the CAML version, for comparison.

CAML Source Code for Single-Unit Implementation and Training

```
(* file: annUnit.caml *)
(* rev 11-18-03  *)

(* follows structure of CommonLISP solution *)
(* uses recursion, no local variables, etc.
   tuple form of arguments (vs. currying) used *)

(* data and functions for unit *)

let h = [[[0.0; 0.0]; [0.25]];
         [[0.0; 1.0]; [0.50]];
         [[1.0; 0.0]; [0.75]];
         [[1.0; 1.0]; [1.00]]];;

let hBias = [[[0.0; 0.0; 1.0]; [0.25]];
             [[0.0; 1.0; 1.0]; [0.50]];
             [[1.0; 0.0; 1.0]; [0.75]];
             [[1.0; 1.0; 1.0]; [1.00]]];;

(* initialization w/o and w/ bias *)

let weightInit () = [0.1; -0.1];;

let weightInitBias () = [0.1; -0.1; 0.2];;

(* unit net activation computation *)
```

```
let rec calcNet = fun (inputs, weights) ->
if inputs==[] && weights==[] then 0.0
   else
   List.hd(inputs) *. List.hd(weights)
                  +. calcNet (List.tl(inputs), List.tl(weights));;

(* artificial neuron activation (squashing) function *)

let squash net =
1.0 /. (1.0 +. exp(-1.0*.net));;

let unit (inputs, weights) =
 squash(calcNet(inputs, weights));;

(* the constant part of the correction, delta *)

let delta (output, target) =
  (target -. output) *. output *. (1.0 -. output);;

let rec trainUnitInputRecur (input, weights, delta, rho)  =
if weights==[] then []
              else
    (List.hd(weights) +. (rho *. delta *. List.hd(input))) ::
    trainUnitInputRecur(List.tl(input), List.tl(weights), delta, rho);;

let trainUnitPattern(input, target, inWeights, rho) =
 trainUnitInputRecur(input, inWeights, delta(unit(input,inWeights),target),rho);;

(* we're almost there *)

(* one pass over h *)

let rec trainUnitAll (h, inWeights, rho) =
if
  not(h==[])
then
  trainUnitAll(List.tl(h), trainUnitPattern(List.hd(List.hd(h)),
                                    List.hd(List.hd(List.tl((List.hd(h))))),
                                    inWeights,rho), rho)
else
  inWeights;;


(* n passes over h *)

let rec trainMultiple (h, inWeights, rho, n) =
if
n > 0 then
      trainMultiple(h, trainUnitAll(h,inWeights,rho),rho,n-1)
      else
      inWeights;;
```

CAML Results for Single Unit

```
$ ocaml
        Objective Caml version 3.07+2

# #use "annUnit.caml";;
```

```
val h : float list list list =
  [[[0.; 0.]; [0.25]]; [[0.; 1.]; [0.5]]; [[1.; 0.]; [0.75]];
   [[1.; 1.]; [1.]]]
val hBias : float list list list =
  [[[0.; 0.; 1.]; [0.25]]; [[0.; 1.; 1.]; [0.5]]; [[1.; 0.; 1.]; [0.75]];
   [[1.; 1.; 1.]; [1.]]]
val weightInit : unit -> float list = <fun>
val weightInitBias : unit -> float list = <fun>
val calcNet : float list * float list -> float = <fun>
val squash : float -> float = <fun>
val unit : float list * float list -> float = <fun>
val delta : float * float -> float = <fun>
val trainUnitInputRecur :
  float list * float list * float * float -> float list = <fun>
val trainUnitPattern : float list * float * float list * float -> float list =
  <fun>
val trainUnitAll : float list list list * float list * float -> float list =
  <fun>
val trainMultiple :
  float list list list * float list * float * int -> float list = <fun>
# trainMultiple(h,weightInit(),0.25,5000);;
- : float list = [1.77202999340092293; 0.21115629107139175]
# trainMultiple(hBias,weightInitBias(),0.25, 5000);;
- : float list =
[2.49834802226194563; 1.32339097977067288; -1.24917390227968572]
# let weights1 =  trainMultiple(h,weightInit(),0.25,5000);;
val weights1 : float list = [1.77202999340092293; 0.21115629107139175]
```

The results should be compared with previous values using Lisp and ML.

11.3.7 What's CAML Light?

In the early 1990s, a smaller version of the CAML language called CAML Light was developed. CAML Light is available for a number of platforms, including Windows and Linux.

CAML Light Example

Consider the CAML implementation of factorial that follows.

```
(* factorial example in CAML *)

let rec fact x = if x=0 then 1
 else x*fact(x-1);;
```

Use in CAML Light for Windows is shown in Figure 11.3.

11.3.8 Overview of Objects in CAML

This section provides a quick, example-oriented overview of the object-oriented features of (O)CAML. Portions of the CLOS example of Chapter 10, Section 10.2, are used.

Consider first the declaration of two CAML objects in the source file of Figure 11.4.

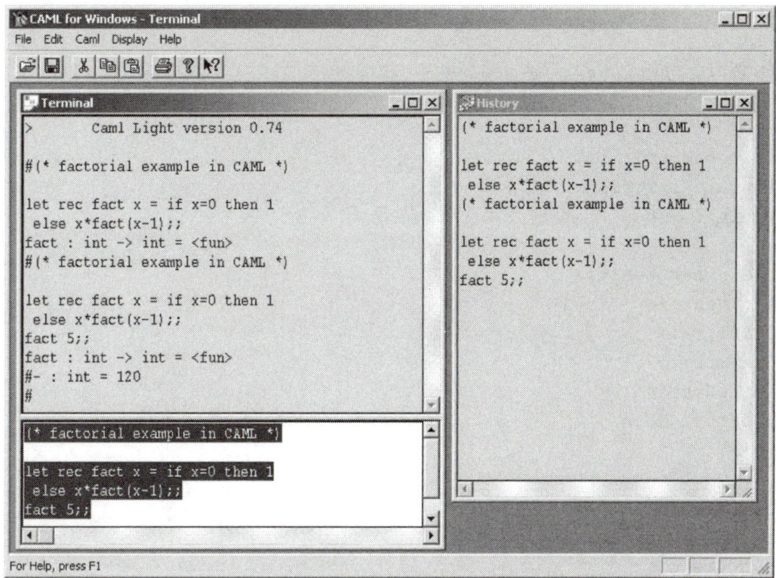

Figure 11.3 Example of CAML Light Use (Factorial).

```
(* vehicle.caml *)

class vehicle =
object
val mutable name = "batmobile"
method print_name = name
end;;

class boat =
object
val mutable name = "leaky"
val mutable capacity = 4
method how_big = capacity
end;;
```

Figure 11.4 A Pair of CAML Objects.

```
# #use "vehicle.caml";;
class vehicle :
  object val mutable name : string method print_name : string end
class boat :
  object
    val mutable capacity : int
    val mutable name : string
    method how_big : int
  end
# let my_vehicle = new vehicle;;
val my_vehicle : vehicle = <obj>
# my_vehicle#print_name;;
- : string = "batmobile"
# let my_boat = new boat;;
val my_boat : boat = <obj>
# my_boat#how_big;;
- : int = 4
# my_vehicle#how_big;;
This expression has type vehicle
It has no method how_big
# my_boat#print_name;;
This expression has type boat
It has no method print_name
#
```

Figure 11.5 Creating and Using Objects from the Class Definitions of Figure 11.4.

When this file is used, the sample behavior is shown in Figure 11.5. Note the specialization of the class methods.

Instead, consider the modification of the class definitions to create a hierarchy and employ inheritance. This is shown in Figures 11.6 and 11.7.

```
(* vehicle2.caml
   employs inheritence *)

class vehicle =
object
val mutable name = "batmobile"
method print_name = name
end;;

class boat =
object
inherit vehicle
val mutable capacity = 4
method how_big = capacity
end;;
```

Figure 11.6 Extension of the Class Structure of Figure 11.4 to Allow Inheritance.

```
# #use "vehicle2.caml";;
class vehicle :
  object val mutable name : string method print_name : string end
class boat :
  object
    val mutable capacity : int
    val mutable name : string
    method how_big : int
    method print_name : string
  end
# let my_vehicle = new vehicle;;
val my_vehicle : vehicle = <obj>
# let my_boat = new boat;;
val my_boat : boat = <obj>
# my_vehicle#print_name;;
- : string = "batmobile"
# my_boat#print_name;;
- : string = "batmobile"
#
```

Figure 11.7 Behavior of the OO System of Figure 11.6.

11.4 Scanning and Parsing in CAML

11.4.1 Introduction

In a manner similar to `flex` and `bison`, `CAML` provides utilites to create scanning and parsing functions using input files to specify the respective lexical syntax as regular expressions and the grammar productions. These functions are `ocamllex` and `ocamlyacc`. The structure for the input to each is similar to that of `flex` and `bison`. A few changes are noteworthy, however.

A good source of information is found in the `CAML` interactive calculator (`calc`) example included in `CAML` examples and available from:

`http://caml.inria.fr/pub/old_caml_site/Examples/`

11.4.2 CAML Scanners (Lexers)

The License Plate Example Revisited

Lexer Input Lexing functions created by `ocamllex` take as an argument a lexer buffer containing the input to be scanned. For this reason, it is necessary to define the lexer input using one of a family of functions from the Lexing module. This includes `Lexing.from_string` and `Lexing.from_channel`.

The lexing function returns the semantic attribute of a recognized token, if one is defined. In addition, an action may be specified.

Specifying Rules to Recognize Tokens Like `flex`, regular expressions are used to specify the tokens to be recognized in the scanning process. We show a simple example of this.

ocamllex Input File for Valid License Plates The `ocamllex` input file `license1.mll` follows. Note specification:

```
(* ocaml lexical analyzer (lexer) example *)
(* recognizing license plates revisited *)
(* no need to define semantic attributes *)

(* create scanning function license *)

rule license =
parse ['a'-'z']['a'-'z']['a'-'z']['1'-'9']['0'-'9']['0'-'9']
      {print_string "valid license plate"}
```

From this file, the `CAML` lexing or scanning function, `license`, is created in file `license1.ml` via:

```
$ ocamllex license1.mll
7 states, 309 transitions, table size 1278 bytes
```

It is illustrative to look at the contents of `license1.ml`.

11.4.3 Creating a Free-Standing Scanner (Interactive CAML Mode)

First, we start CAML and use the scanning function built by `ocamllex`.

```
$ ocaml
        Objective Caml version 3.08.1

# #use "license1.ml";;
```

We now show two ways to pass input to the scanning function and the corresponding results.

Using a String to Hold Scanner Input

We set up the string to be scanned in a lexer buffer as follows.

```
# let lexbuf = Lexing.from_string "abc123";;
```

and then invoke the scanning function:

```
# license lexbuf;;
valid license plate- : unit = ()

# let lexbuf = Lexing.from_string "ab1234";;
(... some snipped ...)
# license lexbuf;;
Exception: Failure "lexing: empty token".
#
```

Obtaining Scanner Input from `sdtin`

An alternative is to pass input to the scanning function from `stdin` (much like our previous `flex` efforts) via:

```
# let lexbuf = Lexing.from_channel stdin;;
```

Subsequent operation is as follows:

```
# license lexbuf;;   (* now reading from stdin *)
abc123
valid license plate- : unit = ()

(* need to reload lexing buffer *)

# license lexbuf;;
123asc
Exception: Failure "lexing: empty token".
#
```

11.5 CAML Compilation with `ocamlc`

The `ocaml` distribution provides the `ocamlc` compiler. `ocaml` produces CAML bytecode suitable for use with `ocamlrun`. Note that CAML source files to be compiled have the extension `ml`. We show a few simple examples. More sophisticated features and use of the `ocaml` bytecode (and native) compilers are documented in the reference manual.

11.5.1 `ocamlc` Compilation Example

CAML Source

Consider the simple CAML source file that follows.

```
(* random number generation/compilation example *)
(* file: randex.ml *)
(* note: Random.int bound returns a random integer
                    between 0 (inclusive) and bound (exclusive)  *)

print_newline();;
print_string("Here's a random number");;
print_string(" between 0 and 51 -> ");;
print_newline();;
print_string((string_of_int (Random.int 52)));;
print_newline();;
print_newline();;
```

Compilation and Use

The previous file is compiled into bytecode via:

```
ocamlc -o randex randex.ml
```

This produces file `randex`, which may be run using the `ocamlrun` bytecode interpreter, `ocamlrun`, as shown:

```
$ ocamlrun randex

Here's a random number between 0 and 51 ->
6

$
```

On Unix systems, the bytecode file may be executed directly:

```
$ ./randex

Here's a random number between 0 and 51 ->
6

$
```

11.5.2 Compiling with Libraries

To compile a program that uses functions in modules other than the core and standard libraries,[6] the library name(s) must be input to `ocamlc`. For example, suppose the previous random-number generation example in Section 11.5.1 were modified to use module `Unix`, which is contained in the `unix` library. The compilation command would be modified to:

```
ocamlc -o randex unix.cma randex.ml
```

11.5.3 `ocaml` Compilation Extensions

Free-Standing Executables

To execute the compiled bytecode, `ocamlrun` is necessary. However, if the `-custom` option is used, `ocamlc` produces a stand-alone executable. In this case, the output file contains both the run-time system and the program bytecode. This file can then be executed directly or on another machine (using the same CPU/operating system). As might be expected, the resulting executable file size is considerably larger.

The Debugger (`ocamldebug`)

If the source files are compiled with the `-g` switch, debug information is added to the bytecode. The `ocaml` debugger (`ocamldebug`) may then be used with this bytecode file for low-level debugging. An example follows.

```
$ ocamldebug randex
        Objective Caml Debugger version 3.09.0

(ocd) run
Loading program... done.

Here's a random number between 0 and 51 ->
6

Time : 68
Program exit.
(ocd)
```

In addition, events, or "interesting source code locations" may be marked[7] in the source code. Thereafter, the debugger may be used to single-step between events and debugger breakpoints may be set at events.

---

[6] Modules from the standard library are automatically linked with the user's object code files by the `ocamlc` command.

[7] See the reference manual for notation and locations that may be marked.

11.6 Bibliographical Remarks and References

11.6.1 Books and Journals

The ML language is specified in Harper, Milner, Tofte, and MacQueen (1997). A very readable introduction is Paulson (1996).

11.6.2 Web-Based Resources

General ML Resources

The on-line ML FAQ is available at:

`http://www.faqs.org/faqs/meta-lang-faq/`

A tutorial on ML may be found at:

`http://www.dcs.napier.ac.uk/course-notes/sml/manual.html`

Other useful resources are:

`comp.lang.ml  (moderated newsgroup)`

`http://www.csci.csusb.edu/dick/samples/ml.syntax.html  (the syntax)`

SML/NJ Resources

The current on-line SML resource is:

`http://www.smlnj.org/`

Installation details for various platforms are described at:

`http://www.smlnj.org/install/index.html`

The SML basis libraries are documented on-line at:

`http://www.standardml.org/Basis/index.html`

Finally, the SML FAQ is available at:

`http://www.smlnj.org/doc/FAQ/index.html`

The original page for SML/NJ, with documentation, is at:

```
http://cm.bell-labs.com/cm/cs/what/smlnj/
(Bell Labs/Lucent Main SML Page)

http://cm.bell-labs.com/cm/cs/what/smlnj/doc/interact.html
(overview of interactive system)

http://cm.bell-labs.com/cm/cs/what/smlnj/doc/basis/index.html
(** Basis Library **)
```

CAML Resources

For learning CAML after SML, a good reference on the distinctions between the ML dialects is found at:

http://www.ps.uni-sb.de/~rossberg/SMLvsOcaml.html

(O)CAML-specific references may be found at:

http://caml.inria.fr/

and

http://www.ocaml.org/

In addition, the FAQ contains significant information for programmers familiar with functional programming (and perhaps ML) who desire a quick start.

A CAML user's manual is available at:

http://caml.inria.fr/ocaml/htmlman/index.html

Haskell Resources

More details are available at the Haskell home page: http://www.haskell.org/

11.7 Exercises

1. Suppose a CAML user defined a function using curried arguments, as shown:

```
# let calc input input2 = List.hd(input)*List.hd(input2);;
val calc : int list -> int list -> int = <fun>
```

   What is the effect of the following tuple-based use of the function?

```
# calc([1;2;3],[2;3;4]);;
```

2. What is returned by the following CAML function?

```
let rec quizFunction = function x ->
  if (List.tl x) == [] then List.hd x
   else quizFunction (List.tl x);;
```

3. CAML allows the definition of anonymous functions, for example:

```
# (fun x -> 2 * x) 3;;
- : int = 6
```

   Can anonymous functions be used recursively in CAML?

4. Compare the computational speed for the training of the ANN unit of Section 11.2.14 with 500K iterations using:

   - SML in interpreted mode
   - A compiled version of the file, using mlton

5. As noted in Section 11.3.1, there is more than one way to define a CAML function. Consider the following two CAML functions:

```
let rec calcNet = fun (inputs, weights) ->
if inputs==[] && weights==[] then 0.0
   else
   List.hd(inputs) *. List.hd(weights)
                   +. calcNet (List.tl(inputs), List.tl(weights));;

let rec calcNet2 (inputs, weights) =
if inputs==[] && weights==[] then 0.0
   else
   List.hd(inputs) *. List.hd(weights)
                   +. calcNet2 (List.tl(inputs), List.tl(weights));;
```

   What is the difference between the two functions?

6. CAML provides functions related to random-number generation in the `Random` module. An example was shown in Section 11.5. However, `ocaml` does not automatically reseed the random number generator, so repeated use of the compiled file (Section 11.5.1) results in the following behavior:

```
$ ./randex

Here's a random number between 0 and 51 ->
6

$ ./randex

Here's a random number between 0 and 51 ->
6

$ ./randex

Here's a random number between 0 and 51 ->
6
```

   Modify the program so that each pseudorandom sequence generated starts with a randomly generated seed.

7. Like many languages, CAML distinguishes between several types of equality. For example, the Pervasives module provides the = function, which tests for structural equality, as well as ==, which tests for physical equality. Using the `ocaml` system, develop some examples to show the behavior of, and difference between, these functions.

8. This problem continues the list reversal example of Section 11.3.3 and should give you some additional experience with `ocaml` lists and recursive function definitions. For each of the three alternative `rev` function definitions shown in parts (a) thru (c):

   - Is the function definition syntactically correct?
   - If so, is the value returned the reverse of the input list?
   - If not, how would you modify the function definition?

(a)
```
(* attempted list reversal function in ocaml *)

(* file: revprob.caml *)

let rec rev = fun aList -\TEXTsymbol{>}

if (aList == []) then aList

else (rev (List.tl aList)) @ [List.hd aList];;
```
(b)
```
(* another attempted list reversal function in ocaml *)

(* file: revprob2.caml *)

let rec rev = fun aList -\TEXTsymbol{>}

if (aList == []) then aList

else (rev (List.tl aList)) @ [aList];;
```
(c)
```
(* a final attempted list reversal function in ocaml *)

(* file: revprob3.caml *)

let rec rev = fun aList -\TEXTsymbol{>}

if (aList == []) then aList

else (rev (List.tl aList)) @ aList;;
```

9. Design and implement a recursive function to return *the last element of an input list* in:

   (a) ML
   (b) CAML

10. (This data is used in the next two problems). Consider the following `ocaml` lists, which are used as global data structures to index playing card values:

```
(* the cards data structure and related *)

let cards =
[''2S'';''3S'';''4S'';''5S'';''6S'';''7S'';''8S'';''9S'';''10S'';''JS'';''QS'';''KS'';''AS'';

"2C";"3C";"4C";"5C";"6C";"7C";"8C";"9C";"10C";"JC";"QC";"KC";"AC";

"2D";"3D";"4D";"5D";"6D";"7D";"8D";"9D";"10D";"JD";"QD";"KD";"AD";

"2H";"3H";"4H";"5H";"6H";"7H";"8H";"9H";"10H";"JH";"QH";"KH";"AH"];;

let ranks = ["2";"3";"4";"5";"6";"7";"8";"9";"10";"J";"Q";"K";"A"];;

let suits = ["spades"; "clubs"; "diamonds"; "hearts"];;
```

Develop and implement an `ocaml` function (and auxiliary functions, if required) that generates a list of seven, nonrepeated random integers between 0 and 51. Use this function's returned value as the basis for a "card-dealing" game, with output as follows:

```
# play1();;
- : string = "3H  9H  6S  4H  8H  9C  AS  That's All Folks!"
# play1();;
- : string = "QS  JS  10H  8C  QH  7D  AS  That's All Folks!"
# play1();;
- : string = "10S  6S  3C  8S  6D  JC  QD  That's All Folks!"
```

11. The result of the previous problem should provide a basis for this problem. Here, we gain some experience with the `Printf` module. Revise and extend the output of the card game to yield the required game display, which follows.

```
#play2();;

********  Welcome to the ocaml Poker Simulator ************

The first (hole) card is:  4H
The second (hole) card is:  10C

Here comes the flop ...

The first community card is:  KC
The second community card is:  KH
The third community card is:  KS

The turn card is:  QH
The river card is:  3D

The 7-card hand is:
4H, i.e., a 4 of hearts
10C, i.e., a 10 of clubs
KC, i.e., a K of clubs
KH, i.e., a K of hearts
KS, i.e., a K of spades
QH, i.e., a Q of hearts
3D, i.e., a 3 of diamonds

That's All Folks!
```

CHAPTER 12

Abstract Syntax and Formal Approaches to Programming Language Semantics

Indecision may or may not be my problem.

—J. Buffett

12.1 Programming Language Semantics

12.1.1 What Are Semantics and Why Study Them?

As noted in Chapter 1, a programming language is characterized by syntax and semantics. In this chapter, we focus on semantics. The formal semantics of a programming language relates the language syntax to meaning, which in many cases is a quantitative description of the underlying computation. There are a number of different approaches to formally quantifying semantics.

In this chapter, the primary emphasis is on the semantics of imperative languages. `minic` is used for the examples.

The specification of the syntax of any language, including programming languages, is an important part of the study of the language. However, if a complete understanding of the language is desired, this step alone is insufficient. Whereas the syntax of the language indicates the exact form and structure of elements that may be produced or recognized (parsed), the underlying meaning of these elements is not inherent in nor conveyed by the syntax.[1]

A Look Back and A Look Ahead

Up to this point, our interpretation of a formal process for investigating programming languages might be as shown in Table 12.1. A revised or enhanced interpretation of the process, which incorporates semantics, might be as shown in Table 12.2.

A More Complete View of a Programming Language

There are two main aspects to a programming language: the language syntax and its associated semantics.

[1]Although we noted that attribute grammars could be used for this purpose.

Concept	Process	Resulting Mapping
Lexical analysis	Scanning	Input file → tokens
Syntactic analysis (correctness)	Parsing	Tokens → concrete parse tree

Table 12.1 Previous Interpretation Processes for a Programming Language.

Concept	Process	Resulting Mapping
Syntactic analysis	Parsing	Tokens → abstract parse tree
Semantic analysis	Parse interpretation	Abstract parse tree → semantic objects[2]

Table 12.2 Enhanced Interpretation Processes for a Programming Language.

- The **syntax** of a programming language defines the correct form for legal programs (or program building blocks).
- The **semantics** of a programming language determines what programs (or program building blocks) mean, produce, compute, return, and so forth.

In what follows, we describe "program building blocks" as "syntactic fragments." Combining syntax and semantics leads to the oft-cited result:

Programming Language = Syntax + Semantics

A More Precise Mathematical Characterization of a Programming Language

Formal approaches to semantics extend the informal approaches with the goal of *achieving a precise, mathematical characterization of the behavior of an assumed syntactically correct program in a specific language.* A standardized and generally accepted mathematical formalism for this purpose has been an elusive goal. There are a number of formal approaches to characterizing semantics. In this chapter, we look at a few of the current approaches.

The specification of a formal semantic description of a programming language does not imply that the language is imperative. However, the vast majority of methods and approaches are designed for this case.

Why Formalize Syntax and Semantics?

A modern (and quantitative) approach to programming languages involves formalizing both syntax and semantics. There are very good reasons for both, which we will explore next.

Why Formalize Syntax?

We have shown a number of quantitative approaches to formalizing a language's syntax, including:

- Syntax diagrams (Pascal)
- BNF/EBNF[3]

[2]Shown later in this chapter.

[3]This is the most common; such a formalization is found in almost every "Introduction to Language xxx Reference Manual."

- Regular expressions
- Formal grammars

Note that formalization of the syntax is necessary and useful for a number of things, including:

1. programmers who require a guide to writing syntactically correct programs.
2. language implementers, who develop parsers as a part of a compiler for the language.
3. formal analysis of language syntax properties, such as whether the language is context-free, is LL(k),[4] LR(k), or ambiguous.

Why Formalize Semantics?

Similarly, a formal characterization of the semantics of a programming language is useful for:

1. programmers, who in the process of generating useful software, must understand the meaning of programs that they write, and convey this meaning, via the language semantics (see the following remark regarding specifications and correctness).
2. implementers, who must write a correct code generator for the language compiler, following a successful or correct parse. This is often thought of as the "back end" of the language's compiler. Formal descriptions of semantics may be used for **validation** of the translation.
3. In addition, semantics formalization permits a formal analysis of other language properties, such as whether the language is strongly typed or block structured.
4. Perhaps most importantly, semantics provides a way to facilitate high-level specifications of the overall task the program is intended to accomplish, and in limited instances, verification as to whether these tasks are correctly accomplished. This spawns the topics of formal methods and program correctness.

Let's Start with a Simple Example

Given the following syntactically correct `minic` (or C) program,

```
int main(void)
{
int t1;
t1=10;
return(t1);
}
```

the basic question is: What is the **meaning** of this program? To answer this, we must define *meaning*, in a programming language sense.

[4]The LL(k) grammars constitute the largest subclass of context-free grammars that permit deterministic top-down parsing using a k-symbol lookahead. The notation LL describes the parsing strategy for which these grammars are designed: the input string is scanned in a left-to-right manner and the parser generates a leftmost derivation.

Application to `minic`

The syntax of a number of `minic` syntactic constructs has been introduced, including assignment of a value to a variable, as well as the `for`, `while`, and `printf` constructs. In some cases, the syntax has been accompanied with informal descriptions of the corresponding semantics (or meaning) of these constructs. For example, we introduced `while` by noting:

> More specifically, the `while` BNF syntax is as follows:
>
> ```
> <command> ::= while(<boolean-expr>) <command>
> ```
>
> The semantics of `while` are that `<command>` is executed repeatedly as long as `<boolean-expr>` is `true`. The test on `<boolean-expr>` takes place before each execution of `<command>`.

In other cases, semantics was not addressed, and it was simply left to the reader to ascribe semantics to the syntactic fragments based upon familiarity with C.

12.1.2 A Brief History of "Reasoning About Programs"

The history of formal programming language semantics is intertwined with the notions of reasoning about programs and program verification, or proving program correctness (Jones, 2003). Early computing pioneers, including Charles Babbage (Randell, 1975) and, much later, John von Neumann (Taub, 1963), John McCarthy (1963), and Alan Turing (Morris and Jones, 1984), addressed this issue. Much of the impetus for this early work was not to overcome the limitations of testing, but rather to develop a "science" to explain the emerging automata. Interestingly, and related to topics in this chapter:

- Von Neumann suggested the use of "assertion boxes" to record the effect of "operation boxes" on program fragments.
- Turing suggested the use of "a number of definite assertions" that can be checked individually, and from which the correctness of the whole program easily follows.
- McCarthy (although focused on the capabilities of recursive functions) suggested that a relationship between mathematical logic and computation would be fruitful.

In the more recent past, Floyd (1967) and Naur (1966) independently suggested the association of a proposition with a "connection" in the flow of control through a program, or as we see in axiomatic semantics, the annotation of a program with assertions (propositions) that relate program variable values to proposition variables. The observation that this technique was independent of "all processors for that language" was also noted. At about the same time, Hoare (1969) published one of the most widely cited works related to this strategy. This yielded Hoare "triples"—pre- and postconditions placed around a program fragment. In addition, a number of "rules of consequence" (axioms) accompanied the approach to facilitate reasoning about assignment and conditional statements.

Program Correctness

Practically, a program cannot be judged as correct (or not) through testing. At issue is the lack of scalability of the exhaustive testing approach. To see this, consider a program with

n branch or decision points. This yields 2^n possible branches that must be checked. For $n = 1000$, which might be considered a relatively modest application program, $2^{1000} = 1.071510^{301}$. Thus, alternative approaches to proving correctness are necessary.

Alternately, correctness may be established using an independent specification of what the program should accomplish. These specifications may be developed and handled in a straightforward manner using operational, denotational, axiomatic, or algebraic semantics.

12.2 Semantics, Semantics, Semantics

There are many definitions and objectives for the realm we're about to enter. Our overall motivation is to be both quantitative and to describe:

- what a program does or produces (usually by description of *components* of the program).
- what happens during the execution of a program (or program component).
- the *meaning* of statements in a programming language.
- what a syntactic fragment should produce via machine translation.

Typically, any approach to studying semantics has the following characteristics:

- In general, a divide-and-conquer, or **compositional** approach, is taken. We decompose a program into syntactic/semantic fragments and consider these individually. Therefore, we usually consider the tightly coupled syntax → semantics descriptions of these fragments.
- In addition, an "abstract" syntax (described in Section 12.5) typically is employed for simplicity and clarity.

The utility of any formal approach to semantics varies with the particular approach and overall objectives of the semantic formalization. Although the approaches we present are "formal" and usually quantitative, in some sense they are also:

- (usually) in a form that allows manipulation.
- not one approach, but a family of strategies.
- not fully accepted—that is, possibly controversial.

Although there is widespread adoption of BNF as a standard method for formalizing syntax, it appears unlikely that a single method will suffice for semantics. Semantics is harder to formalize than syntax, and also has a wider variety of objectives or applications to satisfy. What has developed are families of approaches to formalizing semantics, as outlined in Section 12.3.

12.2.1 Semantics for Specific Language Types

Recall that a language may be declarative, imperative, functional, another type, or a hybrid. The choice of a semantics formalization approach is also strongly related to the language type. Suitability and ease of use vary. For example, employing axiomatic semantics with imperative languages can be quite challenging, whereas purely functional languages make some semantics formalization approaches quite straightforward.

12.2.2 How to Do Semantics Informally

Informal operational semantics, as the name implies, is an approach based upon specifying the operation of code fragments on an assumed machine. This is the most commonly encountered form of attempted semantic formalization and probably should be considered informal. This approach is typical of "How to Program in xxx" and "Introduction to xxx" type programming language references and documentation.

An Example in C or C++

Here's a typical example of this approach. In this form, the semantic description is often preceded by a quasiformal syntactic description or prototype such as:

```
if (<expression>) <statement>
if (<expression>) <statement> else <statement>
```

This is then followed with an (informal) semantic description; for example:

> *In an* `if` *statement, the first (or only) statement is executed if the expression is nonzero and the second statement (if it is specified) is executed otherwise. This implies . . . .*

Interestingly, this is the way most programming is initially learned.

12.2.3 Another Simple Example

Consider the following semantic representation example:

> *Describe the semantics of a syntactically correct arithmetic statement program fragment as the value of the statement.*

Consider the statement fragment[5]:

```
1101
```

This fragment could be:

1. interpreted syntactically as a string of digits (assuming it is syntactically correct).

2. interpreted or describe semantically as a *value*; that is, the semantics or meaning could be 1101_{10} or 1101_2.

[5]Which might be part of a more complex (and complete) assignment statement such as

$$E = V1 + 1101;$$

The semantic interpretation or evaluation still requires that we understand the positional notation used in the syntactic specification. To formalize the semantic specification (in this case, determining value), we could develop a function `evaluate`:

`evaluate`$[1101] =$
`evaluate`$[1 \times 10^3 + 1 \times 10^2 + 0 \times 10^1 + 1 \times 10^0] =$
1101

Unfortunately, the simplicity of this "value" example obscures some difficult questions in formalizing semantics. For example, what about control statements, the machine environment, and so on?

12.2.4 Semantics of Classes and Class Members

In OOP, semantics of class instances (objects) may depend on their class. For example, a `String` class could be defined to have either value semantics or pointer semantics.

12.3 A Quick Overview of Approaches to Semantics Formalization

Before looking at a few of the approaches in detail and using `minic`, we present a short overview.

12.3.1 Self-Definition

An operational self-definition of the language is given by defining the interpretation of the language *in the language itself*; for example, by showing an implementation of a Lisp interpreter in Lisp, or a Prolog interpreter written in Prolog. To many, this appears to be circular reasoning.

12.3.2 Translational Semantics

Sometimes translational semantics is considered a part of operational semantics; here we treat it separately. In the translational approach, semantics is conveyed by showing the translation of program fragments (syntactically correct statements) into another (e.g., assembly language) language called the target language. This requires an actual or hypothetical machine (model), the target machine.

A `minic` Example of Translational Semantics

To illustrate translational semantics, we return to the simple `minic` program:

```
int main(void)
{
int t1;
t1=10;
return(t1);
}
```

Recall that our scanner/parser produces the following (abbreviated) output.

```
Parse Results

transunit(maindecl(int, mainarg(void)),
```

```
body([decl(int, [t1])],
statseq([sassign(ide(t1), num(10))],
retstat(ide(t1)))))
```

The translated (scanned/parsed) output provides an alternative representation for the `minic` source, and may be thought of as conveying translational semantics. More importantly, if the `minic` source file is renamed `minicex1.c` and processed by `gcc` using the command `gcc -S minicex1.c`, the result is the assembly code that follows.

```
     .file     "minicex1.c"
     .version     "01.01"
gcc2_compiled.:
.text
     .align 4
.globl main
     .type      main,@function
main:
     pushl     %ebp
     movl     %esp, %ebp
     subl     $4, %esp
     movl     $10, -4(%ebp)
     movl     -4(%ebp), %eax
     movl     %eax, %eax
     leave
     ret
.Lfe1:
     .size      main,.Lfe1-main
     .ident     "GCC: (GNU) 2.96 20000731 (Red Hat Linux 7.1 2.96-98)"
```

Another viewpoint of translational semantics is that the semantics of the language is conveyed by defining an interpreter or compiler for the language. Translational semantics is a significant approach for compiler writers, but is of limited general utility in learning or expressing semantics.

12.3.3 Operational Semantics

Operational semantics approaches programming language semantics by defining *how a computation is performed*, that is, by describing the **actions** of the program fragment in terms of an actual or hypothetical machine. Operational semantics is also referred to as *intensional semantics*, because the sequence of internal computation steps (the intension) is most important. As mentioned in Section 12.2.2, *informal* operational semantics is the typical means of describing programming languages. It is noteworthy that in operational semantics:

- an actual or hypothetical machine (model)—the target machine—is required.
- a **precise** description of the machine is required.
- the machines used tend to be simple.

The point is that the execution of a program (or program fragment) written in a high-level language provides an operational specification of the program (or program fragment). At a macroscopic scale the semantics indicates: "This is what this fragment does" to the machine.

Operational semantics for a functional language may be shown using a SECD ("reduction machine") machine for the lambda calculus reductions.

A Note Concerning the Real, Virtual, or Simulated Machine

Note that the human reader of the code may be the "virtual" machine, and is often assumed to be able to correctly interpret and execute the statement. This is typically assumed in informal operational semantics. Furthermore, this machine:

- could be used to show the semantics of an imperative, functional, or declarative language.
- is usually simple, executing machine-level instructions.
- is typically comprised of registers, memory locations, and operations.

An Example of Operational Semantics

To illustrate the approach, suppose the state of the machine consists of the values of all registers, memory locations, condition codes, and status registers. We show the semantics with the following steps:

1. Record the machine state prior to execution/evaluation of the code fragment.
2. Execute/evaluate the code fragment (assume termination).
3. Examine the new machine state.

Thus, the semantics of the code fragment is conveyed by the change in the machine state.

12.3.4 Denotational Semantics

The denotational representation of semantics is a very popular and important approach. *The semantics of an assumed syntactically correct program is represented by a mathematical mapping.* The steps taken to calculate the output are unimportant; it is the functional relationship of input to output that matters. Denotational semantics is also called *extensional semantics*, because the "extension" or relation between input and output is the focus.

Specifically, denotational semantics is used to map syntactic objects into domains of mathematical objects. An overall function is postulated with:

$$\texttt{meaning} : \texttt{Syntax} \rightarrow \texttt{Semantics}$$

The divide-and-conquer approach is important in denotational semantics, in the sense that the overall functional mapping is subdivided into a composition of functions and each of the composite functions is related to a program fragment.

Simple Denotational Semantics Example

Recall our previous simplistic example, the semantic interpretation of the string 1101, that is, the value 1101. Denotational semantics approaches this by defining a semantic function, D, with the corresponding mapping as follows:

$$D : digit|digit - string \rightarrow integer\ value$$

Notice that the domain of this function is a syntactic construct and the range is a semantic concept.

12.3.5 Axiomatic Semantics

Axiomatic semantics employs logic to convey meaning. In axiomatic semantics, the meaning of a syntactically correct program is formalized as a logical proposition or assertion (sometimes used as a program specification) that constrains the mapping between program input and output. More specifically, in the axiomatic approach, the program semantics is based on assertions about logical relationships that remain the same each time the program executes. The basic strategy is:

$$\{logical\ preconditions\} \cap \{syntactic\ fragment\} \rightarrow \{logical\ postconditions\}$$

Axiomatic semantics is more abstract than denotational semantics, and involves assertions and logical formulas from the predicate logic. Axiomatic semantics is **machine independent**.

12.3.6 Algebraic Semantics

In algebraic semantics, an algebraic specification of data and language constructs is developed. This approach is noteworthy because it leads to the notion of abstract data types, which in turn could be thought of as implying OO programming.

12.4 Semantic Equivalence

It is possible (and often desirable) that two different program fragments, possibly written using two different programming languages, have exactly the same meaning or semantics. An overly simple example is the two `minic` fragments:

```
t1 = 5 + 4;
```

and

```
t1= 27 / 3;
```

More often, we notice the similarity between constructs such as

```
for(;;)
```

and

```
while(true)
```

This raises the often important issue of *semantic equivalence*. The exact definition of semantic equivalence depends upon the specific semantic formalism used, and is shown in the following detailed investigations of each approach.

12.5 Semantic Descriptions Using an Abstract Syntax

12.5.1 Abstract Syntax

Up to this point we have been considering the so-called concrete syntax of a programming language. Note the following:

1. The BNF specifies the *concrete syntax* of the language.

2. The concrete syntax is precise, and necessary for designing syntactically correct programs. *Programming is not a fuzzy concept.*

3. A parser must be based upon the *concrete syntax.* However, parse trees based upon the concrete syntax are often cluttered with details that, while important in parsing, are superfluous in semantic analysis.

4. The concrete syntax does not indicate "essential" concepts of the language.

5. The concrete syntax should be unambiguous.

6. It is challenging to learn programming just by looking at the concrete syntax.

7. Derivation or parse trees built from the concrete syntax are often cluttered with details that, although important in parsing, are superfluous in *semantic analysis.* It is this observation that suggests a modification (or perhaps a simplification) of the concrete syntax and leads to the notion of an abstract syntax.

12.5.2 Why "Abstract" Syntax?

There are two major uses of an abstract syntax:

1. Abstract syntax specification is an attempt to show the semantics of phrases and make the syntax simpler than the concrete syntax. Semantic specifications based upon the abstract syntax are simpler and often much clearer. Another objective is to simply communicate the structure of language phrases (substrings) in terms of the semantics of the language and reduce language constructs to "essential" representation.

2. Using an abstract syntax can facilitate comparison of elements of programming languages, at a somewhat higher level than (concrete) or BNF. For example, some language constructs in different programming languages have the same conceptual (abstract) structure. Consider the two program fragments shown in Table 12.3. Notice these fragments basically only differ at the lexical level,[6] but the structure and consequently the semantics are the same.

Note also that:

- Abstract syntax, as a topic, is somewhat controversial and the concept itself is ambiguous.
- Abstract syntax trees may be used to show the hierarchical structure of a language (if one exists).
- Often, ambiguity results in the abstract syntax. This is acceptable, because we assume that parsing will or has been done using the concrete syntax.

12.5.3 From Concrete to Abstract Syntax

There is usually no unique mapping or conversion of the concrete syntax of a programming language into an abstract syntax. Recall that the goal is to determine, or highlight, the essential constructs of the language.

---

[6]Although to be precise the concrete syntax is different.

C	Pascal

`while (x != y) {`
`.`
`.`
`.`
`};`
	`while (x <> y) do`
	`begin`
	`.`
	`.`
	`.`
	`end`

Table 12.3 Similarity of Two Constructs in Different Programming Languages.

A Paradigm for Conversion

Consider the following basic two-step paradigm:

1. Determine which nonterminals are fundamental. This is subjective.
2. Determine the basic forms the language constructs may take. In an imperative language, this often results in "promoting" terminals that represent important operations or constructs. This is best shown by examples.

12.5.4 Abstract Syntax Examples for `minic`

A Simple Example

A portion of the syntax of `minic` Version 2 follows:

```
<expr> ::= <integer-expr> | <boolean-expr>
<integer-expr> ::= <simple-integer-expr> | <comp-integer-expr>
<boolean-expr> ::= <simple-boolean-expr> | comp-boolean-expr
<comp-integer-expr> ::= <integer-expr> <int-oper> <integer-expr>
<comp-boolean-expr> ::= <integer-expr> <bool-oper> <integer-expr>
<simple-integer-expr> ::= <identifier> | <integer-const>
<simple-boolean-expr> ::= <identifier> | <boolean-const>
<integer-const> ::= <numeral>
<numeral> ::= <digit> | <digit> <numeral>
<digit> ::= 0|1|2|3|4|5|6|7|8|9
```

Consider the sequence of productions that leads from nonterminal **<expr>** to nonterminal **<numeral>** using the concrete syntax:

```
<expr> =>
<integer-expr> =>
<simple-integer-expr> =>
<integer-const> =>
<numeral>
```

In the abstract syntax, the significant aspect of this sequence is that **<expr>** may be replaced by **<numeral>**, resulting in the much briefer derivation sequence in the abstract syntax:

```
<expr> => <numeral>
```

that is, the production in the abstract syntax:

```
<expr> ::= <numeral>
```

A More Realistic Example

Refer to the `minic` Version 2.1 BNF syntax description in Section 12.5.4. Note that this version of the syntax does not (yet) contain the control structures such as **`if`**, **`for`**, or `while`.

Consider the use of productions starting with **`<expr>`**. Specifically, consider the production of string `3+4*5`.

Derivation Using the Concrete Syntax A derivation sequence for this string might be:

```
<expr>
<integer-expr>
<comp-integer-expr>
<integer-expr> <int-oper> <integer-expr>
<simple-integer-expr> <int-oper> <integer-expr>
<integer-const> <int-oper> <integer-expr>
<numeral> <int-oper> <integer-expr>
<digit> <int-oper> <integer-expr>
3 <int-oper> <integer-expr>
3 <int-oper> <comp-integer-expr>
3 + <integer-expr> <int-oper> <integer-expr>
3 + <simple-integer-expr> <int-oper> <integer-expr>
3 + <integer-const> <int-oper> <integer-expr>
3 + <numeral> <int-oper> <integer-expr>
3 + <digit> <int-oper> <integer-expr>
3 + 4 <int-oper> <integer-expr>
3 + 4 * <integer-expr>
3 + 4 * <simple-integer-expr>
3 + 4 * <integer-const>
3 + 4 * <numeral>
3 + 4 * <digit>
3 + 4 * 5
```

This derivation is also shown in Figure 12.1.

On the basis of the previous derivation, consider the set of possible productions in an abstract syntax shown here:

```
<op> ::= * | / | + | - | < | =< | == | !=
<expr> ::= true | false | <numeral>
<expr> ::= <expr> <op> <expr>
<numeral> ::= 0|1|2|3|4|5|6|7|8|9
```

Derivation Using An Abstract Syntax A derivation sequence for the preceding example based upon the abstract syntax might be:

```
<expr>
<expr> <op> <expr>
<numeral> <op> <expr>
3 <op> <expr>
3 + <expr>
3 + <expr> <op> <expr>
3 + <numeral> <op> <expr>
3 + 4 <op> <expr>
3 + 4 * <expr>
3 + 4 * <numeral>
3 + 4 * 5
```

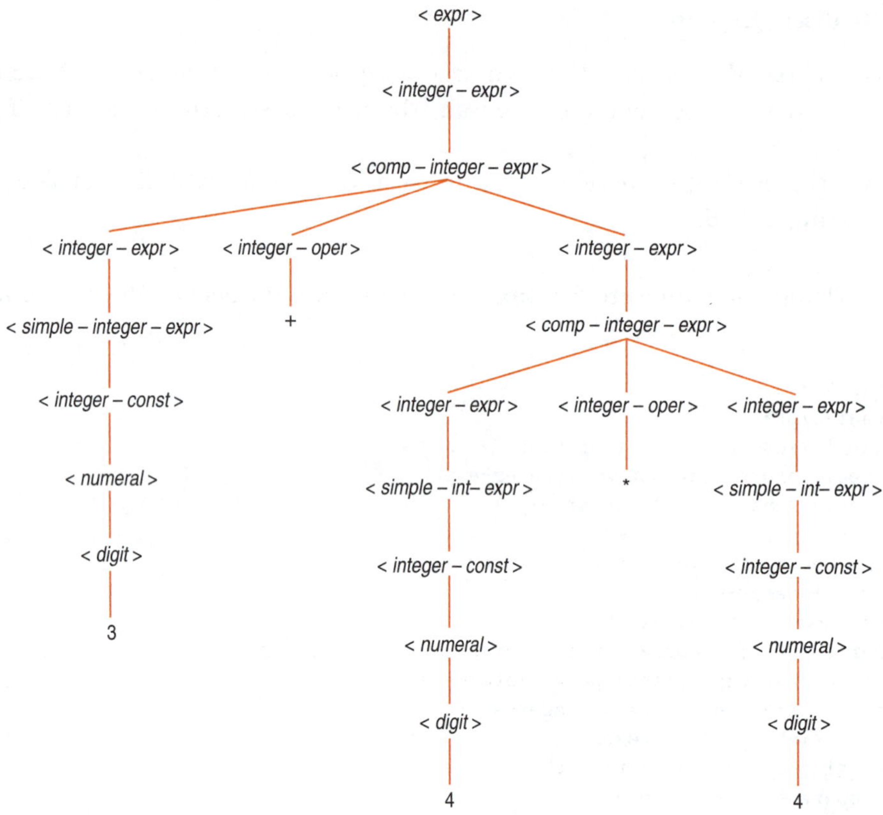

Figure 12.1 Derivation Tree Example Using Concrete Syntax.

This derivation is also shown in Figure 12.2. The simplicity, clarity, and emphasis on the fundamental operation shown in the abstract derivation and abstract derivation tree is evident.

`minic` Derivation Trees Using Abstract Versus Concrete Syntax

Derivation and parse trees based upon the abstract syntax are used to show the significant structure of a derivation or parse. Abstract syntax-based trees are often much simpler because they are not cluttered with the details of the concrete syntax. This is shown in the derivation trees corresponding to the example of Section 12.5.4 in Figures 12.1 and 12.2.

12.6 Denotational Semantics

Using the approach of denotational semantics, the semantics of a syntactically correct program may be determined. Denotational semantics is based upon a program having a mathematical meaning or interpretation.

12.6.1 Concept and Examples

The denotational semantic description or *denotation* is based upon functions that map from syntactic to semantic domains, and thus *denote* the meaning of the syntactic construct. Thus, the denotational semantics approach is more abstract than operational se-

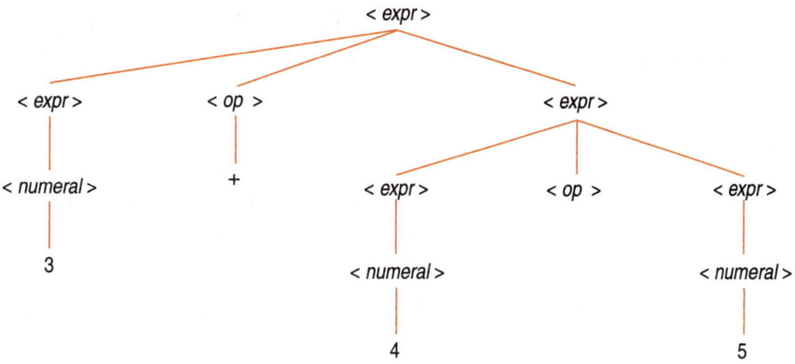

Figure 12.2 Derivation Tree Example Using Abstract Syntax.

mantics, and does not involve specification of the computational steps. In other words, the denotational semantics of a program or fragment is independent of the computational strategy used to implement the program or fragment.

Denotational semantics is also more explicit than axiomatic semantics, in the sense that a rigorous definition of mathematical objects corresponding to each syntactic entity in the language and definition of the mapping function is required. The challenge in this approach is the determination of the mathematical objects and functions and the corresponding syntactic "fragments" from the abstract syntax. In addition, auxiliary functions, as shown, are also developed and used. As in other approaches, the overall program meaning is almost always determined by a composition of mappings—the divide-and-conquer approach, as described in Section 12.6.3.

Specifically, denotational semantics is used to map *syntactic objects* (program 'fragments', including entire programs) into domains of *mathematical objects.* For example, an overall semantic function is postulated with the form:

```
program_meaning : Syntax → Semantics
```

Example 1

Consider the case of arithmetic expressions and assume base 10. For the example arithmetic expression derived from the syntactic construct `<expr>`:

$$2 + 4 - 5$$

The goal of denotational semantics is to develop a set of *semantic functions* that map this input **string** to produce the *denotation*, or meaning, as the mathematical object (integer) with **value** 1.

Example 2

Recall our previous simplistic example, the string (syntactic interpretation) 1101 or the value (semantic interpretation) 1101. The value is given by some semantic function that maps strings of digits, derived from the `minic` syntactic entity `<numeral>`, into semantic values (such as integers). This implies a semantic function, D, as follows:

$$D : digit|digit - string \rightarrow integer\ value$$

For example, the digit 6 maps to the value 6.[7] The details of function D are not given here; rather, only the *signature* of function D is shown.

12.6.2 Semantic Functions

The basis of denotational semantics is the notion of semantic functions. These functions are defined and implemented using *signatures* and *semantic equations*. A **semantic function** maps a syntactic construct (program, code fragment) into a mathematical object. This mapping is the **denotation** of the syntactic construct. Examples of semantic equations follow.

Nomenclature

Because it is clear that a **semantic function** maps a syntactic construct (program, code fragment) into a mathematical object, no special notation is needed in the function signature to indicate domain and range. However, in semantic equations used to implement semantic functions, it is possible to confuse (as was shown in Example 2) syntactic and semantic entities.[8] Therefore we use the double (emphatic) brackets ([[ ]]) to indicate syntactic entities.

Syntactic and Semantic Domains

Let's Not Confuse Domain and Range Recall that any function, shown by its signature:

$$f : R \times R \rightarrow I \tag{12.1}$$

maps from its domain set, or simply domain ($R \times R$ in Equation 12.1), into its range set, or simply range (I in Equation 12.1). Also note that Equation 12.1 does not indicate how this mapping occurs or is implemented; thus more information on the precise mapping is necessary.

In a number of previous descriptions, we have used the terms "syntactic domain" and "semantic domain." Specifically, a semantic function maps from the syntactic domain to the semantic domain. What is meant is that the semantic domain is the range of the semantic function.

Syntactic Domains The syntactic domain consists of the $L(G)$. Usually, however, it is based upon selected constructs from the abstract syntax. For example, the collection of syntactic objects representing the syntactic domain might be:

```
<digit>
<numeral>
<op>
<command>
<command-seq>
<expr>
```

[7] Or any other value we may choose.

[8] For example, is 1101 a string or an integer?

Semantic Domains As noted, the semantic domain contains "mathematical objects." For instance, they may be values or functions. Perhaps the simplest `minic` example could be based upon the translational unit returned value,[9]

$$T : < \texttt{transunit} > \rightarrow (evaluation\ of\ return\ statement) \tag{12.2}$$

For example, the reader should verify that using Equation 12.2, the denotational semantics of the syntactically correct `minic` Version 2 program:

```
int main(void)
{
int t1;
for(t1=10;t1<20;t1=t1+1)
return(t1);
}
```

maps to the value 20.

Consider the case where `minic` has been augmented to allow program input and output. In this case, a more general signature for the `minic` `<transunit>` fragment might be:

$$T : < \texttt{transunit} > \rightarrow (input \rightarrow output) \tag{12.3}$$

The semantic function (T) of Equation 12.3 maps all `minic` programs derived from `<transunit>` into the semantic domain of input-to-output mappings. Thus, in this interpretation, the semantics, or meaning, of a `minic` program is given in terms of an input-to-output mapping implemented by the program.

Command Sequences and the Concept of an Environment or Store

In imperative languages such as `minic`, *the basis for computation is usually a sequence of commands derived from* `<command-seq>`. For example, consider the command sequence in the `minic` code fragment shown in Figure 12.3. The first three `minic` statements are derived from `<command>` and represent (simple) assignment statements. To facilitate development of semantic functions for this syntactic construct, we introduce the notion of a *program environment* or what is commonly referred to as the store, denoted `sto`. `sto` represents the system environment before and after a command is executed. For example, consider an initially empty `sto` followed by execution of the code fragment:

```
a = 10;
```

Afterward, `sto` must be updated to record the existence of a variable a with value 10. In

[9]Assuming that the returned value in the syntax is not optional, that is, void.

```
a = 10;
b = 6;
c = a + b;
for (a;b;b+1) d = c + 2;
```

Figure 12.3 Example of `minic` Sequence.

the example of Figure 12.3, this `sto` is the `sto` that exists prior to execution of the next command, namely:

```
b = 6;
```

Following this, `sto` contains information on the existence of variables `a` and `b`, as well as their respective values. Determination of the semantics of the third command, namely the expression

```
c = a + b;
```

requires, among other things, the use of this `sto`.

The `sto` Environment Mapping

Recall from Section 12.5.4 the sample abstract syntax corresponding to nonterminal `<expr>` in `minic`:

```
<op> ::= * | / | + | - | < | =< | == | !=
<expr> ::= true | false | <numeral>
<expr> ::= <expr> <op> <expr>
<numeral> ::= 0|1|2|3|4|5|6|7|8|9
```

Augmenting this abstract syntax with

```
<identifier> = <expr>
```

it is apparent the `sto` contains mappings from identifiers to the set of values

```
true|false|0|1|2|3|4|5|6|7|8|9
```

On the basis of this abstract syntax, we define the *environment* function:

$$environment : \texttt{<identifier>} \rightarrow \{true, false, 0, 1, 2, 3, 4, 5, 6, 7, 8, 9\}$$

Note that the range of *environment* is the semantic domain consisting of values in the set $\{true, false, 0, 1, 2, 3, 4, 5, 6, 7, 8, 9\}$. Commonly, this value set is augmented by another valued, termed "undefined," to allow the case of an identifier whose value is undefined.

The Semantic Function *assign*

On the basis of the previous sections, we could introduce a semantic function *assign*, with signature:

$$assign : \texttt{<simple-assignment>} \rightarrow (sto \rightarrow sto)$$

that is, *assign* produces or outputs a `sto` to `sto` mapping. *assign* uses an auxiliary function *update_sto* to facilitate this mapping. We show the effect of *update_sto* on the current `sto` in the sample case of assignment

$$m = 5$$

using the notation:

$$\mathit{update\_sto}(\mathit{sto}, m, 5) = \{m \rightarrow 5\}\mathit{sto}$$

meaning that the previous `sto` is modified to include the mapping (m,5).

The Semantic Functions *evaluate* and *execute*

evaluate The simplest form of semantic function *evaluate*, using the sample `minic` abstract syntax, would be application to syntactic constructs derived from `<numeral>`, that is,

$$\begin{aligned} \mathit{evaluate}[[0]] &= 0 \\ \mathit{evaluate}[[1]] &= 1 \\ \mathit{evaluate}[[2]] &= 2 \end{aligned}$$

and so forth. When the expression involves identifiers, we can get the semantics—the value of each identifier from the `sto`—using *environment*[[`<identifier>`]]

More generally,

$$\mathit{evaluate} : \texttt{<expr>} \rightarrow (\texttt{sto} \rightarrow \mathit{value})$$

where the notation *evaluate*[[`<expr>`]]`sto` is used to indicate the evaluation of `<expr>` with the current environment recorded in `sto`.

Sample use of the function *evaluate* for two expressions of `<expr>` involves the recursive semantic equation as follows:

$$\mathit{evaluate}[[\texttt{<expr1>+<expr2>}]]\texttt{sto} = \mathit{plus}(\mathit{evaluate}[[\texttt{<expr1>}]]\texttt{sto}, \mathit{evaluate}[[\texttt{<expr2>}]]\texttt{sto})$$

where *plus* is not a semantic function but rather another auxiliary function. Notice the recursive use of *evaluate*.

execute For a single `<command>`, this is straightforward:

$$\mathit{execute} : \texttt{<command>} \rightarrow (\texttt{sto} \rightarrow \texttt{sto})$$

that is, *execute* is a `sto` to `sto` mapping. For example, in the case of an assignment command, *execute* could invoke *assign* to produce this mapping.

12.6.3 Composition

The assignment of meaning to programs in the denotational semantics approach (as well as other semantic approaches) occurs in a compositional manner. In other words, the meaning of a program fragment is determined from the meanings of its subfragments. We can see this in the denotational semantics of arithmetic statements. From the simple arithmetic example presented in Section 12.6.1, notice that the meaning of this phrase or fragment may be deduced by reduction.

When an imperative program is considered, recall that the major syntactic constructs involve assignment and sequences of statements. In this case, denotational semantics descriptions typically follow the program statement sequence, and produce an overall (composite) mapping from input (or program start) to output (or program halt).

We therefore develop semantic functions whose denotations are decomposable. First, consider the form:

$$execute[[\texttt{<command1>}; \texttt{<command2>}]]$$

that is, consider the syntactic fragment

```
c1 ; c2
```

derived from nonterminal `<command-seq>`. `c1` and `c2` are commands derived from nonterminal `<command>` and are to be executed sequentially. We are interested in the semantics of $[[c1; c2]]$. Suppose the initial `sto` is denoted `sto1`.

$$execute[[c1]]\texttt{sto1} \rightarrow (\texttt{sto1} \rightarrow \texttt{sto2})$$

produces a new `sto`, denoted `sto2`. `sto2` is the `sto` that exists prior to execution of c2. Thus,

$$execute[[c2]]\texttt{sto2} \rightarrow (\texttt{sto2} \rightarrow \texttt{sto3})$$

The overall mapping is

$$execute[[c1; c2]]\texttt{sto1} \rightarrow (\texttt{sto1} \rightarrow \texttt{sto3})$$

which could be written as:

$$execute[[c1; c2]]\texttt{sto1} = execute[[c2]](execute[[c1]]\texttt{sto1}) \tag{12.4}$$

because *execute* produces a `sto`. It is important to note the order shown. The composition in **??** is often denoted:

$$execute[[c1; c2]] = execute[[c2]] \circ execute[[c1]] \tag{12.5}$$

This example may be continued to show the decomposition of a `<command-seq>` of arbitrary length.

12.6.4 Denotational Semantic Equivalence

Definition

Two code fragments are semantically equivalent (using denotational semantics) if they have the same denotation.

Semantic Equivalence Example

Hopefully, to put things all together, we show an example. We prove, using denotational semantics, the semantic equivalence of execution of the following two `minic` code fragments:

```
p=6;
q=p-1
```

and

```
q=5;
p=q+1
```

Notice that both will involve *composition*. More specifically, this means we must prove the overall semantic value is the same for each. Because they are code fragments, we use semantic function ***execute***. Recall the signature on ***execute***:

```
execute: command → (sto → sto)
```

Let `sto` be an arbitrary store. Thus the goal is to prove:

```
execute[[p=6; q=p-1 ]] = execute [[ q=5; p=q+1 ]]
```
(12.6)

We show this with two sketches of the process of determining denotational semantics for each sequence. Notice that composition is involved.

Consider first the left-hand side of Equation 12.6. The steps to achieve the denotational semantics of this syntactic fragment are as follows (notice that the intermediate steps involving *assign* and *evaluate*[[`<expr1>` + `<expr2>`]]`sto` are omitted, for illustration):

$$
\begin{aligned}
execute[[p = 6; q = p - 1]]sto \\
&= execute[[q = p - 1]](execute[[p = 6]]sto) \\
&= execute[[q = p - 1]](update\_sto(sto, p, (evaluate[[6]]))) \\
&= execute[[q = p - 1]]\{p \to 6\}sto \\
&= update\_sto(\{p \to 6\}sto, q, (evaluate[[p - 1]]\{p \to 6\}sto)) \\
&= update\_sto(\{p \to 6\}sto, q, 5) \\
&= \{p \to 6, q \to 5\}sto
\end{aligned}
$$

Thus, the semantics of this command sequence are the mapping of the (arbitrary) initial `sto` to $\{p \to 6, q \to 5\}sto$.

Looking at the second sequence, the denotational semantics are determined as follows:

$$
\begin{aligned}
execute[[q = 5; p = q + 1]]sto \\
&= execute[[p = q + 1]](execute[[q = 5]]sto) \\
&= execute[[p = q + 1]](update\_sto(sto, q, (evaluate[[5]]sto))) \\
&= execute[[p = q + 1]]\{q \to 5\}sto \\
&= update\_sto(\{q \to 5\}sto, p, (evaluate[[q + 1]]\{q \to 5\}sto)) \\
&= update\_sto(\{q \to 5\}sto, p, 6) \\
&= \{q \to 5, p \to 6\}sto
\end{aligned}
$$

Finally, to show denotational semantic equivalence, note that

$$\{p \rightarrow 6, q \rightarrow 5\}sto = \{q \rightarrow 5, p \rightarrow 6\}sto$$

for any arbitrary initial `sto`. Although it may seem like formalization of what is intuitively obvious, the example captures the essence of denotational semantics and semantic equivalence.

12.7 Axiomatic Semantics

The development of axiomatic semantics is more abstract than denotational semantics, and involves assertions and logical formulas from predicate logic. Axiomatic semantics provides a machine-independent formalism for quantifying semantics. This section presents a brief introduction to the concept, together with a number of simple examples.

12.7.1 Using Logic to Formalize Semantics

In axiomatic semantics, the meaning of a syntactically correct program is formalized by developing a *predicate logic transformation* that occurs when a syntactic fragment is executed.[10] More specifically, in the axiomatic approach, the program semantics are based on assertions about logical relationships among values of program variables at various points[11] in a program that remain the same each time the program executes.

12.7.2 Axiomatic Semantics Development

Assume an imperative language. In axiomatic semantics, the program semantics reduces to the semantics of a statement (derived from `<command>`), which is itself usually a sequence of commands derived from `<command-seq>`. The statement semantics is described by the addition of assertions that are always TRUE when control of the program reaches the assertions. In this sense, *program meaning=program correctness* with respect to a specification given by pre- and postcondition assertions.

As with denotational semantics, several aspects of the development process are similar:

1. The divide-and-conquer approach is also important here. In other words, the development of an axiomatic description of program meaning is done incrementally and a composition-like structure results.

2. As in denotational semantics, we also assume that any program for which an axiomatic specification is desired has been previously checked for syntactic correctness.

3. The abstract syntax is used.

Furthermore, there is a concept of "machine state" necessary in the axiomatic semantics approach.

---

[10] Although it is beyond the scope of this discussion, we are actually studying a branch of axiomatic semantics called *relational semantics*.

[11] Typically these points are before and after major syntactic fragments or "constructs" are executed.

12.7.3 Application of Axiomatic Semantics

Axiomatic semantics is commonly used for two primary objectives:

1. Proving programs "correct."

2. Providing formal specification from which programs may be derived.

Our objective involves a tertiary use, namely to develop a formal and quantitative description of the semantics of syntactically correct program fragments.

12.7.4 The Basic Premise

The relation between an initial logical assertion and a final logical assertion following a code fragment captures the essence of the code semantics.

Assertions and Axioms

An **assertion** (or predicate) is a well-formed formula in predicate calculus. An **axiom** is a well-formed formula that is taken to be true. For example, an axiom from the mathematics of real numbers might be:

$$\forall \textit{ real numbers } x, y, \quad xy = yx$$

A Sample Assertion A typical assertion (where $\cap$ indicates conjunction or AND) might look like:

$$\{m < 5 \ \cap \ k = n^2\}$$

where m, n, and k are *variables in a predicate that are related to program variables.* The truth value of the sample assertion depends upon the values of m, n, and k.

As noted, we are concerned with two types of assertions:

1. Assertions about entities that are TRUE just before execution of the code fragment. These are represented using a set of preconditions, $\{P\}$.

2. Assertions about entities that are TRUE just after the execution of the code fragment. These are represented using a set of postconditions, $\{Q\}$.

Using these yields an axiomatic semantics description of a code fragment of the form:

$$\{P\} \texttt{ <code fragment> } \{Q\}$$

Thus, in terms of axiomatic semantics, given the preceding `<code fragment>`, the pre- and postcondition assertion set (P,Q) determines the semantics of the code fragment. On a more theoretical level, in axiomatic semantics

A program, P, with variables and other symbols, maps into statements in first-order predicate logic.

A Note about Notation

We use the notation $\{P\}S\{Q\}$, whereas some authors use $\{Q\}S\{P\}$. The former (our representation) provides a useful mnemonic in that P is "preconditions" and Q is "consequent" or result.

A Review of Predicate Calculus

The mathematics of logic is familiar to most computer engineering/science students through an introduction to digital logic circuits and perhaps a first course in discrete mathematics. Because axiomatic semantics is based upon predicate logic, we review a few simple concepts here.

Predicate Logic Related to Axiomatic Semantics

In predicate logic, we are interested in developing well-formed expressions using logical connectives such as AND, OR, and NOT. Less familiar logical connectives are equality (=, which is *not* assignment) and implication ($\rightarrow$). Furthermore, as we saw in Prolog, the notion of a logical *predicate* is important. Predicates have variables, and the truth value of a predicate depends upon the values these variables take on.

Well-formed formulas (wffs) in predicate calculus are comprised of predicates, variables, constants, and connectives. With respect to axiomatic semantics:

- variables in predicates correspond to program (fragment) variables. Variables in the logical description get values from the corresponding program (fragment) variables.
- function symbols (connectives) in the logical description include all the operations available in the programming language. This includes $<$, $>$, $*$, and so forth. Note that a significant distinction is made between $=$ in logic and the use of `=` (assignment) in the programming language. This is treated in Section 12.7.8.
- the truth value of a wff in predicate logic is dependent upon the values of component variables. Another viewpoint is that the wff, to be TRUE, constrains variable values.

Implication Review

Implication is another important logical connective and plays a role in the rules that accompany axiomatic semantics, as shown in Section 12.7.7. *Implication is not the same as equality.* The truth table for implication is shown here:

p	q	$p \rightarrow q$	$\neg p \cup q$
T	T	T	T
T	F	F	F
F	T	T	T
F	F	T	T

A very important equivalence is:

$$\{(p \rightarrow q) = (\neg p \cup q)\} = T$$

12.7.5 Developing Axiomatic Semantics Descriptions

We may think of developing axiomatic semantics as a three-step process:

1. Describe the semantics of a code fragment by specifying assertions (in $\{P\}$) that must be true *prior to execution* of the fragment.
2. Show the code fragment (call it `C`) and assume it executes (and terminates).[12]
3. Develop assertions that are true after execution ($\{Q\}$).

As noted, the axiomatic semantics of `C` are given by the ordered pair:

$$(\{P\}, \{Q\})$$

Alternately, $(\{P\}, \{Q\})$ provides a **specification** for code (fragment) `C`.

`minic` Example

A simple `minic` code fragment follows. Note that the semicolon is only shown to illustrate the termination of the statement. It is *not* part of the string derived from `<command>`.

```
x = 1 / y;
```

One axiomatic representation for this code fragment in the form $\{P\}$ `<code fragment>` $\{Q\}$ is:

$$\{y \neq 0\} \ \ \texttt{x = 1 / y} \ \{x = \frac{1}{y}\}$$

It is critical to note in the preceding example that `x` and `y` are **program variables** whereas x and y are variables in the predicate calculus.

Invariant Relations Note that although specific values of program variables may change during execution of a code fragment, as well as each time the code fragment is executed, we develop axiomatic semantics by developing assertions (pre- and postfragment) using **invariant relations.** Note this situation in the previous examples.

12.7.6 Partial and Total Correctness in Axiomatic Semantics

Partial Correctness

First, we characterize the logical constraint underlying an axiomatic semantics representation of the form:

$$\{P\}\texttt{C}\{Q\}$$

which uses implication. A program (fragment) is partially correct if the following compound statement in predicate logic is true:

$$\{P\} \cap \texttt{C} \text{ executes } \rightarrow \{Q\}$$

[12]More on this in Section 12.7.6.

Total Correctness

Total correctness extends partial correctness with the additional requirement that the program (fragment) is guaranteed to terminate. In other words,

Partial Correctness + Termination = Total Correctness

Proving Termination

Proving termination is generally considered an advanced topic and beyond our scope. However, we should say that termination is not an issue with many types of commands. Exceptions are `for`- and `while`-based fragments and recursively defined procedures and functions.

12.7.7 Lack of Uniqueness of the Axiomatic Specification

In Section 12.7.5, we were careful to show *one* axiomatic representation. Axiomatic representations are not unique, and this is perhaps the Achilles heel of the technique. We expand upon this in the following section.

Axiomatic Descriptions Using `minic`

Consider the `minic` program fragment involving assignment and an expression:

```
x = y + 1;
```

Suppose further that we are given an axiomatic specification corresponding to this fragment as:

$$\{y = -3\}\ \texttt{x = y + 1}\ \{x < 0\} \tag{12.7}$$

Correctness of the Sample Specification

Given the specification $\{y = -3\}$ `x = y + 1` $\{x < 0\}$, note that y and x are logical variables and `y` and `x` are program variables. We proceed in the following manner:

1. Assume that $\{y = -3\} = \text{TRUE}$. This requires that y (the logical variable) has the value -3. Note this is not assignment, but rather $=$ is used as a logical connective, in this case the test for equality. This also constrains the corresponding program variable, `y`.

2. Assume that `x = y + 1` executes.

3. Because `y` is constrained by the value of y, use the substitution indicated in the program fragment to get the value of `x`, and consequently x. Note that we are not done.

4. $\{y = -3\}$ and the substitution $\rightarrow \{x = -2\}$ (is TRUE).

5. Observe that $\{x = -2\} \rightarrow \{x < 0\}$. Now we are done, except for the following important observation.

In the previous example, be careful to note

$$\{x = -2\} \rightarrow \{x < 0\}$$

This is implication, not equality, and the converse

$$\{x < 0\} \rightarrow \{x = -2\}$$

is not true.

Alternative Specifications for the Same Fragment

We note there are other valid axiomatic specifications for the example of Section 12.7.7 (Equation 12.7). For example, an alternate is

$$\{y = 3\}\ \texttt{x = y + 1}\ \{x > 0\} \tag{12.8}$$

Thus (so far), the axiomatic specification of program fragment `x = y + 1` is either the pair

$$(\{y = -3\}, \{x < 0\})$$

or

$$(\{y = 3\}, \{x > 0\})$$

Furthermore, *another* possible precondition *for the same code fragment and* $\{Q\}$ in Equation 12.8 is:

$$\{P\} = \{y \geq 0\} \tag{12.9}$$

Actually, given only a choice between the two possible preconditions in Equations 12.8 and 12.9, the latter (12.9) is the weakest precondition, as will now be defined.

Standardization: The Weakest Precondition

Formal Definition Given `C` and $\{Q\}$, the **weakest precondition**, denoted $\{W\}$, is defined as follows. Suppose that $\{P\}$ is any precondition for which

$$\{P\}\ \texttt{C}\ \{Q\}$$

holds. If

$$\{P\} \rightarrow \{W\}$$

(note that this is logical implication), then $\{W\}$ is the weakest precondition.

Informal Definition Among all possible preconditions for the pair `C`,$\{Q\}$, $\{W\}$ specifies the fewest constraints.[13]

[13]Consequently, it is the "weakest."

12.7.8 Rules of Inference: Adjunct Tools for Axiomatic Specification

Up to this point, examples of code "fragment" `C` have been simple statements derived from `<command>`. Suppose, however, that `C` is as follows:

```
t1=10;
t2=3;
t3=t2*t1;
b1=t2<t3;
```

Notice that this was derived, from a syntactic viewpoint, from the `minic` nonterminal `<command-seq>`, which in turn was comprised of replacements involving `<command>`. It might be cumbersome to develop an axiomatic specification for this fragment as given. However, suppose some *logic-based* technique were available that allowed a (perhaps more convenient) reformulation of the specification. In this example, a formal rule to allow decomposition might be desirable.

It is for this reason (and others) that axiomatic semantics also provides axioms and proof rules that facilitate the specification of code. They are used as adjunct tools for axiomatic semantics descriptions and proofs.

Notation

There are many tools and notational devices used to facilitate logical proofs. Consider the logic embedded in the following notation:

```
All men are mortal
Socrates is a man
------------------
Socrates is mortal.
```

The meaning of the preceding axiom or rule is that if you have established the truth of the two predicates above the line (conjunction or AND is used), then the conclusion below the line is TRUE. In the simplest form:

```
    p
---------
    q
```

is used to represent the first row of the truth table for implication (see Section 12.7.4, namely:

$$p \rightarrow q = T \tag{12.10}$$

Example: Modus Ponens Using the previous notation, we can show one of the fundamental tools of rule-based inference, namely modus ponens or MP.

$$\begin{array}{ll} p & (=T) \\ \underline{p \rightarrow q} & \underline{(=T)} \\ q & (=T) \end{array} \tag{12.11}$$

Axiom for Command Sequencing

This applies to a `minic` command sequence of the form `C1;C2`, where `C1` and `C2` are commands.

$$\frac{\{P\}\ \mathrm{C1}\ \{Q1\} \cap \{Q1\}\ \mathrm{C2}\ \{Q2\}}{\{P\}\ \mathrm{C1;C2}\{Q2\}} \tag{12.12}$$

For clarity or to avoid possible ambiguity, we write this as:

$$\frac{[\{P\}\ \mathrm{C1}\ \{Q1\}] \cap [\{Q1\}\ \mathrm{C2}\ \{Q2\}]}{\{P\}\ \mathrm{C1;C2}\{Q2\}} \tag{12.13}$$

Axiom for Assignment

As noted previously, the semantics of syntactic constructs using `=` (assignment) must be carefully considered in order to avoid developing nonsensical axiomatic semantics descriptions. Consider two formulations for the axiomatic semantics of an assignment statement:

Formulation 1

$$\{true\}\ \texttt{x = x + 1}\ \{x = x + 1\} \tag{12.14}$$

Notice the direct mapping of program variables and connectives to logical variables and connectives in Equation 12.14, most importantly the (erroneous) mapping of $=$. Note that the postcondition *must be false*, that is, there is no value of x such that $x = x+1$ is TRUE in logic. We are attempting to convey the intuitive notion that augmenting the value of program variable `x` before execution of the fragment by 1 yields the value of program variable `x` after execution. The attempt to capture the axiomatic semantics of assignment via logical variable x and the $=$ connective in logic fails.

Formulation 2 We try to improve upon the previous axiomatic semantics description with the following specification:

$$\{x = A\}\ \texttt{x = x + 1}\ \{x = A + 1\}$$

Whereas this captures the intuitive notion of assignment in a logically correct manner, it is not very general. Thus, we present the axiom for assignment:

$$\{[e/v]Q\}\ \texttt{v = e}\ \{Q\} \tag{12.15}$$

where `v` is derived from `<identifier>` and `e` is derived from `<expr>`. Furthermore, the notation $[e/v]$ means the substitution of e for all free occurrences of v in postcondition Q.

For example, consider the `minic` fragment `y = x + y`. An axiomatic semantics description might be:

$$\{x = 1, x + y > 2\}\ \texttt{y = x + y}\ \{x = 1, y > 2\}$$

where we have used $[x + y/y]\{x = 1, y > 2\}$ to produce $\{x = 1, x + y > 2\}$.

12.7.9 Proof Direction

A commonly asked question in using axiomatic semantics for formal proofs of correctness is the following:

> *Given the axiomatic specification*[14]*:*
>
> $$\{P\}\ \mathtt{C}\ \{Q\}$$
>
> *to prove correctness should I work from* $\{P\}$*, via* C*, to* $\{Q\}$*, or backward, from* $\{Q\}$*, via* C*, to* $\{P\}$*?*

The simple answer is that it depends. Given the objective of showing that $\{P\} \cap$ C executes $\rightarrow \{Q\}$ is a tautology, we may start with $\{P\}$, use C, and show that the result contains $\{Q\}$. Alternately, we might assume that $\{Q\}$ holds (is TRUE), and work backward, through "inversion" of C to determine what must hold prior to C. If this is contained in $\{P\}$, the proof also succeeds. In some cases more effort is required in one direction than in the other. As an aside, this issue parallels the notions of forward and backward chaining in rule-based systems.

12.8 Functional Programming: Semantics and Correctness

Because a functional approach to programming emphasizes function design and implementation, we consider the associated semantics and correctness separately. In addition, we indicate how a proof of program correctness is straightforward.

Consider a program intended to implement the function a^b. This example provides an interesting example for (recursive) function design. It could also be solved using iteration and in most imperative languages. However, consider the following decomposition:

$$a^b = \begin{cases} 1 & \text{if } b = 0 \\ (a^2)^{b/2} & \text{if } b \text{ is even and } > 0 \\ aa^{b-1} & \text{if } b \text{ is odd and } > 0 \end{cases}$$

A CommonLisp implementation is shown here:

```
;;file: expr1.l
;; a^b
;; no side effects

(defun expr (a b)
(if (zerop b) 1
        (if (evenp b) (expr (* a a) (/ b 2))
              (* a (expr a (- b 1))))))
```

The behavior of this function is shown here with a sample CommonLisp session, where we have used `trace` to show the recursive solution.

```
> (load './expr1.l)
;; Loading file .\expr1.l ...
;; Loading of file .\expr1.l is finished.
t
> (expr 2 3)
```

[14] *With code fragment* C *given in detail.*

```
8
> (expr 3 2)
9

> (trace expr)
;; Tracing function expr.
(expr)
> (expr 2 3)

1. Trace: (expr '2 '3)
2. Trace: (expr '2 '2)
3. Trace: (expr '4 '1)
4. Trace: (expr '4 '0)
4. Trace: expr ==> 1
3. Trace: expr ==> 4
2. Trace: expr ==> 4
1. Trace: expr ==> 8
8
> (expr 3 2)

1. Trace: (expr '3 '2)
2. Trace: (expr '9 '1)
3. Trace: (expr '9 '0)
3. Trace: expr ==> 1
2. Trace: expr ==> 9
1. Trace: expr ==> 9
9
```

12.8.1 Proving Correctness Is Much Easier

Correctness of programs in imperative languages is difficult to prove because:

- execution depends on the contents of each memory cell (each stored program variable).
- loops (iteration) must be handled.
- the progress of the computation is measured by snapshots of the state of the computer after each fragment is executed.

On the other hand, purely functional languages are much easier to reason about because of the concept of **referential transparency**, which means that only those values involved in a function application need be considered. These are the variables used to define function input. In other words, the concept of stored program variables does not exist in a purely functional language.

Programs defined as recursive functions usually can be proved correct by an induction proof.[15] An example follows.

12.8.2 Example Proof

```
(defun expr (a b)
(if (zerop b) 1
        (if (evenp b) (expr (* a a) (/ b 2))
              (* a (expr a (- b 1))))))
```

[15]Induction proofs are useful when recursive definitions are employed. The basis for an induction proof is to show that $P(n)$ is true for $n = k$ (the "basis" step) and $n = k + 1$ (the "induction" step). On this basis we may show that $P(n)$ is true for $n \geq k$. For example, suppose $P(n)$ is true for $n = k = 1$ and $n = k + 1$. Then $P(n)$ is true for $n = 1$ and the induction step forces $P(2)$ to be true. If $P(2)$ is true, the induction step requires $P(3)$ to be true, and so forth, thus proving $P(n)$ is true for $n \geq 1$.

The basis step is to show when $b = 0$, `expr(a b)`=`expr(a 0)`$= a^0 = 1$. For any $b > 0$, we then show that `expr(a (+ 1 b))`$=a^{b+1}$ =`a * expr(a b)`$=aa^b$.

Proof

If b is even, $b+1$ is odd, and therefore `expr(a (+ 1 b))=a * (expr(a b))`$= aa^b$. If b is odd, $b+1$ is even and $(b+1)/2$ may be even or odd. If $(b+1)/2$ is odd, `expr(a (+ 1 b))`$=$ `a*expr(a b)`. If $(b+1)/2$ is even `expr(a (+ 1 b))`=`expr(a*a (b+1)/2)`$= (a^2)^{(b+1)/2} = a^{b+1} = aa^b$=`a*expr(a b)`.

12.8.3 Interpreting Functional Programming Using Axiomatic Semantics

The previous example is handled directly in axiomatic semantics (especially in light of the induction proof) by the following description:

- precondition: $b \geq 0$
- postcondition: `(expr a b)` $= a^b$
- proof by induction on b

12.9 Algebraic Semantics

Algebraic semantics, as the name implies, convey programming language semantics through development of an algebra. A major distinguishing feature of this approach, however, is that syntax and semantics are comingled. Furthermore, there is no concept of "machine state" necessary in this approach.

Algebraic semantics are important because they:

1. provide another mechanism for the specification of both syntax and semantics.
2. are related to the concept of abstract data types (ADTs).
3. suggest many of the attributes of object-oriented (OO) programming.

12.9.1 What Is an "Algebra?"

Most readers are familiar with the concepts of "algebra" and an algebra. However, formal definitions are sometimes more elusive.

Informal Definitions

There are many informal definitions, including:

- a branch of mathematics in which arithmetical operations and relationships are generalized by using alphabetic symbols to represent unknown numbers or members of specified sets of numbers.
- any abstract calculus, a formal language in which functions and operations can be defined and their properties studied. Thus the algebra of clauses is another name for set theory and the algebra of logic for formal logic.[16]

[16]From the *Collins English Dictionary, 2000.*

- a branch of mathematics that deals with operations on sets of numbers or other elements that are often represented by symbols. Algebra is a generalization of arithmetic that deals symbolically with elements and operations and relationships connecting the elements.
- the first mathematics, usually encountered in middle or high school, that is significantly more abstract and more challenging than arithmetic.

Formal Definition

An algebra consists of two interrelated entities:

1. A domain of values.
2. A set of operations defined on these values.

These entities usually allow a much richer development of the algebra by developing algebraic relationships and operations that are described by axioms and equations.

Most readers are familiar with certain, well-studied algebras, including Boolean algebra, linear algebra, and the algebra of sets.

12.9.2 Algebraic Formalization for Programming Language Semantics

An algebraic formalization for the semantics of a programming language consists of two parts: a syntactic specification and a semantic specification.

The syntactic specification lists the names of the type, its operations and the types of the arguments, and of the result of the operations. It is often referred to as an *algebraic specification.* Conversely, the semantic specification consists of an algebra defined by a set of algebraic equations. These equations describe the properties of the operations in an implementation-independent manner. Typically, this is done by stating a number of algebraic axioms the operations and sorts must satisfy. Thus, the language syntax is conveyed by the algebraic specification and the language semantics are conveyed by the algebras developed from the algebraic specification.

12.9.3 Vocabulary: Sorts, Operations, and Signatures

Sorts

As mentioned, the syntax of the language is defined by an algebraic specification, which itself is based upon a set of values with defined operations on the values. Fundamental to this specification is the concept of a type or "sort." A sort is a data type specified by a name. Sorts may be predefined (e.g., `integer` and `boolean` in `minic`), or user defined, in which case they are built from built-in types with type constructors. Note that in the specification of sorts we assume no inherent operations other than accessing; the operations on the sorts must be defined separately.

Operations

Operations are functions whose domain is either a subset of the set of sorts or empty. In the case of an empty domain, the operation is considered a constant.

Signatures

The signature of the algebraic specification describes the language syntax and constrains the types of data (sorts) and what operations (by name) may be applied to the data. Signatures only indicate *how* we may use operations on sorts, *but do not describe the behavior of the operation.* Note that this is much like a C function declaration,[17] which is only a prototype of the actual function, specified computationally by the function definition.

12.9.4 An Example Syntax via Algebraic Specification: Booleans

An example is overdue, and may help to bring the previously defined concepts into focus. Consider the development of the algebraic semantics for a programming language intended to implement Boolean logic, and thus one in which the algebraic semantics would be that of Boolean algebra.

Example Sorts

The only sort we will use in the specification is named Boolean.

Example Operations

The corresponding operation names are:

true

false

not

and

or

implies

equal

Example Signatures

Notice that the first two signatures have empty domains and thus comprise constants. Furthermore, no indication is given on how the operation is performed nor any constraints on the resulting values or properties.

true: Boolean

false: Boolean

not: Boolean $\rightarrow$ Boolean

and: Boolean $\times$ Boolean $\rightarrow$ Boolean

or: Boolean $\times$ Boolean $\rightarrow$ Boolean

implies: Boolean $\times$ Boolean $\rightarrow$ Boolean

equal: Boolean $\times$ Boolean $\rightarrow$ Boolean

[17] Often found in header or *.h files.

12.9.5 Corresponding Example Semantics for Booleans

Given the signature for the type or sort Boolean, we now develop the corresponding semantics via a set of equations that constrain the operations and also indicate algebraic properties of the language—that is, the algebra. For illustration, assume variables a_1 and a_2 are of type Boolean.

Equations

The equations that follow define the semantics of this language.

$$
\begin{aligned}
&\text{not(true)} = \text{false}\\
&\text{not(false)} = \text{true}\\
&\text{and}(\text{true},a_1) = a_1\\
&\text{and}(\text{false},a_1) = \text{false}\\
&\text{and}(a_1,a_2) = \text{and}(a_2,a_1)\\
&\text{or}(a_1,a_2) = \text{not}(\text{and}(\text{not}(a_1),\text{not}(a_2)))\\
&\text{implies}(a_1,a_2) = \text{or}(\text{not}(a_1),a_2)\\
&\text{equal}(a_1,a_2) = \text{or}(\text{and}(a_1,a_2),\text{and}(\text{not}(a_1),\text{not}(a_2)))
\end{aligned}
$$

12.10 Concluding Remarks

The techniques in this chapter are useful for defining programming language semantics. In addition, the notion of program correctness has been introduced. Many challenging issues remain in a number of areas, including:

- describing the semantics of languages using the object-oriented programming paradigm.
- distinguishing between static and dynamic semantics, that is, those that may be established on the basis of the code and those that are evident at run-time.
- developing semantics that include parallelism and associated interprocess communication as in a parallel programming paradigm. Operational semantics has been adapted to formalize systems of processes and the communication the processes might undertake.

Finally, a long-standing research topic is the relationship between the different forms of semantic representations. For example, given denotational semantics and axiomatic semantics for a programming language, how could they be unified? This is an important and open question, because a programmer might use axiomatic semantics to reason about the properties of programs, whereas a compiler writer might use denotational semantics to implement the language.

12.11 Bibliographical Remarks and References

Overviews of multiple approaches to formal semantic descriptions of programming languages are given in Ledgard, Marcotty, and Bochman (1976) and Pagan (1981). Algebraic semantics are considered in depth in Goguen and Malcolm (1996). The role of attribute grammars in conveying semantics was introduced in Chapter 5 (Knuth, 1968).

Although we have emphasized formal approaches to the description of imperative languages, these techniques are applicable to other paradigms. For example, the operational and denotational semantics of Prolog have been considered in Arbab and Berry (1987) and Debray and Mishra (1988).

12.12 Exercises

1. Use the `minic` BNF shown to develop an abstract syntax representation.

```
/* minic translational unit grammar w/ o inf. recursion */
/* Version 4.1 with many new constructs */
/* for use in parser development  */
/* file: transunit-bnf4r1nir.txt  */

<transunit> ::= <main-decl> <body>
<main-decl> ::= <type> main <arg>
<type> ::= int | void | boolean
<arg> ::= lparens <type> rparens
<body> ::= lbrace <dec-seq> <statseq> rbrace

<dec-seq> ::= e | <decl> <dec-seq>
<decl> ::= <type> <variable-list>;
<variable-list> ::= <variable> | <variable> , <variable-list>
<variable> ::= <identifier>

<statseq> ::= <return-stat> | <command-seq>; <return-stat>
<command-seq> ::= <command> | <command> ; <command-seq>

/* new commands */

<command> ::= <simple-assignment> | <while> | <for> | <if>

<while> ::= while lparens <boolean-expr> rparens <command>
/* note arguments to for optional */

<for> ::= for lparens <for-simple-assignment> ;
                        <for-boolean-expr>  ;
                        <for-simple-assignment>
                        rparens <command>

<if> ::= if lparens <expr> rparens <command>

<for-simple-assignment> ::= <simple-assignment> | e
<for-boolean-expr> ::= <boolean-expr> | e

<simple-assignment> ::= <lvalue> = <expr>
<expr> ::= <integer-expr> | <boolean-expr>

<integer-expr> ::= <simple-integer-expr> | <comp-integer-expr>
<boolean-expr> ::= <simple-boolean-expr> | <comp-boolean-expr>

<comp-integer-expr> ::= <simple-integer-expr> <int-oper> <rest-integer-expr>
<rest-integer-expr> ::= <simple-integer-expr> | <comp-integer-expr>
/* note to disambiguate need operator precedence rules */

<comp-boolean-expr> ::= <simple-integer-expr> <bool-oper> <simple-integer-expr>
/* not fancy but usable  */

<simple-integer-expr> ::= <identifier> | <integer-const>
```

```
<simple-boolean-expr> ::= <identifier> | <boolean-const>
<integer-const> ::= <numeral>
<int-oper> ::= * | / | + | -
<bool-oper> ::= < | <= | == | !=
<boolean-const> ::= true | false
<lvalue> ::= <identifier>
/* end of updated syntax  */

<return-stat> ::= return <return-arg>;
<return-arg> ::= lparens <variable> rparens   |
                          lparens <numeral>  rparens

/* lexical part for identifiers and numerals */

<identifier> ::= <letter> | <identifier> <letter> |  <identifier> <digit>
<letter> ::= a | b | c | d | e | f | g | h | i | j | k | l | m
                     | n | m | o | p | q | r | s | t | u | v | w | x | y | z
<numeral> ::= <digit> | <digit> <numeral>
<digit> ::= 0|1|2|3|4|5|6|7|8|9
```

2. Develop denotational semantics for the following `minic` syntactic elements:

   (a) <if> ::= if lparens <expr> rparens <command>

   (b) <while> ::= while lparens <boolean-expr> rparens <command>

   (c) <return-stat> ::= return <return-arg>;

3. Using denotational semantics, show that the following are semantically equivalent:

```
execute[[ m=5; n=m+3 ]] = execute [[ n=8; m=n-3 ]]
```

4. Develop denotational semantics for the evaluation of `<numeral>` where:

```
<numeral> ::= <digit> | <digit> <numeral>
<digit> ::= 0|1|2|3|4|5|6|7|8|9
```

5. Continuing the previous problem, using your semantic description, show that the denotation of each of the following is equivalent:

   `[[00233]]`

   `[[0233]]`

   `[[233]]`

6. Given the axiomatic specification for the `minic` fragment:

$$\{y \neq 0\} \;\; \texttt{x = 1 / y;} \; \{x = \frac{1}{y}\}$$

   (a) Prove the correctness of this fragment.

   (b) Suggest alternatives $\{P\}$ and $\{Q\}$.

   (c) With the specification given, would you say the specification is partially or totally correct?

7. This problem is intended to help you see the concept of implication and the definition of the "weakest" precondition. Consider the following set of logical statements involving implication. Each is of the form $P \to W$.

$$(a \cap b \cap c \cap d) \to a$$
$$(a \cap b) \to a$$
$$(a \cap b \cap c \cap d) \to a \cap b$$
$$(a \cap b \cap c \cap d) \to a \cap c$$

   (a) Prove that each of these statements is a tautology.
   (b) Notice in every case that the antecedent contains *more* constraints than the consequent—that is, it is weaker. Suppose in an axiomatic specification of the form $\{P\}$C$\{Q\}$ you have a choice of the following possible $\{P\}$:
      i. $\{a \cap b \cap c \cap d\}$
      ii. $\{a \cap b\}$
      iii. $\{a \cap c \cap d\}$
      iv. $\{a \cap b \cap d\}$
      v. $\{a\}$
      vi. $\{b\}$

   Which is the weakest precondition?

8. Suppose we have added `scanf` to the syntax of `minic`, with the prototype:

```
scanf(''scan-format-string'',\ name1,\ name2,\ ...,\ namen);
```

   where `"scan-format-string"` consists of lowercase alphabetical characters, digits, spaces, and special designators to indicate the reading of integer or boolean values. These were designated by `\i` and `\b`, respectively.[18] *In this problem, we explore the semantics of this code fragment.*

   (a) Based upon your understanding of `scanf` in C, state the *informal operational semantics of this construct.*
   (b) Develop the *denotational* semantics of this construct. Be quantitative. Significant aspects include the semantic function (with signature) and associated semantic equations and auxiliary functions.

9. The following are five attempted axiomatic semantics representations for `minic` code fragments. Determine those that are correct.

$$\{x+1 = y+z\}\texttt{x = x + 1}\{x = y+z\}$$
$$\{y+z > 0\}\texttt{x = y + z}\{x > 0\}$$
$$\{true\}\texttt{x = 6}\{x = 6\}$$
$$\{x = 1, y = 2\}\texttt{x = x + 1}\{x = 2, y = 2\}$$
$$\{x = 1, y = 2\}\texttt{x = x + 1}\{x = y\}$$

[18]Note that the semantics varies from its C counterparts.

10. This problem extends our exploration of **bison** from Chapter 5. Specifically, we investigate the incorporation of semantics into the parsing process. As noted in Section 12.6.2, a simple denotational semantic description of **minic** could be based upon the translational unit returned value, that is,

$$T : \texttt{<transunit>} \rightarrow (evaluation\ of\ return\ statement)$$

    Assume that the returned value in the syntax is not optional, that is, **void** is not a return type.

    Show the **bison** parser revisions necessary to accomplish this rudimentary implementation of denotational semantics. Your effort should build upon extending the use of the symbol table as the **sto**.

11. This exercise makes an excellent term project. The objective is to use **bison** actions to pass semantic values. In the initial effort, consider only simple semantics—for example, those of expression evaluation and assignment. Assume that all variables have been declared, as in Chapter 5. For example, for the two simple assignments:

```
t1=10;
b1=true;
```

    the updated symbol table would appear as shown in Table 12.4. The subsequent parse of a sample expression

Updated Symbol Table Entries		
t1	integer	10
b1	boolean	true

Table 12.4 Implementing Semantics for Expression Evaluation and Assignment in **bison**: Symbol Table Following Assignment of Values to Variables.

```
t1=5*t1+6;
```

    would yield the symbol table shown in Table 12.5.

Updated Symbol Table Entries		
t1	integer	56
b1	boolean	true

Table 12.5 Symbol Table Following Evaluation of an Expression Involving Previously Assigned Variable Values and Assignment.

    Notice that expression evaluation requires checking the symbol table for the previous value of t1 and assignment requires updating the table with the new value.

12. Expand the `bison`-based semantics implementation of the previous problem to include the `if` statement:

```
if(b1)\ t1=5*t1+6;
```

13. (a) Define informal operational semantics and translational semantics.

    (b) Distinguish between informal operational semantics and translational semantics.

    (c) Does one or both of these approaches require a hypothetical machine? If so, which one(s)?

14. In Section 12.6.2, it was suggested that the denotation of a `minic` program could be the translational unit returned value. To this end, consider the following `minic` (Version 2) example:

```
int main(void)
{
int t1;
t1=10;
while(t1<20)
t1=t1+1;
return(t1);
}
```

    (a) With this definition of semantics, what is the semantic value of the program?

    (b) Verify your result using `gdb`.

    (c) Further verify your result using `printf("%d \n", t1);`.

CHAPTER 13

Event-Driven Programming, Part 1: Introduction and (Various) Windows Examples

Change is inevitable . . . except from vending machines.

—From the Web

13.1 Introduction

In this chapter, we begin our look at a very timely and popular programming paradigm: **event-driven programming**. We first explore the programming mindset and underlying principles, and then consider three common development domains–MS Windows, X windows, and wxWidgets. Please note that these examples, by themselves, will not make the reader a competent X Windows, wxWidgets, or MS Windows programmer. Although detailed and self-contained, the sample applications are only intended to illustrate the respective programming approach. Finally, we consider the event-driven paradigm in detail (with hands-on experience) on a PDA, using the Palm OS API, in the next chapter.

13.1.1 A Long Time Ago . . .

A long time ago, in a galaxy far, far away . . .

When a program executed, the program code controlled what happened through the sequence of program statements. The program might go so far as to occasionally prompt the user for input and print output, but the user had little or no control over the order in which events took place while the program was running.

The Typical Sequence of Events

In the "old days" of command-line interface-based programs, the program followed a deterministic sequence of events:

`input (read)` → `compute` → `output (print)` → `halt`

We refer to this paradigm as "programmer-driven control flow," because the programmer decides which part of the program will be run and when. Input is solicited from the user under program control.

An Example

Historically, (sequential) programming is characterized by lack of a graphical user interface (GUI[1]), wherein the program solicits user input through a **polling loop**. A good example is shown in the following snippet of C code.[2]

```
do {
   printf(" 1) Calculate Gas Mixture.\n");
   printf(" Q) Quit.\n");
   printf("\nCHOICE: ");
   fflush(stdin);
   scanf("%s", &ans);
   switch(ans[0]) {
      case '1': main_computation(); break;
                 }
   } while((strcmp("Q",ans) != 0) && (strcmp("q",ans) != 0));
```

13.1.2 Event-Driven Programming

The Paradigm Shift

Many modern systems are developed with user interfaces that respond to user-generated "events" and facilitate more complex program–user interaction. They require a revision of the programmer-driven control flow programming style and lead to new programming paradigms (and operating systems), including **event-driven programming**. Because they most often occur in a single application, we will consider the GUI and event-driven paradigms together.

Fundamental to the event-driven paradigm is the fact that in the process of executing the program,[3] the program doesn't (directly) solicit input. Alternately, in a typical event-driven implementation, the OS or window manager detects that an event has happened (e.g., there's input) and sends a message to the program. The program then decides how to respond to the message or event.

We characterize the situation with the following attributes:

- Event-driven programs have a structure that is quite different from batch programs.
- In event-driven programming, the program is written so that the program can respond to a number of different external and asynchronous events, usually initiated by the user.
- This represents a basic paradigm shift, because the program itself has little or no control over the processing sequence; rather, it simply responds by carrying out the appropriate action in response to events that occur.

---

[1]Pronounced "goo-ey."

[2]This is from a gas blender application.

[3]Note that the programming paradigm (e.g., parallel, imperative, functional) has not been specified.

Thus, the event-driven paradigm turns the programming mindset around:

> *Instead of prompting for user input, it is the job of the program to listen for and respond to user actions (events) that may occur.*

Typical events include mouse movements, engaging push buttons and sliders, menu selections, and data entry in prespecified fields on the GUI.

This basic programming change required in event-driven programming leads to a number of conceptual changes on the part of the programmer. Specifically:

- Event-driven programs have an event loop that waits for and handles events.
- Program control is "given up" to this loop. When run under a window(ing) system, event-driven systems rely on window(ing) software libraries and utilities. Event-driven programming underlies all modern window systems such as X Windows and the various Microsoft Windows versions. Relatively speaking, programs tend to be quite complex. Microsoft Windows makes this even more complicated when programming to the MFC API programming interface. In this case, the programmer must consider a model-view controller architecture on top of an OO programming approach.

Key Aspects of Creating Event-Driven (and GUI) Software

From a programming perspective, reactive or event-driven programming with a GUI requires the following considerations, which are usually common to MS Windows, X Windows, and Palm applications:

1. We must determine what the graphical or visual user interface looks like. More to the point, we must provide code that specifies the GUI on the chosen hardware display device. Often this is facilitated through libraries and other platform-specific tools.

2. We must anticipate all possible events. Otherwise, at best, the user may create inputs that the program cannot "see."

3. We must associate each possible event with some code that reacts to or handles the event. This mapping of events to handling code is often referred to as "registering the handlers for events." In many applications, registering handlers involves mapping events (possibly with associated parameters) to functions.

4. We usually interact with the OS or libraries. In fact, the OS may serve as an intermediary between the event and our code handler.

5. Typically, we program to an API, which in most cases is a library (e.g., Xlib or Motif) or an OS (e.g., PalmOS).

An Important Threesome

The paradigm we consider is comprised of three components:

1. A graphical resource, known to the application user and to the program.

2. An event (or events) related to user (or program) interaction with the graphical resource.

3. A function in the application that reacts or responds to the event.

```
int main(int argc, char** argv)
{
   glutInit(&argc, argv);
// single buffer RGB color model
   glutInitDisplayMode (GLUT_SINGLE | GLUT_RGB);
   glutInitWindowSize (500, 500);
   glutInitWindowPosition (100, 100);
   glutCreateWindow ("ECE847 Calib Pts - Ver 6");
   init ();
// register handlers
   glutDisplayFunc(display); // register callback functions
   glutReshapeFunc(reshape);
   glutKeyboardFunc(keyboard);
   glutMainLoop(); // the 'infinite' loop
   return 0;
}
```

Figure 13.1 Fragment of OpenGL Code Showing Event Loop.

Other Event-Driven Programming Environments

Although the examples in this chapter and the next involve Microsoft Windows, X Windows (X), wxWidgets, and the Palm OS, numerous other programming environments employ event loops. For example, Figure 13.1 shows a fragment of code from an OpenGL application. Most noteworthy is the function `glutMainLoop();` here the infinite (event) loop is realized.

13.2 Example: Microsoft Windows and the MFC

13.2.1 C++ Preliminaries and Relevant Review Topics

Prior to considering event-driven programming for MS windows using the Microsoft Foundation Classes (MFC) and wxWidgets, we highlight a few aspects of the C++ programming language. This is useful because both the MFC and wxWidgets are C++-based frameworks for GUI development. We digress to stress the point:

> *If you do not fully understand object-oriented programming in C++ (as opposed to simply using a C++ compiler with C code and a few C++ extensions), development using the MFC or wxWidgets tools will most likely be very frustrating.*

C++ is a general-purpose, mixed object-oriented and procedural (imperative) programming language. It is strongly typed; you must declare everything. Furthermore, C++ is a compiled language. This probably makes it faster than interpreted languages, and often yields a smaller executable. Arguably, C++ is a de-facto standard for program development.

Another noteworthy attribute of the C++ programming language is the program structure: It is designed for separate compilation prior to linking. In addition, a C (or C++) program, as opposed to a library or DLL, requires a function `main()`, which takes over once the program is loaded and executed. In what follows, we summarize some of the key elements of C++ (and, to some extent, C) that are related to our look at event-driven programming. *This is not a tutorial on C++.*

Types

A type is a concrete representation of a concept (e.g., integers). Common built-in types in C++ include `char`, `int`, `double`, `enum`, `void` (used to signify the absence of information), and arrays (e.g., `char[]`).

Pointers

The use of pointers and dereferencing (e.g, `int *`) is prevalent in C++ and very useful. Referencing is accomplished using the operator &.

Structures and Pointers

C++ allows user-defined types; two especially important ones are structures and classes.

```
struct info { char * name
              int grade}
```

We may declare pointers to structures:

```
info * infoptr;
```

Accessing structure objects through pointers is achieved as follows:

```
infoptr -> grade = 30; //out of 30, of course
```

> *Easy mnemonic 1:* If `p` is a pointer, `p -> n` is equivalent to `(*p).n`.
> *Easy mnemonic 2:* A `struct` is simply a class whose members are public by default.

Classes

As shown in CLOS (Lisp), classes may be viewed as extensions to structures. Classes allow the programmer to create new types and associated operations for use like those built in. A sample class declaration is of the form:

```
class Date {
// ... data  and functions ... more later
Date(void)  // constructor; same name as class
// can be overloaded just like other funs.
~Date()       // destructor
            };
```

Methods

Methods are associated with classes, as shown in the following example. First, the class declaration with associated methods:

```
class tank {
   double length;
   double diameter;
public:
   tank(void);              // tank class constructor declaration
   void set(int new_length, int new_diameter);
   double get_volume(void);
};
```

We then show the respective method implementations:

```
tank::tank(void)        //tank class constructor implementation
{
   length = 30;
   diameter = 8; // all units in inches
}

// method to set a tank size, given input parameters of length and diameter

void tank::set(int new_length, int new_diameter)
{
   length = new_length;
   diameter = new_diameter;
}

// This method will calculate and return the volume of a tank instance
double tank::get_volume(void)
{
   return (length * (3.14159 * (diameter * diameter)/4));
}
```

Accessing methods in class instances[4] is straightforward. For example:

```
   tank small, medium, large;          //three tank instances
   small.set(18, 6);                   // use of class methods
   large.set(35, 20);
   cout << "The small tank volume is " << small.get_volume() << "\n";
   cout << "The medium tank volume is " << medium.get_volume() << "\n";
   cout << "The large tank volume is " << large.get_volume() << "\n";
```

Pointers and Classes

Recall that C++ has no `malloc`. When using pointers to classes, class instances (objects) are created and freed using `new` and `delete`. The following is an example of pointers to class instances and using class methods.

```
tank *point;                          // pointer to a tank

point = new tank;    // uses defaults supplied by constructor

cout << ''The new tank volume is '' << point->get_volume() << ''\n'';

point->set(12, 12);       // use method set in class instance (object)
                                       // pointed to by point

cout << ''The new tank volume is '' << point->get_volume() << ''\n'';

delete point;
```

[4]See also `closex3.cpp` in Chapter 10.

13.2.2 OO: Object-Oriented Thinking/Design

OO goals include flexibility and reusability. Fundamental questions in OO program design are:

What are the classes?

What should they be?

What (data and methods) should they provide?

The simple answer is that often, such as when programming to an API library, many classes have been chosen for you. When you get to define classes (and as we'll see shortly, the class hierarchy), the simple answer is *the choice of classes is problem or application dependent*. However, we try to make class design meaningful to the programmer and to take advantage of OO services.

Another important question is:

What are the relationships between classes?

This illustrates the potential *class hierarchy:*

- In general, a class is constructed from a *lattice* of base classes.
- This means we can represent interclass structure as a directed acyclic graph (DAG).
- If the lattice is a tree, the class lattice is a class hierarchy (ordering).
- Classes obey an inheritance mechanism borrowed from Simula.
- Inheritance attempts to facilitate representational commonality.

In the following example, the base class is `tank`; the derived class is `alum_tank`. In other words, `alum_tank` and `tank` are subclass and superclass, respectively, via:

```
class alum_tank : public tank {
                // class stuff}
```

Notice that derived classes may be base classes for other derived classes. In analysis and design of our MFC-based event-driven program with a GUI, a good heuristic for understanding the overall program structure is:

Follow the base class(es).

Other relevant questions include:

- What are the services (available methods) and attributes of each class, and which ones are inherited from the base class?
- What about multiple inheritance problems? The answer to this is simple: it is beyond our interest.

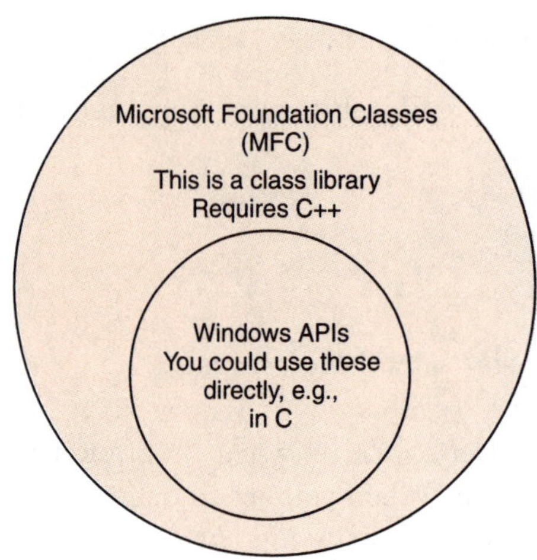

Figure 13.2 Structure of the MFC-Windows API.

13.2.3 Using Classes/Methods You Did Not Write

The MFC

Suppose the objective is to create an MS Windows application. There are numerous ways to approach this effort, some of which require little insight into the overall event-driven/GUI situation. A number of development languages (Visual Basic, Visual C++, and so on) and accompanying integrated development environments (IDEs) are available.

The notion of programming to an Application Programming Interface (API) is familiar to most programmers. Here we consider event-driven programming in the context of Windows APIs and the MFC. In a nutshell, the MFC-based Windows development strategy allows the programmer to take advantage of the tens of thousands of lines of prebuilt, pretested code in the MFC library. Thus, reinvention of the wheel is avoided. The relationship of the MFC to the API is shown in Figure 13.2.

As a final note, use of the MFC may be **far more sophisticated** than the simple functionality example shown here. However, regardless of the complexity of the overall application, the following must be stressed:

> *You must appreciate the Microsoft Foundation Class (MFC) hierarchy. This class hierarchy encapsulates the user interface portion of the Windows API, and makes it possible to create Windows applications in an object-oriented way.*

Design Procedure (Windows)

Historically, the procedure has been[5]:

Design application code
↓
Design user interface
↓
Write code to put together
↓
Notice that it looks a lot like code from last interface

[5]Note that the first two steps may be reversed.

The last remark suggests reusability may be important. MFC was designed with this in mind. Note that:

1. MFC allows code created under Windows 95 to be easily ported to Windows 2000 or Windows XP, and is therefore a popular method for developing Windows applications.

2. MFC encapsulation of "boilerplate" code allows modification (e.g., for new versions of Windows) without the application needing to be rewritten.

3. when using the MFC, you write code that creates the desired user interface (often customization of available building blocks). You also write code that responds when the user interacts with the interface.

Where's `main` (or `WinMain`)?

In the analysis or modifications of C or C++ programs, most programmers look for these functions first. In event-driven programming, a related question is: *Where's the event loop?*

The answer is somewhat surprising: programs that use the MFC do not **explicitly** contain a `main` function or event loop. However, as shown next, we use a class and the message map to interact with the event loop.

MFC Base Class

Most classes in the MFC are derived from a base class `CObject`,[6] which contains the data and methods common to most MFC classes.

How Do Instances of Classes Implement My Application?

This answer is very important:

- *An instance of the application class initializes the application and hooks it to Windows. Recall the role of the class constructor in C++.*
- *An instance of the window class provides the main application window.*

Event Handling and Classes

All event handling occurs through part of the `CWinApp` or application class. This class is number one on the list of important classes. The event loop interacts with user-initiated events of interest to the application through the **message map**, which indicates events and corresponding functions to invoke in response to those events. This accomplishes the registering of events with functions (methods). Note that `CWinApp` is instantiated only once in any program.

Windows and Classes

The `CWnd` class incorporates all the common features typically found in windows, dialog boxes, and controls. The derived class `CFrameWnd` (from `CWnd`) typically implements

[6]Which seldom actually appears in our code.

the framed application window. This class is second on the list of important classes. Finally:

- `CDialog` is used to handle dialogs.
- `CView` is used to give a user access to a document through a window (more on this later).

As the application example that follows shows, every program created via MFC must contain instances of the application and window classes.

13.2.4 Hello, World (File: `static1.cpp`)

The following code represents the basis for a working Windows program. We dissect the code into fragments that indicate the major conceptual underpinnings of a Windows application written using the MFC.

```
//static1.cpp
#include <afxwin.h>
```

The preceding header contains all the types, classes, functions, and variables used in the MFC. It includes other header files. For someone interested in Windows programming, this is moderately interesting reading.

```
// Declare the application class
class CTestApp : public CWinApp
{
public:
  virtual BOOL InitInstance();
};

// Create an instance of the application class
// global - after loading program,
//    instance creation causes the constructor
//    for CWinApp to execute
CTestApp TestApp;

// Declare the main window class
class CTestWindow : public CFrameWnd
{
  CStatic* cs;     // point to single user interface control
public:
  CTestWindow(); // constructor (see below)
};

// The InitInstance function is called
// once when the application first executes
// by the (inherited) constructor of CWinApp
// it is virtual so we can override it

BOOL CTestApp::InitInstance()
{
  m_pMainWnd = new CTestWindow();
       // "handle" to main window
       // creates instance of CHelloWindow
       // and points to it
```

```
      // constructor invoked here
  m_pMainWnd->ShowWindow(m_nCmdShow);
     // m_nCmdShow is based upon conditions at application
     // start up
  m_pMainWnd->UpdateWindow();
  return TRUE;
}

// The constructor for the window class
CTestWindow::CTestWindow()
{
  CRect r;
  // Create the window itself
// Create is method from CFrameWnd class
  Create(NULL,
    "CStatic Tests",
    WS_OVERLAPPEDWINDOW,
    CRect(0,0,200,200));

  // Get the size of the client rectangle
  GetClientRect(&r);
  r.InflateRect(-20,-20);

  // Create a static label
  cs = new CStatic();  // like malloc in c
  cs->Create("hello world",
    WS_CHILD|WS_VISIBLE|WS_BORDER|SS_CENTER,
    r,
    this);
}
```

The executable (so far) is shown in Figure 13.3.

Figure 13.3 Example Windows Application.

13.2.5 A Simple Extension: A Button-Based Application

Adding the Button

First, we revise the previous application so that the GUI contains a single button. The code follows.

```
// button1.cpp
#include <afxwin.h>
#define IDB_BUTTON 100
// Declare the application class
class CButtonApp : public CWinApp
{
public:
  virtual BOOL InitInstance();
};
// Create an instance of the application class
CButtonApp ButtonApp;
// Declare the main window class
class CButtonWindow : public CFrameWnd
{
  CButton *button;
public:
  CButtonWindow();
};
// The InitInstance function is called once
// when the application first executes
BOOL CButtonApp::InitInstance()
{
  m_pMainWnd = new CButtonWindow();
  m_pMainWnd->ShowWindow(m_nCmdShow);
  m_pMainWnd->UpdateWindow();
  return TRUE;
}
// The constructor for the window class
CButtonWindow::CButtonWindow()
{
  CRect r;
  // Create the window itself
  Create(NULL,
    "CButton Tests",
    WS_OVERLAPPEDWINDOW,
    CRect(0,0,200,200));

  // Get the size of the client rectangle
  GetClientRect(&r);
  r.InflateRect(-20,-20);

  // Create a button
  button = new CButton();
  button->Create("Push me",
    WS_CHILD|WS_VISIBLE|BS_PUSHBUTTON,
    r,
    this,
    IDB_BUTTON);
```

Handling the Button

We now extend the simple example to allow our first real look at user interaction with the application. This requires that we explore the Windows Message Map concept.

Message Maps

In the following code, notice that the class declaration for `CButtonWindow` is modified. It now contains a new member function, `HandleButton()`, as well as a macro that indicates a message map is defined for the class. The `HandleButton` function is identified as a message handler by the use of the `afx_msg tag`. The `HandleButton` function is created in the same way as any member function. In this function, we invoke the `MessageBeep` function available from the Windows API.

```
 // button2.cpp
// only significant changes shown

// Declare the main window class
  class CButtonWindow : public CFrameWnd
  {
          CButton *button;
  public:
          CButtonWindow();
          afx_msg void HandleButton();
          DECLARE_MESSAGE_MAP()
  };
  // The message handler function
  void CButtonWindow::HandleButton()
  {
          MessageBeep(-1);
  }
  // The message map
  BEGIN_MESSAGE_MAP(CButtonWindow, CFrameWnd)
          ON_BN_CLICKED(IDB_BUTTON, HandleButton)
  END_MESSAGE_MAP()
```

Creating Message Maps

MFC macros are used to create a message map. The `BEGIN_MESSAGE_MAP` macro accepts two parameters. The first is the name of the specific class to which the message map applies. The second is the base class from which the specific class is derived. It is followed by an `ON_BN_CLICKED` macro, which accepts two parameters: the ID of the control and the function to call whenever that ID sends a command message. Finally, the message map ends with the `END_MESSAGE_MAP` macro.

Button Interaction

When a user clicks the button, it sends a command message containing its ID to its parent, which is the window containing the button. The parent window intercepts this message and uses the message map to determine the function to call. MFC handles the routing, and whenever the specified message is seen, the indicated function gets called.

Ultimately, the program generates a beep whenever the user clicks the button. The previous example application, although simplistic in function, nonetheless involves a great deal of code, as well as a new programming mindset.

13.3 Example: The X Windows System

13.3.1 The X (Windows) Concept

What Is X?

Many GUIs, especially on Unix and Linux systems, are built upon X Windows (X). Unlike MS Windows, *X is not part of an operating system*, but is instead a set of user programs and supporting function libraries. User programs include X display servers and associated window managers (e.g., `twm`) and utilities such as terminal emulators (e.g., `xterm`).

Conceptually, X embodies a client/server architecture that allows computers (often networked) to share GUI-based applications. In X, the X **server** receives the graphical output from the application (produced by the X **client**) and provides the display (and consequently interaction) on the server hardware. Often the X client and the X server are the same machine, such as a desktop running Linux. A useful URL for X development is the home page `http://www.x.org/`.

X Toolkits and Libraries

From a programming viewpoint, X is implemented from a programming toolkit. The lowest level of supporting functions is referred to as `Xlib`. `Xlib` is a C library of low-level graphics functions that may be called by the client or the server. Relevant header files include `X11/Xlib.h`, the main header file for `Xlib`, and `X11/X.h`, wherein types and constants for the X protocol are declared. There are many others.

`Xlib` provides quite a few useful constructs to both increase productivity and portability. For example, `Xlib` provides basic functions for responding to user interface events and drawing graphical output to the display. The Xt Toolkit is built upon `Xlib` and provides a higher-level API for many of the routine functions of a GUI. The so-called Xt "Toolkit Intrinsics" provide a framework for building widgets, which are the GUI building blocks that are implemented with calls to the `Xlib` and `Xt` libraries.

What Is Motif?

Motif is an example of an even higher-level toolkit that builds upon the Xt Toolkit. It is uncommon to build applications from scratch using `Xlib`; thus toolkits such as Motif (and Lesstif) are popular.

Motif is a widely accepted set of user interface guidelines developed by the Open Software Foundation (OSF) that specify how an X Windows system application should "look and feel." In addition to widgets, Motif includes a Motif Style Guide document, which indicates how a Motif user interface should look and behave to be considered Motif compliant. Although it is possible to create a Motif-style GUI without X, Motif, as supplied from the Open Software Foundation (OSF), implements Motif using the `Xt` library as part of the Motif API.

A recent trend in open-source development is to circumvent the `Xt` intrinsics and instead build other, open-source libraries upon `Xlib`. For example, KDE is a toolkit that is built upon the Qt Toolkit, and the Qt Toolkit is built upon `Xlib`. KDE is familiar to many Linux programmers because it defines a graphical desktop environment for Unix/Linux workstations. Similarly, GDK and GDK+ are toolkits built upon `Xlib` that form the basis for GNOME, an entirely free desktop environment.

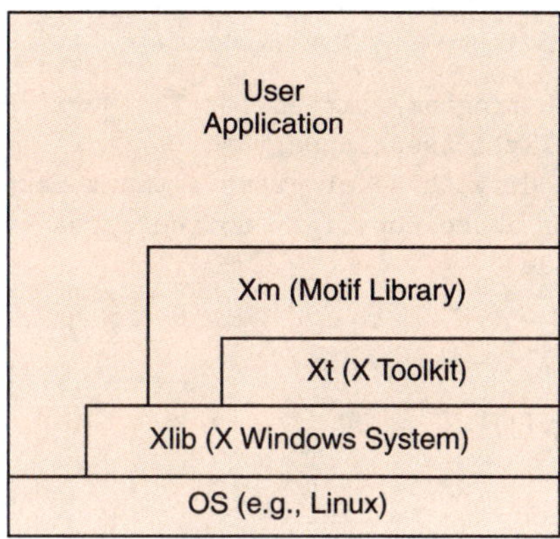

Figure 13.4 Software Library Relationships for X/Motif Development.

Xt, `Xm`, and Widgets

Reusable and configurable building blocks for the GUI are provided by Motif and `Xt` and are called **widgets**. The Motif library (`Xm`) contains a widget set arranged in an object-oriented or class-based format. Commonly used widgets include labels, buttons, and scrollbars. The Motif library defines widget behavior. More importantly, the widget class hierarchy allows widgets to inherit properties from objects above them. As in other OO paradigms, an instance of some widget class—that is, the widget object—is created by *instantiating* it.

Overall Software Architecture

Figure 13.4 shows the interrelationships among the user application, operating system, and various X and Motif libraries.

13.3.2 An Example of Programming in X/Motif

Source Code for Example

This X/Motif example is straightforward and only involves a pair of widgets, a simple "partial GUI," and a single callback function. The C source code is shown in Figure 13.5. Notice that the development process embodies:

- GUI creation using X Windows
- the notion of an event handler
- programming to libraries (X/Motif)

Execution: A Two-Step Process

Basically the execution of an X Windows program involves a two-step process.

1. The application sets up and "exposes" the graphical interface. This is built from widgets.

2. The application then turns control over to the loop that handles events. Once the event loop is invoked, code will only be called in response to a user-entered event. Thus, the program generally waits to receive messages indicating that events such as mouse movement, window resizing, and key presses, have occurred.

```
/* hello-motif.c

This is a modifed version of a program written for The Motif Programming
Manual, Copyright 1994, O'Reilly & Associates, Inc.
Permission to use, copy and modify these programs without restriction is
hereby granted, as long as the above copyright notice appears in each
copy of the program source code.

#include <Xm/PushB.h>

int main (int argc, char *argv[])
{
Widget       toplevel, button;
XtAppContext app;
void         button_pushed(Widget, XtPointer, XtPointer);
XmString     label;
Arg          args[2];

XtSetLanguageProc (NULL, NULL, NULL);

toplevel = XtVaOpenApplication (&app, "Hello", NULL, 0, &argc, argv, NULL,
 sessionShellWidgetClass, NULL);

label = XmStringCreateLocalized ("Push here for 'hello' printf");
XtSetArg(args[0], XmNlabelString, label);
button = XmCreatePushButton (toplevel, "pushme", args, 1);
XmStringFree (label);

XtAddCallback (button, XmNactivateCallback, button_pushed, NULL);
XtManageChild (button);

XtRealizeWidget (toplevel);
XtAppMainLoop (app); // the Xt infinite loop (shown in the text)
        return(0);
}

void button_pushed (Widget widget, XtPointer client_data, XtPointer call_data)
{
printf ("Button Pushed --> hello!\n");
}
```

Figure 13.5 "Hello" in X Source Code.

Application Functionality

The (running) application displays a new X window with a labeled push button, and the action of pushing the button is shown in the calling window (Fig. 13.6).

Compiling the Program

The X Windows source is compiled with (paths may vary on specific machines):

```
gcc hello-motif.c -Wall -L/usr/X11R6/lib -lXm -lXt -lX11 -o hello-motif
```

Detailed Code Analysis

We outline the role of each code fragment in the example.

```
Push here for 'hello' printf
```

```
$ gcc hello-motif.c -Wall -L/usr/X11R6/lib -lXm -lXt -lX11 -o hello-motif
$ ./hello-motif
Button Pushed --> hello!
Button Pushed --> hello!
Button Pushed --> hello!
```

Figure 13.6 Window Created by Hello Application (Top) and Output for Three Successive Button Presses (Bottom).

`XtVaOpenApplication` and the Top-Level Widget First, the return value of `XtVaOpenApplication` in

```
toplevel = XtVaOpenApplication (&app, "Hello", NULL, 0, &argc, argv, NULL,
 sessionShellWidgetClass, NULL);
```

is assigned to widget **`toplevel`**, a so-called "shell widget" or shell-class widget. This widget defines the top-level window of the application and handles interaction with the user's chosen window manager. The first argument to **`XtVaOpenApplication`** is the address of an application context, that is, a structure used by **`Xt`** to manage the application. The second argument is a string defining the application class name. Here this string merely serves as the name of a file used to hold application defaults. The third, fourth, fifth, and sixth arguments are for handling application command line arguments (which are not used in this application). The seventh argument (NULL in the example) is used for fallback resources (see the problems). The eighth argument, **`sessionShellWidgetClass`**, specifies the type of shell to be used for the top level. The last argument (again, not used here) is used to specify a list of resource-value pairs for the top-level widget returned by the function.

Callback Routines Callback routines are functions intended to be invoked by the event loop in response to a window message. In our simple example, function **`XtAddCallback`** registers a user-defined function (**`button_pushed`**) to handle events generated by the button press via:

```
XtAddCallback (button, XmNactivateCallback, button_pushed, NULL);
```

Building the GUI Note the following:

- In X Windows, some widgets handle layout and event management for other widgets (so-called "manager widgets").
- A child–parent relationship exists between many widgets (hierarchy).
- Widgets are not seen (exposed) until they are managed.

In this application, functions **`XmStringCreateLocalized`** and **`XmCreatePushButton`** create the labeled push-button widget.

Exposing the GUI Function **`XtRealizeWidget`** "exposes" the top-level widget. The action of this function is to display all of the managed widgets in the hierarchy beginning with the parent. This is where we "expose the GUI."

```
void XtAppMainLoop (XtAppContext appContext)
{
   XEvent event;

   for(;;) {
     XtAppNextEvent(appContext,&event);
     XtDispatchEvent(&event);
            }
}
```

Figure 13.7 `XtAppMainLoop` Function, Which Implements Infinite Loop for Event Handling.

The Event Loop Finally, a call to `XtAppMainLoop` turns over control to the event dispatch loop. This function, as shown in Figure 13.7, implements an infinite loop that employs the `Xt` event handler function `XtAppNextEvent` and then `XtDispatchEvent`. The only way for the application's code to be executed beyond this point is in response to an event. This is through the callback functions.

The Window Manager

The window manager is another X program that controls the general operation of the window system. It controls the "look and feel" of the X Window application. Note that the window manager and the X server are responsible for interacting with the user's video hardware.

13.3.3 Concluding Remarks

We summarize our experience with this programming paradigm by noting that X Windows program development is not a 10-minute endeavor, nor a subtle extension of command-line-interface (CLI) programming. It embodies the concepts presented in the introduction, namely:

1. the notion of code responding to window-based messages and "registering" handler functions.
2. the task of specification and generation of a GUI.
3. the availability of toolkits or libraries of functions that facilitate the programming process. The references at the end of the chapter include many X Windows books that list the available functions.

13.4 Cross-Platform and Multi-Platform Software Development

Cross-platform development of software involves developing software on one type of machine to run on another type of machine. It is both necessary and common. In fact, the Palm application development we undertake (on either Linux or Windows platforms) is a good example.

<table>
<tr><td colspan="7">wxWindows API</td></tr>
<tr><td>wxMSW</td><td>wxGTK</td><td>wxX11</td><td>wxMotif</td><td colspan="2">wxMac</td><td>wxOS2</td></tr>
<tr><td>WIN32</td><td>GTK+</td><td>Xlib</td><td>Motif/Lesstif</td><td>Classic or Carbon</td><td>Carbon</td><td>PM</td></tr>
<tr><td>Windows</td><td colspan="3">Unix/Linux</td><td>MacOS 9</td><td>MacOS X</td><td>OS/2</td></tr>
</table>

Figure 13.8 Relationship of the wxWidgets API to Platform-Specific Graphics Libraries.

Often it is necessary to develop applications that run on multiple platforms. It is somewhat inefficient to develop separate applications for each platform. Software developed in this manner requires platform-specific maintenance. A good example of this is developing GUI-based applications for use with Linux (using various toolkits, including X), MacOS, and Windows.

13.4.1 Cross-Platform Development Tools

Numerous tools exist to facilitate multiplatform and cross-platform software development. For example, wxWidgets[7] is a tool based upon a class library for developing GUI-oriented C++ programs on a variety of different platforms. wxWidgets defines a common API across platforms, but uses the native graphical user interface (GUI) on each platform. Thus, programs developed with wxWidgets exhibit the native "look and feel" for each platform, yet have common functionality. In theory, a programmer should be able to design a wxWidgets-based application once and have it execute on any platform that has a wxWidget library.

Distributions of wxWidgets and documentation are available at:

`http://wxidgets.org/`

Note that wxWidgets is not a translator from one GUI from another. Instead, wxWidgets defines a common API for all platforms. Once a program is written to the wxWidgets API, the platform-specific libraries are invoked by the wxWidgets API. This is shown in Figure 13.8.

13.4.2 Similarity to MFC-based Coding

Skeletal code for a wxWidgets application is shown in Figure 13.9. As the example indicates, there is a strong similarity of the coding of a wxWidgets application to that of an MFC application. Tables 13.1 and 13.2 summarize the class and macro similarities between these two object-oriented development environments.

---

[7] wxWidgets was formerly known as wxWindows. After a polite request from Microsoft, the name was changed.

```
#include "wx/wx.h"

class HelloWorldApp : public wxApp
{
public:
        virtual bool OnInit();
};

bool HelloWorldApp::OnInit()
{
       wxFrame *frame = new wxFrame((wxFrame*) NULL, -1, "Hello World");
       frame->CreateStatusBar();
       frame->SetStatusText("Hello World");
       frame->Show(TRUE);
       SetTopWindow(frame);
       return true;
}

// this creates main

IMPLEMENT_APP(HelloWorldApp)
```

Figure 13.9 Skeleton Code for a wxWidgets Application.

MFC	wxWidgets
CWinApp	wxAPP
CObject	wxObject
CFrameWnd	wxFrame
CToolBar	wxToolBar
CDialog	wxDialog
CFileDialog	wxFileDialog
Cbutton	wxButton
CBitmap	wxBitmap, wxImage
CFont	wxFont
CPaintDC	wxPaintDC
CDocument	wxDocument
CView	wxView

Table 13.1 Similarity of Class Elements in MFC and wxWidgets (Selected Samples).

MFC	wxWidgets
BEGIN_MESSAGE_MAP	BEGIN_EVEN_TABLE
END_MESSAGE_MAP	END_EVENT_TABLE

Table 13.2 Similarity of Macros in MFC and wxWidgets (Selected Samples).

13.4.3 wxWidgets Fundamentals

General Notes

1. All wxWidgets applications need a derived `wxApp` class and to override the constructor `wxApp::OnInit`.

2. Every application must have a top-level `wxFrame` or `wxDialog` window, derived from the respective class.

   - Each frame may contain one or more instances of classes such as `wxPanel`, `wxSplitterWindow`, or other windows and controls.
   - A frame can have a `wxMenuBar`, a `wxToolBar`, a status line, and a `wxIcon` (used when the frame is "iconized"). `wxPanel` is used to place controls (classes derived from wxControl), which are used for user interaction.
   - Examples of controls are `wxButton`, `wxCheckBox`, `wxChoice`, `wxListBox`, and `wxSlider`.

3. An instance of `wxDialog` can be used for implementing controls. This strategy has the advantage of not requiring a separate frame. This is shown in the "button" example of Section 13.4.4.

4. For dialogs, the use of `wxBoxSizer`, for simple windows, may produce acceptable layouts with a minimum of design effort and coding.

5. Argument default values may be omitted from a function call. In addition, size and position arguments may usually be given a value of -1 (the default), in which case wxWidgets will choose a suitable value.

6. Like the MFC, windows (frames and dialogs) and controls in `wxWidgets` programs are referenced by pointers to objects and thus created using `new`.[8]

7. An event table is used to map events to (handler) functions. Registering events with user-written functions is achieved using one or more

   `BEGIN_EVENT_TABLE . . . END_EVENT_TABLE` macros. An example (from Section 13.4.4) is:

   ```
   BEGIN_EVENT_TABLE(ButtonDlg, wxDialog)
     EVT_BUTTON(BUTTON_SELECT, ButtonDlg::ButtonSelect)
     EVT_CLOSE(ButtonDlg::OnCloseWindow)
   END_EVENT_TABLE()
   ```

   Note that the event table is *specific to a frame*. In the preceding example, the `BEGIN_EVENT_TABLE` macro indicates that events from the ButtonDlg frame (derived from the `wxDialog` class) are intercepted and handled. Also note that a `DECLARE_EVENT_TABLE` macro must be included in the corresponding class definition.

[8]Note that `delete` is not used to free these resources because `wxWidgets` takes care of this.

Where's `main`?

Like MS Windows, wxWidgets C++ source files for applications *do not explicitly contain the* `main` *function.* In wxWidgets, the `IMPLEMENT_APP` macro creates an application instance and starts the wxWidgets program. The prototype is:

```
IMPLEMENT_APP(theApp)
```

where class `theApp` is derived from class `wxApp`. Recall that `wxApp::OnInit()` is called upon class instance creation (startup) and is used to start the wxWidgets program.

Example of Macro Conversion

The `HelloWorldApp` example of Section 13.4.2 contains the macro:

```
IMPLEMENT_APP(HelloWorldApp)
```

The following is a snippet of the translated (temporary) file created by g++ for this macro:

```
// this is the code resulting from the
// IMPLEMENT_APP(HelloWorldApp) macro
// in HelloWorldApp.cpp
// it is contained in the temporary file
// HelloWorldApp.ii and saved by using the
// -save-temps switch in the g++ compilation, i.e.,
// $ g++ -c -save-temps 'wx-config --cxxflags'
//                        -o HelloWorld App.o HelloWorldApp.cpp


wxAppConsole *wxCreateApp()
{
wxAppConsole::CheckBuildOptions
("2" "." "6" " (" "no debug" "," "ANSI" ",compiler with C++ ABI " "1002" ",
wx containers" ",compatible with 2.4" ")", "your program");
return new HelloWorldApp;
}

wxAppInitializer wxTheAppInitializer((wxAppInitializerFunction) wxCreateApp);

HelloWorldApp& wxGetApp()
{
return *(HelloWorldApp *)((wxApp *)wxApp::GetInstance());
}

// here's main:

int main(int argc, char **argv)
{
return wxEntry(argc, argv);
}
```

Events and Handling

Event handling is clearly a major concern. The mapping of events to functions is achieved using a `BEGIN_EVENT_TABLE . . . END_EVENT_TABLE` macro block. Between these macros, specific event macros corresponding to specific resources are defined. These map the event (e.g., a button press or a mouse click) to an event-handling function.

For example, consider the use of a button. The **EVT_BUTTON** macro may be used. The basic prototype is:

```
EVT_BUTTON(id, func)
```

which indicates that `func` is invoked when a user clicks the button with identifier `id`. A unique identifier for the button is required, and as the following example shows, this is defined using an enumeration in the class definition. Note also that the argument of the event-handling function must be of type wxCommandEvent.

Compilation

Normally, in Unix-like environments, a makefile is used. However, a simple **wxWidgets** application (`foo`) may be compiled and linked via:

```
g++ foo.cpp 'wx-config --libs --cxxflags' -o foo
```

where `wx-config --libs --cxxflags` returns the *platform-specific* switches to `gcc` for compilation. For example:

```
$ wx-config --libs --cxxflags
-I/usr/local/lib/wx/include/motif-ansi-release-2.6 -I/usr/local/include/wx-2.6 -D__WXMOTIF__
-I/usr/X11R6/include -D_FILE_OFFSET_BITS=64 -D_LARGE_FILES -D_LARGEFILE_SOURCE=1 -DNO_GCC_PRAGMA
-L/usr/local/lib -pthread  -L/usr/X11R6/lib  -lwx_motif_xrc-2.6 -lwx_motif_qa-2.6 -lwx_motif_html-2.6
-lwx_motif_adv-2.6 -lwx_motif_core-2.6 -lwx_base_xml-2.6 -lwx_base_net-2.6 -lwx_base-2.6
```

On an MS Windows programming platform, if `gcc` is used (under `cygwin`), the makefile is also applicable. If another compiler (e.g., Visual C++) is used, project files or makefiles for that compiler must be used.

13.4.4 A Dialog and Button-Based `wxWidgets` Example

The following source illustrates a simple wxWidgets dialog example using a single button.

```
// A wxWidgets Button/Dialog example
// upgraded for window/application closing

#include "wx/wx.h"

class ButtonApp : public wxApp
{
public:
// Initialize the application
        virtual bool OnInit();
};

//main window is from wxDialog
class ButtonDlg : public wxDialog
{
public:
// constructor
  ButtonDlg();

  void ButtonSelect(wxCommandEvent &event);
  void ButtonDlg::OnCloseWindow(wxCloseEvent &event);
private:
```

```
  DECLARE_EVENT_TABLE()
  // ID of only event
  enum
  {
    BUTTON_SELECT = 1000
  };
};

ButtonDlg::ButtonDlg() : wxDialog((wxDialog *)NULL, -1, "ButtonDialog",
                                  wxDefaultPosition, wxSize(150, 150))
{
  wxButton *button = new wxButton(this, BUTTON_SELECT, "Select", wxDefaultPosition);
  // Setting the button in the middle of the dialog.
  wxBoxSizer *dlgSizer = new wxBoxSizer(wxHORIZONTAL);
  wxBoxSizer *buttonSizer = new wxBoxSizer(wxVERTICAL);
  buttonSizer->Add(button, 0, wxALIGN_CENTER);
  dlgSizer->Add(buttonSizer, 1, wxALIGN_CENTER);
  SetSizer(dlgSizer);
  dlgSizer->SetSizeHints(this);
}
void ButtonDlg::ButtonSelect(wxCommandEvent &command)
{
  wxMessageBox("The button was pressed!");
}

// here's the event table

BEGIN_EVENT_TABLE(ButtonDlg, wxDialog)
  EVT_BUTTON(BUTTON_SELECT, ButtonDlg::ButtonSelect)
// terminate the dialog when the 'x' window button is clicked
  EVT_CLOSE(ButtonDlg::OnCloseWindow)
END_EVENT_TABLE()

bool ButtonApp::OnInit()
{
// create instance of the dialog
  ButtonDlg *button = new ButtonDlg();
// Show it
  button->Show(TRUE);
// Tell the application that it's our main window
  SetTopWindow(button);
  return true;
}

void ButtonDlg::OnCloseWindow(wxCloseEvent &event)
{
// close using Destroy rather than Close.
this->Destroy();
}

IMPLEMENT_APP(ButtonApp)
```

Noteworthy aspects of the previous example include:

1. the use of "sizers," which relieves the programmer of much of the detailed manual layout decisions (see the `wxWidgets` manual).

2. the creation of a button resource via:

   ```
   new wxButton(this, BUTTON_SELECT, "Select", wxDefaultPosition)
   ```

3. the association of the event resulting from clicking on this button and a user-defined method:

```
EVT_BUTTON(BUTTON_SELECT, ButtonDlg::ButtonSelect)
```

4. an illustration of the proper way to terminate an application if the main window is closed.

13.5 Bibliographical Remarks and References

13.5.1 Windows Programming References and Related Resources

Recommended references for Windows programming include the following:

- The Microsoft Developer Network (MSDN). This resource includes a set of online references for developers who write applications using Microsoft products and technologies. The URL is:

  `http://msdn.microsoft.com/`

  In addition, the MSDN provides access to newsgroups related to development using Visual C++ and the MFC. Two are:

  `microsoft.public.vc.mfc`

  `microsoft.public.dotnet.languages.vc`

- A good online reference for C++ programmers is the C/C++ Users Journal:

  `http://www.cuj.com/`

- Finally, there are numerous USENET groups dedicated to this topic; a starting point is:

  `comp.os.ms-windows(programmer)`

13.5.2 X and Motif References and Related Resources

The world of Motif and X Windows-based development can be complicated and daunting to the newcomer (as well as experienced developers). Recommended references include:

- Motif websites:

  `http://www.opengroup.org/openmotif/`

  `http://www.ist.co.uk/motif/`

  The latter provides pointers to two O'Reilly books: volume 6A, the Motif Programming Manual; and volume 6B, the Motif Reference Manual. Volume 6A outlines Motif-based GUI development from the basics. Volume 6B is an invaluable reference for the `Xm` and `Xt` functions. Both are available for download as PDF files under the terms of the Open Publication license. Volume 6A is also available as an html file for browsing. The example programs from Volume 6A are also available for download.
- The USENET groups:

  `comp.windows.x.motif`

  `comp.windows.x`

13.5.3 wxWidgets Programming and Related Resources

A prerequisite for wxWidgets application development is the availability of the wxWidgets C++[9] libraries (including `c++` header files). Although binaries for some platforms are available, customizing and building the `wxWidgets` libraries from source on the development platform is recommended.

The `wxWidgets` home page (`wxwidgets.org`) is probably the best starting place for `wxWidgets` resources. For beginners, the following are probably the most useful resources (as of November 2005):

1. The "Documentation" section contains several versions of the `wxWidgets` reference manual: 'wxWidgets 2.6.2: A portable C++ and Python GUI toolkit.' This document is available as a single pdf file (`wx.pdf`) or set of html files (`wx.html` and related). Both of these formats are downloadable as archives in the "Downloads" section. Installing the html version on the development platform is strongly recommended, because the user may easily jump to linked parts of the document during program development and debugging.

2. The "Documentation" section of the homepage contains pointers to a number of technical references and tutorials. Noteworthy entries within the tutorials section include:

   (a) A tutorial: "wxWindows 2 Programming Cross-Platform GUI Applications in C++," written by Franky Braem (also contained in `wxTutorial.pdf`).

   (b) "Programming with wxWindows—First Steps," by Bavid Beech (also contained in file `wxTutorial.pdf`).

   (c) Robert Roebling's "Hello World" example.

   (d) "Introduction to wxWidgets," by Priyank Bolia.

3. A useful Wiki (community-maintained website) exists for wxWidgets: `wxWiki`. Furthermore, the wxWidgets distribution contains an abundance of programming samples. This includes the C++ source and other files necessary for building and exploring over 50 complete sample applications. These are contained in the `/samples` and `/demos` subdirectories of the distribution.

13.6 Exercises

1. `(Event-driven/Windows)`. The following code uses the MFC, and compiles without warning. However, it does not run. Indicate what you think the problem(s) are. Be clear and concise.

```
// ece352q4.cpp
#include <afxwin.h>
#define IDB_BUTTON 100
// Declare the application class
class CButtonApp : public CWinApp
{
```

[9] We only consider C++-based program development. A wxWidgets API is also available to Python, Perl, and C# developers.

```
public:
        virtual BOOL InitInstance();
};

// Declare the main window class
class CButtonWindow : public CFrameWnd
{
        CButton *button;
public:
        CButtonWindow();
        afx_msg void HandleButton();
        DECLARE_MESSAGE_MAP()
};

// The message map
BEGIN_MESSAGE_MAP(CButtonWindow, CFrameWnd)
        ON_BN_CLICKED(IDB_BUTTON, HandleButton)
END_MESSAGE_MAP()
// The InitInstance function is called once
// when the application first executes
BOOL CButtonApp::InitInstance()
{
        m_pMainWnd = new CButtonWindow();
        m_pMainWnd->ShowWindow(m_nCmdShow);
        m_pMainWnd->UpdateWindow();
        return TRUE;
}
// The constructor for the window class
CButtonWindow::CButtonWindow()
{
        CRect r;
        // Create the window itself
        Create(NULL,
  "CButton Tests",
  WS_OVERLAPPEDWINDOW,
  CRect(0,0,200,200));
        // Get the size of the client rectangle
        GetClientRect(&r);
        r.InflateRect(-20,-20);
        // Create a button
        button = new CButton();
        button->Create("Push me",
  WS_CHILD|WS_VISIBLE|BS_PUSHBUTTON,
  r,
  this,
  IDB_BUTTON);
}
```

2. There are numerous X utilities, some of which provide deeper insight into X application and X server behavior. Readers with access to a Motif/X development environment should use X utility `xwininfo` on the executable versions of the X examples in this chapter. Specifically, get the application's window ID. Having this information, use utility `xev` to watch the generation of X events in the running application.

3. In wxWidgets programming using C++, what is the role of the `IMPLEMENT_APP()` macro?

4. A wxWidgets program, contained in file `wxBasicB2Test.cpp`, follows. The program is syntactically correct (i.e., it **compiles** without errors or warnings). However, it has a big problem.

   (a) State clearly and unambiguously what you think the problem is.

   (b) Verify your assumption by compiling and trying to link the program.

   (c) Fix the problem and verify the program operation.

```
// Basic Window with 2 buttons
// file: wxBasicB2test.cpp

#include <wx/wx.h>

// resource IDs of buttons

#define BUTTON_NUMBER1 1000
#define BUTTON_NUMBER2 2000

// the application
class BasicApplication : public wxApp
{
   public:
         virtual bool OnInit();
};

// a frame
class BasicFrame : public wxFrame
{
   public:
         BasicFrame( const wxChar *title,
                 int xpos, int ypos,
                 int width, int height);
         ~BasicFrame();
   private:
   DECLARE_EVENT_TABLE()
};

// a button
class BasicButton : public wxButton
{
   public:
       BasicButton(wxWindow *parent,
             wxWindowID id,
             const wxString& label,
             const wxPoint& pos,
             const wxSize& size);
       ~BasicButton();
  void ButtonSelect1(wxCommandEvent &event);
  void ButtonSelect2(wxCommandEvent &event);
};

bool BasicApplication::OnInit()
{
   BasicFrame
    *frame = new BasicFrame("Basic Frame Buttons", 50, 50, 800, 400);
   BasicButton
```

```
     *button1 = new BasicButton(frame, BUTTON_NUMBER1, "Button1",
                                wxPoint::wxPoint(50,50), wxSize::wxSize(50,50));
    BasicButton
     *button2 = new BasicButton(frame, BUTTON_NUMBER2, "Button2",
                                wxPoint::wxPoint(50,250), wxSize::wxSize(50,50));
    frame->Show(TRUE);
    SetTopWindow(frame);
    return TRUE;
}

BasicButton::~BasicButton()
{
}

BasicFrame::BasicFrame
              (const wxChar *title,
                      int xpos, int ypos,
                      int width, int height)
              : wxFrame
                 ( (wxFrame *) NULL,
                    -1,
                    title,
                    wxPoint(xpos, ypos),
                    wxSize(width, height)
                 )
{
}

BasicFrame::~BasicFrame()
{
}

void BasicButton::ButtonSelect1(wxCommandEvent &command)
{
  system("ls");
}
void BasicButton::ButtonSelect2(wxCommandEvent &command)
{
  system("pwd");
}

IMPLEMENT_APP(BasicApplication)

// event table
BEGIN_EVENT_TABLE(BasicFrame, wxFrame)
  EVT_BUTTON(BUTTON_NUMBER1, BasicButton::ButtonSelect1)
  EVT_BUTTON(BUTTON_NUMBER2, BasicButton::ButtonSelect2)
END_EVENT_TABLE()
```

5. In X Windows programming, what are "fallback" resources? Why and how are they used?

6. In our X Windows example of Section 13.3.2, the function `XtVaOpenApplication` was used. An alternative is to use function `XtAppInitialize`.

   (a) What is the difference in the use of these two functions?

   (b) Rewrite the example of Section 13.3.2 using `XtAppInitialize`.

CHAPTER 14

Event-Driven Programming, Part 2: PDA Programming with the Palm OS

The surest sign of intelligent life in the universe is that they haven't attempted to contact us.
—Bill Watterson

14.1 Overview

14.1.1 Event-Driven Programming and the Palm OS

In this chapter, we begin a hands-on look at (relatively simple) event-driven programming. Specifically, we consider development of simple applications for an embedded system, namely a PDA (personal digital assistant) based upon the Palm Operating System, or Palm OS.

The Palm OS is not restricted to Palm hardware devices. For example, the following devices employ the Palm OS:

- SONY Color Clie PEG NZ90 handheld with digital camera and MP3 player.
- Kyocera 7135 Smartphone.
- Samsung Mobile Internet Phone SPH-i330.
- Garmin iQue3600-PDA with integrated GPS technology.
- Fossil Wrist PDA with Palm OS.

Palm refers to these devices as "Palm powered."

Development Environments

We will use a coupled set of development tools called the `gcc` tool chain (or the `prc`-tools) for this development. This cross-development software is supported on Windows and Linux platforms. Alternative Palm development tools exist, such as Code Warrior and the Palm OS Developer Suite.[1]

[1]This software provides a comprehensive IDE for Palm development by integrating a tool chain from PalmSource into the Eclipse development environment. Unfortunately, it is only available for Windows environments.

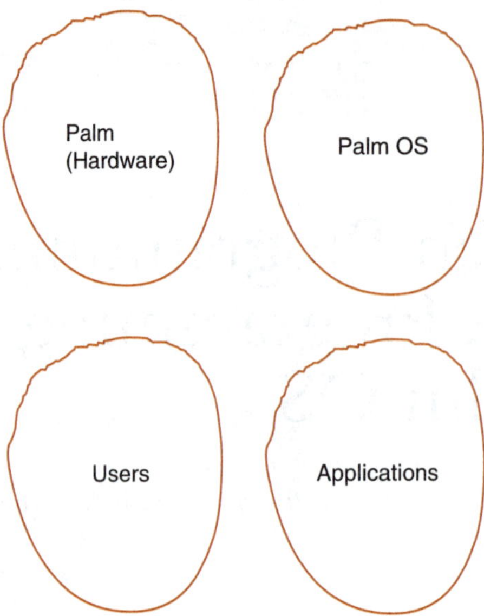

Figure 14.1 Four Entities Involved in the Overall Development.

Scope of the Palm Development Effort in This Chapter

Palm programming is introduced gradually in this chapter using a series of example applications with increasing complexity. The first are two "hello world" variants (`ece352`[2]), after which we introduce other resources such as menus and buttons (`ece352v2`), as well as switching forms. Then the concept of editable fields is introduced using two additional applications (`ece352v4` and `ece352v6b`). Finally, data alerts (`dataalert`) and Palm OS databases (`automaint2`) are introduced.

In each case, relevant C source code and resource specification files are shown. In addition, the pragmatics of building the application, and related tools, are illustrated. The exercises at the end of the chapter (as well as those on the book's webpage) contain many more opportunities for Palm application development. Relevant Palm OS functions are summarized at the end of each section.

Finally, note that there are many aspects of Palm software development that are beyond the scope of our introduction. For example, the development of software that allows the PDA to communicate through a serial or USB port is quite involved and concerns the concept and programming of a *conduit*. Other features facilitate the development of multimedia and wireless applications, as well as enhanced security.

14.1.2 The Confluence of Four Entities

Figure 14.1 shows how hardware, the Palm OS, users, and application software are merged in this effort.

14.1.3 Understanding (and Achieving) Palm Programming

There are a number of challenges for beginning Palm OS developers, including the seemingly simple task of getting a Palm OS development system installed and functioning.

[2]Some of the applications use nonintuitive names, resulting from the course in which they were developed.

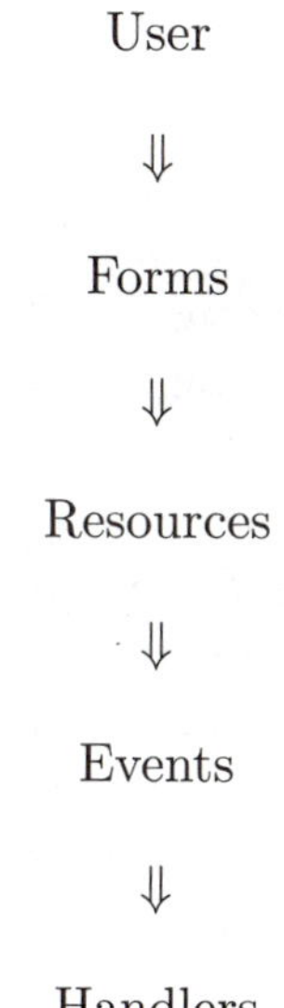

Figure 14.2 Interaction in Event-Driven Programming.

More importantly, it is necessary to understand the relationships among:

- the GUI design (specifying forms and other resources).
- the tool chain used to develop the final application.
- the code interface to the forms and other resources, especially event-handling (see Figure 14.2).
- the role of the Palm OS.

14.1.4 Installation Details and Important References

The `gcc` tool chain is under continuous development. In addition, the Palm OS library continues to evolve.

Basic Elements of the (`gcc`) Tool chain

The basic tools required are:

- `Cygwin` (for Win32 development environments only), a Unix-like environment for `gcc` (see note below).
- PRC-Tools (a port or version of `gcc` for m68k-Palm OS development).
- `Pilrc` (the resource compiler; also recommended are `pilrcui` or `pilrcEdit`, resource previewers).
- Palm OS System Development Kit or SDK. (These are C libraries for use with the Palm OS; versions 4.0 or 5.0r3 are used here.)
- The Palm OS Emulator and a ROM (to see your application results).
- Documentation (lots).

Of course, if you have a real Palm OS-compatible PDA, you can do even more. You are now fully equipped to enter the lucrative and time-consuming world of Palm development.

Important Documentation

Three of the most important documents are:

1. *The Palm OS Programmer's Companion.* This is an excellent tutorial reference on Palm OS programming, resources, events, and so on. Volume I is all that is required for our efforts.

2. *The Palm OS Programmer's API Reference.* This contains a succinct description, by function, of the Palm OS functions and data structures. Although not a teaching document, it is nonetheless invaluable as a programming resource. Each of the examples we develop is followed by a section of abbreviated and annotated function description excerpts for the related functions. It is recommended that a copy of this pdf document be left open while developing Palm applications.

3. *The PilRC User Manual.* This summarizes `pilrc` use and switches, and, most importantly, the syntax of the language used for specifying Palm resources (Resource Language Reference). This includes forms, fields, and alerts.

The Development Steps (or Cycle)

Building the sample Palm application using the prc-tools tool chain involves the following basic steps.[3] Each is annotated for illustration.

`$ pilrcui ece352.rcp`: After you design the form(s), you can (optionally) view them.

`$ m68k-Palm OS-gcc -c -g -PalmOS4.0 -Wall ece352.c`: Compile, but no linking of the main C file. "std" debugging with Palm OS-specific switch on `gcc`. Verbose and picky error reporting.

`$ m68k-Palm OS-gcc ece352.o -g -PalmOS4.0 -Wall -o ece352`: Link and place in the named output file.

`$ pilrc -q ece352.rcp`: Compile the resources in the resource specification file (quietly).

`$ build-prc ece352.def ece352 *.bin`: The big step—put it all together. `build-prc` does what the name implies—it reads resources from the input files given and combines them into one `.prc` resource data file.

Finally, run the emulator, install the initial rom, and load the sample application `ece352.prc`. If you own a Palm or Visor, you can download it and see it function on real hardware.[4]

[3] You might also want to start out in a "clean" subdirectory and look at the new files created after each step. Even more interesting is the use of a binary editor on these files. Basically these are huge structs.

[4] Warning: You are on your own here. Memory leaks, and so forth, can result in the required use of a paper clip inserted in the back of your device. At the very least, back up anything of importance on the hardware PDA first.

14.1.5 Viewing Resources

The Palm application look is determined by the GUI. The GUI may consist of a number of interrelated forms, each containing numerous resources. These are conveyed to the tool chain by one or more `*.rcp` files. One straightforward approach to specifying and modifying the application resources is to simply use an editor and `pilrcui` in an interactive cycle.

Resource Editors

`pilrcEdit` is a Java-based resource editor for any Palm development environment with a java2 runtime environment. Another useful application (Linux only) is the `guikachu` resource editor.

14.2 Palm Programming Specifics, Part I

14.2.1 Palm Programming and Running an Application

Palm OS *applications* are generally single-threaded, event-driven programs. Only one program runs at a time.

Launching an Application

We start at the (temporal) beginning. Each application has a `PilotMain` function that is equivalent to `main` in C programs. To launch a specific application, the system calls `PilotMain` for the application and sends it a *launch code*. Thereafter, `PilotMain` responds. Launch codes are a means of communication between the Palm OS and the application. In addition, applications can send launch codes to each other, but that is beyond our scope.

14.2.2 Palm Programming Is Event-Driven Programming with a Graphical User Interface (GUI)

We have two fundamental concerns:

1. What should the application look like (to the user)? This concerns the *GUI design*.

2. How should the application interact with the user, through the GUI? This concerns *event handling*.

14.2.3 The Event Loop

The Palm OS is an event-based operating system. Palm OS applications contain a software event loop. *Once in the event loop, the application continuously fetches events from the event queue and deals with (or "handles") them.* Some events just require built-in system functionality. Typically, events are "offered" to the system, which many times knows how to handle them. For example, the system knows how to respond to pen taps on forms or menus, or switching applications. The application typically remains in the event loop until the system tells it to shut itself down by sending an `appStopEvent` (not a launch code) through the event queue.

14.2.4 Creating the GUI: Specifying and Viewing Resources

pilrc is used to specify Palm GUI components. This section briefly illustrates a subset of the available resource file constructs commonly used with pilrc. Note that the full description of the pilrc syntax accompanies the pilrc distribution.

pilrc Syntax Notes

In the following, items in all CAPS appear as literals in the file. Items enclosed in < and > are required, whereas items enclosed in [and] are optional. Comments follow the C or C++ convention; single-line comments begin with //, whereas multiline comments are defined with /* and */.

Field Types

```
.i     identifier
.c     character
.s     string
.ss    multiline string
.n     number
.p     position co-ordinate
       may be a number, expression, or one of the following keywords.

          AUTO                Automatic width or height.
                              Value is computed based on the text in
                              the item.
          CENTER              Centers the item either horizontally
                              or vertically.
          CENTER@<coord.n>    Centers the item at the co-ordinate
                              following.
          RIGHT@<coord.n>     Aligns the item at the right
                              co-ordinate following.
          BOTTOM@<coord.n>    Aligns the item at the bottom
                              co-ordinate following.
          PREVLEFT            Previous items left co-ordinate.
          PREVRIGHT           Previous items right co-ordinate.
          PREVTOP             Previous items top co-ordinate.
          PREVBOTTOM          Previous items bottom co-ordinate.
          PREVWIDTH           Previous items width.
          PREVHEIGHT          Previous items height.
```

Resource Specification File The .rcp file may contain the following object definitions:

```
FORM                  Form Resource
MENU                  Form Menu Bar
ALERT                 Alert Dialog Resource
VERSION               Version String
STRING                String Resource
STRINGTABLE           String List Resource
CATEGORIES            Default Category Names
APPLICATIONICONNAME   Application Icon Name
APPLICATION           Application Creator Identification
LAUNCHERCATEGORY      Default Launcher Category Name
ICON
```

```
ICONFAMILY              Icon Bitmap Resource
SMALLICON
SMALLICONFAMILY         Small Icon Bitmap Resource
BITMAP
FONT                    User-Defined Font Resource
```

FORM Specification

```
FORM (tFRM)

     FORM ID <FormResourceId.n> AT (<Left.p> <Top.p> <Width.p> <Height.p>)
       [FRAME] [NOFRAME]
       [MODAL]
       [SAVEBEHIND] [NOSAVEBEHIND]
       [USABLE]
       [HELPID <HelpId.n>]
       [DEFAULTBTNID <BtnId.n>]
       [MENUID <MenuId.n>]
     BEGIN
       <OBJECTS>
     END
```

Where `<OBJECTS>` is one or more of:

```
TITLE                 <Title.s>
BUTTON                <Label.s> ID <Id.n> AT (<Left.p> <Top.p>
                      <Width.p> <Height.p>)
                      [USABLE] [NONUSABLE] [DISABLED] [LEFTANCHOR]
                      [RIGHTANCHOR]
                      [FRAME] [NOFRAME] [BOLDFRAME] [FONT
                      <FontId.n>]
                      [GRAPHICAL] [BITMAPID <BitmapId.n>]
                      [SELECTEDBITMAPID <BitmapId.n>]
PUSHBUTTON            <Label.s> ID <Id.n> AT (<Left.p> <Top.p>
                      <Width.p> <Height.p>)
                      [USABLE] [NONUSABLE] [DISABLED] [LEFTANCHOR]
                      [RIGHTANCHOR]
                      [FONT <FontId>] [GROUP <GroupId.n>]
                      [GRAPHICAL] [BITMAPID <BitmapId.n>]
                      [SELECTEDBITMAPID <BitmapId.n>]
CHECKBOX              <Label.s> ID <Id.n> AT (<Left.p> <Top.p>
                      <Width.p> <Height.p>)
                      [USABLE] [NONUSABLE] [DISABLED] [LEFTANCHOR]
                      [RIGHTANCHOR]
                      [FONT <FontId.n>] [GROUP <GroupId.n>]
                      [CHECKED]
POPUPTRIGGER          <Label.s> ID <Id.n> AT (<Left.p> <Top.p>
                      <Width.p> <Height.p>)
                      [USABLE] [NONUSABLE] [DISABLED] [LEFTANCHOR]
                      [RIGHTANCHOR]
                      [FONT <FontId.n>]
                      [GRAPHICAL] [BITMAPID <BitmapId.n>]
                      [SELECTEDBITMAPID <BitmapId.n>]
SELECTORTRIGGER       <Label.s> ID <Id.n> AT (<Left.p> <Top.p>
                      <Width.p> <Height.p>)
                      [USABLE] [NONUSABLE] [DISABLED] [LEFTANCHOR]
                      [RIGHTANCHOR]
                      [FONT <FontId.n>]
                      [GRAPHICAL] [BITMAPID <BitmapId.n>]
                      [SELECTEDBITMAPID <BitmapId.n>]
```

```
REPEATBUTTON        <Label.s> ID <Id.n> AT (<Left.p> <Top.p>
                    <Width.p> <Height.p>)
                    [USABLE] [NONUSABLE] [DISABLED] [LEFTANCHOR]
                    [RIGHTANCHOR]
                    [FRAME] [NOFRAME] [BOLDFRAME] [FONT
                    <FontId.n>]
                    [GRAPHICAL] [BITMAPID <BitmapId.n>]
                    [SELECTEDBITMAPID <BitmapId.n>]
LABEL               <Label.s> ID <Id.n> AT (<Left.p> <Top.p>)
                    [USABLE] [NONUSABLE] [FONT <FontId.n>]
FIELD               ID <Id.n> AT (<Left.p> <Top.p> <Width.p>
                    <Height.p>)
                    [USABLE] [NONUSABLE] [DISABLED] [LEFTALIGN]
                    [RIGHTALIGN]
                    [FONT <FontId.n>] [EDITABLE] [NONEDITABLE]
                    [UNDERLINED]
                    [SINGLELINE] [MULTIPLELINES] [DYNAMICSIZE]
                    [MAXCHARS <MaxChars.n>]
                    [AUTOSHIFT] [NUMERIC] [HASSCROLLBAR]
POPUPLIST           ID <Id.n> <ControlId.n> <ListId.n>
LIST                <Item.s> ... <Item.s>
                    ID <Id.n> AT (<Left.p> <Top.p> <Width.p>
                    <Height.p>)
                    [USABLE] [NONUSABLE] [DISABLED] [VISIBLEITEMS
                    <NumVisItems.n>]
                    [FONT <FontId.n>]
FORMBITMAP          AT (<Left.p> <Top.p>)
                    [BITMAP <BitmapId.n>] [USABLE] [NONUSABLE]
GADGET              ID <Id.n> AT (<Left.p> <Top.p> <Width.p>
                    <Height.p>)
                    [USABLE] [NONUSABLE]
TABLE               ID <Id.n> AT (<Left.p> <Top.p> <Width.p>
                    <Height.p>)
                    [ROWS <NumRows.n>] [COLUMNS <NumCols.n>]
                    [COLUMNWIDTHS <Col1Width.n> ...
                    <ColNWidth.n>]
SCROLLBAR           ID <Id.n> AT (<Left.p> <Top.p> <Width.p>
                    <Height.p>)
                    [USABLE] [NONUSABLE] [VALUE <Value.n>] [MIN
                    <MinValue.n>]
                    [MAX <MaxValue.n>] [PAGESIZE <PageSize.n>]
```

Relating the GUI Form Parameters to C Code

The following (abbreviated) description of field attributes is provided.

`usable`: If not set, the field object is not considered part of the current interface of the application, and it doesn't appear on screen.

`visible`: Set or cleared internally when the field object is drawn with `FldDrawField` or `FrmShowObject`, and erased with `FldEraseField` or `FrmHideObject`.

`editable`: If not set, the field object doesn't accept text input or editing commands and the insertion point cannot be positioned with the pen. The text can still be selected and copied.

`singleLine`: If set, the field is a single line of text high and the text does not wrap when it exceeds the width of the field. If not set, the text wraps to fill multiple lines.

`underlined`: If set each line of the field, including blank lines, is underlined.

Alternately, one could just look at the field data structures in Palm OS header file `field.h` (in `/.../sdk/include/Core/UI`). This is shown in the excerpt that follows.

```
typedef struct FieldAttrTag
{
UInt16 usable :1; // Set if part of ui
UInt16 visible :1; // Set if drawn, used internally
UInt16 editable :1; // Set if editable
UInt16 singleLine :1; // Set if only a single line is displayed
UInt16 hasFocus      :1;    // Set if the field has the focus
UInt16 dynamicSize :1;    // Set if height expands as text is entered
UInt16 insPtVisible :1; // Set if the ins pt is scrolled into view
UInt16 dirty :1; // Set if user modified
UInt16 underlined :2; // text underlined mode
UInt16 justification :2; // text alignment
UInt16 autoShift :1; // Set if auto case shift
UInt16 hasScrollBar :1; // Set if the field has a scroll bar
UInt16 numeric :1; // Set if numeric, digits and decimal separator only
UInt16 reserved :1; // Reserved for future use
} FieldAttrType;
```

14.2.5 The First Palm GUI

We illustrate the process with a simple example. Consider the content of the resource specification file `ece352.rcp` shown here and in Figure 14.3.

```
#include "ece352.h"

FORM ID MainForm AT ( 0 0 160 160 )
NOFRAME
USABLE
BEGIN
    TITLE "Main Form Title"
    LABEL "Goodbye, Cruel World!" ID MainGoodbyeWorldLabel AT (30 40) FONT 2
END
```

Figure 14.4 shows how it actually looks (on the emulator). This simple GUI design contains a single form, identified as `MainForm`. It has a title and a single label containing text and

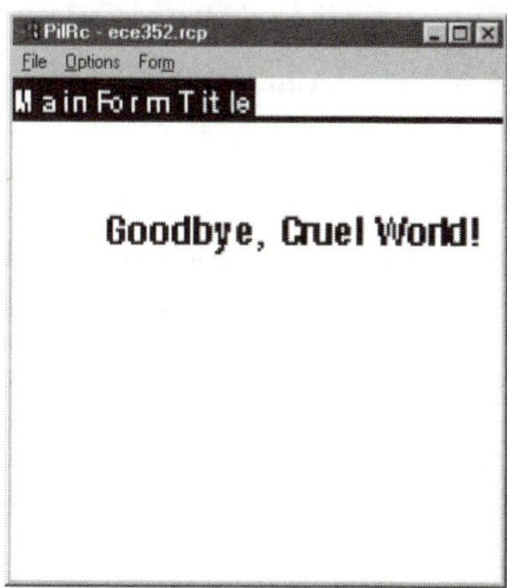

Figure 14.3 Using `pilrcui` to display `ece352.rcp` with command string `pilrcui ece352.rcp`.

Figure 14.4 Emulator Form Corresponding to Definitions in `ece352.rcp`.

located at a specified position on the Palm screen. There are no additional forms, menus, popups (alerts), or any other resources. Subsequent examples change this. `pilrcui` (or the Handspring utility) allows us to view this resource specification, as shown in Figure 14.4. *Note that at this point all we have is a specification for a GUI.* There is no functioning application. To make the application functional, we must design the application executable (in C here). First we develop the link between the application and the GUI resources.

Linking Resources with Code

Now let's begin the integration of this layout of resources with code. `pilrc` allows symbolic constants to be used to define resources. The (minimal) content of `ece352.h`, which must be included in **both** `ece352.c` and `ece352.rcp`, is shown here:

```
#define MainForm                   1400
#define MainGoodbyeWorldLabel        1401
```

Note that we have not addressed the much larger issue of linking events with handlers.

14.2.6 The First Palm Application: C Code and Analysis

All of the C code for this application is contained in the file `ece352.c`.

Where's `main`?

In confronting new code, many C programmers learn to look for function `main`. Note that this function does not exist in our application. Instead, it is replaced by `PilotMain`.

```
 UInt32 PilotMain(UInt16 cmd, MemPtr cmdPBP, UInt16 launchFlags)
{
// just check for a normal launch
if (cmd == sysAppLaunchCmdNormalLaunch) {
if (!StartApplication()) {
EventLoop();
StopApplication();
}
```

```
}
return 0;
}
```

A Note Concerning Code Structure

Many readers, in perusing the simple example code that follows, will immediately observe that the same functionality could be obtained with fewer additional functions and as a part of `PilotMain`. Although this is true, the following structure is presented in order to accommodate larger, more sophisticated applications, and application startup.

Application Startup

Application startup is facilitated by our function `StartApplication` as shown here. Note that `StartApplication` invokes Palm OS function `FrmGotoForm` with specified resource `MainForm`. It is crucial to note (see Section 14.2.9) that `FrmGotoForm` generates two events: `frmLoadEvent` and `frmOpenEvent`. These events are of significant interest to us, and subsequently handled by event handlers in our code:

```
Boolean StartApplication(void)
{
FrmGotoForm(MainForm); //MainForm in *.rcp, *.h
return false;
}


void StopApplication(void)
{
FrmCloseAllForms();
}
```

14.2.7 Events

Events and event handling are key concepts in Palm application development. The simple example includes several functions related to handling events (and in one case, a function-generating event). These involve the passing of a pointer to a struct of type `EventPtr`, namely `event`. As a prelude, we look a little deeper into Palm OS events and related header files.

What Events May Occur?

C Background Review The reader is encouraged to review C, concepts related to structs, pointers, pointers to structs, enumerations (`enum`), and `typedef`. In the Palm OS library header file `Event.h`, the possible events specific to the Palm OS are enumerated via:

```
typedef enum { ... } eventsEnum;
```

which is then part of a struct declared as type `EventType`:

```
typedef struct EventType {
  eventsEnum eType;
...
                  } EventType;
```

Then

```
typedef EventType *EventPtr;
```

declares a pointer to type `EventType` (the struct that contains an `eventsEnum` field). One last note: Recall that accessing elements of a structure referred to by a pointer uses the C syntax ->, that is, in the event-handler examples we use:

```
Boolean MainFormHandleEvent(EventPtr event)
{...
switch (event->eType) ...
```

to enable event-specific handling.

Some Snippets from `Event.h`

```
// snippets of event.h for illustration

typedef enum {
nilEvent = 0,// system level
penDownEvent,// system level
penUpEvent,// system level
penMoveEvent,// system level
...
appStopEvent = 22,// system level
frmLoadEvent,
frmOpenEvent,
frmGotoEvent,
frmUpdateEvent,
...
menuOpenEvent,
menuCloseEvent,
...
} eventsEnum;


// The event record.
typedef struct EventType {
   eventsEnum eType;
...
   union {
...
      struct frmLoad {
         UInt16            formID;
         } frmLoad;

      struct frmOpen {
         UInt16            formID;
         } frmOpen;

      struct frmGoto {
         UInt16            formID;
         UInt16            recordNum;        // index of record that contain a match
         UInt16            matchPos;         // position in record of the match.
         UInt16            matchLen;         // length of match.
         UInt16            matchFieldNum;    // field number string was found int
```

```
        UInt32            matchCustom;       // application-specific info
        } frmGoto;
    } data;

} EventType;

typedef EventType *EventPtr;
```

The Event Loop and Related Code

The event loop in our sample application is implemented via our function `EventLoop`, as shown here.

```
void EventLoop(void)
{
EventType event;
Err error;
do {
EvtGetEvent(&event, evtWaitForever);
if (! SysHandleEvent(&event))
if (! MenuHandleEvent(0, &event, &error))
if (! ApplicationHandleEvent(&event))
FrmDispatchEvent(&event);
}
while (event.eType != appStopEvent);
}
```

Examples of the use of functions that handle events are shown here.

```
Boolean ApplicationHandleEvent(EventPtr event)
{
FormPtr frm;
int formId;
Boolean handled = false;

if (event->eType == frmLoadEvent) {

formId = event->data.frmLoad.formID;
frm = FrmInitForm(formId);
FrmSetActiveForm(frm);
switch (formId) {
case MainForm:
FrmSetEventHandler(frm, MainFormHandleEvent);
break;
}
handled = true;
}
return handled;
}
Boolean MainFormHandleEvent(EventPtr event)
{
Boolean handled = false;
FormPtr frm;
```

```
switch (event->eType) {

case frmOpenEvent:
frm = FrmGetActiveForm();
FrmDrawForm(frm);
handled = true;
break;



          default:              //all other events
             break;
       }
return(handled);
}
```

Of particular note in the preceding code is the handling of the two events `frmLoadEvent` and `frmOpenEvent` generated by function `FrmGotoForm` in Section 14.2.7. Also note that the code handles *all other events* by default.

The Format of a prc File

The PRC Tools application `build-prc` generates the file that is loaded into the Palm device (or the emulator). This file is an "archive" of the Palm application components, including the application resource specifications and executable code. In addition, bitmaps and databases may be included. Interested readers will find descriptions of the format and contents of this file at the Palm developer's site.

14.2.8 Some Important Palm OS Functions

These descriptions are taken from the `Palm OSReference.pdf`.

EvtGetEvent

```
Purpose: Return the next available event.

Prototype: void EvtGetEvent (EventType *event, Int32 timeout)

Parameters:

event: Pointer to the structure to hold the event
returned

timeout: Maximum number of ticks to wait before an
event is returned (-1 means wait indefinitely)

Comments:
 Pass timeout= -1 in most instances. When running on the device,
this makes the CPU go into doze mode until the user provides
input. For applications that do animation, pass timeout >= 0.

Result: Returns nothing.
```

FrmDispatchEvent

```
Purpose: Dispatch an event to the applications handler for the form.
```

Prototype

```
Boolean FrmDispatchEvent (EventType *eventP)
```

Parameters
eventP: Pointer to an event.

Result: Returns the Boolean value returned by the forms event handler or FrmHandleEvent. (If the forms event handler returns false, the event is passed to FrmHandleEvent.) This function also returns false if the form specified in the event is invalid.

Comments:

The event is dispatched to the current forms handler unless the form ID is specified in the event data, as, for example, with frmOpenEvent or frmGotoEvent. A forms event handler (FormEventHandler) is registered by FrmSetEventHandler.
Note that if the form does not have a registered event handler, this function causes a fatal error.

FrmGetActiveForm

Purpose: Return the currently active form.
Prototype:

```
FormType *FrmGetActiveForm (void)
```

Parameters: None.
Result:
Returns a pointer to the form object of the active form.
See Also FrmGetActiveFormID, FrmSetActiveForm

FrmSetActiveForm

Purpose: Set the active form. All input (key and pen) is directed to the active form and all drawing occurs there.

Prototype:

```
void FrmSetActiveForm (FormType *formP)
```

Parameters:
formP: Pointer to the form object (FormType structure).

Result Returns nothing.

Comments A penDownEvent outside the form but within the display area is ignored.

FrmInitForm

Purpose: Load and initialize a form resource.

Prototype: FormType *FrmInitForm (UInt16 rscID)

Parameters:
rscID: Resource ID of the form.

Result: Returns a pointer to the form data structure.

Displays an error message if the form has already been initialized.

FrmSetEventHandler

Purpose: Registers the event handler callback routine for the specified form.

Prototype:

```
void FrmSetEventHandler (FormType *formP,FormEventHandlerType *handler)
```

Parameters:

formP: Pointer to the form object (FormType structure).

handler: Address of the form event handler function, FormEventHandler.

Result: Returns nothing.

FrmGotoForm

Purpose: Send a frmCloseEvent to the current form; send a frmLoadEvent and a frmOpenEvent to the specified form.

Prototype

```
void FrmGotoForm (UInt16 formId)
```

Parameters:
formId: ID of the form to display.

Result: Returns nothing.

FrmDrawForm

Purpose: Draw all objects in a form and the frame around the form.

Prototype:

```
void FrmDrawForm (FormType *formP)
```

Parameters:

formP: Pointer to the form object (FormType structure).

Result: Returns nothing.

```
m68k-Palm OS-gcc -c -g -Wall $1.c
m68k-Palm OS-gcc $1.o -lm -g -Wall -o $1
pilrc -q $1.rcp
build-prc $1.def $1 *.bin
```

Figure 14.5 Sample Shell Script to Build Palm Application.

Figure 14.6 Emulator Main Form with `ece352.prc` Installed.

14.2.9 How to Compile the First Application

Usually, a Palm application is built more than once. Because the same set of commands is often used,[5] a makefile or shell script may be desirable. A sample `bash` shell script[6] is shown in Figure 14.5.[7] Of course, a Makefile may also be used. Note there is no explicit specification of the SDK to be used; the default (usually the only) SDK will be used.

The form of a `*.def` file used by `build-prc` in Figure 14.5 is treated in Section 14.6.3.

14.2.10 Resultant Appearance (via the Emulator)

Figure 14.6 shows how our first application actually looks (on the emulator).

14.2.11 Adding Bitmaps to the Palm Application

Approaches to Adding Bitmaps

The graphical interface provided by the Palm hardware makes the inclusion of bitmapped images (bitmaps) both desirable and important. Bitmaps may be added to applications in two ways:

1. By incorporating them in forms. These are so-called Form Bitmap objects. The bitmap is drawn when the form is drawn, and thus no extra code is required. This section shown is an example of this approach.

---

[5]Note that if you add or remove application resources, it will be necessary to revise or regenerate the `*.h` file.

[6]Usable with either `Linux` or `cygwin`.

[7]Your commands may vary depending upon paths you have previously set, where you have put the various components, and which tools you are using.

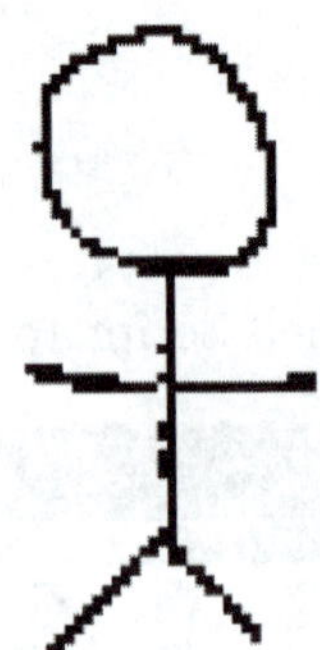

Figure 14.7 Bitmap File for Incorporation in Palm Form (Contained in File hangmeb.bmp).

```
#include "bitmap1.h"

FORM ID OnlyForm AT ( 0 0 160 160 )
NOFRAME
USABLE
BEGIN
    TITLE "Hangme (Static Form)"
    FORMBITMAP AT (30 40) BITMAP bitmapID
    LABEL "Bitmap display example" ID labelID AT (30 130)
END

BITMAP  ID bitmapID "hangmeb.bmp"
```

Figure 14.8 Resource Specification File for Bitmap Inclusion.

2. By drawing the bitmap in software. This requires that we load the bitmap (or, as is commonly used, the bitmap *family*) from a resource database and then invoke either the `WinDrawBitmap` or `WinPaintBitmap` Palm OS functions. This is a more advanced topic. Note that the form manager uses `WinDrawBitmap` to draw Form Bitmap objects.

A Simple Example

Consider the simple "hangman" bitmap shown in Figure 14.7. A resource specification file that includes this bitmap on the main (or only) form is shown in Figure 14.8. The resulting application (Palm screen only) is shown in Figure 14.9. Note that the C source for this application is identical[8] to that of the previous application.

14.3 A More Elaborate Example (Buttons, Multiple Forms, and a Menu)

14.3.1 Adding and Handling Resources

We now enhance our original design and explore other PalmOS features. Specifically, we add the following to our original application to change the "look and feel":

- A menu bar to the main form with a pulldown menu.
- A menu entry on this menu.

[8]With the exception of renaming of resource IDs.

Hangme (Static Form)

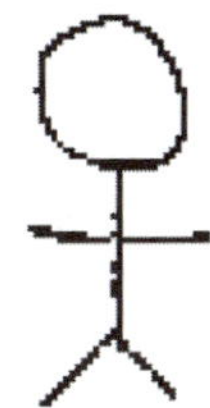

Bitmap display example

Figure 14.9 Resulting Palm Main (Only) Form Screen.

- A button on the main form.
- Display of a text string on the main form after the button is pressed.
- Another "About" form, treated as a *dialog*.
- Another button on the "About" form.
- The same menu (available on the main form) also available on the "About" form.

These enhancements will lead to the generation and consequent handling of many more resources and events, including switching forms, responding to buttons, and so forth.

14.3.2 Specifying and Viewing Resources for the Modified Application

We proceed in the same manner as before, namely:

1. Define the necessary resources.

2. Design the code to display resources and respond to events.

Thus, the contents of the revised resource specification `ece352v2.rcp` are shown here:

```
#include "ece352v2.h"

FORM ID MainForm AT ( 0 0 160 160 )
NOFRAME
USABLE
MENUID MainFormMenuBar
BEGIN
    TITLE "Main Form Title"
        LABEL "Goodbye, Cruel World!" ID MainGoodbyeWorldLabel AT (30 40) FONT 2
    BUTTON "Main Form Btn" ID MainGoodbyeAgainButton AT ( 46 129 68 14) USABLE FRAME FONT 0
END

MENU ID MainFormMenuBar
BEGIN
    PULLDOWN "Menu Bar Stuff"
    BEGIN
```

```
        MENUITEM "Menu Item" ID MainOptionsAbout
        MENUITEM SEPARATOR
    END
END

FORM ID AboutForm AT ( 2 18 156 140 )
FRAME
MODAL
USABLE
MENUID MainFormMenuBar
BEGIN
    TITLE "Menu Item"
        LABEL "Goodbye World" ID AboutAppNameLabel AT (51 22) FONT 1
        LABEL "Version 1 e +07" ID AboutVersionLabel AT (52 32) FONT 1
        LABEL "Modified by rjs 3-29-01" ID AboutAuthorLabel   AT (4 50) FONT 0
        BUTTON "Menu Btn" ID AboutGetOutButton AT ( 62 125 37 12) USABLE FRAME FONT 0
END
```

Again, to get a preview of the design (not the actual functionality of the application), we use `pilrcui` (Figure 14.10).

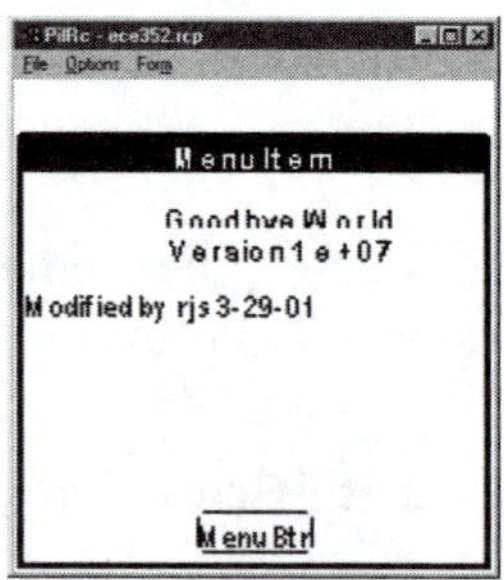

Figure 14.10 `pilrc` Rendition of Forms Corresponding to Definitions in Revised `ece352.rcp`.

14.3.3 Revised Resource File Specification

The following code is the revised `ece352v2.h`, which must be included in **both** `ece352v2.c` and `ece352v2.rcp`. Note it was generated by `pilrc` (see Section 14.3.8).

```
/* pilrc generated file.  Do not edit!*/
#define AboutGetOutButton 9990
#define AboutAuthorLabel 9991
#define AboutVersionLabel 9992
#define AboutAppNameLabel 9993
#define AboutForm 9994
#define MainOptionsAbout 9995
#define MainGoodbyeAgainButton 9996
#define MainGoodbyeWorldLabel 9997
#define MainFormMenuBar 9998
#define MainForm 9999
```

14.3.4 Modified C Code and Analysis

Only the revisions to the initial file (used previously) are shown.

```
Boolean MainFormHandleEvent(EventPtr event)
{
Boolean handled = false;
FormPtr frm;
char * pStr;


switch (event->eType) {
    case ctlSelectEvent:
    if (event->data.ctlEnter.controlID == MainGoodbyeAgainButton) {
    pStr = "I said get lost!";
    WinDrawChars(pStr, StrLen(pStr), ((160-FntCharsWidth(pStr,
StrLen(pStr)))/2), 80);
handled = true;
}
break;


case frmOpenEvent:
frm = FrmGetActiveForm();
FrmDrawForm(frm);
handled = true;
break;

case menuEvent:       // the only menu event
MenuEraseStatus(0);
frm = FrmInitForm(AboutForm);
FrmDoDialog(frm);
FrmDeleteForm(frm);
handled = true;
break;

            default:
                        break;
}
return(handled);
}
```

Note that the About form is accessed via the menu and treated as a *dialog*. Later, we show how to treat alerts the same way. In addition, we discover another technique for displaying or switching to other forms in the application.

14.3.5 Switching Forms

Most Palm applications involve multiple forms for input, display, settings, and so on. The dialog-based approach of Section 14.3 is not the preferred way to switch forms when we want the new form to have its own set of events (usually handled by a form-specific event handler) due to input and display, controls, and so forth. To accomplish this, we make the new form the active form and register a handler function for it. The sample code shown in Figure 14.11 accomplishes this.

```
if (event->data.ctlEnter.controlID == NewFormButton)
         {
           FrmSetActiveForm(FrmInitForm(NewForm));
           frm = FrmGetActiveForm();
           FrmSetEventHandler(frm, FormHandleEvent);
           FrmDrawForm(frm);
          }
```

Figure 14.11 Sample Code for Switching Palm Application Forms.

14.3.6 New Functions (from PalmOSReference.pdf)

WinDrawChars

```
Purpose: Draw the specified characters in the draw window.

Prototype: void WinDrawChars (const Char *chars, Int16 len,
                              Coord x, Coord y)

Parameters:
            chars Pointer to the characters to draw.
            len Length in bytes of the characters to draw.
            x x coordinate of the first character to draw (left
                 bound).
            y y coordinate of the first character to draw (top
                 bound).

Result: Returns void

Comments: This function is useful for printing non-editable status or warning
messages on the screen.
```

MenuEraseStatus

```
Purpose: Erase the menu command status.

Prototype: void MenuEraseStatus (MenuBarType *menuP)

Parameters: menuP Pointer to a MenuBarType, or NULL for the
                   current menu.

Result:   Returns void

Comments: When the user selects a menu command using the command
keystroke, the command toolbar or status message is displayed at
the bottom of the screen. MenuEraseStatus erases the toolbar or
status message.
```

FrmDoDialog

```
Purpose: Display a modal dialog until the user taps a button in the dialog.

Prototype: UInt16 FrmDoDialog (FormType *formP)

Parameters: formP Pointer to the form object (FormType
                  structure).

Result: Returns the resource ID of the button the user tapped.
```

```
FrmDeleteForm

Purpose: Release the memory occupied by a form. Any memory allocated to
objects in the form is also released.

Prototype: void FrmDeleteForm (FormType *formP)

Parameters: formP Pointer to the form object (FormType
                  structure).

Result Returns void.
```

14.3.7 The Finished (Revised) Application

For the revised application, it is difficult to show the dynamic nature of the application with static images, but we'll try. Figures 14.12 to 14.16 show how the Palm application actually looks (on the emulator).

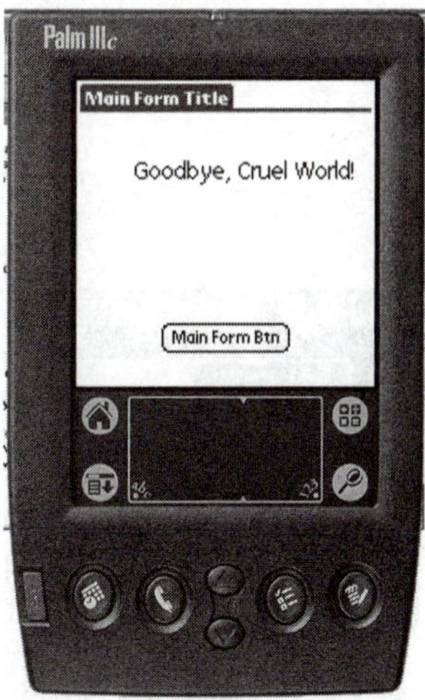

Figure 14.12 Version 2 Palm Application: Main Form.

Figure 14.13 After Main Form Button Is Pressed.

Figure 14.14 Drop-Down Menu.

Figure 14.15 Version 2 Application: Main Form.

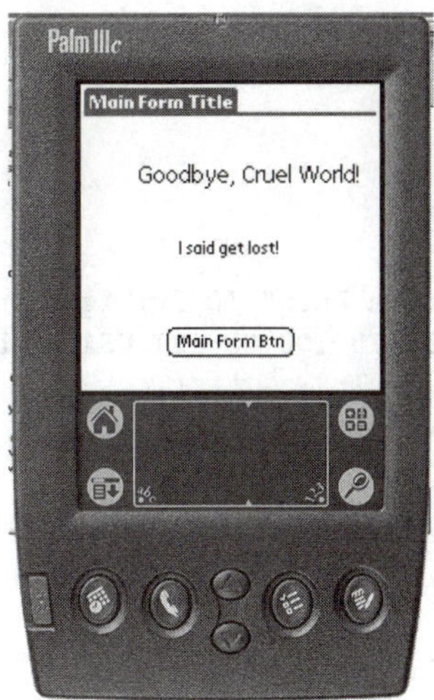

Figure 14.16 Version 2 Application: After Menu Button Is Pressed.

14.3.8 Using `pilrc` to Generate the Header File from a Resource Specification

Motivation

Up to this point we have been generating the `*.h` file with resource specifications from the corresponding `*.rcp` file by hand. This is doable and practical only for small GUI designs. `pilrc` will automatically generate this file, given the *.rcp file.[9]

Example Resource Specification File

Consider the following resource specification file `ece352v3.rcp`:

```
#include "ece352v3.h"

FORM ID MainForm AT ( 0 0 160 160 )
NOFRAME
USABLE
MENUID MainFormMenuBar
BEGIN
    TITLE "MainForm Title"
        LABEL "Goodbye, Cruel World!" ID MainLabel1 AT (20 40) FONT 2
        LABEL "Version 3" ID MainLabel2 AT (20 70) FONT 2

    BUTTON "LeftBtn" ID MFLeftBtn AT ( 20 120 30 15) USABLE FRAME FONT 0
    BUTTON "RightBtn" ID MFRightBtn AT ( 80 120 30 15) USABLE FRAME FONT 0
END

MENU ID MainFormMenuBar
BEGIN
    PULLDOWN "Menu"
    BEGIN
        MENUITEM "Item #1"  MenuID1
        MENUITEM "Item #2"  MenuID2
    END
END
```

[9]It appears to be necessary that the header file already exist and be empty.

```
FORM ID RightBtnForm AT ( 2 18 156 140 )
FRAME
MODAL
USABLE
BEGIN
    TITLE "From Right Btn"
        LABEL "Form From Right Button Push" ID FrmRightBtn AT (05 40) FONT 1
        BUTTON "Back" ID GoBack AT (75 100 35 12) USABLE FRAME FONT 0
END
```

pilrc Operation on Sample File

The following shows the operation of pilrc; the directory shows the generated file.

```
bash-2.02$ /PalmDev/pilrc-2.7b/pilrc -H ece352v3.h ece352v3.rcp
PilRC 68k v2.7b
  Copyright 1997-1999 Wes Cherry   (wesc@ricochet.net)
  Copyright 2000-2001 Aaron Ardiri (ardiri@palmgear.com)

Writing ./tFRM270f.bin
244 bytes
Writing ./MBAR270e.bin
103 bytes
Writing ./tFRM2707.bin
182 bytes
writing include file: ece352v3.h
```

Resulting Header File

The pilrc-generated file appears as follows:

```
/* pilrc generated file.  Do not edit!*/
#define GoBack 9989
#define FrmRightBtn 9990
#define RightBtnForm 9991
#define MenuID2 9992
#define MenuID1 9993
#define MFRightBtn 9994
#define MFLeftBtn 9995
#define MainLabel2 9996
#define MainLabel1 9997
#define MainFormMenuBar 9998
#define MainForm 9999
```

14.4 Interaction with User-Entered Data and the "Echo" Application

A GUI-based design usually implies user interaction with the program. In this section we begin our look at user interaction through fields. The initial application is quite simple. In the subsequent example, we address a number of practical and realistic programming concerns.

14.4.1 Input and Output Fields Are ASCII Text

It is very important to note that all interaction with the user through fields *occurs as (ASCII) text*. Although we may wish to have the user input integers or floating-point numbers, it is imperative to reiterate that these are read as text by the appropriate Palm OS functions. Thus we may be interested in converting input text into integers or floats. Similarly, all output field values are text, so we may be interested in converting floats or integers to text.

14.4.2 Specifying the Application "Look and Feel"

First, we state the desired behavior of the application:

> *In the main form, the user types in (Graffiti) text in an upper field, presses an "echo" button, and the text appears in the lower field.*

Although this application may seem simplistic, it forms the basis for more sophisticated applications that actually process the data and display results.

14.4.3 Specifying and Viewing Resources for the GUI Design

Here's the content of the revised resource specification `ece352v4.rcp`:

```
#include "ece352v4.h"

FORM ID MainForm AT ( 0 0 160 160 )
NOFRAME
USABLE
BEGIN
    TITLE "Interaction Example"
    FIELD ID fieldID_inText AT (30 25 100 20) USABLE LEFTALIGN FONT 0 EDITABLE
                          UNDERLINED SINGLELINE MAXCHARS 20
    BUTTON "Echo Above" ID EchoButton AT (60 60 50 20) USABLE FRAME FONT 0
    FIELD ID fieldID_outText AT (30 100 100 20) USABLE LEFTALIGN FONT 0
NONEDITABLE
                          UNDERLINED SINGLELINE MAXCHARS 20
END
```

Again, to get a preview of the GUI design, we use `pilrcui`, as shown in Figure 14.17.

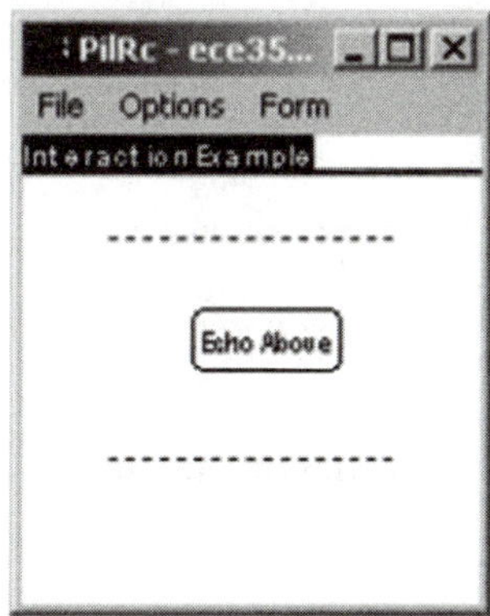

Figure 14.17 `pilrc` Rendition of Form Corresponding to `ece352v4.rcp`.

Now we continue the integration of this layout of resources with code. Here's a revised `ece352v4.h`, which must be included in **both** `ece352v4.c` and `ece352v4.rcp`:

```
// file: ece352v4.h

//      Resource: MainForm
#define MainForm                    1400
#define fieldID_inText              1000
#define fieldID_outText             1001
#define EchoButton                  1002
```

14.4.4 Analysis of Revised C Code for the "Echo" Application

Note that all C code is in the file `ece352v4.c`, shown here.

```
#include <PalmOS.h>
#include "ece352v4.h"

FieldPtr fieldptr_intext;
FieldPtr fieldptr_outtext;

void echo()
{
char *textpointer;

textpointer = FldGetTextPtr(fieldptr_intext);
// does not check if FldGetTextPtr returns NULL
FldSetTextPtr(fieldptr_outtext, textpointer);
FldDrawField(fieldptr_outtext);
// note: only redraws the field, not the form
// does not deallocate the old handle
}

Boolean StartApplication(void)
{
FrmGotoForm(MainForm);
return true;
}


void StopApplication(void)
{
FrmCloseAllForms();
}

Boolean MainFormHandleEvent(EventPtr event)
{
Boolean handled = false;
FormPtr frm;



switch (event->eType) {
    case ctlSelectEvent:
           if (event->data.ctlEnter.controlID== EchoButton) // button pressed
           {
            echo();
            }
```

```
            handled = true;
            break;

case frmOpenEvent:
frm = FrmGetActiveForm();
// need these for echoing
fieldptr_intext = FrmGetObjectPtr(frm, FrmGetObjectIndex(frm, fieldID_inText));
fieldptr_outtext = FrmGetObjectPtr(frm, FrmGetObjectIndex(frm,
fieldID_outText));
FrmDrawForm(frm);
handled = true;
break;

       default:
            break;
}
return(handled);
}


Boolean ApplicationHandleEvent(EventPtr event)
{
FormPtr frm;
int formId;
Boolean handled = false;

if (event->eType == frmLoadEvent) {

formId = event->data.frmLoad.formID;
frm = FrmInitForm(formId);
FrmSetActiveForm(frm);
switch (formId) {
case MainForm:
FrmSetEventHandler(frm, MainFormHandleEvent);
break;
}
handled = true;
}
return handled;
}


void EventLoop(void)
{
EventType event;
Err error;

do
{
EvtGetEvent(&event, evtWaitForever);
if (! SysHandleEvent(&event))
if (! MenuHandleEvent(0, &event, &error))
if (! ApplicationHandleEvent(&event))
FrmDispatchEvent(&event);
}
while (event.eType != appStopEvent);
}
```

```
UInt32 PilotMain(UInt16 cmd, MemPtr cmdPBP, UInt16 launchFlags)
{

// just check for a normal launch

if (cmd == sysAppLaunchCmdNormalLaunch) {
if (StartApplication()) {
EventLoop();
StopApplication();
}
}

return 0;
}
```

The heart of the revision is based upon the following (immature and incomplete) C code fragment. The effort is somewhat simplified, because there is only one form in the application.

```
if (event->data.ctlEnter.controlID== EchoButton) // button pressed
 .
 .
 .
 // here's the actual echo
 textpointer = FldGetTextPtr(fieldptr_intext);
 // does not check if FldGetTextPtr returns NULL
 FldSetTextPtr(fieldptr_outtext, textpointer);
 FldDrawField(fieldptr_outtext);
 // note: only redraws the field, not the form
 // does not deallocate the old handle
 }
```

14.4.5 New Palm OS Functions

FrmGetObjectIndex

```
Purpose: Return the index of an object in the form's objects list.

Prototype: UInt16 FrmGetObjectIndex (const FormType *formP,
                UInt16 objID)

Parameters: formP Pointer to the form object (FormType
                structure).
            objID ID of an object in the form.

Result: Returns the index of the object (the index of the first object is 0).
```

FrmGetObjectPtr

```
Purpose: Return a pointer to the data structure of an object in a form.

Prototype: void *FrmGetObjectPtr (const FormType *formP,
               UInt16 objIndex)

Parameter: formP Pointer to the form object (FormType
            structure).
```

objIndex: Index of an object in the form. You can obtain
this by using FrmGetObjectIndex.

Result: Returns a pointer to an object in the form.

FldGetTextHandle

Purpose: Return a handle to the block that contains the text string of a field.

Prototype: MemHandle FldGetTextHandle (const FieldType* fldP)

Parameters: fldP Pointer to a field object (FieldType structure).

Result: Returns the handle to the text string of a field or NULL if no handle has been allocated for the field pointer.

FldGetTextPtr

Purpose: Return a locked pointer to the field's text string.

Prototype: Char* FldGetTextPtr (FieldType* fldP)

Parameters: fldP Pointer to a field object (FieldType structure).

Result: Returns a locked pointer to the field's text string or NULL if the field is empty.

Comments: The pointer returned by this function can become invalid if the user edits the text after you obtain the pointer.

FldGetTextLength

Purpose: Return the length in bytes of the field's text.

Prototype: UInt16 FldGetTextLength (const FieldType* fldP)

Parameters: fldP Pointer to a field object (FieldType structure).

Result: Returns the length in bytes of a field's text, not including the terminating null character. This is the textLen field of FieldType.

FldSetTextPtr

Purpose: Set a noneditable field's text to point to the specified text string.

Prototype: void FldSetTextPtr (FieldType* fldP, Char* textP)

Parameters: fldP Pointer to a field object (FieldType structure).
textP Pointer to a null-terminated string.

Result: Returns void. May display an error message if passed an editable text field.

Comments: Do not call FldSetTextPtr with an editable text field. Instead, call FldSetTextHandle for editable text fields.

FldRecalculateField

```
Purpose: Update the structure that contains the word-wrapping information
for each visible line.

Prototype: void FldRecalculateField (FieldType* fldP,
                     Boolean redraw)

Parameters: fldP Pointer to a field object (FieldType structure).
            redraw If true, redraws the field.
```

FldDrawField

```
Purpose: Draw the text of the field.

Prototype: void FldDrawField (FieldType* fldP)

Parameters: fldP Pointer to a field object (FieldType structure).

Result: Returns void.
```

14.5 Example: Numerical Input and Computations and Interaction with Fields

14.5.1 Field Handles and Dynamic Memory Allocation

In Palm programming, there is no `malloc` (or `free`). Palm OS functions are available for dynamic memory allocation. Their use is illustrated in the following function. Note that the function is considered the "safe" way to modify fields.

```
/* routine below is 'generic'; just use it */

static void SetFieldHandle(FieldPtr ptrToField, MemPtr ptrToText)
{
 MemHandle  newTextH; // new field text
 MemHandle  oldTextH; // text that may already be in the field
 MemPtr   tempPtr; // pointer to newTextH.

 // Allocate handle to store the new text + 1 extra
 newTextH = MemHandleNew(StrLen(ptrToText)+1);
 // Get pointer to memory and lock.
 tempPtr = MemHandleLock(newTextH);
 // Copy text to pointer
 StrCopy(tempPtr, ptrToText);

 // get old text handle
 oldTextH = FldGetTextHandle(ptrToField);

 // Set the field's new text.
 FldSetTextHandle(ptrToField, newTextH);
 // unlock the new text handle
 MemHandleUnlock(newTextH);
 // update the field
 FldDrawField(ptrToField);

 // Free the old text handle to prevent a memory leak
 if (oldTextH != NULL)
  MemHandleFree(oldTextH);
}
```

```
#include "ece352v6b.h"

FORM ID MainForm AT ( 0 0 160 160 )
NOFRAME
USABLE
BEGIN
    TITLE "ECE352: Num. Conv. (Ex6b)"

    LABEL "input number:" ID InputLabel AT (15 15) FONT 1
    FIELD ID fieldID_inText AT (90 15 30 20) USABLE LEFTALIGN FONT 0 EDITABLE
                      UNDERLINED SINGLELINE MAXCHARS 20
    BUTTON "Convert It" ID MainButton AT (40 35 60 15) USABLE BOLDFRAME FONT 2

    LABEL "squared:" ID OutLabel1 AT (15 60) FONT 1
    FIELD ID fieldID_outText1 AT (70 60 60 20) USABLE LEFTALIGN FONT 0 NONEDITABLE
                      UNDERLINED SINGLELINE MAXCHARS 40

    LABEL "cubed:" ID OutLabel2 AT (15 80) FONT 1
    FIELD ID fieldID_outText2 AT (70 80 60 20) USABLE LEFTALIGN FONT 0 NONEDITABLE
                      UNDERLINED SINGLELINE MAXCHARS 40

    LABEL "sqrt:" ID OutLabel3 AT (15 100) FONT 1
    FIELD ID fieldID_outText3 AT (70 100 60 20) USABLE LEFTALIGN FONT 0 NONEDITABLE
                      UNDERLINED SINGLELINE MAXCHARS 40
END
```

Figure 14.18 Palm Resource Specification File `ece352v6b.rcp`.

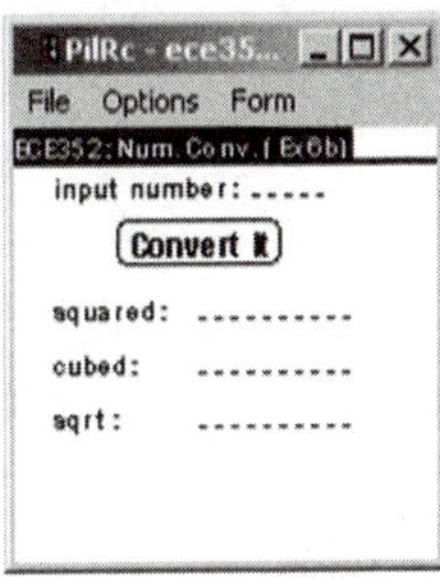

Figure 14.19 `pilrc` Rendition of Main Form Specified by `ece352v6b.rcp`.

We will show the use of this function in the next section.

14.5.2 Specifying and Viewing Resources for the Modified Design

The content of the revised resource specification file `ece352v6b.rcp` is shown in Figure 14.18. The corresponding single-form GUI using `pilrcui` is shown in Figure 14.19. The corresponding `*.h` file may be generated by hand or using `pilrc`.

14.5.3 Analysis of the Revised C Code

Code Listing

Note that the code uses function `SetFieldHandle`, described in Section 14.5.1.

```
// file: ece352v6b.c

#include <PalmOS.h>
```

```
#include "ece352v6b.h"
#include <StringMgr.h>
#include <FloatMgr.h>
#include <math.h>

// prototypes
double my_atof(const char* pc);
void SetFieldHandle(FieldPtr ptrToField, MemPtr ptrToText);
Boolean ApplicationHandleEvent(EventPtr event);
void EventLoop(void);
Boolean MainFormHandleEvent(EventPtr event);


Boolean StartApplication(void)
{
FrmGotoForm(MainForm);
return true;
}


void StopApplication(void)
{
FrmCloseAllForms();
}


double my_atof(const char* pc)
{
  FlpCompDouble fcd;
  FlpBufferAToF(&fcd.fd, pc);
  return fcd.d;
}


void SetFieldHandle(FieldPtr ptrToField, MemPtr ptrToText)
{
 MemHandle  newTextH; // new field text
 MemHandle  oldTextH; // text that may already be in the field
 MemPtr   tempPtr; // pointer to newTextH.

 // Allocate handle to store the new text + 1 extra
 newTextH = MemHandleNew(StrLen(ptrToText)+1);
 // Get pointer to memory and lock.
 tempPtr = MemHandleLock(newTextH);
 // Copy text to pointer
 StrCopy(tempPtr, ptrToText);

 // get old text handle
 oldTextH = FldGetTextHandle(ptrToField);

 // Set the field's new text.
 FldSetTextHandle(ptrToField, newTextH);
 // unlock the new text handle
 MemHandleUnlock(newTextH);
 // update the field
 FldDrawField(ptrToField);
```

```
 // Free the old text handle to prevent a memory leak
 if (oldTextH != NULL)
  MemHandleFree(oldTextH);
}


Boolean MainFormHandleEvent(EventPtr event)
{
Boolean handled = false;
FormPtr frm;
      FieldPtr          fieldout;
      char *            infield_txt;
  char tmpPtr[20];
  FlpCompDouble theCompDouble;
  double in,r1,r2,r3;

switch (event->eType)
      {

    case ctlSelectEvent:
           if (event->data.ctlEnter.controlID == MainButton)
           {
            frm = FrmGetActiveForm();

// get pointer to the input field and corresp text
infield_txt =
   FldGetTextPtr(FrmGetObjectPtr(frm, FrmGetObjectIndex(frm,fieldID_inText)));

// do the actual conversions here; could be separate function

           in = my_atof(infield_txt);
           r1 = in * in;
           r2 = r1 * in;
           r3 = sqrt(in);


// get pointer to each of the output fields and set output text
// the handle to the first output field:
fieldout = FrmGetObjectPtr(frm, FrmGetObjectIndex(frm,fieldID_outText1));

// form outputs as strings
        theCompDouble.d = r1;
        FlpFToA(theCompDouble.fd, tmpPtr);
// call SetFieldHandle with modified output text
        SetFieldHandle(fieldout,tmpPtr);
// get next output field handle
fieldout = FrmGetObjectPtr(frm, FrmGetObjectIndex(frm,fieldID_outText2));

        theCompDouble.d = r2;
        FlpFToA(theCompDouble.fd, tmpPtr);

// call SetFieldHandle again with modified output text
        SetFieldHandle(fieldout,tmpPtr);
// and so forth
fieldout = FrmGetObjectPtr(frm, FrmGetObjectIndex(frm,fieldID_outText3));

theCompDouble.d = r3;
FlpFToA(theCompDouble.fd, tmpPtr);
```

```
SetFieldHandle(fieldout,tmpPtr);

            }// MainButton
            handled = true;
            break;

case frmOpenEvent:
frm = FrmGetActiveForm();
FrmDrawForm(frm);
            handled = true;
            break;

default:
            break;

}
return(handled);
}



Boolean ApplicationHandleEvent(EventPtr event)
{
FormPtr frm;
int formId;
Boolean handled = false;

if (event->eType == frmLoadEvent)
           {
formId = event->data.frmLoad.formID;
frm = FrmInitForm(formId);
FrmSetActiveForm(frm);
       FrmSetEventHandler(frm, MainFormHandleEvent);
handled = true;
      }
return handled;
}


void EventLoop(void)
{
EventType event;
Err error;

do
{
EvtGetEvent(&event, evtWaitForever);
if (! SysHandleEvent(&event))
if (! MenuHandleEvent(0, &event, &error))
if (! ApplicationHandleEvent(&event))
FrmDispatchEvent(&event);
}
while (event.eType != appStopEvent);
}
```

```
UInt32 PilotMain(UInt16 cmd, MemPtr cmdPBP, UInt16 launchFlags)
{
if (cmd == sysAppLaunchCmdNormalLaunch) {
if (StartApplication()) {
EventLoop();
StopApplication();
}
}

return 0;
}
```

Including the Numerical/Math Libraries

Using math functions like `exp`, `log`, and `sqrt` requires the math libraries. Remember that including `math.h` requires adding a switch to `gcc` for linking with the math library. This switch is of the form `-lm` and is shown in the following "makeshell" script:

```
m68k-palmos-gcc -c -g -Wall $1.c
m68k-palmos-gcc $1.o -lm -g -Wall -o $1
pilrc -q $1.rcp
build-prc $1.def $1 *.bin
```

14.5.4 Sample Operation of the Resulting Application

This is shown in Figures 14.20 and 14.21.

14.5.5 New Palm OS Functions

The new functions of interest are from the Palm OS Float Manager. Notice that these functions are declared in `FloatMgr.h`, which must be included in our C source.

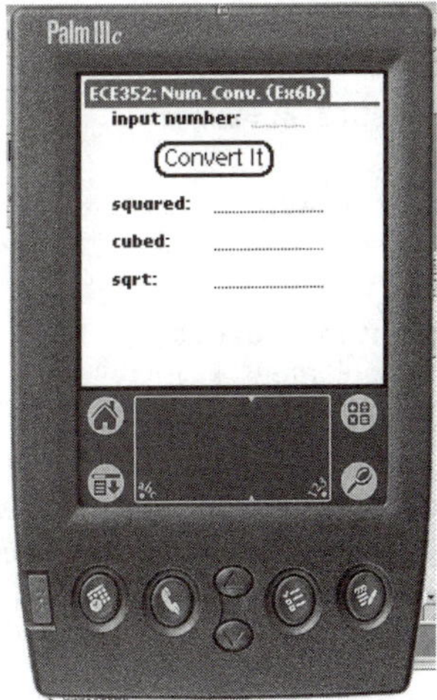

Figure 14.20 Initial Palm Display.

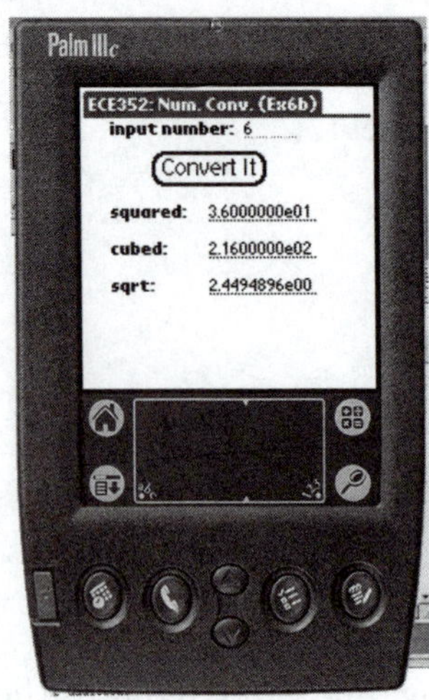

Figure 14.21 Palm Display after Input and Button Press.

```
FlpAToF

Purpose: Convert a null-terminated ASCII string to a
         64-bit floating-point
         number. The string must have the format:
         [+|-][digits][.][digits][e|E[+|-][digits]]

Prototype: FlpDouble FlpAToF (const Char *s)

Parameters: s Pointer to the string to be converted

Result: Returns the value of the string as a floating-point number

Comments: The mantissa of the number is limited to 32 bits.


FlpBufferAToF

Purpose: Convert a null-terminated ASCII string
          to a floating-point number.
          The string must be in the format:
          [-]x[.]yyyyyyyy[e[-]zz]

Prototype: void FlpBufferAToF (FlpDouble *result,
                               const Char *s)

Parameters: result Pointer to the structure into which the return
                   value is placed. result returns the value
                   of the string as a floating-point number.
                 s Pointer to the null-terminated ASCII string to
                   be converted.

Comments: See FlpAToF for a complete description of this function.
          GCC users must use this function instead of FlpAToF.
```

FlpFToA

```
Purpose: Convert a floating-point number to a
         null-terminated ASCII string
         in exponential format: [-]x.yyyyyyye[-]zz

Prototype: Err FlpFToA (FlpDouble a, Char *s)

Parameters: a Floating-point number.
            s Pointer to buffer to contain the ASCII string.

Result: Returns 0 if no error, or flpErrOutOfRange if the supplied value
        is infinite or is not a number. See Also FlpAToF.
```

14.6 Additional Palm OS Programming Notes and Features

14.6.1 Data Alerts

Data Alerts are one of the most programmer-friendly ways to incorporate an impromptu dialog with the user. Usually this is necessary when the program has (or should have) detected missing inputs, erroneous or out-of-range values, or other anomalies in the use of the Palm program. We illustrate the basic usage with a simple example.

An alert is actually a very limited form that displays an icon, a message, and one or more buttons that both provide user input and "dismiss" the dialog (i.e., close the form). In the resource specification file, as shown here, an `ALERT` resource is specified. Further customization of the alert with messages and buttons is shown. Note that in our example, we specify three buttons labeled `Restart`, `Stop`, and `Fire Coach`.

```
#include "dataalertex.h"

FORM ID MainForm AT ( 0 0 160 160 )
NOFRAME
USABLE MODAL
BEGIN
    TITLE "Data Alert Example"
    LABEL "Press The Button" ID AppLabel AT (30 60) FONT 1
    LABEL "* For Non-Academic Use Only *" ID WarnLabel AT (20 25) FONT 0
    BUTTON "Try Me   :-)" ID Button AT (50 130 80 15) USABLE BOLDFRAME FONT 0

END

ALERT ID DataAlert
CONFIRMATION
BEGIN
TITLE "Alert Example..."
MESSAGE "-- \n" \
         " Restart button restarts application (Duh)\n" \
         " Any other button stops it"
BUTTONS "Restart" "Stop" "Fire Coach"
END
```

From a programming viewpoint, the alert-based dialog is initiated using function `FrmAlert` with the ID of the desired `ALERT` resource as the argument (`DataAlert` in our example), as shown in the sample C code that begins on the next page.

```
// file: dataalert.c
// example of alert

#include <PalmOS.h>
#include "dataalertex.h"
#include <StringMgr.h>
#include <FloatMgr.h>


Boolean StartApplication(void)
{
FrmGotoForm(MainForm);
return true;
}


void StopApplication(void)
{
FrmCloseAllForms();
}


Boolean MainFormHandleEvent(EventPtr event)
{
Boolean handled = false;
FormPtr frm;
switch (event->eType)
      {
    case ctlSelectEvent:
           if (event->data.ctlEnter.controlID == Button)
              {
                if(FrmAlert(DataAlert) == 0) StartApplication();
                else StopApplication();
               } // Button

            handled = true;
            break;

case frmOpenEvent:
frm = FrmGetActiveForm();
FrmDrawForm(frm);
            handled = true;
            break;

default:
            break;

}
return(handled);
}



Boolean ApplicationHandleEvent(EventPtr event)
{
FormPtr frm;
int formId;
Boolean handled = false;
```

```
if (event->eType == frmLoadEvent)
          {
formId = event->data.frmLoad.formID;
frm = FrmInitForm(formId);
FrmSetActiveForm(frm);
          FrmSetEventHandler(frm, MainFormHandleEvent);
handled = true;
      }
return handled;
}


void EventLoop(void)
{
EventType event;
Err error;

do
{
EvtGetEvent(&event, evtWaitForever);
if (! SysHandleEvent(&event))
if (! MenuHandleEvent(0, &event, &error))
if (! ApplicationHandleEvent(&event))
FrmDispatchEvent(&event);
}
while (event.eType != appStopEvent);
}

/**************** main *********************************/

 UInt32 PilotMain(UInt16 cmd, MemPtr cmdPBP, UInt16 launchFlags)
{
if (cmd == sysAppLaunchCmdNormalLaunch) {
if (StartApplication()) {
EventLoop();
StopApplication();
}
}

return 0;
}
```

Once invoked, the `FrmAlert(DataAlert)` function waits for the user to press one of the displayed buttons. Notice, in our example, that pressing the main form "try me" button generates the event that invokes `FrmAlert(DataAlert)` and thus starts the dialog.

The key to reactive programming for this resource is the following observation:

> `FrmAlert(DataAlert)` *returns an integer corresponding to the button pressed. The leftmost button returns 0, the next button returns 1, and so forth. Once a button is pressed, the alert is removed.*

In the preceding example, when `FrmAlert(DataAlert)` returns 0, corresponding to the leftmost (i.e., `Restart`) button press, the application is restarted. When `FrmAlert(DataAlert)` returns 1 or 2 (corresponding to presses of the other two buttons), the application is stopped. Figure 14.22 shows the appearance of the alert on the emulator.

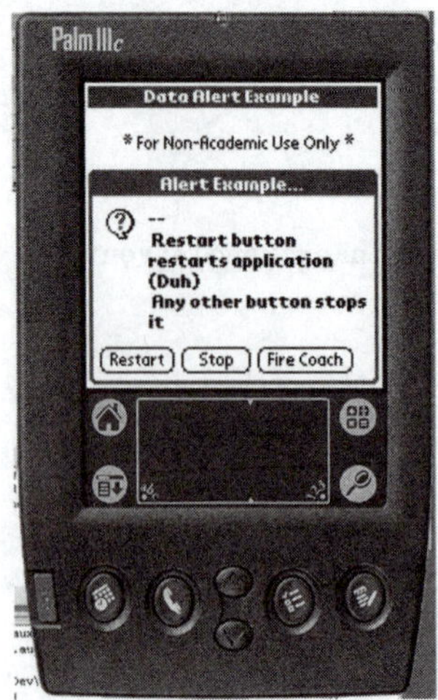

Figure 14.22 Sample Use of Alert-Based Dialog.

14.6.2 Local, Global, and Static Designators

The reader will note the frequent use of the C `static` descriptor in the examples. C provides this to allow control of *scope*. Recall that when applied to local function variables, the `static` descriptor requires the compiler to retain local variable values after the function exits.[10] This is sometimes useful in Palm application functions. Note that this does not have the effect of making variables global.[11] Global variables are known to all functions *and* global variable values are retained, whereas the scope of static variables is restricted to the block in which the function is defined and values are retained.

When `static` is applied to functions, we are implementing a form of "information hiding," wherein functions are unknown outside of the file in which they are defined.

14.6.3 The Application *.def File

Concept and Resources

When using the `prc-tools` development tools, application parameters may be specified to `build-prc` using an optional definition file. This approach has been used in all the examples in this chapter. The definition file may be used to specify various properties of the application, such as the application name, type of the application, whether the application is "beamable" (copy protection), database attributes, and requested stack space. A more complete description of `def` file syntax is available at:

`http://prc-tools.sourceforge.net/doc/`

An Example

The contents of the `def` file for the database application of Section 14.7.2 is shown here:

```
application { ``Auto Maint2'' AutoMaint2 stack=4096 }
```

[10]Otherwise, these values are lost, as local variables are destroyed.

[11]Global variables were dangerous in earlier versions of `prc- tools`.

This specification indicates, in order, the application name, the application creator ID, and 4K of stack space.[12]

14.6.4 Debugging

Although it may seem obvious, we restate one of the fundamental difficulties of debugging Palm applications: In Palm applications, you cannot use `printf` for debugging. Whereas many C programs may be debugged with a judicious sprinkling of `printf` throughout the source code to report and allow checking of intermediate quantities, this is not possible with the Palm. The reason is somewhat obvious: the Palm device has to have predefined "output" and the Palm OS does not recognize a `printf` function. All output must be displayed in or on forms and fields and other resources.

One (somewhat inelegant) approach to Palm application debugging is the judicious use of alerts to indicate impending or completed fundamental or important operations. This is shown in the database example of Section 14.7.2.

The available Palm emulator and associated debugger is quite useful for debugging. Readers are encouraged to investigate its use.

14.6.5 C Functions Versus the Palm OS Library

In many of the previous examples, C library functions were available to (presumably) accomplish the same objective as Palm OS library functions. An example is `atof`, from the C math library. Notice that the Float Manager function `FlpBufferAToF` was used instead (with corresponding Palm OS-defined data type `FlpCompDouble`). In general, it is good policy to use the Palm OS-supplied data structures and functions.

14.6.6 String Manager Functions

Some applications may require the input and output of integers (our previous example illustrated floating-point values). In line with the remarks made in Section 14.6.5, we note that the following Palm OS library functions are available in the String Manager library (declared in `StringMgr.h`) for the input and display of integer values.

```
StrAToI

Purpose:       Convert a string to an integer.

Prototype:   Int32 StrAToI (const Char *str)

Parameters: str Pointer to a string to convert.

Result:  Returns the integer representation (Int32 type)

Comments: Use this function instead of the standard atoi routine.
```

[12] 4K stack space is the default.

```
StrIToA

Purpose:  Convert an integer to ASCII.

Prototype:  Char *StrIToA (Char *s, Int32 i)
Parameters: s Pointer to a string of size maxStrIToALen in
               which to store the results.
            i Integer to convert.
Result: Returns a pointer to the result string.
```

Note that many other useful string manipulation functions are available, including `StrCat`, `StrCompare`, and `StrCopy`.

14.7 Implementing Databases on the Palm

The Palm OS has no inherent "traditional" file structure. In this section, we show the creation and updating of a Palm database for very simple automotive records. The relevant functions to facilitate this effort are summarized; many more are available. We will assume a simple Palm device configuration, that is, one memory card. In addition, we ignore the consequences of several applications sharing a database.

14.7.1 Dealing with Palm Databases

Overview

A database is a set of records of the same type. For purposes of the Palm, a record is a chunk of managed memory (managed by the Memory Manager set of functions). Databases are accessed by name, and individual records are indexed. The Palm OS (through the Data Manager set of functions) provides functions (see Section 14.7.3) that allow creating, opening, closing, deleting, and modifying databases. Be sure to include `<DataMgr.h>` in the source code to allow this. In summary:

1. A database is created or deleted, respectively, by functions `DmCreateDatabase` and `DmDeleteDatabase`.
2. A (usually) global variable of type `DmOpenRef` implements a handle to the (open) database.
3. `DmGetRecord` (or the "read-only" version `DmQueryRecord`) takes an index to and returns a handle to the database record.
4. As shown by the sample code in Section 14.7.2, database records are easily coded using `structs`.
5. Applications are responsible for closing their own databases upon termination.

Palm Documentation

The Palm OS developer's website has a useful overview (with examples) of database development at:

`www.palmos.com/dev/support/docs/recipes/recipe_basic_db_operations.html`

14.7.2 An Automotive Database Application

The code shown in this section implements a Palm application consisting of three interrelated forms that creates (or simply opens, if one exists) a Palm database for automotive maintenance record keeping. The structure of individual records in the database is:

```
UserName
last_interval
last_mileage (mileage at last service)
```

The overall strategy is simple and a number of the functions are familiar. Upon startup, the application displays a (login) form with a username login field and login button. Once the user provides (any) login name, a database is either created or opened. Following this, a second (choice) form lets the user go to a third (setup) form to edit database mileage fields or return to the login form.

Database Application Resource Specification

The following file defines the application resources:

```
#include "automaint2.h"

// Forms and Alerts
FORM ID MainForm AT (0 0 160 160)
MODAL
BEGIN
  TITLE "Auto Maintenance dB"
  LABEL "Welcome to the Auto" ID AppLabel1 AT (20 18) FONT 1
  LABEL " Maint. Database" ID AppLabel2 AT (20 36) FONT 1
  LABEL "Name:" ID loginLabel AT (20 60) FONT 0
  FIELD ID login_inText AT (60 60 60 13) UNDERLINED MAXCHARS 30
  BUTTON "Log In (reqd)" ID LoginButton AT (40 100 70 15) FONT 0 BOLDFRAME
END

FORM ID ChoiceForm AT (0 0 160 160)
MODAL
BEGIN
  TITLE "Auto Maintenance dB"
  FIELD ID welcomeField AT (25 15 120 15) FONT 0 NONEDITABLE
  LABEL "Enter Your Choice:" ID ChoiceLabel AT (25 40) FONT 1
  BUTTON "Setup Form" ID SetupButton AT (45 65 60 15) FONT 0 BOLDFRAME
  BUTTON "Back to Login Screen" ID ChoiceBackButton AT (35 95 85 15) FONT 0
BOLDFRAME
END

FORM ID SetupForm AT (20 20 160 160)
MODAL
BEGIN
  TITLE "Data Setup Form"
  LABEL " Enter/Modify Service Interval:" ID intervalLabel AT (0 20) FONT 0
  FIELD ID IntervalText AT (20 40 80 15) FONT 0 UNDERLINED MAXCHARS 70 NUMERIC
  LABEL " Enter/Modify Last Service Miles" ID mileageLabel AT (0 60) FONT 0
  FIELD ID LastMileageText AT (20 80 80 15) FONT 0 UNDERLINED MAXCHARS 70
NUMERIC
  BUTTON "Save to dB" ID SetupSaveButton AT (35 110 60 15) FONT 0 BOLDFRAME
END
```

```
ALERT ID dataAlert
CONFIRMATION
BEGIN
  TITLE "Forgot to Input Data?"
  MESSAGE "One or both input\n"\
          "fields are empty\n"\
          "OK Uses BOTH Default(s)\n"\
          "(0000 and 3000 mi)"
  BUTTONS "OK" "Restart"
END

ALERT ID loginAlert
INFORMATION
BEGIN
  TITLE "No Login Name ..."
  MESSAGE "Both New and \n"\
          "Old Users Must\n"\
          "Log In"
  BUTTONS "OK"
END

ALERT ID in_DBAlert
INFORMATION
BEGIN
  TITLE "Welcome Back"
  MESSAGE "You're in the dB!"
  BUTTONS "OK"
END

ALERT ID problem_openDBAlert
INFORMATION
BEGIN
  TITLE "Big Problem"
  MESSAGE "This database isn't going to open"
  BUTTONS "%^$&#(@!!!!"
END

ALERT ID exists_DBAlert
INFORMATION
BEGIN
  TITLE "Notice -- Database Exists"
  MESSAGE "A database already exists. I'll use it."
  BUTTONS "Sounds Good!"
END

ALERT ID name_problem_openDBAlert
INFORMATION
BEGIN
  TITLE "Name Problem"
  MESSAGE "DB Name No Good"
  BUTTONS "Shucks"
END
```

```
ALERT ID no_card_problem_openDBAlert
INFORMATION
BEGIN
  TITLE "No Card Problem"
  MESSAGE "Card Not Present"
  BUTTONS "Gosh"
END

ALERT ID memErrInvalidParameter_problem_openDBAlert
INFORMATION
BEGIN
  TITLE "Memory Problem"
  MESSAGE "Invalid Memory Parameter"
  BUTTONS "Darn"
END

ALERT ID closedDBAlert
INFORMATION
BEGIN
  TITLE "Closing Database"
  MESSAGE "Closed the DB -- Bye!"
  BUTTONS "OK"
END

ALERT ID badDBWrite
INFORMATION
BEGIN
  TITLE "DB Write Problem"
  MESSAGE "DmWrite != errNone"
  BUTTONS "Rats"
END
```

Using `pilrcedit`, a sample preview of two of the three GUI forms is shown in Figure 14.23.

Sample Database Application Code

The code shown here implements the application. The software has a few noteworthy features:

1. A number of alerts are used to illustrate database-related operations (and problems).
2. Each form has a separate event-handling function for events generated by resources within the form.
3. Users are required to log in (by simply providing a user name) or the application remains on the login form.
4. Default values for user-chosen or user-modifiable values are provided, following an alert.
5. When the application is stopped, the database is closed.

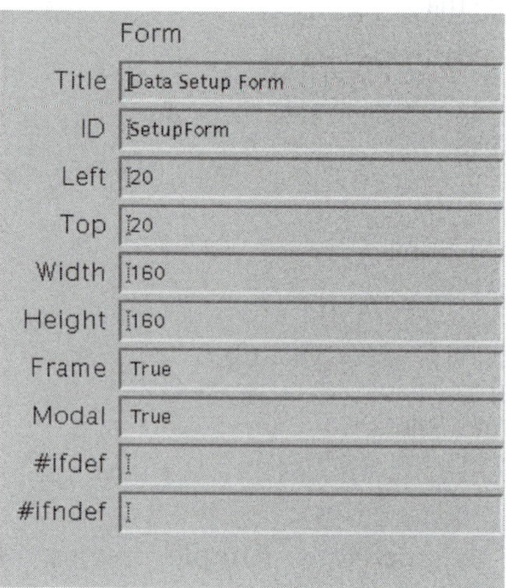

Figure 14.23 Example of Using `pilrcedit` for the Palm Database Application of Section 14.7.2.

```
#include <PalmOS.h>
#include "automaint2.h"
#include <StringMgr.h>
#include "stdio.h"
#include "string.h"
#include <DataMgr.h>

/* auto maintenance database example
   (simplified version)  11-24-03
   for automotive maintenance records
*/

DmOpenRef gDB;
typedef struct
{
  char UserName[20];
  Int32 last_interval;
  Int32 last_mileage;
} DBRecord;
```

```
typedef DBRecord DBRecordType;
typedef DBRecord *DBRecordPtr;
DBRecordType dbrec;
DBRecordPtr s;
MemHandle h;
MemPtr p;
Err err;
UInt16 index;
int in_DB;
FormPtr frm;
FieldPtr current_field;
char tmpPtr[80];
char *login_txt;
Int32 interval, mileage;
char *interval_txt;
char *mileage_txt;

/* function prototypes  */
static void SetFieldHandle (FieldPtr ptrToField, MemPtr ptrToText);
static Boolean StartApplication (void);
static void StopApplication (void);
static Boolean MainFormHandleEvent (EventPtr event);
static Boolean ApplicationHandleEvent (EventPtr event);
static Boolean ChoiceFormHandleEvent (EventPtr event);
static Boolean SetupFormHandleEvent (EventPtr event);
static void EventLoop (void);
Int32 check_user (char *user, DmOpenRef db);

static Boolean StartApplication (void)
{
/* database opening/creation here
   see if DB exists; create if not */
  err = DmCreateDatabase (0, "automDB1", 'Robt', 'DATA', false);

// check for some (serious) errors
  if (err == dmErrInvalidDatabaseName)
    FrmAlert (name_problem_openDBAlert);
  if (err == memErrCardNotPresent)
    FrmAlert (no_card_problem_openDBAlert);
  if (err == dmErrMemError)
    FrmAlert (memErrInvalidParameter_problem_openDBAlert);

// DB already exists
  if (err == dmErrAlreadyExists)
    {
      FrmAlert (exists_DBAlert);
      gDB = DmOpenDatabaseByTypeCreator ('DATA', 'Robt', dmModeReadWrite);
      if (!gDB)
FrmAlert (problem_openDBAlert); // big problem
    }

// check successsful opening of DB
  if (err == errNone)
    {
      gDB = DmOpenDatabaseByTypeCreator ('DATA', 'Robt', dmModeReadWrite);
      if (!gDB)
FrmAlert (problem_openDBAlert); // big problem
    }
```

```
// start MainForm display (generate 2 events)
  FrmGotoForm (MainForm);
  return true;
}

void
StopApplication (void)
{

// close the DB
  if (gDB)
    DmResetRecordStates (gDB); // good policy
  if (gDB)
    DmCloseDatabase (gDB);
  FrmAlert (closedDBAlert);

// close open forms
  FrmCloseAllForms ();
}

static Boolean
ApplicationHandleEvent (EventPtr event)
{
  FormPtr frm;
  int formId;
  Boolean handled = false;
  if (event->eType == frmLoadEvent)

    {
      formId = event->data.frmLoad.formID;
      frm = FrmInitForm (formId);
      FrmSetActiveForm (frm);
      FrmSetEventHandler (frm, MainFormHandleEvent);
      handled = true;
    }
  return handled;
}

static Boolean
MainFormHandleEvent (EventPtr event)
{
  Boolean handled = false;
  switch (event->eType)

    {
    case ctlSelectEvent:
      if (event->data.ctlEnter.controlID == LoginButton)

{
  frm = FrmGetActiveForm ();

  /* get pointer to the login name field and corresp text */
  login_txt =
    FldGetTextPtr (FrmGetObjectPtr
   (frm, FrmGetObjectIndex (frm, login_inText)));
```

```
// check on empty login name field before proceeding
  if (login_txt == NULL)
    FrmAlert (loginAlert);
  else
    {

// now get pointer to (new) output form and go there
      FrmSetActiveForm (FrmInitForm (ChoiceForm));
      frm = FrmGetActiveForm ();
      FrmSetEventHandler (frm, ChoiceFormHandleEvent);
// setup ChoiceForm
      strcpy (tmpPtr, "Welcome,  ");
      strcat (tmpPtr, login_txt);
      strcat (tmpPtr, " !");
      current_field =
FrmGetObjectPtr (frm, FrmGetObjectIndex (frm, welcomeField));
      SetFieldHandle (current_field, tmpPtr);
      FrmDrawForm (frm);
    } //else
} // if LoginButton


      handled = true;
      break;

    case frmOpenEvent:
      frm = FrmGetActiveForm ();
      FrmDrawForm (frm);
      handled = true;
      break;

    default:
      break;
    }
  return (handled);
}

static Boolean
ChoiceFormHandleEvent (EventPtr event)
{
  Boolean handled = false;
  switch (event->eType)
    {
    case ctlSelectEvent:
      if (event->data.ctlEnter.controlID == SetupButton)

{
  FrmSetActiveForm (FrmInitForm (SetupForm));
  frm = FrmGetActiveForm ();
  FrmSetEventHandler (frm, SetupFormHandleEvent);

/* see if user has an interval in the DB. If so, display it
  (for possible user modification)
  otherwise, just wait for one to be entered */

  if ((index = check_user (login_txt, gDB)) != -1)
    { // there is a matching record
      if (FrmAlert (in_DBAlert))
```

```
h = DmQueryRecord (gDB, index);
      s = MemHandleLock (h);
      interval = s->last_interval;
      StrIToA (tmpPtr, interval);
      current_field =
FrmGetObjectPtr (frm, FrmGetObjectIndex (frm, IntervalText));
      SetFieldHandle (current_field, tmpPtr);
      mileage = s->last_mileage;
      StrIToA (tmpPtr, mileage);
      current_field =
FrmGetObjectPtr (frm,
 FrmGetObjectIndex (frm, LastMileageText));
      SetFieldHandle (current_field, tmpPtr);
      MemHandleUnlock (h);
    } //if a matching record exists
  FrmDrawForm (frm);
} //SetupButton

      if (event->data.ctlEnter.controlID == ChoiceBackButton)
{
  FrmSetActiveForm (FrmInitForm (MainForm));
  frm = FrmGetActiveForm ();
  FrmSetEventHandler (frm, MainFormHandleEvent);
  FrmDrawForm (frm);
}
    default:
      break;
    }
  return (handled);
}


static Boolean
SetupFormHandleEvent (EventPtr event)
{
  Boolean handled = false;
  switch (event->eType)
    {
    case ctlSelectEvent:


      if (event->data.ctlEnter.controlID == SetupSaveButton)

{

// get pointers to the interval and last service mileage fields and corresp text
  frm = FrmGetActiveForm ();
  interval_txt =
    FldGetTextPtr (FrmGetObjectPtr
   (frm, FrmGetObjectIndex (frm, IntervalText)));
  mileage_txt =
    FldGetTextPtr (FrmGetObjectPtr
   (frm, FrmGetObjectIndex (frm, LastMileageText)));

// check on empty data fields first
// defaults are 0000 miles and 3000 interval
  if ((mileage_txt == NULL) || (interval_txt == NULL))
```

```
    {
      if (FrmAlert (dataAlert) == 1) // user wants to restart
{
  // close the DB
  if (gDB)
    DmResetRecordStates (gDB);
  if (gDB)
    DmCloseDatabase (gDB);
  FrmAlert (closedDBAlert);
  // then restart
  StartApplication ();
}

      else
{
  mileage = 0000;
  interval = 3000;
}
    }

  else
    {
      interval = StrAToI (interval_txt);
      mileage = StrAToI (mileage_txt);
    }
// put new or modified user info in DB
  if (check_user (login_txt, gDB) == -1) // not in DB
    {
      h = DmNewRecord (gDB, &index, sizeof (dbrec));
      StrCopy (dbrec.UserName, login_txt);
      dbrec.last_interval = interval;
      dbrec.last_mileage = mileage;

// now write it
      if (h) // could fail due to out of memory
{
  p = MemHandleLock (h);
  if (DmWrite (p, 0, &dbrec, sizeof (dbrec)) != errNone)
    FrmAlert (badDBWrite); // might need to check returned value
  MemPtrUnlock (p);
  DmReleaseRecord (gDB, index, true);
}
    }
  else // in DB
    {
      index = check_user (login_txt, gDB);
      h = DmGetRecord (gDB, index); // existing
      StrCopy (dbrec.UserName, login_txt);
      dbrec.last_interval = interval;
      dbrec.last_mileage = mileage;
      p = MemHandleLock (h);
      if (DmWrite (p, 0, &dbrec, sizeof (dbrec)) != errNone)
FrmAlert (badDBWrite); // might need to check returned value
      MemPtrUnlock (p);
      DmReleaseRecord (gDB, index, true);
    } // revision of record (old user)
```

```
  // now go to choice form
  FrmSetActiveForm (FrmInitForm (ChoiceForm));
  frm = FrmGetActiveForm ();
  FrmSetEventHandler (frm, ChoiceFormHandleEvent);
  FrmDrawForm (frm);
} // SetupSaveButton
    default:
      break;
    }
  return (handled);
}


static void
EventLoop (void)
{
  EventType event;
  Err error;

  do

    {
      EvtGetEvent (&event, evtWaitForever);
      if (!SysHandleEvent (&event))
if (!MenuHandleEvent (0, &event, &error))
  if (!ApplicationHandleEvent (&event))
    FrmDispatchEvent (&event);
    }
  while (event.eType != appStopEvent);
}

/***************** main **********************************/

UInt32
PilotMain (UInt16 cmd, MemPtr cmdPBP, UInt16 launchFlags)
{
  if (cmd == sysAppLaunchCmdNormalLaunch)
    {
      if (StartApplication ())
{
  EventLoop ();
  StopApplication ();
}
    }
  return 0;
}

// database auxiliary functions
Int32
check_user (char *user, DmOpenRef db)
{

/* returns index of record for user; else -1
   only used for finding index; does not lock record
   assumes DB open and UserName appears at most once in DB
*/
```

```
  Int32 index;
  Int32 found = -1;
  UInt16 numrecs;

// first, how many records in DB
  numrecs = DmNumRecords (gDB);
// note: record 0 is first record
  if (numrecs > 0)
    {
      for (index = 0; index < numrecs; index++)
{
  h = DmQueryRecord (gDB, index); // 'read-only' version
  s = MemHandleLock (h); // now have pointer to struct
  if (!StrCompare (s->UserName, user))
    {
      found = index;
      MemHandleUnlock (h);
      return found;
    }
  MemHandleUnlock (h);
}
    } // numrecs>0
  return found;
}

static void
SetFieldHandle (FieldPtr ptrToField, MemPtr ptrToText)
{
  MemHandle newTextH; // new field text
  MemHandle oldTextH; // text that may already be in the field
  MemPtr tempPtr; // pointer to newTextH.

  // Allocate handle to store the new text + 1 extra
  newTextH = MemHandleNew (StrLen (ptrToText) + 1);
  // Get pointer to memory and lock.
  tempPtr = MemHandleLock (newTextH);
  // Copy text to pointer
  StrCopy (tempPtr, ptrToText);
  // get old text handle
  oldTextH = FldGetTextHandle (ptrToField);
  // Set the fields new text.
  FldSetTextHandle (ptrToField, newTextH);
  // unlock the new text handle
  MemHandleUnlock (newTextH);
  // update the field
  FldDrawField (ptrToField);
  // Free the old text handle to prevent a memory leak
  if (oldTextH != NULL)
    MemHandleFree (oldTextH);
}


// that's all folks!
```

14.7.3 Relevant Palm OS Database Functions

DmCreateDatabase

Purpose: Create a new database on the specified card with the given name, creator, and type

```
Prototype: Err DmCreateDatabase (UInt16 cardNo,
                                 const Char *nameP, UInt32 creator, UInt32 type,
                                 Boolean resDB)
```

```
Parameters: cardNo The card number to create the database on
            nameP Name of new database
            creator Creator of the database
            type Type of the database
            resDB If true, create a resource database
```

Result: Returns errNone if no error, or one of a number of predefined error codes

DmOpenDatabaseByTypeCreator

Purpose: Open the most recent revision of a database with the given type and creator

```
Prototype: DmOpenRef DmOpenDatabaseByTypeCreator
                               (UInt32 type, UInt32 creator, UInt16 mode)
```

```
Parameters: type Type of database.
            creator Creator of database.
            mode Which mode to open database in
```

Result: DmOpenRef to open database (if succeeds)

DmCloseDatabase

Purpose: Close a database.

Prototype Err DmCloseDatabase (DmOpenRef dbP)
Parameters: dbP Database access pointer

Result: Returns errNone if no error, or dmErrInvalidParam if an error occurs

Comment: This routine doesn't unlock any records that were left locked.

DmQueryRecord

Purpose: Return a handle to a record for reading only

```
Prototype: MemHandle DmQueryRecord (DmOpenRef dbP,
                                    UInt16 index)
```

```
Parameters: dbP DmOpenRef to open database.
            index Which record to retrieve.
```

Result: Returns a record handle. If an error occurs, this function returns NULL, and DmGetLastErr returns an error code indicating the reason for failure

DmNewRecord

```
Purpose: Return a handle to a new record in the database and mark the
         record busy

Prototype: MemHandle DmNewRecord (DmOpenRef dbP, UInt16 *atP,
                                  UInt32 size)

Parameters: dbP DmOpenRef to open database
            atP Pointer to index where new record should be placed
            size Size of new record

Result: Handle to record data
```

DmWrite

```
Purpose: Copies a specified number of bytes to a record within a database
          that is open for writing

Prototype: Err DmWrite (void *recordP, UInt32 offset,
                        const void *srcP, UInt32 bytes)

Parameters: recordP Pointer to locked data record (chunk pointer)
            offset Offset within record to start writing
            srcP Pointer to data to copy into record
            bytes Number of bytes to write

Result: Returns errNone if no error
```

DmGetRecord

```
Purpose: Return a handle to a record by index and mark the record busy

Prototype: MemHandle DmGetRecord (DmOpenRef dbP, UInt16 index)

Parameters dbP DmOpenRef to open database
           index Which record to retrieve

Result: Returns a handle to record data

Comment: Returns a handle to given record and sets the busy bit for the
record
```

14.8 Bibliographical Remarks and References

14.8.1 Books

An excellent introduction to Palm OS programming is Rhodes and McKeehan (2001). Another is Foster (2000). Both of these books include background material on the Palm OS, as well as coverage of development using *both* the `gcc` tool chain and the commercial "Codewarrior" IDE.

14.8.2 Palm Web-Based Resources

There are very important resources for Palm development and installation instructions at:

`http://www.PalmOS.com/dev/tools/gcc/`

Here you will find the gcc-based tools for Windows and Linux development platforms. Moreover, significant documentation, tutorials, and examples are downloadable.

14.9 Exercises

1. Readers may initially feel that the code structure used in the very simple example of Section 14.2.7 is overly structured and unnecessary. To this end:

   (a) revise the formulation so that all code is contained in the `PilotMain` function.

   (b) discuss the suitability of this revised formulation with respect to readability, extendability, and efficiency.

2. This exercise helps the understanding (and debugging) of Palm applications. Revise the second Palm programming example from Section 14.3 so that an alert is generated before and after each event is handled.

3. This exercise is similar to the previous exercise. Revise the Palm programming example from Section 14.5 so that an alert is generated before and after each number is input and the corresponding conversion.

4. This problem illustrates how the simple database example may be expanded into a true automotive service advisor application. Revise the application of Section 14.7.2 to include a field on the setup form where the user enters the current vehicle mileage. In addition, provide an additional button "Advise" that, when pressed, takes the user to a fourth form that indicates the following:

   (a) The difference between the last service mileage (from the database) and the current mileage.

   (b) Whether this difference exceeds the user's chosen service interval (from the database).

   (c) If the interval is exceeded, a popup indicates immediate service is required. If not, the mileage remaining is displayed on the fourth form.

5. Further enhance the revised application in the previous problem by adding another field to the database that holds a user-entered string indicating any specific maintenance done at the last service. Note this requires some thought regarding how to efficiently implement a variable-length string. Provide a default (e.g., "none") entry if the user does not provide one.

6. Section 14.2.7 indicates a rudimentary technique to switch forms in a Palm application. Extend this technique (and code example) to the commonly encountered case where it is necessary to be able to return to the last-encountered form.

7. Palm provides several references on the structure and contents of a `prc` file. Look up the format of the `prc` file and, using a binary editor (see Chapter 1), check the contents of the files generated by the examples in this chapter.

8. This problem considers the development of software for a "hangman" (character guessing in a phrase) game. Three phases are used for the software development, resulting in three applications. One is text based (Win32 **or** Linux); two are Palm applications with different complexity. Specifically, the figures show examples of the desired functionality for:

   (a) Version 0: The Win32 or Linux text version (Fig. 14.24).

   (b) Version 1: The simplest Palm version (Fig. 14.25).

   (c) Version 2: The Palm version with bitmaps and more functionality (Fig. 14.26).

9. This problem summarizes our look at event-driven programming in the previous and present chapters.

   (a) What is the event loop, and why is it important?

   (b) How (specifically) is the event loop implemented in each of the following programming approaches:

      i. Microsoft Windows (using the MFC)

      ii. X Windows (X11)

      iii. Palm OS

      iv. OpenGL

10. **Note: Numerous additional examples and exercises are available on the book website.**

```
$ ./txt_hangman

Welcome to hangman; you get 6 misses

Here's the problem:
---- --- ----

input guess as a single character, then press Enter  --> a
For guess number 1
    you guessed a

previous guesses are: a

here's the revised problem:
---- --- ----
You currently have 1 misses

input guess as a single character, then press Enter  --> e
For guess number 2
    you guessed e

previous guesses are: ae
```

Figure 14.24 Text Version of Hangman as Prelude to Palm Development.

```
here's the revised problem:
__e_ __e e__e
You currently have 1 misses

input guess as a single character, then press Enter  --> r
For guess number 3
    you guessed r

previous guesses are: aer

here's the revised problem:
__er __e e__e
You currently have 1 misses

input guess as a single character, then press Enter  --> t
For guess number 4
    you guessed t

previous guesses are: aert

here's the revised problem:
__er t_e e__e
You currently have 1 misses

input guess as a single character, then press Enter  --> h
For guess number 5
    you guessed h

previous guesses are: aerth

here's the revised problem:
__er the e__e
You currently have 1 misses

input guess as a single character, then press Enter  --> o
For guess number 6
    you guessed o

previous guesses are: aertho

here's the revised problem:
o_er the e__e
You currently have 1 misses

input guess as a single character, then press Enter  --> v
For guess number 7
    you guessed v

previous guesses are: aerthov

here's the revised problem:
over the e__e
You currently have 1 misses
```

Figure 14.24 (continued)

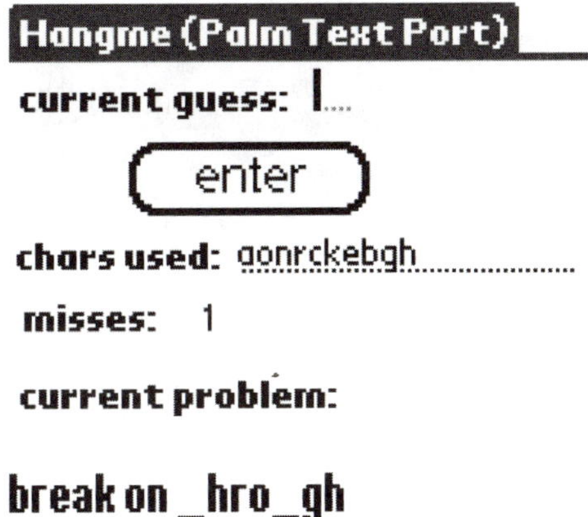

Figure 14.25 First Palm Version of Hangman; Basically a Text Port.

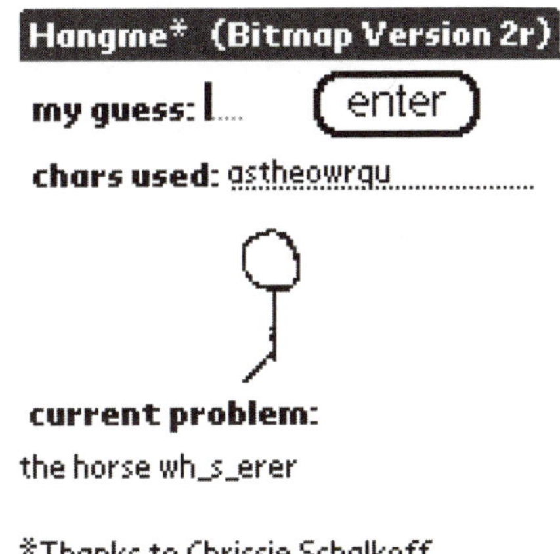

Figure 14.26 Final Palm Version of Hangman Incorporating Bitmaps.

CHAPTER 15

Parallel Computing and Parallel Programming

Applying computer technology is simply finding the right wrench to pound in the correct screw.
—Unknown

15.1 Introduction

There is both significant interest in and a significant need for developing parallel algorithms and parallel implementations for many computational tasks. For example, algorithms for search, optimization, constraint satisfaction, production systems, and pattern and graph matching are excellent candidates for parallel implementation. Note that the subject of how a parallel machine is to be designed and/or programmed is an open question at this point in time.

This chapter presents the rudiments of parallel programming. Advanced topics, such as distributed and parallel file systems and distributed I/O, are not addressed.

15.1.1 Problems, Algorithms, and Implementations

The issues of parallel programming involve the concepts of parallel algorithm decomposition and parallel hardware development and subsequent processing. This, of course, is a function of the language(s) chosen. Most importantly, we stress that the achievement of parallel processing is not simply the consequence of producing massively parallel computing architectures. Figure 15.1 shows a number of possible approaches.

In describing parallel computer architectures, the development of parallel programming languages to accompany these hardware devices must be considered. A very real and significant problem is how to (perhaps automatically) decompose a given processing task into one that may be executed in parallel segments. It is this task that currently borders on being more of an art than an exact science, although as we show, there are some engineering guidelines and current successes.

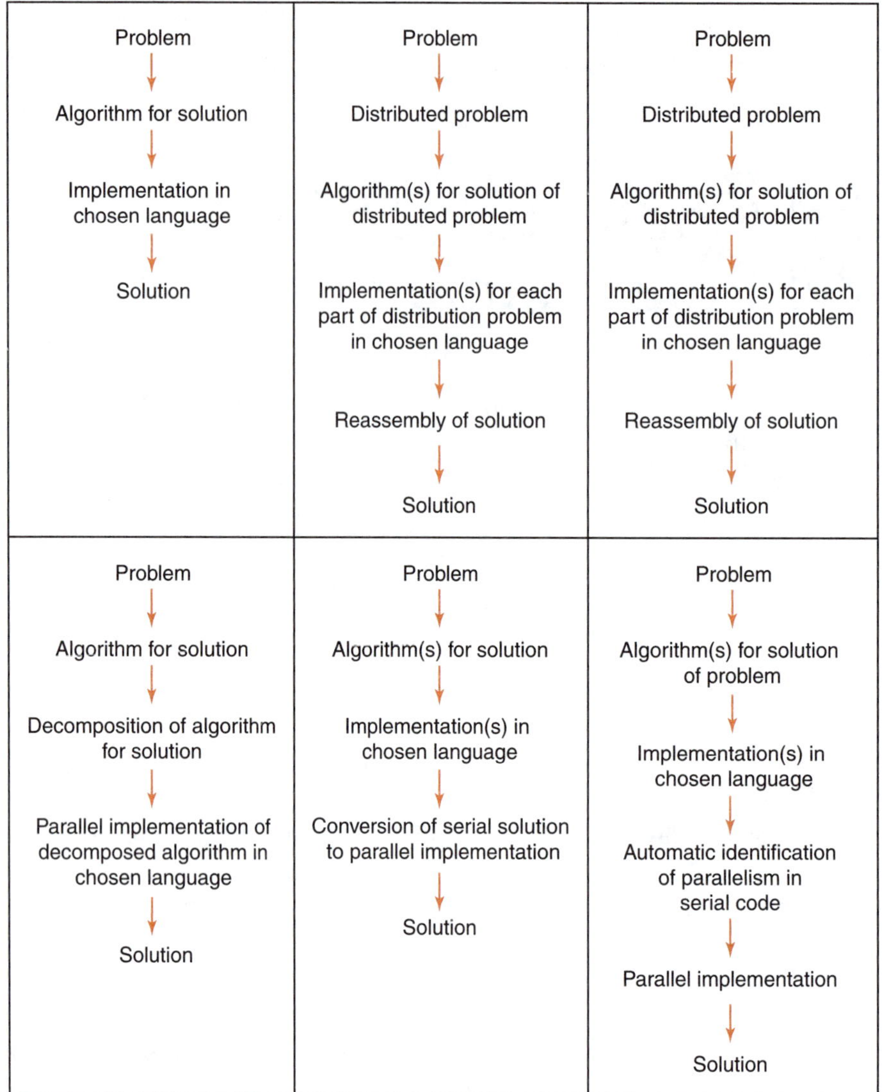

Figure 15.1 Various Problem-Solving Approaches.

15.1.2 Why Is Parallel Programming a Separate Programming Issue?

There are two main reasons we consider the topic of parallel programming as a separate issue:

1. Most of us are accustomed to a serial programming mindset.

   In most cases, the first, if not all, programming languages that we learn are serial (and imperative). We are taught to use the syntax and semantics of a programming language to articulate (to the compiler) *WHAT* computation is desired, with implied serial evaluation of statements. Seldom, if ever, do we consider *WHEN* the computation could be performed, perhaps in concert with others.

   As time passes, the availability of parallel processing paradigms and programming languages may change this.

```
a=10;
b=sqrt(a);
c=a+b;
d=6;
e=sqrt(d);
f=d+e;
g=f+c;
```

Figure 15.2 Simple `minic` Code Fragment for Potential Parallelism Analysis.

2. Much of the effort in developing a parallel processing-based solution to a problem requires an effort to *decompose* the problem into a form amenable for parallelism. Specifically:

    (a) Where is the parallelism?

    (b) How do I articulate/exploit it in my program?

    This effort usually requires some consideration of the underlying computational architecture. For example, interprocess(or) communication costs or overhead must be considered.

15.1.3 A Simple `minic` Example

Consider the simple `minic` code fragment shown in Figure 15.2. Most readers should be able to informally identify parts of this code that are suitable for parallel execution. For example, two blocks:

```
a=10;                d=6;
b=sqrt(a);           e=sqrt(d);
c=a+b;               f=d+e;
```

could be computed concurrently. However, the computation required by

```
g=f+c;
```

must necessarily follow these computations.

Another serious obstacle to parallelization of imperative languages involves the use of control or conditional constructs. For example, consider the code in Figure 15.3. Clearly identifying parallelism in this case is more challenging.

```
scanf(''\i '', a);
b=sqrt(a);
if (b<4) then
    if (a==1) b=4;
c=a+b;
d=6;
if (c>a) then d=1;
e=sqrt(d);
if (e>a) then e=1;
f=d+e;
g=f+c;
```

Figure 15.3 `minic` Code Fragment with Conditional Constructs.

15.1.4 Interrelated Parallel Concepts

This chapter provides an introduction to a number of concepts associated with parallel computing, including:

- parallel processing architectures.
- parallel processing applications.
- parallel algorithm decomposition.
- parallel program decomposition.
- parallel programming and parallel programming tools and environments.

15.1.5 "Can't We Just Increase the Clock Speed?"

It is assumed that the reader is familiar with the concept of the Von Neumann (sequential) computing model.

Despite amazing gains in processing speed[1] and available memory size, there are reasons to expect that real-time processing requirements will be met not simply via faster hardware. Rather, this goal will be achieved using different hardware and software architectures. In the near future, it may not be possible to speed up a particular processor by simply increasing clock speed. This is due to the fact that propagation delays of integrated circuit gates are approaching the speed of electricity in a wire, which is a theoretical limit. Thus, an obvious approach to overcome this obstacle is based upon the following observation:

> *In implementing a given algorithm, if we are unable to increase processor speed to meet requirements, an alternative is to distribute the algorithm or computation over an ensemble of processors and thereby achieve speedup (over the single-processor implementation) due to the concurrency of the implementation.*

This is the principal area subset of parallel processing that we explore. On the basis of this, we identify three issues related to the design of parallel solutions:

1. The design of programming languages with a parallel capability (either under the control of—or alternately, transparent to—the programmer).
2. The programmer's efficient use of these languages or language extensions.
3. The implementation of these languages on suitable hardware architectures.

15.1.6 Computational Complexity

In order to study the efficiency and behavior of algorithms and corresponding implementations, two entities are required:

1. A model of the computation
2. A complexity measure

[1] See the section on Moore's Law in Chapter 1.

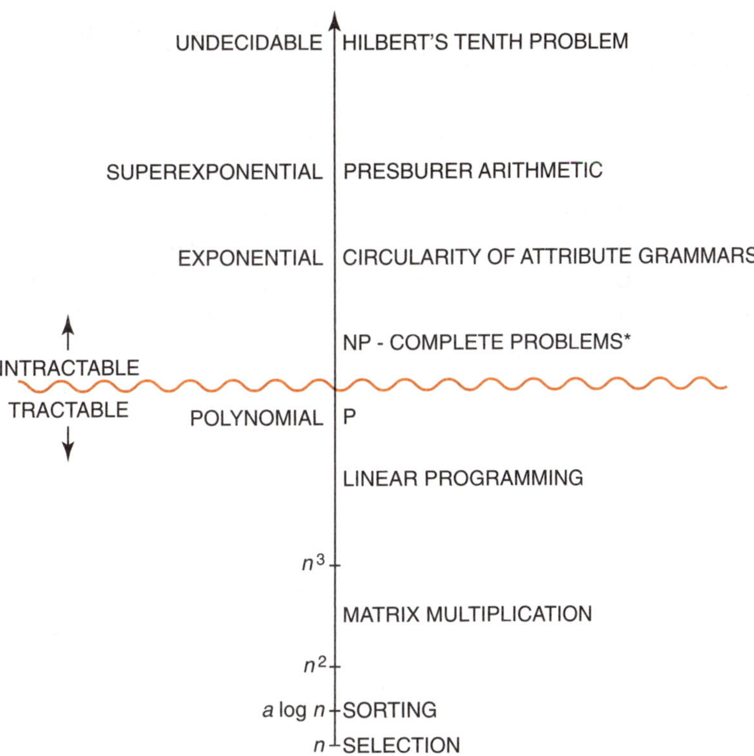

Figure 15.4 The Spectrum of Computational Complexity.

A hierarchy of complexity functions exists. Following the approach of Tarjan (1983), we denote an efficient algorithm as one whose worst-case running time is bounded by a polynomial function of the problem size. Tractable problems have efficient algorithms; intractable problems do not. We note that even tractable problems become gradually unusable. This is shown in Figure 15.4.

In computing program execution time estimates on the basis of operations per second and total required operations, it is useful to note that 10^8 seconds = 3 years. From Figure 15.5, observe how the complexity of seemingly innocuous problems, when scaled to a larger n, often results in unacceptable computing times.

Growth	1	20	50	100	1,000	10,000	100,000	1,000,000
n	1×10^{-6} sec	20×10^{-6} sec	50×10^{-6} sec	1×10^{-4} sec	1×10^{-3} sec	1×10^{-2} sec	0.1 sec	1 sec
n^2	1×10^{-6} sec	4×10^{-4} sec	2.5×10^{-2} sec	1×10^{-2} sec	1.0 sec	1.67 min	2.78 hours	11.6 days
n^3	1×10^{-6} sec	8×10^{-3} sec	2.5×10^{-3} sec	1.25×10^{-1} sec	16.8 min	11.6 days	3.17×10^5 CENT	—
2^n	2×10^{-6} sec	1.05 sec	35.7 years	4.02×10^{14} CENT	—	—	—	—
$\exp(n)$	2.7×10^{-6} sec	8.10 min	1.65×10^6 CENT	—	—	—	—	—

Figure 15.5 Sample Growth of Problem Complexity.

We define an algorithm as polynomial time (P) if its complexity function is polynomial. A nonpolynomial time (NP) algorithm has a complexity function that dominates every polynomial function.

Referring to Figure 15.5, for example, we note that the exponential function dominates any polynomial, and is thus nonpolynomial. A useful consequence of this categorization is that NP functions, when n increases, get large (unmanageable) at an alarming rate. Mathematicians have discovered a large class of problems that are NP-complete.[2] Using the best methods known, the complexity of NP-complete problems grows exponentially. An example is the so-called "traveling salesman" problem. From this figure, it is clear that the modification of algorithms (with reasonable heuristics, for example) to avoid NP-complete (or worse) complexities is desirable. This may lead to algorithms that do not guarantee a solution, but may run with P complexity.[3]

15.1.7 Space (Area)–Time Tradeoffs

Even very fast uniprocessor architectures are inadequate for many current or projected computing tasks. This has generated significant interest into the area of parallel processing, that is, identifying subtasks that may be independently implemented in a time-parallel manner. Usually, this process assumes replication of the spatial or physical hardware, therefore leading to space–time tradeoffs.

In numerical applications the identification of potential processing concurrency is often quite obvious. For example, operations involving vector quantities suggest the obvious desirability of emulating this data structure in hardware; hence the creation of array processors (not to be confused with arrays of processors). In contrast, problems in symbolic manipulation often do not suggest any obvious decomposition.

15.1.8 Parallel Performance and Limitations

Measures of the performance of parallel computing architectures are of fundamental importance to their systematic, structured development and application. Intuitively, one might hope that an n processor implementation of an algorithm or parallelized program will achieve the result in $1/n$ of the time required by a single processor working on the same problem. In this case, the product of the overall processing time and hardware complexity is constant. Unfortunately, this is at best an upper bound on the achievable speedup; the actual performance increase is less impressive. This result is due to the result of:

- the processing time necessary for communication (e.g., sharing of data or results) between processors.
- the fact that processors may have to wait for the results of other processors (i.e., the process was not completely decomposable into a parallel algorithm).
- the fact that some area of data memory may need to be shared by several processors (and therefore contention for memory resources may occur).

[2] We'll ignore what "complete" means.
[3] An interesting trade-off!

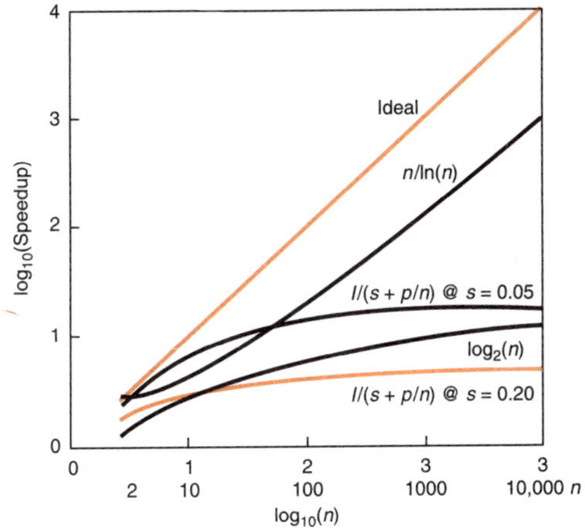

Speed Comparisons

n(# processors (Ideal Speedup)	Minsky $\log_2(n)$	Optimistic (Hwang/Briggs) ($n/\ln(n)$)	Amdahl's Law ($1/(s+p/n)$) $s = 0.05$	$s = 0.20$
4	2.0	2.9	3.5	2.5
10	3.3	4.3	6.9	3.6
100	6.6	21.7	16.8	4.8
1,000	10.0	144.8	19.6	5.0
10,000	13.3	1,086.0	20.0	5.0

Figure 15.6 Speedup Measures.

15.1.9 Metrics for Measuring or Predicting Speedup

Defining Speedup

For a parallel implementation, we define *speedup* as the following ratio:

$$speedup = \frac{\text{processing time with single processor}}{\text{processing time with } n \text{ processors}} = \frac{t_s}{t_p} \tag{15.1}$$

On this basis, the theoretically achievable maximum speedup for an n-processor implementation of an algorithm is n. Due to reasons cited previously, actual speedup may be observed and/or predicted to be less than this value.

Minsky's Conjecture

One historically significant measure is Minsky's conjecture, which states that the actual speedup is $\log_2(n)$. This, as Figure 15.6 indicates, is somewhat disappointing, especially for large processor numbers. Consequently, the economics of large processor implementations, in cases where Minsky's conjecture holds, favor fewer but faster processors. An alternate speedup measure, proposed as an upper bound (Hwang and Briggs, 1984), is $\frac{n}{ln(n)}$. This is a more optimistic bound. Minsky's conjecture and the Hwang/Briggs bound assume some (unstated) amount of necessary serial computation.

Amdahl's Law

Another approach, which is known as Amdahl's law, explicitly predicts speedup as a function of the fraction of required serial computations in a given algorithm. Defining the following quantities:

s: The fraction of computations that are necessarily serial.

p: The fraction of computations that may be done in parallel (note $s + p = 1$).

n: Number of processors over which p is distributed.

Amdahl's law predicts speedup as:

$$speedup = \frac{(s+p)}{(s+p/n)} = \frac{1}{(s+p/n)} \tag{15.2}$$

In general, Amdahl's law is a pessimistic bound on achievable speedup, even for small values of s ($< 5\%$). Note that, according to Amdahl's law, speedup approaches $\frac{1}{s}$ for large n. Figure 15.6 compares these measures. The measure of speedup, therefore, is highly dependent upon the desired overall operation, the decomposition chosen, and the specific architecture chosen to implement the decomposed algorithm.

15.2 Algorithm Decomposition Techniques and Tools

15.2.1 Types of Parallelism

Parallelism is defined in several ways. *Algorithmic parallelism* (AP) involves decomposition of an algorithm into component operations, which in turn may be executed in parallel. *Data parallelism* (DP) involves decomposition of the input data into partitions over which the operation may be carried out independently, and thus in parallel. A similar taxonomy attributed to Flynn (1972) is that of partitioning the process according to instructions (I) and data (D). By considering the manner in which a given architecture treats these entities to achieve concurrency, several classes of processors result. A processor architecture that executes a single instruction on a single datum is a single instruction/single data stream (SISD) architecture. This architecture is typified by the familiar uniprocessor or Von Neumann paradigm. An architecture wherein a single instruction is executed on more than one datum is referred to as a single instruction/multiple data stream (SIMD) machine. An architecture wherein independent instructions may be applied to a multiple data stream is termed a multiple instruction/multiple data stream (MIMD) machine.

15.2.2 Data Flow Graphs

The heart of any parallelization effort is the identification of potential concurrency for the algorithm implementation.

15.2.3 Data Dependency

Consider the following `minic` program fragment consisting of a four-command sequence:

```
a:=b+c (i)

d:=a+c (ii)

e:=5d+a (iii)

a:=d+e (iv)
```

As the DFG shows (this is left to the reader), the algorithm portion defined by statements (i) and (ii) (as written) cannot be executed in parallel due to data dependency. Specifically, the value of `a` must be computed prior to its use in (ii). Similarly, (iii) is data dependent upon (i) and (ii). Another common type of data dependence is shown in (i) and (iv); here a parallel decomposition would attempt to assign potentially conflicting values to `a`.

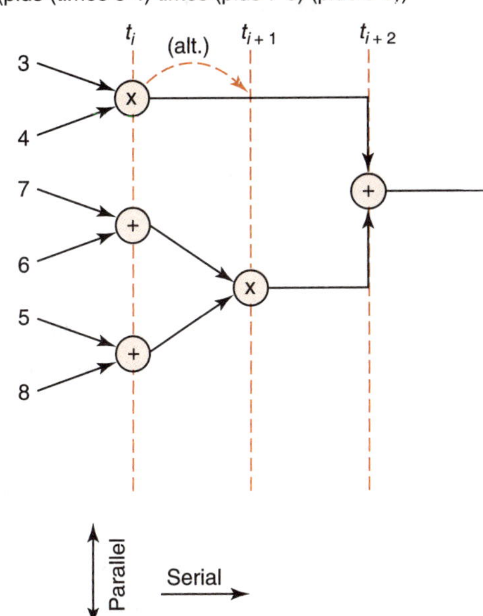

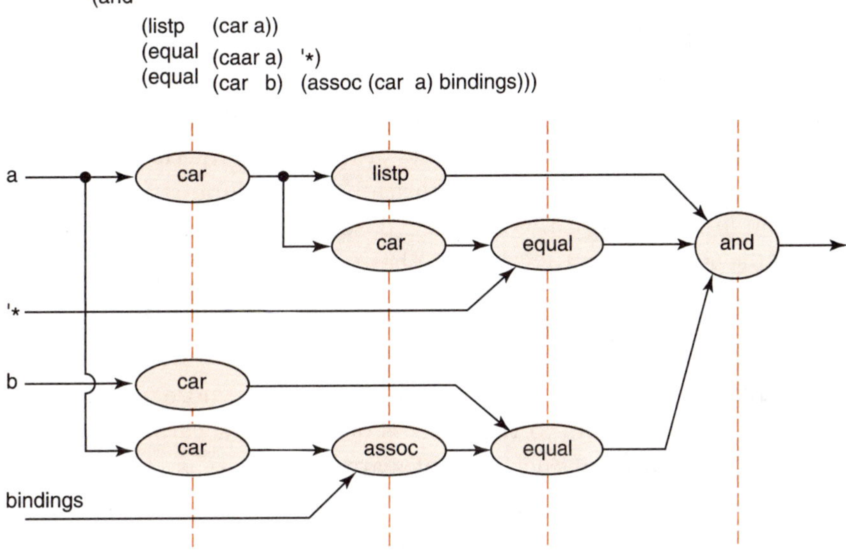

Figure 15.7 Data Flow Graphs (DFGs) for Lisp Fragments.

15.3 Parallelism in Declarative Programming (Prolog)

In Prolog, the goal formulation and ordering of clauses in the database determine the (sequential) order in which unification-guided search occurs. However, parallelism is possible.

15.3.1 AND and OR Parallelism

Two types of parallelism that may impact Prolog parallel execution are AND parallelism and OR parallelism.

```
p(X) :- p1(X), p2(X)
```

AND Parallelism Example
(one shared variable)

```
q(X) :- q1(X) ; q2(X).
```

(i) Original Clause

```
q(X) :- q1(X).

q(Y) :- q2(Y).
```

(ii) Clause Rewritten for Parallel Unification

OR Parallelism Example

Figure 15.8 AND/OR Parallelism in Prolog.

In the case of two or more clauses in the tail of a rule that are AND-ed, the simultaneous verification of these clauses is referred to as AND parallelism. Recalling the scoping of variables in Prolog, two or more of these clauses with common variables require communication between the parallel unification processes to ensure that a successful unification (if possible) occurs with consistent variable binding. This communication or checking represents overhead that works against the potential speedup benefits of the parallel formulation.

Similarly, OR-parallelism may be achieved by concurrently attempting unification on clauses that represent alternate solution paths. OR-ed clauses, in contrast to their AND-ed counterparts, do not require checks for consistency in variable bindings. This is relatively easy to see, because a rule with n OR-ed tail clauses may be rewritten as n (independent) rules. However, the nondeterminism of algorithms based upon the unification process combined with large numbers of possible OR-based solution paths may quickly lead to combinatorial explosion. Figure 15.8 depicts these concepts in Prolog.

15.3.2 Argument Dependence and Parallelism

Another concern, so called argument parallelism, is one of the more interesting and difficult concepts to implement and refers to the process of unifying several predicates containing one or more variables in parallel. Such variables are referred to as *shared variables.* Checking consistency of bindings (particularly if variables may be bound to other variables) is a nontrivial problem. Two extremes to realizing AND-parallelism in clauses with shared variables are possible:

1. None-shared-variable (NSV) schemes, wherein the presence of shared variables in subgoals forces these subgoals to be explored serially. This may be implemented during the unification process by dynamically creating and updating a dependency network to control subgoal exploration.

2. Reconciliation schemes, where all subgoals are explored in parallel, and possible conflicts are reconciled using an additional unification step.

A more moderate approach is to annotate shared variables in one of a variety of ways to restrict the binding of variables in satisfying subgoals. A specific example is where only one subgoal is allowed to determine the value of a specific variable. This subgoal is referred to as a producer of its respective variable binding.

15.3.3 Parallel Implementation of Unification

Consider the simple Prolog rule:

```
f(X) :- p1(X), p2(X).
```

If, during unification, predicate `f` is invoked as a subgoal with variable `X` unbound, we could attempt to spawn two parallel unification processes, one for `p1(X)` and one for `p2(X)`. However, `p1` and `p2` may yield unifications with different values bound to the shared variable `X`. Of course, one approach is to let this occur, and then discard the solution in search of other independently obtained solutions with different bindings for `X`. If a consistent solution (i.e., one in which `X` is bound to the same value) is found, the unification process succeeds. Unfortunately, it is more likely that binding conflicts or inconsistencies arise.

The "Reconciliation" Approach

Suppose a set of possible bindings on variable X is produced in the unification of p1(X) and another (possibly different) set of bindings on X is produced in the unification of p2(X). Denote these sets of bindings as SX1 and SX2, respectively. A consistent solution is the intersection of SX1 and SX2. Thus, after SX1 and SX2 are produced, a reconciliation of (possibly disparate) bindings is undertaken. Such a scheme is inefficient, for example, when the cardinality of SX1 is small and SX2 is large and their intersection is small. In this case, computational resources are wasted in computing SX2.

A "Producer-Consumer" Approach

This approach is an alternative to the reconciliation approach. It makes sense to "communicate" members of SX1, as they are produced, to the parallel unification process producing SX2. By restricting values of X in the p2(X) unification to SX1 (note here that p1(X) is a "producer" of variable bindings), the set of common unifications (still explored in parallel, but with interprocess communications) is efficiently obtained. One of the difficulties, however, is determining which clauses should be producers.

15.3.4 Parallel Prolog

Paralogic (http://www.plogic.com/) has released a parallel implementation of the Prolog language called *n-parallel Prolog*. Their approach uses MPI (described in Section 15.5) for distribution of the Prolog computation over a cluster of processors.

15.4 Extension of Languages to Allow Concurrent Programming

Many parallel programming languages are modified conventional or sequential programming languages with some parallel extensions. One of the major advantages of standardization on a parallel language is that the user is not required to understand the details of the underlying parallel architecture. Therefore the parallel machine is abstracted into a programming model. This allows access to a much larger audience of programmers, and enables some portability of code from one parallel machine to another (or its successor).

15.4.1 Necessary Parallel Programming Language Extensions

We may think of individual code segments as defining a set of computing processes. Fundamental to any consideration of parallel programming languages are two entities:

1. A means to delineate a process or code segment as parallel,[4] serial, or some combination thereof.

2. A means to allow synchronization or communication between processes (particularly when the run times of independent processes are not constant and unknown *a priori*) as well as overall input/output (I/O).

15.4.2 Processes

Definition of a Process

There are numerous definitions of a process. For our purposes, a **process** is an instance of a program running in a computer, and is synonymous with the term *task*.

A process has an associated set of data used to keep track of the process. A process can initiate a subprocess, which is termed a *child* process. The initiating process is referred to as the *parent* process. Processes can exchange information or synchronize their operation through several methods of interprocess communication (IPC).

Processes and Unix

In Unix and similar (e.g., Linux) operating systems, a process is started when a program is initiated (either by a user entering a shell command or by another program). In Unix and Linux-like systems, `init` is the original or originating process for the operating system and is used to spawn others. For example, Linux provides numerous commands for monitoring system processes. `ps` is used to show system processes, `system` is used to start a new process, `exec` is used to replace a process, `fork` is used to duplicate[5] a process, and `wait` is used for process synchronism.

Creating Multiple Processes

To allow programming with multiple (concurrent) processes, a technique is needed to spawn multiple parallel processes. This is one role of `mpirun`, as shown in Section 15.5.4.

Using `fork`

A more complete description of the `fork` construct (system call) may be found in the associated man pages. Basically, the `fork` creates a new child process that is identical to the parent (calling) process, except that the new process has a unique process ID (PID). The new process inherits a copy of the data space belonging to the parent process, including variables and open file descriptors. The parent and child processes are distinguished by process IDs, as shown in the following example.

---

[4] That is, allowing execution in parallel.

[5] Duplication consequently creates a new process.

Example Source

```
#include <sys/types.h>
#include <unistd.h>
#include <stdio.h>

int main(void)
{
pid_t pid;
char *message;
int n;

printf("\n *** Demo of process fork program*** \n\n");
pid=fork(); // get new pid from fork
switch(pid)
{
case -1:
exit(1); //fork failed
case 0:  // 0 returned in child's thread
message = "      Hello World from the child process";
n = 5;
break;
default:  // PID of child returned in parent's thread
message = "    Hello World from the parent process";
n = 3;
break;
}

for(; n > 0; n--) {
puts(message);
// printf(message);
sleep(1);
  }

sleep(2); // to delay prompt
exit(0);
}
```

Results

```
$ ./forkex

*** Demo of process fork program***

    Hello World from the parent process
      Hello World from the child process
      Hello World from the child process
    Hello World from the parent process
    Hello World from the parent process
      Hello World from the child process
      Hello World from the child process
      Hello World from the child process
$
```

15.5 MPI and Beowulf Cluster Programming

15.5.1 The Beowulf Concept

A Beowulf computing cluster is an attempt to build a low-cost, scalable supercomputer using common, off-the-shelf (COTS) components. It consists of a network of PCs and is built from commodity components (often referred to as a "pile of PCs"). Beowulf-class computing offers supercomputer performance at an attractive and (relatively) affordable price/performance ratio.

Beowulf PCs currently use a Unix-like (e.g., Linux) OS and thus leverage existing low-cost computing techniques and tools (e.g., Linux, GNU tools, MPI). The clusters are scalable, but it appears that they may be pushing the limits of COTS hardware scalability, especially in the area of high-speed networking. Message-passing execution and programming models are employed and based upon available supporting software. A Beowulf programmer may implement conceptual architectures such as SI(SP)MD, MIMD, and tree-structured architectures via control of interprocess communications.

There is active Beowulf R&D within many organizations. Science and engineering applications for Beowulf clusters abound, including computational fluid dynamics, image processing, genomic research, and computer science/engineering education.

15.5.2 MPI

MPI stands for the Message Passing Interface. It is a standardized and portable message-passing system designed by researchers from academia and industry and is available on a wide variety of parallel computers.

MPI From a Programming Viewpoint

From a programming viewpoint, MPI is a common API for parallel programming. The MPI standard defines the syntax and semantics of a library of functions and runtime routines for writing and executing portable message-passing programs in Fortran, C, or C++. The MPI specification is one of the leading standards for message-passing libraries for parallel computers.

MPI Implementations

There are a number of freely available MPI implementations for heterogeneous networks of workstations and symmetric multiprocessors, based upon both Unix (Linux) and Windows NT. Currently, the most common hardware platform seems to be Linux machines in Beowulf clusters. MPI is intended to be efficient and portable. The commonly used Linux implementation of MPI is `mpich`.

Communication = Passing Messages

MPI facilitates processes communication and synchronization using a library of functions. Note that MPI allows the overlap of interprocess communication and computation. This is achieved by the use of nonblocking communication calls, which separate the initiation of a communication from its completion.

The basic communication primitive in MPI is the transmittal of data between a pair of processes, that is, "point-to-point communication." There are many variations on this point-to-point operation. MPI provides a set of send and receive functions that allow the communication of typed data with an associated tag that allows selectivity of messages at the receiving end. Finally, the last communication function parameter is a *communicator*, which specifies a communication domain. A communicator thus serves to define a set of processes for which communication is possible. `MPI\_COMM\_WORLD` is a default communicator and defines an initial communication domain for all the processes that participate in the computation.

Process Rank: "Who Am I?"

Each process is identified by a process rank. Process ranks are integers and are returned by a call to a communicator using `MPI_Comm_rank( )`. In the examples that follow, one process is denoted `ROOT`. This is merely a convenient programming convention and identifies one process responsible for distributing and accumulating processing results.

The Significance of Process Rank and the MPI Programming Mindset

Recall the taxonomy given in Section 15.2.1. The typical application developed using MPI embodies an extension of the SIMD type, denoted as the single program/multiple data (SPMD) computational model. The program is distributed (using `mpirun`) to each the *np* processes, and is executed on each.

As the MPI coding examples that follow show, knowledge of process rank for each process provides a way for the behavior of the distributed program to be tailored to each process. In addition, interprocess communication is facilitated.

15.5.3 Basic MPI Function Summaries

The most commonly used (introductory) MPI functions are summarized in Section 15.7.

15.5.4 MPI "Hello World" Example

Source Code (C)

```
#include <stdio.h>
#include "mpi.h"

main(int argc, char** argv) {
        int p; /* Rank of process */
        int n; /* Number of processes */
        int source; /* Rank of sender */
        int dest; /* Rank of receiver */
        int tag = 50; /* Tag for messages */
  char message[100]; // storage for message
        MPI_Status status; /* Return status for receive */


        MPI_Init(&argc, &argv);
        MPI_Comm_rank(MPI_COMM_WORLD, &p);
        MPI_Comm_size(MPI_COMM_WORLD, &n);

        if (p != 0) {
                sprintf(message, "Hello World from process %d",
                               p);
                dest = 0;
```

```
                MPI_Send(message, strlen(message)+1, MPI_CHAR, dest,
                                tag, MPI_COMM_WORLD);
}
        else  { // p == 0
                for (source = 1; source < n; source++) {
                MPI_Recv(message, 100, MPI_CHAR, source, tag,
                                MPI_COMM_WORLD, &status);
                printf("%s\n", message);
}
}
        MPI_Finalize();
}       /* main */
```

Sample Results

Using the commands below, a 16-process version of the program was run:

```
$gcc hello-mpi.c -lmpi -o hello-mpi
$mpirun -np16  hello-mpi
```

with the following results:

```
Hello World from process 1
Hello World from process 2
Hello World from process 3
Hello World from process 4
Hello World from process 5
Hello World from process 6
Hello World from process 7
Hello World from process 8
Hello World from process 9
Hello World from process 10
Hello World from process 11
Hello World from process 12
Hello World from process 13
Hello World from process 14
Hello World from process 15
```

Later, we show a more sophisticated assessment of MPI performance using graphical tools.

15.5.5 MPI and Lisp

MPI procedures may be specified in a language-independent notation, thus making MPI functionality potentially available using a number of programming languages. For example, GCL/MPI is a free software package built on top of MPI and GCL Lisp. It combines the GCL or AKCL dialect of Lisp with the the use of MPI to yield an SPMD architecture. The distribution[6] is available at:

`ftp://ftp.ccs.neu.edu/pub/people/gene/starmpi/`

[6]This version is still experimental.

15.6 Extended MPI Examples

15.6.1 1-NNR Computations and Parallel (Cluster) Processing

The 1-NNR, or 1-nearest neighbor algorithm, is a popular pattern-recognition algorithm. It is based on the concept of finding the minimum distance from a vector to be classified, denoted $\underline{x}$, to a set of points denoted the training set, or H. In H, we assume each sample is labeled. For this problem, we assume the vector distance measure is Euclidean distance.[7]

The 1-NNR computation alludes to a ubiquitous problem in many computations:

> *Given a set of points, H, a vector $\underline{x}$, and a measure of distance in vector space, find the point in H that is closest to $\underline{x}$.*

Other Computationally Efficient Strategies

Although we show a solution to speed up the 1-NNR computation, note that other strategies exist that lead to reduced computation. The most popular are those based upon *binning*, or preordering of the data in H to facilitate first searching parts of H that are closer to $\underline{x}$ than others.

Serial Implementation in C

Relevant Data Structures

```
#define MAXTRAINPTS 3000 // number of samples in H
#define MAXTESTPTS 3000 // number in test set

typedef float vector[2];
struct labsamp {
    char class[3];
    vector value;
    } h[MAXTRAINPTS];

float dist[MAXTRAINPTS];
```

Distances and Minimum Distances

```
float distance (vector v, struct labsamp w)
{
/*compute distance between vector and h */
    float v_distance;
    int i;
    float ldist, int1;
    ldist = 0.0;
    for (i = 0; i<2; i++)
        {
        int1 = v[i] - w.value[i];
        ldist = int1 * int1 + ldist;
        }
    v_distance = ldist;
    return(v_distance);
}
```

[7]Note that we could also work with the square of distance.

```
void findmindist(void)
{
    int i;
    float minl;
    minl = dist[0];
    for (i = 0; i < MAXTRAINPTS; i++)
        if (dist[i] <= minl)
            {
            minl = dist[i];
            res = minl;
            vectorindex = i;
            }
}
```

The Main Computation over S_T

```
for(i=0;i<MAXTESTPTS;i++)
    {
    for(j=0;j<MAXTRAINPTS;j++)
       {
        dist[j] = sqrt(distance(x,h[j])); // could work with d^2
       }
    findmindist();
    ...}
```

Parallel (MPI) Implementation

Decomposition Strategy The basic strategy employed in this problem decomposition is partitioning of H. Thus, the process is to use nonoverlapping subsets of H, to reduce the time needed for the overall number of distance computations, because processes may compute concurrently. Specifically:

1. Each process figures, and communicates to root, its boundaries in H—that is, the subset of samples in H to be considered. In the code that follows, each process only computes from elements `sampl_start` to `sampl_end` in H.

2. Using this subset of H, each process computes distances of each test set (S) sample to the process-specific subset of H.

3. Each process then computes the **minimum** distance for all samples in S and stores the result as `lowest[MAXTESTPTS][]`, where `lowest[MAXTESTPTS][0]` is the minimum distance found by the process and `lowest[MAXTESTPTS][1]` is the corresponding class. Note that each process classifies *all* points in S before sending the result to `ROOT`; otherwise communication overhead will overwhelm the computation and result in limited speedup.

4. All processes then send the minimum distance and class for *all* processed samples in S (`MAXTESTPTS`) to `ROOT`.

5. Using this data, `ROOT` then computes the minimum overall or global distance over H. In the code that follows, `min_proc[i]` is the minimum (over all processes) distance for sample i.

MPI-Based Source Code in C

```
/* 1-NNR classification*/
// compile: gcc <file>.c -lm -Wall -lmpi -lmpe -o <file>
// run: mpirun -np <no proc> <file>

#include <stdio.h>
#include <stdlib.h>
#include <string.h>
#include <math.h>
#include "mpi.h"
#include "mpe.h"

#define MAXTRAINPTS 3000 // number of samples in H
#define MAXTESTPTS  3000 // number in test set
#define NMAX 256 // no more than 256 processes
#define ROOT 0

typedef float vector[2];
struct labsamp {
    char class[3];
    vector value;
    };
struct labsamp h[MAXTRAINPTS];
double dist[MAXTRAINPTS];
double res;
int i,j,k;
vector x;
int min_index;
int min_proc[MAXTESTPTS];
int current_min_proc;
double lowest[MAXTESTPTS][2];  // proc-specific distance and class (as double)
double rlowest[MAXTESTPTS][NMAX][2]; // assumes n<NMAX-- root's working data
FILE *h_fileptr, *s_fileptr, *a_fileptr;

// MPI globals
int p; // process 'me'
int n; // number of processes requested by mpirun
MPI_Status status; // return status for MPI_Recv
int ds,increm,sampl_start,sampl_end; /* process domains */
int proc;
int count;
int event1s,event1f,event2s,event2f; //for logging
int event3s,event3f,event4s,event4f;

// auxiliary MPI functions
void setup_domains()
{
char message[100];
int tag = 5;
ds = ceil((double)MAXTRAINPTS/(double)n);    // use a more direct fn?
increm = ds-1;
if(p==ROOT) // let root figure and print this
      { if(increm*n > MAXTRAINPTS) printf("\n*** you have unused process(es )***\n");
        printf("\nfor training  set cardinality %d and %d processes, the \
                 slice increment is %d samples\n\n",
               MAXTRAINPTS,n,ds);
      }
```

```
// each process figures, and communicates to root, its boundaries in H
// this is just an example of communication, not MPI performance
// would not include in 'real' code
sampl_start = p*ds;
sampl_end = (p+1)*increm + p;
if(sampl_end >=  MAXTRAINPTS) sampl_end=MAXTRAINPTS-1;
sprintf(message,"for process %d => \
        start sample in H is %d and end sample is %d\n",p,sampl_start,sampl_end);

MPI_Send(message, strlen(message)+1, MPI_CHAR, ROOT,
              tag, MPI_COMM_WORLD);  // send it to root

if(p==ROOT) {
         printf("each process computes and communicates:\n\n");
         for(proc=0;proc<n;proc++){
              MPI_Recv(message, 100, MPI_CHAR, proc, tag,
                          MPI_COMM_WORLD, &status); // root receives it
              printf("%s", message);
                          }
         printf("\n\n");
         }
} // setup_domains

void send_to_root()
{
/* all processes send the min distance and class
   for ALL processed samples in S (MAXTESTPTS) to root */
if(p != ROOT) {
       MPI_Send(lowest,2*MAXTESTPTS,MPI_DOUBLE,ROOT,33,MPI_COMM_WORLD);
       printf("process %d just sent array to ROOT\n",p);
               }
// now receive it all
if(p==ROOT) {
for(i=0;i<MAXTESTPTS;i++){
               rlowest[i][0][0] = lowest[i][0];
               rlowest[i][0][1] = lowest[i][1];
                          }
         for(proc=1;proc<n;proc++)            {
                MPI_Recv(lowest,2*MAXTESTPTS, MPI_DOUBLE, proc, 33,
                                 MPI_COMM_WORLD, &status);
       printf("ROOT just received array from process %d\n",proc);
       for(i=0;i<MAXTESTPTS;i++){
                      rlowest[i][proc][0]=lowest[i][0];
                      rlowest[i][proc][1]=lowest[i][1];
                   }
                                                    }
             }
} //send_to_root


float distance (vector v, struct labsamp w)
{
/*compute distance between vector and h */
    float v_distance;
    int i;
    float ldist, int1;
    ldist = 0.0;
    for (i = 0; i<2; i++)
```

```
        {
        int1 = v[i] - w.value[i];
        ldist = int1 * int1 + ldist;
        }
    v_distance = ldist;
    return(v_distance);
}

void examine_sample(struct labsamp ts)
{
    printf("   x1              x2        class");
    printf("\n");
    printf("%8.3f          ", ts.value[0]);
    printf("%8.3f          ", ts.value[1]);
    printf("%2s          ", ts.class);
    printf("\n");
}


void writex(int p)
{
printf("process %d has vector to classify: %f %f \n",p,x[0],x[1]);
printf("\n");

}

void find_min_dist(void)
{
    int i;
    double minl;
    minl = dist[sampl_start];
    for (i = sampl_start; i <= sampl_end; i++)
        if (dist[i] <= minl)
            {
            minl = dist[i];
            min_index = i;
    res=minl;
            }
}

void root_find_min_dist(void)
{
    int j,proc;
    double min_overall;
    for(j=0;j<MAXTESTPTS;j++){
    min_overall = rlowest[j][0][0];
    for (proc = 0; proc < n; proc++)
        if (rlowest[j][proc][0] <= min_overall)
            {
            min_overall = rlowest[j][proc][0];
            min_proc[j] = proc;
// corresp min distance for point j is rlowest[j][min_proc[j]][0];
// corresp class (double) is rlowest[j][min_proc[j]][1];
            }
                                }
}
```

```
void open_and_load_training_set(void)
{
if((h_fileptr = fopen("train.dat", "r")) != NULL)
          printf("process %d opened training set file\n",p);
  for(i=0 ; i<(MAXTRAINPTS/3) ; i++)
    {
     if(fscanf(h_fileptr, "%f %f", &h[i].value[0], &h[i].value[1]) != 2)
           printf("Error occurred while reading data");
     strcpy (h[i].class,"w1");
    }
  for(i=(MAXTRAINPTS/3) ; i<(2*MAXTRAINPTS)/3 ; i++)
    {
     if(fscanf(h_fileptr, "%f %f", &h[i].value[0], &h[i].value[1]) != 2)
           printf("Error occurred while reading data");
     strcpy (h[i].class,"w2");
    }
  for(i=(2*MAXTRAINPTS)/3 ; i<MAXTRAINPTS ; i++)
    {
     if(fscanf(h_fileptr, "%f %f", &h[i].value[0], &h[i].value[1]) != 2)
           printf("Error occurred while reading data");
     strcpy (h[i].class,"w3");
     }
fclose(h_fileptr);
}

void open_test_set()
{
if((s_fileptr = fopen("test.dat", "r")) != NULL)
   printf("process %d opened test file\n", p);
}

/********  main  ****************/

int main(int argc, char** argv) {
// MPI obligatory stuff
MPI_Init(&argc, &argv);
// find out how many and who I am
MPI_Comm_rank(MPI_COMM_WORLD, &p);
MPI_Comm_size(MPI_COMM_WORLD, &n);
MPE_Init_log();
// get event numbers for event logging
event1s = MPE_Log_get_event_number();
event1f = MPE_Log_get_event_number();
event2s = MPE_Log_get_event_number();
event2f = MPE_Log_get_event_number();
event3s = MPE_Log_get_event_number();
event3f = MPE_Log_get_event_number();
event4s = MPE_Log_get_event_number();
event4f = MPE_Log_get_event_number();

setup_domains();
open_and_load_training_set(); // all processes
open_test_set(); // all processes
MPE_Describe_state(event1s,event1f,"proc-min","red");
MPE_Log_event(event1s,0,"proc-min-start");
// now actual processing
for(i=0;i<MAXTESTPTS;i++)
```

```
   {
    if(fscanf(s_fileptr, "%f %f", &x[0], &x[1]) != 2)
           printf("Error occurred while reading data");
/* compute distances of each sample to
   process-specific subset of H, i.e.,
   each process only computes from
   sampl_start to sampl_end  */
    for(j=sampl_start;j<=sampl_end;j++)
       {
        dist[j] = sqrt(distance(x,h[j])); // NOTE: work with d^2 !!
//      printf("process %d  point    %d       %f\n",p,j,dist[j]);
       }
    find_min_dist();

/* each process computes lowest[MAXTESTPTS][]
    where
      lowest[MAXTESTPTS][0] is min distance found by process
      lowest[MAXTESTPTS][1] is corresp class
    note each process classifies ALL points in S before sending
  otherwise communications will overwhelm computation
*/
 lowest[i][0]=res;
 if(strcmp("1", &h[min_index].class[1])==0)  lowest[i][1] = 1.0;
 if(strcmp("2", &h[min_index].class[1])==0)  lowest[i][1] = 2.0;
 if(strcmp("3", &h[min_index].class[1])==0)  lowest[i][1] = 3.0;
    } // MAXTESTPTS loop
MPE_Log_event(event1f,0,"proc-min-fin");
printf("process %d just computed all min. distances\n",p);
fclose(s_fileptr);
MPE_Describe_state(event2s,event2f,"root-trans","blue");
MPE_Log_event(event2s,0,"send-start");
send_to_root();
MPE_Log_event(event2f,0,"send-fin");
// root now has rlowest[MAXTESTPTS][proc][2]
if(p==ROOT){
MPE_Describe_state(event3s,event3f,"root-min","green");
MPE_Log_event(event3s,0,"start");
root_find_min_dist();
MPE_Log_event(event3f,0,"done");
printf("ROOT just computed min. overall distance\n");
// min_proc[i] is min (over all processes) distance for sample i
if((a_fileptr = fopen("answer.dat", "w")) != NULL)
             printf("process %d opened answer file\n",p);
for(i=0;i<MAXTESTPTS;i++) {
               current_min_proc=min_proc[i];
               fprintf(a_fileptr,"%d\n",(int)rlowest[i][current_min_proc][1]);
          }
fclose(a_fileptr);
          }//if p=ROOT
MPE_Finish_log("1nnrlog");
return(MPI_Finalize());
}
```

Checking Results An early check on the validity of our implementation is obtained by reducing H to $n = 3$ samples and S to $n = 2$ samples and printing selected vectors, distances, and computed minima. These are shown on the next page.

```
for training  set cardinality 3 and 1 processes, the
slice increment is 3 samples

each process computes and communicates:

for process 0 =>        start sample in H is 0 and end sample is 2


process 0 opened training set file
   x1              x2         class
 -28.845          18.789          w1
   x1              x2         class
  -1.354         -10.603          w2
   x1              x2         class
  -6.802           7.725          w3
process 0 opened test file
process 0 has vector to classify: -7.494012 3.056125

process 0  point    0       26.521125
process 0  point    1       14.975972
process 0  point    2       4.720250
 for process 0, min_index is 2
point      process       distance         class
0             0            4.720250                3.000000
process 0 has vector to classify: -4.558779 -22.050310

process 0  point    0       47.514615
process 0  point    1       11.887502
process 0  point    2       29.860030
 for process 0, min_index is 1
point      process       distance         class
1             0            11.887502               2.000000
process 0 just computed all min. distances
point      process       distance         class
0             0            4.720250                3.000000
1             0            11.887502               2.000000
ROOT just computed min. overall distance
process 0 opened answer file
```

Sample Terminal Session, $np = 5$ Processors

Although a better visualization of the overall process parallelism in the computation is probably obtained through `upshot` (described in the next section), we show a log of the screen session that results from the command line string `mpirun -np 5 1nnrmpi`. This spawns five copies of our program on the cluster, that is, five processes to compute the 1NNR. Hopefully, the role of the various `printf` statements in the source code is now clear.

```
[rjschal@thymine 1nnr]$ mpirun -np 5 1nnrmpi

for training  set cardinality 3000 and 5 processes, the
slice increment is 600 samples

each process computes and communicates:

for process 0 =>        start sample in H is 0 and end sample is 599
process 1 opened training set file
```

```
process 4 opened training set file
for process 1 =>        start sample in H is 600 and end sample is 1199
process 2 opened training set file
process 1 opened test file
for process 2 =>        start sample in H is 1200 and end sample is 1799
for process 3 =>        start sample in H is 1800 and end sample is 2399
for process 4 =>        start sample in H is 2400 and end sample is 2999


process 2 opened test file
process 3 opened training set file
process 0 opened training set file
process 4 opened test file
process 3 opened test file
process 0 opened test file
process 1 just computed all min. distances
process 1 just sent array to ROOT
process 4 just computed all min. distances
process 4 just sent array to ROOT
process 3 just computed all min. distances
process 3 just sent array to ROOT
process 0 just computed all min. distances
ROOT just received array from process 1
process 2 just computed all min. distances
process 2 just sent array to ROOT
ROOT just received array from process 2
ROOT just received array from process 3
ROOT just received array from process 4
ROOT just computed min. overall distance
process 0 opened answer file
[rjschal@thymine 1nnr]$
```

Process Logging and Graphical Parallel 1NNR Results Using `upshot`

Process Logging `upshot` is an X-based graphics tool for visualization of log files produced by parallel programs. Note the numerous MPI logging functions appearing throughout the source code. For example, we log the time for `ROOT` to compute the overall minimum distance using the code fragment:

```
MPE_Describe_state(event3s,event3f,"root-min","green");
MPE_Log_event(event3s,0,"start");
root_find_min_dist();
MPE_Log_event(event3f,0,"done");
```

The consequence of this is generation of a log file[8] of the processes. A sample corresponding to the $np = 5$ case is shown in Figure 15.9.

Sample Graphical Results

Using a Single Process This is shown in Figure 15.10. Note in this case that interprocess communication is not required.

[8]The `alog` format is shown here.

```
-1 0 0 0 0 0 Me
-2 0 0 25 0 0
-3 0 0 5 0 0
-4 0 0 1 0 0
-5 0 0 7 0 0
-6 0 0 0 0 0
-7 0 0 0 0 669731
-8 0 0 1 0 0
-11 0 0 0 0 0
-13 0 500 501 0 0 red proc-min
-13 0 500 501 0 0 red proc-min
-13 0 500 501 0 0 red proc-min
-13 0 500 501 0 0 red proc-min
-13 0 500 501 0 0 red proc-min
-13 0 502 503 0 0 blue root-trans
-13 0 502 503 0 0 blue root-trans
-13 0 502 503 0 0 blue root-trans
-13 0 502 503 0 0 blue root-trans
-13 0 502 503 0 0 blue root-trans
-13 0 504 505 0 0 green root-min
-201 0 0 -1 0 0 MPI_PROC_NULL
-201 0 0 -2 0 3 MPI_ANY_SOURCE
-201 0 0 -1 0 6 MPI_ANY_TAG
500 4 0 0 0 9440 proc-min-start
500 1 0 0 0 11748 proc-min-start
500 2 0 0 0 12433 proc-min-start
500 3 0 0 0 14656 proc-min-start
500 0 0 0 0 15647 proc-min-start
501 4 0 0 0 547510 proc-min-fin
502 4 0 0 0 547605 send-start
501 2 0 0 0 548935 proc-min-fin
502 2 0 0 0 549030 send-start
501 1 0 0 0 552433 proc-min-fin
502 1 0 0 0 552508 send-start
501 3 0 0 0 554750 proc-min-fin
502 3 0 0 0 554857 send-start
503 4 0 0 0 581907 send-fin
503 2 0 0 0 581910 send-fin
503 3 0 0 0 582260 send-fin
503 1 0 0 0 591925 send-fin
501 0 0 0 0 639567 proc-min-fin
502 0 0 0 0 639726 send-start
503 0 0 0 0 668275 send-fin
504 0 0 0 0 668286 start
505 0 0 0 0 669731 done
```

Figure 15.9 alog-Format Log File for $np = 5$ Case.

Using 5 and 9 Processes Results using 5 and 9 processes are more interesting. The $np = 5$ and $np = 9$ process results are shown in Figures 15.11 and 15.12. In the $np = 5$ process case, observe that considerable process temporal overlap occurs, and communications overhead is reasonable.

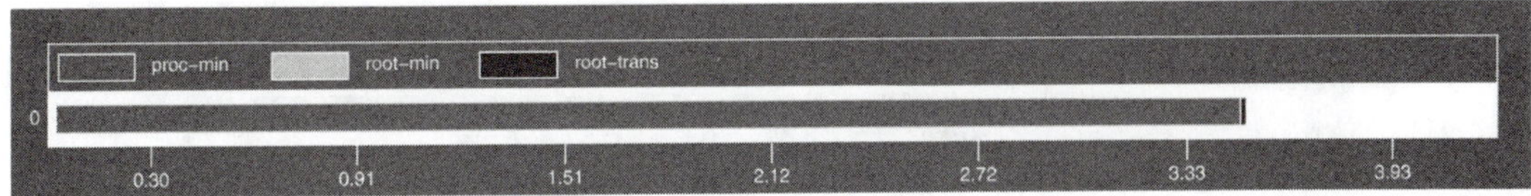

Figure 15.10 Parallel 1NNR Results Using a Single Process.

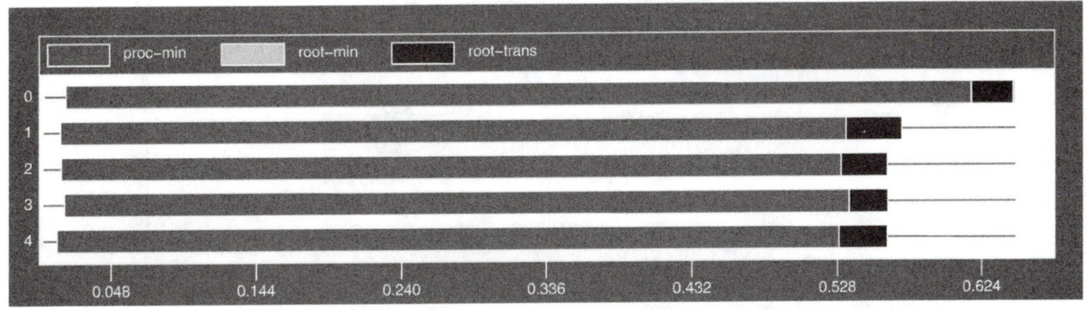

Figure 15.11 Parallel 1NNR Results Using $np = 5$ Processes.

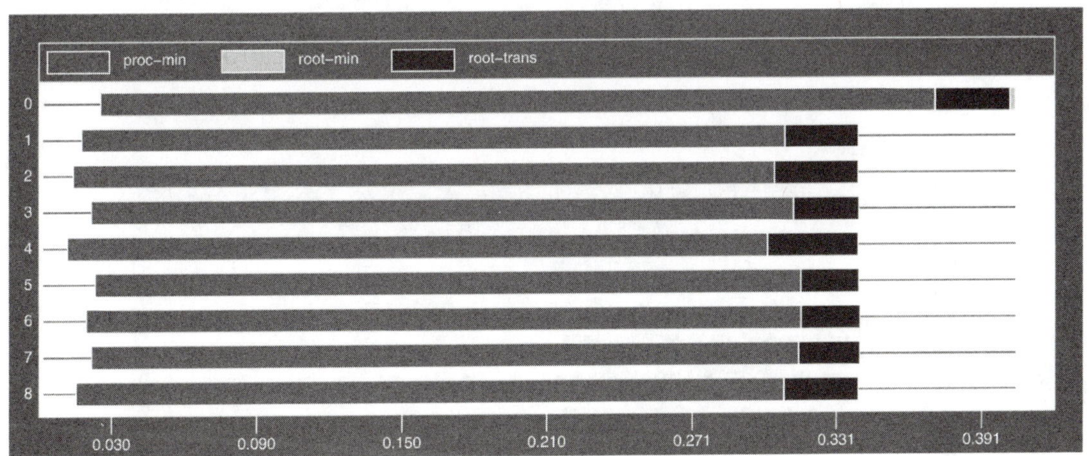

Figure 15.12 Parallel 1NNR Results Using $np = 9$ Processes.

Using 21 and 35 Processes The $np = 21$ and $np = 35$ process cases are shown in Figures 15.13 and 15.14, respectively. These cases illustrate the diminishing benefit of using additional processors as well as substantial degradation due to interprocess communications costs (i.e., 20 and 34 processes sending data to `ROOT`).

15.6.2 Image Processing (Binary Morphology)

Digital image processing is the processing of two-dimensional (2-D) image data to produce other images. One particularly important family of 2-D processing operations is morphological transformations (Schalkoff, 1989). We use the morphological `dilation` operator (and later erosion—see the problems) as applied to binary images as an example of parallel processing/programming. This operator may be implemented in a number of ways; we show a "template-based" approach here. For simplicity, we use a 200×200 pixel image. Particularly noteworthy in this example is the parallel decomposition used.

Figure 15.13 Parallel 1NNR Results Using $np = 21$ Processes.

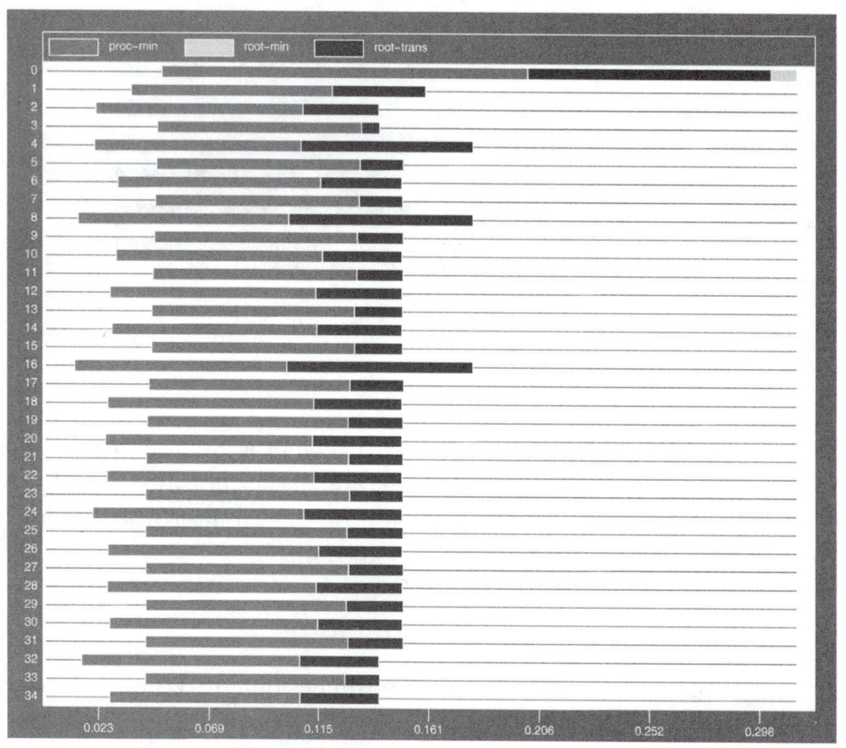

Figure 15.14 Parallel 1NNR Results Using $np = 35$ Processes.

Development Issues

Some questions we should ask first:

1. What's the morphological operator (e.g., dilation, erosion)?
2. How do I represent/store images (file format)?
3. What are the key elements of the implementation?
4. What is the computational complexity?

The last question is left to the exercises.

Defining the Dilation Operator

In binary morphology, images and structuring elements are represented using point sets. An ON (intensity = 1) pixel location in an image is simply represented by its corresponding 2-D coordinate location in the point set. All other locations or coordinates are assumed to be OFF or 0 in intensity. For display purposes, we convert ON pixel intensities to the integer value 255.

The Minkowski addition (dilation) operator is denoted [+] and may be implemented via template matching as defined by the following operation:

$$A[+]B = \{\underline{x} | [((-B) + \underline{x}) \cap A] \in A\} \tag{15.3}$$

In other words, the dilation of image A by structuring element or template B is comprised of all pixels where the shifted or translated structuring element and image A have at least one nonzero element (or pixel) in common.

$-B$ corresponds to the negated entries in the structuring element point set B. Viewing B as an image, with the origin assumed at the center of B, observe that this corresponds to a 180-degree rotation of image B. In many realistic applications, B is invariant with respect to a 180-degree rotation; thus $-B = B$.

Corresponding Implementation in C The following code fragment shows the heart of the dilation computation used to implement Equation 15.3.

```
/* now actually compute interior */
/* assumes a binary {0,255} input image */

for(i=bM/2;i<dim_m-bM/2;i++)
   for(j=bN/2;j<dim_n-bN/2;j++)
/* arbitrary sized B (bM,bN) loop */
   {
    overlap=0; // initial condition
    for(bi=0;bi<bM;bi++)
       for(bj=0;bj<bN;bj++)
          overlap=(imagein[i-bM/2+bi][j-bN/2+bj] && minusB[bi][bj]) || overlap;
                // lazy evaluation potential -- if overlap ==1, break
    if(overlap) imageout[i][j]=255;  //for display
          else imageout[i][j]=0;
   }
```

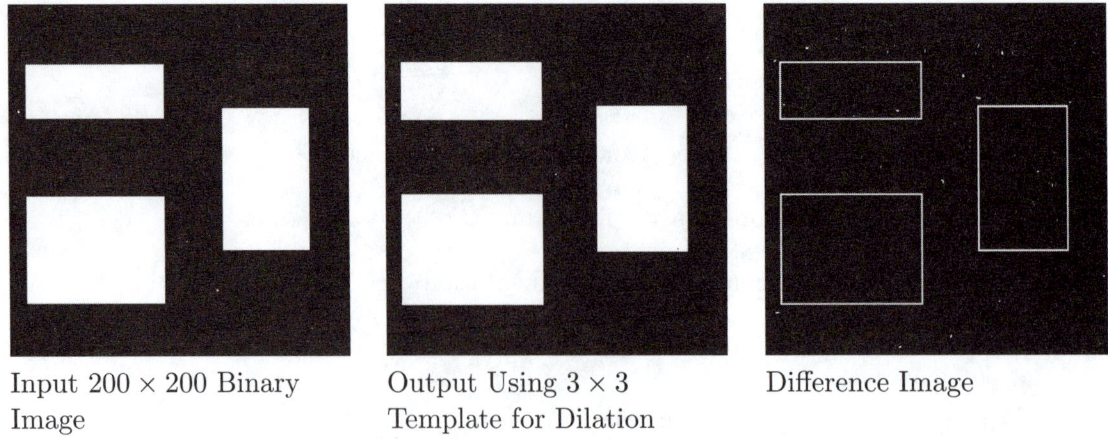

Input 200 × 200 Binary Image | Output Using 3 × 3 Template for Dilation | Difference Image

Figure 15.15 Dilation Example.

Dilation Utility and Examples

We first show an example of images processed using a 3 × 3 structuring element. Notice how the regions in the processed image are dilated by the 3 × 3 element (Figure 15.15). Computing the absolute value of the intensity difference between the images, on a pixel-by-pixel basis, yields the rightmost difference image shown. Note the extraction of region edges.

Second Dilation Example

We now show an example of images processed (dilated) using a 5 × 5 structuring element, B (Figure 15.16). Notice how the regions in the processed image are dilated by the 5 × 5 element. Computing the absolute value of the difference between the images, on a pixel-by-pixel basis, yields the "thicker" edge image shown. Notice the effect of dilation in closing small holes in image regions. This problem is continued in the exercises.

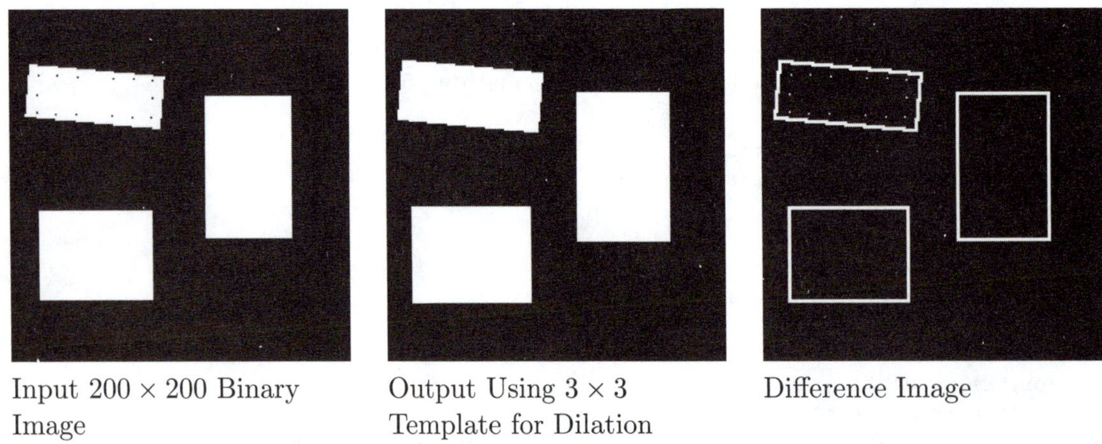

Input 200 × 200 Binary Image | Output Using 3 × 3 Template for Dilation | Difference Image

Figure 15.16 Second Dilation Example.

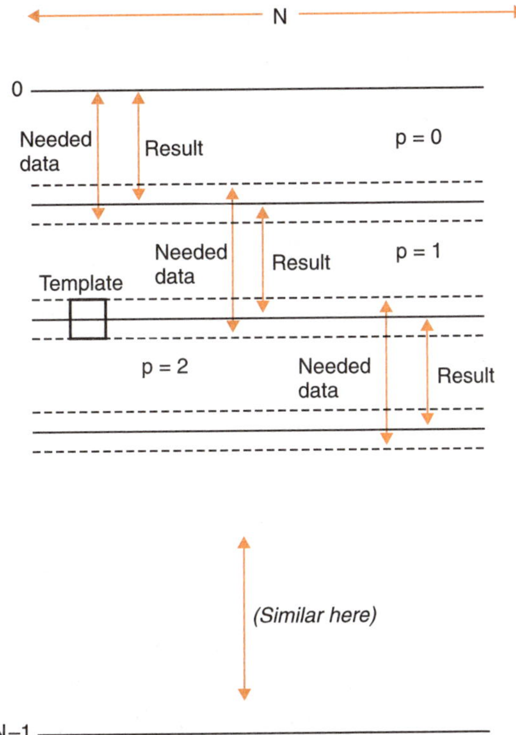

Figure 15.17 Image Data Decomposition for Parallel Implementation of Dilation. Note Overlapping Image Slices Required by Each Process.

Parallel Decomposition

The decomposition we employ is relatively straightforward: We "slice" the image into "stripes" and compute the dilation results for each slice. Complicating this decomposition are two factors:

1. To compute a result along a slice border, data from the adjacent image slice is needed. The amount of data depends upon the width of the structuring element.

2. The result of the individual processes must be reassembled to form the output (dilated) image. This requires communication.

The data decomposition strategy is shown in Figure 15.17.

Skeletal MPI Implementation

```
int main(int argc, char** argv)
{
// obligatory stuff
MPI_Init(&argc, &argv);

// find out how many and who I am
MPI_Comm_rank(MPI_COMM_WORLD, &p);
MPI_Comm_size(MPI_COMM_WORLD, &np);
last = np-1;
```

```
// root opens file
// and communicates parts to processes
if(p==ROOT)
  {open_image_file("image1.pgm");
   setup_domains();
  }

process();
// each process works on part of image data

// communicate process results back to root
(if p != ROOT) send_to_root();

if(p==ROOT) output_image("outputfile1p.pgm");
/* obligatory stuff */

        return(MPI_Finalize());
} /* main */
```

Computational Strategy

The MPI implementation shown uses a 1-D slice decomposition of the 2-D input data. Implementation of the decomposition is along index `i` where `i` $\in [0, N-1]$ for an image containing N lines of data. The (basic) idea is that with np processes (note process `ROOT` computes here), there are $ds = (N/np)$ rows per process. Because this is a discrete problem, we need to adjust the size of the last region.

The overall computational strategy implemented in the accompanying source code is as follows:

1. Process `ROOT` opens the input image file.
2. Process `ROOT` sends the respective input image data to all the processes using data structure `pin`.
3. Each process computes the dilation on its data and produces data structure `pout`.
4. Each process sends the resulting data to process `ROOT`.
5. Process `ROOT` assembles the received data and puts the result in the output file.

Complete MPI Implementation with Process Logging

```
/* example of image dilation using MPI*/
/* includes process logging for UPSHOT */
/* assumes:
0. root process is process 0
1. MPI_INT is c's int
2. slice width > bM
*/

#include <stdio.h>
#include <math.h>
#include <stdlib.h>
#include <string.h>
#include "mpi.h"
#include "mpe.h"
```

```
#define ROOT 0
#define ERR -1
#define N 200
#define bN 5
#define bM 5

// globals

int n=N;
int p; // process 'me'
int np; // number of processes requested by mpirun
int last;
MPI_Status status; // return status for MPI_Recv
int blocksize, endblocksize, rootblocksize;
int ds,increm,ipstart,ipend; /* process domain extent and 1D borders */
int proc;
int diff;
int es;
int kp,count;
int dim_m, dim_n;
int (*pin)[N]; // process in and out images
int (*pout)[N];
int (*imagein)[N]; // the whole images
int (*imageout)[N]; // only used and malloced by ROOT
int (*block)[N]; // some number of lines in a slice

// for logging
int event1s,event1f,event2s,event2f; //for logging
int event3s,event3f,event4s,event4f;
int event5s,event5f,event6s,event6f;

// function prototypes

void setup_domains(void);
void domains_comm(void);
void receive(void);
int receive_and_assemble(void);
int open_image_file(char *infilename);
int process(void);
int output_image(char *outfilename);


//+++++++++++++++++++++++++++++++++++++++++++++++++++++++++++++++++++++++++++++++++++
void setup_domains()
{
// uses global parameters from main

int fi,fj;
// malloc the biggest block (interior)
if(!(block=malloc(blocksize*sizeof(int)))) printf("malloc failure\n");

printf("ROOT has pin data; nothing to send\n");

for(kp=1;kp<np-1;kp++)
   {
/* note that each interior process needs 2* es edge data where es=bM/2
   we fill up block with this and send it */
```

```
ipstart = kp*ds;
ipend = (kp+1)*increm + kp;
printf("for process %d => \
        start row is %d and end row is %d\n",kp,ipstart,ipend);

// fill up block for interior slices
for(fi=ipstart-es;fi<=ipend+es;fi++) // assumes slice width>bM
  for(fj=0;fj<N;fj++)
     block[fi-ipstart+es][fj]=imagein[fi][fj];

MPI_Send(block,blocksize,MPI_INT,kp,11,MPI_COMM_WORLD);
printf("ROOT sent image slice to process %d\n",kp);
   } //for interior processes

// handle last block, <= blocksize worth of data
kp=last;
ipstart = kp*ds;
ipend = (kp+1)*increm + kp;
if(ipend >=  N)
  {diff=ipend-(N-1); // diff fewer elements in last block
   ipend=N-1;
  }
printf("for process %d => \
        start row is %d and end row is %d\n",kp,ipstart,ipend);
for(fi=ipstart-es;fi<=ipend;fi++)
  for(fj=0;fj<N;fj++)
    block[fi-ipstart+es][fj]=imagein[fi][fj];
MPI_Send(block,endblocksize,MPI_INT,np-1,11,MPI_COMM_WORLD);
printf("ROOT sent last image slice to  process %d\n",kp);

} // setup_domains
//++++++++++++++++++++++++++++++++++++++++++++++++++++++++++++++++++++++++++++++++
```

```
//++++++++++++++++++++++++++++++++++++++++++++++++++++++++++++++++++++++++++++++++
void receive()
{
int ti,tj;
if(p==ROOT) // ROOT processes the first slice; doesn't really 'receive'
   if(!(pin=malloc(rootblocksize*sizeof(int)))) printf("malloc failure\n");
   else
       {
       for(ti=0;ti<rootblocksize/N;ti++)
         for(tj=0;tj<N;tj++)
            pin[ti][tj]=imagein[ti][tj];
       printf("ROOT has pin\n");
       }

if(p>0 && p<np-1)
   if(!(pin=malloc(blocksize*sizeof(int)))) printf("malloc failure\n");
   else
      {
        if(MPI_Recv(pin,blocksize,MPI_INT,ROOT,11,MPI_COMM_WORLD,&status) != MPI_SUCCESS)
printf("problem with MPI_Recv in process %d\n",p);
       } // interior region else
```

```
if(p==last)
   if(!(pin=malloc(endblocksize*sizeof(int)))) printf("malloc failure\n");
    else
    {
      if(MPI_Recv(pin,endblocksize,MPI_INT,ROOT,11,MPI_COMM_WORLD,&status) != MPI_SUCCESS)
printf("problem with MPI_Recv in process %d\n",p);
    } // last region else
} //receive
//++++++++++++++++++++++++++++++++++++++++++++++++++++++++++++++++++++++++++++++++++


//++++++++++++++++++++++++++++++++++++++++++++++++++++++++++++++++++++++++++++++++++
int process(void){
int i,j,bi,bj;
int b[bM][bN]={1,1,1,1,1,
       1,1,1,1,1,
       1,1,1,1,1,
       1,1,1,1,1,
       1,1,1,1,1}; // b not minusB
int minusB[bM][bN];
int overlap;
/* now  process data  */
/* dilation example */
/* 3 cases: ROOT, interior and last */

/* NOTE: image extension is not handled, i.e., just
   work from i=j=start to i=j=end, where start and end
   depend upon bN and bM (assume both are ODD), and zero
   the image 'frame' to get the same size output image
*/

// initialization by individual processes
// form minusB (reflected B)

for(i=0;i<bM;i++)
   for(j=0;j<bN;j++)
     minusB[i][j]=b[bM-1-i][bN-1-j];

/* compute; assumes a binary {0,255} input image */

if(p==ROOT)
{

MPE_Describe_state(event2s, event2f, "root comp", "blue");
MPE_Log_event(event2s,0," root start");

if(!(pout=malloc(rootblocksize*sizeof(int)))) printf("malloc failure\n");
printf("ROOT has malloced pout\n");
for(i=0;i<ds+es;i++) // initialization
  for(j=0;j<dim_n;j++)
          pout[i][j]=0;
for(i=es;i<=increm+es;i++)
   for(j=bN/2;j<N-bN/2;j++)
/* arbitrary sized B (bM,bN) loop */
   {
    overlap=0; // initial condition
    for(bi=0;bi<bM;bi++)
```

```
       for(bj=0;bj<bN;bj++)
          overlap=(pin[i-bM/2+bi][j-bN/2+bj] && minusB[bi][bj]) || overlap;
// note lazy evaluation potential (not used) -- if overlap ==1, break
    if(overlap) pout[i][j]=255;  //for display
          else pout[i][j]=0;
   }
printf("ROOT processed image\n");

MPE_Log_event(event2f,0," root fin");

} //ROOT

if(p>0 && p<np-1) // interior
{

MPE_Describe_state(event3s, event3f, "process", "red");
MPE_Log_event(event3s,0,"process start");

if(!(pout=malloc(blocksize*sizeof(int)))) printf("malloc failure\n");
for(i=0;i<ds+2*es;i++) // initialization
  for(j=0;j<dim_n;j++)
          pout[i][j]=0;
for(i=es;i<=increm+es;i++)
   for(j=bN/2;j<N-bN/2;j++)
/* arbitrary sized B (bM,bN) loop */
   {
    overlap=0; // initial condition
    for(bi=0;bi<bM;bi++)
       for(bj=0;bj<bN;bj++)
          overlap=(pin[i-bM/2+bi][j-bN/2+bj] && minusB[bi][bj]) || overlap;
    if(overlap) pout[i][j]=255;  //for display
          else pout[i][j]=0;
   }
/* here just 3 x 3 for illustration:
      {
      overlap=(imagein[i-1][j-1] && minusB[0][0]) ||
              (imagein[i-1][j] && minusB[0][1]) ||
              (imagein[i-1][j+1] && minusB[0][2]) ||
              (imagein[i][j-1] && minusB[1][0]) ||
              (imagein[i][j] && minusB[1][1]) ||
              (imagein[i][j+1] && minusB[1][2]) ||
              (imagein[i+1][j-1] && minusB[2][0]) ||
              (imagein[i+1][j] && minusB[2][1]) ||
              (imagein[i+1][j+1] && minusB[2][2]);
      if(overlap) imageout[i][j]=255;  //for display
                else imageout[i][j]=0;
      }
end illustration */
printf("process %d processed image\n",p);

MPE_Log_event(event3f,0,"process finish");
} // interior

if(p==last) // last
{

MPE_Describe_state(event4s, event4f, "last comp", "yellow");
MPE_Log_event(event4s,0," last start");
```

```
if(!(pout=malloc(endblocksize*sizeof(int)))) printf("malloc failure\n");
for(i=0;i<endblocksize/N;i++) // initialization
  for(j=0;j<dim_n;j++)
          pout[i][j]=0;
for(i=es;i<increm+es-diff;i++)
   for(j=bN/2;j<N-bN/2;j++)
/* arbitrary sized B (bM,bN) loop */
   {
    overlap=0; // initial condition
    for(bi=0;bi<bM;bi++)
       for(bj=0;bj<bN;bj++)
          overlap=(pin[i-bM/2+bi][j-bN/2+bj] && minusB[bi][bj]) || overlap;
    if(overlap) pout[i][j]=255;  //for display
          else pout[i][j]=0;
   }
printf("process %d processed image\n",p);

MPE_Log_event(event4f,0," last fin");
} // last
free(pin);
return(0);
}
//++++++++++++++++++++++++++++++++++++++++++++++++++++++++++++++++++++++++++++++++++++




//++++++++++++++++++++++++++++++++++++++++++++++++++++++++++++++++++++++++++++++++++++
int send_to_root(void)
{
// ROOT already has pout; no communication nec. here

if(p>0 && p<last) // interior
{
// note only send valid parts of pout back, not es
printf("process %d is sending pout to ROOT\n",p);
MPI_Send(pout+es,blocksize-2*N*es,MPI_INT,ROOT,11,MPI_COMM_WORLD);
//MPI_Send(pout+es,blocksize-2*N*es,MPI_INT,ROOT,11,MPI_COMM_WORLD);
} //interior

if(p==last) // last
{
// note only send valid parts of pout back, not es
printf("process %d is sending pout to ROOT\n",p);
MPI_Send(pout+es,endblocksize-N*es,MPI_INT,ROOT,11,MPI_COMM_WORLD);
} // last

free(pout); // every pout except ROOT
return 0;
} // send_to_root()
//++++++++++++++++++++++++++++++++++++++++++++++++++++++++++++++++++++++++++++++++++++




//++++++++++++++++++++++++++++++++++++++++++++++++++++++++++++++++++++++++++++++++++++
int receive_and_assemble(void)
{
```

```
int row,col;
printf("ROOT now executing function 'receive and assemble'\n");
// ROOT already has pout corresp to 1st rows of imageout

for(row=0;row<=increm;row++)
for(col=0;col<N;col++)
imageout[row][col]=pout[row][col];

// ROOT assembles rest of imageout from the individual pout(p) p>0

  for(kp=1;kp<last;kp++)
  {
   printf("ROOT ready to receive pout data from process %d\n",kp);
   if(MPI_Recv(block,blocksize-2*N*es,MPI_INT,kp,11,MPI_COMM_WORLD,&status)
       != MPI_SUCCESS) printf("problem with ROOT receive from process %d\n",kp);
   for(row=kp*ds;row<=increm+kp*ds;row++)
for(col=0;col<N;col++)
imageout[row][col]=block[row-kp*ds][col];
   }
// last slice
   printf("ROOT ready to receive pout data from process %d\n",last);
   if(MPI_Recv(block,endblocksize-N*es,MPI_INT,last,11,MPI_COMM_WORLD,&status)
       != MPI_SUCCESS)
  printf("problem with ROOT receive from process %d\n",last);
for(row=last*ds;row<N;row++)
for(col=0;col<N;col++)
imageout[row][col]=block[row-last*ds][col];
return 0;
}
//+++++++++++++++++++++++++++++++++++++++++++++++++++++++++++++++++++++++++++++++++++++


//+++++++++++++++++++++++++++++++++++++++++++++++++++++++++++++++++++++++++++++++++++++
int output_image(char *outfilename)
{
int i,j;
FILE *imagefileptr;

imagefileptr = fopen(outfilename, "w");
    if ( !imagefileptr ) {
        fprintf( stderr, "Unable to open output file '%s'\n", outfilename );
return ERR;  }
/* write the header */
fprintf(imagefileptr,"P2\n");
fprintf(imagefileptr,"#sample dilation image\n");
fprintf(imagefileptr,"%d  %d\n",n,n);
fprintf(imagefileptr,"%d \n",255);
/* be careful about order and coordinate system */
for(i=0;i<N;i++)
  {
   for(j=0;j<N;j++)
       fprintf(imagefileptr,"%d ",imageout[i][j]);
   fprintf(imagefileptr,"\n ");
   }
fclose(imagefileptr);
printf("wrote output file %s \n", outfilename);
return(0);
}
```

```
//++++++++++++++++++++++++++++++++++++++++++++++++++++++++++++++++++++++++++


//++++++++++++++++++++++++++++++++++++++++++++++++++++++++++++++++++++++++++
int open_image_file(char *infilename)
{
FILE *infileptr;
char type[20];
char comment[128];
int i,j;
int dim_m,dim_n,max_val;
/* open input file  */
infileptr = fopen(infilename, "r");
    if ( !infileptr ) {
        fprintf( stderr, "Unable to open input file '%s'\n", infilename );
return ERR;  }
/* read header */
printf("opened input file;");
/* should be
   P2
   #ece847 (or some other comment)
   200 200
   255
   then data
   below checks this (uncomment printfs if necessary)
*/
fscanf(infileptr,"%s\n",type);
//printf("type is %s\n",type);
fscanf(infileptr,"%s\n",comment);
//printf("comment is %s\n",comment);
fscanf(infileptr,"%d  %d\n",&dim_m,&dim_n);
//printf("dimensions are %d  %d\n",dim_m,dim_n);
fscanf(infileptr,"%d \n",&max_val);
//printf("max intensity is: %d\n",max_val);
//printf("successfully read header \n");

/* now read data */
for(i=0; i<dim_m;i++)
{
   for(j=0;j<dim_n;j++)
       fscanf(infileptr,"%d ",&imagein[i][j]);
       fscanf(infileptr,"\n");
}
fclose(infileptr);
printf(" read %s\n\n",infilename);
return(0);
}
//++++++++++++++++++++++++++++++++++++++++++++++++++++++++++++++++++++++++++


//++++++++++++++++++++++++++++++++++++++++++++++++++++++++++++++++++++++++++
void domains_comm()
/* more a test of communication than a utility */
{
char message[100];
int tag = 5;
```

```
ds = ceil((double)N/(double)np);    // use a more direct fn?
increm = ds-1;

if(p==ROOT) // let root print this
        printf("\nfor height of %d and %d processes, the slice size is %d rows\n\n",
               N,np,ds);

// process boundaries
ipstart = p*ds;
ipend = (p+1)*increm + p;
if(ipend >=  N) ipend=N-1;
sprintf(message,"for process %d => \
        start row is %d and end row is %d\n",p,ipstart,ipend);

MPI_Send(message, strlen(message)+1, MPI_CHAR, ROOT,
              tag, MPI_COMM_WORLD);  // send it to root

if(p==ROOT) {
         printf("each process computes and communicates:\n\n");
         for(proc=0;proc<np;proc++){
              MPI_Recv(message, 100, MPI_CHAR, proc, tag,
                          MPI_COMM_WORLD, &status); // root receives it
              printf("%s", message);
                          }
         printf("\n\n");
         }

} // domains_comm
//+++++++++++++++++++++++++++++++++++++++++++++++++++++++++++++++++++++++++++++++++++



//+++++++++++++++++++++++++++++++++++++++++++++++++++++++++++++++++++++++++++++++++++
int main(int argc, char** argv)
{
MPI_Init(&argc, &argv);

// find out how many and who I am
MPI_Comm_rank(MPI_COMM_WORLD, &p);
MPI_Comm_size(MPI_COMM_WORLD, &np);

// logging
MPE_Init_log();

// get event numbers
event1s = MPE_Log_get_event_number();
event1f = MPE_Log_get_event_number();
event2s = MPE_Log_get_event_number();
event2f = MPE_Log_get_event_number();
event3s = MPE_Log_get_event_number();
event3f = MPE_Log_get_event_number();
event4s = MPE_Log_get_event_number();
event4f = MPE_Log_get_event_number();
event5s = MPE_Log_get_event_number();
event5f = MPE_Log_get_event_number();
event6s = MPE_Log_get_event_number();
event6f = MPE_Log_get_event_number();
```

```
last=np-1;
// parameters each process must know
// let ROOT do the printing

ds = ceil((double)N/(double)np);    // use a more direct fn?
increm = ds-1;
es=bM/2; // extra data needed for width of B>1 element
blocksize=(ds+2*es)*N;// ELEMENTS for interior slices
rootblocksize=blocksize-es*N; // == (ds+es)*N ?simpler?
// last block, <= blocksize worth of data
kp=last;
ipstart = kp*ds;
ipend = (kp+1)*increm + kp;
if(ipend >=  N)
  {diff=ipend-(N-1); // diff fewer elements in last block
   ipend=N-1;
  }
endblocksize=(ipend-ipstart+1+es)*N;

if(p==ROOT) // print decomposition used
   {
printf("for height of %d and %d processes, a data slice is %d rows\n",
               N,np,ds);
printf("the increment is %d rows and last block is short %d rows\n",increm,diff);
printf("for bM= %d, es is %d\n",bM,es);
printf("(interior) blocksize is %d ELEMENTS\n",blocksize);
printf("rootblocksize is %d ELEMENTS\n",rootblocksize);
printf("endblocksize is %d ELEMENTS\n",endblocksize);
   }

// below is just reality/communications check/example

if(p==ROOT) {
   if(!(imagein=malloc(N*N*sizeof(int)))) printf("malloc failure\n");
   open_image_file("image1.pgm");
MPE_Describe_state(event1s, event1f, "setup domains", "green");
MPE_Log_event(event1s,0,"send slices start");
   setup_domains();
MPE_Log_event(event1f,0,"send slices done");
           }

receive(); // includes ROOT

process(); // each process computes output image slice, i.e., part of image data
// communicate process results back to root
if(p!=ROOT) send_to_root();
if(p==ROOT) {
     if(!(imageout=malloc(N*N*sizeof(int)))) printf("malloc failure\n");
//     printf("ROOT has malloced imageout\n");

MPE_Describe_state(event6s, event6f, "ROOT assemble", "pink");
MPE_Log_event(event6s,0,"assemble start");
     receive_and_assemble();
MPE_Log_event(event6f,0,"assemble fin");

     output_image("out1p.pgm");
     free(block);
     free(pout); // just ROOT
```

```
    free(imagein);
    free(imageout);
    printf("That's All Folks!\n\n");
          }
MPE_Finish_log("dil6");
return(MPI_Finalize());
} /* main */
```

MPI-Based Processing Results and Performance (Fig. 15.18)

Output Image Produced with 3×3 Structuring Element and $np = 8$ Processor Decomposition

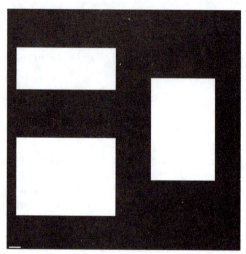

Output Image Produced with 5×5 Structuring Element and $np = 8$ Processor Decomposition

Figure 15.18 Parallel (MPI) Output Images—Dilation Example.

Sample Output Images

Sample Log File This corresponds to the $np = 8$ processor case.

```
-1 0 0 0 0 0 Me
-2 0 0 19 0 0
-3 0 0 6 0 0
-4 0 0 1 0 0
-5 0 0 11 0 0
-6 0 0 0 0 0
-7 0 0 0 0 57372
-8 0 0 1 0 0
-11 0 0 0 0 0
-13 0 500 501 0 0 green setup domains
-13 0 504 0 0 0 red process
-13 0 504 0 0 0 red process
-13 0 504 0 0 0 red process
-13 0 504 0 0 0 red process
-13 0 506 507 0 0 yellow last comp
-13 0 502 503 0 0 blue root comp
-13 0 510 511 0 0 pink ROOT assemble
-201 0 0 -1 0 0 MPI_PROC_NULL
-201 0 0 -2 0 2 MPI_ANY_SOURCE
-201 0 0 -1 0 3 MPI_ANY_TAG
500 0 0 0 0 28082 send slices sta
504 1 0 0 0 32261 process start
```

```
504 2 0 0 0 35146 process start
0 1 0 0 0 37209 process finish
504 3 0 0 0 37789 process start
0 2 0 0 0 39867 process finish
504 4 0 0 0 40384 process start
0 3 0 0 0 42815 process finish
501 0 0 0 0 43206 send slices don
506 5 0 0 0 43522  last start
502 0 0 0 0 43574  root start
0 4 0 0 0 45284 process finish
507 5 0 0 0 47366  last fin
503 0 0 0 0 48155  root fin
510 0 0 0 0 48206 assemble start
511 0 0 0 0 57372 assemble fin
```

Sample Performance for 200 $\times$ 200 Image Figures 15.19 to 15.22 show results using the `upshot` graphical tool on log files generated by MPE. In this case, the input image size is 200 $\times$ 200 and the number of (parallel) processes spawned (np) varies from 2 to 20.

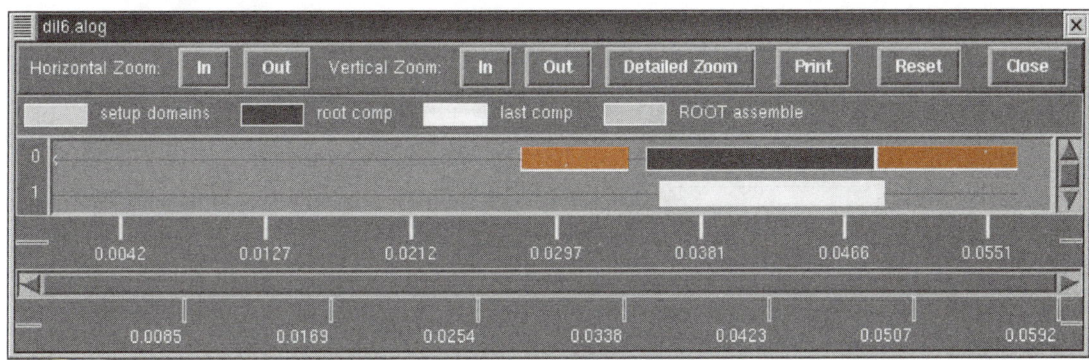

Figure 15.19 Process Logging—$np = 2$ Processes for Image Dilation.

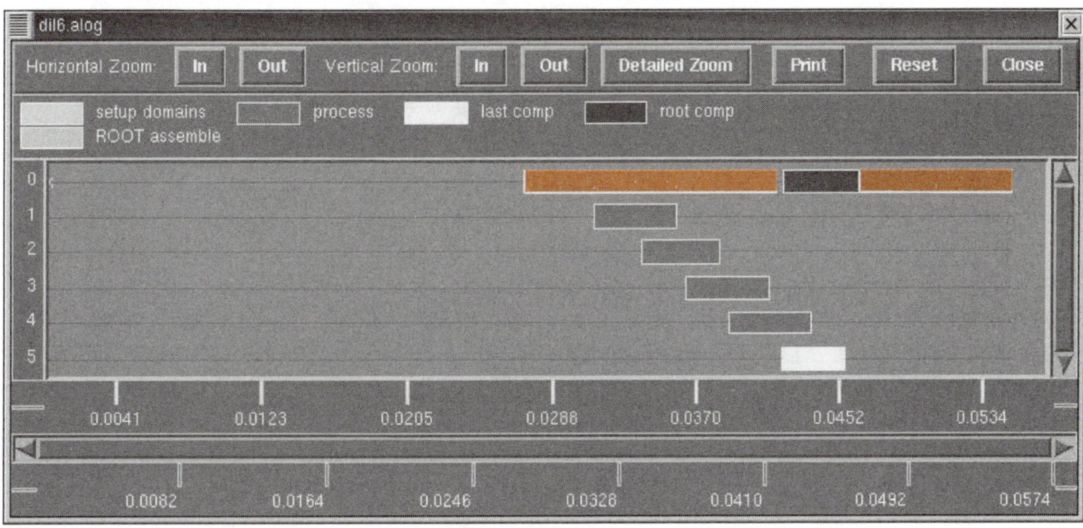

Figure 15.20 Process Logging—$np = 6$ Processes for Image Dilation.

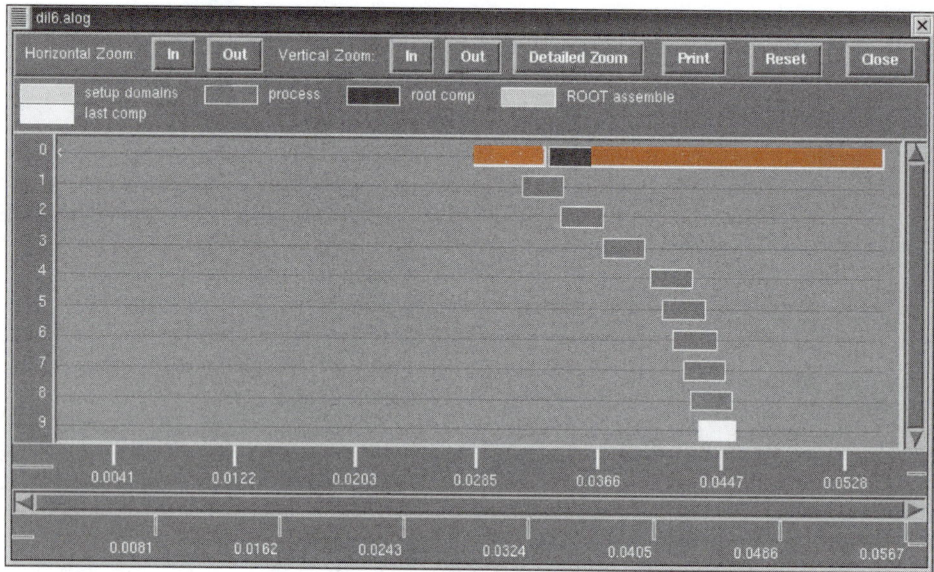

Figure 15.21 Process Logging—$np = 10$ Processes for Image Dilation.

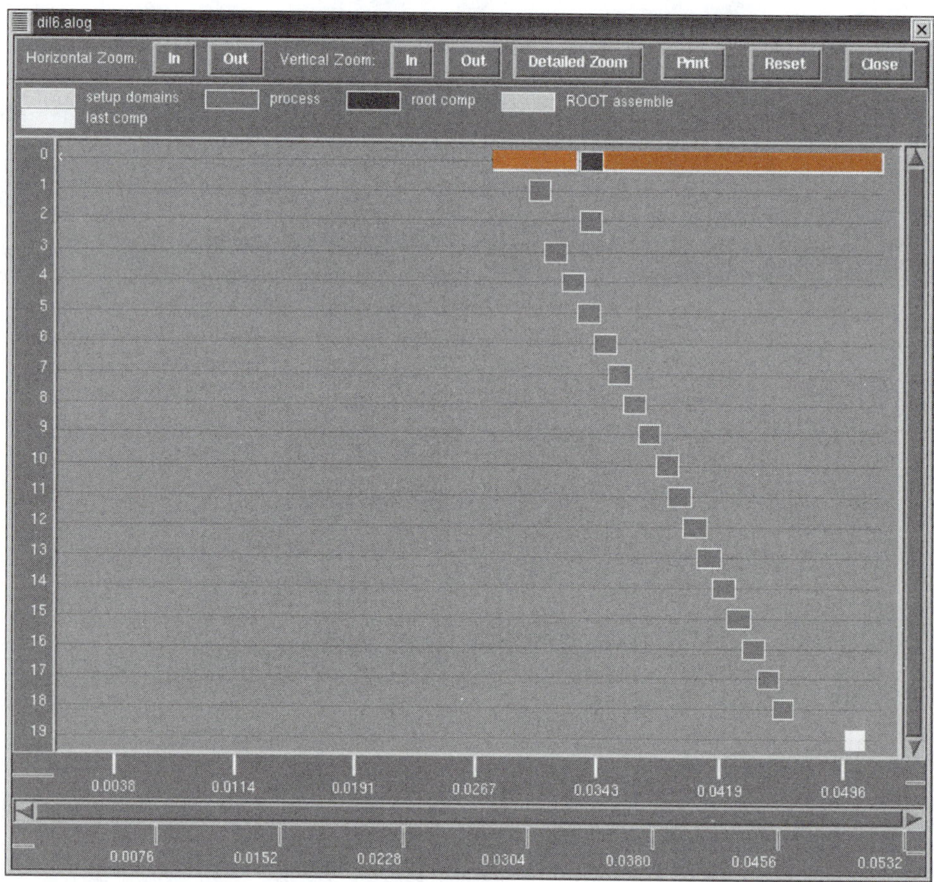

Figure 15.22 Process Logging—$np = 20$ Processes for Image Dilation.

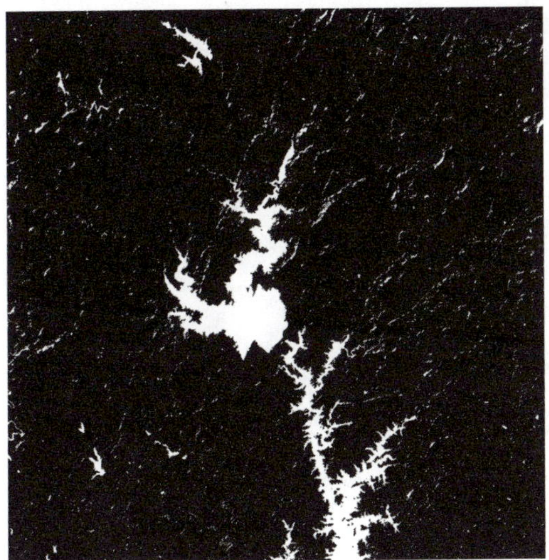

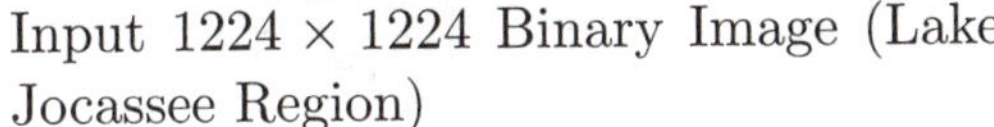

Input 1224 × 1224 Binary Image (Lake Jocassee Region)

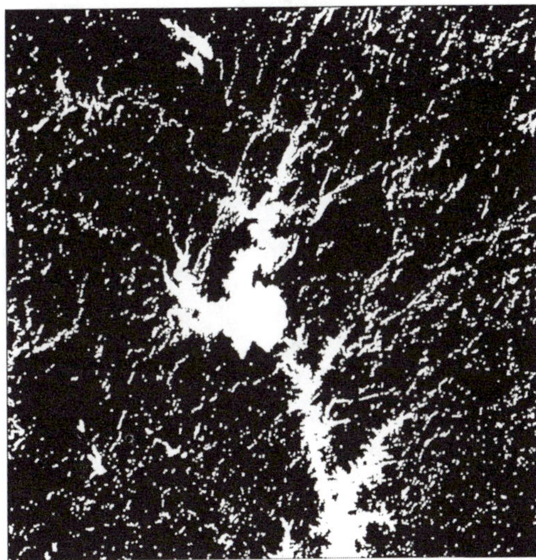

Output Using 5×5 Template for Dilation

Figure 15.23 Dilation Example with Larger (Landsat) Image.

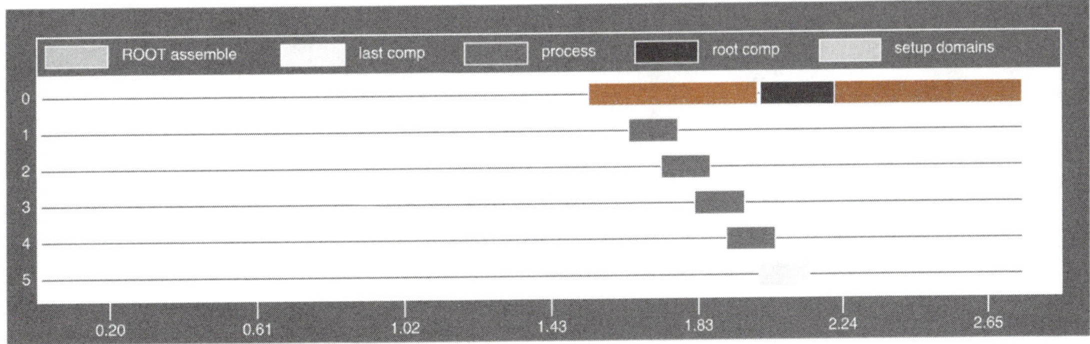

Figure 15.24 Parallel Dilation Results Using 1224×1224 Image and $np = 6$ Processes.

Sample Performance for 1224 × 1224 Image To further illustrate MPI and performance measures, consider the dilation of a significantly larger (1224×1224) image, as shown in Figure 15.23. Using this data, dilation results for $np = 6$ are shown in Figure 15.24.

15.6.3 Concluding Remarks

The preceding MPI-based parallel computing examples are intended to illustrate basic MPI programming concerns. Noteworthy are the data decompositions used, implementation of interprocess communications, and the process-specific execution of multiple copies of the distributed program. Although illustrative, these examples are relatively simple MPI applications. More advanced concepts include:

- parallel input/output
- derived datatypes
- alternative communicators and send/receive variants
- tuning the parallel program performance

15.7 Selected (Abbreviated) MPI and MPE man Pages

15.7.1 MPI

MPI_Init

```
NAME
       MPI_Init -  Initialize the MPI execution environment

SYNOPSIS
       #include "mpi.h"
       int MPI_Init(int *argc, char ***argv)

INPUT PARAMETERS
       argc   - Pointer to the number of arguments
       argv   - Pointer to the argument vector


COMMAND LINE ARGUMENTS
       MPI  specifies no command-line arguments but does allow an
       MPI implementation to make use of them.

       -mpiqueue
              - print out the state of the  message  queues  when
              MPI_FINALIZE  is called.  All processors print; the
              output may be hard to decipher. This is intended
              as a debugging aid.

       -mpiversion
              - print out the version of the implementation ( not
              of MPI), including the  arguments  that  were  used
              with configure.

       -mpinice nn
              -  Increments  the  nice  value by nn (lowering the
              priority of the program by nn).  nn must be  posi-
              tive  (except  for  root).  Not all systems support
              this argument; those that do not will ignore it.

       -mpedbg
              - Start a debugger in an xterm window if  there  is
              an  error  (either  detected  by  MPI or a normally
              fatal signal).  This works only if MPICH  was  con-
              figured with -mpedbg .  CURRENTLY DISABLED.  If you
              have TotalView, -mpichtv or mpirun  -tv  will  give
              you a better environment anyway.

       -mpimem
              -  If  MPICH was built with -DMPIR_DEBUG_MEM , this
              checks all malloc and free operations (internal  to
              MPICH) for signs of injury to the memory allocation
              areas.

       -mpidb options
              - Activate various debugging options.  Some require
              that  MPICH  have  been built with special options.
              These are intended for  debugging  MPICH,  not  for
              debugging  user  programs.   The  available options
              include:
```

```
mem     - Enable dynamic memory tracing of internal MPI objects
memall  - Generate output of all memory allocation/deallocation
ptr     - Enable tracing of internal MPI pointer conversions
rank n  - Limit subsequent -mpidb options to on the process with
the specified rank in MPI_COMM_WORLD.  A rank of -1
selects all of MPI_COMM_WORLD.
ref     - Trace use of internal MPI objects
reffile filename - Trace use of internal MPI objects with output
to the indicated file
trace   - Trace routine calls
```

NOTES

On exit from this routine, all processes will have a copy of the argument list. This is not required by the MPI standard, and truely portable codes should not rely on it. This is provided as a service by this implementation (an MPI implementation is allowed to distribute the command line arguments but is not required to).

ERRORS

All MPI routines (except MPI_Wtime and MPI_Wtick) return an error value; C routines as the value of the function and Fortran routines in the last argument. Before the value is returned, the current MPI error handler is called. By default, this error handler aborts the MPI job. The error handler may be changed with MPI_Errhandler_set; the predefined error handler MPI_ERRORS_RETURN may be used to cause error values to be returned. Note that MPI does not guarentee that an MPI program can continue past an error.

MPI_SUCCESS
- No error; MPI routine completed successfully.

MPI_ERR_OTHER
- This error class is associated with an error code that indicates that an attempt was made to call MPI_INIT a second time. MPI_INIT may only be called once in a program.

MPI_Comm_rank

NAME

MPI_Comm_rank - Determines the rank of the calling process in the communicator

SYNOPSIS

```
#include "mpi.h"
int MPI_Comm_rank ( MPI_Comm comm, int *rank )
```

INPUT PARAMETERS

comm - communicator (handle)

OUTPUT PARAMETER

rank - rank of the calling process in group of comm (integer)

ERRORS

All MPI routines (except MPI_Wtime and MPI_Wtick) return an error value; C routines as the value of the function and Fortran routines in the last argument. Before the value is returned, the current MPI error handler is called. By default, this error handler aborts the MPI job. The error handler may be changed with MPI_Errhandler_set; the predefined error handler MPI_ERRORS_RETURN may be used to cause error values to be returned. Note that MPI does not guarantee that an MPI program can continue past an error.

MPI_SUCCESS
- No error; MPI routine completed successfully.

MPI_ERR_COMM
- Invalid communicator. A common error is to use a null communicator in a call (not even allowed in MPI_Comm_rank).

MPI_Comm_size

NAME

MPI_Comm_size - Determines the size of the group associated with a communicator

SYNOPSIS

```
#include "mpi.h"
int MPI_Comm_size ( MPI_Comm comm, int *size )
```

INPUT PARAMETER

comm - communicator (handle)

OUTPUT PARAMETER

size - number of processes in the group of comm (integer)

ERRORS

All MPI routines (except MPI_Wtime and MPI_Wtick) return an error value; C routines as the value of the function and Fortran routines in the last argument. Before the value is returned, the current MPI error handler is called. By default, this error handler aborts the MPI job. The error handler may be changed with MPI_Errhandler_set; the predefined error handler MPI_ERRORS_RETURN may be used to cause error values to be returned. Note that MPI does not guarentee that an MPI program can continue past an error.

MPI_SUCCESS
- No error; MPI routine completed successfully.

MPI_ERR_COMM
- Invalid communicator. A common error is to use a null communicator in a call (not even allowed in MPI_Comm_rank).

MPI_ERR_ARG
- Invalid argument. Some argument is invalid and is not identified by a specific error class (e.g., MPI_ERR_RANK).

MPI_Send

```
NAME
       MPI_Send - Performs a basic send

SYNOPSIS
       #include "mpi.h"
       int MPI_Send(void *buf, int count, MPI_Datatype datatype, int dest,
       int tag, MPI_Comm comm)

INPUT PARAMETERS
       buf - initial address of send buffer (choice)
       count - number of elements in send buffer (nonnegative
       integer)
       datatype
       - datatype of each send buffer element (handle)
       dest - rank of destination (integer)
       tag - message tag (integer)
       comm - communicator (handle)


NOTES
       This routine may block until the message is received.

ERRORS
       All MPI routines (except MPI_Wtime and MPI_Wtick) return
       an error value. Note that MPI does not guarentee that an MPI
       program can continue past an error.

       MPI_SUCCESS
              - No error; MPI routine completed successfully.
       MPI_ERR_COMM
              - Invalid communicator. A common error is to use a
              null communicator in a call (not even allowed in
              MPI_Comm_rank).
       MPI_ERR_COUNT
              - Invalid count argument. Count arguments must be
              non-negative; a count of zero is often valid.
       MPI_ERR_TYPE
              - Invalid datatype argument. May be an uncommitted
              MPI_Datatype (see MPI_Type_commit).
       MPI_ERR_TAG
              - Invalid tag argument. Tags must be non-negative;
              tags in a receive (MPI_Recv, MPI_Irecv,
              MPI_Sendrecv, etc.) may also be MPI_ANY_TAG. The
              largest tag value is available through the
              attribute MPI_TAG_UB.

       MPI_ERR_RANK
              - Invalid source or destination rank. Ranks must
              be between zero and the size of the communicator
              minus one; ranks in a receive (MPI_Recv,
              MPI_Irecv, MPI_Sendrecv, etc.) may also be
              MPI_ANY_SOURCE.

SEE ALSO
       MPI_Isend, MPI_Bsend
```

MPI_Recv

NAME

    MPI_Recv - Basic receive

SYNOPSIS

```
#include "mpi.h"
int MPI_Recv(void *buf, int count, MPI_Datatype datatype, int source,
             int tag, MPI_Comm comm, MPI_Status *status )
```

OUTPUT PARAMETERS

    buf   - initial address of receive buffer (choice)
    status - status object (Status)

INPUT PARAMETERS

    count - maximum number of elements in receive buffer
             (integer)
    datatype
           - datatype of each receive buffer element (handle)
    source - rank of source (integer)
    tag   - message tag (integer)
    comm   - communicator (handle)

NOTES

The count argument indicates the maximum length of a message; the actual number can be determined with MPI_Get_count .

ERRORS

All MPI routines (except MPI_Wtime and MPI_Wtick) return an error value; C routines as the value of the function and Fortran routines in the last argument. Before the value is returned, the current MPI error handler is called. By default, this error handler aborts the MPI job. The error handler may be changed with MPI_Errhandler_set ; the predefined error handler MPI_ERRORS_RETURN may be used to cause error values to be returned. Note that MPI does not guarantee that an MPI program can continue past an error.

MPI_SUCCESS
- No error; MPI routine completed successfully.

MPI_ERR_COMM
- Invalid communicator. A common error is to use a null communicator in a call (not even allowed in MPI_Comm_rank).

MPI_ERR_TYPE
- Invalid datatype argument. May be an uncommitted MPI_Datatype (see MPI_Type_commit).

MPI_ERR_COUNT
- Invalid count argument. Count arguments must be non-negative; a count of zero is often valid.

MPI_ERR_TAG
- Invalid tag argument. Tags must be non-negative; tags in a receive (MPI_Recv , MPI_Irecv , MPI_Sendrecv , etc.) may also be MPI_ANY_TAG . The largest tag value is available through the attribute MPI_TAG_UB .

```
MPI_ERR_RANK
        - Invalid source or destination rank. Ranks must
        be between zero and the size of the communicator
        minus one; ranks in a receive ( MPI_Recv ,
        MPI_Irecv , MPI_Sendrecv , etc.) may also be
        MPI_ANY_SOURCE .
```

MPI_Finalize

```
NAME
       MPI_Finalize - Terminates MPI execution environment

SYNOPSIS
       #include "mpi.h"
       int MPI_Finalize()

NOTES
       All processes must call this routine before exiting. The
       number of processes running after this routine is called
       is undefined; it is best not to perform much more than a
       return rc after calling MPI_Finalize .
```

15.7.2 MPE

With the exception of the general description of MPE, the following are shown in the order in which they are likely to be used in a program.

MPE

```
NAME
       MPE - MultiProcessing Environment

DESCRIPTION
       The Multi-Processing Environment (MPE) attempts to provide
       programmers with a complete suite of performance analysis
       tools for their MPI programs based on post processing
       approach. These tools include a set of profiling
       libraries, a set of utility programs, and a set of graphi-
       cal visualization tools.

       The first set of tools to be used with user MPI programs
       is profiling libraries, which provide a collection of rou-
       tines that create log files. These log files can be cre-
       ated manually by inserting MPE calls in the MPI program,
       or automatically by linking with the appropriate MPE
       libraries, or by combining the above two methods.
```

MPE_Init_log

```
NAME
       MPE_Init_log - Initialize for logging

SYNOPSIS
       int MPE_Init_log()
```

NOTES

Initializes the MPE logging package. This must be called before any of the other MPE logging routines. It is collective over MPI_COMM_WORLD.

SEE ALSO

MPE_Finish_log

MPE_Log_get_event_number

NAME

MPE_Log_get_event_number - Gets an unused event number

SYNOPSIS

```
int MPE_Log_get_event_number( )
```

RETURNS

A value that can be provided to MPE_Describe_event or MPE_Describe_state which will define an event or state not used before.

MPE_Describe_state

NAME

MPE_Describe_state - Create log record describing a state

SYNOPSIS

```
int MPE_Describe_state( start, end, name, color )
int start, end;
char *name, *color;
```

INPUT PARAMETERS

start - event number for the start of the state
end - event number for the end of the state
name - Name of the state
color - color to display the state in

NOTES

States are added to a log file by calling MPE_Log_event for the start and end event numbers.

SEE ALSO

MPE_Log_get_event_number

MPE_Log_get_event_number

NAME

MPE_Log_get_event_number - Gets an unused event number

SYNOPSIS

```
int MPE_Log_get_event_number( )
```

```
RETURNS
       A value that can be provided to MPE_Describe_event or
       MPE_Describe_state, which will define an event or state not
       used before.
```

MPE_Log_event

```
NAME
       MPE_Log_event -  Logs an event

SYNOPSIS
       int MPE_Log_event(event,data,string)
       int event, data;
       char *string;

INPUT PARAMETERS
       event  - Event number
       data   - Integer data value
       string - Optional string describing event
```

MPE_Finish_log

```
NAME
       MPE_Finish_log -  Send log to master, who writes it out

SYNOPSIS
       int MPE_Finish_log( filename )
       char *filename;

NOTES
       This routine dumps a logfile in alog or clog format.  It
       is collective over MPI_COMM_WORLD .  The default is alog
       format.  To generate clog output, set the environment
       variable MPE_LOG_FORMAT to CLOG.
```

15.8 Bibliographical Remarks and References

15.8.1 Books and Journals

Computational complexity is well-discussed by Tarjan (1983). Flynn's taxonomy is described in Flynn (1972). Useful references for parallel processing concepts are Hwang and Briggs (1984) and Quinn (1994, Chapter 4).

The classic MPI reference is Lusk, Gropp, and Skjellum (1999). Cluster computing concepts are covered in Buyya (1999).

15.8.2 Web-Based Resources

The `mpich` MPI implementation is available at:

http://www-unix.mcs.anl.gov/mpi/

This site also contains pointers to references and tutorials. For `mpich` installation on a Linux box, see:

http://www-unix.mcs.anl.gov/mpi/mpich/

15.9 Exercises

1. Referring to the example of Section 15.2.3, draw the DFG.

2. This is almost a philosophical problem. Consider the development of parallel scanning and parsing software.

   (a) Where would you find potential computations for parallel decomposition?

   (b) Which parts are necessarily serial?

3. Draw the DFG for the sample minic code in Figure 15.2, Section 15.1.3.

4. The text considers parallel implementation of dilation; however, it is probably necessary to fully appreciate the details of the serial implementation first. Implement the (serial) dilation operator on the 200×200 input image shown in Section 15.6.2. B is arbitrary.

   As a second test, show an example of images processed (dilated) using a different 5×5 structuring element, namely the "cross":

$$B = \begin{pmatrix} 00100 \\ 00100 \\ 11111 \\ 00100 \\ 00100 \end{pmatrix}$$

   and the following image `image3.pgm`. Apply the dilation operation and compute the absolute value of the difference between the images, on a pixel-by-pixel basis, and show the resultant image.

Figure 15.25 Input 200×200 Binary Image for Second Dilation Example to Further Test the (Serial) Software Development Effort (`image3.pgm`).

5. Another important and useful operator is erosion. Erosion is a morphological operator based upon *Minkowski subtraction* (Schalkoff, 1989). The Minkowski subtraction operator of image A using structuring element B is denoted as $A[-]B$ and, using the so-called "template" interpretation, the locus of ON pixels in the output image is determined using:

$$A[-]B = \{\underline{x} | (-B) + \underline{x} \in A\}$$

Recall $(-B)$ denotes reflected (180-degree rotation in 2-D case) B, where each element of the set $-B$ is defined as:

$$-B = \{\underline{x} | \underline{x} = -\underline{\xi} \; where \; \underline{\xi} \in B\}$$

Erosion of image A by structuring element B, denoted $A(--)B$, is simply Minkowski subtraction using $-B$, that is:

$$A(--)B = A[-](-B) = \{\underline{x} | B + \underline{x} \in A\}$$

For implementation, notice that this simply requires that we find all image locations where (shifted) B is (entirely) contained within a region of ON pixels.

An example of erosion is shown in Figure 15.26, using `image2` from Figure 15.16. In addition to the output image produced, the difference image is given.

Input 200×200 Binary Image (`image2`)

Erosion Result Using 5×5 Template

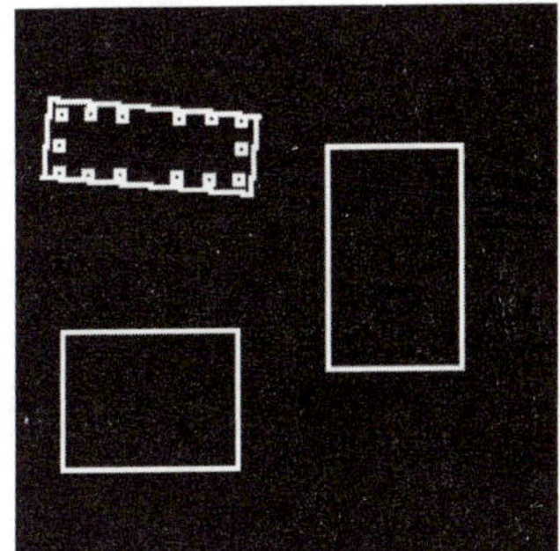

Difference Image for Erosion Example

Figure 15.26 Erosition Example—Note the Visual Effect.

For this problem, implement the erosion operator (serial version) and compare your results with the example given.

6. (This makes an excellent project.) Decompose your serial erosion implementation for MPI and discuss the results.

7. The computational complexity of the erosion and dilation operators warrants investigation. Consider the following major loop of the dilation computation (without lazy evaluation). Pay particular attention to the line noted.

```
for(i=bM/2;i<dim_m-bM/2;i++)
   for(j=bN/2;j<dim_n-bN/2;j++)
   {
```

```
    overlap=0; // initial condition
    for(bi=0;bi<bM;bi++)
       for(bj=0;bj<bN;bj++)
    /* the next line is the heart of the computation */
          overlap=(imagein[i-bM/2+bi][j-bN/2+bj] && minusB[bi][bj])
                   || overlap;
    if(overlap) imageout[i][j]=255;
          else imageout[i][j]=0;
   }
```

Show for a square image and structuring element template where `bM/2=bN/2=B` and `dim_m=dim_n=dim` that the total number of computations is given by:

$$\left[\texttt{dim} - 2 \times int\left(\frac{B}{2}\right)\right]^2 \times B^2$$

where the `int` function implements integer division as in C, that is, the effect is that the noninteger remainder is truncated. Thus, $\texttt{int}(\frac{5}{2}) = 5/2 = 2$.

Determine this number for the following cases:

(a) dim = 200; $B = 5$

(b) dim = 1000; $B = 11$

(c) dim = 3000; $B = 21$

8. The analysis for the previous problem is often facilitated by profiling tools. One of the more popular is the GNU `gprof` utility. For example, consider the results of `gprof` on the following annotated fragment of code for image erosion:

```
            void compute_contained(void)
  960400 -> {
  960400 ->           contained=(imagein[i-bM/2+bi][j-bN/2+bj]
                             && b[bi][bj]) && contained;
  960400 -> }


1 -> int process(void){
        1 -> for(i=bM/2;i<dim_m-bM/2;i++)
        1 ->    for(j=bN/2;j<dim_n-bN/2;j++)
            /* arbitrary sized B (bM,bN) loop */
               {
        1 ->     contained=1; // initial condition
        1 ->     for(bi=0;bi<bM;bi++)
        1 ->        for(bj=0;bj<bN;bj++)
            // for gprof example
        1 ->           compute_contained();
        1 ->     if(contained) imageout[i][j]=255;
        1 ->           else imageout[i][j]=0;
               }

        1 -> printf("processed image\n");
        1 -> return(0);
        1 -> }
```

Note that **gprof** indicates the number of times each function was used. For illustration, **gprof** also provides flat profiles and call graph information; a sample is shown here:

```
Flat profile:

Each sample counts as 0.01 seconds.
  %   cumulative   self              self     total
 time   seconds   seconds    calls  Ts/call  Ts/call  name
 50.00      0.02     0.02                             compute_contained (eroserial.c:115 @ 80488f5)
 25.00      0.03     0.01                             process (eroserial.c:143 @ 8048a44)
 12.50      0.04     0.01                             process (eroserial.c:143 @ 8048a5e)
 12.50      0.04     0.01                             process (eroserial.c:142 @ 8048a66)
  0.00      0.04     0.00   960400     0.00     0.00  compute_contained (eroserial.c:114 @ 80488ea)
  0.00      0.04     0.00        1     0.00     0.00  open_image_file (eroserial.c:74 @ 80486ec)
  0.00      0.04     0.00        1     0.00     0.00  output_image (eroserial.c:40 @ 8048583)
  0.00      0.04     0.00        1     0.00     0.00  process (eroserial.c:119 @ 8048970)

Call graph


granularity: each sample hit covers 4 byte(s) for 25.00% of 0.04 seconds

index % time    self  children    called     name
                0.00    0.00  960400/960400      process (eroserial.c:145 @ 8048a59) [89]
[5]      0.0    0.00    0.00  960400         compute_contained (eroserial.c:114 @ 80488ea) [5]
-----------------------------------------------
                0.00    0.00       1/1           main (eroserial.c:156 @ 8048b0f) [33]
[6]      0.0    0.00    0.00       1         open_image_file (eroserial.c:74 @ 80486ec) [6]
-----------------------------------------------
                0.00    0.00       1/1           main (eroserial.c:158 @ 8048b24) [35]
[7]      0.0    0.00    0.00       1         output_image (eroserial.c:40 @ 8048583) [7]
-----------------------------------------------
                0.00    0.00       1/1           main (eroserial.c:158 @ 8048b24) [35]
[8]      0.0    0.00    0.00       1         process (eroserial.c:119 @ 8048970) [8]
-----------------------------------------------
```

Check this result using your serial implementation and the results of the previous problem.

9. Another useful tool in assessing computational costs of a problem as a function of data size is the **time** function. **time** records elapsed real time, user CPU time, and system CPU time, for execution of a program. Figure 15.27 shows sample results. Based upon this result, the question is relatively simple: How does computation time scale with data size in this case?

10. It is not hard to see the utility of parallel implementations when the computation grows as the size of the data. Both the total number of computations as well as memory requirements may become intolerable with reasonable linear dimensions. Often the dimensionality of the computational domain may obscure this. For example, consider 3D computational grids of the following dimensions. Assume one computation and one word of memory is required per grid point. Determine the total number of computations and size of the memory structure necessary.

    (a) Linear dimension = 32 (i.e., a $32 \times 32 \times 32$ grid).

    (b) Linear dimension = 128 (i.e., a $128 \times 128 \times 128$ grid).

    (c) Linear dimension = 2048 (i.e., a $2048 \times 2048 \times 2048$ grid).

```
$ time ./morph dilation image2.pgm image2dil5x5.pgm
operator is dilation
opened input file
type is P2
comment is #ece847
dimensions are 200  200
max intensity is: 255
successfully read header
read image2.pgm
processed image
wrote output file image2dil5x5.pgm

real 0m0.153s
user 0m0.070s
sys 0m0.010s
```

Timing Results for 200 × 200 Image

```
$ time ./bigmorph dilation landsatn.pgm landsatn-dil5x5.pgm
operator is dilation
opened input file
type is P2
comment is #ece847big
dimensions are 1224  1224
max intensity is: 255
successfully read header
read landsatn.pgm
processed image
wrote output file landsatn-dil5x5.pgm

real 0m2.516s
user 0m2.380s
sys 0m0.050s
```

Timing Results for 1224 × 1224 Image

Figure 15.27 Example of Using `time` with Varying Image Size (Serial Image Dilation Implementation).

11. Suppose a computation is defined on a 3D grid, and it is desired to decompose the computation for implementation using MPI. Assume that each point on the 3D grid must communicate with its six nearest neighbors. Discuss how you would partition this grid for communication using MPI.

12. Suppose you are given a computation defined on a 3D grid of dimensions `WIDTH` × `HEIGHT` × `DEPTH`. Your major computational loop is implemented using a form:

```
for(i=1;i<WIDTH-1;i++){
  for(j=1;j<HEIGHT-1;j++){
    for(k=1;k<DEPTH-1;k++){
      <the actual computation>
      }}}
```

Discuss how you would use MPI to **partition** the grid points and therefore convert this computation into one suitable for *np* processes, where each process performs the computation on a subset of the grid consisting of a smaller number of points.

13. Assume that you have been given a 3D computation on a grid of points as described in the previous two problems. Furthermore, assume that the 3D grid is to be partitioned for processing by np processes. Most importantly, assume:

    - the number of computations performed by each process is proportional to the volume of each subdivision.
    - the interprocess communication necessary is proportional to the "surface area" of this volume.

    The goal is to maximize the number of computations performed in parallel, while simultaneously minimizing interprocess communications overhead or cost. In other words, the partitioning of the 3D grid should minimize the ratio

    $$\frac{communications\ time}{processing\ time}$$

    or

    $$\frac{subgrid\ surface\ area}{subgrid\ volume}$$

    On this basis, what would you expect would be the optimal decomposition? What geometries would you consider?

14. The parallel 1NNR program was run using $np = 99$ processes (on a cluster with 256 nodes), and the results are shown in Figure 15.28. Comment on the results, and speculate what might be the cause of this behavior.

15. (a) Using the logs from the 1NNR example of Section 15.6.12, compute the speedup in each case and plot speedup versus np.

    (b) Is the speedup linear?

16. Speedup was defined in Section 15.1.9. Sometimes, due to computation and memory limitations with a single processor, it is not possible to determine the execution time, t_s, for a serial implementation ($np = 1$) by actually performing the computation. However, suppose overall computation times, t_p, for varying values of np, are known. Call these corresponding quantities $t_p^{(n)}$ and $np^{(n)}$ for $np > 1$. Some questions are:

    (a) On the basis of these quantities, can we extrapolate or estimate t_s?

    (b) On the basis of these quantities, can we determine the speedup for any np? If so, how?

    (c) On the basis of these quantities, can we determine if the speedup is linear in np, that is, if $speedup = k \times np$?

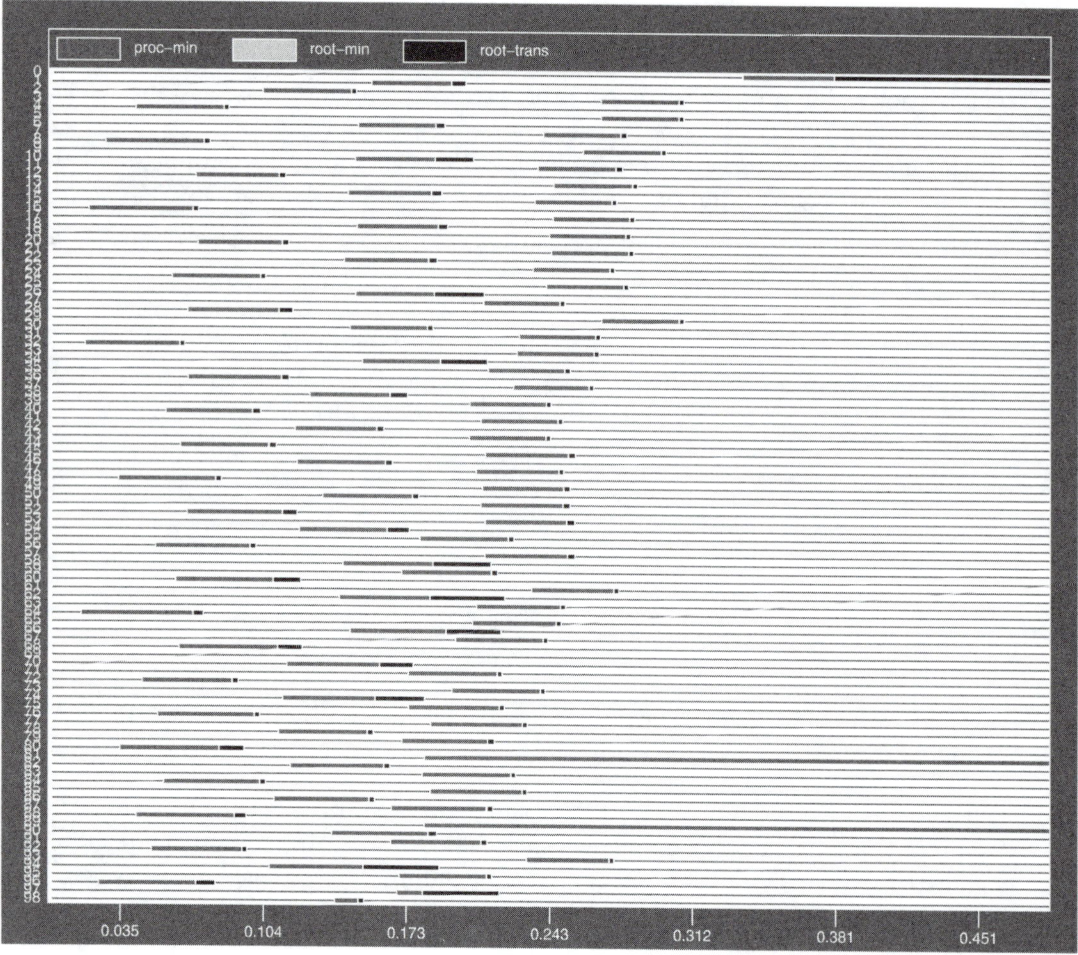

Figure 15.28 Parallel 1NNR Results Using $np = 99$ Processes.

0

Bibliography

Aho, A. V., and S. C. Johnson. Lr parsing. *ACM Computing Surveys (CSUR)*, 6(2):99–124, June 1974.

Aho, A. V., and J. D. Ullman. *The Theory of Parsing, Translation and Compiling.* Vol. I: *Parsing*. Prentice-Hall, 1972.

Aho, A. V., and J. D. Ullman. *The Theory of Parsing, Translation, and Compiling.* Vol. II. Prentice-Hall, 1973.

Appel, A., and M. Ginsburg. *Modern Compiler Implementation in C.* Cambridge University Press, 1998. Note: also available are *Modern Compiler Implementation in ML* and *Modern Compiler Implementation in Java.*

Arbab, B., and B. M. Berry. Operational and denotational semantics of prolog. *Journal of Logic Programming*, 4:309–330, 1987.

Arbib, M. A., R.N. Moll, and A.J. Kfoury. *An Introduction to Formal Language Theory*. Springer-Verlag, 1988.

Backus, J. Can programming be liberated from the Von Neumann style? A functional style and its algebra of programs. *Communications of the ACM*, 21(8): 613–641, August 1978.

Bergin, T. J., and R. G. Gibson. *History of Programming Languages*. Addison-Wesley, 1996.

Borger, E., and D. Rosensweig. A mathematical definition of full prolog. *Science of Computer Programming*, 24:249–286, 1994.

Buyya, R. *High-Performance Cluster Computing: Programming and Applications*. Prentice Hall, 1999.

Charette, R. Why software fails. *IEEE Spectrum*, 42–49, September 2005.

Chomsky, N. *Syntactic Structures*. Mouton, 1957.

Clocksin, W. F., and C. S. Mellish. *Programming in Prolog Using the ISO Standard*, ed. 5. Springer-Verlag, 2003.

Debray, S., and P. Mishra. Denotational and operational semantics in prolog. *Journal of Logic Programming*, 5:61–91, 1988.

DeRemer, F., and T. Pennello. Efficient computation of lalr(1) look-ahead sets. *ACM Transactions on Programming Languages and Systems (TOPLAS)*, 4(4):615–649, October 1982.

Doets, H. C. *From Logic to Logic Programming*. MIT Press, 1994.

Ed-Dbali, A., P. Deransart, and L. Cervoni. *Prolog: The Standard*. Springer-Verlag, 1996.

Eischen, K. Software development: An outsider's view. *IEEE Computer*, 35(5):36–44, May 2002.

Enderton, H. B. In memoriam: Alonzo Church (1903–1995). *Bulletin of Symbolic Logic*, 1(4):486–488, 1995.

Floyd, R. W. Assigning meaning to programs. *Proc. Symp. in Applied Mathematics.* Vol. 19: *Mathematical Aspects of Computer Science*, 19–32, 1967.

Flynn, M. J. Some computer organizations and their effectiveness. *IEEE Trans. on Computers*, C-21(9):948–960, Sept. 1972.

Foster, L. R. *Palm OS Programming Bible* (with CD-ROM). John Wiley & Sons, 2000.

Frakes, W. B., and K. Kang. Software reuse research: Status and future. *IEEE Trans. on Software Engineering*, 31(7):529–536, July 2005.

Fu, K. S. *Syntactic Methods in Pattern Recognition*. Academic Press, 1974.

Fu, K. S., and T.L. Booth. Grammatical inference: Introduction and survey–part I. *IEEE Trans. Pattern Analysis and Machine Intelligence*, PAMI-8(3):343–375, May 1986.

Goguen, J., and G. Malcolm. *Algebraic Semantics of Imperative Programs*. MIT Press, 1996.

Harper, R., R. Milner, M. Tofte, and D. MacQueen. *The Definition of Standard ML (Revised)*. MIT Press, 1997.

Hoare, C. A. R. An axiomatic basis for computer programming. *Comm. ACM*, 12:576–580, October 1969.

Hogger, C. J. *Introduction to Logic Programming*. Academic Press, 1984.

Hopcroft, J. E., and J.D. Ullman. *Formal Languages and Their Relation to Automata*. Addison-Wesley, 1969.

Hudak, P. Conception, evolution and application of functional programming languages. *ACM Computing Surveys*, 21(3):359–411, September 1989.

Hwang, K., and F. A. Briggs. *Computer Architecture and Parallel Processing*. McGraw-Hill, 1984.

Jones, C. B. The early search for tractable ways of reasoning about programs. *IEEE Annals of the History of Computing*, 26–49, April–June 2003.

Kennedy, K., and J. Ramanathan. Deterministic attribute grammar evaluator based on dynamic sequencing. *ACM Transactions on Programming Languages and Systems*, 1(1):142–160, July 1979.

Kleene, S. C. Origins of recursive function theory. *Annals of the History of Computing*, 3(1):52–67, 1981.

Knuth, D. E. Semantics of context-free languages. *Mathematical Systems Theory*, 2(2):127–146, 1968.

Knuth, D. E. Examples of formal semantics. *Lecture Notes in Mathematics, No. 188*, 212–235, 1971.

Kristensen, B., and O. Madsen. Methods for computing lalr(k) lookahead. *ACM Transactions on Programming Languages and Systems*, 3(1), January 1981.

Ledgard, H. F., M. Marcotty, and G.V. Bochmann. A sampler of formal definitions. *ACM Computing Surveys*, 8(2):191–276, 1976.

Lloyd, J. W. *Foundations of Logic Programming*. Springer-Verlag, 1984.

Lusk, E., W. Gropp, and A. Skjellum. *Using MPI: Portable Parallel Programming with the Message-Passing Interface*, ed. 2. MIT Press, 1999.

Manzano, M. Life, work and some miracles of alonzo church. *Journal of History and Philosophy of Logic*, 18(4), 1997.

McCarthy, J. Recursive functions of symbolic expressions and their computation by machine, part 1. *Communications of the ACM*, 4(3):184–195, April 1960.

McCarthy, J. Towards a mathematical science of computation. *Computer Programming and Formal Systems*, 33–70, 1963.

Morris, F. L., and C.B. Jones. An early program proof by Alan Turing. *Annals of the History of Computing*, 6(2):139–144, April 1984.

Naur, P. Proof of algorithms by general snapshots. *BIT*, 6(4):310–316, 1966.

Pagan, F. G. *Formal Specifications of Programming Languages*. Prentice-Hall, 1981.

Paulson, L. C. *ML for the Working Programmer*, ed. 2. Cambridge University Press, 1996.

Quinn, M. J. *Parallel Computing Theory and Practice*. McGraw-Hill, 1994.

Randell, B. *The Origins of Digital Computers: Selected Papers*, ed. 2. Springer Verlag, 1975.

Rhodes, N., and J. McKeehan. *Palm OS Programming: The Developer's Guide*, ed. 2. O'Reilly & Associates, 2001.

Roads, C. Grammars as representations for music. *Computer Music Journal*, 3(1):48–55, 1979.

Robinson, J. A. A machine-oriented logic based on the resolution principle. *Journal of the Association for Computing Machinery*, 12(1):23–41, 1965.

Rosser, J. B. Highlights of the history of the lambda-calculus. *Annals of the History of Computing*, 6(4):337–349, 1984.

Schalkoff, R. J. *Digital Image Processing and Computer Vision*. John Wiley, 1989.

Schalkoff, R. J. *Pattern Recognition: Statistical, Structural and Neural Approaches*. John Wiley, 1992.

Schalkoff, R. J. *Artificial Neural Networks*. McGraw-Hill, 1997.

Steele, G. Thoughts on language design. *Dr. Dobb's Journal*, 31–32, January 2006.

Tarjan, R. E. *Data Structures and Network Algorithms*. SIAM Publications, 1983.

Taub, A. H. *John Von Neumann: Collected Works (Design of Computers, Theory of Automata and Numerical Analysis)*, Vol. V. Pergamon Press, 1963.

Trembly, J. P., and P. G. Sorenson. *The Theory and Practice of Compiler Writing*. McGraw-Hill, 1985.

Wegner, P. Programming languages—the first 25 years. *IEEE Transactions on Computers*, 1207–1225, December 1976.

Wexelblat, R. L. *History of Programming Languages*. Academic Press, 1981.

Wilner, W. T. Formal semantic definition using synthesized and inherited attributes. *Formal Semantics of Programming Languages*, 25–40, 1972.

Index

`bison`, 141, 169, 170, 176, 232
`c++`, 383
`c++`-style comments, 234
`c++`-style comments (in `minic`), 246
`clisp`, 321
`c`, 135
`c`-style comments, 234
`flex`, 141, 169, 170, 232
`fun`, 398
`lex`, 170
`mapcar`, 346
`mpich`, 582
`protocol` predicate, 81
`setf`, 369
`use`, 399
`yacc`, 169
1-nearest neighbor, 585

abstract syntax, 446
abstraction (lambda calculus), 308
algebraic semantics, 446, 468
algebraic specification, 469
algorithm decomposition, 569, 572
algorithmic parallelism, 576
alphabet, 49
ambiguity, 91, 212
ambiguous grammar (minic example), 212
Amdahl's law, 575
analytic mode (grammar), 52
AND and OR parallelism (Prolog), 577
anonymous function, 307
anonymous variable, 79
API, 484, 495
Artificial Intelligence, 319
ASCII, 140
assertion, 459
attribute grammar, 257
attributes, 260
axiom, 459
axiomatic semantics, 446, 458

back end (compiler), 146
backtracking, 99
base class, 485
basic function groups (Lisp), 329
Beowulf cluster, 582
BNF, 30, 60, 151, 210
bottom-up parsing, 143
branching(minic), 227

c++, 480
c-style comments (in `minic`), 229
callback routines, 493
CAML, 393, 410
Chomsky Normal Form, 141, 143
class hierarchy, 377, 483, 491
class instance, 485
classes, 481
clause, 78
clause (Prolog), 76
client-server architecture, 490
closure set, 50
cluster computing, 582
combination (lambda calculus), 308

command-line interface, 477, 494
Common Lisp, 321
CommonLisp Object System (CLOS), 369, 376, 481
compiler, 49, 146
compiler-compilers, 169
complexity function, 573
composite function, 314
composition, 457
computational complexity, 572
concrete syntax, 446
concurrency, 572
cond, 337
cons, 333
constraint satisfaction problems (CSPs), 75
context constraints, 259
context-free, 177
context-free (T_2) grammar, 53
context-free grammar, 55, 57, 257, 261
context-sensitive (T_1) grammar, 53
contextual constraints, 262
contextual constraints (in programming languages), 257
contextual constraints (see also type checking), 256
cross-platform development, 495
currying, 311, 404
CWinApp class, 485
CWnd class, 485
CYK Parse Table, 144, 145
CYK parsing algorithm, 143

data flow graph, 576
data parallelism, 576
declarative languages, 20
declarative programming, 2, 75
defun, 329
denotation, 450
denotational semantics, 445, 450
derivation tree, 52, 57, 139, 142, 447, 450
disambiguation rules, 211
dual-use characters (in scanning), 222

empty string, 50
environment, 453
event handling, 485
event loop, 479, 480, 491
event-driven programming, 2, 477, 478
exception, 397
expert system, 82

fact, 78
fact (Prolog), 78
finite-state machine, 306
flex input file, 170
flex rules section, 171
formal grammar, 3, 47, 51
formal grammars, 30
formal proof of correctness, 353
formal specification, 459
free (T_0) grammar, 53
functional language, 19, 467
functional programming, 2, 305, 369, 391

generative mode (grammar), 52
goal, 77, 79
grammar ambiguity, 60
grammar equivalence, 57
grammatical ambiguity, 60
GUI, 478, 479, 488, 494, 495

head, 93
head (clause), 78

imperative language, 18, 82, 571
imperative programming, 2, 87
implication, 460
informal operational semantics, 442
inheritance, 374
integrated development environment (IDE), 484
interpreter, 49
iteration, 344

lambda calculus, 305, 317, 444
lambda functions (in Lisp), 312
language, 48, 52
let, 344
lexical analysis, 141
lexical structure, 139
LGN, 151
linear grammar, 55
Lisp, 319
list (in Prolog), 93
list manipulation functions, 321
lists (SML), 405

Logic Grammar Notation (LGN), 104
lookahead, 156

mathematical objects, 451
Message map, 489
Message Passing Interface (MPI), 582
methods, 378, 481
Microsoft Foundation Classes (MFC), 479, 480, 485, 489
Microsoft Windows, 479, 484
Minsky's Conjecture, 575
ML, 391, 394
Modus Ponens, 104
Moore's Law, 11
morphological operator, 595
Motif, 490
MPI communicator, 583
MSDN, 501

negation-as-failure, 102
nil, 327
nonterminal, 145

object oriented, 20
Object Oriented (OO) Computing, 20
Object Oriented Programming (OOP), 20, 443
Objective CAML (OCAML), 393
OCAML, 391
Open Software Foundation (OSF), 490
OpenGL, 480
operation, 469
operational semantics, 444
operator precedence, 60

parallel hardware, 569
parallel programming, 2, 569
parallel programming languages, 570
Parallel Prolog, 579
parse, 142
parse tree, 57, 142, 447
parser, 139, 176
parsing, 49, 141
partial correctness, 461
phrase structure grammar, 54
pointers to class objects, 482
polymorphic behavior, 404
polymorphic function, 313
postconditions, 459
preconditions, 459
predicate, 77
predicate functions, 261
predicate logic, 460
predicates, 77, 336
prefix notation, 309
process, 580
process rank (MPI), 583
productions, 52, 137, 139
progn, 342
program correctness, 458, 466
programming language, 1
programming paradigms, 18
Prolog, 75, 151

query, 77
quote (Lisp), 327

read-eval-print loop (EVAL), 323
recursion, 84, 111, 306, 320, 338
recursion (in Prolog), 95
recursive function, 467
recursive production, 308
reduction (lambda calculus), 310
referential transparency, 315, 353
regular (finite-state or T_3) grammars, 54
regular expression, 61
regular expressions, 170, 234
regular language, 55
relation, 307
reserved words, 153
reserved words and symbols, 137, 141
rule (Prolog), 78
rule-based programming, 23

s-expression, 326
self-embedding productions, 222
semantic domain, 453
semantic equivalence, 446, 457
semantic function, 452
semantic functions, 261
semantic rules, 261
semantic value, 177
semantics, 1, 29, 75, 259, 437, 441
sentence, 52, 142
side effect, 77, 314
signature, 470
SIMD, 576

Single Program, multiple Data (SPMD), 583
SISD, 576
slot values, 372
software reuse, 10
sort, 469
source code comments (scanning), 227
speedup, 575
stream, 347
subgoal, 80
symbol table, 262
syntactic 'fragments', 438
syntactic ambiguity, 60
syntactic domain, 452
syntax, 1, 29, 48, 49, 56, 60, 63, 75, 77, 437, 438

tail, 93
tail (clause), 78
terminal, 145
terminals, 136
tokens, 139, 141, 169, 176
top-down parsing, 142
total correctness, 462
translational semantics, 443
Turing machine, 306
type checking, 228, 257

unification, 76, 79, 578
uniprocessor architecture, 574

variable declaration, 211, 257

weakest precondition, 463
whitespace, 140
widgets, 491
window manager, 493

X, 490
X Toolkit Intrinsics, 490
X windows system, 479
Xlib, 490